Perceptual Expertise

OXFORD SERIES IN VISUAL COGNITION

Series Editors
Gillian Rhodes
Mary A. Peterson

Perception of Faces, Objects, and Scenes: Analytic and Holistic Processes
Edited by Mary A. Peterson and Gillian Rhodes

Fitting the Mind to the World: Adaptation and After-Effects in High-Level Vision
Edited by Colin W. G. Clifford and Gillian Rhodes

Human Body Perception from the Inside Out
Edited by Günther Knoblich, Ian M. Thornton, Marc Grosjean, and Maggie Shifrar

Understanding Events: From Perception to Action
Edited by Thomas F. Shipley and Jeffrey M. Zacks

Visual Memory
Edited by Steven J. Luck and Andrew Hollingworth

Perceptual Expertise: Bridging Brain and Behavior
Edited by Isabel Gauthier, Michael J. Tarr, and Daniel Bub

Perceptual Expertise

Bridging Brain and Behavior

Edited by

ISABEL GAUTHIER, MICHAEL J. TARR,
AND DANIEL BUB

OXFORD
UNIVERSITY PRESS

2010

OXFORD
UNIVERSITY PRESS

Oxford University Press, Inc., publishes works that furthers
Oxford University's objective of excellence
in research, scholarship, and education.

Oxford   New York
Auckland   Cape Town   Dar es Salaam   Hong Kong   Karachi
Kuala Lumpur   Madrid   Melbourne   Mexico City   Nairobi
New Delhi   Shanghai   Taipei   Toronto

With offices in
Argentina   Austria   Brazil   Chile   Czech Republic   France   Greece
Guatemala   Hungary   Italy   Japan   Poland   Portugal   Singapore
South Korea   Switzerland   Thailand   Turkey   Ukraine   Vietnam

Published by Oxford University Press, Inc.
198 Madison Avenue, New York, New York 10016

www.oup.com

Oxford is a registered trademark of Oxford University Press

Library of Congress Cataloging-in-Publication Data
Perceptual expertise : bridging brain and behavior / edited by Isabel Gauthier,
    Michael J. Tarr, and Daniel Bub.
      p.   cm.
    Includes bibliographical references and index.
    ISBN 978-0-19-530960-7 (cloth : alk. paper)
    1. Visual perception.   2. Face perception.   3. Categorization (Psychology)
    I. Gauthier, Isabel.   II. Tarr, Michael J.   III. Bub, Daniel.
    BF241.P438 2010
    152.14—dc22

                                                2009015045

9   8   7   6   5   4   3   2   1

Printed in the United States of America
on acid-free paper

Foreword

Robert L. Goldstone
rgoldsto@indiana.edu
Department of Psychological and Brain Sciences
Indiana University

Having observed the Perceptual Expertise Network (PEN) in action, I can attest to its importance and uniqueness. The PEN group has been a highly tight-knit and intellectually vibrant community, self organized in a grass-roots manner by researchers intrinsically interested in a common topic—the scientific understanding of perceptual learning leading to expert performance. Their efforts were jump-started by a McDonnell Foundation grant, and to my mind, the resulting workshops and research synergies are simply the best example that I know of for how to successfully foster true cross-laboratory collaboration. The PEN group is now a large community, not organized around a single individual, but rather around a core group of about 10 large research teams. The PEN group is itself integrated into other groups such as the National Science Foundation Science of Learning Center on Temporal Dynamics.

As to the topic itself, perceptual learning is important for two reasons—because it is perceptual and because it is learning. Changes to perception are particularly important because they affect all subsequent cognitive processes that occur downstream. There is good evidence, both neurophysiological and behavioral, that perceptual learning can involve early changes to the primary visual, auditory, and somatosensory cortices. One might feel that the early perceptual system ought to be hardwired—it is better not to mess with it if it is going to be depended upon by all processes later in the information processing stream. There is something right with this intuition, but it implicitly buys into a "stable foundations make strong foundations" assumption that it is appropriate for houses of cards, but probably not for flexible cognitive systems. For better models of cognition, we might turn to Birkenstock shoes and suspension bridges, which provide good foundations for their respective feet and cars by flexibly deforming to their charges. Just as a suspension bridge provides better support for cars by conforming to the weight loads, perception supports problem solving and reasoning by conforming to these tasks. Many of the chapters in this book attest to the advantage of having a flexible perceptual system that customizes itself to its needed tasks. Avoiding both the Scyllae of requiring all perceptual discriminations to be "preloaded" into the brain/mind, and the Charybdis of assuming that all sophisticated discriminations require the explicit concatenation of many elementary perceptual features, the contributions contained herein point to a third middle route. Namely, new perceptual representations can be constructed because of their diagnosticity for a personally relevant task. These representations do not have to be hardwired, and in fact, it is difficult to see how all personally relevant representations (e.g., cars for mechanics, pitches for umpires, birds for naturalists, or X-rays for radiologists) *could* be hardwired. These representations do not have to be processed as concatenations assembled from a set of generic elemental detectors. The chapters provide solid evidence that many pertinent perceptual representations functionally act as holistically registered, acquired detectors. Accordingly, the representations are genuinely perceptual, acting as the components for later cognitive representations.

If perceptual learning is crucially perceptual, it is also crucially learning. Consistent with the ripples of downstream influence that early perceptual changes exert, perceptual systems should generally be designed to change slowly and conservatively, so as not to disrupt their downstream consumers. For this reason, this book's focus on perceptual *expertise* is appropriate. Expertise typically requires at least 10 years to attain (Ericsson, Krampe, & Tesch-Römer, 1993), sufficient time to influence perception, not simply decision trees or explicitly memorized strategies. The protracted time course of acquiring new perceptual tools is certainly frustrating for those in the business of judging wines, rock samples, cell structures, dives, or manufacturing flaws. One of the reasons why wisdom can't be simply told (Bransford, Franks, Vye, & Sherwood, 1989) but rather must be lived is that wisdom is frequently perceptual and thus must be built into one's neurological wiring. Doctors with years of clinical experience frequently experience surprise that their verbal descriptions have little value to second-year residents. The lecturer knows what she means by "spiky" tumors or "aggravated" tissue, but these words are not transmittable in the same way that "isosceles" can be simply verbally communicated as "a triangle having two sides of equal length." The doctor's terminology is not easily communicated because the words are just the tip of the iceberg. The iceberg below the surface is the years of experience needed to connect perceptual information to the words. Understanding the words is largely a matter of acquiring perceptual skills of segmentation, highlighting, differentiation, and unitization. Although the doctor's terminology takes years to master because its perceptual basis must also be learned, the final product of this mastery is that the newly forged expert sees a new world. Thomas Kuhn (1962) described how scientists, when exposed to a particular theoretical paradigm, see physical phenomena in new ways: "Though the world does not change with a change of paradigm, the scientist afterward works in a different world." (p. 121). A similar transformative experience accompanies expertise and justifies the hard and long work necessary to establish this "see change" in perception.

One might suppose that perceptual learning and perceptual expertise have strictly limited spheres of application because evolution has already tuned our perceptual systems to be sensitive to the most important elements of the world in which we live (Olshausen & Field, 1996). Having an adaptive perceptual system is advantageous when the world is variable. However, at least at a first pass, isn't the world fairly stable? We are all exposed to the same wavelengths of light thanks to the sun's spectral class. The gravitational constant is . . . constant. However, I would reply that there is an important sense in which different people face different environments. Namely, to a large extent, a person's environment consists of animals, people, and things made by people. All of these things have been designed by evolution or people to show local and regional variation. We *might* have been built by evolutionary R&D to be adept at processing faces (but see Chapters 1, 2, and 3 for persuasive arguments against strong forms of even this claim), but we could never have been prebuilt to be expert at processing particular faces such as Barack Obama's and John McCain's because there are simply too many possible faces. If we develop the need to identify a face or discriminate among faces, then these perceptual skills need to be acquirable. It is vital that perceptual systems be tunable because differences between faces are critical for the social animals that we are. Furthermore, our very identities are connected with the objects for which we become experts. Our vocations, avocations, and values are revealed by whether we become experts at distinguishing wines, words, or warplanes.

Although certain aspects of our world are shared by all of us, many of the most important identifications that we make cannot be universal and hardwired. When a domain becomes important to us, differences among the objects in that domain necessarily become important to us. To be a bird expert is to cease treating all birds alike, and to make distinctions between them (Tanaka & Taylor, 1991). The same is true for expertise with food, disease, art, music, or sport. One of the most striking regularities of learning is that the expert cannot help but make distinctions that they could not originally make at all as novices. Cognitive psychologists have rightly emphasized the cognitive equipment that all people share, but a powerful piece of this equipment is the ability to differentiate ourselves so that we are each unique. We can employ domain-general processes to become specialized for domains and particular instances within the domains.

A corollary of this ironically universal tendency to become unique is that what becomes highly specialized processing need not have started that way. As the chapters in this book demonstrate, the presence of neuroanatomically compact regions with distinct functional specializations does not sanction the inference that these regions were innately wired to perform those functions. The functional specializations of brain regions adapt over an organisms' lifetime and often span multiple object domains. Cognitive scientists have traditionally linked domain specificity and constraints. To learn, we must have constraints. Gold (1967) and Chomsky (1965) showed that there are too many possible grammars to learn a language in a finite amount of time, let alone 2 years, if there were no constraints on what those grammars look like. Psychologists applied these formal results to development and learning, concluding that different domains (including language, but also physics, biology, quantitative reasoning, social relations, and face perception perhaps) have their own special structures which should be exploited for learning. To efficiently exploit these kinds of structures entails having different kinds of constraints for different domains.

An exciting possibility pursued by the contributions to this book is that some constraints may be acquired rather than built in. Computational modeling suggests that the eventual specialization of a neural module often belies its rather general origins (Jacobs, Jordan, & Barto, 1991). Very general neural differences, such as whether a set of neurons has a little or a lot of overlap in their receptive fields, can cause the two populations of neurons to spontaneously specialize for handling either categorical or continuous judgment tasks, or snowball small initial differences into "what" versus "where" visual systems (Jacobs & Jordan, 1992). Empirical evidence from these pages, as well as developmental psychology (Sloutsky & Fisher, 2008; Smith, Jones, & Landau, 1996), has begun to support this modeling work, showing that we do not need to start with domain-specific constraints. The specific domains can emerge from more domain-general principles of association, contingency detection, statistical learning, and clustering.

Figure F.1 An illustrated allegory of the human bias to see the world filtered through a perceptual system that has been tuned to the same world. [Conceived by Robert Goldstone and Joe Lee, illustrated by Joe Lee.]

This computational and developmental work fits well with this book's leitmotif that particular domains, such as faces and letters, are indeed special for people, but that the process by which they became special may in large part be general. We learn about faces, and this learning changes how we learn about new faces. We develop constrained expectations about what faces should look like by being exposed to faces. Constraints both shape learning, and are shaped by learning. The promise of this work is that it will elaborate on how an intelligent system can create at least some of its own constraints—constraints that were not originally there before the brain organized itself to reflect important domains. The classic work on formal language learning is still correct. A system that aspires to learn needs to have constraints on what it can learn. There is no such thing as a system that is good at learning absolutely anything that it is presented. Efficient learning depends on making good assumptions about the kinds of things that will be presented. However, it still may be the case that many of these assumptions can be acquired by exposure to what the world has to offer. The functional and neurophysiological specializations explored in the following papers attest to the power of acquired constraints. Our perceptual systems enforce strong constraints on what we extract from the world, but they are also adapted to what we extract (see Figure F.1). If we must be constrained in order to learn, there is nonetheless substantial consolation in having those constraints themselves be flexibly tuned.

REFERENCES

Bransford, J., Franks, J. J., Vye, N. J., & Sherwood, R. D. (1989). New approaches to instruction: Because wisdom can't be told. In S. Vosniadu & A. Ortony, *Similarity and Analogical Reasoning* (pp. 470–497). New York: Cambridge University Press.

Chomsky, N. (1965). *Aspects of the theory of syntax*. Cambridge: The MIT Press.

Ericsson, K. A., Krampe, R. T., & Tesch-Römer, C. (1993). The role of deliberate practice in the acquisition of expert performance. *Psychological Review, 100(3)*, 363–406.

Gold, E.M. (1967). Language identification in the limit. *Information and Control, 16*, 447–474.

Jacobs, R. A., Jordan, M. I., & Barto, A. G. (1991). Task decomposition through competition in a modular connectionist architecture: The what and where vision tasks. *Cognitive Science*, 15, 219–250.

Jacobs, R. A., & Jordan, M. I. (1992). Computational consequences of a bias towards short connections. *Journal of Cognitive Neuroscience*, 4, 323–336.

Kuhn, T. S. (1962). *The structure of scientific revolutions*. Chicago: University of Chicago Press.

Olshausen B. A., & Field, D. J. (1996). Emergence of simple-cell receptive field properties by learning a sparse code for natural images. *Nature, 381*, 607–609.

Sloutsky, V. M., & Fisher, A.V. (2008). Attentional learning and flexible induction: How mundane mechanisms give rise to smart behaviors. *Child Development, 79,* 639–651.

Smith, L. B., Jones, S. S., & Landau, B. (1996). Naming in young children: A dumb attentional mechanism? *Cognition, 60,* 143–171.

Tanaka J, & Taylor, M. (1991). Object categories and expertise: Is the basic level in the eye of the beholder? *Cognitive Psychology, 23,* 457–482.

Preface—Lessons from PEN: Scientific Collaboration and the Search for Synergy

Susan M. Fitzpatrick, Ph.D.
Vice President, James S. McDonnell Foundation

Synergy, according to the open-source, online encyclopedia Wikipedia (http://en.wikipedia.org/wiki/Main_Page) is defined as follows:

> Synergy or synergism (from the *Greek* synergos meaning working together, circa 1660) refers to the phenomenon in which two or more discrete influences or agents acting together create an effect greater than the sum of the effects each is able to create independently.

When, in 2000, the James S. McDonnell Foundation (JSMF) announced that support for collaborative activities would be a major component of its new 21st Century Research Initiative, JSMF staff spent a fair amount of time and energy discussing the specific qualities that would make proposals successful. In reality, much of the scientific research, especially in areas that are by their very nature multidisciplinary, involves collaborations. Collaborations span the scale from individuals working together in a laboratory to multiinstitutional networks. Even a casual glance at the names and affiliations of the authors of journal articles in, for example, *Nature Neuroscience* indicates that team-based research is increasingly the norm. So in what way would the JSMF collaborative activity awards recognize and encourage a type of collaboration differing from the norm?

Central to our thinking, and derived from the foundation's prior experience with study panels, networks, and centers, was the notion of "synergy." Of course, to seek synergy leaves one open to charges of unacademic trendy thinking or susceptibility to management guru-ese. In our minds, though, there is a difference between the traditional forms of scientific collaboration and what we hope to seed through a new funding initiative. The advantages of standard scientific collaboration tend to be additive. X with expertise Y contributes Z, and A with expertise B contributes C, and so forth. The final product is roughly equivalent to the sum of the parts. Each party contributes what they already know how to do, and the different pieces are stitched together. What JSMF envisioned was supporting collaborative activities whose core characteristic was bringing together carefully selected groups of researchers around a shared problem. In fact, the shared problem, the core set of questions around which the proposed team was centered, had to require that the combined expertise and knowledge of the group would transcend the sum of the parts. In other words, the proposal would make clear why already too-busy people were willing to take on yet another commitment of time, energy, and resources. Our intent was that the collaborative activity awards would not support the ongoing work each of the collaborators was likely to pursue (and secure funding for) in her or his own laboratory. Rather, the funds would deliberately support the infrastructure required for deeper collaboration to emerge (more on this below) and provide seed money for experimental questions arising in response to group interactions. The colla-borative activity award funding was intended to support the "more."

In the years since first announcing the collaborative activity awards program, JSMF has steadily refined the criteria for evaluating collaborative proposals. In addition to the "sum being greater than the parts," the founda-tion now looks more carefully at not only how synergy emerges from colla-boration, but how synergy comes to characterize the very nature of the collaborative group itself. Synergy (continuing with the language of Wikipedia) can create a dynamic state in which combined action is favored over the sum of individual component actions and behavior of whole systems unpredicted by the behavior of their parts taken separately. A willingness to be open and accepting of the unpredictability component is a particularly vital characteristic, in the foundation's experience, of truly successful collaborations.

We still marvel that one of the very first letters of inquiry received by JSMF fulfilled both the letter and the spirit of the collaborative activity initiative. It was submitted by Vanderbilt University on behalf of Isabel Gauthier and the Perceptual Expertise Network (PEN). JSMF anticipated that granting colla-borative activity awards would be akin to spotting rare birds—we expected infrequent sightings but ready recognition. PEN is a *rara avis*.

The description of the collaborative activity awards posted on the JSMF website were (and still are) deliberately vague. If, as we hoped, collaborative activities were to be shaped around a particular issue, then it followed that the fabric of each collaborative group proposed would be uniquely woven to fit the need. JSMF intended to leave it up to the investigators to tell us what it was that they needed and how they wanted to structure the work. An attribute of PEN that struck us as remarkable, although less so now in retrospect, was the professional youth of the proposed collaborative's principal investiga-tors, several of whom were, at the time, untenured assistant professors. We had assumed that the risks associated with working collaboratively on difficult problems with unpredictable courses and outcomes would more likely appeal to established scientists seeking opportunities for undertaking new challenges. In hindsight, it makes sense that a group of young scientists would welcome the opportunity to explore new ways of doing science—and to seek funding that would make it possible to both formalize and scale up the ways of working together that they were, informally, already pursuing. PEN was one of the very first collaborative activity awards approved for funding by JSMF. As the papers in this volume attest, PEN represents a remarkably successful way of doing science. PEN also offers some important lessons for those interested in fostering collaboration.

The various public and private institutions funding science are not immune to following trends, and at the moment supporting collaboration is "in." At science policy forums and scientific meetings there is a fair amount of discussion on why answering many of today's pressing research questions requires teams of people with differing areas of expertise working together. In principle, this may very well be true. In practice, it is not that easy to accomplish primarily because we really do not have a good definition of what it is we mean by "collaboration." As mentioned above, collaboration of a certain kind is typical of how most science gets done. The organizational structure of laboratories, departments, schools, institutes, professional societies, and so on encourages the sharing and dissemination of techniques, tools, information, and personnel. Despite the powerful cultural image of the lone wolf genius, most scientific research is carried out by teams and small groups. It is when the attempt is made to reach across broad disciplinary boundaries or to span levels of analysis that collaboration, and encouraging collaboration via incentives such as grants, becomes tricky. Recognizing variations in experimental traditions, developing a shared language, uncovering hidden assumptions, valuing another's expertise, sharing credit, and trusting one's colleagues takes tremendous commitment. This kind of effort must be driven by the needs of the problem to be solved, it cannot be mandated by institutional administrators or by funding agencies.

PEN's success can be credited, in part, to the problem the group identified. Understanding how the brain acquires perceptual expertise requires the work of cognitive psychologists, neuropsychologists, cognitive neuroscientists, computational modelers, and others. It requires that data obtained from human and animal subjects with a variety of different methods and at different levels of analysis be meaningfully integrated. Members of PEN had to be comfortable constraining one another's explanations and questioning one another's assertions. The research questions were not all mapped out at the beginning of the project; instead, the research questions evolved, new directions unfolded, and new possibilities for experiments were decided on by the group as a whole. Developing the trust that makes shared work possible among researchers occupying physical locations all over the map takes leadership and it takes time. The PEN members recognized this and made it an explicit component of their project. They explored how best to use face to face meetings, web conferences, visits to laboratories, and shared resources to achieve the three aspects of synergy ("more", dynamic action, and unpredictability) discussed above. The evolution of the interactions across laboratories is evidenced by the graphs displayed in the first figure of the Introduction (see page 4). Initially, the formal interactions across laboratories form rather sparse connections but were quickly diversified and strengthened. It is also noteworthy that the connections across laboratories do not resemble a hub and spoke design. The PEN members are not held together because of individual connections with one central group.

What has JSMF learned about supporting collaborations? First and foremost, the fundamental nature of the problem to be solved must require the proposed collaboration. It should be clear how bringing together a group of people is going to achieve more than what could be achieved if the Foundation simply funded each researcher to go on doing what it is they do and share their knowledge through traditional academic routes such as publications and lectures. Second, there must be funds explicitly provided for administrative support, meetings, travel, sharing information, and for pilot experiments so new ideas can be tested quickly. The grant should be flexible in terms of how the funds are expended. Funding should be provided for a reasonable period of time: not less than 5 years, and often as long as a decade. Most importantly, we have found that these awards can be used to encourage the asking of deep questions, tackling difficult problems with uncertain outcomes, pushing the limits of knowledge, and creating new frameworks for the doing of science.

The work in this volume fully attests to the novelty and excitement of both the work being done and with the very process of doing that work. Best of all, this is only the beginning. Expect more.

Contents

Contributors

Galia Avidan
Department of Psychology
Ben-Gurion University of the Negev
Beer Sheva, Israel

Marlene Behrmann
Department of Psychology and
Center for the Neural Basis of Cognition (CNBC)
Carnegie Mellon University
Pittsburgh, Pennsylvania

Daniel Bub
Department of Psychology
University of Victoria
Victoria, British Columbia,
Canada

Cindy M. Bukach
Department of Psychology
University of Richmond
Richmond, Virginia

Olivia S. Cheung
Department of Psychology
Vanderbilt University
Nashville, Tennessee

Garrison W. Cottrell
Department of Computer Science and Engineering
University of California, San Diego
La Jolla, California

George S. Cree
Department of Psychology
University of Toronto Scarborough
Toronto, Ontario
Canada

Kim M. Curby
Department of Psychology
Temple University
Philadelphia, Pennsylvania

Tim Curran
Department of Psychology
University of Colorado, Boulder
Boulder, Colorado

Susan M. Fitzpatrick
The James S. McDonnell Foundation
Saint Louis, Missouri

Isabel Gauthier
Department of Psychology
Vanderbilt University
Nashville, Tennessee

Robert L. Goldstone
Department of Psychological and Brain Sciences
Indiana University
Bloomington, Indiana

Kate Humphreys
Department of Psychology & CNBC
Carnegie Mellon University
Pittsburgh, Pennsylvania

Karin H. James
Department of Psychological and Brain Sciences
Indiana University
Bloomington, Indiana

Thomas W. James
Department of Psychological and Brain Sciences
Indiana University
Bloomington, Indiana

Gael Jobard
Sciences du Vivant
Université de Caen Basse-Normandie
Basse-Normandie, France

Richard Le Grand
Department of Psychology
Kwantlen Polytechnic University
Surrey, British Columbia
Canada

Daphne Maurer
Department of Psychology
McMaster University
Hamilton, Ontario
Canada

Catherine J. Mondloch
Department of Psychology
Brock University
St. Catharines, Ontario
Canada

Thomas J. Palmeri
Department of Psychology
Vanderbilt University
Nashville, Tennessee

Jessie J. Peissig
Department of Psychology
California State University, Fullerton
Fullerton, California

Bruno Rossion
Faculté de Psychologie
Université Catholique de Louvain
Louvain-la-Neuve, Belgium

Robert T. Schultz
Department of Pediatrics,
University of Pennsylvania School of Medicine
Center for Austin Research, Children's
Hospital of Philadelphia
Philadelphia, Pennsylvania

Lisa S. Scott
Department of Psychology
University of Massachusetts, Amherst
Amherst, Massachusetts

David L. Sheinberg
Department of Neuroscience
Brown University
Providence, Rhode Island

James W. Tanaka
Department of Psychology
University of Victoria
Victoria, British Columbia
Canada

Michael J. Tarr
Department of Cognitive and Linguistic Sciences
Brown University
Providence, Rhode Island and
Center for the Neural Basis of Cognition
Department of Psychology
Carnegie Mellon University
Pittsburgh, Pennsylvania

Cibu Thomas
Department of Psychology and
Center for the Neural Basis of Cognition
Carnegie Mellon University
Pittsburgh, Pennsylvania

Verena Willenbockel
Department of Psychology
University of Victoria
Victoria, British Columbia
Canada

Alan C.-N. Wong
Department of Psychology
The Chinese University of Hong Kong
Shatin, New Territories
Hong Kong, China

Perceptual Expertise

Introduction

Isabel Gauthier, Daniel Bub, and Michael J. Tarr

This book represents a snapshot of an ongoing scientific collaboration among 10 labs over 8 years[1]. At one level, the included chapters present an overview of what we have learned so far about two related questions. First, how does learning influence perception and categorization? Second, how is such learning reflected in the plasticity and functional organization of neural structures? Our intention is that these chapters serve as an introduction to anyone interested in this topic. However, at another level, this book bears additional significance. For as participants in the Perceptual Expertise Network ("PEN"), these chapters provide an opportunity for us to review and celebrate how much we have gained by working together on difficult problems, instead of confronting them independently and alone.

Our collaborations are as diverse as the individuals they bring together. As PEN members, we are, of course, subject to the same in-group biases prevalent in the social world around us: we naturally consider our group to be special (as evidenced by the exponential growth of our collaborative activities over the course of the last 8 years, Figure I.1). Beyond such self-congratulation, we are still convinced that we have cultivated a successful collaborative model unlike almost anything we have experienced before. Yet, like any successful project, hindsight is 20-20, and it is now much easier to note what has worked and what hasn't worked, than it would have been to make these observations at the start. At the inaugural meeting of our network, Susan Fitzpatrick from the McDonnell Foundation (who wrote the preface to this book) expressed amusement and surprise that the oldest member of our group was (at the time!) likely to be younger than the youngest member of any other collaborative the foundation had previously supported[2]. Indeed, many of us were relatively "newly minted" PhDs, and one factor that certainly helped us forge our collaborations was our lack of preconception about how to run a research program, collaborative or otherwise. As such, we built much of the PEN structure on the enthusiasm of our students—a principle that remains to this day.

---

[1] Yet, there would have been no book if John Herrington had not posted "Send Isabel your book chapter" on Bob Schultz' water bottle on Nov 13, 2008. Thank you John!
[2] Susan was being generous. . .

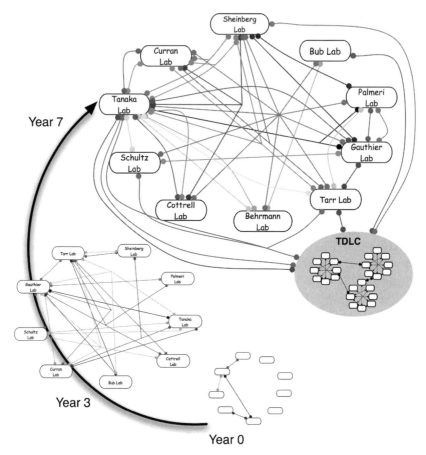

Figure I.1 The growth of collaborative activities between PEN labs. Before PEN, only a few of collaborated. Now, PEN is one of four research networks that is part of the Temporal Dynamics Learning Center headed by Gary Cottrell and funded by NSF. Each group of lines connecting different labs represents one ongoing collaborative project (this is not cumulative; completed projects do not appear in any given year).

A BRIEF HISTORY OF PEN

PEN is a group of scientists who have been working together since 2000 to explore how different kinds of minds and brains—of children, of adults, of people with brain dysfunctions, of monkeys, and even of computers—acquire or lose class-specific visual categorization abilities. By "class-specific" we mean visually delineated object domains: faces, shoes, chairs, birds, cars, Greebles[3], and so forth... This central theme has given rise to many

---

[3] If you don't know what a Greeble is now, you will by the end of this book!

questions, such as: how does one learn to discriminate similar objects in a visually similar category, for example, different models of cars, or different species of birds? Although an interesting question in its own right, the issue of fine-level discrimination within visually homogeneous categories is made even more intriguing by the fact that the category of human faces requires this degree of perceptual ability. Do the same neural and functional mechanisms used for face recognition play some role in how we learn to tell apart objects in other categories? And if so, many new questions emerge. For instance, are people suffering from autism less able to acquire the skills necessary to efficiently recognize individual faces? Does brain injury to neural mechanisms responsible for face processing also impact the processing of nonface objects? And so on. Of course, in practice the questions addressed by participants in PEN are varied and constantly evolving based on both our own findings and the tremendous progress being made in the wider fields of cognitive science, psychology, and neuroscience.

We should acknowledge that this sort of collaboration is a luxury that we are fortunate to enjoy. It has only been possible because of the generosity and long-term support of the James S. McDonnell Foundation. In 2000, the foundation—recognizing the difficulty of relying on traditional sources to fund highly collaborative and risky research—initiated a new program emphasizing interdisciplinary efforts, "Bridging Brain, Mind, and Behavior". Two of us, Isabel Gauthier and Michael Tarr (her PhD mentor) had been seeking a means to bring together colleagues working on issues relevant to those explored in Gauthier's dissertation, completed in 1998. Her thesis focused on the question: why does face recognition appear to be special? The beginnings of an answer to this question emerged from converging evidence based on multiple techniques, and the help of many creative minds. Recruiting Isabel as a graduate student, Mike's overture was both adventurous and honest: "I don't currently do cognitive neuroscience, but I can find the right people and we can learn together." At the time PEN was created, Mike and Isabel had already teamed up with many of the current PEN members to work on specific projects. Jim Tanaka[4], on a trip to Yale, provided critical advice in the creation of the Greeble training paradigm, suggesting as a criterion for expertise training the entry-level shift. Marlene Behrmann[5] had been collaborating with them on testing the role of level of categorization for the deficits observed in visual agnosia. Daniel Bub was conducting exciting work with an intriguing prosopagnosic patient who at the time (and for a long time) defied every account. Bob Schultz had asked

---

[4] Who Mike knew from his visits home, which happened to be right next to Carnegie Mellon University, where Tanaka was working as a postdoc with Martha Farah.

[5] Who Mike *also* knew from his visits to CMU, where Behrmann had been hired to replace Farah. So in the end it is probably a good thing Mike's father left his job in beautiful Santa Barbara, California and moved to Pittsburgh. (Footnote to Mike's footnote: Isabel originally wanted to work with Martha Farah and only learned of Mike's work by looking at papers that Martha cited).

Isabel for help with the first fMRI study demonstrating hypoactivity of the face-selective brain regions in autism, performed at Yale with the help of John Gore[6], with whom Isabel was working as a postdoc after a collaboration as a graduate student.

In order to more broadly represent the wide variety of possible approaches, we identified several other scientists who seemed interested in similar questions, but who were pursuing them using complementary methods: Tim Curran (who had already collaborated with Jim Tanaka on electrophysiological markers of perceptual expertise); David Sheinberg (a neurophysiologist whom Mike had known for several years); and Gary Cottrell (a computational modeler who had already built a model explaining the modularity of face processing through environmental influences[7]). Several years later, we also added Tom Palmeri (who now codirects PEN activities within the NSF-funded Temporal Dynamics Learning Center based at UCSD).

The motivation behind PEN, in response to the challenge posed by the McDonnell Foundation, was (and is) based on two principles: first, to do science guided by a question-driven framework rather than one motivated by techniques. PEN members do not ask themselves what should be the next fMRI or ERP experiment, just because those happen to be the techniques with which they are most familiar or in which they have invested their lab resources. Instead, they brainstorm and later capitalize on the diversity of their group to select the tool or tools[8] that best suit that particular question. Second, PEN members believe that students can benefit by grounding their education in a highly collaborative experience. In particular, because cognitive neuroscience inherently requires collaboration, scientists who master this challenge early in their training should be better equipped in their future careers.

DEVELOPING A NEW COLLABORATIVE MODEL

At present, PEN is comprised of approximately 30 people, including principal investigators, postdoctoral fellows, graduate students, and undergraduate research assistants at seven institutions in both the United States[9] and Canada. An administrative assistant based at Vanderbilt coordinates the

---

[6] We are forever indebted to John and his generosity in providing scan time to us at Yale for absolutely nothing for many of our early research projects, including Isabel's dissertation work. John, although trained as an MR physicist, had (and has) an abiding curiosity for the nature of the human mind and brain. He was a true collaborator with us in thinking about how to design, run, and analyze these studies.

[7] Gary also cited more of Isabel's papers in a 1999 Neural Networks article than she remembers having published at the time.

[8] We mean the research methods, not the PEN PIs!

[9] Including both blue and red states.

activities of the meeting (we've had four, with Suzie Dukic as the longest, making her mark on the group and recently replaced by Emilia McCann). The entire group meets face-to-face twice a year, generally with two outside researchers invited to present their work and interact with the group. After being generously supported through two cycles by the James S. McDonnell Foundation, PEN partly inspired the Temporal Dynamics of Learning Center, an NSF Science of Learning Center directed by Gary Cottrell, where it is the flagship network in a new network-of-networks approach to large-scale collaboration.

PEN workshops are unlike most scientific meetings; in fact, they all begin with a warning to invited guests: expect to be interrupted—a lot[10]. New results are presented, studies are proposed, and concepts are debated—and many of the interactions occur over dinners and extended lunchtimes, when members are encouraged to form smaller groups to discuss specific projects. In the first workshops, PEN members discussed how to approach the problem of perceptual expertise—the ability to efficiently and reliably discriminate between objects within a visually similar class, reviewed those effects, behavioral or neural, that seem to be associated with expertise, identified the many empirical and theoretical holes in the expertise literature, and discussed the importance of multiple techniques in the group's collaborative efforts.

Once we had established a common background, each workshop since then has been organized by a rotating pair of PIs and trainee group who together establish a theme and select guest speakers for each meeting, as well as define any "wrinkles" in how participants presented their work at that particular gathering. Notable innovations have included the deliberate omission of a schedule[11] for speakers, an agreement to eschew common background information that serves as filler in most talks, "blitzes" of several sequential 5 minute talks, and turning off Wi-Fi in the meeting room. As of October 2008, PEN has held 17 meetings (Table I–1), and it is a measure of

Table I–1 PEN Workshops as of November 2008

Workshop	Location	Guests
PEN I - February 2001	Nashville	Susan Fitzpatrick, Chuck Nelson, Jon Kaas
PEN II - June 2001	Glasgow	Philippe Schyns, Koen Lamberts,
PEN III - November 2001	Providence	Francesca Simion, Viola Macci Cassia
PEN IV - April 2002	Napa Valley	Valerie Goffaux, Mike Dixon
PEN V - July 2002	Victoria	Roberto Caldara, Allison Sekuler,
PEN VI - February 2002	Boulder	Yuko Munakata, Tom Palmeri

Continued

---

[10] Particularly by Gary.

[11] Ensuring that everybody (but Gary) shows up to the workshop ready to present.

Table I–1 (Continued)

Workshop	Location	Guests
Modeling workshop - March 2003	Nashville	Alice O'Toole, David Noelle
PEN VII - July 2003	Cape Cod	Bruce McCandliss, Bosco Tjan
PEN VIII - January 2004	Nashville	Dan Levin, Rob Goldstone
PEN IX - October 2004	San Diego	Shlomo Bentin
PEN X - April 2005	Pittsburgh	Uri Hasson, Marcel Just
PEN XI - October 2005	Montreal	Avi Chaudhuri, Javid Sadr, René Marois
PEN XII - May 2006	Sarasota	Virginia De Sa, Alex Petrov
PEN XIII - October 2006	Tucson	Mary Peterson, Dan Kersten
PEN XIV - April 2007	New Haven	Marvin Chun, Michael Frank
PEN XV - October 2007	Cambridge	Mahzarin Banaji, Marc Hauser
PEN XVI - May 2008	Banff	Brad Love, Jim DiCarlo
PEN XVII - October 2008	Chicago	Max Riesenhuber, Kalanit Grill-Spector

the dedication and enthusiasm of PEN participants that many PIs have only missed one or two of these meetings. We have also introduced a variety of motivations and challenges to the group, relying on the inherent tendency of humans[12] to compete. Consequently, PEN workshops now include prizes such as the "Bubbly award" given by Isabel for the presentation that most surprises us with its format (and succeeds!), and the "TimTom award" (Figure I.2) for the person who interacts positively (or just interacts) with the most people at a given meeting. We have also tried to invite guest speakers who may disagree with us, and, hopefully, surprise them by how much we, ourselves, disagree with one another. And not trivially, we enjoy good food in sometimes pleasant locations[13], and some of us[14] have been spotted dancing to various kinds of music at local bars after tiring workshop days. Although the details of our meetings are numerous and each on its own may appear trivial, science, like any human endeavor, is accomplished by individuals developing and striving together within a social system. In PEN we hope that we have nurtured a positive environment for doing good science, and in doing so, we have equipped ourselves to effectively face scientific challenges, bringing out the best in ourselves. Finally, we would like to thank Catharine Carlin, Mallory Jensen and everyone else at Oxford University Press who worked on the book, as well as the project manager, Padmapriya Ramalingam from Integra Software Services. The book would not have been possible without them.

---

[12] And particularly academics.
[13] Excepting Nashville, Pittsburgh, and Providence.
[14] Always led by Gary.

Figure I.2 The TimTom award consists of a bear the winner keeps until the next meeting, as well as a random item (e.g., clock, deck of cards) with the picture of TimTom that she/he can keep forever. TimTom was named in honor of the surprising discovery that a composite of Tim Curran and Tom Palmeri's face looks better than each of them alone.

PEN is (past and current members):

Britt Anderson	Gary Cottrell	David Grelotti
Karen Anderson	Rosie Cowell	AfmZakaria Haque
Luke Barrington	George Cree	Karin Harman James
Marlene Behrmann	Tim Curran	John Herrington
Caroline Blais	Matthew Dailey	Kari Hoffman
Danielle Brown	Chris D'lauro	Janet Hui-wen Hsiao
Daniel Bub	Casey DeBuse	Elinora Hunyadi
Cindy Bukach	Daniel Fiset	Tom James
Serena Butcher	Heather Flowe	Gael Jobard
Sean Butler	Jonathan Folstein	Carrie Joyce

Yi Cheng
Olivia Sin Chi Cheung
Jeff Cockburn
Chun-Chia Kung
Brenden Lake
Rick Le Grand
Sophie Lebrecht
Mike Mack
Tom McKeeff
James McPartland
Linda Moya
Jonathan Nelson
Adrian Nestor
Nam Nguyen
Mayu Nishimura
Erika Nyhus
Tom Palmeri
Jessie Peissig
Carley Piatt
Lara Pierce

Alex Foss
Isabel Gauthier
Iris Gordon
Matt Pierce
Jenn Richler
Giulia Righi
Bruno Rossion
Suzy Scherf
Robert Schultz
Lisa Scott
Honghao Shan
David Sheinberg
Christine Shin
Sarah Shomstein
Heida Maria Sigurdardottir
Jed Singer
Mikle South
Lars Strother
Jim Tanaka
Mike Tarr

Martha Kaiser
Cheryl Klaiman
Kathy Koenig
Katherine Tepe
Marc Thioux
Cibu Thomas
Bernie Till
Matt Tong
Ana Beth Van Gulick
Jean Vettel
Brian Wagar
Verena Willenbockel
Rankin Williams
Julie Wolf
Luke Woloszyn
Alan Chun-Nang Wong
Yetta Kwailing Wong
Lingyun Zhang

1

How Faces Became Special

Cindy M. Bukach and Jessie J. Peissig

The perceptual expertise network (PEN) was created to study how the brain becomes specialized for *different* types of object recognition, but its foundations are based on a large body of research demonstrating specificity for *one* class of objects in particular. In this chapter, we pay tribute to studies of face specificity as the basis and motivation for our research. This brief review is intended to provide a context for the work presented in the following chapters and thus will focus on studies of face recognition conducted prior to PEN's formation, including some work published in the first few years of PEN's existence, but omitting detailed discussion of more recent findings that were unknown at the beginning of our collaboration.

An overview of the face recognition literature prior to the beginning of PEN reveals a tremendous amount of research that demonstrated functional and cortical specialization for faces in a variety of populations, including normal adults, patients, infants, and monkeys; these studies used a variety of methodologies, including behavioral, imaging, electrophysiological, and single-cell recording techniques. This evidence has been widely interpreted as supporting a modular system for face recognition that is functionally distinct and anatomically segregated from general object recognition. According to this interpretation, faces are considered to be different from other object categories both because of the sociobiological necessity for humans to differentiate members of their own group, and because of the differences in cognitive demands for face perception relative to general object recognition (Sergent, Ohta, & MacDonald, 1992). For example, face recognition requires a level of individuation not necessary for most other objects, and is more complex because of the large number of exemplars that need to be individuated and because of their common general configuration. Face identity must also be generalized across different physiognomic expressions. This modular perspective is also reflected in the early models of face recognition (e.g., Bruce & Young, 1986; Burton, Bruce, & Johnston, 1990). Consistent with this modular approach, face recognition was primarily studied either independently from, or in contrast to, general object recognition. After reviewing this impressive body of research, we will end the chapter with a discussion of the motivation for integrating the study of face and object recognition with the purpose of testing the possibility that face specialization represents one instance of a more general perceptual tuning mechanism that is characteristic of the object recognition system as a whole.

PROSOPAGNOSIA

The earliest evidence for face specificity comes from case studies of individuals who have a selective or disproportionate impairment for face recognition relative to the recognition of nonface objects. This phenomenon is known as prosopagnosia. Despite intact elementary visual processing, individuals with prosopagnosia can no longer recognize familiar individuals on the basis of the face alone, but must rely on other information, such as voice, distinctive markings, hairstyles, or gait. The term "prosopagnosia" was first coined in 1947 by Joachim Bodamer (as cited in Ellis, 1996) in a study documenting two soldiers who could no longer recognize familiar faces following head trauma. Although these were not the first cases of face recognition impairment to be described (for a review, see Ellis, 1996), Bodamer's work is important because he made a strong argument for the selectivity of face recognition deficits. The existence of an impairment that primarily affects face recognition and leaves recognition of other types of objects mainly intact raised the possibility that there may be an anatomically segregated system dedicated to the recognition of faces. This argument had a profound influence on theories of face and object recognition and to a great extent shaped the way that research on face and object recognition was designed and interpreted.

Not surprisingly, subsequent studies of prosopagnosia were dominated by issues concerning the specificity of face recognition deficits and the locus of the "face-specific" neural substrate. Reviews of individual cases identified occipitotemporal regions, and particularly the fusiform gyrus in the right hemisphere, as being critical regions for face recognition (Damasio, Damasio, & Van Hoesen, 1982; De Renzi, 1986b). Another such issue was the relationship of concomitant deficits to prosopagnosia. Prosopagnosia is frequently associated with other cognitive impairments, such as achromatopsia, alexia without agraphia, visual field deficits, and occasionally with visuospatial defects such as neglect. By selecting the appropriate brain-injured control subjects, Damasio et al. demonstrated that these associated impairments could exist in the absence of any face recognition deficits and thus were not functionally related to prosopagnosia.

More controversial has been the question of whether nonface object recognition is completely spared in patients with prosopagnosia. In fact, the original Bodamer cases that first inspired the notion of a face-specific recognition system showed some recognition difficulties for nonface object classes: Case 1 could no longer recognize animals and Case 2 had several perceptual difficulties including a slight agnosia and simultanagnosia (as cited in Ellis, 1996). Although there have since been several cases of prosopagnosia who show no such difficulty on basic tasks of nonface object recognition, the specificity of prosopagnosia has continued to be challenged on the basis of methodological grounds. As early as 1955, Faust (as cited in Hecaen, 1981) pointed out that face and nonface categories were tested at different levels of classification: Whereas nonface object recognition involved discrimination between visually dissimilar object classes (a chair vs. a table), face recognition involved discrimination of individuals within a single, visually homogeneous object class. Faust documented a prosopagnosic who could not discriminate between individual exemplars of chairs, and on this basis postulated that prosopagnosia was a deficit in making within-class discriminations. This hypothesis generated considerable debate. Several studies were published supporting Faust's conceptualization of prosopagnosia as a domain-general within-class impairment. For example, prosopagnosic cases were published who had difficulty discriminating birds (Bornstein, 1963), animals (Gloning & Quatember, 1966; Lhermitte & Pillon, 1975), cars (Damasio et al., 1982; Gloning & Quatember, 1966; Lhermitte & Pillon, 1975), cows (Bornstein, Sroka, & Munitz, 1969); clothing (Damasio et al., 1982), and coins (Blanc-Garin, 1984). Yet other cases were reported to have no difficulty on specific tasks of within-class discrimination (Bruyer et al., 1983; De Renzi, 1986b; Farah, Levinson, & Klein, 1995; McNeil & Warrington, 1993). Lending considerable weight to the domain-specific notion was the publication of a case with preserved face recognition in the presence of impaired object recognition (Moscovitch, Winocur, & Behrmann, 1997). This case was considered particularly important because it provided the first neuropsychological evidence for a possible double dissociation between face and object recognition, but so far has been the only documented case with complete sparing of face recognition.

Several issues complicate the resolution of the face specificity controversy. One issue is the heterogeneity of cases with prosopagnosia. Prosopagnosia can be present from early childhood (congenital or developmental prosopagnosia), or it can be acquired after normal face recognition skills have developed (for example, through traumatic brain injury, stroke, or degenerative disease such as encephalitis). Not only do cases differ in etiology, they also vary in the severity, locus, and cognitive mechanisms affected. A common way of classifying cases of prosopagnosia is along a perceptive-mnestic dimension (De Renzi, 1986a; Hecaen, 1981). Apperceptive prosopagnosia tends to have a more posterior locus, usually involving the temporal-occipital junction, including or posterior to the fusiform gyrus. As the locus would suggest, these cases often have impairments of a more perceptual nature. Amnestic agnosia, on the other hand, tends to have a more anterior locus, including the anterior temporal lobes, leaving low-level perceptual functions primarily intact (Damasi, Tranel, & Damasio, 1990). Other regions may also play an important role in how well face recognition is carried out, such as systems involved in social cognition or attention (e.g., the amygdala, Schultz, 2005). All of these factors may interact with category specificity in a different way.

A second issue is the multiplicity of strategies that can be used to perform a recognition task. For example, the most commonly used neuropsychological test for diagnosing prosopagnosia, the Benton Facial Recognition Test (Benton, Sivan, Hamsher, Varney, & Spreen, 1994), can be performed successfully by individuals with prosopagnosia using an abnormal feature-matching strategy (Duchaine, Dingle, Butterworth, & Nakayama, 2004). Thus, simple accuracy is not always enough to demonstrate intact recognition ability without considering the particular strategy that the individual has engaged to complete the task. Often an assessment of speed–accuracy trade-off or the imposition of a limited exposure duration or response deadline can help to assess and limit the strategies used, but even these methodologies may allow for a well-practiced abnormal strategy. When possible, tasks are designed to test a particular strategy or processing style.

Finally, it is difficult to equate different object categories on all of the potential factors that might influence recognition performance, such as within-class visual similarity, complexity, familiarity, level of classification, or expertise. For example, faces are visually very similar, are typically identified at a more subordinate level than other objects (John vs. Fred compared to chair vs. table), and differ in the amount of expertise that individuals have at identifying these objects. Gauthier, Behrmann and Tarr (1999) suggested that manipulating the level of categorization within object classes is a better way to assess impairments across object categories.

From this brief review of prosopagnosia, it is clear that the domain specificity debate has been around at least since Faust's 1955 article. Currently, evidence continues to accrue on both sides of the debate, though it is undeniable that in everyday life deficits in face recognition are the most obvious consequence for individuals with prosopagnosia. Despite the difficulties inherent in resolving the controversies surrounding the implications of prosopagnosia for other objects, research on this important topic has led to new discoveries and the development of more sophisticated methodologies and models of face recognition. Current studies of prosopagnosia employ a broader and more sophisticated battery of tests that attempt to assess specific processes thought to be necessary for face recognition. For example, recent studies have examined the ability of prosopagnosics to learn to recognize new objects or faces (Bukach, Bub, Gauthier, & Tarr, 2006; Duchaine, Yovel, Butterworth, & Nakayama, 2006). Regardless of whether impairments are specific to faces or to a cognitive process that happens to be more necessary for faces than for other objects, prosopagnosia continues to be one of the strongest sources of evidence for specialization within the visual recognition system. The study of face recognition deficits therefore promises to yield important findings and will continue to inform theories of face recognition and cortical specialization in general.

BEHAVIORAL AND COGNITIVE EFFECTS

Behavioral signatures of face specificity in neurologically intact individuals have likewise been noted from an early date. Knowledge of the inversion effect for faces (poor recognition of inverted faces relative to upright faces) is evident as early as the sixteenth century in the reversible paintings of Arcimboldo (see Figure 1.1). It was noted as a psychological phenomenon

Figure 1.1 Arcimboldo's *The Vegetable Gardener*, circa 1590. Upright, the face formed by this configuration of vegetables is easily perceived as a face, but inverted it looks merely like a bowl of vegetables randomly arranged. Used with permission from Bridgeman Art Library (See color Plate 1).

as early as 1940 (Kohler, 1940), but its specificity to faces was not objectively tested until 1969 when Yin compared the size of the inversion effect for faces to that for other mono-oriented objects (Yin, 1969). He found that although all mono-oriented objects showed some degree of advantage for the upright orientation, faces had a *disproportionately large* inversion effect relative to nonface objects. Yin concluded that there are two inversion factors: a general factor relevant to all mono-oriented stimuli related to familiarity with a single orientation, and a second face-specific factor that applied only to upright faces. Although Yin's conclusion has been challenged on the basis of the need to control potential confounding stimulus factors such as stimulus complexity and upright performance between object classes (Goldstein & Chance, 1981), disproportionate effects of inversion remain one of the most cited pieces of evidence for face specificity, and inversion continues to be widely used as a control condition to test for the specificity of a particular process (see Carey & Diamond, 1977, for early replications of a disproportionate effect of inversion for faces compared to houses, buildings, and dog faces; Scapinello & Yarmey, 1970; Valentine & Bruce, 1986; Yarmey, 1971). Indeed, the Margaret Thatcher Illusion (Thompson, 1980) continues to be a most striking demonstration of the powerful effect of inversion on face recognition and a popular way to introduce the concept of face specificity to new students (see Figure 1.2).

Yin's (1969) study was important because it introduced the idea that upright faces were processed in a *qualitatively* different way than other objects or inverted faces. As Yin himself pointed out, the inversion effect alone does not reveal what that qualitative difference might be. However, based on subject feedback, Yin speculated that the face-specific factor might be due to a whole-based strategy for upright faces, in contrast to a distinguishing feature-based strategy for inverted faces and other objects. Yin's work inspired a new field of inquiry that aimed to uncover the special process(es) engaged by upright faces in contrast to a more "component-based" process employed by nonface objects and inverted faces. Two possibilities have emerged as the most likely candidates to explain the qualitative difference in cognitive processing between faces and nonface objects: holistic and relational processing. Holistic processing refers to a "gestalt-like" representation or the interactive processing of multiple parts. Relational processing refers to the encoding of information about the spatial relation between

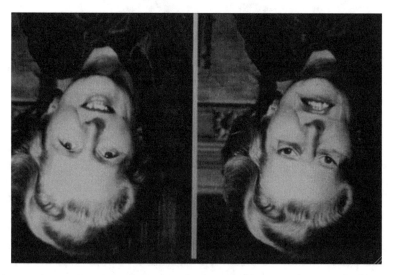

Figure 1.2 The Margaret Thatcher Illusion (Thompson, 1980). The differences between these two faces is much more noticeable when the two faces are perceived upright than when they are inverted. Used with permission from P. Thompson, "Margaret Thatcher: A new illusion," 1980, *Perception, 9,* pp. 483–484, Pion Limited, London.

parts. Unfortunately, the term "configural processing" has been used to describe both of these processes, thus this term will be avoided in the present review (see Maurer, Le Grand, & Mondloch, 2002, for a discussion of the different ways that "configural" processing has been used).

Holistic Processing

Early attempts to understand face "gestalt" examined whether or not a face was processed and/or stored as a template of integrated features (Bradshaw & Wallace, 1971; Matthews, 1978; Smith & Nielsen, 1970; Tversky & Krantz, 1969). One method used to study holistic processing was to match faces that varied on different combinations of features to determine if multiple features are processed interactively (suggesting a template) or as independent features in either a parallel or serial fashion. For example, Smith & Neilson (1970) used multidimensional face schemas in a recognition task and found evidence for simultaneous self-terminating feature comparisons (RTs increased on different trials as the number of differences between face pairs increased, but did not depend on the number of relevant features to be compared, suggesting the fastest feature determined RT, not the number to be searched). Other researchers approached the gestalt question by examining part judgments. For example, Homa, Haver, and Schwartz (1976) likened gestalt perception to the word superiority effect. He found evidence that face parts (eyes, nose, and mouth) were processed better in an intact face than in a scrambled face in which the parts were disordered in terms of their location.

Other researchers used interference between parts as a measure of holistic processing. Young, Hellawell, and Hay (1987) found evidence for interference from the top and bottom halves of composite faces (faces made from the top and bottom of two different faces). In this study, participants were slow to identify the top of a famous face when it was paired with the bottom of a different face. Response times for identification of face halves improved when face halves were misaligned with respect to one another. Furthermore, this "composite alignment" effect was absent for inverted faces. The authors argued that aligned face composites "fused together" to form a new and unfamiliar identity, suggesting faces are processed as wholes. This effect was later replicated with unfamiliar faces (Hole, 1994) and is now a common measure of holistic processing.

None of the above-mentioned studies explicitly tested the specificity of holistic processing to faces. Whereas Smith & Neilson (1970) and Homa et al. (1976) considered faces as an example of a "well integrated object class" (Smith & Neilson) or a class that had a "well defined form or structure" (Homa et al.), Young, Hellawell, & Hay (Young et al., 1987) and Hole (1994) explored holistic processing of faces with no reference to other object types. The first study to directly test the specificity of holistic processing to faces was Tanaka and Farah (1993). In this influential study, Tanaka and Farah (1993) developed the whole–part paradigm, in which a face or object is studied, and recognition of a part is later tested in the context of the whole or in isolation.

This is a forced-choice procedure in which the distractor is similar in all aspects to the studied face or object with the exception of the target feature. Tanaka and Farah reasoned that if parts were represented independently, then part recognition should be easier for the isolated condition (a part–whole advantage); conversely, if parts were not differentiated, then recognition should be better in the context of the whole (a whole–part advantage). Tanaka & Farah found a whole–part advantage for upright faces, but not for inverted faces, scrambled faces, or houses (Tanaka & Sengco, 1997). They concluded that faces were processed more holistically than other objects, and defined a holistic representation as a template in which parts are undifferentiated. This interpretation of holistic processing as an undifferentiated template can be viewed as the extreme end of a holistic continuum that represents degrees of interdependence between face parts.

Relational Processing

The first studies to specifically manipulate the spatial relations between face parts were a study by Haig (1984) and a study by Sergent (1984) published in the same year. Haig compared sensitivity to small displacements of eyes, nose, and mouth in upright faces and found that individuals were very sensitive to vertical movements of mouth, eyes, and nose, and narrowing of the distance between eyes. Sergent's study compared component and relational properties of upright and inverted faces. She manipulated three aspects of a set of schematic faces: the outer contour, component information (e.g., eye shape), and the spacing of the internal features. Using a simultaneous matching task, she found that the three sources of information were processed interactively in upright faces, and that inversion disrupted both relational and component information. Although these two studies were the first to manipulate spatial relations in faces, it is Diamond and Carey (1986) who can be credited with developing the concept of relational processing as it is most typically used today. They identified two types of relational properties: (a) First-order relational properties refer to the overall configuration of parts (eyes above nose above mouth); (b) second-order relational properties refer to the metric distances between features (how widely spaced the eyes are, how far above the mouth the nose is placed), and this is what is now commonly referred to simply as "relational processing." Diamond and Carey argued that faces are special because of three properties: faces share common first-order relations between parts; people rely on second-order relations to individuate faces, and people have a lot of experience individuating faces. They tested these claims by examining inversion effects for dogs, another category that shares first-order relations. They found a large inversion effect for dogs, but only for dog experts who have the necessary experience individuating dogs, not dog novices. They interpreted the inversion effect as disrupting the processing of second-order spatial relations. Further evidence supporting the role of expertise in face recognition came from a study that found a greater inversion effect for own race than other race faces (Rhodes, Brake,

Taylor, & Tan, 1989; but see Valentine & Bruce, 1986). These authors likewise concluded that greater expertise leads to greater reliance on relational processing, and thus a greater inversion effect.

Diamond and Carey's (1986) study was widely influential not only because it initiated the expertise debate by suggesting that facelike processing can occur for nonface objects under certain circumstances, but also because it associated inversion with the disruption of second-order relational processing in particular. It should be noted, however, that neither the study by Diamond and Carey nor the study by Rhodes et al. (1989) manipulated spatial relations between parts, and so did not actually test whether inversion disrupted second-order spatial relations specifically. Rather, their claims were based on the evidence presented by Sergent (1984) mentioned above. In the 1990s following these landmark studies, researchers began to manipulate the spatial relations within faces to determine whether relational properties were indeed more disrupted by inversion than local component properties such as shape or color. Although some studies found that local information could be disrupted by inversion (e.g., Rhodes, Brake, & Atkinson, 1993), the majority of studies found that component information was either insensitive to inversion or less sensitive to inversion than relational information (e.g., Bruyer & Coget, 1987; Cabeza & Kato, 2000; Freire, Lee, & Symons, 2000; Leder & Bruce, 1998; Searcy & Bartlett, 1996). Regardless of whether relational processing is the only process that is disrupted by face inversion (see Bukach, Le Grand, Kaiser, Bub, & Tanaka, 2008, for more recent evidence on this question), it is clear from a survey of these studies that the majority of research on relational processing was carried out in the context of face recognition, with little or no reference to relational processing in nonface objects. This sentiment is captured in Leder and Bruce's statement that despite evidence for inversion effects with other mono-oriented objects, "it seems justified to speak of a special face-inversion effect (FIE)" (Leder & Bruce, 2000, p. 513).

FACE CELLS IN NONHUMAN PRIMATES

Another origin of the domain-specific hypothesis for faces that is of particular importance is the discovery and continued testing of cells that respond preferentially to faces in nonhuman primates. Perhaps the most well-known version of the face cell is the popularized hypothetical "grandmother cell," which according to Barlow (1995) originated in an amusing story told by Jerry Lettvin while introducing neural coding of objects to his students in 1969. However, reality soon imitated fiction, and researchers began reporting face-selective cells in the macaque (for a more complete history of the term "grandmother cell," see Gross, 2002). These data have shaped theories of face recognition and guided the research on humans and nonhumans. In the following paragraphs, we will review several important historical papers studying face cells and their influence on the current study of face recognition.

Gross and colleagues (Gross, Bender, & Rocha-Miranda, 1969; Gross, Rocha-Miranda, & Bender, 1972) were the first to demonstrate that the inferotemporal cortex (IT) in the rhesus macaque responded to complex objects. Prior to Gross's studies, recording from single cells was concentrated primarily in earlier visual areas (e.g., V1 and V2) where very simple stimuli such as bars and spots of light were used to stimulate individual neurons. Gross's data were initially met with skepticism. One criticism included speculation that these cells actually responded to simpler stimuli that had not been properly tested. Continued testing by Gross and colleagues and other research groups, such as Tanaka and colleagues (see Tanaka, 1996, for a review), has shown that at least a portion of cells in IT do respond best to complex stimuli and that reducing these stimuli to simpler versions or parts leads to significant decreases in responding.

It is now widely accepted that IT and nearby brain areas in the temporal cortex are critically involved in object recognition, and that cells in these areas respond preferentially to complex stimuli, such as hands. Not surprisingly, faces were among some of the first complex stimuli used to test object selectivity in IT (Gross et al., 1972). However, a special significance for faces within the brain was not noted until a few years later, when several different groups of researchers reported finding larger numbers of neurons that seemed to respond preferentially to faces (Desimone, 1991). For example, Bruce, Desimone, and Gross (1981) tested cells in an area of the temporal cortex referred to as the superior temporal polysensory area (STP). A portion of the recorded cells (7 out of 59) responded preferentially to whole faces, and a number of the remaining cells (14 out of 59) responded preferentially to specific face features, suggesting this area of the temporal cortex contained "face cells."

In another landmark study, Perrett, Rolls, and Caan (1982) tested cells in the superior temporal sulcus (STS) for face specificity. This study is significant because Perrett et al. tested a larger pool of "face" cells and looked more closely at the characteristics of the neuronal activation. They selected a subgroup of cells that were more responsive to faces than to other tested stimuli (between 2 and 10 times as much). These "face" cells were further tested to determine if their response was sustained or whether the cells would habituate with sustained exposure. Most cells did not habituate but showed continued responding as long as the monkey was fixating the face. Only a small number of cells showed a declining response to sustained exposure. Visual selectivity was also tested using complex visual stimuli and simple geometric stimuli. Only a very small number of the face-selective cells showed any activation to these other stimuli. Perrett et al. then tested face-selective cells with arousing stimuli, to determine whether face activation might be due to the arousing nature of faces. They found that very few cells showed any significant response to the arousing stimuli (they tested both aversive and reward-related). Next, the researchers tested different image transformations such as 2-D representations, grayscale faces, and various face sizes and orientations (including inverted and profile). Cell responses were largely unaffected by these transformations, with the exception of the profile faces. Faces shown in profile exhibited a significant response decrement or a complete elimination of the response. Finally, Perrett et al. tested the response of the "face" cells to parts of faces. They found a variety of different responses. Some cells showed a response for eyes, others responded to the mouth or hair, and still others only responded to the whole face. Most cells exhibited a larger response to stimuli containing multiple face features than to stimuli containing a single face feature. These data provided additional evidence that the "face" cells in the temporal lobe were specific to faces and not merely responding to arousing stimuli.

Perrett et al. (1984) looked more closely at the organization of face cells in the temporal cortex, specifically the STS. Understanding the organization of these areas is particularly useful for making theoretical assumptions about the organization and role of these cells in face recognition. However, the single-cell recording technique does not easily lend itself to this type of inquiry. Perrett et al. looked for response consistency in nearby cells to discern whether the face cells were randomly dispersed among cells that responded to other visual stimuli, or whether cells were organized systematically. They found that vertical cortical minicolumns of face-selective cells in the STS were more likely to respond to similar head views when compared with deviations of 50 microns or more from the column. Horizontally, they were more likely to find cells that responded to similar classes of stimuli within 2 mm, a result that suggests that face cells are organized systematically in visual areas. Perrett et al. also tested numerous perceptual manipulations, such as contrast reversal and spatial frequency filtering. In their perceptual tests, Perrett et al. found that when the face was easy to perceive, the majority of the cells tested generally showed very little or no change in responding. If the faces were difficult or impossible to perceive, however, cell activity disappeared or was significantly reduced. The data published by Perrett et al. demonstrated that there is an underlying organization of face cells in the brain, and that these cells appear to respond specifically to the *perception* of a face.

These and the many other studies of "face" cells in monkeys provided the impetus for many researchers to look for similar face-specific neuronal activity and brain areas in humans. The existence of face cells also provided one of the most oft-cited arguments for the "special" nature of faces. Face cells are consistently found in the monkey higher-visual areas and give the impression that faces have a special status within visual areas in the primate brain. However, it is important to keep in mind that these studies do not give any indication as to how and when these face cells develop. Primates have a significant amount of social experience with faces, which could very likely lead to a large representation of those stimuli in visual areas. More recent data (Sigala & Logothetis, 2002) indicate that cell activity in the temporal cortex can be driven by experience with particular classes of stimuli and the relative importance of particular features during training. Thus, the prevalence of face cells and their characteristic activation may be directly related to a primate's face experience.

INFANT FACE PREFERENCE

Face perception has also been studied extensively in infants, and much of this research has centered on the question of whether infants perceive or attend to faces differently than other objects. Although it is clear that infants do not display the distinctive behavioral markers for face recognition shown by a mature visual system, a remarkable amount of evidence has accrued that suggests that from a very early age, faces capture the visual attention of infants. Several studies have found that infants display a visual preference for faces over other objects. Visual preference for faces refers to the finding that infants will spend more time looking or will orient to and track a moving target longer or farther when the target is a face compared to other visual stimuli. Earliest studies using schematic face stimuli found that by 2 months of age infants look longer at schematic faces than they look at a variety of nonface stimuli, including black and white concentric circles, newsprint, and solid circular patches of color (Fantz, 1963). Even more impressive was the finding by Goren, Sarty, and Wu (1975) that newborn infants as young as 9 minutes track a schematic face farther than a scrambled schematic face (see Figure 1.3). Since then, there have been many replications of infant face preference (e.g., Johnson, Dziurawiec, Ellis, & Morton, 1991; Maurer & Young, 1983; Morton & Johnson, 1991; Umiltá, Simion, & Valenza, 1996; Valenza, Simion, Cassia, & Umiltá, 1996), though some have failed to replicate this preference (e.g., Easterbrook, Kisilevsky, Hains, & Muir, 1999).

The interpretation of face preference in infants has been a subject of much debate. Fantz (1963) interpreted this phenomenon as evidence for an innate mechanism that facilitates responsiveness to socially relevant stimuli, rather than an innate face processor per se, leaving open the possibility that preference for socially relevant objects other than faces may exist. Goren et al. (1975) postulated a more restricted adaptive theory, interpreting infant preference for intact faces over scrambled faces as evidence for an evolved "unlearned" mechanism specialized for faces in particular. This interpretation became known as the "structural hypothesis" (Kleiner, 1987), as it emphasized the structural properties of faces as an object class. Perhaps the most influential structural theory of an innate face module is the CONSPEC/ CONLEARN theory (Morton & Johnson, 1991). According to Morton and Johnson, early infant preference reflects the operation of the CONSPEC process: an innate subcortical mechanism that contains structural information about faces and is responsible for orienting infants to any stimulus that matches the innately specified structure of a face. Based primarily on a replication and extension of Goren et al. (1975), they further suggested that the innately prespecified structural information includes information about the relative spatial location of elements within the face pattern (similar to the first-order configuration of Diamond & Carey, 1986). CONSPEC is responsible for face preference in infants from birth to about 2 months. After 2 months of age, a different process, CONLEARN, begins to operate. In contrast to CONSPEC, CONLEARN is not face specific but represents a general

Figure 1.3 Example of stimuli used by Goren et al. (1975) to test infant preference. Infants as young as 9 days old tracked the schematic face (first panel) farther than any of the other stimuli. Used with permission from C. C. Goren, M. Sarty, and P. Y. Wu, "Visual following and pattern discrimination of face-like stimuli by newborn infants," 1975, *Pediatrics* 56 (4), pp. 544–549, Copyright 1975 American Academy of Pediatrics.

mechanism that is necessary to learn the specific visual characteristics of faces, and relies upon the full primary cortical visual pathway. This two-stage theory of infant face recognition is widely accepted among theorists who favor the domain-specific view of face recognition.

In contrast to structural explanations of infant face preference, other researchers interpreted this phenomenon as reflecting general properties of the early visual system. According to this approach, an object will capture the attention of an infant if its visual properties are optimal for the visual capabilities of the infant's sensory system (Banks & Salapatek, 1981). This view is known as the "sensory hypothesis." Thus, infants show a preference for faces over scrambled faces or other objects not because faces are a special class of objects, but because their general physical properties render them highly visible to the infant visual system. For example, faces are symmetrical and contain high-contrast, low-frequency features that are ideally suited to the infant visual system (Kleiner & Banks, 1987). Kleiner and Banks further argued that rearranging facial features changes fundamental visual properties such as spatial frequency, and these properties might account for infant preference of intact faces over scrambled faces. One sensory hypothesis model that generated much debate is the linear systems model, proposed by Banks and colleagues (Banks & Ginsburg, 1985; Banks & Salapatek, 1981). This model first decomposes visual patterns by a Fourier transform to determine the spatial frequency, contrast, orientation, and phases of the constituent sine wave gratings that make up the pattern. The model then predicts infant preference based on the resulting amplitude spectrum (the amplitude and orientation of the component spatial frequencies) and the contrast sensitivity function of a particular age group. Other types of general visual properties, such as a preference for horizontal over vertical arrangements of elements (Farroni, Valenza, Simion, & Umiltá, 2000) and acuity differences between upper and lower visual fields (Simion, Cassia, Turati, & Valenza, 2001), have also been proposed to account for face preferences.

Another source of evidence supporting early specialization for faces is the finding that infants show visual preference for their own mother's face over the faces of strangers. The discrimination of mothers over strangers is particularly impressive given the poor visual acuity, contrast sensitivity, and spatial frequency range of the newborn (Nelson, 2001; see Figure 1.4).

Figure 1.4 Demonstration of the perception of a face to a newborn infant (left) relative to an adult (right). Used with permission from A. Slater and R. Kirby, "Innate and learned perceptual abilities in the newborn infant," 1998, *Experimental Brain Research, 123* (1), pp. 90–94, Copyright 1998 Springer Science + Business Media.

The first study to show that infants could discriminate mother from stranger on the basis of visual information alone was a study by Field, Cohen, Garcia, & Greenberg (1984). They showed that infants ranging from 22 to 93 hours looked longer at the live face of their own mother than that of a stranger. Moreover, after habituating to the mother's face over several trials, the neonates looked longer at a stranger's face than the mother's face at test. This novelty response is only possible if neonates can discriminate between the two faces. Bushnell, Sai, & Mullin (1989) later replicated this finding in an improved design that eliminated olfactory cues. Other researchers found that infants produce significantly more sucking responses to a video image of their mother over that of a stranger (Walton, Bower, & Bower, 1992), and further that infants suck more to view a previously trained face than an unfamiliar face, even when the trained face was shown in a different orientation, size, or in the photonegative (Walton, Armstrong, & Bower, 1997). This remarkable ability of infants to discriminate face stimuli within hours of birth is typically interpreted as supporting a domain-specific view of face recognition, though a comparison to discrimination ability for nonface objects is notably absent from these studies. This opinion is expressed by Slater & Kirby (1998), who state that mother preference is evidence for a "head start" for faces over other objects.

The debate over the interpretation of infant preference has generated a great deal of research, and these studies form an important part of the context from which PEN emerged. We wish to thank Franacesca Simion, in particular, who graciously appeared at one of our earliest PEN meetings to discuss issues related to infant preference. As with all great debates, the controversy regarding face preference in infants has not only resulted in improved paradigms with better control conditions, it has also broadened our knowledge of the visual system for both faces and objects and continues to generate new questions for future research.

BRAIN IMAGING

With the rapid advancement of brain imaging technology in the 1990s, new sources of evidence for cortical specialization emerged. Although there are now at least three face-selective regions identified (a region in the superior temporal sulcus (STS), a region in the occipital fusiform region (OFA), and one in the lateral fusiform gyrus (FFA), this discussion will focus on face selectivity in the FFA as this region has received the most attention. The first study to identify face-selective brain regions using functional imaging techniques was a Positron Emission Tomography (PET) study by Sergent, Ohta, and MacDonald (1992). PET measures brain activity indirectly by tracking regional blood flow through a radioactive tracer (^{15}oxygen) injected into the blood stream. In Sergent et al.'s groundbreaking study, participants performed several tasks with different objects while their cerebral blood flow was being measured, including discrimination of gratings, objects, face genders, and face identities. By subtracting activation patterns for face gender from activation patterns for face identity, Sergent et al. were able to localize regions that were involved in face recognition. These areas included the fusiform gyrus and anterior temporal cortex bilaterally, and the right parahippocampal gyrus and adjacent areas. In contrast, areas associated with object recognition (objects–gratings) included the left occipitotemporal cortex. Importantly, the ventromedial regions of the right hemisphere associated with face recognition were not involved in the object recognition task. Sergent et al. concluded that whereas the left hemisphere is involved in both face and object recognition, the additional perceptual processes necessary for face recognition are performed in the right fusiform gyrus (See also Haxby et al., 1994; Sergent et al., 1994).

Researchers soon turned to a new imaging technique, functional magnetic resonance imaging (fMRI), because of the many advantages that fMRI offers over PET. fMRI measures neural activity through the magnetic properties of naturally occurring oxygenated hemoglobin carried in the bloodstream. As a result, fMRI does not require injection of radioactive isotopes. Furthermore, fMRI has a greater spatial and temporal resolution than PET. Similar to Sergent's PET study described above, researchers localized regions selective for face processing by subtracting a variety of control conditions from face activation, including activation to scrambled faces, letter strings, textures, and objects (Clark et al., 1997; Kanwisher, Chun, McDermott, & Ledden, 1996; McCarthy, Puce, Gore, & Allison, 1997; Puce, Allison, Asgari, Gore, & McCarthy, 1996; Puce, Allison, Gore, & McCarthy, 1995). These studies consistently identified a small face-specific region in the lateral fusiform gyrus, particularly in the right hemisphere (though it has also been found bilaterally and in the left hemisphere). Although two other face-selective regions have also been identified (Halgren et al., 1999; Haxby et al., 1999; Kanwisher, McDermott, & Chun, 1997; Puce, Allison, Bentin, Gore, & McCarthy, 1998), the majority of research continues to focus on this region in the fusiform gyrus.

All of the studies listed above contributed to the localization of face processing to the fusiform gyrus, but it is the fMRI study by Kanwisher, McDermott, & Chun (1997) that has had the greatest impact in establishing the specificity of this region for faces. Kanwisher et al.'s study was influential for a number of reasons. First, the authors named this face-specific region in the lateral fusifom gyrus the "fusiform face area (FFA)," a label that is now universally used (see Figure 1.5). This study also established the technique of first localizing face-specific regions in individuals with a face localizer task before using other task manipulations to explore the function of the individually localized regions. The localizer task used by Kanwisher et al. involved a subtraction of activity to passively viewed common objects from activity to passively viewed faces (though a 1-back task in which subjects respond to an immediate repeat of a stimulus is now more commonly used as a localizer task). This localizer technique reduced the number of voxelwise statistical comparisons to be made in the subsequent tasks and thus significantly

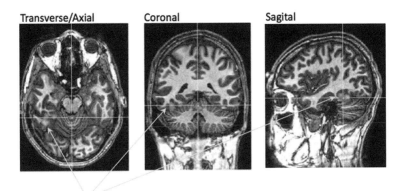

Right FFA

Figure 1.5 The right fusiform face area (FFA, in yellow-red), as defined in an individual subject using a typical functional localizer (contrast between perception of faces vs. objects) (See color Plate 2).

increased statistical power. It also avoided the problems associated with group analyses due to individual variability in the location of face-specific regions. Finally, this method allowed researchers to go beyond localization to focus their research on the function of the localized regions. Using this technique, researchers began to examine how factors such as inversion affected face processing in the FFA (Haxby et al., 1999; Kanwisher, Tong, & Nakayama, 1998). Researchers began to examine the effect of category membership, level of categorization, and expertise on nonface object processing in the FFA as well (Chao, Martin, & Haxby, 1999; Gauthier, Tarr, Anderson, Skudlarski, & Gore, 1999; Gauthier et al., 2000). These studies sparked a debate on the specificity of the FFA for face recognition that was aptly captured in the pair of 2000 *Nature Neuroscience* papers, one by Kanwisher (2000) and the other by Tarr and Gauthier (2000), and gave impetus to the formation of the Perceptual Expertise Network. Since these seminal papers, imaging technology and methodologies have continued to advance, opening exciting new ways to approach the face specificity debate. For example, Tsao, Freiwald, Tootell & Livingston (Tsao, Freiwald, Tootell, & Livingstone, 2006) combined fMRI and single-cell recordings in the macaque and found that the majority (97%) of cells in the face area as determined through fMRI were also face selective at the single-cell level. In humans, high-resolution fMRI techniques (now with voxel sizes as small as 1 X 1 X 1 mm) suggest a more heterogeneous picture of the FFA, with areas of high face selectivity interspersed with regions that are not face selective (Grill-Spector, Sayres, & Ress, 2006).

ELECTROPHYSIOLOGY

The localization of face-selective regions in the brain is apparent from the neurophysiology studies of both humans and nonhuman primates reviewed above. However, both brain imaging and lesion studies have very poor temporal resolution and thus are not well suited to examine the time course of cognitive processes. Event-related potentials (ERPs) have been explored as a way to look at face activation with greater temporal precision than is possible using brain imaging or lesion studies and also use a higher level of analysis than single-cell recordings (recording from large groups of cells, not just one at a time). ERPs average the time course of electrical activity measured on the scalp in response to an event across many trials. The resulting waveform produces ERP components (positive and negative deflections in electrical potential) that reflect underlying cognitive processes with millisecond resolution. Using a subtraction technique similar to that used in fMRI studies, differences in waveforms across conditions can be used to infer modulation of the underlying cognitive processes.

Jeffreys and colleagues published some of the earliest evidence of an ERP component that appeared to be specific to faces (Jeffreys, 1989, 1996; Jeffreys & Tukmachi, 1992; Jeffreys, Tukmachi, & Rockley, 1992). In particular, they looked at a component they called the "vertex positive potential" or VPP, and another potential called the "vertex negative potential" or VNP. They found that the VNP seemed to vary more than the VPP and was smaller in magnitude. Jeffreys and colleagues thus studied the VPP to a greater extent. The VPP is a relatively early component, with a latency of approximately 150 to 200 ms. Jeffreys (1989) tested many of the same parameters as those tested in single-cell recordings of the monkey brain, hoping to find parallels between these face-specific mechanisms. For example, he found that the VPP was not affected by changing the size or the retinal placement of the face image, as long as the clarity of the image was not compromised. The magnitude of the VPP is smaller, however, if the face stimulus is reduced in size to the point where it is difficult to identify it as a face. Other types of changes did affect the latency of the VPP and in many cases the amplitude as well. For example, showing the face against a patterned background, showing the face to a single eye rather than both eyes, and showing the face in negative contrast (a photographic negative) all resulted in an increase in the latency of the VPP and in some instances also resulted in a reduction in amplitude. Jeffreys also found an increase in latency for rotating or inverting the face and for the removal of various face parts, such as the nose or mouth. Jeffreys' results correspond to some of the data recorded from single cells in the monkey temporal cortex (Perrett, Mistlin, & Chitty, 1987), which provided some evidence that ERPs could bridge the gap between studies of faces using neurophysiology in the monkey and human studies of faces. Additional studies by Jeffreys and colleagues (Jeffreys, 1996; Jeffreys & Tukmachi, 1992; Jeffreys et al., 1992) further explored the properties that affect the VPP, showing that the VPP responds to a wide variety of facelike stimuli, including faces of animals, and that the amplitude is greatest for faces presented at fixation, regardless of stimulus size.

Several years after Jeffreys first published his account of the VPP (Jeffreys, 1989), Bentin, Allison, Puce, Perez, and McCarthy (1996) published evidence for a negative component approximately 170 ms after stimulus presentation. This component, called the N170, was present for faces, but not for cars or butterflies, suggesting that it was specific to faces. They also found a positive component approximately 190 ms after stimulus presentation, which Bentin et al. propose may be similar to the VPP reported by Jeffreys. The N170, however, exhibited substantial differences from the VPP. For example, the VPP responded to animal faces as well as human faces whereas Bentin et al. show that the N170 does not show activation for animal faces (but see Carmel & Bentin, 2002). Due to the more face-specific responding of the N170, the N170 continues to be explored extensively, while the VPP is not. Bentin et al. also explored the effects of inversion on the N170. They compared faces and inverted faces to cars, inverted cars, and butterflies. They found an N170 for both faces and inverted faces, indicating that the N170 may not reflect face recognition processes (which are impaired when a face is inverted). From this evidence, Bentin et al. concluded that the N170 more likely reflects the categorization of a stimulus as a face. The N170 for inverted faces did have a slightly longer latency than upright faces, perhaps reflecting that the categorization mechanism was at least somewhat affected by inversion.

Bentin et al. (1996) also tested how face parts would affect activity of the N170 compared to an intact face. They found longer latencies and smaller amplitude for the N170 when presenting just the mouth or nose compared to the whole face. In contrast, the N170 was actually larger for isolated eyes compared to the whole face. These results raised the possibility that the N170 may reflect mechanisms that are specialized for detecting eyes rather than whole faces. In a final test, Bentin et al. looked at the N170 response to faces in which the internal parts were misplaced (i.e., not in the expected configuration). This test would indicate whether the holistic integrity of the face is required for activation of the N170, or if the presence of facial features alone (in particular the eyes) is enough for activation. They found that the faces with misplaced parts elicited a substantial N170, similar in magnitude to the N170 for eyes alone.

Eimer (1998) further explored whether the N170 reflected an eye processor or if this component is specialized for detecting face parts. To do this, Eimer tested participants using faces, houses, and faces in which the eye region had been removed. He found a significant difference between houses and faces, regardless of whether or not the faces included the eye region. A comparison of the faces with and without the eye regions showed that the amplitude of the N170 was nearly identical. The only difference between the two stimulus types was that faces without eyes elicited an N170 with a slightly longer latency than faces with eyes. These results indicated that the N170 was not specific to detecting and processing eyes alone and instead was more generally for detection of faces.

Eimer and colleagues went on to test the N170 in more detail in subsequent papers (Eimer, 2000a, 2000b; Eimer & McCarthy, 1999). For example, Eimer and McCarthy (1999) found that the N170 was significantly impaired in prosopagnosic individuals, compared to individuals with no face recognition deficit. This finding provides additional evidence that the N170 reflects in some way the accurate identification and recognition of faces. Eimer (2000a) compared N170 activation for familiar versus unfamiliar faces. They found no difference between familiar and unfamiliar faces, indicating that the N170 does not reflect processing specific to the identity of the face. Rather, this component more likely reflects structural encoding of the face. Finally, Eimer (Eimer, 2000b) compared N170 activation for frontal face views, profile views, views of the back of the head including the cheek, and back views of the head. Eimer found that the amplitude of the N170 was significantly smaller for the back view and the back view showing cheek compared to the profile and frontal views. He also compared intact face stimuli to faces in which the internal or external features were eliminated. Eimer again found that the N170 was significantly smaller for the stimuli in which either the external or internal features had been eliminated. These data support Eimer's previous findings indicating that the N170 reflected processing the structure of the whole face, not just specific internal features such as eyes.

These ERP studies and others provided additional evidence that faces are processed differently from other object categories. Even though it is likely that several cognitive processes necessary for face recognition may be reflected in the N170 (including face detection and structural encoding), the mechanism does appear to be specific to the type of processing required for face recognition and not for the recognition of other categories, such as butterflies. Thus, the N170 data are another piece of evidence used to support the idea that faces are indeed "special."

Taking the study of event-related potentials directly into the human brain, McCarthy and colleagues published a unique series of studies in which evoked potentials were recorded directly from the electrodes implanted into the brains of human participants diagnosed with epilepsy. They found results that were quite similar to those published using scalp-recorded electrodes but were able to test a wide variety of comparisons while recording directly from visual areas, allowing them to determine more precisely where in the visual system these signals originated.

In the first of this series of papers, Allison, Puce, Spencer, and McCarthy (1999) tested participants with a variety of visual stimuli, including unfamiliar faces, flowers, cars, and butterflies. They found an ERP that appeared to be face specific, the N200 (negative waveform approximately 200 ms after stimulus presentation), which was recorded from electrodes placed ventrally in the occipitotemporal cortex. The authors proposed that the N200 reflected an early stage of perceptual processing.

In a subsequent paper, McCarthy, Puce, Belger, and Allison (1999) tested the robustness and specificity of the N200 face response. McCarthy et al. compared normal color face images to face images that were grayscale, blurred, and line drawings. They found that the responses to these different face types did not significantly differ. The N200 was also relatively unaffected by variations in size:

regardless of the size of the face image, the N200 was larger for faces than for nonface stimuli (gratings in this case), and although large faces evoked a larger N200 than small faces, these differences were fairly small. Finally, McCarthy et al. found that both the amplitude and latency of the N200 to human faces differed significantly from responses to dog and cat faces. McCarthy et al. argued these data support the idea that these areas are most responsive to human faces, regardless of changes made to the face stimuli, and that responding to other types of stimuli was significantly different.

McCarthy et al. (1999) also tested whether the face-specific N200 would demonstrate sensitivity to holistic versus parts processing for faces. The N200 showed only very small differences for both amplitude and latency of the response to faces that were upright (holistic processing) and inverted (part processing). However, they did find hemisphere differences between upright and inverted faces; the right hemisphere appeared to be efficient at processing upright faces holistically, and the left hemisphere appeared to be more efficient at the inverted faces. In a similar vein, McCarthy et al. also compared N200 responses for whole faces compared to face parts. They found that although the N200 responses to face parts elicited a smaller amplitude than to whole faces, it was still significantly greater than the amplitude to other objects. These results suggest that the N200 does show some sensitivity to holistic versus part processing, but these differences are fairly small and hemispheric in nature.

In the third installment of the series of papers, Puce, Allison, and McCarthy (1999) tested whether face activation of the N200 was due to emotional arousal by comparing faces to erotic and aversive images. They found that activation to faces was significantly greater than to the erotic and aversive images, indicating that N200 activation was not due to emotional valence. Next, Puce et al. tested familiar and unfamiliar faces by comparing famous faces to unknown faces and found no significant differences. Finally, they tested whether semantic priming would affect the N200 by comparing conditions in which a name preceding an image of a famous face matched the face (priming condition) or did not match the face (nonpriming condition). They found no significant difference between the priming and the non-priming conditions. The results of this study indicate that the N200 is unaffected by top-down processes such as familiarity and priming, and that it reflects recognition that a stimulus is a face rather than face identity.

The electrophysiological studies reviewed above, recorded both directly from the brain and from the scalp, added another dimension to the study of face recognition and the "special" status of faces relative to other objects. Evidence for face-specific ERP components argued for the uniqueness of faces in the visual system and provided information regarding timing of face-specific processes. These studies also provided a new way to examine *how* faces become special and thus inspired a number of more recent studies that have begun to uncover factors that modulate the amplitude or latency of face-specific components such as the N170 (Rossion, Gauthier, Goffaux, Tarr, & Crommelinck, 2002; Tanaka & Curran, 2001). Recent ERP studies have also examined whether expertise for nonface objects recruits face-specific processes by examining evidence for interference in the N170 component (Gauthier, Curran, Curby, & Collins, 2003; Rossion, Collins, Goffaux, & Curran, 2007). These studies show that the N170 is sensitive to expertise level, and the results have been interpreted as evidence that expertise for faces and nonface objects rely on similar perceptual mechanisms.

CONCLUSION

It is clear from this brief survey of research leading up to the formation of PEN that there is ample evidence for the specialization of cognitive and neural mechanisms for face recognition. It is also evident that a vigorous debate had begun to form over the *explanation* of specialization for faces. On one side of the debate, the evidence was interpreted as support for a domain-specific, modular system dedicated to face recognition. This approach produced models of face recognition independent of object recognition, and tended to focus on the structural properties of faces as an object class and their biological and social relevance, as well as the role of innately prespecified mechanisms. On the other side of the debate, researchers began to question *how* faces come to be specialized, and whether mechanisms of specialization for faces could also explain specialization for nonface objects and general principles of neural specialization. This approach emphasized the processes underlying face specialization and the role of experience.

In the late 1990s, researchers began to focus more on the role of expertise as one of the potential factors underlying specialization for visual recognition. In a series of foundation papers, Tarr, Gauthier, and colleagues trained individuals to become experts with a class of homogenous novel objects known as Greebles (see Figure 1.6). They found a remarkable similarity in the behavioral and neural mechanisms underlying expert Greeble recognition to those underlying face recognition (Gauthier & Tarr, 1997; Gauthier, Williams, Tarr, & Tanaka, 1998). Following these publications, PEN formed to explore the possibility that face specificity was one example of a more general type of neural specialization, and to explore more general issues related to category specialization and cortical plasticity.

There are many benefits of moving beyond a face recognition system and the question of whether faces are special (see Bukach, Gauthier, & Tarr, 2006, for a detailed discussion). One benefit is that the knowledge derived from the study of face specificity can be generalized to the object recognition system as a whole. A second benefit is that factors underlying cortical specialization can be determined. By using nonface objects to modulate neural activity and behavioral effects, we can determine the relationship between neural biases, task demands, and experience in both face and object recognition. Finally, by studying both real-world and lab-trained experts, we can plot the trajectory of neural and behavioral changes that underlie the development of specialization within the object recognition system, and beyond.

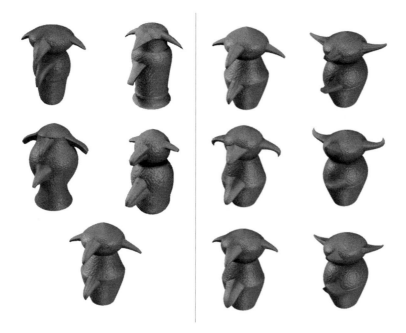

Figure 1.6 Example of Greebles used in studies of perceptual expertise training (e.g., Gauthier & Tarr, 1997). On the left are samples of Greebles from five different families. On the right are samples of six individuals from one family.

REFERENCES

Allison, T., Puce, A., Spencer, D. D., & McCarthy, G. (1999). Electrophysiological studies of human face perception. I: Potentials generated in occipitotemporal cortex by face and non-face stimuli. *Cerebral Cortex, 9*(5), 415–430.

Banks, M. S., & Ginsburg, A. P. (1985). Infant visual preferences: a review and new theoretical treatment. *Advances in Child Development and Behavior, 19*, 207–246.

Banks, M. S., & Salapatek, P. (1981). Infant pattern vision: A new approach based on the contrast sensitivity function. *Journal of Experimental Child Psychology, 31*(1), 1–45.

Barlow, H. (1995). The neuron doctrine in perception. In M. S. Gazzaniga (Ed.), *The cognitive neurosciences.* (pp. 415–435). Cambridge, MA: The MIT Press.

Bentin, S., Allison, T., Puce, A., Perez, E., & McCarthy, G. (1996). Electrophysiological studies of face perception in humans. *Journal of Cognitive Neuroscience, 8*(6), 15.

Benton, A. L., Sivan, A. B., Hamsher, K. D., Varney, N. R., & Spreen, O. (1994). *Contributions to neuropsychological assessment.* New York: Oxford University Press.

Blanc-Garin, J. (1984). Perception des visages et reconnaissance de la physionomie dans l'agnosie des visages. *L'année Psychologique, 84*(4), 573–598.

Bornstein, B. (1963). Prosopagnosia. In L. Halpern (Ed.), *Problems of dynamic neurology* (pp. 283–318). Jerusalem, Israel: Hebrew University Hadassah Medical School.

Bornstein, B., Sroka, H., & Munitz, H. (1969). Prosopagnosia with animal face agnosia. *Cortex, 5*(2), 164–169.

Bradshaw, J. L., & Wallace, G. (1971). Models for the processing and identification of faces. *Perception & Psychophysics, 9*(5), 443–448.

Bruce, C., Desimone, R., & Gross, C. G. (1981). Visual properties of neurons in a polysensory area in superior temporal sulcus of the macaque. *Journal of Neurophysiology, 46*(2), 369–384.

Bruce, V., & Young, A. (1986). Understanding face recognition. *British Journal of Psychology, 77*(3), 305–327.

Bruyer, R., & Coget, M. C. (1987). Features of laterally displayed faces: Saliency or top-down processing? *Acta Psychologica, 66*(2), 103–114.

Bruyer, R., Laterre, C., Seron, X., Feyereisen, P., Strypstein, E., Pierrard, E., et al. (1983). A case of prosopagnosia with some preserved covert remembrance of familiar faces. *Brain and Cognition, 2*(3), 257–284.

Bukach, C. M., Bub, D. N., Gauthier, I., & Tarr, M. J. (2006). Perceptual expertise effects are NOT all or none: Spatially limited perceptual expertise for faces in a case of prosopagnosia. *Journal of Cognitive Neuroscience, 18*, 48–63.

Bukach, C. M., Gauthier, I., & Tarr, M. J. (2006). Beyond faces and modularity: the power of an expertise framework. *Trends in Cognitive Sciences, 10*, 159–166.

Bukach, C. M., Le Grand, R., Kaiser, M., Bub, D. N., & Tanaka, J. W. (2008). Preservation of mouth region processing in two cases of prosopagnosia. *Journal of Neuropsychology, 2*, 227–244.

Burton, A. M., Bruce, V., & Johnston, R. A. (1990). Understanding face recognition with an interactive activation model. *British Journal of Psychology, 81 (Pt. 3)*, 361–380.

Bushnell, I. W., Sai, F., & Mullin, J. T. (1989). Neonatal recognition of the mother's face. *British Journal of Developmental Psychology, 7*(1), 3–15.

Cabeza, R., & Kato, T. (2000). Features are also important: Contributions of featural and configural processing to face recognition. *Psychological Science, 11*(5), 429–433.

Carey, S., & Diamond, R. (1977). From piecemeal to configurational representation of faces. *Science, 195*(4275), 312–314.

Carmel, D., & Bentin, S. (2002). Domain specificity versus expertise: factors influencing distinct processing of faces. *Cognition, 83*(1), 1–29.

Chao, L. L., Martin, A., & Haxby, J. V. (1999). Are face-responsive regions selective only for faces? *Neuroreport, 10*(14), 2945–2950.

Clark, V. P., Parasuraman, R., Keil, K., Kulansky, R., Fannon, S., Maisog, J. M., et al. (1997). Selective attention to face identity and color studied with fMRI. *Human Brain Mapping, 5*(4), 293–297.

Damasio, A. R., Tranel, D., & Damasio, H. (1990). Face agnosia and the neural substrates of memory. *Annual Review Neuroscience, 13*, 89–109.

Damasio, A. R., Damasio, H., & Van Hoesen, G. W. (1982). Prosopagnosia: Anatomical basis and behavioral mechanisms. *Neurology, 32*, 331–341.

De Renzi, E. (1986a). Current issues on prosopagnosia. In H. Ellis, M. A. Jeeves, F. Newcombe, & A. Young (Eds.), *Aspects of face processing* (pp. 243–253). Boston: Martinus Nijhoff Publishers.

De Renzi, E. (1986b). Prosopagnosia in two patients with CT scan evidence of damage confined to the right hemisphere. *Neuropsychologia, 24*(3), 385–389.

Desimone, R. (1991). Face-selective cells in the temporal cortex of monkeys. *Journal of Cognitive Neuroscience, 3*(1), 1–8.

Diamond, R., & Carey, S. (1986). Why faces are and are not special: An effect of expertise. *Journal of Experimental Psychology: General, 115*(2), 107–117.

Duchaine, B. C., Dingle, K., Butterworth, E., & Nakayama, K. (2004). Normal greeble learning in a severe case of developmental prosopagnosia. *Neuron, 43*(4), 469–473.

Duchaine, B. C., Yovel, G., Butterworth, E. J., & Nakayama, K. (2006). Prosopagnosia as an impairment to face-specific mechanisms: Elimination of the alternative hypotheses in a developmental case. *Cognitive Neuropsychology, 23*(5), 714–747.

Easterbrook, M. A., Kisilevsky, B. S., Hains, S. M. J., & Muir, D. W. (1999). Faceness or complexity: Evidence from newborn visual tracking of facelike stimuli. *Infant Behavior & Development, 22*(1), 17–35.

Eimer, M. (1998). Does the face-specific N170 component reflect the activity of a specialized eye processor? *Neuroreport: An International Journal for the Rapid Communication of Research in Neuroscience, 9*(13), 2945–2948.

Eimer, M. (2000a). Event-related brain potentials distinguish processing stages involved in face perception and recognition. *Clinical Neurophysiology, 111*(4), 694–705.

Eimer, M. (2000b). The face-specific N170 component reflects late stages in the structural encoding of faces. *Neuroreport: For Rapid Communication of Neuroscience Research, 11*(10), 2319–2324.

Eimer, M., & McCarthy, R. A. (1999). Prosopagnosia and structural encoding of faces: evidence from event-related potentials. *Neuroreport, 10*(2), 255–259.

Ellis, H. D. (1996). Bodamer on prosopagnosia. In C. Code, C.-W. Wallesch, Y. Joanette, & A. R. Lecours (Eds.), *Classic cases in neuropsychology* (pp. 69–74). Hove, England: Psychology/Erlbaum (UK) Taylor & Francis Ltd.

Fantz, R. L. (1963). Pattern vision in newborn infants. *Science, 140*(3564), 296–297.

Farah, M., Levinson, K. L., & Klein, K. L. (1995). Face perception and within-category discrimination in prosopagnosia. *Neuropsychologia, 33*(6), 661–674.

Farroni, T., Valenza, E., Simion, F., & Umiltà, C. (2000). Configural processing at birth: Evidence for perceptual organisation. *Perception, 29*(3), 355–372.

Field, T. M., Cohen, D., Garcia, R., & Greenberg, R. (1984). Mother-stranger face discrimination by the newborn. *Infant Behavior & Development, 7*(1), 19–25.

Freire, A., Lee, K., & Symons, L. A. (2000). The face-inversion effect as a deficit in the encoding of configural information: Direct evidence. *Perception, 29*(2), 159–170.

Gauthier, I., Behrmann, M., & Tarr, M. J. (1999). Can face recognition really be dissociated from object recognition? *Journal of Cognitive Neuroscience, 11*(4), 349–370.

Gauthier, I., Curran, T., Curby, K. M., & Collins, D. (2003). Perceptual interference supports a non-modular account of face processing. *Nature Neuroscience, 6*(4), 428–432.

Gauthier, I., & Tarr, M. J. (1997). Becoming a "greeble" expert: Exploring mechanisms for face recognition. *Vision Research, 37*(12), 1673–1682.

Gauthier, I., Tarr, M. J., Anderson, A. W., Skudlarski, P., & Gore, J. C. (1999). Activation of the middle fusiform "face area" increases with expertise in recognizing novel objects. *Nature Neuroscience, 2*(6), 568–573.

Gauthier, I., Tarr, M. J., Moylan, J., Skudlarski, P., Gore, J. C., & Anderson, A. W. (2000). The fusiform "face area" is part of a network that processes faces at the individual level. *Journal of Cognitive Neuroscience, 12*(3), 495–504.

Gauthier, I., Williams, P., Tarr, M. J., & Tanaka, J. (1998). Training "greeble" experts: A framework for studying expert object recognition processes. *Vision Research, 38*(15–16), 2401–2428.

Gloning, K., & Quatember, R. (1966). Methodischer Beitrag zur Untersuchung der Prosopagnoise. *Neuropsychologia, 4*, 133–141.

Goldstein, A., & Chance, J. (1981). Laboratory studies of face recognition. In G. Davies, H. Ellis, & J. Shephard (Eds.), *Perceiving and remembering faces* (pp. 81–104). New York: Academic Press.

Goren, C. C., Sarty, M., & Wu, P. Y. (1975). Visual following and pattern discrimination of face-like stimuli by newborn infants. *Pediatrics, 56*(4), 544–549.

Grill-Spector, K., Sayres, R., & Ress, D. (2006). High-resolution imaging reveals highly selective nonface clusters in the fusiform face area. *Nature Neuroscience, 9*(9), 1177–1185.

Gross, C. G. (2002). Geneology of the "Grandmother Cell." *The Neuroscientist, 8*, 512–518.

Gross, C. G., Bender, D. B., & Rocha-Miranda, C. E. (1969). Visual receptive fields of neurons in inferotemporal cortex of the monkey. *Science, 166*(3910), 1303–1306.

Gross, C. G., Rocha-Miranda, C. E., & Bender, D. B. (1972). Visual properties of neurons in inferotemporal cortex of the macaque. *Journal of Neurophysiology, 35*(1), 96–111.

Haig, N. D. (1984). The effect of feature displacement on face recognition. *Perception, 13*(5), 505–512.

Halgren, E., Dale, A. M., Sereno, M. I., Tootell, R. B. H., Marinkovic, K., & Rosen, B. R. (1999). Location of human face-selective cortex with respect to retinotopic areas. *Human Brain Mapping, 7*(1), 29–37.

Haxby, J. V., Horwitz, B., Ungerleider, L. G., Maisog, J. M., Pietrini, P., & Grady, C. L. (1994). The functional organization of human extrastriate cortex: A PET-rCBF study of selective attention to faces and locations. *Journal of Neuroscience, 14*(11, Pt. 1), 6336–6353.

Haxby, J. V., Ungerleider, L. G., Clark, V. P., Schouten, J. L., Hoffman, E. A., & Martin, A. (1999). The effect of face inversion on activity in human neural systems for face and object perception. *Neuron, 22*, 189–199.

Hecaen, H. (1981). The neuropsychology of face recognition. In G. Davies, H. Ellis, & J. Shephard (Eds.), *Perceiving and remembering faces* (pp. 39–54). New York: Academic Press.

Hole, G. J. (1994). Configurational factors in the perception of unfamiliar faces. *Perception, 23*(1), 65–74.

Homa, D., Haver, B., & Schwartz, T. (1976). Perceptibility of schematic face stimuli: Evidence for a perceptual Gestalt. *Memory & Cognition, 4*(2), 176–185.

Jeffreys, D. A. (1989). A face-responsive potential recorded from the human scalp. *Experimental Brain Research, 78*(1), 193–202.

Jeffreys, D. A. (1996). Evoked potential studies of face and object processing. *Visual Cognition, 3*, 1–38.

Jeffreys, D. A., & Tukmachi, E. S. (1992). The vertex-positive scalp potential evoked by faces and by objects. *Experimental Brain Research, 91*(2), 340–350.

Jeffreys, D. A., Tukmachi, E. S., & Rockley, G. (1992). Evoked potential evidence for human brain mechanisms that respond to single, fixated faces. *Experimental Brain Research, 91*(2), 351–362.

Johnson, M. H., Dziurawiec, S., Ellis, H., & Morton, J. (1991). Newborns' preferential tracking of face-like stimuli and its subsequent decline. *Cognition, 40*(1), 1–19.

Kanwisher, N. (2000). Domain specificity in face perception. *Nature Neuroscience, 3*(8), 759–763.

Kanwisher, N., Chun, M. M., McDermott, J., & Ledden, P. J. (1996). Functional imaging of human visual recognition. *Cognitive Brain Research, 5*(1), 55–67.

Kanwisher, N., McDermott, J., & Chun, M. M. (1997). The fusiform face area: A module in human extrastriate cortex specialized for face perception. *Journal of Neuroscience, 17*(11), 4302–4311.

Kanwisher, N., Tong, F., & Nakayama, K. (1998). The effect of face inversion on the human fusiform face area. *Cognition, 68*(1), B1–B11.

Kleiner, K. A. (1987). Amplitude and phase spectra as indices of infants' pattern preferences. *Infant Behavior & Development, 10*(1), 49–59.

Kleiner, K. A., & Banks, M. S. (1987). Stimulus energy does not account for 2-month-olds' face preferences. *Journal of Experimental Psychology: Human Perception and Performance, 13*(4), 594–600.

Kohler, W. (1940). *Dynamics in psychology*. Oxford, England: Liveright.

Leder, H., & Bruce, V. (1998). Local and relational aspects of face distinctiveness. *Quarterly Journal of Experimental Psychology: Human Experimental Psychology, 51A*(3), 449–473.

Leder, H., & Bruce, V. (2000). When inverted faces are recognized: The role of configural information in face recognition. *Quarterly Journal of Experimental Psychology: Human Experimental Psychology, 53A*(2), 513–536.

Lhermitte, F., & Pillon, B. (1975). La prosopagnosie, role de l'hemisphere droit dans la perception visuelle (A propos d'un cas consecutif a une lobectomie occipitale droite). *Revue Neurologique, 131*, 791–812.

Matthews, M. L. (1978). Discrimination of Identikit constructions of faces: Evidence for a dual processing strategy. *Perception & Psychophysics, 23*(2), 153–161.

Maurer, D., Le Grand, R., & Mondloch, C. J. (2002). The many faces of configural processing. *Trends in Cognitive Sciences, 6*(6), 255–260.

Maurer, D., & Young, R. E. (1983). Newborn's following of natural and distorted arrangements of facial features. *Infant Behavior and Development, 6*, 127–131.

McCarthy, G., Puce, A., Belger, A., & Allison, T. (1999). Electrophysiological studies of human face perception. II: Response properties of face-specific potentials generated in occipitotemporal cortex. *Cerebral Cortex, 9*(5), 431–444.

McCarthy, G., Puce, A., Gore, J. C., & Allison, T. (1997). Face-specific processing in the human fusiform gyrus. *Journal of Cognitive Neuroscience, 9*(5), 605–610.

McNeil, J. E., & Warrington, E. K. (1993). Prosopagnosia: A face-specific disorder. *Quarterly Journal of Experimental Psychology: Human Experimental Psychology, 46*(1), 1–10.

Morton, J., & Johnson, M. H. (1991). CONSPEC and CONLERN: A two-process theory of infant face recognition. *Psychological Review, 98*(2), 164–181.

Moscovitch, M., Winocur, G., & Behrmann, M. (1997). What is special about face recognition? Nineteen experiments on a person with visual object agnosia and dyslexia but normal face recognition. *Journal of Cognitive Neuroscience, 9*(5), 555–604.

Nelson, C. A. (2001). The development and neural bases of face recognition. *Infant and Child Development, 10*(1), 3–18.

Perrett, D. I., Mistlin, A. J., & Chitty, A. J. (1987). Visual neurones responsive to faces. *Trends in Neurosciences, 10*(9), 358–364.

Perrett, D. I., Rolls, E. T., & Caan, W. (1982). Visual neurones responsive to faces in the monkey temporal cortex. *Experimental Brain Research, 47*(3), 329–342.

Perrett, D. I., Smith, P. A., Potter, D. D., Mistlin, A. J., Head, A. S., Milner, A. D., et al. (1984). Neurones responsive to faces in the temporal cortex: studies of functional organization, sensitivity to identity and relation to perception. *Human Neurobiology, 3*(4), 197–208.

Puce, A., Allison, T., Asgari, M., Gore, J. C., & McCarthy, G. (1996). Differential sensitivity of human visual cortex to faces, letterstrings, and textures: A functional magnetic resonance imaging study. *Journal of Neuroscience, 16*(16), 5205–5215.

Puce, A., Allison, T., Bentin, S., Gore, J. C., & McCarthy, G. (1998). Temporal cortex activation in humans viewing eye and mouth movements. *Journal of Neuroscience, 18*(6), 2188–2199.

Puce, A., Allison, T., Gore, J. C., & McCarthy, G. (1995). Face-sensitive regions in human extrastriate cortex studied by functional MRI. *Journal of Neurophysiology, 74*(3), 1192–1199.

Puce, A., Allison, T., & McCarthy, G. (1999). Electrophysiological studies of human face perception. III: Effects of top-down processing on face-specific potentials. *Cerebral Cortex, 9*(5), 445–458.

Rhodes, G., Brake, S., & Atkinson, A. P. (1993). What's lost in inverted faces? *Cognition, 47*(1), 25–57.

Rhodes, G., Brake, S., Taylor, K., & Tan, S. (1989). Expertise and configural coding in face recognition. *British Journal of Psychology, 80*(3), 313–331.

Rossion, B., Collins, D., Goffaux, V., & Curran, T. (2007). Long-term expertise with artificial objects increases visual competition with early face categorization processes. *Journal of Cognitive Neuroscience, 19*(3), 543–555.

Rossion, B., Gauthier, I., Goffaux, V., Tarr, M. J., & Crommelinck, M. (2002). Expertise training with novel objects leads to left-lateralized facelike electrophysiological responses. *Psychological Science, 13*(3), 250–257.

Scapinello, K. F., & Yarmey, A. D. (1970). The role of familiarity and orientation in immediate and delayed recognition of pictorial stimuli. *Psychonomic Science, 21*(6), 329–331.

Schultz, R. T. (2005). Developmental deficits in social perception in autism: the role of the amygdala and fusiform face area. *International Journal of Developmental Neuroscience, 23*, 125–141.

Searcy, J. H., & Bartlett, J. C. (1996). Inversion and processing of component and spatial-relational information in faces. *Journal of Experimental Psychology: Human Perception and Performance, 27*, 904–915.

Sergent, J. (1984). An investigation into component and configural processes underlying face perception. *British Journal of Psychology, 75*(2), 221–242.

Sergent, J., Ohta, S., & MacDonald, B. (1992). Functional neuroanatomy of face and object processing. A positron emission tomography study. *Brain, 115 (Pt. 1)*, 15–36.

Sergent, J., Ohta, S., MacDonald, B., Zuck, E., Bruce, V., & Humphreys, G. W. (1994). Segregated processing of facial identity and emotion in the human brain: A PET study. In *Object and face recognition. Special issue of visual cognition, Vol. 1, No. 2/3.* (pp. 349–369). Hillsdale, NJ: Lawrence Erlbaum Associates, Inc.

Sigala, N., & Logothetis, N. K. (2002). Visual categorization shapes feature selectivity in the primate temporal cortex. *Nature, 415*(6869), 318–320.

Simion, F., Cassia, V. M., Turati, C., & Valenza, E. (2001). The origins of face perception: Specific versus non-specific mechanisms. *Infant and Child Development, 10*(1), 59–65.

Slater, A., & Kirby, R. (1998). Innate and learned perceptual abilities in the newborn infant. *Experimental Brain Research, 123*(1–2), 90–94.

Smith, E. E., & Nielsen, G. D. (1970). Representations and retrieval processes in short-term memory: Recognition and recall of faces. *Journal of Experimental Psychology, 85*(3), 397–405.

Tanaka, K. (1996). Inferotemporal cortex and object vision. *Annual Review of Neuroscience, 19*, 109–139.

Tanaka, J. W., & Curran, T. (2001). A neural basis for expert object recognition. *Psychological Science, 12*(1), 43–47.

Tanaka, J. W., & Farah, M. J. (1993). Parts and wholes in face recognition. *Quarterly Journal of Experimental Psychology A, 46*(2), 225–245.

Tanaka, J. W., & Sengco, J. A. (1997). Features and their configuration in face recognition. *Memory and Cognition, 25*(5), 583–592.

Tarr, M. J., & Gauthier, I. (2000). FFA: A flexible fusiform area for subordinate-level visual processing automatized by expertise. *Nature Neuroscience, 3*(8), 764–769.

Thompson, P. (1980). Margaret Thatcher: A new illusion. *Perception, 9*(4), 483–484.

Tsao, D. Y., Freiwald, W. A., Tootell, R. B. H., & Livingstone, M. S. (2006). A cortical region consisting entirely of face-selective cells. *Science, 311*(5761), 670–674.

Tversky, A., & Krantz, D. H. (1969). Similarity of schematic faces: A test of interdimensional additivity. *Perception & Psychophysics, 5*(2), 124–128.

Umiltá, C., Simion, F., & Valenza, E. (1996). Newborn's preference for faces. *European Psychologist, 1*(3), 200–205.

Valentine, T., & Bruce, V. (1986). The effect of race, inversion and encoding activity upon face recognition. *Acta Psychologica, 61*(3), 259–273.

Valenza, E., Simion, F., Cassia, V. M., & Umiltá, C. (1996). Face preference at birth. *Journal of Experimental Psychology: Human Perception and Performance, 22*(4), 892–903.

Walton, G. E., Armstrong, E. S., & Bower, T. G. R. (1997). Faces as forms in the world of the newborn. *Infant Behavior & Development, 20*(4), 537–543.

Walton, G. E., Bower, N. J., & Bower, T. G. (1992). Recognition of familiar faces by newborns. *Infant Behavior & Development, 15*(2), 265–269.

Yarmey, A. D. (1971). Recognition memory for familiar "public" faces: Effects of orientation and delay. *Psychonomic Science, 24*(6), 286–288.

Yin, R. K. (1969). Looking at upside-down faces. *Journal of Experimental Psychology, 81*, 141–145.

Young, A. W., Hellawell, D., & Hay, D. C. (1987). Configurational information in face perception. *Perception, 16*(6), 747–759.

2

Objects of Expertise

David L. Sheinberg and Michael J. Tarr

> *. . . a set of stimuli composed of three rounded parts—a base, body, and head—one on top of the other, with protrusions that are readily labeled penis, nose, and ears. Unfortunately, these rounded, bilaterally symmetrical creatures closely resemble humanoid characters, such as the Yoda (in Return of the Jedi).*
> —Biederman & Kalocsai (1997).

Why is face recognition so interesting? Within the realm of visual cognition, faces have been afforded a degree of analysis that surpasses most other object categories. There are several reasons for this intense scrutiny. First, faces are critical to us as social beings. Thus, we are inherently interested the mental and neural processes responsible for our ability to recognize, interpret, and remember faces. Second, face recognition is one of the most difficult visual discrimination tasks we routinely (and almost universally) perform. As such, vision researchers often view face recognition as the most extreme task our visual systems can support. Third, in part motivated by the first two reasons, face recognition is often considered a likely candidate for cognitive and neural specialization. Consequently, face processing makes an interesting litmus test with regard to the nature versus nurture debate. Although these factors do make faces an interesting subject, here we argue that the study of face recognition in and of itself is not nearly as informative as face recognition studied in the context of the recognition of nonface objects.

Reviewing the literature, one would not get this impression. Faces have often been specifically studied for two independent reasons. First, they constitute a convenient, complex stimulus category that can be used to probe questions about object processing and recognition. For example, important questions of viewpoint and illumination invariance have been studied using faces (Braje, Kersten, Tarr, & Troje, 1998; Hill, Schyns, & Akamatsu, 1997), not because these problems are unique to faces, but because face stimuli satisfy the need for objects that are not trivially discriminable and because they are convenient to researchers in terms of availability (e.g., http://www.face-rec.org/databases/). To be clear, we are not suggesting that this is necessarily a bad thing. As we have already acknowledged, faces are highly relevant objects and present a challenging recognition problem worthy of study in its own right. However, research motivated by such logic should not be construed as an attempt to "prove" that faces are "special." In contrast, the second reason that faces have been targeted as objects of study is intrinsically tied to faces qua faces. That is, there is an extensive body of research predicated on the idea that faces are processed and recognized in a way that sets them apart from other objects (Liu & Chaudhuri, 2003). Our concern is that studies motivated by such logic place an extreme emphasis on faces, thereby lending themselves to self-fulfilling research. For example, in many studies that explore the "specialness" of faces, the nonface control stimuli may be incommensurate with face stimuli along many dimensions (Gauthier & Tarr, 1997), leading to ambiguous conclusions. Thus, it behooves us to consider a more general framework for object processing in which face recognition is but a subset.

A more general framework that includes nonface objects as full partners provides the strongest means for evaluating the functional and/or neural independence (or lack thereof) between face and object processing. In studies that take this approach, the question of independence is typically addressed by looking for common behavioral effects or neural substrates. However, such comparisons are difficult to make if the task demands are different between object classes. Put another way, one must be careful to include appropriate nonface comparison objects. Comparing face recognition to the basic-level recognition of nonface objects confounds object *category* with the particular task demands evoked by that category (Gauthier & Tarr, 1997). As emphasized throughout this volume, faces are typically recognized, by default, at the *individual level* due to expertise with a visually homogeneous object class. The same cannot be said for most other object classes—although we may have more or less experience with various object categories, we are rarely experts for any of them and, more often than not, do not need to individuate between different exemplars within each class. Thus, nonface comparison classes for faces should share the unique properties that happen to be true of faces.

It is, of course, easy to lay down this stricture but somewhat more difficult to realize it in actual experimental design. How does one ensure that comparison classes have the same functional properties as faces but are not somehow "facelike" in terms of appearance? That is, meaningful comparisons should isolate specific factors while controlling for others, in particular, image geometry. For example, if a comparison class "looks like faces," then it is possible that any commonalities with face processing may be due to a "face processor" stretching to accommodate the recognition of this new class (Kanwisher, 2000). The problem with this argument is that it is sometimes hard to define what it means to look like a face. Like Senator Jesse Helms' definition of pornography—"I know it when I see it"—it is possible to apply a loose definition to what counts as a face. Thus, facelike geometry has been claimed for everything from Greebles (Gauthier & Tarr, 1997) to birds to dogs to cars. Are such objects really facelike in terms of image geometry (Figures 2.1 and 2.2)? In some sense, yes. The original Greebles have two horizontally arranged parts above two vertically arranged parts. Birds have an eye and a beak that might count as a nose or mouth. Cars have two headlights and a grill. However, it is difficult to imagine that proponents of face

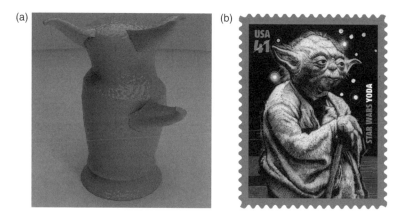

Figure 2.1 Greebles and Yoda: Separated at birth?

specificity counted such objects as within the domain of a specialized face module until new results required it. The point here is not to belabor this ongoing debate, but to illustrate the fact that defining a nonface comparison class by image geometry alone is perilous at best. That is, without some principled definition of "facelike," it is a tautology to apply this label post hoc to any object category that elicits behavior or neural responses that are similar to those elicited by faces (i.e., a category is "facelike" if it happens to show "facelike" effects). In the end, different definitions of what counts as a face are likely to persist, and there is no clear means for resolving this question at the present time. All that can be said is that, to date, there is no set recipe that clearly delineates those combinations of geometries that will produce "facelike" behavioral or neural effects. In contrast, particular manipulations of expertise, independent of image geometry, have consistently yielded such effects.

At the same time, it is possible that many of the nonface comparison classes used in expertise studies share properties with faces beyond expertise. In particular, "looking like a face" may encompass two notions that help make faces faces. First, nonface comparison classes (and the tasks used over them) often emphasize objects as individual entities. As humans we are much more likely to anthropomorphize individuals as compared to undifferentiated classes (Figure 2.3). Second, nonface comparison classes often appear to be animate (e.g., birds or Greebles). Animacy is a critical component of rendering faces as socially relevant stimuli (e.g., expression and eye gaze interpretation). If objects in a nonface comparison class appear to have the potential for self-generated movement, then it is much easier for us to imagine them as unique individuals (Heider & Simmel, 1944). Thus, subjects, partly in response to these two factors, may be more inclined to invoke the same mechanisms used for identifying faces for the individuation of nonface objects.

Figure 2.2 Do these objects "look like faces"? (See color Plate 3)

How then, should one proceed in evaluating the relationship between face and nonface object processing? One view—the theme of this volume—is that the critical property that makes face processing "special" is our extreme visual expertise with faces as an object class (Tanaka, 2001). As such, beyond trying to use reasonable nonface object classes when assessing face and nonface object processing, manipulating expertise provides a potential dimension for explaining why certain behavioral and/or neural effects arise. To be fair, much as with the argument that something is "facelike," defini-tively stating that a given object class is being processed at the expert level is an ill-defined concept. That is, expertise is much more than simply training subjects to discriminate between visually similar objects using "second-order," "holistic," or "configural" information. First, expertise is more likely a continuous dimension: we are all, more or less, experts with every object class we know about. For some we have little interest and experience

Figure 2.3 It is human nature to anthropomorphize individual objects?

and, consequently, are relatively more novice; for others we have greater interest and experience and, consequently, are relatively more expert. Indeed, even within groups of experts we find great variation in individual abilities (Kung, Ellis, & Tarr, 2007; Gauthier, Skudlarski, Gore, & Anderson, 2000). Second, although specific criteria have been proposed for what endpoint is associated with expert-level processing (Tanaka & Taylor, 1991), such criteria do not tell us anything about the particular mechanisms recruited to reach such a level. Thus, an individual could attain nominal expertise, yet not do so using the same mechanisms as used in other expertise domains (Bukach, Bub, Gauthier, & Tarr, 2006). With this caveat in mind, we turn to specific studies of expert-level recognition with nonface objects.

The first study we review demonstrates our point that nominal expertise says little about mechanism. In their entertaining study, Biederman and Shiffrar (1987) examined the strategies used by experts in a task that requires "years of extensive practice for its mastery"—of sexing day-old chicks. Remarkably, Biederman and Shiffrar found that attending to a simple shape contrast (convex vs. concave or flat) was sufficient to render novices' sexing performance comparable to that of experts. Moreover, although expertise in this domain is associated with the ability to correctly classify extremely rare configurations, Biederman and Shiffrar found that, post-training, novices and experts tended to miss on the same images. At the same time, expertise does confer some improvement in performance: experts learn particular "types" (really subtypes) of configurations that vary from the most common examples. That is, they learn a "look-up table" of exceptions (much as been argued for English speakers learning irregular verb forms; Pinker, 1999).

Consider that no one would hesitate to call expert chicken sexers "experts": with years of experience, they perform a difficult, subordinate-level, visual discrimination with a high degree of accuracy and with great speed. Such characteristics mark most manifestations of visual expertise, including face expertise (Tanaka, 2001), dog expertise (Diamond & Carey, 1986), bird expertise, car expertise (Gauthier, Skudlarski, et al., 2000), chess expertise (Chase & Simon, 1973), and laboratory-created expertise (Gauthier & Tarr, 1997; Gauthier et al., 1998). Yet in contrast to Biederman and Shiffrar's results, experts in all of these domains appear to rely on implicit, nonverbalizable perceptual strategies. That is, individual experts are incapable of articulating how they accomplish expert-level recognition (e.g., Dodson, Johnson, & Schooler, 1997). Moreover, even if persistent and insidious cognitive scientists managed to uncover the perceptual principles being used by such experts, it would be impossible to simply convey these principles to novices, allowing them to suddenly achieve expert-level performance. As the old adage goes, "Q: How do you get to Carnegie Hall? A: Practice, practice, practice." For most instances of expertise, this is exactly the case.

The aforementioned joke raises a somewhat more serious scientific question: Is practice alone sufficient to create expertise? That is, what sort of experience is necessary to achieve expert-level performance in a given

THE FAR SIDE® By GARY LARSON

Figure 2.4 We are all more or less experts with every object class depending on our interests (Used with permission from Creators Syndicate.).

domain? Think about the fact that we all see 100's of cars on a daily basis. Yet few of us are car experts. Expertise seems to require both experience *and* motivation (provided through interest in a domain or through rewards from an experimenter; Tarr & Cheng, 2003). Chicken sexing is the exception to this rule: Expert-level performance may arise from years of training or from a short-course in the relevant contrast that covers most instances of the task. This distinction leads to the deeper distinction between mechanisms of expertise. That is, what particular functional and neural visual mechanisms are recruited by experts in order to achieve expert-level performance? In the case of chicken sexing, the answer is somewhat mundane and transparent: Attention to a single qualitative shape contrast is sufficient. Moreover, sensitivity to this shape contrast may be a fundamental property of the primate visual system (Jacobs, 2003; Vogels, Biederman, Bar, & Lorincz, 2001). One might be tempted to label this example the exception and all other cases of expertise as the "rule." This, however, would be a mistake. Much as there is an ongoing debate about the degree to which mechanisms are shared between faces and nonface objects in domains of expertise (e.g., Kanwisher, 2000; Tarr & Gauthier, 2000), one should ask whether *any* two domains of expertise share the same functional and neural mechanisms. With regard to expert chicken sexing relative to most other (studied) domains of expertise, the assumption is that there are few shared mechanisms (other than basic visual processes). As mentioned, with regard to faces relative to most other domains of expertise, there is, as yet, no clear answer. However, our working assumption is that there are many shared mechanisms—often collected under the umbrella of "holistic" or "configural" processes. It is the examination of such domains that we discuss next.

In contrast to Biederman and Shiffrar's study, Diamond and Carey's (1986) classic study of dog show judges suggests that it may take a decade or more to become an expert with even one subgroup of dogs (and presumably this expertise cannot be easily transferred to novices). Diamond and Carey's critical finding was that, in a forced-choice recognition memory task, dog show judges exhibited a picture-plane inversion effect for dogs comparable to that exhibited for faces. In contrast, dog novices showed no inversion effect for dogs, but a comparable face inversion effect. Interestingly, Diamond and Carey did not find this pattern when they used a set of dog breeds that fell outside of the judges' particular domains of expertise (Experiment 2). That is, if a given judge was an expert with setters (and potentially the larger group of sporting dogs), they still showed novice-like effects when remembering poodles (and more generally nonsporting dogs and toys). This unintended result highlights another point from our earlier discussion: One must be careful to isolate specific factors that may contribute to a given effect. Thus, nominal studies of expertise should ensure that the particular stimuli are within the subject population's domain of expertise. In Diamond and Carey's (1986) study, inversion effects are attributable to expertise with a constrained object class—a given dog breed or visually similar subgroup—and not to generic visual properties of dogs or generic expertise with all dogs.

This conclusion is relevant to the larger discussion of objects of expertise in two ways. First, as discussed earlier, some researchers have attributed results that suggest shared behavioral or neural mechanisms between faces and nonface objects to the nonface stimuli "looking like faces." However, in Diamond and Carey's study, no particular subgroup of dogs looks more or less like faces—obtaining a facelike inversion effect was predicated entirely on a given dog show judge's domain of expertise (and not on the image geometry of the stimuli). Thus, the degree to which dogs generically "look like faces" cannot explain their specific results (although it is possible that some base level similarity to faces is necessary to acquire expertise in the first place)—it was only the concatenation of the visual homogeneity of a given dog breed *with* expertise for that specific breed that led to facelike inversion effects. Second, even within the domain of faces, there are expertise effects. The "other-race effect" (ORE) describes the fact that observers tend to exhibit larger behavioral effects (Rhodes, Tan, Brake, & Taylor, 1989) and neural responses (Golby et al., 2001) for face stimuli that are from their own race. The most recent evidence suggests that the ORE advantage stems from exposure to faces of a particular race and not to some genetic predisposition to faces of that race (Bar-Haim et al., 2006). The point here is that even within the domain of faces, much as within nonface object categories, there are degrees of expertise. Moreover, this variation appears to have little to do with the specific appearance of the objects within a domain, but everything to do with the particular experience of the individual. Finally, we should note that although we have discussed Diamond and Carey's results in the context of the sort of experience it takes to become an expert, because they studied extant experts (and did not predicate their results on an individual measure of expertise), their results do not actually address the question of how expertise is acquired.

Although it is possible to use individual variation within a subject population to study, indirectly, the acquisition of expertise, a more direct method involves creating experts in the laboratory. Given Diamond and Carey's conjecture that expertise may take a decade or more to acquire, this seems a daunting task. On the other hand, sheer duration of experience may not be the critical variable in how one attains expert-level recognition performance. The right kind of experience, for example, massed training with feedback, might be sufficient to create experts in considerably less than 10 years. At the same time, mere exposure to a range of examples and to many image variants may lay down representational scaffolding on which to expertise may be built. Indeed, recent work has revealed that extensive exposure, even in the absence of expertise training, can have profound influences on neural substrates involved in learning (Peissig et al., 2007; Sheinberg & Logothetis, 2002). From a functional point of view, this idea is quite old. Bruner (1957) introduced the idea of *perceptual readiness*, arguing that what we call categorization is directly tied to accumulated perceptual experience. A corollary of this proposal is that in the process of becoming an expert, experience within the original training domain may severely limit the generality of that acquired expertise. For example, as already mentioned, breed-specific dog show judges (Diamond & Carey, 1986), modern car experts (Grill-Spector et al., 2004), and Australian butterfly experts (Rhodes et al., 2004) behave like novices when presented with other breeds, classic cars, and unfamiliar butterfly species, respectively.

Although it might seem as if this problem could be remedied after the fact, for example, by remedial training on the new, unfamiliar exemplars (e.g., classic cars; for evidence that the ORE may be reversed, at least during development, see McKone, Brewer, et al., 2007; and Sangrigoli, Pallier, Argenti, Ventureyra, & de Schonen, 2005), it may be that the neural traces laid down during first experience are inviolate and constrain the extent of future expertise in that domain. Indeed, we have some evidence that the first objects within a new category learned by monkeys maintain, even long after many other instances have been learned, a special status in terms of their neural realization (Peissig et al., 2007). This kind of perceptual primacy for items learned early (age of acquisition) is well documented in the language domain (see, e.g., Ghyselinck, Lewis, & Brysbaert, 2004, for review). In vision, it is thus worth understanding how raw experience may shape generalization of expertise across examples within a known category. Interestingly, the same problem arises with regard to changes in objects across viewpoint, illumination, and pose (Tarr & Vuong, 2002), as experts within a domain are often surprisingly specific in their abilities with regard to identifying objects from a given viewpoint, lighting, and configuration. Thus, face and dog experts are significantly impaired when recognizing inverted faces and dogs (Diamond & Carey, 1986; Yin, 1969). Similar specificity has been found for lighting conditions and is likely to occur for part configurations as well. Again, there is the open question as to whether remedial training is sufficient to overcome this specialization once it is locked down by initial experiences and the subsequent acquisition of expertise (for evidence that the face inversion effect can be ameliorated with training, see Ashworth Vuong, Rossion, & Tarr, 2008).

At the same time, as discussed above, although the nature of one's raw experience is not without implications, massed previous familiarity with a category does not seem to be a necessary prerequisite for acquiring expertise. Even without known "perceptual readiness," and contrary to the conjectures of researchers such as Diamond and Carey (1986), it appears as if neural and functional markers often considered to be indicative of expertise may develop rather quickly. Gauthier and Tarr (1997; see also Gauthier et al., 1998; Gauthier, Tarr, Anderson, Skudlarski, & Gore, 1999) explored this possibility using novel objects known as "Greebles" (the top right object in Figure 2.2 is a Greeble[1]).

---

[1] For purposes of posterity, readers might be interested in knowing that "Greeble" is a nonsense name suggested by the psychologist, Robert P. Abelson. Also, Greebles might be the only psychophysical stimulus set to have their own entry in Wikipedia.

Leaving aside the specific question as to whether Greebles actually look like faces, Greebles do appear as animate creatures and exhibit bilateral symmetry. Of course, as much as Greebles do look like little beings, as discussed earlier, their appearance probably stretched most researchers' previous intuitions about what it meant to be "facelike" (for some evidence that Greebles are not facelike, see Gauthier, Behrmann, & Tarr, 2004).

Two key findings emerge from Gauthier and Tarr's study. First, using Tanaka and Taylor's (1991) criterion for expertise—being able to recognize objects in a given domain at the subordinate level as fast as they are recognized at the basic/entry level—Gauthier and Tarr found that they could create experts with about 7-0 hours of training. Second, Greeble experts, but not novices, exhibited sensitivity to "configural" changes similar to those observed in face processing (Tanaka & Farah, 1993), but only for upright Greebles. More specifically, posttraining, moving certain parts of a Greeble affected the processing of its other, untransformed, parts. The logic here is quite similar to that of Diamond and Carey: Experts in a nonface object domain show an effect associated with face processing. The difference here is that subjects served as their own controls. The novices who did not show such effects were the same subjects as the experts, pretraining. Leaving aside the issue of whether faces are or are not "special," these data demonstrated the remarkable fact that a relatively brief laboratory training regimen was sufficient to develop expertise by two criteria: equivalent recognition times at different levels of specificity and sensitivity to configural manipulations.

A fair question at this point is whether this sort of laboratory training really creates experts or simply prompts subjects to show, as mentioned, those behavioral effects often associated with expertise. Beyond specific criteria, one of the hallmarks of perceptual expertise is the ability to rapidly learn and accurately recognize new instances within an expertise domain. That is, expertise allows generalization to previously unknown members of an expert object class. For example, a single experience with a person is often adequate to allow us to remember having seen that individual when we encounter them again (even if we never learned their name). Thus, a particular constellation of effects may emerge indicating expertise, but unless these effects generalize to new exemplars within the domain, expertise may not actually be the underlying cause of these effects. Critically, in Gauthier and Tarr's study the particular Greebles used to assess sensitivity to configural manipulations were *new* individuals unknown to the subjects until this assessment (the same is true for the behavioral and neural assessments used in other Greeble studies). The need to test experts with novel exemplars of an expert class places additional constraint on stimuli suitable for studying visual expertise. Above we discussed the argument that objects in a domain of interest should not "look like faces." That is, nonface objects should not be too visually similar to an extant domain of expertise, be it faces or some other category[2]. At the same time, to study expertise and not simply image memory, objects should look *a lot* like known objects within the domain interest yet not be individually familiar to the experts in question.

This latter constraint raises a new issue—when do objects "count" as exemplars within a domain of expertise? One intuitive answer to this question is that domains of expertise are bounded by the basic (or entry) level. Because basic-level categories (for count nouns at least) are typically consequences of visual similarity (Rosch et al., 1976), expertise occurs naturally at this level. However, we already know from Diamond and Carey's (1986) study that dog show judges are experts only for particular subgroups of dogs. Thus, it appears that visual expertise tends to cover a tighter notion of visual similarity than does the basic level (Tanaka, Curran, & Sheinberg, 2005). Of course, it is possible that dogs are a particularly bad example of a basic-level category: Other than genetics and a basic mammalian body plan, what do Chihuahuas and Saint Bernards really have in common? Perhaps inadvertently, two recent studies have answered this question (Grill-Spector et al., 2004; Rhodes et al., 2004). In each study the authors were attempting to address a somewhat different and controversial issue: the degree to which the neural mechanisms recruited by face recognition are also recruited by expert recognition of nonface objects (respectively, cars and butterflies). Putting this issue aside, both of these studies used fMRI to examine the neural activity of experts while processing objects nominally within their domains of expertise. As discussed below, based on earlier studies of expertise (Gauthier et al., 1999; Gauthier, Skudlarski, et al., 2000) one might expect category selectivity (for the domain of expertise) in the part of the ventral stream known as the fusiform gyrus (see Chapter 1). Interestingly, in both cases the authors found little evidence for such category selectivity. One interpretation of these results is that neural category selectivity for nonface domains of expertise is a variable phenomenon that is difficult to replicate—roughly the conclusion reported in both papers. An alternative, however, is that the specific expertise of the experts under study was somewhat narrower than the authors assumed. That is, much as with Diamond and Carey's dog show judges, expertise may be limited to a particular subgroup within a basic-level category. Further examination of both studies suggests that this is indeed the case (Bukach, Gauthier, & Tarr, 2006). In the case of the butterfly experts, they were tested with unfamiliar species of butterflies (p. 198, Rhodes et al., 2004); in the case of car experts, they were modern car experts, but the majority of the test stimuli were antique cars (Grill-Spector et al., 2004). Thus, dogs seem to be the rule rather than the exception with regard to the coverage of

---

[2] Presumably this same constraint would hold if one happened to be studying subjects with expertise in a nonface object category. For example, if one were interested in training subjects to be experts with a novel stimulus class, and those subjects happened to be bird experts, then it would be prudent to ensure that the novel stimuli did not "look like birds."

expertise within a domain. That is, when studying visual expertise, objects should be unfamiliar to subjects, but not so unfamiliar that they define a different subgroup within the larger basic-level category.

Interestingly, experience with specific objects within a class can interact with the nature of basic-level categories. The specific definition often ascribed to the basic level is that it is the first and fastest label applied to an object (Brown, 1958; Rosch et al., 1976). Yet this can change with experience. For example, birders will naturally identify familiar birds at the species level, and we all immediately identify faces at the individual level (Tanaka, 2001). Moreover, the actual labels applied by default vary from individual to individual, based on their own experiences with object categories. Critically, the influence of experience on labeling behavior is not limited to cases where expertise has been attained. Rather, experience is a continuous variable that modulates the processing of all objects, whether they are in a domain of expertise or not. As discussed above, perceptual readiness refers to the degree to which experience in and of itself affects categorization. Thus, in this view, we are more are less experts with all categories we have experienced (Figure 2.4). That is, expertise is a *general* property of object representation, not something limited to special cases such faces or Greebles.

To some degree, this observation has been known to neuroscientists for over 40 years. That is, single cells in the monkey temporal lobes reveal sensitivity for a variety of visual patterns—faces, hands, geometric figures, wirelike objects, butterflies, mountain lions, parrots, trees, backpacks, and so forth (Anderson, Sanderson, & Sheinberg, 2007; Desimone et al., 1984; Logothetis, Pauls, & Poggio, 1995; Mruczek & Sheinberg, 2007; Schwartz, Desimone, Albright, & Gross, 1983; Sheinberg & Logothetis, 1997, 2001). Such responses are almost surely a consequence of experience. In this context, at least at the single-cell level, there is nothing particularly unique about face-selective neurons (Figure 2.5). That is, selectivity to specific objects is ubiquitous. Thus, if we are to accept the argument that neural specificity is associated with expertise (or with domain-specific processing, Kanwisher, 2000), then we must also accept that similar object-selective responses are indicative of some modicum of expertise or domain-specific processing (broadly defined). Similarly, as discussed below, neuroimaging reveals object-selective responses to a wide range of domains of expertise, including cars, birds, handwriting, chess boards, and Greebles (Gauthier et al., 1999; Gauthier, Skudlarski, et al., 2000; Righi & Tarr, 2004; Sugita, Tsukiura, Suzuki, & Manaka, 2006; Xu, 2005). The obvious interpretation of this body of results is that neural specialization at the systems level is likewise a product of experience, and specialization per se is an adaptive property of complex perceptual systems.

The alternative to a generalized model of expertise is that the mechanisms underlying face specialization and the specialization seen for all other object categories are separable from one another (McKone, Kanwisher, & Duchaine, 2007). Arguments in favor of this alternative rest largely on the lower magnitudes and differential locations of neural responses to nonface object

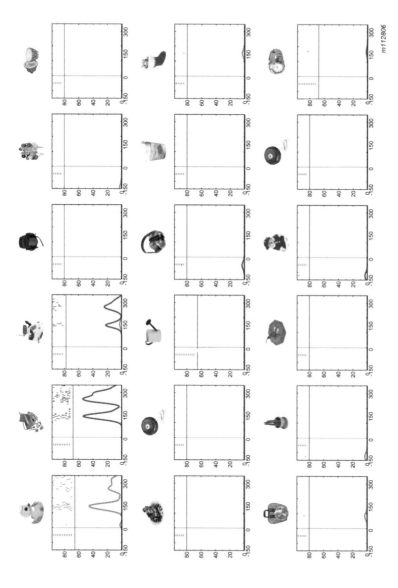

m112806

Figure 2.5 Simultaneous recording from two nearby cells (electrodes approximately 0.5 mm apart) in monkey inferior temporal cortex reveals high selectivity for a variety of objects during a passive viewing task. The 18 panels each indicate the response of the two neurons to the images shown above. One cell responds almost exclusively to the figure of the rubber duck and the other to the wheelchair and, to a lesser extent, the robot. Each horizontal tick left of the vertical line at zero marks a single trial (necessary, as many trials include no spikes). Data from Anderson and Sheinberg (unpublished) (see color Plate 4).

categories (McKone, Kanwisher, et al., 2007; similar "magnitude" arguments have been made regarding behavioral effects, McKone & Kanwisher, 2005). However, our position is that such arguments misstate the so-called "expertise hypothesis" as a binary set of conditions. Under this view, one is either an expert or not and anything less is unspecialized. In contrast, we consider the expertise hypothesis to be a general account of specialization across all stages of perceptual knowledge—from the neonate's earliest encounters with objects to the most extreme examples of expert visual processing, including adults individuating faces, birders with decades of experience recognizing passerine bird species, and highly trained radiologists spotting minute tumors in X-ray films.

Does this view of the expertise hypothesis weaken it? We believe just the opposite. In a world where expertise is a special case, applying only to faces, then there is not much else to be said. Accounts of how we learn about objects over experience would have little to do with neural specialization or the recruitment of holistic mechanisms. On the other hand, taking expertise as the norm opens a world of possibilities. That is, experience is continuously modulating both the functional and physiological organization of our visual systems—plasticity is inherent in how we process and learn about objects and, as stated earlier, we are all, to some degree, experts with *all* object categories of which we have knowledge. Evidence for this plasticity, as reviewed next, comes from neurophysiology, neuroimaging, and neuropsychology. Interestingly, such evidence may be dissociated from behavioral data. Thus, for nonface domains, it is not always the case that neural specialization for objects maps directly to measurable differences in how we recognize objects. Indeed, as we shall see, recent evidence suggests that this same claim may be made about faces—neural face selectivity is necessary, but not sufficient for face recognition. As such, there appear to be few reasons to assume separable mechanisms for faces and objects. Rather, a unified general process that is sensitive to experiential factors *and* intrinsic category biases (e.g., social relevance) can be postulated and serve as a framework for understanding a wide array of results.

Physiological explorations of visually responsive cells selective for face and nonface objects have proceeded in peace and in parallel. In fact, the earliest report of microelectrode recordings from the primate temporal lobe made no mention of facelike sensitivity in single cells. Instead, Gross and colleagues (1969) hinted that they encountered a particularly interesting cell responsive to visual patterns that looked like hands—a result detailed in their 1984 report (Desimone et al., 1984).

Even so, one of the most compelling reasons for considering the study of face processing separate from the study of object processing can be traced to the striking discovery that single cells in the primate visual system can respond selectively, and sometimes apparently exclusively, to face stimuli (Desimone et al., 1984; Perrett, Rolls, & Caan, 1982). It is important to understand why these findings, which have stood the test of time, should not be mistaken for evidence that faces are apportioned a privileged set of neurons in the visual system. In contrast, we believe that the very existence of specialized neural elements selective for faces supports the view that understanding the relationship between face and nonface object processing in the visual system is a fruitful avenue for understanding how complex visual objects are processed both physiologically and behaviorally.

Why, then, have faces garnered so much attention? We offer a few explanations, none of which should be taken as evidence that faces ought to be considered as inherently unique. First, given that neuroscientists still have only a primitive understanding of how shapes are encoded by cells in the visual system, any stimulus set that can reliably activate even a small proportion of cells makes a welcome addition to the physiologist's test arsenal. Note that this represents experimenter bias and not some underlying principle of brain organization. It is true that for this bias to propagate, it must prove effective. But as indicated above, there is no doubt that face cells can be found, and recent advances in functional neuroimaging may improve the odds of locating face-selective clusters of cells (Tsao, Freiwald, Tootell, & Livingstone, 2006). Bear in mind, however, that while the exact percentage of such cells is not known, this number, at least for the rhesus inferior temporal cortex, is quite low, perhaps 2%–5%.

A second rationale for focusing entire studies on response properties of face cells is that they provide a very useful starting point for investigations of object invariance. The problem of how observers recognize objects despite transformations in scale, position, and orientation has a long history in computational vision. Biologically inspired solutions, based on properties of neurons involved in the process, have led many research groups to investigate how individual cells respond to these same transformations. Faces, like other any other object, can be presented in standard and transformed states, but it is clearly advantageous to explore invariance in controlled conditions. By studying a collection of cells where each exhibits similar selectivity from the outset (i.e., high sensitivity to facelike stimuli), some degree of control can be achieved. Here again, however, this methodological consideration should not be mistaken for proof that this subpopulation of cells is unique. As an analogy, consider Golgi's indispensable silver stain for nervous tissue, wherein single cells are impregnated with crystallized silver chromate. The usefulness of this technique, made famous by Ramón y Cajal, derives from the fact that only a tiny subset of neurons are actually stained in the process, making it possible to study these individual cells in great detail. To this day, however, no one knows why so few cells are stained. Of relevance here is the fact that the stained sample is assumed to be representative of a much larger sample. In this way, we see the use of an experimentally selected set of face-selective neurons to be informative not just in and of themselves, but also as proxies for a much richer collection of intermingled visual cells that may have different, undiscovered, selectivities.

Finally, beyond the possibility of understanding the brain's solution to solving the invariance problem, investigators have focused attention on face cells because they also provide a method for exploring the challenging problem of stimulus differentiation. Composed of like parts, both in number and global configuration, faces are the "poster child" when it comes to the problem of object individuation. Indeed, there is no question that faces are recognized by normal observers at this level, so the notion that studying cells selective for faces may help uncover underlying computation principles for individuation is well founded. However, we once again emphasize the logic of this approach, and its implications. It assumes that because faces are hard to individuate and because we have a neural substrate for investigating this process, it makes sense to explore this neural population in detail. What it does not imply, though, is that either the stimulus domain for individuation or the cells in question are unique.

A similar point may be made regarding the larger-scale neural systems that support visual object recognition. In particular, faces have certainly served as a canonical stimulus in the neuroimaging domain (a search on PubMed for "face and fMRI" identifies 350 target articles!). In parallel with the neurophysiological results reviewed above, there is apparent category selectivity for faces at the level of millions of neurons. This was first established by Sergent, Ohta, & MacDonald (1992) and, later, by Kanwisher, McDermott, & Chun (1997), both of whom identified a small region of the right fusiform gyrus within the ventral temporal lobe that shows higher neural activity (i.e., the summed responses of many neurons) for face stimuli as compared to stimuli from other object categories. This functionally defined brain region has been dubbed the "fusiform face area" or FFA (Kanwisher et al., 1997)—a label consistent with the belief that the specific task demands of face recognition (as reviewed at the beginning of this chapter) imply a domain-specific face "module." However, the claim that the FFA is actually a neural module (Fodor, 1983; Kanwisher, 2000) for face recognition appears problematic when considered in the context of the recognition of other objects. Putting aside for the moment the issue of expertise, the FFA and the regions around it are highly active during most visual recognition tasks (Gauthier, Anderson, Tarr, Skudlarski, & Gore, 1997; Gauthier, Tarr, Moylan, Anderson et al., 2000). Moreover, when neuroimaging data are used to argue for face specialization, they are predicated on *higher* FFA activity for faces as compared to objects, not on absolute face exclusivity (Kanwisher et al., 1997; McKone & Kanwisher, 2005). Put another way, does a quantitative difference between the neural response seen for faces and the neural responses seen for other objects warrant a qualitative separation in how we think about the processing of the two domains?

We think not. At the same time, there are good reasons to believe that faces are "special" in terms of their social importance and level of individuation (Tarr, 2005). Thus, it is not surprising that the neural systems tasked with the object recognition problem show some bias for faces relative to socially less critical and computationally less complex stimuli. However, this bias does not necessarily translate into domain specificity. That is, regardless of the evolutionary pressures that might have led to the *ability* to individuate faces, the mere fact of this ability does not imply that this ability is realized by a distinct neural system exclusive to faces. All that need be true is that a domain-general system be capable of supporting the particular task of face individuation.

Consider also that, until recently, standard neuroimaging methods have had a resolution of about 3 mm^3; consequently, so-called category-selective regions such as the FFA are actually the result of the summed activation of millions[3] of individual neurons, some of which are likely to prefer faces and some of which may prefer other objects. Again, facts about face "specialness" must carry some weight in how our visual systems come to be organized. That is, it would unsurprising to find that within a network of neurons dedicated to some component of the object recognition process, there is overrepresentation of faces relative to other object categories, even more so if this component realizes computations that are critical for object individuation, for example, "holistic" mechanisms (Gauthier & Tarr, 2002). Thus, the quantitative "advantage" observed in the FFA for faces relative to other objects may simply reflect a similar quantitative advantage in how many individual neurons preferentially respond to faces as opposed to other object categories.

Supporting the idea that variations in neural population size across object categories underlie differences in measured fMRI responses, a recent study found that within the FFA there exists a wide range of face selectivity (Grill-Spector, Sayres, & Ress, 2006, 2007). The use of high-resolution fMRI to interrogate the microstructure of the FFA and surrounding neural areas will be crucial in extending previous standard resolution fMRI studies of category selectivity. For example, Haxby et al. (2001) explored the neural coding of faces, cats, houses, bottles, scissors, shoes, and chairs across a wide area of ventral-temporal cortex. An information-theoretic analysis revealed that categories could be reliably identified using only the responses of the category-selective subregions that were *not* preferential for the category in question. Put another way, nonmaximal responses were sufficient for category identification (Haxby et al., 2001). Such findings led Haxby and colleagues to conclude that the neural population codes used to represent object categories are widely distributed and overlapping (see also, Haxby, 2006). Building on this conclusion, O'Toole, Jiang, Abdi, & Haxby (2005) used a pattern-based classification algorithm to explore the organization of ventral-temporal cortex. Using the data from Haxby et al. (2001), they compared the confusability matrices generated by their pattern classifier when run on neural response patterns as measured by fMRI to the confusability matrices generated when run on images of the visual stimuli. Consistent with the view that ventral-temporal cortex is organized on the basis of geometric differences among object categories (and not processing differences), they found high

---

[3] Estimates of neuronal cell density suggest that a 3 mm^3 voxel would encompass more than one million neurons, although this figure depends on cortical area and species (Chow, Blum, & Blum, 1950; O'Kusky & Colonnier, 1982).

correlations between the confusability of object categories and the confusability of the empirically derived neural response maps from Haxby's earlier study (O'Toole et al., 2005).

Taken together, fMRI studies in humans suggest that category selectivity is a ubiquitous characteristic of how *all* objects are coded in ventral-temporal cortex. It is interesting to compare those studies that focus specifically on the FFA—a small, functionally defined region—with those exploring much larger expanses of visual cortex and ask to what functional role the clustering of specialized subunits such as the FFA may play. First, there is some evidence that the FFA is involved in holistic processing of complex, homogeneous stimuli (Gauthier & Tarr, 2002), a process critical for face individuation (Tanaka & Farah, 1993). One possibility is that the task of individuating between highly similar exemplars within a category relies on local interactions between cells with overlapping stimulus sensitivities. If this interaction is competitive, then as one acquires expertise with faces, they may come to be overrepresented in the FFA relative to other object categories for which recognition relies less on individuating between visually similar exemplars (Gauthier & Tarr, 1997). Second, while the task of discriminating between different object categories may rely on information drawn from all candidate categories (Ullman, Vidal-Naquet, & Sali, 2002), the task of individuating between category members relies exclusively on within-category information (Zhang & Cottrell, 2005). Thus, brain regions associated with basic-level categorization may code category information in a manner that allows across-category comparison (in that information from other categories provides information about how to tell one category from another). In contrast, brain regions associated with individual-level recognition are likely to code category information in a manner that maintains distinct category boundaries (in that information from other categories does not provide information about how to differentiate between two within-category exemplars). This is precisely the pattern we observe across the ventral-temporal cortex: the wider regions of the "recognition" pathway showing overlap in neural representations of categories (Haxby et al., 2001) and the narrow, within-category individuation mechanism dubbed FFA showing distinct boundaries between neural representations of categories (Grill-Spector et al., 2006, 2007).

Note that in our discussion of how the brain codes object categories at the resolution of millions of neurons, we have, to this point, almost entirely omitted the issue of expertise. Now let's factor expertise into the mix. Our account of the relationship between the neural coding of object categories within the wider ventral-temporal cortex and within the FFA makes three specific predictions regarding what happens when observers acquire a second domain of visual expertise (e.g., in addition to faces).

Within the FFA, the acquisition of a new domain of expertise will lead to more neurons specifically coding for that domain. A consequence is that high-resolution fMRI may reveal a larger number of distinct category-selective subregions for the domain in question. This prediction follows naturally from the principle that domains of interest—socially relevant categories, hobbies, etc.—come to be overrepresented relative to less interesting domains because of the desire to differentiate between exemplars within the domain of interest. For most of us, faces inherently have this property. For some of us, new object categories—birds, cars, etc.—can come to have great importance in our lives. In such cases, we begin to attend to more subtle features, and we recruit holistic shape recognition mechanisms, for instance, as realized in the FFA (Gauthier & Tarr, 2002). Supporting this prediction, it is already established that standard resolution fMRI shows, across the FFA, higher neural responses for new expertise domains. Numerous studies have found that both extant (Gauthier Skudlarski et al., 2000; Righi & Tarr, 2004; Xu, 2005) and lab-created experts (Gauthier et al., 1999; Kung, Peissig, & Tarr, 2007), when processing objects in their domain of expertise, show neural responses in the FFA proportional to their level of expertise with that domain. That is, increasing expertise is correlated with increasing category-selective activity in the fusiform gyrus. Of course, it is still an open question whether this is due to an increasing population of distinct category-selective voxels for the new expertise domain, or whether this increase is the result of higher activity among pre-existing neural representations.

Second, given that our first prediction is born out, within the distinct FFA subregions coding for the new domain of expertise, the neural representations of individual exemplars within the expertise domain will be distributed and overlapping, as found by Haxby et al. (2001) for object categories more generally across ventral-temporal cortex. Because the task of individuating exemplars within a homogeneous category relies on information across those exemplars, more localized neural representations (possibly finer than the resolution of even high-resolution fMRI) should overlap. This prediction follows the general principle used in the "20 questions" game that when differentiating between geometrically more similar items (i.e., item exclusion helps refine your search), knowing what something *is not* is useful; however, such information is less useful when differentiating between highly dissimilar items (i.e., item exclusion does not significantly narrow your search space). Of course, it is still unclear at what resolution we might observe the neural coding of individual exemplars within a category, thus high-resolution fMRI may be incapable of addressing this question. At the same time, there are several fMRI adaptation studies that hint at precisely this sort of organization within the FFA. For example, in Gauthier Tarr, Moylan, Skudlarski et al. (2000), greater adaptation in the neural response within the FFA was found for repetitions of the same individual as compared to repetitions of different faces. Such results suggest that codes for individual faces in the FFA have overlapping, but not identical, neural populations.

Third, the acquisition of a new domain of expertise may result in a decrease in the neural response of FFA to previously acquired expertise categories. Why should this be the case? Consider a fully connected network implementing a process critical to the identification of exemplars within a domain. If someone is an expert in only one domain, that domain is likely to predominate in the neural representation space of that network. Indeed, the singular domain of expertise may be heavily overrepresented relative to the minimal neural resources needed to successfully support expert-level recognition for the domain. In particular, Grill-Spector et al.'s (2006, 2007) finding of a preponderance of distinct face-selective subregions in the FFA may simply reflect this fact. However, if a second domain of expertise is introduced into the network, some of the resources previously devoted to face individuation will either: (1) be shared between the two domains, leading to neurons that show preferential responses for both domains; or, (2) be captured by the new domain, leading to neurons that were once face selective but that become selective for the new domain. Note that neither of these alternatives speaks to how the acquisition of new expertise will impact task—either account allows for maintenance of good performance if that domain simply garnered more neural resources than were actually necessary (because it had no competitors in the network).

Grill-Spector et al.'s (2006, 2007) finding of highly distinct face-selective subregions within the FFA speaks to this question. Specifically, any new expertise domain that comes to be represented in the FFA is likely to likewise show distinct, highly selective subregions preferential for that domain. That is, given that the distinctiveness seems to govern the neural codes present in the FFA, neural resource competition will result in some of the previously face-selective subregions being captured by the new domain, producing new distinct domain-selective subregions. At standard-resolution fMRI, the consequences of this redistribution are both an increase in the summed neural response of the FFA to the new expertise domain (as discussed above), *and* a decrease in the summed neural response of the FFA to the first domain of expertise—almost always faces. As surprising as this prediction might seem, it is actually born out by a recent study. Across two fMRI studies using different groups of bird experts, Kung, Ellis, & Tarr (2007) found that higher *behaviorally measured* bird expertise predicts both higher category-selective neural responses to birds (as in Gauthier, Skudlarski et al., 2000), and, concomitantly, *lower* category-selective neural responses to faces in the FFA. Interestingly, this inverse relationship between bird expertise and face selectivity in FFA is also consistent with similar results obtained with laboratory-trained experts—both Gauthier et al. (1999) and Behrmann, Marotta, Gauthier, Tarr, & McKeeff (2005) found that as individuals acquired expertise with Greebles, they showed a decrease in their measured neural response to faces within the FFA. Unfortunately, subjects in these studies were almost always at ceiling on face recognition *performance,* therefore it was impossible to assess whether this decrease in neural response is reflected in behavior. The exception to this is the single prosopagnosic subject reported in Behrmann et al.'s (2005) study who did show a diminution in his face recognition abilities over training. However, it is difficult to conclude anything from this case in that he clearly has impaired neural resources relative to nonbrain-injured subjects. Based on the rough model we outlined above, our conjecture is that individuals without brain injury will *not* show any variation in their face recognition abilities as it relates to their expertise in other domains. That is, any capacity limits for the FFA fall well beyond expertise in two domains.

Conclusions. We are struck by the trend towards assuming that faces and objects should be studied separately. Our feeling is that until otherwise proven (and most of the field would probably agree that the jury is still out), there are good theoretical and empirical reasons to keep faces and objects in the same scientific bin. Where there are differences between these two categories, they seem to arise from the unique task demand of individuating faces. That is, the need to individuate leads to differential experience early in development and continued reliance on computational resources that may otherwise be untapped in categorical object recognition. Obviously, the "expertise approach" is an attempt to assess whether these resources are recruited when "facelike" task demands are imposed on nonface object domains. Regardless of how one interprets the results of such studies, it is clear that a complete picture of the visual recognition process will include experiments using both faces and nonface stimuli.

REFERENCES

Anderson, B., Sanderson, M. I., & Sheinberg, D. L. (2007). Joint decoding of visual stimuli by IT neurons' spike counts is not improved by simultaneous recording. *Experimental Brain Research, 176*(1), 1–11.

Anderson, B., & Sheinberg, D. L. (2008). Effects of temporal context and temporal expectancy on neural activity in inferior temporal cortex. *Neuropsychologia, 46*(4), 947–957.

Ashworth III, A. R. S., Vuong, Q. C., Rossion, B., & Tarr, M. J. (2008). Recognizing rotated faces and Greebles: What properties drive the face inversion effect? *Visual Cognition, 16*(6), 754–784.

Bar-Haim, Y., Ziv, T., Lamy, D., & Hodes, R. M. (2006). Nature and nurture in own-race face processing. *Psychological Science: A Journal of the American Psychological Society / APS, 17*(2), 159–163.

Behrmann, M., Marotta, J., Gauthier, I., Tarr, M. J., & McKeeff, T. J. (2005). Behavioral change and its neural correlates in visual agnosia after expertise training. *Journal of Cognitive Neuroscience, 17*(4), 554–568.

Biederman, I., & Kalocsai, P. (1997). Neurocomputational bases of object and face recognition. *Philosophical Transactions of the Royal Society B: Biological Sciences, 352*(1358), 1203–1219.

Biederman, I., & Shiffrar, M. M. (1987). Sexing day-old chicks: A case study and expert systems analysis of a difficult perceptual-learning task. *Journal of Experimental Psychology: Learning, Memory, and Cognition, 13*(4), 640–645.

Braje, W. L., Kersten, D., Tarr, M. J., & Troje, N. F. (1998). Illumination effects in face recognition. *Psychobiology, 26*(4), 371–380.

Brown, R. W. (1958). *Words and things.* Glencoe, IL: The Free Press.

Bruner, J. S. (1957). On perceptual readiness. *Psychological Review, 64,* 123–152.

Bukach, C. M., Bub, D. N., Gauthier, I., & Tarr, M. J. (2006). Perceptual expertise effects are NOT all or none: Local perceptual expertise for faces in a case of prosopagnosia. *Journal of Cognitive Neuroscience, 18*(1), 48–63.

Chase, W. G., & Simon, H. A. (1973). Perception in chess. *Cognitive Psychology, 4*, 55–81.

Chow, K., Blum, J. S., & Blum, R. A. (1950). Cell ratios in the thalamo-cortical visual system of macaca mulatta. *Journal of Comparative Neurology, 92*(2), 227–239.

Desimone, Albright, Gross, & Bruce (1984). Stimulus-Selective properties of inferior temporal neurons in the macaque. *The Journal of Neuroscience, 4*(8), 2051–2062.

Diamond, R., & Carey, S. (1986). Why faces are and are not special: An effect of expertise. *Journal of Experimental Psychology: General, 115*(2), 107–117.

Dodson, C. S., Johnson, M. K., & Schooler, J. W. (1997). The verbal overshadowing effect: Why descriptions impair face recognition. *Memory & Cognition, 25*(2), 129–139.

Fodor, J. A. (1983). *Modularity of Mind*. Cambridge, MA: MIT Press.

Gauthier, I., Anderson, A. W., Tarr, M. J., Skudlarski, P., & Gore, J. C. (1997). Levels of categorization in visual recognition studied with functional Magnetic Resonance Imaging. *Current Biology, 7*, 645–651.

Gauthier, I., Behrmann, M., & Tarr, M. J. (2004). Are Greebles like faces? Using the neuropsychological exception to test the rule. *Neuropsychologia, 42*, 1961–1970.

Gauthier, I., Skudlarski, P., Gore, J. C., & Anderson, A. W. (2000a). Expertise for cars and birds recruits brain areas involved in face recognition. *Nature Neuroscience, 3*(2), 191–197.

Gauthier, I., & Tarr, M. J. (1997). Becoming a "Greeble" expert: Exploring the face recognition mechanism. *Vision Research, 37*(12), 1673–1682.

Gauthier, I., & Tarr, M. J. (2002). Unraveling mechanisms for expert object recognition: Bridging brain activity and behavior. *Journal of Experimental Psychology: Human Perception and Performance, 28*(2), 431–446.

Gauthier, I., Tarr, M. J., Anderson, A. W., Skudlarski, P., & Gore, J. C. (1999). Activation of the middle fusiform "face area" increases with expertise in recognizing novel objects. *Nature Neuroscience, 2*(6), 568–573.

Gauthier, I., Tarr, M. J., Moylan, J., Anderson, A. W., Skudlarski, P., & Gore, J. C. (2000b). Does visual subordinate-level categorisation engage the functionally defined Fusiform Face Area? *Cognitive Neuropsychology, 17*(1/2/3), 143–163.

Gauthier, I., Tarr, M. J., Moylan, J., Skudlarski, P., Gore, J. C., & Anderson, A. W. (2000c). The fusiform "face area" is part of a network that processes faces at the individual level. *Journal of Cognitive Neuroscience, 12*(3), 495–504.

Gauthier, I., Williams, P., Tarr, M. J., & Tanaka, J. (1998). Training 'greeble' experts: A framework for studying expert object recognition processes. *Vision Research, 38*(15–16), 2401–2428.

Ghyselinck, M., Lewis, M. B., & Brysbaert, M. (2004). Age of acquisition and the cumulative-frequency hypothesis: a review of the literature and a new multi-task investigation. *Acta Psychologica (Amst.), 115*(1), 43–67.

Golby, A. J., Gabrieli, J. D., Chiao, J. Y., & Eberhardt, J. L. (2001). Differential responses in the fusiform region to same-race and other-race faces. *Nature Neuroscience, 4*(8), 845–850.

Grill-Spector, K., Knouf, N., & Kanwisher, N. (2004). The fusiform face area subserves face perception, not generic within-category identification. *Nature Neuroscience, 7*(5), 555–562.

Grill-Spector, K., Sayres, R., & Ress, D. (2006). High-resolution imaging reveals highly selective nonface clusters in the fusiform face area. *Nature Neuroscience, 9*(9), 1177–1185.

Grill-Spector, K., Sayres, R., & Ress, D. (2007). Corrigendum: High-resolution imaging reveals highly selective nonface clusters in the fusiform face area. *Nature Neuroscience, 10*(1), 133.

Gross, Bender, & Rocha-Miranda (1969). Visual receptive fields of neurons in inferotemporal cortex in the monkey. *Science, 166*, 1303–1306.

Haxby, J. V. (2006). Fine structure in representations of faces and objects. *Nature Neuroscience, 9*(9), 1084–1086.

Haxby, J. V., Gobbini, M. I., Furey, M. L., Ishai, A., Schouten, J. L., & Pietrini, P. (2001). Distributed and overlapping representations of faces and objects in ventral temporal cortex. *Science, 293*, 2425–2430.

Heider, F., & Simmel, M. (1944). An experimental study of apparent behavior. *American Journal of Psychology, 57*, 243–259.

Hill, H., Schyns, P. G., & Akamatsu, S. (1997). Information and viewpoint dependence in face recognition. *Cognition, 62*(2), 201–222.

Jacobs, D. W. (2003). What makes viewpoint-invariant properties perceptually salient? *Journal of the Optical Society of America A, Optics, Image Science & Vision, 20*(7), 1304–1320.

Kanwisher, N. (2000). Domain specificity in face perception. *Nature Neuroscience, 3*(8), 759–763.

Kanwisher, N., McDermott, J., & Chun, M. M. (1997). The fusiform face area: A module in human extrastriate cortex specialized for face perception. *Journal of Neuroscience, 17*, 4302–4311.

Kung, C.-C., Ellis, C., & Tarr, M. J. (2007). *Dynamic reorganization of fusiform gyrus: Long-Term bird expertise reduces face selectivity.* Paper presented at the Annual Meeting of the Cognitive Neuroscience Society. New York, NY.

Kung, C., Peissig, J. J., & Tarr, M. J. (2007). Is region-of-interest overlap comparison a reliable measure of category specificity? *Journal of Cognitive Neuroscience, 19*(12), 2019–2034.

Liu, C. H., & Chaudhuri, A. (2003). What determines whether faces are special? *Visual Cognition, 10*(4), 385–408.

Logothetis, N. K., Pauls, J., & Poggio, T. (1995). Shape representation in the inferior temporal cortex of monkeys. *Current Biology, 5*(5), 552–563.

McKone, E., Brewer, J. L., MacPherson, S., Rhodes, G., & Hayward, W. G. (2007). Familiar other-race faces show normal holistic processing and are robust to perceptual stress. *Perception, 36*(2), 224–248.

McKone, E., & Kanwisher, N. (2005). Does the human brain process objects of expertise like faces? A review of the evidence. In S. Dehaene, J.-R. Duhamel, M. D. Hauser, & G. Rizzolatti (Eds.), *From monkey brain to human brain.* Cambridge, MA: The MIT Press.

McKone, E., Kanwisher, N., & Duchaine, B. C. (2007). Can generic expertise explain special processing for faces? *Trends in Cognitive Sciences, 11*(1), 8–15.

Mruczek, R. E. B., & Sheinberg, D. L. (2007). Activity of inferior temporal cortical neurons predicts recognition choice behavior and recognition time during visual search. *Journal of Neuroscience, 27*, 2825–2836.

O'Kusky, J., & Colonnier, M. (1982). A laminar analysis of the number of neurons, glia, and synapses in the adult cortex (area 17) of adult macaque monkeys. *Journal of Comparative Neurolology, 210*(3), 278–290.

O'Toole, A. J., Jiang, F., Abdi, H., & Haxby, J. V. (2005). Partially distributed representations of objects and faces in ventral temporal cortex. *Journal of Cognitive Neuroscience, 17*(4), 580–590.

Peissig, J. J., Singer, J., Kawasaki, K., & Sheinberg, D. L. (2007). Effects of Long-Term Object Familiarity on Event-Related Potentials in the Monkey. *Cerebral Cortex, 17,* 1323–1334.

Perrett, D. I., Rolls, E. T., & Caan, W. (1982). Visual neurones responsive to faces in the monkey temporal cortex. *Experimental Brain Research, 47,* 329–342.

Pinker, S. (1999). *Words and rules: The ingredients of language.* New York, NY: Basic Books Inc.

Rhodes, G., Byatt, G., Michie, P. T., & Puch, A. (2004). Is the fusiform face area specialized for faces, individuation, or expert individuation? *Journal of Cognitive Neuroscience, 16*(2), 189–203.

Rhodes, G., Tan, S., Brake, S., & Taylor, K. (1989). Race sensitivity in face recognition: An effect of different encoding processes. In A. F. Bennett & K. M. McConkey (Eds.), *Cognition in Individual and Social Contexts* (pp. 83–90). Amsterdam: North-Holland.

Righi, G., & Tarr, M. J. (2004). Are chess experts any different from face, bird, or Greeble experts? *Journal of Vision, 4*(8), 504a.

Rosch, E., Mervis, C. B., Gray, W. D., Johnson, D. M., & Boyes-Braem, P. (1976). Basic objects in natural categories. *Cognitive Psychology, 8,* 382–439.

Sangrigoli, S., Pallier, C., Argenti, A. M., Ventureyra, V. A. G., & de Schonen, S. (2005). Reversibility of the other-race effect in face recognition during childhood. *Psychological Science, 16*(6), 440–444.

Schwartz, E. L., Desimone, R., Albright, T. D., & Gross, C. G. (1983). Shape recognition and inferior temporal neurons. *Proceedings of the National Academy of Sciences U S A, 80*(18), 5776–5778.

Sergent, J., Ohta, S., & MacDonald, B. (1992). Functional neuroanatomy of face and object processing: A positron emission tomography study. *Brain, 115,* 15–36.

Sheinberg, D. L., & Logothetis, N. K. (1997). The role of temporal cortical areas in perceptual organization. *Proceedings of the National Academy of Sciences U S A, 94*(7), 3408–3413.

Sheinberg, D. L., & Logothetis, N. K. (2001). Noticing familiar objects in real world scenes: the role of temporal cortical neurons in natural vision. *Journal of Neuroscience, 21*(4), 1340–1350.

Sheinberg, D. L., &Logothetis, N. K. (2002) Perceptual learning and the development of complex visual representations in temporal cortical neurons. In M. Fahle and T. Poggio (Eds.), *Perceptual learning* (95–124). Cambridge, MA: MIT Press.

Sugita, Y., Tsukiura, T., Suzuki, C., & Manaka, Y. (2006). *Handwriting analysis activates the fusiform face area.* Paper presented at the Society for Neuroscience. Atlanta, GA.

Tanaka, J. W. (2001). The entry point of face recognition: Evidence for face expertise. *Journal of Experimental Psychology: General, 130*(3), 534–543.

Tanaka, J. W., Curran, T., & Sheinberg, D. L. (2005). The training and transfer of real-world perceptual expertise. *Psychological Science: A Journal of the American Psychological Society / APS, 16*(2), 145–151.

Tanaka, J. W., & Farah, M. J. (1993). Parts and wholes in face recognition. Quarterly Journal of Experimental Psychology, 46A, 225–245.

Tanaka, J. W., & Taylor, M. (1991). Object categories and expertise: Is the basic level in the eye of the beholder? Cognitive Psychology, 23, 457–482.

Tarr, M. J. (2005). How experience shapes vision. *APA Science Briefs,* (July).

Tarr, M. J., & Cheng, Y. D. (2003). Learning to see faces and objects. *TRENDS in Cognitive Sciences, 7*(1), 23–30.

Tarr, M. J., & Gauthier, I. (2000). FFA: A flexible fusiform area for subordinate-level visual processing automatized by expertise. *Nature Neuroscience, 3*(8), 764–769.

Tarr, M. J., & Vuong, Q. C. (2002). Visual object recognition. In S. Yantis, & H. Pashler (Eds.), *Stevens' handbook of experimental psychology: Vol. 1. Sensation and perception.* (pp. 287–314). New York, NY: John Wiley & Sons, Inc.

Tsao, D. Y., Freiwald, W. A., Tootell, R. B., & Livingstone, M. S. (2006). A cortical region consisting entirely of face-selective cells. *Science, 311*(5761), 670–674.

Ullman, S., Vidal-Naquet, M., & Sali, E. (2002). Visual features of intermediate complexity and their use in classification. *Nature Neuroscience, 5,* 682–687.

Vogels, R., Biederman, I., Bar, M., & Lorincz, A. (2001). Inferior temporal neurons show greater sensitivity to nonaccidental than to metric shape differences. *Journal of Cognitive Neuroscience, 13*(4), 444–453.

Xu, Y. (2005). Revisiting the role of the fusiform face area in visual expertise. *Cerebral Cortex, 15,* 1234–1242.

Yin, R. K. (1969). Looking at upside-down faces. *Journal of Experimental Psychology, 81*(1), 141–145.

Zhang, L., & Cottrell, G. W. (2005). Holistic processing develops because it is good. In B. G. Bara, L. Barsalou, & M. Bucciarelli (Eds.), *Proceedings of the 27th Annual Cognitive Science Conference*: Mahwah, NJ: Lawrence Erlbaum.

3

Development of Expertise in Face Recognition

Catherine J. Mondloch, Richard Le Grand, and Daphne Maurer

INTRODUCTION

The ability to recognize individual faces is a highly specialized skill that emerges during infancy, continues to develop throughout childhood, and becomes adult-like in late adolescence. In this chapter we explore the developmental progression of face recognition and consider possible mechanisms that underlie it. Specifically, we evaluate the role of visual experience in driving the developmental changes and consider other potential factors that could account for the slow development of adult-like expertise. To begin, we describe the properties of the fully developed adult system for face processing.

Adults are experts at face processing. They have the remarkable ability to detect faces, even in the absence of normal facial features. They readily detect faces in paintings in which faces are composed of objects such as an arrangement of fruit, vegetables, or rocks (Bruce & Young, 1986), or when presented with a two-tone Mooney face (Kanwisher, Tong, & Nakayama, 1998), at least when the stimuli are upright. Face detection is facilitated by the fact that all faces share the same first-order relations: two eyes aligned horizontally above a nose and mouth. As a result, face images can be superimposed, or averaged, and the resulting stimulus remains recognizably face-like (Diamond & Carey, 1986). While adults are proficient at face detection, they recognize faces less often at this basic level (i.e., "that's a face") and more often at the subordinate level (e.g., "that's Wayne Gretzky") and can do so rapidly and accurately (Tanaka, 2001). This tendency to identify faces more often at the subordinate level is considered a marker of perceptual expertise (Tanaka & Gauthier, 1997). In fact, adults can recognize thousands of individual faces, even when the person is at a distance, in poor lighting, has a new hairdo, or is a former schoolmate who has not been seen for over 20 years (Bahrick, Bahrick, & Wittlinger, 1975).

How do newborn infants, who have never before perceived faces, eventually acquire the expert ability to recognize thousands of individual faces in adulthood? Here we outline the developmental pattern of face recognition during infancy and childhood, and examine the role of experience in driving the development of this expert system.

INFANCY

The Starting Point: Face Detection by Newborns

Newborns are readily engaged by faces: they look at real faces for long periods of time, look longer at drawings of faces than at experimental stimuli like newsprint or bull's-eyes, and, under some circumstances, when presented with patterns matched on low-level visual variables, orient preferentially toward those with more face-like characteristics (cf. Fantz, 1965; Goren, Sarty, & Wu, 1975; Johnson, Dziurawiec, Ellis, & Morton, 1991; Kleiner, 1987; Stechler, 1964; Mondloch et al., 1999; Valenza, Simion, Macchi Cassia, & Umiltà, 1996). These attentional biases ensure that the developing visual system receives input from human faces.

What is less certain is whether newborns' biases reflect the newborn being drawn toward stimuli matching an inborn specific face template or whether they result from more general visual preferences that favor faces. For example, real human faces may be attractive to newborns because they contain high-contrast patterned elements, are dynamic, come within 10–12 inches of the newborn's eyes, and often are accompanied by a voice—properties that engage newborns' attention even when the stimulus is not a face (e.g., Fantz, 1965; Kleiner, 1987). Fourier analyses of drawn faces indicate that they contain a great deal of energy at spatial frequencies visible to the newborn (Kleiner & Banks, 1987). Indeed, when newborns' preference for a face-like pattern over a checkerboard-like lattice was probed by pitting a hybrid stimulus with the visible energy in the face arranged like the lattice (which looks like a lattice to adults) against a hybrid pattern with the visible energy in the lattice arranged like a face (which looks like a face to adults), newborns looked longer at the former—the nonfacelike pattern with the face's energy level (see Figure 3.1d; Kleiner, 1987; Mondloch et al., 1999). These results indicate that overall level of visible energy is more important in determining newborns' looking preferences than whether the energy is arranged spatially to resemble a face. Faces are attractive to newborns, then, in part because they contain an optimal amount of energy that is visible to the newborn. Other objects in the newborn's environment are less attractive because the newborn's poor acuity and contrast sensitivity make many of their properties invisible and/or because they are visible but do not have the optimal amount of visible energy.

Although optimal visible energy influences newborns' preference for faces, it is not the only influence. For example, in the tests with hybrid stimuli, newborns did show sensitivity to facial organization when visible energy was equated: they looked longer at a face (i.e., energy and organization of the face) than at a comparison stimulus with the energy of the face organized like the lattice (Kleiner, 1987; Morton, Johnson, & Maurer, 1990). Similarly, newborns in the first hour after birth look longer at a stimulus (*config*) that has a head outline filled with three black squares in the location of the eyes and mouth than at a stimulus in which the location of the squares is inverted

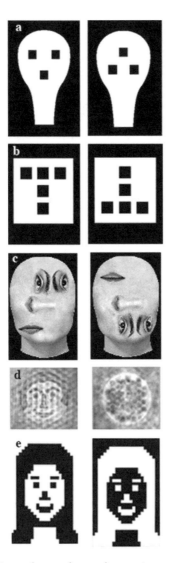

Figure 3.1 Stimulus pairs used to test face preferences in newborns, 6-week-olds, and 12-week-olds. (a) Config and its inverted version; (b) a "T" pattern and its inverted version; (c) a top-heavy scrambled face and a bottom-heavy scrambled face. Newborn infants prefer the leftmost image for pairs a, b, and c. (d) A stimulus with the organization of a face but the visible energy of a lattice, and a stimulus with the organization of a lattice but the visible energy of a face. Newborns prefer the stimulus on the right; 6- and 12-week-olds prefer the stimulus on the left. (e) A positive contrast schematic face and its phase-reversed version. A preference for the positive contrast face emerges between 6 and 12 weeks of age. Used with permission from C. J. Mondloch et al., 1999, "Face perception during early infancy," *Psychological Science*, *10*, pp. 419–422, Copyright 1999 Wiley-Blackwell.

(see Figure 3.1a) (Mondloch et al., 1999; see also Valenza et al., 1996). This early preference supports Johnson and Morton's proposal that there is an innate subcortical mechanism, *Conspec*, that causes newborns to orient toward high-contrast elements with the configuration of facial features (Johnson, 2005; Johnson & Morton, 1991; Morton & Johnson, 1991). They argue that Conspec serves to guarantee that the newborn's developing brain receives a great deal of visual input from faces, and that it then declines postnatally to be replaced by a cortical mechanism, *Conlern*. The experimental results suggest that config may approximate the optimal or minimal stimulus to activate Conspec. As would be expected under Morton and Johnson's hypothesis, the newborn's preference for config is robust if the stimuli are in the temporal visual field but disappears if they are in the nasal visual field, a pattern matching the temporal-nasal asymmetry in input to the subcortical structures likely to be involved (e.g., the superior colliculus, the pulvinar, or both) (Simion, Valenza, Umiltà, & Dalla Barba, 1998). Also, as predicted, the visual preference for the config stimulus disappears at about 6 weeks of age, at the same time that the baby begins to show greater sensitivity to the organizational properties of faces (see below) (Mondloch et al., 1999; see also Johnson & Morton, 1991). Collectively, these results suggest that there is an innate mechanism, possibly subcortical, that attracts babies to faces so that the developing cortex receives the visual experience necessary to drive cortical specialization for faces (but see Acerra, Burnod, & de Schonen, 2002, for evidence that even this preference could result from higher visible energy in config than the inverted stimulus). This innate mechanism is supplemented by general visual preferences for optimal energy level, movement, visual/auditory stimulation, and so forth, that serve the same adaptive function of guaranteeing that the baby pays attention to the faces in the environment.

Although the findings for config suggest that, in addition to general visual properties favoring faces, there is an innate preference for faces, Simion's systematic investigation of the preference suggests an alternative account. She found that newborns look preferentially toward head-shaped figures with more elements in the top over head-shaped figures with more elements in the bottom (see Figure 3.1b and c for examples) (Macchi Cassia, Turati, & Simion, 2004; Simion, Macchi Cassia, Turati, & Valenza, 2001; Simion, Valenza, Macchi Cassia, Turati, & Umiltà, 2002; Turati, Simion, Milani, & Umiltà, 2002; reviewed in Turati, 2004). This is true for photographs of faces, as well as arrangements of black squares like those used originally: newborns look longer at five squares arranged to form an upright T than at its inverted version (Simion et al., 2002), and they look longer at a photograph of a face with its elements rearranged unnaturally to have more elements than normal in the top than at the unadulterated photograph (Macchi Cassia et al., 2004). Thus, the preference for config may be just another example of newborns' preference for head-shaped stimuli with more visible elements in the top half—a general visual preference—and not evidence for an innate face template per se. Like the other general visual preferences, the top-heavy preference will serve the adaptive function of assuring that the human beings who interact with the newborn easily attract and keep the infants' attention. Interestingly, in adults such top-heavy patterns activate the fusiform face area (Caldera et al., 2006) and elicit a face-like event-related N170 (Le Grand, Barrie, & Tanaka, 2005), despite not being perceived as face-like. Thus, the newborn preference for top-heavy patterns may be related to activity in brain areas that later become specialized for face processing—in part because of the face input they receive during early infancy (see the section "The Role of Experience during Infancy").

While there is debate about the mechanisms underlying face preferences at birth, there is agreement that infants' preferences change postnatally. By 2–3 months, infants look preferentially toward stimuli with the internal organization of a face—even when that organization is pitted against a more optimal level of visible energy (Kleiner & Banks, 1987; Mondloch et al., 1999; see Maurer, 1985, for review of earlier studies) and even when it is pitted against a head-shaped pattern with the same number of elements, or even more elements, in the top half (Macchi Cassia, Kuefner, Westerlund, & Nelson, 2006; Turati, Valenza, Leo, & Simion, 2005). Unlike younger infants, they also look longer at a face with the normal polarity of dark elements on a light background than at the reverse negative polarity (see Figure 3.1e; Dannemiller & Stephens, 1988; Mondloch et al., 1999). These postnatal changes are assumed to reflect increasing cortical specialization for faces, although the newly developed selectivity for faces over top-heavy stimuli is not manifest in the components of the event-related potential that signal face detection in adults (potential precursors of the N170) (Machia Cassia et al., 2006). The postnatal changes appear to be driven by visual experience: our results to date from infants treated for bilateral congenital cataract indicate that on the day when they can first see after treatment, their face preferences matched those of newborns rather than age mates (Mondloch, Lewis, Maurer & Levin, unpublished data; see the section "The Role of Experience during Infancy"). Thus, in this rare condition in which visual input is blocked by cataracts, postnatal brain maturation is not sufficient to drive the typical changes in behavioral face preferences.

Recognition of Facial Identity

Newborns can recognize the face of their mother from visual cues alone: infants as young as 3 days old fixate their mother's face longer than the face of a stranger, even when olfactory cues have been eliminated by video presentation or a masking scent (Bushnell, 2001; Bushnell, Sai, & Mullin, 1989; Pascalis, de Schonen, Morton, Deruelle, & Fabre-Grenet, 1995). This looking preference is robust in infants who have had as little as 5.5 hours of exposure to the mother's face over those 3 days (Bushnell, 2001) and in infants who have not seen their mother during the preceding 15 minutes (the longest delay tested) (Bushnell, 2001). After habituation to the photograph of one unfamiliar female, infants 3 to 4 days old look longer at the photograph of a second unfamiliar female even after a 2 minute delay (the longest delay tested) (Pascalis & de Schonen, 1994). Not surprisingly, given their poor visual sensitivity, newborns make the discrimination when the faces are filtered to include information only at very low spatial frequencies (large details; 0–0.5 cycles/degree) but not when the faces are filtered to include only higher spatial frequencies (smaller details) (de Heering et al., 2008). These results indicate that newborns have the ability to perceive large distinguishing features of individual faces and to recognize them after a short delay even when the face (of their mother) is presented in an unfamiliar context (without movement, voice, smell, or contingent interaction; in a two-dimensional format). Thus, even during the period of primitive face detection (see the section "The Starting Point: Face Detection by Newborns"), babies are able to differentiate individual faces and store information about identity. However, the information they use appears to be more limited than it will be later during infancy.

To study the information used to recognize faces, investigators have tested newborns' recognition of the mother's face when various cues are eliminated. When the mother and stranger both wear identical scarves or wigs, thus eliminating most external cues, newborns no longer show a looking preference for mother over stranger (Pascalis et al., 1995), and this failure persists until about 6 weeks of age (Bartrip, Morton, & de Schonen, 2001; Bushnell, 2003). Similarly, following habituation to the photographed face of mother or a stranger, 1-month-olds show recovery of looking to a novel face when the individuals were photographed with either the eyes or mouth occluded but not if the two faces wore identical bathing caps (Bushnell, 1982).[1] This pattern has led researchers to conclude that young infants recognize and differentiate faces based on the external contour—perhaps because the area between the hair and face forms a large, high contrast contour that they can see easily. It fits with evidence of a more general externality bias favoring processing of external contour over internal features (e.g., Milewski, 1976; Salapatek, 1975) and with evidence that 1-month-olds (the youngest age tested) fixate the external contour of faces more than its internal features, even when the face belongs to the baby's own mother and even when it is moving and talking (Hainline, 1978; Haith, Bergman, & Moore, 1977; Maurer & Salapatek, 1976).

However, there are two findings inconsistent with the conclusion that the young infant's recognition of facial identity is based only on the external contour and that there is a change favoring internal features around 2 months of age. First, although it is not until 6 weeks of age that babies can recognize their mother when the external contour is occluded, during the first 4 months of life, infants fail to show a looking preference when the mother and stranger both wear masks occluding the internal features and leaving the hair and external contour visible, perhaps because they fail to recognize the stimulus as a face (Bartrip et al., 2001).

---

[1] The occlusion of eyes or mouth was tested only in the experiment involving mother and stranger.

Second, a recent habituation study revealed that even newborns 1 to 3 days old can discriminate between two strangers, based on the internal features alone (Turati, Macchi Cassia, Simion, & Leo, 2006). Turati et al.'s procedure differed from the studies measuring a looking preference for mother's face (Bartrip et al., 2001; Pascalis et al., 1995) in that there was no change in the features available for recognition between learning and test. Thus, newborns appear to be able to discriminate between unfamiliar faces based on *either* internal or external cues and to recognize something about those cues in an immediate test. Follow-up studies using the same method have revealed that external cues are, nevertheless, more salient for newborns: following habituation to a full face, newborns show a novelty preference on the paired test when shown the familiar and novel face with external features only but not when shown their internal features only. Similarly, following habituation to external features alone, newborns show a novelty preference on the paired test when shown full versions of the two faces, but do not following habituation to internal features alone (Turati et al., 2006). Combined with the scanning data (e.g., Milewski, 1976; Salapatek, 1975) showing a bias to look at external features, the results suggest that newborns learn faces based mainly on their external contour unless that contour has been masked. By 7 months of age, infants show evidence of integrating the internal and external features: following habituation to the faces of two unfamiliar women, they treat a new face that recombines the internal features of one woman with the external features of the other as if it is completely novel, if the faces are presented upright but not if they are inverted (Cashon & Cohen, 2001). Paradoxically, the integrative skill follows a U-shaped function with no sign of integration at 3 months, the integrative pattern for both upright and inverted faces at 4 months, a seeming loss of integration at 6 months, and its re-emergence at 7 months for upright faces only (Cashon & Cohen, 2004). Similarly, 4-month-olds discriminate between strangers' faces following habituation as readily when the faces are both presented inverted as when they are both presented upright unless the baby has to generalize habituation to the face in a novel point of view (Turati, Sangrigoli, Ruel, & de Schonen, 2004).

By 2–3 months, babies switch from an external to an internal bias when scanning faces and geometric patterns (Hainline, 1978; Haith et al., 1977; Hunnius & Geuze, 2004; Maurer & Salapatek, 1976; Salapatek, 1975). They look at the internal features more than the external features with a bias to fixate the eyes, at least in static faces. They also begin to demonstrate the cognitive skills needed to form prototypic representations of faces, a prerequisite to developing the multidimensional face space that appears to underlie adults' expert coding of facial identity (de Haan, Johnson, Maurer, & Perrett, 2001). At 5, but not 3 months, they discriminate between schematic faces that have normal relations among features from those that have been Thatcherized; that is, the relation among the internal features has been altered by rotating the eyes and mouth in an otherwise upright face, leaving each feature in more or less the normal location but making the face look grotesque from the altered relation among features (Bertin & Bhatt,

2004; Bhatt, Bertin, Hayden, & Reed, 2005). At 5 months they also discriminate between two photographed faces that differ only in the space between the two eyes and the space between the eyes and mouth, a configural cue called second-order relations that contributes to adults' face expertise (see the section "Internal Facial Characteristics"): following habituation to one spacing, they show a novelty preference when shown the same face with a change in spacing that spans the normal range of human variability (Hayden, Bhatt, Reed, Corbly, & Joseph, 2007). At 3 months, they fail a similar test with even larger changes in spacing that are outside natural limits (Bhatt et al., 2005). As in adults, 5-month-olds' sensitivity to Thatcherization and to second-order relations decreased when the faces were inverted. Combined with the findings for external and internal features, the results suggest that by 5–7 months of age, similar mechanisms underlie the processing of facial identity in infants and adults. Together, the evidence of parallel changes in scanning for faces and geometric patterns, of emergent skills that can initially be applied readily to either upright or inverted faces, of U-shaped developmental curves, and of later specialization for upright faces suggests that development during infancy may involve general changes in visual processing that are not face specific, but that alter the types of information babies pick up from their many exposures to upright faces in their environment. This exposure may, in turn, tune the emergent skills to upright faces.

A Special Role for Eyes?

Newborns look longer at a face if its eyes are open rather than closed (Batki, Baron-Cohen, Wheelwright, Connellan, & Ahluwalia, 2000) and if the eyes have direct rather than averted gaze (Farroni, Csibra, Simion, & Johnson, 2002; Farroni, Menon, & Johnson, 2006; Farroni, Pividori, Simion, Massaccesi, & Johnson, 2004). The looking preference for direct gaze is present for upright faces, but not for inverted faces or faces turned 45° to the side (Farroni et al., 2006). Although the explanation might be related to differences in the spatial frequencies in the eyes region, the preference nevertheless functions to attract newborns to the faces of individuals interacting with them and may facilitate the learning of the many social cues conveyed by the eye. In addition, a recent study found that newborns' orienting preference for config over the inverted stimulus and for a photographed face with normal rather than inverted internal features occurs only when the polarity matches that of a human face: dark squares (eyes) on a lighter background or a dark spot (pupil) within a lighter square (iris) (Farroni et al., 2005). Moreover, newborns show an orienting preference for a normal face photographed with natural overhead lighting (which creates shadows around the eye sockets so that dark eyes appear on a light background) over the same face photographed with unnatural lighting from below. Combined, these results suggest that newborns' face detection cannot be explained entirely based on visible energy or top-heavy energy within a frame. Rather, newborns appear to have an innate face template that is tuned to structural properties of the face that are associated with the appearance of the eyes. Such a template has the adaptive value of increasing newborns' attention to the faces of people who are interacting with them: in an upright orientation, lit from above, with eyes open and direct gaze. Those are the conditions under which people expect the baby to learn to recognize them and the conditions under which they emit the cues the baby will need to learn about facial expressions and joint attention.

Eye gaze also modulates 4-month-olds' recognition of facial identity: following habituation to a video of an animated face, infants show a novelty preference for a novel face over the familiar face in static, colored photographs when the faces have direct gaze throughout the experiment but not when they have averted gaze (Farroni, Massaccesi, Menon, & Johnson, 2007). It is not known whether averted gaze caused poorer encoding (as suggested by shorter looking time during habituation) or poorer retrieval, nor whether there are similar effects earlier in infancy.

CHILDHOOD

Face Recognition in Children

Despite abundant exposure to faces during infancy and childhood, children do not reach adult levels of expertise in recognizing facial identity until adolescence. Six- and eight-year-olds have difficulty matching facial identity when two versions of the same face differ in facial expression, clothing, or lighting (Benton & Van Allen, 1973, as cited in Carey, Diamond, & Woods, 1980; Bruce et al., 2000; Mondloch, Geldart, Maurer, & Le Grand, 2003) and even 10-year-olds have difficulty when they differ in point of view (Mondloch, Geldart, et al., 2003). Even when the same picture of a face is shown during familiarization and the recognition test, 10- to 14-year-olds make more errors than adults. In one study (Carey et al., 1980), adults and children aged 7 to 14 studied 48 faces; they were asked to indicate the gender of half of the faces and the likeability of the rest. They were then shown 48 pairs of faces and, for each pair, were asked which face had been seen previously. Like adults, children of all ages performed better for faces that had been rated on likeability, presumably because those faces had been processed more deeply; nonetheless, children of all ages made more errors than adults in both conditions.

Children's poor performance on some face recognition tasks may be attributable to general cognitive skills, such as immature memory strategies and attention. However, it is unlikely that general cognitive immaturities offer a complete explanation. First, the extent of the immaturity in face processing varies across manipulations relevant to face processing despite identical task demands (see "Cues to Facial Identity" below), and children perform worse than adults under a variety of conditions, even when memory demands are minimized/eliminated. Mondloch, Le Grand, & Maurer (2002) asked children (6 to 10 years of age) to make same/different judgments about pairs of Caucasian female faces; models wore a surgical cap to cover their hair and ears. Ten-year-olds made more errors than adults when the faces were presented sequentially with only a 300 ms interstimulus interval (Mondloch et al., 2002), and 8-year-olds (the only age group tested) made more errors than adults even when the faces were presented simultaneously for an unlimited amount of time (Mondloch, Dobson, Parsons, & Maurer, 2004; see also Bruce et al., 2000). Thus, although memory demands may contribute to children's poor performance on some tasks, 8-year-olds make more errors than adults even under conditions that minimize memory demands.

Children also perform worse than adults when tested with children's faces. Developmental change is evident in match-to-sample tasks (Bruce et al., 2000) and in same/different discrimination tasks even when the stimuli are children's faces (Mondloch, Maurer, & Ahola, 2006), the category of faces with which they have the most experience. There is also improvement in performance between 6 and 10 years of age when children are tested with familiar faces. Hay and Cox (2000) presented 6- to 7-year-olds and 9- to 10-year-olds with a face for 5 s and then, after a 10 s interstimulus interval, asked them to indicate which of two faces they had just seen. The older group performed better than the younger group regardless of whether the target face was familiar (a schoolmate) or unfamiliar.

In summary, children make more errors than adults at recognizing facial identity on face recognition tasks under a variety of conditions: recognizing highly familiar faces, matching familiar and unfamiliar faces, and making same/different judgments about pairs of unfamiliar faces presented either sequentially or simultaneously. Understanding the slow development of adult-like expertise for face recognition requires isolating components that underlie that expertise and tracing the development of each. In the next few sections, we review what is known about specific skills that play a role in adults' expert face recognition: holistic processing, sensitivity to differences among faces in the shape of external contours, internal features, and the spacing among features, and the ability to recognize faces despite transformations in their appearance.

Holistic Face Processing

Holistic processing is a hallmark of adults' expert face perception. When adults process faces holistically, the parts are integrated into a whole or gestalt-like representation, and information about individual features becomes less accessible (for a review see Maurer, Le Grand, & Mondloch, 2002). A compelling demonstration of holistic processing is the *composite face effect* (Carey & Diamond, 1994; Hole, 1994; Hole, George, & Dunsmore, 1999; Le Grand, Mondloch, Maurer, & Brent, 2004; Michel, Caldara, & Rossion, 2006; Young, Hellawell, & Hay, 1987). Adults find it difficult to recognize the top half of a celebrity's face when it has been aligned with the bottom half of a different face (Young et al., 1987). Presumably holistic processing binds the two halves of the face and creates a novel face, thereby making it difficult to recognize the person in the top half. Adults perform better after manipulations that disrupt holistic processing such as misaligning the two halves or inverting the face (Young et al., 1987). The composite face effect also occurs for same/different judgments about the top halves of unfamiliar faces (Hole, 1994; see Figure 3.2). In addition, adults recognize the features from an individual's face more easily in the context of the whole face (e.g., Larry's nose in Larry's face) than in isolation (*the whole/part advantage*) (Tanaka & Farah, 1993; see also Michel, Rossion, Han, Chung, & Caldara, 2006). These findings demonstrate that facial features are not only represented individually, but are also integrated into a holistic representation that interferes with access to any representation of the individual features.

There is some evidence suggesting that young children may process faces in a more piecemeal fashion than adults. Schwarzer (2000) trained 7-year-olds, 10-year-olds, and adults to place schematic faces into one of two categories that corresponded to an adult face and a child's face. The faces varied in four attributes (eyes, nose, mouth, and outline) and could be sorted successfully based on an individual feature or overall resemblance. Test faces were created to determine which approach had been used during training. For example, one test face had adult eyes, but all of the other features were those of a child. If a participant were classifying faces based on the isolated features of the eyes, he/she would categorize the face as an adult's; if a participant were classifying faces based on overall resemblance, he/she would categorize the face as a child's. Most 7- and 10-year-olds (about 62%) made choices based on isolated features, whereas most adults (56%) made choices based on overall similarity, that is, they categorized the faces holistically. Younger children (aged 3 to 5 years) show

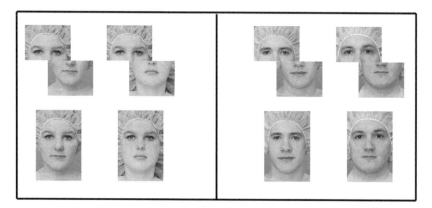

Figure 3.2 Composite face stimuli. Face pairs from the misaligned condition (top row) and the aligned condition (bottom row). For all face pairs, the bottom halves are different. The top halves either have the same (left column), or different (right column) top halves. In the aligned condition, holistic processing creates the impression that the top halves are always different. Reprinted with permission from R. Le Grand et al., 2004, *Psychological Science 15*, p. 763, Copyright 2004 Wiley-Blackwell.

little evidence of holistic processing on this task; instead they categorize faces based on a single feature (20%) or a different attribute on each trial (65%) (Schwarzer, 2002). Thus, under some conditions holistic processing may be slow to develop, at least for schematic pictures that are presented for a prolonged period of time.

However, when photographs of faces are used, both the composite face task and the whole/part task reveal adult-like holistic processing during early childhood. When asked to identify the top half of composite faces depicting classmates or newly familiarized faces, 6- and 10-year-old children, like adults, are faster on misaligned trials than on aligned trials (Carey & Diamond, 1994). Similarly, when 4- and 6-year-olds are asked to make same/different judgments about the top halves of unfamiliar faces, their accuracy is higher on "same" trials when the faces are misaligned (i.e., when interference is reduced by disrupting holistic processing) than when the faces are intact, and the effect is adult-like in magnitude (de Heering, Houthuys, & Rossion, 2007; Mondloch, Pathman, Le Grand, Maurer, & de Schonen, 2007). Similar conclusions can be drawn from studies that use the whole/part advantage to measure holistic processing. Children as young as 4 years show the whole/part advantage with no significant change in the size of the effect between 6 and 10 years of age (Tanaka, Kay, Grinnell, Stansfield, & Szechter, 1998) or between age 4 and adulthood (Pellicano & Rhodes, 2003; Pellicano, Rhodes, & Peters, 2006): at every age tested, subjects were more accurate at picking out a previously seen face from one in which a feature had been altered than they were at discriminating between the isolated parts. This early development of holistic processing may be necessary for the eventual development of adult-like expertise but it is not sufficient; despite evidence of holistic processing under some conditions by 4 years of age, some face processing skills have yet to emerge, and even young adolescents make more errors than adults on a variety of face processing tasks. Below we explore the mechanisms that underlie the slow development of adult-like expertise.

Cues to Facial Identity

Adults are able to recognize facial identity based on a variety of subtle differences among individual faces, including the shape of the external contour, the shape of individual internal features (e.g., eyes, mouth), and differences in the spacing among features (e.g., distance between the eyes) or *second-order relations*. Although each of these cues varies between two faces in the real world, the laboratory affords an opportunity to test sensitivity to each of these cues in isolation.

Facial Contour

Facial contour (hair, chin shape) facilitates face recognition, particularly of unfamiliar faces. Adults and children alike find it easier to recognize an unfamiliar face based only on its external features than only on its internal features (Want, Pascalis, Coleman, & Blades, 2003). Likewise, adults are able to make same/different judgments for pairs of unfamiliar faces that differ only in external contour even when the hair and ears are covered by a surgical cap and clothing cues are removed (Mondloch et al., 2002; See Figure 3.3). Under special conditions, adults can be fooled by external contour; when looking at a picture of Bill Clinton beside another politician, they perceive the second face as belonging to Al Gore even when the internal features are those of Bill Clinton (Sinha & Poggio, 1996). For adults, the external contour is a less salient cue for highly familiar faces: adults are better able to recognize familiar faces from photographs that include only the internal features than from photographs that include only the external features (Ellis, Shepherd, & Davies, 1979). Unlike adults, children younger than 7 years of age are more accurate when asked to identify pictures of classmates if photographs contain only the external features than if photographs contain only the internal features, and it is only when children are between 9 and 11 years of age that they show the adult-like pattern (Campbell & Tuck, 1995; Campbell, Walker, & Baron-Cohen, 1995).

Sensitivity to the external contour of a face develops very early (see also the section "Recognition of Facial Identity"). When asked to recognize a familiar face from a storybook that is paired with a foil that differs only in the external contour, 4-year-old children's (the youngest age tested) performance is virtually errorless (Mondloch, Leis, & Maurer, 2006). The same is true when 4-year-olds are asked to find their own face that is paired with a foil wearing the same clothes but with a different external contour. Notably, 4-year-olds notice that the foil is wearing their own clothing but not that the foil has their internal features (Mondloch, Leis, et al., 2006). By 6 years of age (the youngest age tested), children's accuracy is adult-like when making same/different judgments about pairs of unfamiliar faces that differ only in external contour despite the the fact that the models were wearing a surgical cap (Mondloch et al., 2002). Consistent with findings that children can identify faces based on contour information alone, removing contour information impairs their performance. In a match-to-sample task, children

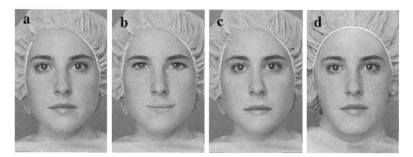

Figure 3.3 An original face (a) and three altered versions: (b) differs in the shape of the eyes and mouth(c) differs in the spacing among features, and (d) differs in the shape of the external contour. Used with permission from C. J. Mondloch et al., 2002, "Configural face processing develops more slowly than featural face processing," *Perception 31* (5), 553–566, Pion Limited, London.

between the ages of 5 and 10 years make more errors when the hair and ears are masked than when these external cues are visible (Bruce et al., 2000); older children have not been tested on this task. This pattern of results is somewhat paradoxical given that by 2 months of age infants look longer at the internal facial features than the external contour and that even newborns can recognize faces based on the internal features alone (see the section "Recognition of Facial Identity").

Children's sensitivity to the external contour is perhaps most evident in studies showing that paraphernalia (e.g., a hat) interferes with their face recognition. Six-year-olds and eight-year-olds are influenced by paraphernalia (e.g., glasses, hats) when matching unfamiliar faces: they are apt to select a match wearing the same hat as the target face rather than the target face without the hat (Carey & Diamond, 1977). This effect is reduced in older children (Carey & Diamond, 1977) and in younger children when the faces presented are less similar (Baenninger, 1994; Flin, 1985). Freire & Lee (2001) trained children between 4 and 7 years of age and 11-year-olds to recognize "Bob" when he was presented among three distracters that differed either in the spacing among facial features or the shape of individual features. Children who successfully completed training were then tested on four additional trials in which all four models (including the target; *uniform trials*) or two models (the target and one foil; *mixed trials*) wore a hat. Accuracy in both conditions increased with age; when the foils differed in the spacing of features (i.e., when paraphernalia should have its maximal effect), only the 11-year-olds performed above chance levels in the mixed trials.

Internal Facial Characteristics

Adults also recognize facial identity based on the shape and color of internal features (e.g., eyes, mouth) and the spacing among them, *second-order relations*. Several studies have isolated these two variables and measured adults' sensitivity to each type of cue. Freire, Lee, & Symons (2000) created eight versions of a single face that differed either in the shape of the eyes and mouth or in the spacing among facial features (e.g., by moving the eyes closer together and the mouth down). Adults made same/different judgments about pairs of faces that were presented simultaneously. Adults' accuracy was very high in both conditions but was about 10% higher in the featural condition ($M = 90\%$) than in the spacing condition. Similar results were obtained by Mondloch et al. (2002); adults' accuracy was about 7% higher in the featural condition ($M = 89\%$) than in the spacing condition, despite the spacing changes covering most of the natural variation among Caucasian female faces. Although scaling issues make it difficult to compare the two conditions directly when set sizes are small, more recent work suggests that adults' accuracy for featural cues was not overestimated in the original studies. Mondloch, Robbins, & Maurer (in press) created 20 versions of a single face that differed only in the appearance of the eyes and mouth; adults were asked to make same/different judgments for pairs of faces that were presented sequentially. Accuracy on "different" trials was high ($M = 93\%$) across the 60 pairs and did not decrease when the 11 pairs in which one face had make-up were removed from the analysis. Furthermore, when the analysis was constrained to the 29 pairs in which there was no striking difference in the color or size of the iris, accuracy remained at 93%. This pattern of results suggests that previous estimates of adults' sensitivity based on smaller face sets (Freire et al., 2000; Mondloch et al., 2002) are representative. Thus, adults are more sensitive to featural changes than they are to spacing changes that cover most of the natural variability among faces in the real world but stay within normal limits (Farkas, 1981), a result leading to the conclusion that adults are adept at using featural differences in recognizing facial identity.

Nonetheless, under some conditions features may not provide a reliable cue: when the face is seen from a new point of view, when the person poses a new facial expression, under poor lighting conditions, and after many years of aging. Under these conditions the appearance of individual features changes, and adults may need to rely on the spacing among facial features that comes from the bone structure of the face. It is not surprising then that adults are exquisitely sensitive to the spacing of facial features (Freire et al., 2000; Mondloch et al., 2002) and that limits in this sensitivity correspond to limits in their visual acuity (Ge, Luo, Nishiura, & Lee, 2003; Haig, 1984). Thus, the slow development of expert face recognition may result from slow development of sensitivity to either the shape of individual features or to the spacing among them.

Several studies suggest that sensitivity to differences among faces in the spacing of features (second-order relations) develops more slowly than sensitivity to differences in the shape of individual features. By 5 years of age (the youngest age tested), children, like adults, are biased toward low spatial frequencies in facial identity tasks. Deruelle & Fagot (2005) showed participants a low-pass face, a high-pass face, or a hybrid face (comprised of lower spatial frequencies from one face and higher spatial frequencies from another); participants were asked which of two filtered faces matched the original model in identity. Adults and children both chose the low-pass face, indicating their bias toward low spatial frequencies. Nevertheless, children appear to be able to use featural information in faces, but they are much less sensitive than adults to second-order relations. Mondloch, Leis, et al., (2006) familiarized 4-year-olds with two faces from a storybook over a 2-week period. The children were then asked to identify unaltered photographs of those children when they were paired with foils that differed either in the shape and color of individual features or in the spacing among features. Four-year-olds' performance was above chance when the foils differed featurally but was at chance levels when the foils differed in the spacing of features. An identical pattern of results was obtained when children were tested with pictures of their own face (Mondloch, Leis, et al., 2006) and with the faces of friends from their daycare center (Mondloch & Thomson, 2008). When tested with unfamiliar faces in a simultaneous match-to-sample task, 4-year-olds' performance was above chance, but only 10 of 18 children were correct on more than three of four test trials (Mondloch & Thomson, 2008). Similarly, when asked to select a target face presented among three foils, 4-year-olds performed at chance levels when the faces differed only in the spacing of features (Freire & Lee, 2001; see analysis of data for separate age groups in McKone & Boyer, 2006, p. 137) whereas they performed above chance when the foils differed in the shape of individual features. Performance improves dramatically by 6 years of age such that children are able to select a target among three foils (Freire & Lee, 2001) and perform above chance when asked to make same/different judgments about pairs of unfamiliar faces that differ only in the spacing of features (Mondloch et al., 2002). Nonetheless, whereas 6-year-olds are nearly adult-like when discriminating faces based on individual features (with no statistical difference by 10 years of age), even 14-year-olds make more errors than adults when discriminating faces based on the spacing of features (Mondloch et al., 2002; Mondloch, Le Grand, & Maurer, 2003). Converging evidence comes from a study in which 7- and 10-year-olds were asked which of two stimuli matched a just-seen target. All groups performed accurately when the task involved isolated features, with no improvement with age; in contrast, 10-year-olds were better than 7-year-olds when it involved the whole face, presumably because they were better able to use second-order relations (Hay & Cox, 2000). Collectively, these data suggest that sensitivity to spacing differences develops more slowly than sensitivity to featural differences, with children not beginning to use spacing cues to recognize facial identity until some time between 4 and 6 years of age. Children's failure to use spacing cues for facial identity appears to be at odds with the finding that 7-month-old infants are able to predict which of two stimuli is about to move when the stimuli differ only in the spacing of features (Hayden et al., 2007). Given that the visual system of infants is able to detect differences in the spacing of facial features, we conclude that the visual system of 4-year-old children is able to do so, but that children do not use that information to judge identity when the spacing of facial features falls within normal limits.

Only one study suggests that 7-year-olds are equally mature for featural and second-order relational changes. Adults recognize distinctive faces more readily than typical faces (Valentine & Bruce, 1986a, 1986b), likely because they reside in a less densely clustered area of face space (Valentine, 1991). Gilchrist and McKone (2003) demonstrated that children as young as 7 years of age show this advantage and that they do so both when faces are made distinctive by altering the appearance of individual features and when faces are made distinctive by altering the spacing among features. These results are consistent with those showing that by 7 years of age children are sensitive to the spacing of features in facial identity tasks (Freire & Lee, 2001; Mondloch et al., 2002), but Gilchrist and McKone (2003) claim that 7-year-olds are adult-like in their sensitivity. The finding of adult-like sensitivity in this task suggests that children are as sensitive as adults when spacing alterations are sufficiently large to make the face distinctive and when performance in adults is equated for the two conditions (but see Mondloch et al., 2004, for evidence that 8-year-olds judge spatially altered faces as less grotesque than adults).

Although 4-year-olds are not sensitive to second-order relations for facial identity, their insensitivity to the spacing of features is not absolute. The usual interpretation of the whole/part paradigm is that poor performance in the isolated features condition indicates that faces are processed holistically and that characteristics of individual features are encoded in the context of this gestalt representation (Tanaka & Farah, 2003). In adults, the whole/part effect is disrupted by changing the spacing of the features within the whole face (Tanaka & Sengo, 1997), presumably because the gestalt is altered when features are moved, making it more difficult to recognize features in their new context. Consequently, adults are less able to identify which of two mouths is "Bob's" when the mouths are presented in the context of "Bob's" face but other features such as the eyes are moved. These data suggest that an implicit representation of second-order relations is incorporated into the facial gestalt. Pellicano et al. (2006) report the same effect in 4-year-old children, suggesting that 4-year-olds' gestalt may also include information about the spacing among features. We note, however, that Pellicano et al. did not present the original face in their study; rather, the model face had eyes moved in one direction (e.g., farther apart) and the test face had eyes moved in the opposite direction (i.e., closer together) (personal communication, 2007). This is in contrast to our studies in which the original, unaltered version of a face was presented with a spatially altered version in which the eyes were moved in one direction. Consequently, differences in the spacing among facial features were twice as large in the study by Pellicano and Rhodes (approximately 5 SDs) (Pellicano & Rhodes, personal communication, 2007) than in our studies (Mondloch, Leis et al., 2006; Mondloch & Thomson, 2008). The implication is that 4-year-olds are sensitive to only large changes in spacing.

Studies of distinctiveness also suggest that 4-year-olds are sensitive to large changes in spacing. McKone & Boyer (2006) created distinctive faces by altering the appearance of individual features or the spacing among them. One group of adults rated each face on distinctiveness, and based on those ratings, McKone and Boyer created pairs with small, medium, or large differences in distinctiveness such that distinctiveness ratings were equated across featural and spacing manipulations. Four-year-olds selected the face adults had rated distinctive for both types of change when the differences in distinctiveness were large, although their success ($M = 63\%$) was less than that of adults ($M = 92\%$). Importantly, they were no more successful for featural changes than spacing changes. These data suggest that 4-year-olds have some sensitivity to second-order relations, at least when adults rate one member of the pair as extremely distinct. However, when spacing changes are small (McKone & Boyer, 2006) and remain within normal limits (Mondloch & Thomson, in press), 4-year-olds perform at chance levels when asked to select the more distinctive member of each pair. Thus, adult-like sensitivity to second-order relations is slow to mature when stimulus sets representative of variability in the real world are used (e.g., Friere et al., 2000; Freire & Lee, 2001; Mondloch et al., 2002; Mondloch, Leis, et al., 2006; Mondloch, Le Grand, et al., 2003; Mondloch & Thomson, 2008).

In summary, children's poor performance on some face recognition tasks, relative to that of adults, appears to be caused by the slow refinement of specific face processing skills. By 4 years of age (the youngest age tested) children are very sensitive to facial contour, and they show evidence of adult-like holistic processing. Sensitivity to facial features is evident by 4 years of age and is adult-like by 10 years of age. Sensitivity to differences among faces in the spacing of features emerges during the preschool years for large differences but continues to be refined until adolescence. Although the underlying cause of the refinement of sensitivity to the spacing of facial features may not be face specific (i.e., may be due to more general development of the visual system), the consequence appears to be a gradual improvement in face recognition skills. Below we discuss factors that account for the slow development of expert face recognition.

WHAT FACTORS ACCOUNT FOR THE SLOW DEVELOPMENT OF FACE RECOGNITION?

Expertise in face recognition develops after years of experience in differentiating among upright human faces. As a result of this extensive experience, by adulthood faces are processed differently than objects for which we are not experts (e.g., houses, landscapes, and animals) (e.g., Diamond & Carey, 1986; Scapinello & Yarmey, 1970; Yin, 1969), at least when faces are upright. A striking demonstration of adults' expertise in face identity is the *face inversion effect*—much poorer accuracy and longer reaction times for discriminating and recognizing faces presented upside-down versus upright (Yin, 1969; for a review, see Rossion & Gauthier, 2002). The magnitude of this inversion effect is much larger for faces than most nonface objects (for reviews see Maurer et al., 2002; Rossion & Gauthier, 2002; Valentine, 1988). A similar inversion effect can also be obtained with nonface objects through extensive experience discriminating among them (Gauthier & Tarr, 1997). The effect of experience on recognition is also evident when comparing human faces and those of other species. Adults are much better able to discriminate among human faces than among faces of another species such as sheep and monkeys (Mondloch et al., 2006; Pascalis, de Haan, & Nelson, 2002). Adults are also much better able to recognize faces of individuals from their own race compared to individuals from another race or cultural group—the *other-race effect* (Meissner & Brigham, 2001), an effect that is modulated by the differential frequency of exposure to own- versus other-race faces (Wright, Boyd, & Tredoux, 2001). Presumably as a result of differential experience, adults process other-race faces less holistically (Michel, Caldara, et al., 2006; Michel, Corneille, & Rossion, 2007; Michel, Rossion, et al., 2006; Tanaka, Kiefer, & Bukach, 2004; but see Elms et al., 2008) and are less sensitive to differences in the appearance of individual features and the spacing among them (Elms et al., 2008; Hayward, Rhodes, & Schwaninger, 2008; Rhodes, Hayward, & Winkler, 2006). Superior face processing for upright own-race faces is unlikely to be innately prespecified; rather, it is more likely to be the result of regularly differentiating faces from particular categories. Below we examine how experience shapes the face recognition system during development, discuss the neural mechanisms that underlie this ability, and identify potential factors that would account for the slow maturation of expertise in face recognition.

The Role of Experience during Infancy

Infancy is characterized by rapid developmental changes in the ability to process faces, changes that are dependent upon visual experience. Because of their own visual biases and the fact that adults and children alike are attracted to them, babies receive abundant exposure to faces during the first few weeks of life. Here we examine converging evidence that early exposure to faces shapes the specificity of the face perception system; in its absence some mechanisms underlying adult expertise are prevented from developing normally.

A unique method that has been employed to examine the role of early experience has been to compare individuals with normal visual experience to patients who were born with cataracts in both eyes that were sufficiently dense to deprive them of visual input early in life. Later in infancy the cataracts were treated by surgical removal of the natural lens and fitting of an optical correction (a contact lens) that provided nearly normal visual input thereafter (see Maurer, Lewis, & Brent, 1989). Because the cataracts deprived these patients of all patterned input, and not just input from faces, such studies are an indirect assessment of whether the development of face perception requires early experience with faces. Our studies on these patients indicate that visual experience during the first few weeks and months of life is critical for the normal development of some, but not all, aspects of face processing.

Although sensitivity to first-order relations (face detection) improves during infancy (see the section "The Starting Point: Face Detection by Newborns"), its eventual perfection does not require early visual input. Individuals aged 9–20 years (mean = 14 years) who were deprived of early visual experience during early infancy by bilateral cataracts (mean length of deprivation = 3.9 months from birth) are as fast and accurate as age-matched controls at detecting facial structure in upright Mooney faces (Mondloch, Le Grand, et al., 2003). The results from deprived patients could reflect an innate programming of sensitivity to first-order relations of faces that is not affected adversely by visual deprivation. Alternatively, and more likely, it reflects a mechanism that can be trained equally well by visual input from birth or after a delay. Several pieces of evidence indicate that experience alters the face preferences of visually normal infants and hence favor the second alternative (see "Infancy" section). In addition, preliminary data from infants treated for congenital cataract after 6 weeks of age indicate that the pattern of face preferences on the day they can first see is like that of newborns, rather than that of infants of the same age who had normal visual experience—a pattern suggesting that the postnatal increase in sensitivity to first-order relations is driven by visual input (Mondloch, Lewis, Maurer, & Levin, unpublished data). In adults, upright Mooney faces activate the face-sensitive FFA (Kanwisher et al., 1998). However, it is unknown whether the neural correlates underlying face detection following early visual deprivation are the same as those found in visually normal individuals or when these neural correlates emerge.

The normal ability to detect faces based on their first-order relations following early visual deprivation contrasts with permanent deficits in other aspects of face processing. Early visual deprivation prevents the later development of holistic processing, as measured by the composite face effect. Visually normal adults and children as young as 4 years of age have difficulty identifying that the top halves of two identical faces are the same when they are aligned with different bottom halves (de Heering et al., 2007; Hole, 1994; Le Grand et al., 2004; Mondloch et al., 2007). This effect is the result of holistic processing of the intact, aligned faces, making it difficult to ignore the bottom halves of the faces. Performance improves when the top and bottom halves are misaligned, a manipulation that disrupts holistic processing. In contrast, patients (age 9 to 23 years) deprived of early visual experience by bilateral cataracts (mean duration of deprivation = 4.6 months from birth) perform just as well when composite faces are aligned as they do when composite faces are misaligned (Le Grand et al., 2004). This result is particularly striking as the patients' impairment in holistic processing is demonstrated by *enhanced* performance relative to normals when the top halves are the same and the faces are aligned. The results demonstrate that this important aspect of processing, which distinguishes face from object processing (reviewed in Maurer et al., 2002), is not prespecified, but rather depends on early visual input to set up or maintain the neural substrates underlying it.

Early visual deprivation has no apparent effect on the later development of recognition of facial identity based on individual features (featural processing). Deprived patients can easily distinguish faces that differ only in the shape of individual features (Le Grand, Mondloch, Maurer, & Brent, 2001), even when there are no striking changes in the color or size of the eyes (Mondloch et al., 2008), and they can match faces based on emotional expression, vowel being mouthed, and direction of eye gaze (Geldart, Mondloch, Maurer, de Schonen, & Brent, 2002)—tasks that can be performed by processing local features. They can also distinguish faces that differ only in the external contour of the face (Le Grand et al., 2001). In contrast, they have deficits in distinguishing faces that differ only in the spacing among features such as the distance between the eyes (Le Grand et al. 2001; Le Grand, Mondloch, Maurer, & Brent, 2003), and in matching faces' identity when the matching face is presented from a novel point of view

(Geldart et al., 2002)—tasks that require sensitivity to second-order relations (Mondloch, Geldart, et al., 2003). Early visual input to specifically the right hemisphere is necessary for the later development of normal sensitivity to second-order relations. Patients deprived of normal input to either the right hemisphere or both hemispheres show impairment at distinguishing faces that differ in the spacing of features, while patients whose early deprivation affected mainly the left hemisphere perform normally (Le Grand et al., 2003). In fact, visual deprivation of normal input to the right hemisphere lasting as little as the first 2 months after birth is sufficient to cause these deficits. This finding is especially interesting given that sensitivity to second-order relations is particularly slow to develop in visually normal children (see the section "Internal Facial Characteristics"). More recent work suggests that the deficit in the spacing among facial features is face specific; patients treated for bilateral congenital cataract perform like visually normal controls when asked to discriminate houses that differ only in the spacing of features (i.e., windows and doors) (Robbins, Maurer, Mondloch, Nishimura, & Lewis, 2008). In contrast, recognition of facial identity based on the shape of internal features or the external contour develops more rapidly and does not require early visual experience.

In sum, visual experience during early infancy, which is effectively limited to low spatial frequencies (see the section "The Starting Point: Face Detection by Newborns"), sets up or maintains the cortical areas that will become responsible for some aspects of expert face processing later in life. It is unclear from the studies of cataract patients whether it is visual input per se, or more specifically experience with faces during early infancy that drives this neural organization. However, a recent study with monkeys suggests that it is visual input during infancy that is necessary to preserve the neural architecture for the later development of face expertise, not experience with faces per se. Sugati (2008) selectively deprived infant monkeys of experience with faces beginning immediately after birth until between 6 and 24 months of age. The infant monkeys were raised in a visually rich environment, but their human caregivers wore masks at all time. When tested during the period of deprivation, the infant monkeys looked preferentially toward both human and monkey faces when they were paired with nonface objects; however they did not look longer at monkey faces than at human faces. Furthermore, following familiarization with one face, they were able to discriminate both novel human and novel monkey faces and could do so based on either the shape of internal features or their spacing. In fact, it was later exposure to either human or monkey faces that led to perceptual narrowing (see next section). As discussed in the next section, several lines of evidence from studies on visually normal infants demonstrate that experience with faces early in life affects the properties of the face processing system. Combined with the results on face detection (see the section "The Starting Point: Face Detection by Newborns"), these results suggest that exposure to faces during infancy is necessary for the refinement of sensitivity to the first-order relations that define a face, but not for the development of sensitivity to the featural and spacing differences that adults use to recognize facial identity. For those identity cues, what is necessary is that the nervous system be exposed to patterned visual input so that the requisite neural substrate is preserved for later refinement by experience with faces. As we discuss in the next section, that refinement normally begins during infancy, but Sugita's study with monkeys suggests that the refinement can be delayed if there is no exposure to faces.

Experience-Based Perceptual Narrowing

The face processing system in infancy normally undergoes a process of refinement based on the specific faces to which the infant is exposed. According to the model proposed by Nelson and colleagues (Nelson, 2001; Pascalis et al., 2002), regions of the temporal cortex that receive information about faces during early infancy are initially broadly tuned to stimuli from a number of categories including inverted faces and nonhuman faces. With increased exposure to upright human faces over the subsequent months and years, these cortical regions become more and more narrowly tuned and eventually become specialized for recognition of such stimuli. The process of specialization is illustrated well by the study of face-deprived monkeys mentioned earlier (Sugita, 2008). At the end of deprivation, the monkeys were housed alone and for a 1-month period were exposed to either human or monkey faces. At the end of 1 month, when they were shown a pair of faces comprised of one human face and one monkey face, they looked longer at the species of face to which they had been exposed. Furthermore, infants exposed to human faces were able to recognize individual human faces, but not individual monkey faces; infants exposed to monkey faces showed the opposite pattern. These visual preferences and differential recognition abilities were maintained even after 1 year of being exposed to both human and monkey faces.

Similar patterns have been revealed in human infants. Perceptual narrowing begins during infancy: 6-month-olds can discriminate between individual monkey faces as readily as between individual human faces, whereas 9-month-olds tested with the same method discriminate between the human but not the monkey faces (Nelson, 1993; Pascalis et al., 2002), a pattern that is paralleled in language (Kuhl, Tsao, & Liu, 2003) and music perception (Hannan & Trehub, 2005). Experience with monkey faces between 6 and 9 months of age can maintain the 6-month-olds' skill: 9-months-olds who were regularly exposed to a picture book of monkey faces during the previous 3 months retain the ability to accurately discriminate monkey faces (Pascalis et al., 2005; see Hannon & Trehub, 2005, for a similar finding in music perception and Kuhl et al., 2003, for a similar finding in phonemic perception). The own-species bias is evident later in childhood, as well. Five-year-olds also show an enhanced ability at recognizing the identity of human faces compared to faces from nonhuman categories such as sheep and monkeys (Pascalis, Demont, de Haan, & Campbell, 2001).

Exposure to predominantly own-race faces during infancy also refines the face processing system and leads to an increase in the ability to discriminate own-race faces compared to other-race faces (i.e., the other-race effect). Newborn infants do not show a preference for own-race compared to other-race faces, but exposure to mainly own-race faces during the first 3 months is sufficient to bias infants' looking preferences. Infants aged 3 months who were raised in a predominantly homogeneous own-race environment show a looking preference for own-race over other-race faces (Bar-Haim, Ziv, Lamy, & Hodes, 2006; Kelly et al., 2005). Consistent with the view that visual experience with specific face categories shapes the infant face recognition system, there is no looking preference for own-race faces in 3-month-olds living in a heterogeneous cross-race environment (e.g., Israeli-born infants of African parents) (Bar-Haim et al., 2006). In addition to a looking preference, 3-month-olds are also better at recognizing the identity of own-race faces than of other-race faces. Caucasian infants who are familiarized with a single Caucasian and Asian face only demonstrate a novelty preference for an unfamiliar own-race face. However, the infant face recognition system remains sufficiently malleable that brief exposure to three Asian faces leads to evidence of discrimination among them (Sangrigoli & de Schonen, 2004b). Nonetheless, by 3.5 months babies are more sensitive to differences among own-race faces than among other-race faces: Caucasian infants can discriminate between an original Caucasian face and a morphed version of that face that is 70% Caucasian/30% Asian, but they show no evidence of discriminating between an original Chinese face and a morphed version that is 70% Asian/30% Caucasian. Between 3 and 9 months of age, face perception continues to be tuned by experience such that by 9 months of age, infants recognize own- but not other-race faces (Kelly et al., 2007). Superior processing for own-race faces is also evident during childhood. It has been demonstrated at 4 years of age and a number of ages thereafter that children are better at identifying individual faces from their own race (Chance, Turner, & Goldstein, 1982; Pezdek, Blandon-Gitlin, & Moore, 2003; Sangrigoli & de Schonen, 2004a). Nevertheless, the face processing system remains sufficiently plastic during childhood to allow for the other-race effect to be reversed: when tested as adults, Korean individuals adopted by Caucasian families in Europe between the ages 3–9 years are better at recognizing Caucasian faces, for which they have extensive experience after the adoption, than Asian own-race faces that they experienced before adoption (Sangrigoli, Pallier, Argenti, Ventureyra, & de Schonen, 2005).

A hallmark of adults' expertise in face recognition is the face inversion effect: adults are much faster and accurate at recognizing upright faces relative to their inverted counterpart. Studies with young infants suggest that experience with faces in the canonical upright orientation is critical to the development of configural face processing. Like newborns (Turati et al., 2006), infants at 3–5 months of age can discriminate between the faces of two strangers as readily upright or inverted (Cashon & Cohen, 2004; Turati & Simion, 2004). However, when the task is modified so as to force the use of configural cues, babies in the same age range may pass with upright faces and fail with inverted faces: this is true for recognizing a familiar face in a new viewpoint at 4 months (Turati et al., 2004), discriminating two faces that differ only in the spacing of internal features at 5 months (Bhatt et al., 2005; Hayden et al., 2007), and integrating internal and external features into a holistic gestalt at 7 months (Cashon & Cohen, 2004).

Paradoxically, studies with children indicate that the inversion effect emerges during the preschool years and continues to increase until middle childhood. Under many conditions, 6- and 8-year-olds' judgments of facial identity are equivalent for upright and inverted faces while 10-year-olds show the adult-like pattern of better performance on upright faces (Carey & Diamond, 1977). Thus, by the age of 10, children clearly show the inversion effect. Tests using a child-friendly procedure involving a picture book of upright and inverted faces reveal an inversion effect by 5 years of age, but even in that study children between the ages of 2 and 4 years show no evidence of an inversion effect (Brace et al., 2001). At first glance these findings appear to contradict evidence showing an inversion effect in infants. However, it is difficult to compare directly face inversion studies with infants to those with children because the methodology and stimuli used with these two groups differ tremendously. For example, whereas studies on children tend to use a relatively large set of photographic face images, infant studies typically use habituation to a single face, and often the images are schematic or cartoon faces. The lack of a face inversion effect in young children suggests that at this age the face processing system is not as specified as in adults, and perhaps additional experience viewing upright faces is necessary for such specificity to emerge. In sum, developmental studies on the face inversion effect provides further evidence that the system underlying face recognition becomes gradually fine tuned during infancy and childhood to the properties of faces present in the individual's visual environment, namely upright human faces. The slow development of the face inversion effect parallels that of sensitivity to second-order relations. Interestingly, while inverting a face affects the ability to encode many types of facial cues, it appears to disproportionately affect sensitivity to second-order relations, and this pattern first emerges at 10 years of age (Mondloch et al., 2002).

Why Is Sensitivity to Second-Order Relations Particularly Slow to Develop?

There are several hypotheses about why children's sensitivity to second-order relations develops so slowly. One hypothesis is that this sensitivity improves as children acquire additional experience differentiating individual faces (Nelson, 2003). Diamond and Carey (1986) argued that children under 10 years of age are like adult novices attempting to recognize individual dogs: both lack expertise in differentiating among individuals based on second-order relations. However, the difference in accuracy between adults and 8-year-olds is of equal magnitude for both human faces (for which adults have expertise) and for monkey faces (for which they do not), suggesting that expertise per se is an inadequate explanation. Mondloch, Maurer, et al. (2006) asked 8-year-olds and adults to make same/different judgments about pairs of monkey faces and pairs of human faces that differed only in the spacing among features; the spacing changes were identical across the two face sets. If the large improvement in sensitivity to the spacing of features in upright human faces that occurs between 8 and 14+ years of age depends on years of experience differentiating individual human faces, then there should have been a greater difference between children and adults for human faces than for monkey faces because additional experience discriminating monkey faces is not acquired after 8 years of age. The results did not match this prediction. Adults were more accurate than 8-year-olds for both face sets, but, like adults, 8-year-olds' accuracy was 9% higher for the human face set than it was for the monkey face set. Furthermore, when asked to discriminate houses that differed in features (houses and doors) or the spacing among features, 8-year-olds were disproportionately worse than adults on the spacing task (Robbins, Shergill, Maurer, & Lewis, 2007). Based on these results, we conclude that the slow development of sensitivity to second-order relations after 8 years of age is caused, at least in part, by age differences in general perceptual abilities rather than in face-specific mechanisms. For example, limits in adults' sensitivity to second-order relations correspond to limits in their acuity (Ge et al., 2003; Haig, 1984). Skoczenski and Norcia (2002) showed that Vernier acuity, a hyperacuity involving sensitivity to slight misalignments between stimuli like abutting lines, continues to improve until 14 years of age. Thus, although the lower spatial frequencies available to infants allow some sensitivity to second-order relations (Hayden et al., 2007; de Schonen & Mathivet, 1989), adult-like expertise may depend on a much more refined visual system. A second visual skill that continues to improve until adolescence is spatial integration—the ability to link small oriented elements into a flowing contour (Kovacs, Kozma, Feher, & Benedek, 1999). Although even 4-year-olds show the whole/part advantage (Pellicano & Rhodes, 2003; Pelicano et al., 2006) and 4-year-olds show an adult-like composite face effect (Carey & Diamond, 1994; de Heering et al., 2007; Mondloch et al., 2007), the ability to integrate separated elements continues to be refined after those ages (see also Schwartzer, 2000). In sum, immaturities in Vernier acuity, spatial integration, or some other visual skill may limit children's sensitivity to second-order relations, at least after 8 years of age.

A second hypothesis is that the "face space" that allows adults to discriminate and recognize hundreds of faces by encoding individual exemplars relative to a face prototype (Valentine, 1991) is slow to develop. Faces vary continuously on multiple dimensions (e.g., eye size, distance between the nose and mouth), each of which can be represented as a vector in "face space." Individual faces are represented as single points in this multidimensional space. The *direction* of the vector joining each individual face to the prototype represents how that face differs from the average face (the identity trajectory); the *distance* between each individual face and the prototype represents how typical/distinctive that face is. Norm-based coding of facial

identity has recently been demonstrated in adults using adaptation paradigms: adapting (exposure) to a face for several seconds biases perception of a
subsequent face, so that an average face, seen correctly as having no particular
identity before adaptation, begins to resemble the computationally opposite
identity (Leopold, O'Toole, Vetter, & Blanz, 2001). Children show
this identity aftereffect by 8 years of age (the youngest age tested;
Nishimura, Maurer, Jeffery, Pellicano, & Rhodes, 2008). Adults also demonstrate attractiveness aftereffects. After being adapted to consistently distorted
faces (e.g., with compressed features), adults' ratings of both facial attractiveness and normality shift in the direction of the adapting stimuli such that
faces with slight distortions are rated as more attractive and more normal
than unaltered faces (Maclin & Webster, 2001; Rhodes, Jeffery, Watson,
Clifford, & Nakayama, 2003; Watson & Clifford, 2003). Children also show
attractiveness aftereffects by 8 years of age (Anzures, Mondloch, & Lackner,
2009). Although infants can form face prototypes (de Haan et al., 2001) and
8-year-olds show adaptation aftereffects, children's face space may be less
refined than that of adults. This was evident when adults and 8-year-olds
were asked to rate the attractiveness of both unaltered and distorted faces
prior to adaptation (Anzures et al., 2009); much larger distortions were
required for children than for adults in order to generate preadaptation
ratings in which unaltered faces were rated as most attractive. Likewise,
although 8-year-olds rate both Thatcherized and spatially distorted faces as
more bizarre than unaltered faces, their bizarreness ratings are much lower
than those of adults (Mondloch et al., 2004). These data suggest that some
aspects of norm-based coding continue to develop during childhood (e.g.,
the number of dimensions represented in face space and the ability to
discriminate small differences within any one dimension; Anzures et al.,
2009; see also Rhodes, Robbins, et al., 2005).

Development of the Neural Markers Underlying Face Processing

As discussed above, there is an abundance of behavioral evidence that face
processing changes during infancy and childhood. Similar change is also
found for the brain mechanisms underlying face processing. In adults, certain
cortical areas are highly responsive to faces as compared to a variety of
nonface objects. Neuroimaging studies in adults have identified face processing regions within the ventral occipitotemporal cortex, particularly an area
of the fusiform gyrus referred to as the *FFA* (fusiform face area) (e.g., Haxby
et al., 2001; Haxby, Hoffman, & Gobbini, 2000). In adults, the FFA responds
more to faces than to a variety of nonface objects (Aguirre, Singh, &
D'Esposito, 1999; Dubois et al., 1999; Haxby et al., 2001; McCarthy, Puce,
Gore, & Allison, 1997). The response to faces is generally bilateral with a
stronger response in the right than left hemisphere (Kanwisher, McDermott,
& Chun, 1997; McCarthy et al., 1997). Activity in the FFA is higher when the
background encourages perception of the stimulus as a face than when it
encourages perception of a vase (the Rubin face–vase illusion; Hasson,

Hendler, Bashat, & Malach, 2001). Similarly, in a binocular rivalry task in which a face and a house are presented to different eyes, face percepts are accompanied by increased FFA responses (Moutoussis & Zeki, 2002; Tong, Nakayama, Vaughan, & Kanwisher, 1998; see also Bentin, Sagiv, Mecklinger, Friederici, & von Cramon, 2002). Inverting two-tone Mooney faces disrupts the ability to detect a face and produces a significant decrease in FFA activation (Kanwisher et al., 1998). The FFA also responds strongly to upright objects for which the observer has expertise, especially when the objects must be categorized at the subordinate level (Gauthier, Skudlarski, Gore, & Anderson, 2000; Gauthier, Tarr, Anderson, Skudlarski, & Gore, 1999). There is considerable debate as to the precise role of the FFA in face processing, including whether it is truly selective for faces or rather mediates the differentiation of objects with which one has developed an expertise (e.g., Gauthier et al., 1999; Grill-Spector, Knouf, & Kanwisher, 2004; Joseph & Gathers, 2002; Rhodes, Byatt, Michie, & Puce, 2004; Tarr & Cheng, 2003). Regardless of whether the processing in the FFA is specific to faces or generalizes to other objects of expertise, there remains the question of the development of its selective response to faces.

To date there is little known about developmental changes in the activation of the FFA during infancy. By 2 months of age, human faces activate a network of cortical areas predominantly in the right inferior-temporal cortex. This network includes regions within the fusiform gyrus that may be the homologue of the adult FFA (Tzourio-Mazoyer et al., 2002). However, the activation is widely distributed and includes cortical areas implicated in language processing. fMRI studies suggest that face-specific neural activity is slow to develop during childhood. Three studies have reported a lack of face-specific activity in the fusiform face area prior to 10 years of age (Aylward et al., 2005; Gathers, Bhatt, Corbly, Farley, & Joseph, 2004; Scherf, Behrmann, Humphreys, & Luna, 2007; see also Passarotti et al., 2003), and in the one study reporting face-specific activity (Golarai et al., 2007) the right fusiform face area was three times larger in adults than in children aged 7 to 11 years. Furthermore, accuracy on a face memory task was correlated with the size of the fusiform face area (Golarai et al., 2007). Together with behavioral studies, studies of the fMRI correlates of face processing in infants and children suggest that there is a gradual process of cortical specialization that emerges early, and with increased experience with faces, continues to develop throughout childhood and into adolescence.

Developmental studies using event-related potentials (ERPs) provide converging evidence of increasing neural specificity with age. Studies of adults have shown that a negative-going deflection occurring at about 170 ms poststimulus (N170) is larger for faces than for many other categories of stimuli (Bentin, Allison, Puce, Perez, & McCarthy, 1996; Carmel & Bentin, 2002) and usually occurs more rapidly when adults view upright faces compared to objects (Caldera et al., 2003; Itier & Taylor, 2004). In adults, the N170 is affected by manipulations that disrupt the basic configuration of the face: its latency is increased when the face is presented without eyes

(Eimer, 1998), the features are scrambled (Jemel, George, Olivares, Fiori, & Renault, 1999), or the face is inverted (Bentin et al., 1996; Rossion et al., 1999; Sagiv & Bentin, 2001). In addition to the temporal delay, inverting a face increases the amplitude of the N170 (Rossion et al., 1999). Based on these findings, it has been proposed that the adult N170 reflects a *structural encoding mechanism* sensitive to the basic configuration of a face (Bentin et al., 2002). In addition, the N170 may reflect specific aspects of face processing, with the N170 in the left hemisphere being larger when the observer is detecting featural differences than spacing differences, and the right hemisphere showing the opposite pattern (Scott & Nelson, 2006). Furthermore, the enhanced N170 seen for faces may reflect expertise, rather than face processing per se; the N170 is also observed for nonface objects with which the observer has extensive expertise. For example, the N170 is greater when dog and bird experts are presented with an object from their category of expertise than for control stimuli (Scott, Tanaka, Scheinberg, & Curran, 2006; Tanaka & Curran, 2001; see also Curran, Tanaka, & Weiskopf, 2002).

In infants as young as 3 months of age, there is an ERP component that is also elicited by faces more than other objects. Some investigators have argued that this component represents a putative infant N170. The component is of similar morphology to the adult N170, although its amplitude is smaller and latency longer—it occurs approximately 290 ms after stimulus onset— and it is commonly referred to as the N290. By 3 months of age, the N290 shows the adult-like pattern of greater amplitude to faces relative to visual noise images containing the amplitude spectra of a face (Halit, Csibra, Volein, & Johnson, 2004), although inversion effects do not emerge until after 6 months of age (de Hann et al., 2002; Halit et al., 2003). At 3 and 6 months, the N290 is larger for human than monkey faces, but it is only at 12 months that the component is sensitive to both the species and orientation of a face (de Haan, Pascalis, Johnson, 2002; Halit, de Haan, & Johnson, 2003). As in adults, at 12 months of age, the amplitude of the ERP is larger for inverted than upright human faces, and there is no difference for inverted compared to upright monkey faces. Even at 12 months, there remain fundamental differences between the infant N290 and the adult N170, such as its longer latency, smaller amplitude, and more medial distribution for upright human faces (Halit et al., 2003). These ERP results are consistent with behavioral studies of the gradual specialization of the face recognition system. They support the idea that initially the mechanisms underlying face processing are relatively broad tuned, and that only later in development with sufficient exposure to upright human faces do they become more specific for that category.

The functional specificity of the N170 continues to become more adult-like throughout childhood. To date there is a marked absence of developmental ERP research on face processing between 12 months and 4 years of age. A face-sensitive N170 is present at 4 years of age with a small amplitude and long latency that extends beyond 270 ms, like the infant N290 (Taylor, Batty, & Itier, 2004). Between 4 and 14 years of age, there is a gradual increase in amplitude and a decrease in latency of the N170 in response to upright human faces (Taylor, Edmonds, McCarthy, & Allison, 2001; Taylor, McCarthy, Saliba, & Degiovanni, 1999). However, even 14-year-olds show an N170 that is smaller in amplitude and longer in latency than that of adults irrespective of whether the stimuli are photographs or schematic faces (Itier & Taylor, 2004; Taylor et al., 1999), a finding consistent with behavioral evidence that expert face recognition remains immature in midadolescence (see the section "Face Recognition in Children").

In summary, early visual experience in conjunction with the newborn's bias to look preferentially toward faces are the starting points for the prolonged development of face processing. Behavioral studies and investigations of the neural correlates of face processing in infants and children suggest that there is a gradual process of perceptual and cortical specialization that emerges early, and with increased experience with faces, continues to develop throughout childhood and into adolescence. The end point of this development is the ability to discriminate and identify faces rapidly, an ability that is limited to the kinds of faces (i.e., upright own-race faces) that are differentiated regularly.

Questions/Issues to Be Resolved

The Starting Point
1) To what extent can the experimental effects that have been shown with eye gaze in newborns be explained by low-level visual variables versus an innate eye detector?
2) When during infancy does holistic processing between internal face parts emerge?
3) How are the newborns' responses and postnatal changes altered in babies who are diagnosed later with autism and other neurodevelopmental disorders? If their responses are abnormal, are there environmental events that can alter the developmental trajectory?
4) What is the developmental relationship between the N290 and the N170? Does the N290 become the N170, or does it disappear to be replaced by the N170?

Development between Infancy and the Preschool Years
5) What changes occur in the sensitivity and morphology of the N170 component between the ages of 12 months and 4 years of age? How do those changes correlate with behavioral changes?
6) Why do infants show evidence of a face inversion effect but 4-year-olds do not? Could a more sensitive measure reveal a face inversion effect in children younger than 5 years?

What Is So Slow to Develop?
7) To what extent are children's poor sensitivity to second-order relations caused by limits in basic visual abilities (e.g., Vernier acuity, spatial integration)?

8) To what extent does the development of expertise for a new stimulus category (e.g., Greebles) in a lab setting mimic the development of expertise with faces during childhood?

Underlying Mechanisms

9) Several characteristics of adult face perception (e.g., distinctiveness effect, inversion effects, the other-race effects) can be interpreted as reflecting adults' face space. What is the nature of children's face space? What characteristics are especially immature during childhood (e.g., the number of dimensions versus sensitivity to differences within dimensions)?

10) As individuals develop expertise for a new face category (e.g., after arriving in a new country), do the various face processing mechanisms emerge in the same order that is evident in normal development?

REFERENCES

Acerra, F., Burnod, I., & de Schonen, S. (2002). Modelling aspects of face processing in early infancy. *Developmental Science, 5,* 98–117.

Aguirre, G. K., Singh, R., & D'Esposito, M. (1999). Stimulus inversion and the responses of face and object-sensitive cortical areas. *NeuroReport, 10,* 189–194.

Anzures, G., Mondloch, C. J., & Lackner, C. (2009) Face adaptation and aftereffects in 8-year-olds and adults. *Child Development, 80,* 1780–0191.

Aylward, E. H., Park, J. E., Field, K. M., Parsons, A. C., Richards, T. L., Cramer, S. C., & Meltzoff, A. N. (2005). Brain activation during face perception: Evidence of a developmental change. *Journal of Cognitive Neuroscience, 17,* 308–319.

Baenninger, M. (1994). The development of face recognition: Featural or configurational processing? *Journal of Experimental Child Psychology, 57,* 377–396.

Bahrick H. P., Bahrick, H. P., & Wittlinger, R. P. (1975). Fifty years of memory for names and faces: A cross-sectional approach. *Journal of Experimental Psychology: General, 104,* 54–75.

Benton, A. L., & van Allen, M. W. *Manual: Test of Face Recognition.* Neuro-Sensory Center Publication No. 287, Department of Neurology, University Hospitals, Iowa City, Iowa, 1973.

Bar-Haim, Y., Ziv, T., Lamy, D., & Hodes, R. M. (2006). Nature and Nurture in own-race face processing. *Psychological Sciences, 17*(2), 159–163.

Bartrip, J., Morton, J., & de Schonen, S. (2001). Responses to mother's face in 3-week to 5-month-old infants. *British Journal of Developmental Psychology, 19,* 219–232.

Batki, A., Baron-Cohen, S., Wheelwright, S., Connellan, J., & Ahluwalia, J. (2000). Is there an innate gaze module? Evidence from human neonates. *Infant Behavior and Development, 23*(2), 223–229.

Bentin, S., Allison, T., Puce, A., Perez, E., & McCarthy, G. (1996) Electrophysiological studies of face perception in humans. *Journal of Cognitive Neuroscience, 8,* 551–565.

Bentin, S., Sagiv, N., Mecklinger, A., Friederici, A., & von Cramon, Y. (2002) Priming visual face-processing mechanisms: Electrophysiological evidence. *Psychological Science, 13,* 190–193.

Bertin, E., & Bhatt, R. S. (2004). The Thatcher illusion and face processing in infancy. *Developmental Science, 7*(4), 431–436.

Bhatt, R. S., Bertin, E., Hayden, A., & Reed, A. (2005). Face processing in infancy: Developmental changes in the use of different kinds of relational information. *Child Development, 76,* 169–181.

Brace, N. A., Hole, G. J., Kemp, R. I., Pike, G. E., Van Duuren, M., & Norgate, L. (2001). Developmental changes in the effect of inversion: Using a picture book to investigate face recognition. *Perception, 30,* 85–94.

Bruce, V., Campbell, R. N., Doherty-Sneddon, G., Import, A., Langton, S., McAuley, S., & Wright, R. (2000). Testing face processing skills in children. *British Journal of Developmental Psychology, 18,* 319–333.

Bruce, V., & Young, A. W. (1986). Understanding face recognition. *British Journal of Psychology, 77,* 305–327.

Bushnell, W. R. (1982). Discrimination of faces by young infants. *Journal of Experimental Child Psychology, 33,* 298–308.

Bushnell, W. R. (2001). Mother's face recognition in newborn infants: Learning and memory. *Infant and Child Development, 10,* 67–74.

Bushnell, W. R. (2003). Newborn face recognition. In O. Pascalis & A. Slater (Eds.), *The development of face processing in infancy and early childhood* (pp. 41–53). New York: Nova.

Bushnell, W. R., Sai, F., Mullin, & J. T. (1989). Neonatal recognition of the mother's face. *British Journal of Developmental Psychology, 7,* 67–74.

Caldera, R., Seghier, M. L., Rossion, B., Lazeyras, F., Michel, C., & Hauert, C. A. (2006). The fusiform face area is tuned for curvilinear patterns with more high-contrasted elements in the upper part. *NeuroImage, 31,* 313–319.

Caldera, R., Thut, G., Servoir, P., Michel, C. M., Bovet, P., & Renault, B. (2003). Face versus non-face object perception and the other-race effect: A spatio-temporal event-related potential study. *Clinical Neurophysiology, 114*(3), 515–528.

Campbell, R., & Tuck, M. (1995) Recognition of parts of famous-face photographs by children: An experimental note. *Perception, 24,* 451–456.

Campbell, R., Walker, J., & Baron-Cohen, S. (1995). The development of differential use of inner and outer face features in familiar face identification. *Journal of Experimental Child Psychology, 59,* 196–210.

Carey, S., & Diamond, R. (1977). From piecemeal to configurational representation of faces. *Science, 195,* 312–313.

Carey, S., & Diamond, R. (1994). Are faces perceived as configurations more by adults than by children? *Visual Cognition, 1,* 253–274.

Carey, S., Diamond, R., & Woods, B. (1980). Development of face recognition: A maturational component? *Developmental Psychology, 16,* 257–269.

Carmel, D., & Bentin, S. (2002). Domain specificity versus expertise factors influencing distinct processing of faces. *Cognition, 83*(1), 1–29.

Cashon, C., & Cohen, L. (2001). Do 7-month-old infants process independent features or facial configurations? *Infant and Child Development, 10,* 83–92.

Cashon, C., & Cohen, L. (2004). Beyond U-shaped development in infants' processing of faces: An information-processing account. *Journal of Cognition and Development, 5*(1), 59–80.

Chance, J. E., Turner, A. L., & Goldstein, A. G. (1982). Development of differential recognition for own- and other-race faces. *Journal of Psychology, 112,* 29–37.

Curran, T., Tanaka, J. W., & Weiskopf, D. M. (2002). An electrophysiological comparison of visual categorization and recognition memory. *Cognitive, Affective, and Behavioral Neuroscience, 2*(1), 1–18.

Dannemiller, J. L., & Stephens, B. R. (1988). A critical test of infant pattern preference models. *Child Development, 59,* 210–216.

de Haan, M., Johnson, M. H., Maurer, D., & Perrett, D. I. (2001). Recognition of individual faces and average face prototypes by 1- and 3-month-old infants. *Cognitive Development, 16,* 659–678.

de Haan, M., Pascalis, O., & Johnson, M. H. (2002). Specialization of neural mechanisms underlying face recognition in human infants. *Journal of Cognitive Neuroscience, 14,* 199–209.

de Heering, A., Houthuys, S., & Rossion, B. (2007). Holistic face processing is mature at 4 years of age: Evidence from the composite face effect. *Journal of Experimental Child Psychology, 96*(1), 57–70.

de Heering, A., Turati, C., Rossion, B., Bulf, H., Goffaux, V., & Simion, F. (2008). Newborns' face recognition is based on spatial frequencies below 0.5 cycles per degree. *Cognition, 106,* 444–454.

Deruelle, C., & Fagot, J. (2005). Categorizing facial identities, emotions, and genders: Attention to high- and low-spatial frequencies by children and adults. *Journal of Experimental Child Psychology, 90,* 172–184.

de Schonen, S., & Mathivet, E. (1989). First come, first served: A scenario about the development of hemispheric specialization in face recognition during infancy. *European Bulletin of Cognitive Psychology, 9,* 3–44.

Diamond, R., & Carey, S. (1986). Why faces are and are not special: An effect of expertise. *Journal of Experimental Psychology: General, 115,* 107–117.

Dubois, S., Rossion, B., Schiltz, C., Bodart, J. M., Michel, C., Bruyer, R., & Crommerlinck, M. (1999). Effect of familiarity on the processing of human faces. *NeuroImage, 9*(3), 278–289.

Eimer, M. (1998). Does the face-specific N170 component reflect the activity of a specialized eye processor? *NeuroReport, 9*(13), 2945–2948.

Ellis, H. D., Shepherd, J. W., & Davies, G. M. (1979). Identification of familiar and unfamiliar faces from internal and external features: Some implications for theories of face recognition. *Perception, 8,* 431–439.

Elms, N., Mondloch C. J., Maurer, D., Hayward, W., Rhodes, G., Tanaka, J., & Zhou, G. (2008). *Limitations of expert face processing.* Poster presented to the Vision Sciences Society, Naples, Florida.

Fantz, R. L. (1965). Visual perception from birth as shown by pattern selectivity. *Annals of the New York Academy of Sciences, 118*(25), 793–814.

Farkas, L. G. (1981). Anthropometry of the head and face in medicine (2nd ed.). New York: Elsevier.

Farroni, T., Csibra, G., Simion, F., & Johnson, M. H. (2002). Eye contact detection in humans from birth. *Proceedings of the National Academy of Sciences, 99,* 9602–9605.

Farroni, T., Johnson, M. H., Menon, E., Zulian, L., Faraguna, D., & Csibra, G. (2005). Newborns' preference for face-relevant stimuli: Effects of contrast polarity. *Proceedings of the National Academy of Sciences, 102*(47), 17245–17250.

Farroni, T., Massaccesi, S., Menon, E., & Johnson, M. H. (2007). Direct gaze modulates face recognition in young infants. *Cognition, 102*(3), 396–404.

Farroni, T., Menon, E., & Johnson, M. (2006). Factors influencing newborns' preference for faces with eye contact. *Journal of Experimental Child Psychology, 95,* 298–308.

Farroni, T., Pividori, D., Simion, F., Massaccesi, S., & Johnson, M. H. (2004). Eye gaze cueing of attention in newborns. *Infancy, 5,* 39–60.

Flin, R. H. (1985). Development of face recognition: An encoding switch? *British Journal of Psychology, 76,* 123–134.

Freire, A., & Lee, K. (2001). Face recognition in 4- to 7-year-olds: Processing of configural, featural, and paraphernalia information. *Journal of Experimental Child Psychology, 80,* 347–371.

Freire, A., Lee, K., & Symons, L. A. (2000). The face-inversion effect as a deficit in the encoding of configural information: Direct evidence. *Perception, 29,* 159–170.

Gathers, A. D., Bhatt, R., Corbly, C. R., Farley, A. B., & Joseph, J. E. (2004). Developmental shifts in cortical loci for face and object recognition. *NeuroReport, 15,* 1549–1553.

Gauthier, I., Skuldarski, P., Gore, J. C., & Anderson, A. W. (2000). Expertise for cars and birds recruits brain areas involved in face recognition. *Nature Neuroscience, 3*(2), 191–197.

Gauthier, I., & Tarr, M. J. (1997). Becoming a "Greeble" expert: Exploring mechanisms for face recognition. *Vision Research, 37,* 1673–1682.

Gauthier, I., Tarr, M. J., Anderson, A. W., Skudlarski, P., & Gore, J. C. (1999). Activation of the middle fusiform "face area" increases with expertise in recognizing novel objects. *Nature Neuroscience, 2,* 568–573.

Ge, L., Luo, J., Nishimura, M., & Lee, K. (2003). The lasting impression of Chairman Mao: Hyperfidelity of familiar-face memory. *Perception, 32,* 601–614.

Geldart, S., Mondloch, C. J., Maurer, D., de Schonen, S., & Brent, H. (2002). The effects of early visual deprivation on the development of face processing. *Developmental Science, 5,* 490–501.

Gilchrist, A., & McKone, E. (2003). Early maturity of face processing in children: Local and relational distinctiveness effects in 7-year-olds. *Visual Cognition, 10,* 769–793.

Golarai, G., Ghahremani, D. G., Whitfield-Gabrieli, S., Reiss, A., Eberhardt, J. C., Gabrieli, J. D., & Grill-Spector, K. (2007). Differential development of high-level visual cortex correlates with category-specific recognition memory. *Nature Neuroscience, 10*(4), 512–522.

Goren, C., Sarty, M., & Wu, P. (1975). Visual following and pattern discrimination of face-like stimuli by newborn infants. *Pediatrics, 56,* 544–549.

Grill-Spector, K., Knouf, N., & Kanwisher, N. (2004). The fusiform face area subserves face perception, not generic within-category identification. *Nature Neuroscience, 7*(5), 555–562.

Haig, N. D. (1984). The effect of feature displacement on face recognition. *Perception, 13,* 505–512.

Hainline, L. (1978). Developmental changes in visual scanning of face and non-face patterns by infants. *Journal of Experimental Child Psychology, 25*(1), 90–115.

Haith, M. M., Bergman, T., & Moore, M. J. (1977). Eye contact and face scanning in early infancy. *Science, 198*(4319), 853–855.

Halit, H., Csibra, G., Volein, A., & Johnson, M. H. (2004). Face-sensitive cortical processing in early infancy. *Journal of Child Psychology and Psychiatry, 45*(7), 1228–1234.

Halit, H., de Haan, M., & Johnson, M. H. (2003). Cortical specialization for face processing: Face-sensitive event-related potential components in 3- and 12-month-old infants. *NeuroImage, 19*(3), 1180–1193.

Hannan, E. E., & Trehub, S. E. (2005). Tuning in to musical rhythms: Infants learn more readily than adults. *Proceedings of the National Academy of Sciences, 102*(35), 12639–12643.

Hasson, U., Hendler, T., Bashat, D., & Malach, R. (2001). Vase or face? A neural correlate of shape-selective grouping processes in the human brain. *Journal of Cognitive Neuroscience, 13*, 744–753.

Haxby, J. V., Gobbini, M. I., Furey, M. L., Ishai, A., Schouten, J. L., & Pietrini, P. (2001). Distributed and overlapping representations of faces and objects in ventral temporal cortex. *Science, 293*, 2425–2430.

Haxby, J. V., Hoffman, E. A., & Gobbini, M. I. (2000). The distributed human neural system for face perception. *Trends in Cognitive Science, 4*(6), 223–233.

Hay, D. C., & Cox, R. (2000). Developmental changes in the recognition of faces and facial features. *Infant and Child Dvelopment, 9*, 199–212.

Hayden, A., Bhatt, R. S., Reed, A., Corbly, C. R., & Joseph, J. E. (2007). The development of expert face processing: Are infants sensitive to normal differences in second-order relational information? *Journal of Experimental Child Psychology, 97*(2), 85–98.

Hayward, W. G., Rhodes, G., & Schwaninger, A. (2008). An own-race advantage for components as well as configurations in face recognition. *Cognition, 106*(2), 1017–1027.

Hole, G. (1994). Configurational factors in the perception of unfamiliar faces. *Perception, 23*, 65–74.

Hole, G., George, P. A., & Dunsmore, V. (1999). Evidence for holistic processing of faces viewed as photographic negatives. *Perception, 28*, 341–359.

Hunnius, S., & Greuze, R. (2004). Developmental changes in visual scanning of dynamic faces and abstract stimuli in infants: A longitudinal study. *Infancy, 6*, 231–255.

Itier, R. J., & Taylor, M. J. (2004). Face recognition memory and configural processing: A developmental ERP study using upright, inverted and contrast-reversed faces. *Journal of Cognitive Neuroscience, 16*, 1–15.

Jemel, B., George, N., Olivares, E., Fiori, N., & Renault, B. (1999). Event-related potentials to structural familiar face incongruity processing. *Psychophysiology, 36*, 437–452.

Johnson, M. H. (2005). Subcortical face processing. *Nature Reviews Neuroscience, 6*(10), 766–774.

Johnson, M. H., Dziurawiec, S., Ellis, H. D., & Morton, J. (1991) Newborns' preferential tracking of face-like stimuli and its subsequent decline. *Cognition, 40*, 1–19.

Johnson, M. H., & Morton, J. (1991). Biology and cognitive development: The case of face recognition. Oxford, UK: Basil Blackwell.

Joseph, J. E., & Gathers, A. D. (2002). Natural and manufactured objects activate the fusiform face area. *NeuroReport, 24*(13), 935–938.

Kanwisher, N., McDermott, J., & Chun, M. (1997). The fusiform face area: A module in human extrastriate cortex specialized for face perception. *Journal of Neuroscience, 17*, 4302–4311.

Kanwisher, N., Tong, F., & Nakayama, K. (1998). The effect of face inversion on the human fusiform face area. *Cognition, 68*, B1–B11.

Kelly, O. J., Quinn, P. C., Slater, A. M., Lee, K., Ge, L., & Pascalis, O. (2007). The other-race effect develops during infancy: Evidence of perceptual narrowing. *Psychological Science, 18*(12), 1084–1089.

Kelly, O. J., Quinn, P. C., Slater, A. M., Lee, K., Gibson, A., Smith, M., Ge, L., & Pascalis, O. (2005). Three-month-olds, but not newborns, prefer own-race faces. *Developmental Science, 8*(6), F31–F36.

Kleiner, K. (1987). Amplitude and phase spectra as indices of infants' pattern preferences. *Infant Behaviour and Development, 10,* 49–59.

Kleiner, K., & Banks, M. (1987). Stimulus energy does not account for 2-month-old infants' face preferences. *Journal of Experimental Psychology: Human Perception and Performance, 13,* 594–600.

Kovacs, P., Kozma, P., Feher, A., & Benedek, G. (1999). Late maturation of visual spatial integration in humans. *Proceedings of the National Academy of Science, 96,* 12204–12209.

Kuhl, P., Tsao, F., & Liu, H. (2003). Foreign language experience in infancy: Effects of short-term exposure and social interaction on phonetic learning. *Proceedings of the National Academy of Sciences, 100,* 9096–9101.

Le Grand, R., Barrie, J., & Tanaka, J. (2005). Testing the face-like versus geometric properties of the N170 component. *Journal of Cognitive Neuroscience, 12 (Suppl.),* 112.

Le Grand, R., Mondloch, C. J., Maurer, D., & Brent, H. P. (2001). Early visual experience and face processing. *Nature, 410,* 890.

Le Grand, R., Mondloch, C. J., Maurer, D., Brent, H. (2003). Expert face processing requires visual input to the right hemisphere during infancy. *Nature Neuroscience, 6*(10), 1108–1112.

Le Grand, R., Mondloch, C. J., Maurer, D., & Brent, H. P. (2004). Impairment in holistic face processing following early visual deprivation. *Psychological Science, 15,* 762–768.

Leopold, D. A., O'Toole, A. J., Vetter, T., & Blanz, V. (2001). Prototype-referenced shape encoding revealed by high-level aftereffects. *Nature Neuroscience, 4,* 89–94.

Macchi Cassia, V., Keufner, D., Westerlund, A., & Nelson, C. (2006). Modulation of face-sensitive event-related potentials by canonical and distorted human faces: The role of vertical symmetry and up-down featural arrangement. *Journal of Cognitive Neuroscience, 18,* 1343–1358.

Macchi Cassia, V., Turati, C., & Simion, F. (2004). Can a nonspecific bias toward top-heavy patterns explain newborns' face preference? *Psychological Science, 15,* 379–383.

Maclin, O. H., & Webster, M. A. (2001). Influence of adaptation on the perception of distortion in natural images. *Journal of Electrical Imaging, 10,* 100–109.

Maurer, D. (1985). Infants' perception of facedness. In T. Field & N. Fox (Eds.), *Social perception in infancy* (pp. 73–100). Norwood, NJ: Ablex.

Maurer, D., Le Grand, R., & Mondloch, C. J. (2002). The many faces of configural processing. *Trends in Cognitive Sciences, 6,* 255–260.

Maurer, D., Lewis, T. L., & Brent, H. P. (1989). The effects of deprivation on human visual development: Studies of children treated for cataracts. In F. J. Morrison, C. E. Lord, & D. P. Keating (Eds.), Applied developmental psychology: Vol. 3. Psychological development in infancy (pp. 139–227). San Diego, CA: Academic Press.

Maurer, D., & Salapatek, P. (1976). Developmental changes in the scanning of faces by young infants. *Child Development, 47*(2), 523–527.

McCarthy, G., Puce, A., Gore, J., & Allison, T. (1997). Face-specific processing in the human fusiform gyrus. *Journal of Cognitive Neuroscience, 9,* 605–610.

McKone, E., & Boyer, B. (2006). Sensitivity of 4-year-olds to featural and second-order relational changes in face distinctiveness. *Journal of Experimental Child Psychology, 94*(2), 134–162.

Meissner, C. A., & Bringham, J. C. (2001). Thirty years of investigating the own-race bias in memory for faces. *Psychology, Public Policy, and Law, 7,* 3–35.

Michel, C., Caldara, R., & Rossion, B. (2006). Same-race faces are perceived more holistically than other-race faces. *Visual Cognition, 14,* 55–73.

Michel, C., Corneille, O., Rossion, B. (2007). Race categorization modulates holistic encoding. *Cognitive Science, 31,* 911–924.

Michel, C., Rossion, B., Han, J., Chung, C.-S., & Caldara, R. (2006). Holistic processing is finely tuned for faces of our own race. *Psychological Science 17,* 608–615.

Milewski, A. (1976). Infants' discrimination of internal and external pattern elements. *Journal of Experimental Child Psychology, 22,* 229–246.

Mondloch, C. J., & Thomson, K. (2008). Limitations in four-year-old children's Sensitivity to the Spacing among Facial Features. *Child Development, 79,* 1514–1524.

Mondloch, C. J., Dobson, K. S., Parsons, J., & Maurer, D. (2004). Why 8-year-olds can't tell the difference between Steve Martin and Paul Newman: Factors contributing to the slow development of sensitivity to the spacing of facial features. *Journal of Experimental Child Psychology, 89,* 159–181.

Mondloch, C. J., Geldart, S., Maurer, D., & Le Grand, R. (2003). Developmental changes in face processing skills. *Journal of Experimental Child Psychology, 86,* 67–84.

Mondloch, C. J., Le Grand, R., & Maurer, D. (2002). Configural face processing develops more slowly than featural face processing. *Perception, 31,* 553–566.

Mondloch, C. J., Le Grand, R., & Maurer, D. (2003). Early visual experience is necessary for the development of some—but not all—aspects of face processing. In O. Pascalis & A. Slater (Eds.), *The development of face processing in infancy and early childhood* (pp. 99–117). New York: Nova.

Mondloch, C. J., Leis, A., & Maurer, D. (2006). Recognizing the face of Johnny, Suzy, and me: Insensitivity to the spacing among features at four years of age. *Child Development, 77,* 234–243.

Mondloch, C. J., Lewis, T. L., Budreau, D. R., Maurer, D., Dannemiller, J. L., Stephens, B. R., & Kleiner-Gathercoal, K.A. (1999). Face perception during early infancy. *Psychological Science, 10,* 419–422.

Mondloch, C. J., Maurer, D., & Ahola, S. (2006). Becoming a face expert. *Psychological Science, 17*(11), 930–934.

Mondloch, C. J., Pathman, T., Le Grand, R., Maurer, D., & de Schonen, S. (2007). The composite face effect in six-year-old children: Evidence of adultlike holistic face processing. *Visual Cognition, 15,* 564–577.

Mondloch, C. J., Robbins, R., & Maurer, D. (in press). Discrimination of facial features by adults, 10-year-olds and cataract-reversal patients. *Perception.*

Mondloch, C. J., & Thomson, K. (in press). Limitations in four-year-old children's sensitivity to the spacing among facial features. *Child Development.*

Morton, J., & Johnson, M. H. (1991). Conspec and Conlearn: A two-process theory of infant face recognition. *Psychological Review, 98,* 164–181.

Morton, J., Johnson, M. H., & Maurer, D. (1990). On the reasons for newborns' responses to faces. *Infant Behaviour and Development, 13,* 99–103.

Moutoussis, K., & Zeki, S. (2002). Responses of spectrally selective cells in macaque area V2 to wavelengths and colors. *Journal of Neurophysiology, 87*(4), 2104–2112.

Nelson, C. A. (1993). The recognition of facial expressions in infancy: Behavioral and electrophysiological evidence. In: B. de Boysson-Bardies, S. de Schonen, P. Jusczyk, P. McNeilage, and J. Morton, (Eds.), *Developmental neurocognition: Speech and face processing in the first year of life,* (pp. 187–198). Dordrecht, The Netherlands: Kluwer Academic Publishers.

Nelson, C. A. (2001). The development and neural bases of face recognition. *Infant and Child Development, 10,* 3–18.

Nelson, C. A. (2003). The development of face recognition reflects an experience-expectant and activity-dependent process. In O. Pascalis & A. Slater (Eds.), *The development of face processing in infancy and early childhood* (pp. 79–97). NY: Nova.

Nishimuru, M., Maurer, D., Jeffrey, L., Pellicano, E., & Rhodes, G. (2008). Fitting the child's mind to the world: Adaptive norm-based coding of facial identity in 8-year-olds. *Developmental Science, 11,* 620–627.

Pascalis, O., de Haan, M., & Nelson, C. A. (2002). Is face processing species specific during the first year of life? *Science, 296,* 1321–1323.

Pascalis, O., Demont, E., de Haan, M., & Campbell, R. (2001). Recognition of faces of different species: A developmental study between 5 and 8 years of age. *Infant and Child Development, 10,* 39–45.

Pascalis, O., & de Schonen, S. (1994). Recognition memory in 3- to 4-day-old human neonates. *NeuroReport, 5*(14), 1721–1724.

Pascalis, O., de Schonen, S., Morton, J., & Deruelle, C., & Fabre-Grenet, M. (1995). Mother's face recognition by neonates: A replication and an extension. *Infant Behavior and Development, 18,* 79–85.

Pascalis, O., Scott, L. S., Kelly, D. J., Shannon, R. W., Nicholoson, E., Coleman, M., & Nelson, C. A. (2005). Plasticity of face processing in infancy. *Proceedings of the National Academy of Sciences, 102,* 5297–5300.

Passarotti, A. M., Paul, B. M., Bussiere, J. R., Buxton, R. B., Wong, E. C., & Stiles, J. (2003). The development of face and location processing: An fMRI study. *Developmental Science, 6*(1), 100–117.

Pellicano, E., & Rhodes, G. (2003). Holistic processing of faces in preschool children and adults. *Psychological Science, 14, 618–622.*

Pellicano, E., Rhodes, G., & Peters, M. (2006) Are preschoolers sensitive to configural information in faces? *Developmental Science, 9,* 270–277.

Pezdek, K., Blandon-Gitlin, I., & Moore, C. (2003). Children's face recognition memory: More evidence for the cross-race effect. *Journal of Applied Psychology, 88*(4), 760–763.

Rhodes, G., Byatt, G., Michie, P. T., & Pruce, A. (2004). Is the fusiform face area specialized for faces, individuation, or expert individuation? *Journal of Cognitive Neuroscience, 16*(2), 189–203.

Rhodes, G., Hayward, W. G., & Winkler, C. (2006). Expert face coding: Configural and component coding of own-race and other-race faces. *Psychonomic Bulletin Review, 13*(3), 499–505.

Rhodes, G., Jeffrey, C., Watson, T. L., Clifford, C. W., & Nakayama, K. (2005). Fitting the mind into the world: Face adaptation and attractiveness aftereffects. *Psychological Science, 14*(6), 558–566.

Rhodes, G., Robbins, R., Jaquet, E., McKone, E., Jeffery, L., & Clifford, C. (2005). Adaptation and face perception: How aftereffects implicate norm-based coding in faces. In C. W. G. Clifford & G. Rhodes (Eds.), *Fitting the mind to the world: Adaptation and afereffects in high-level vision,* (pp. 213–140). Oxford, UK: Oxford University press.

Robbins, R., Maurer, D., Mondloch, C. J., Nishimura, M., Lewis, & T. L. *A house is not a face: The effects of early visual deprivation on the later discrimination on spacing and featural changes in a non-face object.* Poster presented to the Cognitive Neuroscience Society, San Francisco, CA, 2008.

Robbins, R., Shergill, Y., Maurer, D., & Lewis, T. L. (2007). Spaced out: Good discrimination but poor memory for spacing differences in houses [Abstract]. *Journal of Vision, 7*(9):1035, 1035a, http://journalofvision.org/7/9/1035/, doi:10.1167/7.9.1035.

Rossion, B., Delvenne, J. F., Debatisse, D., Goffaux, V., Bruyer, R., Crommelinck, M., & Guérit, J.-M. (1999) Spatio-temporal localization of the face inversion effect: An event-related potentials study. *Biological Psychology, 50,* 173–189

Rossion, B., & Gauthier, I. (2002). How does the brain process upright and inverted faces? *Behavioral and Cognitive Neuroscience Reviews, 1,* 63–75.

Sagiv, N., and Bentin, S. (2001). Structural encoding of human and schematic faces: Holistic and part-based processes. *Journal of Cognitive Neuroscience 13,* 937–951.

Salapatek, P. (1975). Pattern perception in early infancy. In L. B. Cohen & P. Salapatek (Eds.), *Infant perception: From sensation to cognition* (Vol. 1, pp. 133-248). *New York: Academic.*

Sangrigoli, S., & de Schonen, S. (2004a). Effect of visual experience on face processing: A developmental study of inversion and non-native effects. *Developmental Science, 7*(1), 74–87.

Sangrigoli, S., & de Schonen, S. (2004b). Recognition of own-race and other-race faces by three-month-old infants. *Journal of Child Psychology and Psychiatry, 45*(7), 1219–1227.

Sangrigoli, S., Pallier, C., Argenti, A. M., Ventureyra, V. A., & de Schonen, S. (2005). Reversibility of the other-race effect in face recognition during childhood. *Psychological Science, 16*(6), 440–444.

Scapinello, K. F., & Yarmey, A. D. (1970). The role of familiarity and orientation in immediate and delayed recognition of pictorial stimuli. *Psychonomic Science, 21,* 329–330.

Scherf, K. S., Behrmann, M., Humphreys, K., & Luna, B. (2007). Visual category-selectivity for faces, places, and objects emerges along different developmental trajectories. *Developmental Science, 10*(4), F15–F30.

Schwarzer, G. (2000). Development of face processing: The effect of face inversion. *Child Development, 71, 391–401.*

Schwarzer, G. (2002). Processing of facial and non-facial visual stimuli in 2-5-year-old children. *Infant and Child Development, 11,* 253–269.

Scott, C., & Nelson, C. (2006). Featural and configural face processing in adults and infants: A behavioral and electrophysiological investigation. *Perception, 35*(8), 1107–1128.

Scott, C., Tanaka, J. W., Scheinberg, D. L., & Curran, T. (2006). A re-evaluation of the electrophysiological correlates of expert object processing. *Journal of Cognitive Neuroscience, 18,* 1–13.

Simion, F., Macchi Cassia, V., Turati, C., & Valenza, E. (2001). The origins of face perception: Specific versus non-specific mechanisms. *Infant and Child Development, 10,* 59–65.

Simion, F., Valenza, E., Macchi Cassia, V., Turati, C., & Umiltà, C. (2002). Newborns' preference for up-down asymmetrical configurations. *Developmental Science, 5,* 427–434.

Simion, F., Valenza, E., Umiltà, C., & Dalla Barba, B. (1998). Preferential orienting to faces in newborns: A temporal-nasal asymmetry. *Journal of Experimental Psychology: Human Perception and Performance, 24,* 1399–1405.

Sinha, P., & Poggio, T. (1996). I think I know that face... *Nature, 384,* 404.

Skoczenski, A. M., & Norcia, A. M. (2002). Late maturation of visual hyperacuity. *Psychological Science, 13,* 537–541.

Stechler, G. (1964). Newborn attention as affected by medication during labor. *Science, 114,* 315–317.

Sugati, Y. (2008). Face perception in monkeys reared with no exposure to faces. *Proceedings of the National Academy of Sciences, 105,* 394–398.

Tanaka, J. W. (2001). The entry point of face recognition: Evidence for face expertise. *Journal of Experimental Psychology General, 130*(3), 534–543.

Tanaka, J. W., & Curran, T. (2001). A neural basis for expert object recognition. *Psychological Science, 12*(1), 43–47.

Tanaka, J. W., & Farah, M. J. (1993). Parts and wholes in face recognition. *Quarterly Journal of Experimental Psychology, Human Experimental psychology, 46a,* 225–245.

Tanaka, J. W., & Farah, M. J. (2003). Holistic face recognition. In M. Peterson & G. Rhodes, Eds. *Analytic and holistic processes in the perception of faces, objects, & scenes 2,* (pp. 53–91). NY: Oxford University Press.

Tanaka, J. W., & Gauthier, I. (1997). Expertise in object and face recognition. *Psychology of Learning and Motivation, 36,* 83–125.

Tanaka, J. W., Kay, J. B., Grinnell, E., Stansfield, B., & Szechter, T. (1998). Face recognition in young children: When the whole is greater than the sum of its parts. *Visual Cognition, 5, 479–496.*

Tanaka, J. W., Kiefer, M., & Bukach, C. M. (2004). A holistic account of the own-race effect in face recognition: Evidence from a cross-cultural study. *Cognition, 93,* B1–B9.

Tanaka, J. W., & Sengo, J. (1997). Features and their configuration in face recognition. *Memory and Cognition, 25,* 583–592.

Tarr, M. J., & Cheng, Y. D. (2003). Learning to see objects and faces. *Trends in Cognitive Sciences, 7*(1), 23–30.

Taylor, M. J., Batty, M., & Itier, R. J. (2004). The faces of development: A review of early face processing over childhood. *Journal of Cognitive Neuroscience, 16*(8), 1426–1442.

Taylor, M. J., Edmonds, G. E., McCarthy, G., & Allison, T. (2001). Eyes first! Eye processing develops before face processing in children. *NeuroReport, 12,* 1671–1676.

Taylor, M. J., McCarthy, G., Saliba, E., & Degiovanni, E. (1999). ERP evidence of developmental changes in processing of faces. *Clinical Neurophysiology, 100,* 910–915.

Turati, C. (2004). Why faces are not special at birth: An alternative account for newborns' face preference. *Current Directions in Psychological Science, 13,* 5–8.

Turati, F., Macchi Cassia, V., Simion, F., & Leo, I. (2006). Newborns face recognition: Role of inner and outer facial features. *Child Development, 77*(2), 297–311.

Turati, C., Sangrigoli, S., Ruel, J., de Schonen, S. (2004). Evidence of the face-inversion effect in 4-month-old infants. *Infancy, 6,* 275–297.

Turati, C., Simion, F., Milani, I., & Umiltà, C. (2002). Newborns' preference for faces: What is crucial? *Developmental Psychology, 38,* 875–882.

Turati, C., Valenza, E., Leo, I., & Simion, F. (2005). Three month olds' visual preference for faces and its underlying mechanisms. *Journal of Experimental Child Psychology, 90,* 255–273.

Tong, F., Nakayama, K., Vaughan, J. T., & Kanwisher, N. (1998). Binocular rivalry and visual awareness in human extrastriate cortex. *Neuron, 21,* 753–759.

Tzourio-Mazoyer, N., de Schonen, S., Crivello, F., Reutter, B., Aujard, Y., & Mazoyer, B. (2002). Neural correlates of woman face processing by 2-month-old infants. *NeuroImage, 15,* 454–461.

Valentine, T. (1988). Upside-down faces: A review of the effect of inversion upon face recognition. *British Journal of Psychology, 79*(4), 471–491.

Valentine, T. (1991). A unified account of the effects of distinctiveness, inversion, and race in face recognition. *The Quarterly Journal of Experimental Psychology, 43, 161–204.*

Valentine, T., & Bruce, V. (1986a). The effects of distinctiveness in recognising and classifying faces. *Perception, 15,* 525–535.

Valentine, T., & Bruce, V. (1986b). Recognising familiar faces: The role of distinctiveness and familiarity. *Canadian Journal of Psychology, 40,* 300–305.

Valenza, E., Simion, F., Macchi Cassia, V., & Umiltà, C. (1996). Face preference at birth. *Journal of Experimental Psychology: Human Perception and Performance, 22,* 892–903.

Want, S. C., Pascalis, O., Coleman, M., & Blades, M. (2003). Recognizing people from the inner or outer parts of their faces: Developmental data concerning 'unfamiliar' faces. *British Journal of Developmental Psychology, 21,* 125–135.

Watson, T. L., & Clifford, C. W. (2003). Pulling faces: An investigation of the face-distortion aftereffects. *Perception, 32*(19), 1109–1116.

Wright, D. B., Boyd, C. E., & Tredoux, C. G. (2001). A field study of own-race bias in South Africa and England. *Psychology, Public Policy, and Law, 7,* 119–133.

Yin, R. K. (1969). Looking at upside-down faces. *Journal of Experimental Psychology, 81,* 141–145.

Young, A. W., Hellawell, D., & Hay, D. C. (1987). Configurational information in face perception. *Perception, 16,* 747–759.

4

Degrees of Expertise

Lisa S. Scott, James W. Tanaka, and Tim Curran

INTRODUCTION

Visual object recognition and categorization are fundamental abilities required for successful negotiation of the visual world. Humans effortlessly classify and recognize objects and faces within busy scenes thousands of times a day. Thus, understanding how perceptual categorization and learning occur and how such seemingly complicated computations are implemented in brain processes is an important goal in cognitive psychology and cognitive neuroscience. One way of furthering our understanding of category learning is to examine how differences in experience with specific classes of objects (e.g., dogs, cars, faces) influence the speed and level at which these objects are categorized.

Object categorization is arbitrary in the sense that a single object can be classified at multiple levels of abstraction. For instance, the same American Tree Sparrow can be classified as an "animal" at a general or superordinate level, a "bird" at the basic level, and an "American Tree Sparrow" at a specific or subordinate level. In contrast to object categorization, object *recognition* is not arbitrary in that most objects are identified at the same level of abstraction—the so-called basic level (Jolicoeur, Gluck, & Kosslyn, 1984; Murphy & Smith, 1982; Rosch, Mervis, Gray, Johnson, & Boyes-Braem, 1976). Seminal work by Rosch and colleagues demonstrated that the basic level is the optimum level of abstraction at which category members are perceptually most similar to one another and are maximally distinct from other category members. Given its structural advantage, the basic level is the preferred level in initial object recognition.

However, the basic level is typically not the preferred level for experts where recognition often demands a more specific, subordinate level of identification (Johnson & Mervis, 1997; Tanaka, 2001; but see Wong & Gauthier, in press, and Chapter 10, for descriptions of basic-level expertise). For example, face processing is thought to be a universally expert skill where faces are differentiated at the level of the individual (e.g., Bob, Susan) (Tanaka, 2001). Similarly, given the demands of expertise, expert bird watchers and car enthusiasts identify birds or cars at a more subordinate level (e.g., Bachman warbler, BMW Z1) compared to nonexperts (Tanaka & Taylor, 1991). Tanaka & Taylor (1991) suggested that category specificity arises when the demands of expertise require that exemplars within a category be differentiated from one another (as we do with faces). Furthermore, different recognition strategies may be best supported by different parts of the visual system (Scott, Tanaka, Sheinberg, & Curran, 2006). According to this view, face perception and expert perceptual processing differ from nonexpert object perception with respect to the cognitive strategies and neural substrates that are recruited to support subordinate-level recognition. Subordinate-level categorization of vehicles and animals in nonexperts has been found to rely on predominately high–spatial frequency information, whereas basic-level categorization relies on low–spatial frequency information (Collin & McMullen, 2005). However, in face categorization there is a greater reliance on low–spatial frequency information for subordinate-level categorization of faces relative to objects (Harel & Bentin, in press). Thus, the perceptual information used for visual face and object categorization appears to be flexible and dependent on previous experience and whether fine-grained and detailed visual analyses are needed.

Understanding the processes and mechanisms involved in the acquisition of expert object recognition will not only inform the study of perceptual expertise but will also aid in our understanding of how experience influences object perception. Full appreciation of how humans learn to categorize necessarily involves an understanding of expert perceptual processing. This includes the conditions necessary for category learning and perception to occur as well as the neural mechanisms mediating these processes. However, this also includes understanding why and when learning does not occur as well as when perceptual processing is disrupted.

The present chapter will examine perceptual category learning and expertise from a variety of perspectives. First, we consider the naturally occurring perceptual expertise of face recognition and examine specialization involved in the recognition of one's own species, own race, or own face. Second, we will describe work investigating the abilities of real-world experts and draw parallels and contrasts between the acquired forms of expertise and the naturally occurring form of face recognition. Third, we will discuss studies that examine the training of expertise and learning conditions, which promote the acquisition of expert recognition.

EXPERIENCE-DEPENDENT BIASES IN FACE PROCESSING

Humans rely on face processing abilities to accomplish a variety of everyday activities, including identifying and discriminating individuals, emotions, gender, race, attractiveness, and age. Face processing research spans the fields of cognitive, social, clinical, and developmental psychology, as well as the fields of cognitive, affective, and computational neuroscience. Thus, the importance of understanding face processing abilities in humans is reflected in the large number of empirical articles investigating this phenomenon. The purpose of this review is not to discuss the whole of the face processing literature, but to review the research that has looked at increasing levels of subspecialization *within* the domain of face processing, including the recognition of faces from other species, faces from other races, and the recognition of one's own face.

Recognition of Own and Other Species' Faces.

The other-species effect (OSE) is the phenomenon in which subjects exhibit superior recognition of members of their own species (i.e., conspecifics) relative to recognition of members from other species. The OSE has been studied by comparing recognition of primate faces (e.g., monkeys and humans) to non-primates faces (e.g., sheep and cows) (Campbell, Pascalis, Coleman, Wallace, & Benson, 1997; Pascalis, Demont, de Haan, & Campbell, 2001) and by comparing the recognition of human and nonhuman primate monkey faces (Dufour, Pascalis, & Petit, 2006; Pascalis & Bachevalier, 1998; Pascalis, de Haan, & Nelson, 2002; Pascalis et al., 2005; Scott, Shannon, & Nelson, 2005, 2006). Assuming that human infants and adults have little perceptual experience with nonhuman primate faces relative to human faces, the OSE suggests that perceptual experience plays a role in shaping face perception abilities.

In human recognition, a perceptual advantage is found for recognition of primate faces compared to nonprimate faces. For example, in human adults recognition is disproportionately impaired for inverted relative to upright human and monkey faces compared to inverted relative to upright sheep faces (Pascalis & Bachevalier, 1998), the so-called face inversion effect (Yin, 1969). Although the exact source of the inversion effect is controversial (Freire, Lee, & Symons, 2000; Riesenhuber, Jarudi, Gilad, & Sinha, 2004), this effect has been used as a benchmark to gauge the extent to which other stimuli are processed like human faces.

Developmental studies have shown that young (5 years) and older (8 years) children recognized human faces better than monkey faces which, in turn, were better recognized than sheep faces (Pascalis et al., 2001). Critically, similar to adults, children displayed an inversion effect for the primate human and monkey faces, but not for recognition of sheep faces. Pascalis and colleagues suggest that the human face processing system may be tuned to the characteristics of primate (human and monkey) faces by 5 years of age and that subsequent experience with own-species faces tunes this system to better discriminate faces with which we have experience. Although there appears to be an advantage for the recognition of primate faces over nonprimate faces in humans, several studies have found that among primates, there is a preference for faces from one's own species. For example, using looking time measures to infer human and monkey's ability to discriminate same and other species' faces, Pascalis and Bachevalier (1998) found that monkeys looked longer at novel monkey faces than novel human faces whereas humans showed the reverse pattern of looking. These findings suggest better discrimination for own-species compared to other-species faces.

In addition to the behavioral investigations described above, studies using event-related potentials (ERPs) have also reported differential responses while humans recognize and differentiate human versus nonhuman primate faces. ERPs represent the summation of electromagnetic activity generated from synchronously active neurons in the brain, resulting in a series of positive and negative voltage deflections over time. These deflections, referred to as components, are thought to reflect the activity of underlying neural processes. ERP studies have found a negatively peaked component occurring around 170 ms after stimulus onset (called the "N170") that differentiates faces and objects (e.g., Carmel & Bentin, 2002) and is delayed (e.g., Bentin, Allison, Puce, Perez, & McCarthy, 1996) and enhanced (e.g., Rossion et al., 1999) to inverted faces compared to upright faces. In adults, the N170 ERP component has been found to be longer in latency (Carmel & Bentin, 2002) and less susceptible to inversion effects (de Haan, Pascalis, & Johnson, 2002) while participants view monkey faces compared to human faces. Furthermore, a recent investigation of the time course of human and monkey face processing, using both behavioral and ERP measures, suggests that human adults more readily learn and subsequently recognize human compared to monkey faces (Scott, Shannon & Nelson, 2005). More specifically, adult humans are not only better at recognizing human compared to monkey faces but, given the same amount of familiarization to both types of faces, can generalize recognition of frontal familiarized faces to profile views of these same faces for human but not for monkey faces. Importantly, the amplitude of the VPP component, which is thought to arise from the same neural source(s) as the N170 component (Joyce & Rossion, 2005; Rossion, Joyce, Cottrell, & Tarr, 2003), was also found to positively correlate with measures of accuracy for the human but not the monkey faces (See Figure 4.1). Thus, the amplitude of the VPP increased as accuracy increased for the human but not the monkey faces task (even when accuracy to the monkey faces was well above chance). These data support the hypothesis that previous experience with certain types of faces influences subsequent behavioral and neural processing and that this experience generalizes to the recognition of nonhuman primate faces.

One question related to studies of the OSE is whether or not these perceptual biases are genetically determined or whether they can be accounted for solely by experiential factors. As in all of the questions related to the nature or nurture of cognitive or perceptual abilities, these perceptual biases likely reflect a combination of influences including both genetic and experiential factors. However, several recent investigations have begun to elucidate the mechanisms of the development of face processing in the first year of life using human and monkey faces (Pascalis et al., 2002, 2005; Scott & Monesson, 2009). Six-month-old infants have been found to discriminate monkey faces that 9-month-olds and adults do not, suggesting that younger infants exhibit a more broadly tuned face processing system than older infants and adults (Pascalis et al., 2002). Furthermore, 6-month-old infants who were given 3 months of perceptual experience with monkey faces, by sending them home with books of images individually labeled monkey faces, maintain the ability to discriminate monkey faces at 9-months-of age (Pascalis et al., 2005; Scott & Monesson, 2009). These data suggest that, during the first 9 months of life, infants may be particularly sensitive to perceptual differences between different types of faces, and this sensitivity is subsequently decreased for faces not present in their environment.

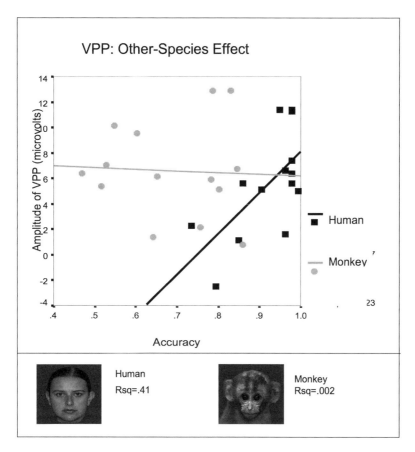

Figure 4.1 Behavioral measures of percent correct for the monkey and human task (Scott, Shannon, & Nelson, 2005) plotted against the maximum amplitude for the VPP component. Responses to monkey faces are shown in gray; responses to human faces are shown in black. Used with permission from the Psychonomic Society/ Journal of Cognitive, Affective, and Behavioral Neuroscience, Copyright 2005.

The electrophysiological time course of human and monkey face processing has also been investigated within the first year of life (de Haan et al., 2002; Halit, de Haan, & Johnson, 2003; Scott & Nelson, 2006; Scott, Shannon, & Nelson, 2006). de Haan et al. (2002) first reported two components (the N290 and the P400) in the 6-month-old infant ERP that both appear to be developmental precursors to the adult N170 component. During the first year of life, differences between upright and inverted faces and between face and nonface objects are spread across both the infant N290 and P400. However, by 12 months of age, the N290 appears to be functionally equivalent to the adult N170 (Halit et al., 2003). Differences between human and monkey face processing have been recently investigated in 9-month-old infants (Scott, Shannon, & Nelson, 2006). In this study, ERPs were collected while 9-month-olds were presented with pictures of familiar and unfamiliar monkey or human faces in two different orientations. Earlier in processing (the infant N290), there was evidence for electrophysiological differentiation of familiar compared to unfamiliar faces, regardless of orientation or species. In contrast, later in processing (the infant P400) the response became more specific for human faces compared to monkey faces. Whereas the P400 to human faces differentiated the orientation of both familiar and unfamiliar faces, the P400 to monkey faces only differentiated at the level of familiarity. These results suggest more specific processing of human compared to monkey faces in 9-month-old humans. However, recall the above-described behavioral results, which suggest that without perceptual experience, 9-month-olds decline in their ability to discriminate monkey faces (Pascalis et al, 2002, 2005). Unlike the behavioral results, ERP data suggest a residual ability, in the brain, to differentiate monkey faces in 9-month-olds.

Face expertise has also been investigated by manipulating the spacing of facial features in both human and monkey faces (Mondloch, Maurer, & Ahola, 2006). In this study adults and 8- year-olds performed a sequential, same–different discrimination task for human and monkey faces. Spacing changes were made to both types of faces. Results reveal that although adults performed better overall, both 8-year-olds and adults were better at detecting changes for human faces compared to monkey faces. This suggests that any advantage adults have over children is due to general, rather than domain-specific, cognitive and perceptual improvements such as spatial integration. The authors conclude that face-specific improvements cannot be accounted for by increased experience with faces after 8 years of age.

Recognition of Own and Other-Race Faces

The other-race effect (ORE), also called the own-race effect/bias or cross-race effect/bias, is a commonly reported phenomenon in which people have more difficultly differentiating and remembering faces of another race compared to faces within their own race (Chance, Turner, & Goldstein, 1982; Meissner & Brigham, 2001; O'Toole, Deffenbacher, Valentin, & Abdi, 1994). The ORE is assumed to reflect differential experience with own- and other-race faces. However, it is currently unclear *how* race-specific information and experience influences face processing abilities. Several developmental and adult investigations have focused on understanding what aspects of face processing are influenced by race information.

The ORE has been shown as early as 3 months of age using both visual preference tasks and visual paired comparison tasks (Bar-Haim, Ziv, Lamy, & Hodes, 2006; Kelly et al., 2005; Sangrigoli & De Schonen, 2004). Although partially present in 3-month-olds, the ORE is not seen in newborns (Kelly et al., 2005) and does not seem to be fully present until 9 months of age (Kelly, Quinn, Slater, Lee, Ge, & Pascalis, 2007). Furthermore, preferences for own-race faces in 3-month-olds have been found to be dependent on the amount of exposure to same- versus other-race faces (Bar-Haim et al., 2006).

Similarly, investigators studying this effect in adults have historically attributed the ORE to greater exposure with faces of one's own race compared to other races (Brigham & Mallpass, 1985; Malpass & Kravitz, 1969). Investigations showing that training with other-race faces can reduce this effect also support the notion that the ORE is experience dependent (Elliott, Willis, & Goldstein, 1973; Lavrakas, Buri, & Mayzner, 1976; Malpass, Lavigueur, & Weldon, 1973). Just 1 hour of visual training significantly reduced the other-race effect, whereas visual training with one's own race did not improve performance (Malpass et al., 1973). Paired-associate training with other-race faces significantly improved later discrimination of other-race faces compared to no training or training with own-race faces (Elliott et al., 1973), but this reduction of the ORE through training does not appear to be long lasting (Lavrakas et al., 1976).

Recent training studies suggests that perceptual exposure by itself might not be sufficient to reduce the other-race effect (Tanaka & Droucker, submitted; Tanaka & Pierce, 2009). In the first phase of this experiment, Caucasian participants who had relatively little experience with non-Caucasian people were given an old/new recognition test comprised of African-American and Hispanic faces as a baseline measure. Next, participants received 2 weeks of training in which they were required to individuate African-American (or Hispanic) faces and categorize Hispanic (or African-American) (See Figure 4.2). Critically, the African-American and Hispanic faces were presented an equal number of times during training, so the faces did not differ with respect to their absolute amount of perceptual exposure. After training, the participants completed an old/new recognition test with a novel set of African-American and Hispanic faces. The central finding was

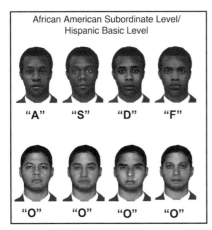 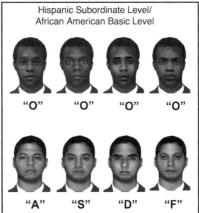

Figure 4.2 Examples of face images used in the other-race training study. Half of the Caucasian subjects completed training with African-American faces at the subordinate or individual level and Hispanic faces at the basic or category level (left box), and the other half did the opposite (right box).

that recognition improved for faces from the racial group that was in the individuating condition, but there were no gains in recognition for faces in the race categorization condition (See Figure 4.3). These results suggest that the ORE is not mediated by amount of absolute exposure to faces from another race, but by the level at which these faces are categorized. Individuation of people from unfamiliar racial groups can help ameliorate the ORE whereas racial categorization serves to perpetuate racial differences in recognition—no matter how many times one sees faces from an other race (Tanaka & Droucker, submitted; Tanaka & Pierce, 2009).

Although it appears that the level of experience with faces helps determine the magnitude of the ORE, these studies do not address *how* race-specific visual experience influences the cognitive mechanisms of the face processing. Other studies suggest that the development of holistic or configural processing is disrupted when viewing other-race faces, leading to a decrement in recognition abilities (Fallshore & Schooler, 1995; Rhodes, Tan, Brake, & Taylor, 1989; Tanaka, Kiefer, & Bukach, 2004). The inversion of faces causes considerable decrements in recognition accuracy and reaction time compared to the inversion of objects (Yin, 1969). Presumably, inverting faces leads a disruption in configural over featural processing (Freire, Lee, & Symons, 2000). The inversion effect has been found to be greater for own compared to other-race faces, suggesting that the strategies for recognizing and discriminating other-race compared to own-race faces may depend on more feature-based processing (Fallshore & Schooler, 1995; Rhodes et al., 1989).

Using the parts and wholes task, Tanaka et al. (2004) examined the relative importance of featural and configural information in the recognition of own versus other-race faces. In this task, participants study an intact face and are then tested for their recognition of face parts presented in the whole face or in isolation. Recognition of the face parts is typically superior in the whole-face condition than in the isolated condition because the whole face provides a better match with the underlying holistic face representation. When shown Caucasian and Asian faces, Caucasian participants were better at recognizing the Caucasian faces when the whole face was presented compared to just the features. However, there was no advantage for holistically presented faces when Caucasians viewed Asian faces. Furthermore, Asian participants were better at identifying the correct face when presented holistically compared to featurally for both Asian and Caucasian faces. Interestingly, Caucasians reported significantly more exposure to Caucasian compared to Asian faces, whereas Asians reported equal exposure to both.

A similar recent investigation also found differences in holistic processing, using composite faces, between own- and other-race faces (Michel, Rossion, Han, Chung, & Caldara, 2006). In the composite paradigm, the top half of a well-known person is paired with the bottom half of another well-known person (Young, Hellawell, & Hay, 1987). When participants are asked to report the identity of the cued top or bottom portion of the

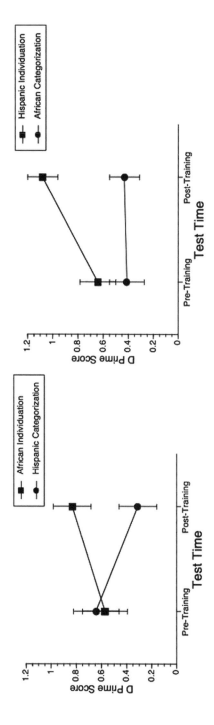

Figure 4.3 Mean d' scores on pre- and postmemory tasks for participants who completed subordinate training with African-American faces (left) and those who completed subordinate level training with Hispanic faces (right).

face, recognition accuracy is impaired when the face halves are aligned relative to when they are misaligned or when the composite face is inverted. In the aligned face condition, the to-be-ignored half of the face interferes with judgments of the to-be-attended cued portion, suggesting that the features of a face are not perceived independently of one another but are integrated in a unitary, holistic representation. Using this paradigm with Chinese and Caucasian faces, Michel and colleagues (2006) found that participants were faster to identify the top part of an aligned face if the face halves were not from the participant's race. That is, Asian participants demonstrated less configural interference for Caucasian faces whereas the Caucasian participants showed less interference for the Asian faces. These findings are consistent with evidence suggesting that the ORE may be due to a deficit in holistic relative to featural face processing when presented with other-race faces (Michel et al., 2006; Tanaka et al., 2004). However, one recent report found evidence for deficits in both featural and configural face processing in Caucasian and Chinese adults (Hayward, Rhodes, & Schwaninger, 2008). More research is needed to reconcile whether the ORE is due to specific deficits in holistic processing of other-race faces or whether there is a general face processing deficit including both featural and configural processing.

A somewhat overlapping perspective of the ORE suggests that impaired processing of other-race faces may be due to the way in which other-race faces are represented and retrieved from memory. For example, Valentine (1991) proposed a model that holds that faces are represented in a hypothetical multidimensional face space. Within this space, faces are stored based on various relevant dimensions, such as features or sets of features. Experience with faces, including learning the conditional probabilities of the feature dimensions of incoming faces, mediates the ability to encode and process various faces. Thus, the ORE results from repeated exposure to own-race faces as well as learning the invariant features, which are diagnostic to recognition and discrimination for own but not other-race faces. Once formed, this representation does not easily generalize to faces of another race (Chiroro & Valentine, 1995; Tollefson, Luxenberg, Valentine, Dunsmore, & Tollefson, 1991).

Alternately, the race-feature hypothesis holds that race information masks processing of faces when viewing other-race faces (Levin, 2000). In other words, race information is explicitly encoded for other- but not own-race faces. This processing specifies race information first, prior to recognition, which then masks processing of other individuating information used in own-race identification. Support for this theory comes from an investigation that improved other-race face recognition by informing participants of the ORE, prior to completion of a study–test recognition paradigm, and instructing them to individuate other-race faces by paying close attention to what differentiates one particular face from another of the same race (Hugenberg, Miller, & Claypool, 2007). Participants without such instructions showed a decreased discrimination of other- compared to same-race faces.

The multidimensional face space and the race-feature hypotheses were tested using both similarity ratings and identification accuracy of same- and other-race faces (Byatt & Rhodes, 2004). The results suggest that participants are more accurate and rate faces as more dissimilar for same- compared to other-race faces. Byatt and Rhodes (2004) also found that although race is an important feature in identification, it is equally important for same- and other-race faces. These data support the multidimensional face space hypothesis and suggest that same- and other-race faces form distinct clusters within face space and that other-race faces are more densely clustered within this space.

Theories of the ORE have been tested using computational models (Furl, Phillips, & O'Toole, 2002). This investigation analyzed the performance of several recognition algorithms to determine conditions in which an ORE can be generated. Results of this modeling suggest that a simple exposure–based algorithm actually leads to a recognition advantage for other- compared to own-race faces. The authors explain that this occurs because in an exposure-only system, other-race faces are seen as more distinctive and therefore more easily recognized. Thus, in order to computationally replicate the ORE, Furl and colleagues implemented a two-stage model of face learning that goes beyond the simple exposure–based algorithm and combines both a feature extraction stage and an identity classification stage. During the classification stage, the perceptual space is warped to emphasize distinctions between exemplars. This, combined with greater experience with own-race faces, leads to an increased ability to discriminate own- versus other-races faces. Thus, results of this modeling are consistent with the "developmental contact" hypothesis and suggest that behavioral differences between own and other-race faces are due to differential experience encoding distinctions between exemplars of own- versus other-race faces (Furl et al., 2002).

Work in neuroimaging has explored the neural substrates of own- and other-race face perception. The fusiform face area is a region of temporal cortex that responds more strongly to faces than to other objects using measures of functional brain activity (fMRI) (Haxby, Hoffman, & Gobbini, 2000; Kanwisher, McDermott, & Chun, 1997; Kanwisher, Stanley, & Harris, 1999; McCarthy, Puce, Gore, & Allison, 1997). This region also exhibits a greater response when experts view objects of expertise (Gauthier, Skudlarski, Gore, & Anderson, 2000; Gauthier, Tarr, Anderson, Skudlarski, & Gore, 1999; Gauthier, Tarr, et al., 2000). Studies have found differential responses to same- versus other-race faces in regions of the fusiform gyrus (Golby, Gabrieli, Chiao, & Eberhardt, 2001; Kim et al., 2006). More specifically, Golby et al. (2001) found superior recognition memory for same- compared to other-race faces, and the difference in performance between these two types of faces correlated with increased activation to own- compared to other-race faces in the left fusiform as well as regions of the hippocampus and parahippocampal gyrus. Additionally, face familiarity appears to modulate the ORE in the fusiform area (Kim et al., 2006). In this study, Korean participants completed a familiarity judgment task while being presented with familiar and unfamiliar Korean and Caucasian faces. Greater activation in the fusiform was found for same-race compared to other-race unfamiliar faces. This differential activation was not found for familiar faces. These data suggest that the ORE can be found using both behavioral and neuroimaging methods. Furthermore, the ORE is more robust for unfamiliar compared to familiar faces, suggesting an interaction between familiarity at the level of the race and familiarity at the level of the individual. This interaction is supported by work suggesting that training with other-race faces reduces the ORE and increases holistic processing of other-race faces (McKone, Brewer, MacPherson, Rhodes, & Hayward, 2007).

Studies using ERPs have also reported differential responses to own and other-race faces (Caldara, Rossion, Bovet, & Hauert, 2004; Caldara et al., 2003; Ito & Urland, 2005b; James, Johnstone, & Hayward, 2001). Caldara and colleagues (2003, 2004) investigated the sensitivity of the N170 to race information in faces. In both of these investigations, the N170 did not differentiate same- versus other-race faces, but modulation of race was seen for a positive component around 240 milliseconds after stimulus onset (Caldara et al., 2004). However, another recent study found the N170 to be sensitive to the race of a face (Ito & Urland, 2005). Tanaka and Pierce (2009) also found that a later ERP component is responsive to the level at which other-race faces are learned. In their study, Caucasian participants were trained to identify African-American or Hispanic faces at either the level of the individual (e.g., Bob, Joe, Frank) or race (African-American, Hispanic). Although faces from both races were presented an equal number of times during training, only faces from the individuated race elicited an enhanced N250, suggesting that this component is sensitive to the level at which other-race faces are categorized and not necessarily the amount of perceptual exposure. More work investigating the role of task context, experience, and the N170 and N250's sensitivity to same- versus other-race faces should further our understanding of the electrophysiological correlates of the ORE.

The above review suggests expertise effects within face recognition and reveals a processing advantage for own- compared to other-race faces. This effect is replicable across a variety of studies and is apparent using behavioral, neuroimaging, computational modeling, and electrophysiological techniques. Furthermore, although the mechanisms responsible for this effect are still debated, differential exposure, differential experience individuating other-race faces at the subordinate level, differences in configural processing, and the early processing of race-specifying information during face perception have all been found to influence this face processing bias.

Self Recognition

In previous sections, we discussed expert recognition of human faces relative to other nonhuman species and other-race faces. The different lines of research suggest that face expertise cuts across many levels of category distinctions and occurs at different scales of perceptual analysis. Here we examine a very narrowly defined kind of face expertise involving the recognition of a single face; namely, the recognition of one's own face. Of all the faces that we see and recognize, none are as familiar to us as our own face. From the moment of birth to the time of death, our own image is an enduring presence and a tangible manifestation of our self-identity (Gallup, 1970).

Tong and Nakayama (1999) demonstrated the special status of the own face representation in a visual search study where the target was either the subject's own face or an unfamiliar face. The subject's task was to locate the target item displayed among an array of unfamiliar distracter faces. The main finding was that search times were reliably faster by 58 ms to 77 ms when the own face was the target compared to the unfamiliar face targets. The own-face advantage was reliable over hundreds of testing trials and across different views (frontal, three-quarter, and profile) and orientations (upright, inverted) of the own face. These findings suggest that own-face representations possess a "robust" quality that differentiates them from other-face and object representations. According to Tong and Nakayama, robust representations: (a) mediate rapid visual analysis, (b) require extensive visual experience, (c) contain view-invariant information, (d) facilitate a variety of visual and decisional processes across tasks and contexts, and (e) demand fewer attentional resources. Tong and Nakayama's criteria of robustness is an apt description of expert processes where specialized perceptual routines are conferred upon the object of expertise, facilitating its fast and accurate recognition. The authors left open the question as to whether robustness can be extended to other overlearned faces (e.g., spouse, sibling) or objects (birds, cars). However, the case of own-face recognition qualifies as the narrowest form of perceptual expertise where privileged access is restricted to the recognition of a single, albeit important, face exemplar.

Other work in own-face recognition has investigated the neural substrates mediating self-recognition. Kircher and colleagues (2001) found interesting differences between the hemodynamic response to the subject's own face versus the face of their partner. Relative to when participants viewed images of their partners, images of the self led to enhanced blood oxygenation in the right limbic, left prefrontal cortex and superior temporal cortex. Viewing images of the partner, but not the self, led to right insula activiation. Thus, the subject's own-face stimulus elicits greater brain activation than even a face of someone who is highly familiar to them and with whom they have formed strong emotional associations. These results suggest that unique affective and semantic processes are triggered by the image of one's self.

The neuroimaging evidence suggests that specific neural substrates are specialized for the recognition of self, and presumably, if these structures are compromised, selective deficits or biases in own-face recognition might occur. Although there are no known cases of selective prosopagnosia for recognition of self, a study by Keenan, Nelson, O'Connor, & Pascual-Leone

(2001) examined the effects of anesthesia of the cerebral hemispheres on the perception of self and others. While undergoing an anaesthetization procedure to evaluate their epilepsy condition, patients were shown a photograph that was a 50/50 morph of their own face and the face of a famous person. After recovery, when asked to recall the photograph, patients whose left hemisphere had been anaesthetized recalled the "self" as the face that had been presented. In contrast, patients receiving right hemisphere anaesthetization were biased toward recalling the famous face. It has also been reported that patients with a right frontotemporal lesion experience a sense of detachment or estrangement from themselves (Sperry, Zaidel, & Zaidel, 1979). Other patients with right hemisphere damage misidentify those own body parts as belonging to others, a condition known as "asomatopagnosia" (Meador, Loring, Feinberg, Lee, & Nichols, 2000). These results indicate that structures in the right hemisphere play a larger role in the "expert" recognition of self.

The neural correlates of own-face effects have also been examined with ERPs. In an early study, Ninomiya, Onitsuka, Chen, Sato, & Tashiro (1998) found that when participants were monitoring a display for a famous face, their own face elicited a larger P3a (or "novelty P3") response than other nontarget stimuli (e.g., red square, unfamiliar face). The P3a is typically observed for salient, low-probability nontarget stimuli (Goldstein, Spencer, & Donchin, 2002). Thus, given the presence of other low-probability nontargets, the stronger P3a to the subject's own face probably reflects its greater salience. Similarly, a greater P300 has been found in response to the self-face in comparison with another familiar face, such as that of a friend (Scott, Luciana, Wewerka, & Nelson, 2005). Interestingly, this effect was not found in 4-year-old children. In 4-year-olds, the ERP response to the self-face is not differentiated from the mother's face, but both are both differentiated from unfamiliar faces (Scott, Luciana, et al., 2005).

Further evidence demonstrating the automaticity of own-face processing was found using the Joe/No Joe task (Tanaka, Curran, Porterfield, & Collins, 2006). In this task, participants completed a familiarization phase during which they studied a target "Joe" face ("Jane" for female subjects). They were then presented with a series of probe faces and indicated whether each probe face was "Joe" or "not Joe." The faces included the subject's own face, a same-sex "Joe" (Jane) face, and several same-sex "other" faces. Despite the fact that subjects were monitoring for Joe's face, their own face elicited an enhanced negative deflection (N250) over right posterior regions of the scalp—an ERP component associated with subordinate-level processing of faces and objects of expertise (Schweinberger, Huddy, & Burton, 2004; Schweinberger, Pickering, Burton, & Kaufmann, 2002; Schweinberger, Pickering, Jentzsch, Burton, & Kaufmann, 2002; Scott, Tanaka, Sheinberg, & Curran, 2006; 2008). The results from the "Joe/No Joe" study show that presentation of the own-face stimulus is sufficient to activate a corresponding face representation even when the own face was not directly task relevant. Although the N250 to the subject's own face was enhanced relative to Joe's face and other

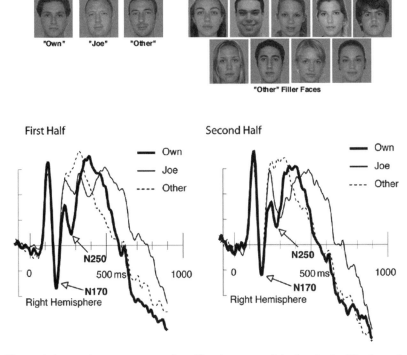

Figure 4.4 Top pictures are examples of face images used during the Joe/No-Joe task. The bottom shows the N170 and N250 response during the first and second halves of the experiment. Note that by the second half of the experiment, the N250 response to Joe's faces is equivalent in amplitude to the N250 response to the participant's own face.

nontarget faces in the first half of the experiment, Joe's face became suffi-ciently familiar over the course of the experiment to elicit an N250 that was equivalent to the own face in the second half of the experiment (See Figure 4.4). Thus, the N250 response was not specific to the subject's own face but seemed to index the familiarity of individual faces and other objects. In contrast to these findings, the N170 appears to be sensitive to the familiarity of basic-level categories (as documented below) in a fashion that does not typically discriminate objects at the individual or subordinate level (Bentin & Deouell, 2000; Eimer, 2000; Scott, Tanaka et al., 2006, 2008). However, using a continuous presentation adaptation paradigm, Jacques and Rossion (2006) report that the N170 can show sensitivity to differences in individual faces. This type of presentation may remove activation from low-level visual properties that might mask identity-level effects on the N170 using a single stimulus design.

In variations of the "Joe/No Joe" experiment, particpants monitored for either Joe's dog or Joe's car intermixed with pictures of their own dog, own car, other unfamiliar dogs, and other unfamiliar cars (Tanaka, Curran, Boddington, & Droucker, 2005). The main finding of these experiments was that images of the subject's own dog and own car stimuli elicited an enhanced N250 component that was similar in magnitude to the ERP produced by their own face. These findings suggest that the N250 is not necessarily restricted to one's own face but can be extended to other highly familiar, self-relevant objects.

Overall, self-recognition seems to represent an extremely specific form of experience-dependent expertise that preferentially engages our core face/object identification mechanisms and also involves other processes that may be integral to processing self-identity. Just as differential experience with our own species or own race facilitates perception of faces falling within these categories, high levels of experience with individual objects such as our own face, own car, or own dog facilitates perception of these particular objects. Later, we will argue that well-controlled training studies suggest that separate neural mechanisms may support recognition at different levels of abstraction (e.g., basic versus subordinate-level) (Scott, Tanaka, et al., 2006, 2008).

This review of experience-dependent biases in face recognition examined different degrees of expertise within the domain of face recognition. Results of studies conducted with other-species faces, other-race faces, and subjects' own faces suggest an important role of perceptual exposure and individuation experience in the tuning of the neural mechanisms underlying face recognition. These results further suggest that the processes involved in the recognition of faces may be similarly recruited for objects of expertise. In the next section, we will examine the kind of acquired expertise that people develop for real-world objects, such as car experts who excel at identifying the precise makes and models of automobiles or expert "birders" who are adept at identifying species of birds. An examination of the cognitive and neurophysiological mechanisms mediating acquired expertise provides an informative contrast to the behavioral and biological processes of natural face recognition.

REAL-WORLD OBJECT EXPERTISE

Real-world perceptual expertise represents the endpoint on the continuum of perceptual category learning. Real-world expertise has been investigated across a variety of domains. For example, studies examining the abilities of dog show judges (Diamond & Carey, 1986; Robbins & McKone, 2006; Tanaka & Curran, 2001), bird watchers (Gauthier, Skudlarski, et al., 2000; Johnson & Mervis, 1997; Palmeri & Blalock, 2000; Tanaka & Curran, 2001; Tanaka & Taylor, 1991; Xu, 2005), car experts (Gauthier, Curran, Curby, & Collins, 2003; Gauthier, Skudlarski, et al., 2000; Grill-Spector, Knouf, & Kanwisher, 2004; Rossion, Collins, Goffaux, & Curran, 2007; Xu, Liu, & Kanwisher, 2005), fingerprint examiners (Busey & Vanderkolk, 2005), radiologists (Myles-Worsley, Johnston, & Simons, 1988; Nodine &

Krupinski, 1998; Nodine, Kundel, Lauver, & Toto, 1996; Nodine et al., 1999), expert fisherman (Boster & Johnson, 1989), and tree experts (Lynch, Coley, & Medin, 2000; Proffitt, Coley, & Medin, 2000) have all investigated the categorization abilities of the expert.

As mentioned previously, everyday object recognition typically occurs at the basic level (Rosch et al., 1976). As described above, the basic level for recognition of an American Tree Sparrow is "bird" whereas the subordinate level would be "American Tree Sparrow." Evidence for increased subordinate-level processing in experts comes from work showing that dog show judges and birdwatchers recognized dogs and birds at the subordinate (species) level as fast as at the basic level (Tanaka & Taylor, 1991). This result, now called the "entry-level shift" of processing has become an index of subordinate-level expertise. More specifically, there is a downward shift in reaction time, with subordinate-level training, from identifying objects at the basic level to the subordinate level with increases in expertise.

To investigate how expertise influences basic-level processing, Johnson & Mervis (1997) conducted a series of expertise studies. In these investigations, three levels of bird expertise (novices, intermediate experts, and advanced experts) were tested. These authors conclude that the basic level does not lose its privileged status as expertise increases. However, subordinate level access to objects increases with expertise. Furthermore, in the more advanced experts, subordinate level processing achieves basic-level privileges. The authors further suggest that increases in expertise leads to an increase in the ability to attend to more fine-grained perceptual features, typically associated with subordinate-level processing.

In addition to increases in the ability to process some objects of expertise at the subordinate level (see Chapter 10 for discussion of expertise that affects other levels of categorization), there is also a trend for greater holistic processing of objects of expertise. In a classic investigation, Diamond and Carey (1986) examined the inversion effect, typically found for faces, in expert dog judges and breeders. Results of this study suggest that when dog experts have sufficient knowledge to individuate dogs within a specific breed, inversion of these dogs significantly impairs subsequent memory. This result is consistent with what is found for inverted faces and led these authors to conclude that faces are not a special class of stimuli. Furthermore, they conclude that any class of stimuli that share the same basic configuration can be individuated at the subordinate level, and those in which expertise is obtained are perceived and remembered similarly to faces. In car experts relative to novices, a visual short-term memory advantage is also found for cars (Curby, Glazek, & Gauthier, 2009). This advantage is similar to what is found for faces and correlates with level of car expertise. Rossion and Curran (in press) found that groups of car experts and novices showed similar car inversion effects, but the magnitude of the inversion effect correlated with degree of expertise within the expert group. This correlation with expertise is similar to what was reported by Curby et al. (2009) and suggests that increased expertise significantly influences perceptual processing of upright versus inverted objects of expertise. In contrast, Robbins and McKone (2006) found no evidence of facelike holistic processing in dog experts viewing images of dogs as measured by the inversion task, the composite paradigm, and sensitivity to contrast reversal (but see Gauthier and Bukach, 2007, for a critical review of their interpretation of null results).

To more closely examine the acquisition of expertise, researchers have utilized different methods for comparing nonexperts and experts at various stages of training. Johnson and Mervis (1997) found that more advanced experts have greater access to subordinate-level object information compared to less advanced experts and novices. Mammographers with different levels of experience have been tested on their ability to detect malignant lesions (Nodine et al., 1999). Participants included expert mammographers (more than 5 years experience), 2nd-, 3rd-, or 4th-year radiology residents, and radiology technologists (who have experience with mammographic imaging but no reading experience). As radiological expertise increased, false positives decreased. Moreover, simply viewing X-ray images, as in the case of the radiology technologists, did not improve diagnostic skills. In a similar investigation, novice controls, 1st- year radiology residents (less than 1 year of radiological experience), junior staff radiologists (average of 4 years experience), and senior radiologists (average of 22 years of experience) were tested on their memory of normal and abnormal chest X-rays (Myles-Worsley et al., 1988). Recognition memory for abnormal X-rays increased with experience, but recognition memory for *normal* X-rays decreased with radiological experience. These results suggest that expertise in radiology increases the ability to remember clinically relevant abnormal X-rays, but that this increase is associated with a concomitant decrease in memory for normal X-rays.

A question of interest when studying expertise is whether being an expert in one domain leads to increased performance in other domains or increases in general abilities. For example, does being a radiologist increase your abilities on other nonradiological visual search tasks? Nodine and Krupinski (1998) looked at the abilities of radiologists and nonradiological experts in two visual search tasks. Specifically, participants completed "WALDO" (from "Where's Waldo" poster books) and "NINA" (from the hidden detection drawings appearing in theatrical scenes of the *New York Times*) visual search tasks. Results suggest no significant differences between experts and nonexperts in the ability to detect targets across both tasks. However, experts took significantly longer to search the image scenes than nonexperts. Furthermore, using eye tracking, the authors determined that the scanning patterns of the radiologists contained more fixations and covered less of the image compared to nonexperts, who used a more circumferential search pattern. In sum, radiological expertise did not increase abilities in new search tasks, with similar requirements. These results are consistent with what is typically found in perceptual learning studies and suggest that increased performance in perceptual learning tasks does not easily transfer to other related tasks (e.g., Ahissar, Laiwand, Kozminsky, & Hochstein, 1998; Fiorentini & Berardi, 1980; Poggio, Fahle, & Edelman, 1992; Sagi & Tanne,

1994). However, recently Green and Bavelier (2003) found generalization of learning in video game experts and in novices trained on an action video game. In this study, habitual video game players were found to have increased visual attentional capacity, enhanced task-switching abilities, and faster temporal processing of visual information. These researchers also trained novices on a single action video game and determined that similar to habitual video game players, training also increased visual attentional processes. Combined, these data suggest that while perceptual skills do not easily transfer, attentional skills may more readily transfer across tasks.

Recent investigations into the neural correlates of perceptual expertise find that long-term expertise with birds and cars recruits face-selective areas within the ventral temporal cortex (Gauthier, Skudlarski, et al., 2000; Xu, 2005). Furthermore, electrophysiological investigations of real-world expertise provide evidence against the notion that the N170 is a specific marker of face processing and suggest that the N170 may be involved in more domain-general processing of objects of expertise (Gauthier et al., 2003; Rossion, Curran, & Gauthier, 2002; Rossion et al., 2007; Tanaka & Curran, 2001). Tanaka and Curran (2001) established the relation between the N170 ERP component and expert object recognition. In this study, bird and dog experts completed a category verification task. Results revealed a significantly enhanced N170 ERP component when bird and dog experts categorized objects within their domain of expertise relative to objects outside their domain. These results suggest that by 170 ms after stimulus onset, objects of expertise are electrophysiologically differentiated from objects with which expertise has not been obtained.

Other research has similarly shown that the amplitude of the N170 increases with car expertise as measured by a perceptual matching task (Gauthier et al., 2003). In addition, both behavioral and electrophysiological research suggest that being an expert in one domain (e.g., cars) may interfere with perceptual processing within another domain (Gauthier & Curby, 2005; Gauthier et al., 2003; Rossion, Kung, & Tarr, 2004; Rossion et al., 2007). In one study, concurrent presentations of faces and cars reduced the N170 amplitude to faces for car experts but not for novices (Rossion et al., 2007). Another study examined interference related to holistic processing of cars and faces (Gauthier et al., 2003). Behavioral results suggested that car experts process upright cars more holistically than novices, and this interfered with holistic processing of faces. Furthermore, electrophysiological results suggest that the difference between the amplitude of the car and face N170 negatively correlates with car expertise. Thus, the greater expertise with cars (as measured by d'), the smaller the N170 difference between cars and faces. The presence of interference between faces and car expertise suggest shared neural mechanisms for processing these stimuli (see Chapter 8 for more on this topic).

A recent report with fingerprint experts found inversion effects, similar to what is found for faces, for images of fingerprints in fingerprint experts compared to novices (Busey & Vanderkolk, 2005). In this study the N170 to inverted fingerprints in fingerprint experts was delayed compared to upright fingerprints. This difference was not found in fingerprint novices. These data suggest that similar to the results described above, as well as ERP studies with faces, increases in fingerprint expertise is accompanied by an increase in configural processing.

It is important to point out that not all studies of real-world experts have found expertise effects for previously identified neural indices of face processing. The M170 component is thought to be the magnetoencephalography (MEG) equivalent to the N170 ERP component. Using MEG, Xu et al. (2005) did not find expertise differences for the M170. More specifically, there was no difference between the M170 to cars and other objects in car experts or car novices. The M170 was correlated with successful face identification but not the identification of objects of expertise. Xu et al. (2005) criticized prior N170 expertise experiments for not using a localizer approach to show that the same channels showing enhanced responses to faces over objects also show expertise effects. In other words, they argue that expertise effects occurring at the time of the N170 are distinct from face-selective effects. However, the force of this argument is weakened by the fact that Xu et al. did not observe any MEG effects of expertise, even when broadly searching other locations and time points.

The above review suggests that similar to face recognition, increases in individuation or subordinate-level processing are seen in real-world experts. While some of the research suggests that real-world experts process objects of expertise holistically, other studies indicate that there may be multiple pathways to perceptual expertise involving both holistic and featural analysis. The reviewed research also reveals overlap of face and expert object processing mechanisms as evidenced by similar electrophysiological increases with bird, dog, and car expertise. Moreover, reported interference effects (Gauthier et al., 2003; Rossion et al., 2007) further supports overlapping neural resources for face and expert object processing. Although not yet directly investigated, evidence of interference also suggests that there may be somewhat limited resources for object processing, and future research should examine the limitations and trade-offs of perceptual expertise.

TRAINING EXPERTS IN THE LABORATORY

One way to mimic the acquisition of a natural expert system like face processing is to train participants to better discriminate different classes of objects. Researchers using training studies do not expect to equate laboratory-trained expertise to real-world expertise. Real-world expertise occurs on the scale of years, whereas typical laboratory training studies require only hours of training. However, training studies allow for the manipulation of different factors that may contribute to the acquisition of expertise, providing better control over variables influencing this process. Some of the important factors that have been manipulated across the different training studies include: level of categorization, supervised training versus unsupervised exposure learning, and stimulus type. Moreover, training studies have allowed for a more precise look at generalization of learning, the relation between changes in the brain and changes in behavior, as well as the flexibility and stability of learning effects.

Face processing is thought to differ from nonexpert object processing in two ways. First, we view hundreds of faces everyday, thus it is thought that the amount of exposure to faces is greater than other object categories. Second, as mentioned previously, faces are typically individuated and thus processed at a more subordinate level than nonexpert object processing. These two differences also hold for the processing of expert stimuli. For example, bird experts not only see more birds than nonexperts, but they also individuate birds at a more subordinate (species) level compared to nonexperts (Tanaka & Taylor, 1991). Although the effects of exposure and subordinate-level processing cannot be precisely dissociated in face processing or in real-world experts, training studies allows for this dissociation. Similarly, training studies also allow for the manipulation of feedback in category learning. For example, one determine how supervised learning, mediated by explicit feedback, differs from unsupervised exposure to stimuli? Furthermore, manipulations of categorization level allow for a better understanding of how increases in basic versus subordinate-level processing are related to category expertise. Finally, generalization of learning occurs when performance improvements with a specific set of trained exemplars generalize or transfer to previously unlearned exemplars. Training studies also allow for better manipulations of the factors that lead to more or less generalization.

The use of training studies to examine the acquisition of perceptual expertise originated with training participants with novel objects called Greebles (Gauthier, Behrmann, & Tarr, 1999; Gauthier & Tarr, 1997, 2002; Gauthier, Tarr, et al., 1999; Gauthier, Williams, Tarr, & Tanaka, 1998). The first of these investigations found that training not only led to faster and more accurate responses, but training also increased the configural (and thus facelike) processing of Greebles (Gauthier & Tarr, 1997), evidenced by increased reaction time to trained Greeble configurations (studied parts, in a studied configuration) compared to transformed Greeble configurations (studied parts, in a different configuration). Tests of generalization of learning after Greeble training suggest that learning generalizes to Greebles that are structurally similar to the training set, but does not generalize to Greebles that are less similar to the training set (Gauthier et al., 1998).

Tanaka, Curran, and Sheinberg (2005) applied the Greeble training protocol to teach bird expertise. In this study, participants learned to classify 10 species of wading birds and 10 species owls at either the subordinate (species, e.g., Snowy Owl) or basic (wading bird) level of abstraction. Participants completed 6 days of training with the amount of training equated for both basic and subordinate-level conditions. Results indicate that participants trained at the subordinate level demonstrated increased discrimination on previously trained wading birds or owls. In addition, an "entry level shift" was observed such that subordinate training led to similar category verification times for basic and subordinate-level judgments. Furthermore, subordinate- but not basic-level training led to greater generalization to novel exemplars within the trained species and to novel (untrained) species within that family (i.e., owls or wading birds). These data suggest that learning to individuate at the subordinate but not the basic level increases discrimination in experts.

Neuroimaging studies have more closely linked behavioral changes due to training with corresponding changes in brain activity as measured by fMRI and ERP methods (Gauthier, Tarr, et al., 1999, 2000; Rossion, Gauthier, Goffaux, Tarr, & Crommelinck, 2002; Scott, Tanaka, et al., 2006, 2008; Tarr & Gauthier, 2000). Using fMRI, two areas of the brain, the right hemisphere "OFA" and "FFA," previously associated with face processing, have also been found to increase in activation after Greeble training (Gauthier, Tarr, et al., 1999; Gauthier, Tarr, et al., 2000; Tarr & Gauthier, 2000). More specifically, these areas are both recruited when Greeble novices become Greeble experts.

As described above, the N170 component has been found to index face processing. Furthermore, an enhanced N170 is found in real-world experts for objects of expertise compared to other nonexpert objects (Gauthier et al., 2003; Tanaka & Curran, 2001). Recently the N170 has also been investigated using training studies with nonface objects. Following Tanaka, Curran, & Sheinberg (2005), the relative contribution of subordinate- and basic-level category experience in the acquisition of perceptual expertise was investigated with both behavioral and electrophysiological measures (Scott, Tanaka et al., 2006). Behavioral results showed that subordinate- but not basic-level training improved subordinate discrimination of trained exemplars, and that this improvement generalized to novel exemplars of trained species and exemplars from novel species within the subordinate-trained family. We hypothesized that if the N170 were related to expert perceptual processing at the subordinate level, as previous findings with real-world experts suggests, then we should see an increased N170 to subordinate- but not basic-level training. However, ERP results indicated that both basic- and subordinate-level training enhanced the early N170 component, but only subordinate-level training amplified the later N250 component (See figure 4.5). These results suggest that perceptual expertise enhances neural responses to both basic and subordinate processing, with basic-level processing proceeding subordinate-level processing in time. However, this study did not address whether the increases seen for the N170 component are specific to basic-level processing or whether they can be accounted for by increased mere exposure to objects of expertise. Moreover, the processes of generalization and maintenance of learning, and whether these behavioral and electrophysiological effects can be replicated with other classes of stimuli, had yet to be determined.

To address these questions, a follow-up to the above investigation was conducted using different classes of cars as training stimuli (Scott, Tanaka, et al., 2008). Antique cars, modern SUVs, and modern sedans served as stimuli classes. For this study ERPs were recorded before, immediately after, and 1 week after each of these classes of cars was trained at either the

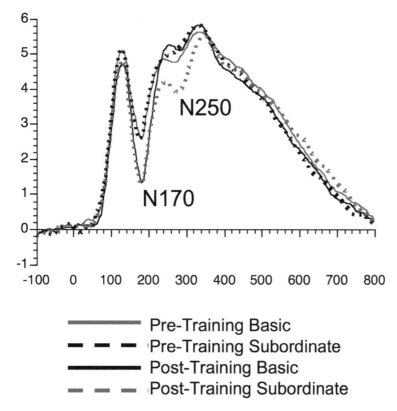

Figure 4.5 This graph pictures the right hemisphere occipital-temporal ERP response during pre and posttraining to birds trained at the subordinate versus the basic level. The N170 increased equally for both types of training, whereas the N250 only increased in response to subordinate-level training.

basic, subordinate, or exposure-only level. Results of this study suggest better behavioral discrimination of cars trained at the subordinate level compared to the basic and exposure-only conditions, and this ability does not degrade after a week without training. Interestingly, basic-level and exposure-only training yields similar later discrimination, both immediately and 1 week later. However, unlike the previous study with birds, there appears to be less generalization of expertise to novel exemplars of trained car models and no generalization to novel car models. Electrophysiologically, the N170 appears to increase equally for all three types of training, but the N250 only increases in response to cars trained at the subordinate level. Similar to the observed behavioral improvements, the increase in N250, but not N170, amplitude continues 1-week posttraining. Overall, these data suggest that expertise training at the subordinate level results in an increased ability to discriminate within-class, trained exemplars and that this change is reflected in increases in the N250 ERP component.

The generalization discrepancy between the bird and car training studies may have important implications for our understanding of general category learning. First, as artifact versus natural kind objects, cars and birds have different features that help specify subordinate-level category membership. For example, color is diagnostic for the subordinate-level categorization for birds, but not diagnostic for subordinate-level categorization of cars. Other features, such as texture and contrast, may also be more diagnostic for categorizing birds compared to cars. Thus, we suggest that the greater the number of features that are diagnostic for subordinate-level category membership, the greater the generalization to unlearned exemplars will be. Identifying how bird expertise differs from car expertise might prove informative for understanding previously reported differences between living and nonliving objects, and natural versus artificial categories. Second, previous verbal experience of participants may differ for cars and birds. It is conceivable that participants' prior verbal knowledge for car labels ("Honda CRV," "Toyota Camry," etc.) is interfering with their ability to learn the new subordinate-level labels we give them during training ("Model A," "Model B," "Model C," etc.). Requiring that participants learn new labels for cars, when they may already have labels for them, might impair performance and generalization. Both of these hypotheses can be tested using novel objects whose features and variability can be manipulated.

The electrophysiological results of the bird (Scott, Tanaka, et al., 2006) and car (Scott, Tanaka, et al., 2008) training studies suggest that the N170 component indexes unsupervised exposure in category learning because the amplitude of this response increases regardless of the type of training (exposure training, subordinate-level training, or basic-level training). These data suggest that previous reports of the N170, which find increased amplitude to faces and to objects of expertise compared to nonexpert objects, may be due to increased exposure to these object categories. Although subordinate-level training does not appear to differentially modulate the early N170 response, the later N250 is significantly greater for objects trained at the subordinate relative to the basic level and exposure-only training. This N250 response to objects trained at the subordinate level is consistent with previous studies investigating the N250 in response to faces (Schweinberger et al., 2004; Schweinberger, Pickering, Burton, et al., 2002). These studies find a larger N250 to repeated and familiar faces compared to novel or unfamiliar faces.

The relative timing of the N170 and N250 responses is consistent with a hierarchical, simple-to-complex view of visual processing whereby later processing become increasingly more stimulus specific (Jiang et al., 2006). This account is supported by studies of face processing, studies using the Joe/No Joe task with the own face, car, and dog, and now results from training studies. Furthermore, this hypothesis is also consistent with a recent neuro-computational model of basic- and subordinate-level training (Nguyen & Cottrell, 2005). Nguyen and Cottrell were able to model the results from the bird training studies (Scott, Tanaka, et al., 2006; Tanaka, Curran, & Sheinberg, 2005) with a two-component model of perceptual expertise.

Following a common series of lower-level visual processing stages, the model contains two separate modules that simultaneously learn basic- and subordinate-level classification tasks. Thus, similar to the electrophysiological data described above, this model depended upon a combination of supervised (back propagation) and unsupervised (autoencoder) mechanisms.

The above-described research highlights similarities between laboratory-trained experts and real-world experts. Research suggests that holistic processing increases with perceptual training (Gauthier & Tarr, 1997; Gauthier et al., 1998). In addition, similar to what is seen in real-world experts (Gauthier et al., 2003), there is also evidence of interference between faces and expert object processing in laboratory-trained experts (Rossion, Gauthier, et al., 2002). For example, Rossion, Kung, and Tarr (2004) trained participants with Greebles and found that, similar to face/car interference effects reported with real-world car experts (Rossion et al., 2007), the N170 to faces viewed concurrently with Greebles was significantly attenuated compared to the N170 to faces viewed concurrently with nonexpert objects of similar complexity. These results imply that car and Greeble expertise compete for the same holistic resources that mediate everyday face recognition.

Results of training studies have further clarified the importance of individuation training as well as unsupervised exposure in the formation of expert perceptual abilities. For example, studies looking at electrophysiological and behavioral changes over time (Scott, Tanaka, et al., 2006, 2008), have refined our understanding of the N170 component and suggest that increases in the N170 are due to increased exposure to object categories (such as faces or objects of expertise). Furthermore, the N250 component appears to be involved in subordinate-level processing of objects and faces. Overall, training studies provide a powerful tool for elucidating the mechanisms involved in the acquisition of perceptual expertise, and the use of these studies for further understanding what makes an expert "expert" is invaluable.

GENERAL CONCLUSIONS

This review was intended to give the reader a general overview of the different types of perceptual expertise currently being investigated. It was meant to underscore the differences and similarities across many different studies, examining face processing and the other-species, other-race, and self-face effects, and expert object recognition in both real-world and laboratory trained experts. Across all of these areas, the role of experience-dependent learning in shaping perceptual abilities has been examined. Results suggest that both unsupervised exposure and supervised, feedback-mediated learning at the subordinate level interact to produce recognition biases, such as the OSE and the ORE. Evidence for these different mechanisms comes from studies utilizing both behavioral and neuroscientific methods. Issues of generalization of learning were reviewed in each of the subsections of this chapter, and although there is evidence of generalization of learning across several studies, there do appear to be limitations to generalization, which are currently not completely understood. Interference effects between objects of expertise and faces have been found in both real-world and laboratory-trained experts—suggesting shared resources for face and expert object processing. Finally, one important avenue for future research is to understand further the multiple pathways to expert perceptual processing.

REFERENCES

Ahissar, M., Laiwand, R., Kozminsky, G., & Hochstein, S. (1998). Learning pop-out detection: Building representations for conflicting target-distractor relationships. *Vision Research, 38*, 3095–3107.

Bar-Haim, Y., Ziv, T., Lamy, D., & Hodes, R. M. (2006). Nature and nurture in own-race face processing. *Psychological Science, 17*, 159–163.

Bentin, S., Allison, T., Puce, A., Perez, E., & McCarthy, G. (1996). Electrophysiological studies of face perception in humans. *Journal of Cognitive Neuroscience, 8*, 551–565.

Bentin, S., & Deouell, L. Y. (2000). Structural encoding and identification in face processing: ERP evidence for separate mechanisms. *Cognitive Neuropsychology, 17*, 35–54.

Boster, J. S., & Johnson, J. C. (1989). Form or function: A comparison of expert and novice judgements of similarlity among fish. *American Anthropologist, 91*, 866–889.

Brigham, J. C., & Mallpass, R. S. (1985). The role of experience and contact in the recognition of faces of own- and other-race persons. *Journal of Social Issues, 41*, 139–155.

Busey, T. A., & Vanderkolk, J. R. (2005). Behavioral and electrophysiological evidence for configural processing in fingerprint experts. *Vision Research, 45*, 431–448.

Byatt, G., & Rhodes, G. (2004). Identification of own-race and other-race faces: Implications for the representation of race in face space. *Psychonomic Bulletin and Review, 11*, 735–741.

Caldara, R., Rossion, B., Bovet, P., & Hauert, C. A. (2004). Event-related potentials and time course of the "other-race" face classification advantage. *NeuroReport, 15*, 905–910.

Caldara, R., Thut, G., Servoir, P., Michel, C. M., Bovet, P., & Renault, B. (2003). Face versus non-face object perception and the 'other-race' effect: A spatio-temporal event-related potential study. *Clinical Neurophysiology, 114*, 515–528.

Campbell, R., Pascalis, O., Coleman, M., Wallace, S. B., & Benson, P. J. (1997). Are faces of different species perceived categorically by human observers? *Proceedings: Biological Sciences, 264*, 1429–1434.

Carmel, D., & Bentin, S. (2002). Domain specificity versus expertise: Factors influencing distinct processing of faces. *Cognition, 83*, 1–29.

Chance, J. E., Turner, A. L., & Goldstein, A. G. (1982). Development of differential recognition for own- and other-race faces. *Journal of Psychology, 112*, 29–37.

Chiroro, P., & Valentine, T. (1995). An investigation of the contact hypothesis of the own-race bias in face recognition. *Quarterly Journal of Experimental Psychology, 48A*, 879–894.

Collin, C. A., & McMullen, P. A. (2005). Subordinate-level categorization relies on high spatial frequencies to a greater degree than basic-level categorization. *Perception & Psychophysics, 67*, 354–364.

Curby, K. M., Glazek, K., & Gauthier, I. (2009). A visual short-term memory advantage for objects of expertise. *Journal of Experimental Psychology: Human Perception and Performance, 35*, 94–107.

de Haan, M., Pascalis, O., & Johnson, M. H. (2002). Specialization of neural mechanisms underlying face recognition in human infants. *Journal of Cognitive Neuroscience, 14*, 199–209.

Diamond, R., & Carey, S. (1986). Why faces are and are not special: An effect of expertise. *Journal of Experimental Psychology: General, 115*, 107–117.

Dufour, V., Pascalis, O., & Petit, O. (2006). Face processing limitation to own species in primates: A comparative study in brown capuchins, tonkean macaques and humans. *Behavioural Processes, 73*, 107–113.

Eimer, M. (2000). Event-related brain potentials distinguish processing stages involved in face perception and recognition. *Clinical Neurophysiology, 111*, 694–705.

Elliott, E. S., Willis, E. J., & Goldstein, A. G. (1973). The effects of discrimination training on the recognition of white and oriental faces. *Bulletin of the Psychonomic Society, 2*, 71–73.

Fallshore, M., & Schooler, J. W. (1995). Verbal vulnerability of perceptual expertise. *Journal of Experimental Psychology: Learning Memory & Cognition, 21*, 1608–1623.

Fiorentini, A., & Berardi, N. (1980). Perceptual learning specific for orientation and spatial frequency. *Nature, 287*, 43–44.

Freire, A., Lee, K., & Symons, L. A. (2000). The face-inversion effect as a deficit in the encoding of configural information: Direct evidence. *Perception, 29*, 159–170.

Furl, N., Phillips, J. P., & O'Toole, A. J. (2002). Face recognition algorithms and the other-race effect: Computational mechanisms for a developmental contact hypothesis. *Cognitive Science, 26*, 797–815.

Gallup, G. G. (1970). Chimpanzees: Self- recognition. *Science, 167*, 86–87.

Gauthier, I., Behrmann, M., & Tarr, M. J. (1999). Can face recognition really be dissociated from object recognition? *Journal of Cognitive Neuroscience, 11*, 349–370.

Gauthier, I. and Bukach, C. (2007). Should we reject the expertise hypothesis? *Cognition, 103*, 322–330.

Gauthier, I., & Curby, K. M. (2005). A perceptual traffic jam on highway n170: Interference between face and car expertise. *Current Directions in Psychological Science, 14*, 30–33.

Gauthier, I., Curran, T., Curby, K. M., & Collins, D. (2003). Perceptual interference supports a non-modular account of face processing. *Nature Neuroscience, 6*, 428–432.

Gauthier, I., Skudlarski, P., Gore, J. C., & Anderson, A. W. (2000). Expertise for cars and birds recruits brain areas involved in face recognition. *Nature Neuroscience, 3*, 191–197.

Gauthier, I., & Tarr, M. J. (1997). Becoming a "greeble" expert: Exploring mechanisms for face recognition. *Vision Research, 37*, 1673–1682.

Gauthier, I., & Tarr, M. J. (2002). Unraveling mechanisms for expert object recognition: Bridging brain activity and behavior. *Journal of Experimental Psychology: Human Learning and Memory, 28*, 431–446.

Gauthier, I., Tarr, M. J., Anderson, A. W., Skudlarski, P., & Gore, J. C. (1999). Activation of the middle fusiform 'face area' increases with expertise in recognizing novel objects. *Nature Neuroscience, 2*, 568–573.

Gauthier, I., Tarr, M. J., Moylan, J., Skudlarski, P., Gore, J. C., & Anderson, A. W. (2000). The fusiform "face area" is part of a network that processes faces at the individual level. *Journal of Cognitive Neuroscience, 12*, 495–504.

Gauthier, I., Williams, P., Tarr, M. J., & Tanaka, J. (1998). Training 'greeble' experts: A framework for studying expert object recognition processes. *Vision Research, 38*, 2401–2428.

Golby, A. J., Gabrieli, J. D., Chiao, J. Y., & Eberhardt, J. L. (2001). Differential responses in the fusiform region to same-race and other-race faces. *Nature Neuroscience, 4*, 845–850.

Goldstein, A., Spencer, K. M., & Donchin, E. (2002). The influence of stimulus deviance and novelty on the P300 and novelty P3. *Psychophysiology, 39*, 781–790.

Green, C. S., & Bavelier, D. (2003). Action video game modifies visual selective attention. *Nature, 423*, 534–537.

Grill-Spector, K., Knouf, N., & Kanwisher, N. (2004). The fusiform face area subserves face perception, not generic within-category identification. *Nature Neuroscience, 7*, 555–562.

Halit, H., de Haan, M., & Johnson, M. H. (2003). Cortical specialisation for face processing: Face-sensitive event-related potential components in 3- and 12-month-old infants. *NeuroImage, 19*, 1180–1193.

Harel, A. & Bentin, S. (in press). Stimulus type, level of categorization and spatial-frequencies utilization: Implications for perceptual categorization hierarchies. *Journal of Experimental Psychology: Human Perception and Performance.*

Haxby, J. V., Hoffman, E. A., & Gobbini, M. I. (2000). The distributed human neural system for face perception. *Trends in Cognitive Sciences, 4*, 223–233.

Hayward, W. G., Rhodes, G., & Schwanginger, A. (2008). An own-race advantage for components as well as configurations in face recognition. *Cognition, 106*, 1017–1027.

Hugenberg, K., Miller, J., & Claypool, H. M. (2007). Categorization and individuation in cross-race recognition deficit: Toward a solution to an insidious problem. *Journal of Experimental Social Psychology, 43*, 334–340.

Ito, T. A., & Urland, G. R. (2005). The influence of processing objectives on the perception of faces: An erp study of race and gender perception. *Cognitive, Affective, and Behavioral Neuroscience, 5*, 21–36.

Jacques, C., & Rossion, B. (2006). The speed of individual face categorization. *Psychological Science, 17*, 485–492.

James, M. S., Johnstone, S. J., & Hayward, W. G. (2001). Event-related-potentials, configural encoding, and feature based encoding in face recognition. *Journal of Psychophysiology, 15*, 275–285.

Jiang, X., Rosen, E., Zeffiro, T., Vanmeter, J., Blanz, V., & Riesenhuber, M. (2006). Evaluation of a shape-based model of human face discrimination using fMRI and behavioral techniques. *Neuron, 50*, 159–172.

Johnson, K. E., & Mervis, C. B. (1997). Effects of varying levels of expertise on the basic level of categorization. *Journal of Experimental Psychology: General, 126*, 248–277.

Jolicoeur, P., Gluck, M. A., & Kosslyn, S. M. (1984). Pictures and names: Making the connection. *Cognitive Psychology, 16*, 243–275.

Joyce, C., & Rossion, B. (2005). The face-sensitive N170 and VPP components manifest the same brain processes: The effect of reference electrode site. *Clinical Neurophysiology, 116*, 2613–2631.

Kanwisher, N., McDermott, J., & Chun, M. M. (1997). The fusiform face area: A module in human extrastriate cortex specialized for face perception. *Journal of Neuroscience, 17*, 4302–4311.

Kanwisher, N., Stanley, D., & Harris, A. (1999). The fusiform face area is selective for faces not animals. *NeuroReport, 10*, 183–187.

Keenan, J. P., Nelson, A., O'Connor, M., & Pascual-Leone, A. (2001). Neurology: self-recognition and the right hemisphere. *Nature, 409*, 305.

Kelly, D. J., Quinn, P., Slater, A., Lee, K., Ge, L., Pascalis, O. (2007). The other-race effect develops during infancy: Evidence of perceptual narrowing. *Psychological Science*, 18, 1084–1089.

Kelly, D. J., Quinn, P. C., Slater, A. M., Lee, K., Gibson, A., Smith, M., et al. (2005). Three-month-olds, but not newborns, prefer own-race faces. *Developmental Science, 8*, F31–F36.

Kim, J. S., Yoon, H. W., Kim, B. S., Jeun, S. S., Jung, S. L., & Choe, B. Y. (2006). Racial distinction of the unknown facial identity recognition mechanism by event-related fMRI. *Neuroscience Letters, 387*, 279–284.

Kircher, T. J., Senior, C., Phillips, M. L., Rabe-Hesketh, S., Benson, P. J., Bullmore, E. T., et al. (2001). Recognizing one's own face. *Cognition, 78*, B1–B15.

Lavrakas, P. J., Buri, J. R., & Mayzner, M. S. (1976). A perspective on the recognition of other race faces. *Perception & Psychophysics, 20*, 475–481.

Levin, D. T. (2000). Race as a visual feature: Using visual search and perceptual discrimination tasks to understand face categories and the cross-race recognition deficit. *Journal of Experimental Psychology: General, 129*, 559–574.

Lynch, E. B., Coley, J. D., & Medin, D. L. (2000). Tall is typical: Central tendency, ideal dimensions, and graded category structure among tree experts and novices. *Memory & Cognition, 28*, 41–50.

Malpass, R. S., & Kravitz, J. (1969). Recognition for faces of own and other race. *Journal of Personality & Social Psychology, 13*, 330–334.

Malpass, R. S., Lavigueur, H., & Weldon, D. E. (1973). Verbal and visual training in face recognition. *Perception & Psychophysics, 14*, 283–292.

McCarthy, G., Puce, A., Gore, J. C., & Allison, T. (1997). Face-specific processing in the human fusiform gyrus. *Journal of Cognitive Neuroscience, 9*, 605–610.

McKone, E., Brewer, J. L., MacPherson, S., Rhodes, G., & Hayward, W. G. (2007). Familiar other-race faces show normal holistic processing and are robust to perceptual stress. *Perception, 36*, 224–248.

Meador, K., Loring, D., Feinberg, T., Lee, G., & Nichols, M. E. (2000). *Neurology, 55*, 816–820.

Meissner, C. A., & Brigham, J. C. (2001). Thirty years of investigating the own-race bias in memory for faces: A meta-analytic review. *Psychology, Public Policy, and Law, 7*, 3–35.

Michel, C., Rossion, B., Han, J., Chung, C.-S., & Caldara, R. (2006). Holistic processing is finely tuned for faces of our own race. *Psychological Science, 17*, 608–615.

Mondloch, C. J., Maurer, D., & Ahola, S. (2006). Becoming a face expert. *Psychological Science, 17*, 930–934.

Murphy, G. L., & Smith, E. E. (1982). Basic-level superiority in picture categorization. *Journal of Verbal Learning and Verbal Behavior, 21*, 1–20.

Myles-Worsley, M., Johnston, W. A., & Simons, M. A. (1988). The influence of expertise on x-ray image processing. *Journal of Experimental Psychology: Learning, Memory & Cognition, 14*, 553–557.

Nguyen, N., & Cottrell, G. W. (2005). *Owls and wading birds: Generalization gradients in expertise.* Paper presented at the 27th Annual Cognitive Science Society, La Stresa, Italy. Mahwah: Lawrence Erlbaum.

Ninomiya, H., Onitsuka, T., Chen, C. H., Sato, E., & Tashiro, N. (1998). P300 in response to the subject's own face. *Psychiatry and Clinical Neuroscience, 52*, 519–522.

Nodine, C. F., & Krupinski, E. A. (1998). Perceptual skill, radiology expertise, and visual test performance with NINA and WALDO. *Academic Radiology, 5*, 603–612.

Nodine, C. F., Kundel, H. L., Lauver, S. C., & Toto, L. C. (1996). Nature of expertise in searching mammograms for breast masses. *Academic Radiology, 3*, 1000–1006.

Nodine, C. F., Kundel, H. L., Mello-Thoms, C., Weinstein, S. P., Orel, S. G., Sullivan, D. C., et al. (1999). How experience and training influence mammography expertise. *Academic Radiology, 6*, 575–585.

O'Toole, A. J., Deffenbacher, K. A., Valentin, D., & Abdi, H. (1994). Structural aspects of face recognition and the other-race effect. *Memory & Cognition, 22*, 208–224.

Palmeri, T. J., & Blalock, C. (2000). The role of background knowledge in speeded perceptual categorization. *Cognition, 77*, B45–B57.

Pascalis, O., & Bachevalier, J. (1998). Face recognition in primates: A cross species study. *Behavioural Processes, 43*, 87–96.

Pascalis, O., de Haan, M., & Nelson, C. A. (2002). Is face processing species-specific during the first year of life? *Science, 296*, 1321–1323.

Pascalis, O., Demont, E., de Haan, M., & Campbell, R. (2001). Recognition of faces of different species: A developmental study between 5 and 8 years of age. *Infant and Child Development, 10*, 39–45.

Pascalis, O., Scott, L. S., Kelly, D. J., Shannon, R. W., Nicholson, E., Coleman, M., et al. (2005). Plasticity of face processing in infancy. *Proceedings of the National Acadamy of Sciences, 102*, 5297–5300.

Poggio, T., Fahle, M., & Edelman, S. (1992). Fast perceptual learning in visual hyperacuity. *Science, 256*, 1018–1021.

Proffitt, J. B., Coley, J. D., & Medin, D. L. (2000). Expertise and category-based induction. *Journal of Experimental Psychology: Learning, Memory, and Cognition, 26*, 811–828.

Rhodes, G., Tan, S., Brake, S., & Taylor, K. (1989). Expertise and configural coding in face recognition. *British Journal of Psychology, 80*, 313–331.

Riesenhuber, M., Jarudi, I., Gilad, S., & Sinha, P. (2004). Face processing in humans is compatible with a simple shape-based model of vision. *Proceedings of the Royal Society of London Series B-Biological Sciences, 271*, S448–S450.

Robbins, R., & McKone, E. (2006). No face-like processing for objects-of-expertise in three behavioural tasks. *Cognition, 103*, 34–79.

Rosch, E., Mervis, C., Gray, W., Johnson, D., & Boyes-Braem, P. (1976). Basic objects in natural categories. *Cognitive Psychology, 8*, 382–439.

Rossion, B., Collins, D., Goffaux, V., & Curran, T. (2007). Long-term visual expertise with artificial objects increases visual competition with early face categorization processes. *Journal of Cognitive Neuroscience, 19*, 543–555.

Rossion, B., & Curran, T. (in press). Visual expertise with pictures of cars correlates with RT magnitude of the car inversion effect. *Perception.*

Rossion, B., Curran, T., & Gauthier, I. (2002). A defense of the subordinate-level expertise account for the N170 component. *Cognition, 85,* 189–196.

Rossion, B., Delvenne, J. F., Debatisse, D., Goffaux, V., Bruyer, R., Crommelinck, M., et al. (1999). Spatio-temporal localization of the face inversion effect: An event-related potentials study. *Biological Psychology, 50,* 173–189.

Rossion, B., Gauthier, I., Goffaux, V., Tarr, M. J., & Crommelinck, M. (2002). Expertise training with novel objects leads to left-lateralized facelike electrophysiological responses. *Psychological Science, 13,* 250–257.

Rossion, B., Joyce, C. A., Cottrell, G. W., & Tarr, M. J. (2003). Early lateralization and orientation tuning for face, word, and object processing in the visual cortex. *NeuroImage, 20,* 1609–1624.

Rossion, B., Kung, C. C., & Tarr, M. J. (2004). Visual expertise with nonface objects leads to competition with the early perceptual processing of faces in the human occipitotemporal cortex. *Proceedings of the National Academy of Sciences, 101,* 14521–14526.

Sagi, D., & Tanne, D. (1994). Perceptual learning: Learning to see. *Current Opinion in Neurobiology, 4,* 195–199.

Sangrigoli, S., & De Schonen, S. (2004). Recognition of own-race and other-race faces by three-month-old infants. *Journal of Child Psychology & Psychiatry, 45,* 1219–1227.

Schweinberger, S. R., Huddy, V., & Burton, A. M. (2004). N250r: A face-selective brain response to stimulus repetitions. *NeuroReport, 15,* 1501–1505.

Schweinberger, S. R., Pickering, E. C., Burton, A. M., & Kaufmann, J. M. (2002). Human brain potential correlates of repetition priming in face and name recognition. *Neuropsychologia, 40,* 2057–2073.

Schweinberger, S. R., Pickering, E. C., Jentzsch, I., Burton, A. M., & Kaufmann, J. M. (2002). Event-related brain potential evidence for a response of inferior temporal cortex to familiar face repetitions. *Cognitive Brain Research, 14,* 398–409.

Scott, L. S., Luciana, M., Wewerka, S., & Nelson, C. A. (2005). Electrophysiological correlates of facial self-recognition in adults and children. *Cognitie, Creier, Comportament, IX,* 211–238.

Scott, L. S. & Monesson, A. (2009). The origin of biases in face perception. *Psychological Science, 20,* 676–680.

Scott, L. S., & Nelson, C. A. (2006). Featural and configural face processing in adults and infants: A behavioral and electrophysiological investigation. *Perception, 35,* 1107–1128.

Scott, L. S., Shannon, R. W., & Nelson, C. A. (2005). Behavioral and electrophysiological evidence of species-specific face processing. *Cognitive, Affective & Behavioral Neuroscience, 5,* 405–416.

Scott, L. S., Shannon, R. W., & Nelson, C. A. (2006). Neural correlates of human and monkey face processing in 9-month-old infants. *Infancy, 10,* 171–186.

Scott, L. S., Tanaka, J., Sheinberg, D. L., & Curran, T. (2006). A reevaluation of the electrophysiological correlates of expert object processing. *Journal of Cognitive Neuroscience, 18,* 1453–1465.

Scott, L. S., Tanaka, J. W., Sheinberg, D. L., & Curran, T. (2008). The role of category learning in the acquisition and retention of perceptual expertise: A behavioral and neurophysiological study. *Brain Research, 1210,* 204–215.

Sperry, R., Zaidel, E., & Zaidel, D. (1979). Self recognition and social awareness in the deconnected minor hemisphere. *Neuropsychologia, 17*, 153–166.

Tanaka, J. W. (2001). The entry point of face recognition: Evidence for face expertise. *Journal of Experimental Psychology: General, 130*, 534–543.

Tanaka, J. W., & Curran, T. (2001). A neural basis for expert object recognition. *Psychological Science, 12*, 43–47.

Tanaka, J. W., Curran, T., Boddington, S., & Droucker, D. T. (2005). *The N250 component as a measure of object and non-human face familiarity effects in ERPs.* Paper presented at the Society for Neuroscience, Washington, DC.

Tanaka, J. W., Curran, T., Porterfield, A., & Collins, D. (2006). Activation of pre-existing and acquired face representations: The N250 component as an index of face familiarity. *Journal of Cognitive Neuroscience, 18*, 1488–1497.

Tanaka, J. W., Curran, T., & Sheinberg, D. (2005). The training and transfer of real-world, perceptual expertise. *Psychological Science, 16*(2), 145–151.

Tanaka, J. W. & Pierce, L. J. (2009). The neural plasticity of other-race face recognition. *Cognitive, Affective and Behavioral Neuroscience, 9*, 122–131.

Tanaka, J.W. & Droucker, Reversing the other race effect in adults through expertise training. Manuscript submitted for publication.

Tanaka, J. W., & Gauthier, I. (1997). Expertise in object and face recognition. In R. L. Goldstone, P. G. Schyns, & D. L. Medin (Eds.), *Psychology of learning and motivation* (Vol. 36, pp. 83–125). San Diego, CA: Academic Press.

Tanaka, J. W., Kiefer, M., & Bukach, C. M. (2004). A holistic account of the own-race effect in face recognition: Evidence from a cross-cultural study. *Cognition, 93*, B1–B9.

Tanaka, J. W. & Pierce, L. J. (2009). The neural plasticity of other-race face recognition. *Cognitive, Affective, and Behavioral Neuroscience, 9*, 122–131.

Tanaka, J. W., & Taylor, M. J. (1991). Object categories and expertise: Is the basic level in the eye of the beholder? *Cognitive Psychology, 23*, 457–482.

Tarr, M. J., & Gauthier, I. (2000). FFA: A flexible fusiform area for subordinate-level visual processing automatized by expertise. *Nature Neuroscience, 3*, 764–769.

Tollefson, G. D., Luxenberg, M., Valentine, R., Dunsmore, G., & Tollefson, S. L. (1991). An open label trial of alprazolam in comorbid irritable bowel syndrome and generalized anxiety disorder. *Journal of Clinical Psychiatry, 52*, 502–508.

Tong, F., & Nakayama, K. (1999). Robust representations for faces: Evidence from visual search. *Journal of Experimental Psychology: Human Perception and Performance, 25*, 1016–1035.

Valentine, T. (1991). A unified account of the effects of distinctiveness, inversion, and race in face recognition. *Quarterly Journal of Experimental Psychology A, 43*, 161–204.

Wong, C.-N., & Gauthier, I. (in press) The basic level as the entry point of expert letter recognition. *Visual Cognition*.

Xu, Y. (2005). Revisiting the role of the fusiform face area in visual expertise. *Cerebral Cortex, 15*, 1234–1242.

Xu, Y., Liu, J., & Kanwisher, N. (2005). The M170 is selective for faces, not for expertise. *Neuropsychologia, 43*, 588–597.

Yin, R. K. (1969). Looking at upside-down faces. *Journal of Experimental Psychology: General, 81*, 141–145.

Young, A., Hellawell, D., & Hay, D. C. (1987). Configural information in face perception. *Perception, 10*, 747–759.

5

Face Processing in Autism: Insights from the Perceptual Expertise Framework

Kim M. Curby, Verena Willenbockel, James W. Tanaka, and Robert T. Schultz

INTRODUCTION

While persons with an autism spectrum disorder (ASD) have a range of cognitive impairments, their performance is sometimes on par with or even superior to that of their age-and IQ-matched peers on tasks of visual perception, such as visual search and embedded figures tests (e.g., Behrmann, Thomas, & Humphreys, 2006; Jolliffe & Baron Cohen, 1997; Mottron, Dawson, Soulieres, Hubert, & Burack, 2006; Shah & Frith, 1983, 1993). One striking, and perhaps revealing, exception is their impaired performance in perceptual tasks that involve face stimuli, such as those requiring the perception of facial identity or identification of facial expressions (Klin et al., 1999; Wolf et al., 2008). This selective impairment in face perception has been the topic of much research, and it has been suggested to potentially contribute to the debilitating social impairment at the core of this disorder (Schultz, 2005). Here we argue that the expertise framework, used to account for the normal development of face perception skills, may have important implications for understanding the face recognition deficit observed among people with ASDs (Tarr & Gauthier, 2000). This framework may also open potential avenues of treatment because, unlike the suggestion that face perception abilities stem from an innate capacity, the expertise framework emphasizes the importance of experience and instruction for skill development (Tarr & Gauthier, 2000). An expertise account of face processing skill offers the possibility that face recognition training programs may improve such skills among people with ASDs (Wolf et al., 2008).

This chapter will first provide a general description of ASDs, a spectrum of disorders that have intrigued psychologists for decades with their striking variability and puzzling combinations of impaired and preserved abilities. Next, it will provide a survey of the literature documenting the face processing deficit in ASDs, including evidence for a role of experience in contributing to this deficit. In this context, we will describe a recent treatment study in which the perceptual expertise framework was applied to the training of face recognition in children with ASDs.

This chapter will then proceed to explore the current literature documenting more general visuocognitive abnormalities in ASDs and their relevance to our understanding of the face perception deficit documented in this group. Some current models of ASDs will be outlined, including both "cold" models that emphasize executive or visuocognitive abnormalities and "hot" models that emphasize affective or sociocognitive processing abnormalities. Next, we discuss a possible contribution, through their impact on experience, of both "cold" visuocognitive abnormalities and "hot" sociocognitive abnormalities to the face perception deficits among people with ASDs.

What Is Autism?

Autism is a complex, behaviorally defined neurodevelopmental disorder characterized by a triad of symptoms including impairments in social reciprocity and communication and the presence of repetitive behaviors and restricted interests (DSM-IV-TR, APA, 2000). Autism and related disorders emerge in the first 3 years of life and are almost always lifelong disabling conditions. The "autism spectrum disorders" (ASDs) encompass the categorical disorders of autism, Asperger's syndrome, and Pervasive Developmental Disorders—Not Otherwise Specified (PDD-NOS). However, it is not clear that using categorical nomenclature, as opposed to conceptualizing a continuum of disability, confers any advantages with respect to basic or applied science. This spectrum is extremely broad, with core symptoms varying from mild to severe, alongside cognitive profiles ranging from profound mental retardation to superior (Volkmar, Lord, Bailey, Schultz, & Klin, 2004; Wing & Gould, 1979). Although the genetic and neurobiological bases of ASD are not yet fully understood, it seems clear that ASD is genetically, neurobiologically, and phenotypically heterogeneous (Anderson, 2008; Geschwind & Levitt, 2007; O'Roak & State, 2008).

The difficulties that people with ASD experience with reciprocal social interaction are the targets of much research; unlike the communication deficits and the restricted interests and behaviors that are shared with other disorders, ASD-related social deficits are relatively unique. People with ASD typically experience difficulties in everyday social activities and often struggle with the use and interpretation of nonverbal communication such as eye gaze, facial expression, body postures, and gestures (Baron-Cohen, Campbell, Karmiloff-Smith, Grant, & Walker, 1999; Celani, Battacchi, & Arcidiacono, 1999; Klin, Jones, Schultz, Volkmar, & Cohen, 2002; Mundy, Sigman, Ungerer, & Sherman, 1986; Pelphrey et al., 2002). These difficulties often lead to problems in the regulation of social interactions critical for establishing and maintaining relationships with others.

One of the most intriguing aspects of ASD is the coupling of frequently severe deficits in social and communication functions with relatively spared abilities in other cognitive and perceptual domains. In some cases these spared capacities can even be superior to those demonstrated by typically developing individuals, as in the case of savants. For example, there have been numerous reports of individuals with uncanny visual discrimination abilities, facility with numbers, and memory for detail (e.g., see Thioux, Stark, Klaiman, & Schultz, 2006; Treffert, 1989). Savants aside, the mean scores for people with ASD on visuospatial tasks, such as the block design or embedded figures tests, tend to be higher than those for matched controls (Shah & Frith, 1993). The combination of intact and impaired abilities in ASD underscores the complexity of the disorder, while at the same time making it of great interest to psychologists.

As suggested by the variability in the severity and nature of the symptoms across individuals, it is generally accepted that even within a subgroup (e.g., Asperger's syndrome), there is unlikely to be a single cause of ASD. In addition, the triad of deficits suggests that a diverse set of neural systems is affected. However, in contrast to cases with comorbid mental retardation, the relative preservation of specific faculties in a large number of individuals with ASD is proof that general impairment in cognitive functioning is not a core feature of the disorders.

The early onset and heritability strongly suggest a biological basis of ASD, but twin studies suggest that both nature and nurture play a role. Such studies have found that the rate at which the broader ASD spectrum co-occurs in fraternal twins is around 10%, but this rate jumps to about 90% among identical twins (Bailey et al., 1995). Notably, the less than perfect co-occurrence of ASD among identical twins speaks convincingly to the role of environment factors as well.

In terms of understanding both the manifestation and underlying cause or causes of ASD, it is important to note the possibility of ongoing interactions between genes and environment throughout development. Specifically, given that ASD is a developmental disorder, rather than it resulting from a number of abnormalities in independent and diverse systems, it is possible that insults to just one or two key nodes alter the development of a diverse range of systems (Schultz, 2005). Thus, an understanding of the normal development of social-perceptual skills, such as face recognition, and how it compares to that of people with ASD, may be critical for understanding this disorder.

AUTISM: AN ABSENCE OF PERCEPTUAL EXPERTISE WITH FACES

Face processing skill likely plays a critical role in supporting normal social development and functioning; the ability to efficiently distinguish friend from stranger and to read others' emotional expressions is not only impor-tant for one's safety, but also for gauging the appropriateness of different social behaviors. Thus, the face processing deficit in ASD may contribute to the social deficits experienced by this group. This possibility, along with the fact that the face processing deficit in ASD is one of the most reliable findings in the literature (although see Jemel, Mottron, & Dawson, 2006), renders it a topic worthy of investigation. The extensive body of empirical work docu-menting this deficit forms the basis of the following section.

Humans typically have prodigious face processing abilities; we can recognize thousands of individual faces accurately even if we have not seen them for many years, and with a single glance we can extract a wealth of social information such as emotional expression, gender, race, and direction of eye gaze/intent. In contrast, individuals with autism are characterized by poor face processing abilities and/or strategies, although they are not considered prosopagnosic per se. The difficulties and atypicalities in face processing that characterize ASD are interesting in two respects: they may provide insights into the deficits in social interaction and nonverbal communication that individuals with ASD experience, and they may reveal factors necessary for efficient face processing that we otherwise take for granted. The following section provides an overview of the literature, including behavioral, ERP, and fMRI studies, documenting the face processing deficit in ASD.

Behavioral Evidence for Atypical Face Processing in ASD

Individuals with ASD have been shown to demonstrate selective impairments in face processing, affecting both their ability to discriminate (Tantam, Monaghan, Nicholson, & Stirling, 1989) and recognize faces (e.g., Boucher & Lewis, 1992; Klin et al., 1999; but see Jemel, Mottron, & Dawson, 2006). Boucher and Lewis (1992) showed that while recognition of buildings among those with ASD was equivalent to that among typically developing individuals, face recognition was impaired. ASD-related deficits in face processing are more common among children and low-functioning individuals, although there are studies documenting similar deficits among high-functioning adults with ASD (Behrmann, Avidan, et al., 2006; Blair, Frith, Smith, Abell, & Cipolotti, 2002). For example, Blair et al. (2002) showed that while adults with autism perform worse on tests of face memory than do matched control groups, they outperform controls on tests of memory for leaves and buildings. In addition, Behrmann, Avidan, et al. (2006) demonstrated that adults with ASD discriminate faces more slowly than do control groups. These results provide evidence that face processing skills are selectively impaired in ASD while nonface object processing remains relatively intact.

The face perception deficit in ASD also affects other aspects beyond identity processing, such as those requiring the processing of emotion, gaze direction, gender, and even lip reading tasks (Deruelle, Rondan, Gepner, & Tardif, 2004). For example, in contrast to typical children, children with ASD were found to sort images of emotional expressions using nonemotional cues (Weeks & Hobson, 1987). Other face processing difficulties include problems discriminating gender (Njiokiktjien et al., 2001) and unusual patterns of eye gaze processing (Pelphrey, Morris, & McCarthy, 2005; Ristic et al., 2005). Given the critical social information conveyed through faces, the widespread face processing abnormalities observed in ASD may contribute to the severe social impairments that are characteristic of this group.

There is further evidence suggesting that individuals with ASD employ face processing strategies that differ from those used by individuals without

ASD. Typical face processing relies on a holistic processing strategy where the features and the spatial relationships of features within a face are integrated as a perceptual "gestalt", or whole face stimulus that emphasizes eye information (Tanaka & Farah, 1993). In contrast, individuals with autism employ a more parts-based approach that focuses on the mouth feature (Joseph & Tanaka, 2002). By six years of age, typically developing individuals are more successful at identifying the top half of a "composite" face (made from the top and bottom of different faces) when it is out of alignment with the bottom than when the two halves are aligned (Carey & Diamond, 1994), a pattern generally interpreted as reflecting automatic processing of faces as wholes rather than as independent features. That is, when the top and bottom halves of different faces are aligned they form a perceptual gestalt, making it difficult to make a judgment about one part without interference from the task-irrelevant part (Carey & Diamond, 1994; Young, Hellawell, & Hay, 1987). When these two halves are misaligned, there is a release from this obligatory holistic processing (Young et al., 1987). In contrast, individuals with autism do not differ in their discrimination performance when the top and bottom halves of the face are aligned versus when they are misaligned (Teunisse & de Gelder, 2003). The absence of this alignment effect suggests that individuals with autism perceive faces more in terms of their individual features than in terms of their constituent.

An abnormality in face encoding and representation is also apparent in the diminished tendency of individuals with ASD to demonstrate the face inversion effect. For typical adults, face recognition, relative to nonface object recognition, is disproportionately impaired by a 180° picture plane rotation (Yin, 1969). Inversion is thought to disrupt holistic/configural processing, which is typically the "default" mode for upright face recognition (Freire, Lee, & Symons, 2000). Yet, individuals with ASD often perform better at recognizing inverted faces than do controls (Hobson, Ouston, & Lee, 1988; Langdell, 1978; Tantam et al., 1989). The lack of a face inversion effect suggests that instead of holistic/configural processing, a more featural processing strategy resembling the strategy used for object perception by typically developing individuals might be at play.

Electrophysiological Evidence for Atypical Face Processing in ASD

Faces elicit a specific pattern of electrical brain activity. When recording EEG during a face processing task, a negative peak in brain waves, occurring about 170 milliseconds after the onset of the face stimulus, can be observed. This N170 component is larger and earlier to faces (and eyes alone) than to other objects, making it a sensitive "marker" of human face processing (e.g. Bentin, Allison, Puce, Perez, & McCarthy, 1996; Eimer, 1998, 2000a, 2000b, 2000c; George, Evans, Fiori, Davidoff, & Renault, 1996). The N170 is recorded over the posterior temporal lobe and is typically greater in the right than in the left hemisphere. One characteristic of the N170 in typically developing individuals is that its amplitude and latency is modulated by face orientation:

inverted faces elicit a delayed, but often larger, N170 than do upright faces (Eimer, 2000b; Rebai, Poiroux, Bernard, & Lalonde, 2001; Rossion et al., 2000). Notably, scrambling of faces reduces the amplitude of the N170, whereas stimulus familiarity has no effect (e.g. Bentin & Deouell, 2000; Eimer, 2000a). These findings together suggest that the N170 reflects structural encoding and plays an important role in the early stages of face processing.

In individuals with ASD, a distorted N170 pattern has been observed. The N170 to faces has been found to be delayed compared to the N170 to furniture in high-functioning individuals with ASD, and their N170 was not sensitive to face inversion (McPartland, Dawson, Webb, Panagiotides, & Carver, 2004). Furthermore, face processing speed, as indicated by the peak latency of the N170, was reported to be linked with face recognition performance (McPartland et al., 2004). These findings suggest that individuals with ASD differ from controls early in the encoding and processing of facial information (see Dawson, Webb, & McPartland, 2005, for a review). Another atypicality has been found with regard to the scalp topography of the N170; in contrast to typically developing individuals, the N170 is more bilaterally than unilaterally (right) distributed in at least some individuals with ASD (McPartland et al., 2004; see also MEG study by Bailey, Braeutigam, Jousmaki, & Swithenby, 2005). The atypical topography of the N170 in individuals with ASD indicates that the delay in the response to faces is not only due to decreased efficiency in the typical face processing circuit, but also to the involvement of an additional or altered neural circuit.

EEG activity in the gamma range is another indicator of early-stage face processing. Gamma activity (between 30 and 80 Hz) is thought to play an important role in binding together stimulus properties (e.g., binding spatially distinct features into a whole; Eckhorn, Reitboeck, Arndt, & Dicke, 1990; Gray, König, Engel, & Singer, 1989; Milner, 1974). Typically, upright face perception is characterized by a larger increase in gamma oscillations than that for inverted face perception (Keil et al., 1999; Rodriguez et al., 1999), and this has been interpreted as reflecting the difference in holistic processing of upright and inverted faces (see Dawson, Webb, & McPartland, 2005, for a review). Individuals with ASD lack this difference—they show similar gamma activation to upright and inverted faces (Grice et al., 2001). Decreased gamma bursts in response to upright faces indicate decreased perceptual binding and thus this finding is consistent with an impairment in holistic/configural processing of faces in ASD.

ERPs also provide insights into the perception of facial expressions. Different facial expressions have been found to elicit different ERP patterns not only in infants and children but also in adults (e.g., Eimer & Holmes, 2002; Nelson & de Haan, 1996). Typically, fearful faces evoke a characteristic N300 and negative slow wave response that is evident in electrophysiological scalp recordings (Dawson, Webb, Carver, Panagiotides, & McPartland, 2004). However, children with ASD demonstrate a significantly delayed N300 to fearful faces compared to typically developing children (Dawson et al., 2004). They also lack the larger-amplitude, negative slow wave response to fearful faces and show an atypical scalp topography of responses. These results suggest that information processing is slowed and that atypical neural circuits are active during the perception of emotional expression in ASD.

ERP components are also informative about the processes mediating face recognition. Typically developing infants and young children show differential ERP responses to familiar and unfamiliar faces and objects (e.g., Carver et al., 2003; de Haan & Nelson, 1999). The posterior P400 and the frontal Nc components in typical children and the slow wave component in developmentally delayed children are sensitive to the familiarity of faces and objects. Children with ASD were found to lack these differential ERP responses to their mother's face versus a stranger's face at the level of the P400 and the Nc. However, the amplitude of both these electrophysiological components were enhanced in response to their favorite toy compared to an unfamiliar toy (Dawson et al., 2002). These findings indicate that ASD is characterized by a selective impairment in face processing. Overall, findings of electrophysiological studies support the view that various face processing deficits in ASD are common and present early in life.

Neuroimaging Evidence for Atypical Face Processing in ASD

Abnormalities in the processing of faces among people with ASD are also evident in studies using fMRI techniques. In typically developing individuals, the lateral part of the middle fusiform gyrus is maximally activated by human faces and is commonly referred to as the fusiform face area (FFA; Kanwisher, McDermott, & Chun, 1997). Decreased activation in the FFA during face perception tasks, relative to that found in typically developing individuals, is arguably one of the most robust and consistently reported findings in the neuroimaging literature on ASD (e.g., Pierce, Müller, Ambrose, Allen, & Courshesne, 2001; Schultz et al., 2000, Critchley et al., 2000). Findings from fMRI studies not only suggest that individuals with ASD fail to recruit the FFA to the same degree as typical controls do when perceiving faces, but some evidence suggests that they may also recruit a different neural system. For example, Schultz and colleagues (2000) found increased inferotemporal gyrus (ITG) activation to faces, along with decreased FFA activation among people with ASD. Notably, while the brain activation pattern during face discrimination differed between groups in this study, the activation during the object discrimination task was consistently found to be maximal in the ITG across both groups (Schultz et al., 2000). This finding is consistent with the claim that the perceptual processing of faces in ASD may be more similar to that for objects in typically developing individuals.

Other regions of the "social brain network" are also functionally atypical in ASD (Bachevalier & Loveland, 2006; Baron-Cohen & Belmonte, 2005; Castelli, Frith, Happé, & Frith, 2002; Pelphrey et al., 2005; Schultz, 2005). Pelphrey et al. (2005) focused on the superior temporal sulcus (STS), which is thought to play an important role in the processing of social information conveyed by gaze direction (Allison, Puce, & McCarthy, 2000). In an fMRI paradigm in which subjects were presented with a small target appearing in an animated character's visual field, they tested whether the STS would show greater activation on trials in which the character moved the eyes toward the target than on incongruent trials in which the character shifted her gaze toward empty space. In contrast to the control group, the group with ASD showed no differential STS activity to the goal-directed versus non-goal-directed eye movements. These findings are consistent with behavioral evidence suggesting that people with ASD have difficulty using information from gaze direction to read the intentions of other people.

Studies have also shown atypical activation of the amygdala in ASD during perceptual judgments involving faces and/or facial expressions. These findings seem to be related to known deficits in emotion perception among people with ASD. Intriguingly, Dalton et al. (2005) found that people with ASD who had longer fixations on the eye region of face stimuli had the greatest amount of amgydala and FFA activation. Dalton et al. (2005) speculated that hyperactivation in the neural circuitry of emotion leads to over-arousal to social stimuli. In order to reduce this heightened sensitivity, or more specifically the resulting anxiety, gaze fixation may be diminished, resulting in hypoactivation of the fusiform gyrus. This model contrasts with that of Schultz (2005), which postulated that the amygdala serves as a detector of socially salient events and upregulates FFA activation; thus, hypoactivation of the FFA would be due in part to the failure of the amygdala to signal to the FFA that socially relevant percepts exist, deserving added information processing and evaluation. Notably, the Dalton study is unusual in finding hyperactivation of the amygdala in ASD, as opposed to the more typical finding of hypoactivation (e.g., Baron-Cohen et al, 1999; Grelotti et al., 2005). Given that anxiety is a frequent comorbid condition, the role of arousal needs to be considered in fMRI studies that measure amygdala activity in ASD (Juranek et al., 2006). In addition, although Dalton et al.'s (2005) finding is important, it cannot be said from those data that when a person with ASD fixates on the eye region, the FFA is engaged normally. A within-subject analysis is needed to address such a question. Unfortunately, we do not yet know what factors mediate FFA activity in real time among people with ASD, although such studies are under way. Findings reported to date about individual differences in FFA activity indicate that weak face identification skills, short fixation on the eye region, and greater social impairment are all correlated with reduced FFA activity (Schultz, Chawarska, & Volkmar, 2006). It seems likely that all three predictors of individual differences at the level of FFA activation share something in common, but the nature of these relationships has not yet been well delineated.

In summary, converging evidence suggests that face processing is atypical in ASD. Behavioral results indicate that people with ASD have difficulties in both face recognition and discrimination while object processing remains relatively intact. Notably, people with ASD appear to use different strategies to process faces than do typically developing controls. These behavioral findings are consistent with electrophysiological results showing that face processing is delayed in ASD, and that the binding of features may be impaired. fMRI studies further support these findings and suggest that the brains of individuals with ASD process faces differently than the brains of typically developing individuals, possibly more like that of nonface objects.

EVIDENCE FOR A ROLE OF EXPERIENCE IN THE FACE PERCEPTION DEFICIT AMONG PEOPLE WITH ASD

There are a number of findings in the literature that suggest that the face perception deficit associated with ASD may result partly from a lack of experience in processing facial information. This insight comes from comparing the development of face perception skills in typically developing children to that in people with ASD, as well as from the perceptual expertise framework used to explain face processing skill within a healthy population. The potential role of experience in contributing to this face processing deficit among people with ASD is discussed in this section.

Reduced Experience with Faces in ASD: A Developmental Perspective

The neural mechanisms underlying face processing are established very early in life, with the visual system of newborns' set up in such a way as to gear their attention to faces (Goren, Sarty, & Wu, 1975; Simion, Valenza, Umilta, & Dalla Barba, 1998); when newborns are presented with face-like patterns and comparably complex nonface patterns, they show a visual preference for the face patterns (Goren et al., 1975; Johnson, Dziurawiec, Ellis, & Morton, 1991). Specifically, newborns show a preference for face-like *configurations*, that is, for items with more elements (e.g., the two eyes) in the top part than the bottom part (Cassia, Turati, & Simion, 2004). In addition, infants only a few days old attend longer to an image of their mother's face than to an unfamiliar face (Bushnell, Sai, & Mullin, 1989), and 1-month-old infants are able to discriminate and rapidly recognize individual faces (de Haan, Johnson, Maurer, & Perrett, 2001). Furthermore, within their first year of life, infants are able to respond to facial gestures, gaze direction, and emotional expressions (see Dawson et al., 2005, for a review). Thus, for typical infants, faces are salient stimuli and increasingly informative during development.

In contrast, infants with ASD may not show the same special attention to the human face. Retrospective studies of young toddlers who were later diagnosed with ASD have revealed that these children can be differentiated from typically developing individuals by having spent comparatively less time looking at people, and at faces in particular, and more time looking at inanimate objects (Baranek, 1999; Osterling & Dawson, 1994; Osterling, Dawson, & Munson, 2002). This difference is so robust that the lack of interest in the faces of others, evident in the first 6 to 12 months of life for many children who go on to express ASD, is one of the better predictors of later diagnosis (Maestro et al., 2002; Osterling & Dawson, 1994).

The reduced attention to faces among toddlers with ASD appears to remain through adolescence and into adulthood (Klin et al., 2002; Trepagnier, Sebrechts, & Peterson, 2002). This has been demonstrated in studies measuring observers' visual scan paths and percent viewing time of different regions of a visual scene (Klin et al., 2002). In one study, the authors showed participants a short excerpt from the movie *Who's Afraid of Virginia Wolf*, during which time they recorded observers' eye movements. Participants with ASD spent significantly less time fixating on the faces of the characters and more time on apparently inconsequential features in the environment, such as the light switch on the wall in the background of the scene (Klin et al., 2002). Thus, reduced attention to faces appears to be a robust symptom among people with ASD.

In addition to evidence that people with ASD spend less time viewing faces, there are findings indicating that even when they do attend to faces, they appear to show an atypical viewing pattern. Typical people tend to focus on the eye region when attending to a face, especially during social interactions, and thus this viewing pattern dominates their experience with faces. In contrast, people with ASD spend relatively more time fixating on the mouth region of a face (Klin et al., 2002; but see van der Geest, Kemner, Verbaten, & van Engeland, 2002). In addition, eye-tracking studies have revealed decreased gaze to facial features (e.g., eyes, nose, mouth) and increased gaze to nonfeatural elements (Pelphrey et al., 2002). Together these findings suggest that people with ASD not only have reduced, but also abnormal, experience with faces relative to their typically developing peers. These differences across the course of development likely impact the ability to establish proficiency or expertise with the processing of facial information.

ASD: A Failure to Develop Perceptual Expertise with Faces

The perceptual expertise account of face processing would suggest that reduced and abnormal experience in processing facial information, the consequence of an early absence of a preference to attend to faces, should lead to reduced face recognition ability (Schultz, 2005; Schultz et al., 2000). This account also makes a number of specific predictions regarding the nature of how the processing of facial information should differ among children with ASD compared to their typically developing peers. Specifically, one consequence of the development of perceptual expertise with faces is that our recognition skill for this category becomes specific to the orientation that dominates our experience, that is the upright orientation (Yin, 1969). Notably, the size of the cost of inversion to face recognition performance is correlated with age (Carey, 1996; Carey & Diamond, 1994). Thus, there appears to be a progressive tuning of the face processing system across development, resulting in the superior performance for the orientation that dominated one's experience with faces. Consistent with the proposed failure to develop perceptual expertise with faces in ASD, there are reports of an absence of the face inversion effect among people with ASD (Langdell, 1978; Teunisse & de Gelder, 2003). As noted above, this disproportionate cost to face recognition performance due to inversion develops over time; during early childhood neither typically developing individuals nor individuals with ASD exhibit a face inversion effect (Carey, 1996; Carey & Diamond, 1994; Langdell, 1978; Teunisse & de Gelder, 2003). At the adult stage, the face inversion effect is very robust for typical individuals. One interpretation of this finding is that children with ASD may not have the degree of perceptual experience and expertise necessary to fine-tune their face processing skill, and as a result they fail to show orientation specificity as measured by the face inversion effect.

If individuals with ASD lack perceptual expertise with faces, then it should be possible to train this type of domain-specific recognition following the training protocols that have been successful in fostering perceptual expertise with other object categories. As a test of this prediction, children with ASD participated in a face training program using the *Let's Face It!* (LFI!) software. *Let's Face It!* leads the child through a series of hierarchically structured exercises intended to address a critical facet of face perception, such as the analytic and holistic perception of facial identity and expression, recognition across viewpoints, and changes in external cues. Results from a recently completed clinical trial indicate that 20 hours of LFI! training was sufficient to improve some aspects of holistic face recognition among children with autism (Wolf et al., 2008). These findings show that face recognition, like other forms of perceptual expertise, can be acquired through direct instruction and systematic training.

An alternative hypothesis is that the extended developmental course of typical face processing reflects processes of maturation rather than experience. But there are many parallels between typical face processing and experience-based expert processing of nonface categories, as well as between face processing among people with ASD and the manner in which novices process nonface categories. For example, like face processing in ASD, novices with nonface object categories tend to process these objects in a more part-based or piecemeal fashion relative to those demonstrating expertise with the same category: car novices, relative to car experts, are better able to make judgments about part of a car without being influenced by the other parts (Gauthier, Curran, Curby, & Collins, 2003). Thus, people with ASD appear to perform more like object novices than object experts when processing faces, with the more parts-based processing style observed among people with ASD being similar to that which is characteristic of novice processing.

In addition, the holistic processing style typically recruited by faces and nonface objects of expertise, but not for faces in ASD, has been linked with activation in the FFA (Gauthier, Tarr, Anderson, Skudlarski, & Gore, 1999; Gauthier, Skudlarski, Gore, & Anderson, 2000; Gauthier, Curby, Skudlarski, & Epstein, 2005). For example, participants who undergo a lab-based expertise training regimen with novel objects show increased FFA activation in response to these objects, and the degree of activation is correlated with measures of holistic processing (Gauthier et al., 1999, Gauthier & Tarr, 2002). In addition, real-world experts such as bird or car experts recruit the FFA for their respective objects of expertise, and the degree to which they recruit this area is correlated with their level of expertise with the category (Gauthier et al., 2000, 2005). Thus, hypoactivation of the fusiform brain region observed in ASD is not only consistent with evidence that such people process faces less holistically, but also with suggestions that they lack the normal perceptual expertise with faces.

A case study involving an individual with ASD, known as DD, who had extensive experience with "Digimon" characters provides further evidence that lack of experience may contribute to face perception deficits in ASD (Grelotti et al., 2005). For this 10-year-old boy, Digimon characters constituted a "restricted interest," which refers to interests that tend to dominate one's thoughts and interactions with others and are common among people with ASD. In this case, the individual's FFA was more active in response to Digimon characters, compared to faces or other nonface objects, suggesting that the FFA may not be impaired perse in individuals with ASD. Instead, it may be possible, with enough experience, to kick-start the FFA's role in face processing among people with ASD.

From a neuroimaging perspective, insight into the possible role of experience in contributing to the face recognition deficits in ASD comes not only from the numerous studies reporting hypoactivation in the FFA, but also from the few studies that fail to find such a result. For example, one such study found equivalent activation in the fusiform region for personally familiar faces among groups of children with ASD and their typically developing peers. When observing familiar faces, such as that of their mother or coworker, adults with ASD showed greater activation in the fusiform compared to when they viewed faces of strangers (Pierce, Haist, Sedaghat, & Courchesne, 2004). The amygdala was also more active to familiar than to unfamiliar faces in ASD (Pierce et al., 2004). Taken together, these results suggest that the fusiform can be recruited by faces, but it may only be recruited for faces that have high emotional value. These findings could fit well with a model emphasizing developed expertise: the development of expertise with faces, and thus the recruitment of the FFA, may start with highly familiar faces and only respond to the whole category after extensive experience. Therefore, the pattern observed in ASD—that is, normal levels of fusiform activation for familiar but not unfamiliar faces—may parallel the beginning stages of the transition from novice to expert.

We have outlined in this section the available evidence suggesting links between altered experience and face processing deficits in ASD. In sum, the processing of faces among people with ASD shares many of the characteristics of the processing of nonface objects among control individuals. This is consistent with suggestions that people with ASD may fail to develop the perceptual expertise that typically distinguishes the processing of faces from that of other object categories. In the following section, we discuss accounts of ASD that focus on socioaffective and visuocognitive abnormalities, as such abnormalities could conceivably underlie altered experience with faces in ASD.

UNDERSTANDING ASD: INSIGHTS FROM SOCIOAFFECTIVE AND VISUOCOGNITIVE ABNORMALITIES

There are a number of accounts of ASD that are relevant to our understanding of how the experience of individuals across development may be altered, with consequences for the development of face processing skills. Proposed accounts that emphasize visuocognitive abnormalities could be (crudely) considered "cold" models of ASD. In contrast, accounts that emphasize socioaffective abnormalities might be considered "hot" models of ASD. One account—referred to here as the amygdala/fusiform modulation model of ASD—can be considered a "hot" account because it emphasizes a central role of socioaffective and reward aspects of stimulus processing (Schultz, 2005). Accounts focusing more on cognitive processing abnormalities in ASD, such as the "weak central coherence" theory (Happé & Frith, 2006) or the "enhanced perceptual functioning" account (Mottron, Dawson, Soulieres, Hubert, & Burack, 2006), can be considered "cold" models because they do not include a direct role of affect processing in such deficits. Combining insights from "hot" and "cold" accounts of ASD may benefit our understanding of this complex syndrome, especially with respect to our understanding of the face processing deficit. Notably, face processing, which requires highly trained and skillful use of visual information, is also socially critical and emotionally significant. These aspects of face processing place it at the junction of both "hot" and "cold" theories. In this section we will first describe the "hot" amygdala/fusiform modulation model of ASD (Schultz, 2005). We will then briefly describe the enhanced visual functioning and the weak central coherence "cold" models of ASD (Happé & Frith, 2006; Mottron et al., 2006). Finally, we will discuss how visuocognitive abnormalities and socioaffective abnormalities may actually be linked in ASD, raising possibilities that they may contribute together to the failure of people with ASD to develop perceptual expertise with faces.

The Amygdala/Fusiform Modulation "Hot" Model of Autism

The amygdala/fusiform modulation model of ASD provides a proposal of how basic abnormalities in socioaffective processing could alter a child's experience throughout development (Schultz, 2005). Specifically, the model posits that this deficit may arise as the result of hardwired abnormalities and their cascading influence on experience-dependent development of brain systems responsible for processing socially relevant stimuli.

The development of face perception skill in typically developing infants is likely fostered by a bias to attend to facelike configurations (e.g., Cassia et al., 2004). Morton and Johnson (1991) propose that this preference for faces is modulated by a subcortical visual processing route that passes incoming information from the retina to the superior colliculus to the pulvinar nucleus of the thalamus, and then to the amygdala. Notably, the amygdala has been implicated in detecting and attributing emotional salience to stimuli (Pasley, Mayes, & Schultz, 2004; Schultz, 2005; Vuilleumier, Richardson, Armony, Driver, & Dolan, 2004). The amygdala/fusiform modulation model of the social deficits in people with ASD, combined with their face perception deficit, suggests that abnormalities in this subcortical visual processing route may be the first stage of a neurodevelopmental process that later includes deficits in FFA-mediated face perception.

The amygdala/fusiform modulation model proposes that the typical early preferences for face-like configurations provide the scaffolding to support social learning. The amygdala, along with other reward centers in the brain, is believed to play a crucial role in reinforcing such preferences, influencing social attention, and in modulating fusiform activation. A key assertion of the amygdala/fusiform modulation model is that the degree to which a face is "emotionally salient," even during the perception of nonemotional aspects such as when determining facial identity, is a core element in explaining the social deficits in ASD. This theory suggests that faces of people are less emotionally engaging to individuals with ASD, and that they do not attract and sustain their attention to the same extent that they do for typically developing individuals. In turn, the resulting deficient experience with faces leads to a failure to acquire normal face perception skill, and more importantly, negatively impacts opportunities for learning about people and their social motives. At a neural level, this is expected to occur because of the lack of the necessary modulatory inputs from the amygdala to the fusiform gyrus during face processing. This proposal is consistent with the expertise framework, which suggests that extensive experience, especially in the case of active processing of stimuli at a subordinate or individual level, is required to support the development of perceptual expertise like that which underlies normal face processing.

Evidence of the importance of interactions between the amygdala and fusiform regions can be found in both structural and functional studies of the human brain. For example, Amaral and Price (1984) documented the extensive reciprocal connections between the amygdala and the fusiform gyrus as well as other ventral visual regions in nonhuman primates. Additionally, patients with lesions to the amygdala show an absence of the normal amplification of activation in the FFA when viewing fearful, relative to neutral, faces (Vuilleumier et al., 2004). Observed inverse correlations between the degree of amygdala damage and the difference in FFA responsivity to fearful versus neutral faces provide yet further evidence that FFA activity is modulated by emotional content.

Abnormalities in the amygdala among individuals with ASD can also be found at both structural and functional levels of analysis. On a functional level, a number of studies employing fMRI have reported hypoactivation in the amygdala during a face perception task (Baron-Cohen et al., 1999; Critchley et al., 2000; Pierce, et al., 2000). At a neuronal level, there are findings of increased neuronal density (Bauman & Kemper, 1985, 1994) and reduced neuronal number (Schumann & Amaral, 2006) in the amygdala. Structural MRI studies have shown enlarged amygdalae in toddlers and young children (Schumann et al., 2004; Sparks et al., 2002), while studies in later childhood have produced inconsistent results, and possibly suggest no overall volume differences after a period of precocious enlargement. For example, some studies have reported increased volume relative to controls (Howard et al., 2000; Sparks et al., 2002), while others have reported decreased volume (Aylward et al., 1999; Pierce et al., 2001; Rojas et al., 2004). More recent studies relating amygdala volume to comorbid anxiety symptoms in ASD suggest a possible explanation for this inconsistency between findings (Juranek et al., 2006). In addition, one study capitalizing on the variability in amygdala volume in ASD reported that those with small amygdalae were slower to distinguish emotional from neutral faces, showed less eye contact, and were more socially impaired than those with larger amygdalae (Nacewicz et al., 2006). Thus, although there is some inconsistency in the literature regarding the exact nature of amygdala abnormalities in ASD there is little doubt that it is a key node in the pathophysiology of autism.

Evidence from the neuroimaging literature supports the usefulness of the fusiform/amygdala theory in accounting for not only the face recognition impairments, but also the social impairments more broadly present in ASD. Recent studies have suggested a role of the fusiform in social cognition beyond the perception of face stimuli (Schultz et al., 2003). Specifically, findings of a small, but significant, relationship between measures of social competency (e.g., the social scale in the ADOS assessment) and fusiform activation provide support for an impact of fusiform abnormalities on general social functioning (Schultz, Hunyadi, Connors, & Pasley, 2005).

Visuocognitive Abnormalities and "Cold" Models of ASD

When pursuing potential accounts of the apparent failure of people with ASD to develop perceptual expertise for facial information, an important consideration is the integrity of the visual system. Abnormalities at early stages along sensory pathways could potentially lie at the source of differences detected at later stages, even in the processing of affective information. Visual processing is considered by many as a relative strength in the cognitive profile of people with ASD (e.g., see Mottron et al., 2006). Thus, the visual system is often overlooked as a potential locus of the face perception deficit in ASD. However, research over the last decade has revealed how the processing of faces, compared to that of nonface objects, may differentially recruit the types of low-level visual information that are processed independently in visual pathways. Thus, abnormalities early in the visual system could impair face processing while leaving the processing of other objects relatively intact. In this section, evidence of visuocognitive abnormalities in ASD will be discussed along with their possible role in contributing to this selective face recognition deficit.

Visuocognitive Abnormalities in ASD: Global versus Local Processing

Abnormal face processing in ASD may be just one symptom of a more fundamental difference in the way visual information is processed in the ASD brain. For
example, people with ASD appear to demonstrate a preference or bias for feature-
level information and local processing (Wang, Mottron, Peng, Berthiaume, &
Dawson, 2007). This preference is not only present in face processing, but it is also
evident more generally in the tendency to attend to minor details or features that
often go unnoticed by their typically developing peers. Frith's (1989) theory of
"weak central coherence" speaks to this difference in cognitive style, suggesting
that a bias toward processing "local" rather than "global" information is characteristic of individuals with ASD. Indeed, some findings suggest that people with
ASD may have difficulty processing global information within a visual scene
(Frith, 1989). In contrast, people with ASD demonstrate a general advantage for
the processing of local information (Jolliffe & Baron Cohen, 1997; Mottron,
Burack, Stauder, & Robaey, 1999; Plaisted, Swettenham, & Rees, 1999; Rinehart,
Bradshaw, Moss, Brereton, & Tonge, 2000; Shah & Frith, 1983). Interestingly, this
proposed local processing bias in ASD may actually underlie the advantage
sometimes observed on tasks where the global information is misleading or
distracting (but see Brian & Bryson, 1996; Jolliffe & Baron Cohen, 1997;
Ozonoff, Rogers, & Pennington, 1991; Shah & Frith, 1983). This suggests that
individuals with ASD may be more inclined to process not only faces, but any
visual input, as fragments rather than as unified wholes.

Evidence of superior processing of fine-detailed or local information among
people with ASD has led others to propose that rather than possessing "weak
central coherence," these individuals possess "enhanced perceptual functioning." For example, Mottron and colleagues (2006) proposed that not only
do individuals with ASD possess superior abilities with respect to the processing
of local visual information, but also that this ability interferes with proficiency in
processing perceptual information at a more global level. The "enhanced perceptual functioning" model suggests that the perceptual processing of people
with ASD is not only enhanced, but by default is also locally oriented (Mottron et
al., 2006). As a result, fine-detailed visual information is extracted and processed
more easily by people with ASD and dominates their perception. Thus, the
"enhanced perceptual functioning" model, like the "weak central coherence"
theory, provides an account of the relative advantage of local over global
information processing observed in people with ASD.

Visuocognitive Abnormalities in ASD: Spatial Frequency Processing

It is possible that this general bias to process local visual information, whether it is
the consequence of "enhanced perceptual functioning" or "weak central coherence" may be especially consequential for face processing: as outlined in the section
"Behavioral Evidence for Atypical Face Processing in ASD," normal face processing is thought to rely on a more holistic, or global, processing strategy while
nonface object processing is that to rely on a more feature-based, or local, strategy
(Farah, Wilson, Drain, & Tanaka, 1998; Tanaka & Farah, 1993; Tanaka & Sengco,

1997). Furthermore, it has been suggested that global visual information and local visual information are best represented by different and separable components of a visual stimulus (Sergent, 1986; Shulman, Sullivan, Gish, & Sakoda, 1986; Shulman & Wilson, 1987). Complex visual stimuli, such as an image of a face, contain a spectrum of information varying along what has been referred to as spatial frequency; spatial frequency is akin to the grain of resolution of an image, with higher spatial frequencies revealing fine local details and lower scales better representing the overall shape and global contours (Sergent, 1986; Shulman et al., 1986; Shulman & Wilson, 1987). In the visual system there is evidence that different "channels" are responsible for processing different bands of spatial frequency information (Blakemore & Campbell, 1969a, 1969b; Campbell & Robson, 1968). It is suggested that these channels arise partly out of the different basic properties of neurons in the visual system (see DeValois & DeValois, 1988, for a review). Thus, selective abnormalities in lower level aspects of visual processing may have distinct consequences for the processing of different stimulus categories, depending on the degree to which processing of these categories relies on different spatial frequency scales.

Consistent with the possibility that face processing relies more on holistic (global) and less on feature-based (local) information, a number of studies have suggested that, among typical individuals, face processing relies more on low spatial frequency (LSF) than on high spatial frequency (HSF) information (Goffaux, Gauthier, & Rossion, 2003; Goffaux & Rossion, 2006; but see Cheung, Richler, Palmeri, & Gauthier, 2008, for evidence that these effects may be the result of a response bias). For example, holistic processing effects, such as the obligatory influence of task-irrelevant parts on face part judgments, are significantly greater for faces containing only LSF information than for those containing only HSF information (Goffaux & Rossion, 2006). In addition, the greater amplitude of the N170 potential in response to faces as compared to nonface objects appears to be driven by LSF face information (Goffaux et al., 2003). Furthermore, the electrophysiological face inversion effect, that is, the 10-ms delay in the N170 response to inverted, relative to upright, faces, is abolished by removing LSF information within faces (Goffaux et al., 2003). The attenuation of these holistic processing markers in the absence of LSF information suggests that holistic processing, which has been credited for our superior skill processing upright faces, may utilize such information.[1]

---

[1] While a number of studies highlight the role of LSF information in holistic face processing, it is important to note that the processing of HSF facial information also recruits face-selective areas to a similar degree (Eger, Schyns, & Kleinschmidt, 2004; Gauthier, Curby, Skudlarski, & Epstein, 2005; Vuilleumier, Armony, Driver, & Dolan, 2003; Winston, Vuilleumier, & Dolan, 2003). Vuilleumier et al. (2003) even reported greater activation in the FFA for faces containing only HSF, relative to those containing only LSF, information. In addition, inconsistent with a preferential role of LSF information in holistic processing, Willenbockel et al. (in press) reported evidence that the same spatial frequency information is used for both upright and inverted face recognition. Cheung et al. (2008) also found equivalent holistic processing for HSF and LSF faces once response biases were taken into account. Therefore, there is evidence that HSF information also plays a role in face processing.

Although evidence suggests that both HSF and LSF information are involved in face processing within typically developing controls, a selective bias to process HSF scales, which best carry local information, may contribute to the face recognition deficit in ASD. Deruelle and colleagues (2004) reported that children with ASD perform better at matching a face containing only HSF information, compared to only LSF information, to a regular image containing the full spectrum of spatial frequency information (see also Deruelle, Rondan, Salle-Collemiche, Bastard-Rosset, & Da Fonséca, 2008). In addition, our own findings, in the form of a detailed case study, are consistent with the existence of a bias toward HSF information when processing faces, both at a behavioral and neurophysiological level (Curby, Schyns, Gosselin, & Gauthier, 2003). Thus, an abnormality in the visual system could potentially underlie the characteristic local processing bias in ASD and also contribute to the face processing deficit in this group.

Integrating the "Hot" and "Cold" Accounts to Understand Face Processing in ASD

There are a number of findings suggesting that the more general visual-cognitive differences observed among people with ASD may be related to the proposed abnormalities in socioaffective processing. For example, recent studies exploring FFA and amygdala activation in response to viewing fearful faces provides a link between processing the emotional content of faces and spatial frequency scale (Vuilleumier, Armony, Driver, & Dolan, 2003; Winston et al., 2003). These studies found that the enhanced response of the amygdala and fusiform cortex to faces with fearful, relative to neutral, expressions is driven by LSF information. Notably, these findings provide an interesting possible interpretation of available data regarding the face processing deficit in ASD: abnormalities at the level of spatial frequency scale processing may lead to difficulties in assessing and detecting emotion in faces. It is possible that this could result in reduced input from the amygdala to the fusiform in response to a facial stimulus and thus potentially account for the reduced motivation to attend to faces in ASD.

Specifically, the general bias to process local, rather than global, information may be related to abnormalities in interactions between the fusiform and amygdala brain regions. The amygdala/fusiform modulation model suggests that the amygdala in the normal brain serves an alerting function, drawing attention to socially rewarding stimuli. Within this context, the typical, preferential response of the amygdala to LSF emotional face information may have significant implications for ASD. In addition, the importance of LSF information for holistic face processing suggests that reduced sensitivity to LSF information may not only have consequences for the development of face recognition skill, possibly through a dysfunction in the amygdala's role in guiding attention to faces, but it may also make the LSF information in faces less available to people with ASD. Further studies should investigate a possible relationship between abnormalities at the perceptual level and the social deficit that is central to ASD.

It is important to note that recent evidence suggests that the FFA may not be characterized as simply an LSF-tuned processor, and that in fact the role of SF information in the processing of faces and in the FFA may be more complex than first thought. It has been proposed that the fusiform gyrus, which is the site of the FFA, may be the locus of integration for the different SF channels that detect and transmit the information embedded in different SF scales through the visual system (Rotshtein, Vuilleumier, Winston, Driver, & Dolan, 2007). Thus, an abnormality in the FFA or in the input to this region may result in difficulties integrating visual information from different SF scales in faces.

In sum, in this section we have speculated about possible points of intersection of visuocognitive and socioaffective accounts of ASD. We outlined how the reported abnormalities in socioaffective and visuocognitive processing in ASD may be related, and that together they may alter the experience of people with ASD in such a way that they impair the development of perceptual expertise with faces. Further work is needed to fully evaluate the potential of this account to inform our understanding of the face perception deficit in ASD as well as more general deficits in social functioning.

WHAT CAN WE LEARN ABOUT FACE PROCESSING AND PERCEPTUAL EXPERTISE FROM AUTISM?

In this chapter we have suggested that both affective ("hot") and more perceptual or cognitive ("cold") factors may play a role in altering experience in ASD, potentially disrupting the development of perceptual expertise with faces. An important question that arises from this proposal pertains to the role of affect in the development of perceptual expertise among the typical population. Experts such as car enthusiasts (who have perceptual expertise identifying cars) typically have great affection for their objects of expertise, and this undoubtedly contributes to their initial motivation to study this category. Intriguingly, some experts demonstrate degrees of interest that rival the often obsessive restricted interests among individuals with ASD. Cases such as DD, the 10-year-old boy with autism who demonstrated a restricted interests in "Digimon" cartoon characters and showed increased fusiform cortex activation to these characters, but not to faces, further suggest that an affective attachment may be necessary for, or facilitate, the development of perceptual expertise, including the related transition to more holistic visual processing strategies. Indeed, some propose that positive emotion may facilitate a more holistic cognitive style more generally (Fredrickson & Branigan, 2005; Johnson & Fredrickson, 2005). An interesting question is whether such affective or reward signals provide critical input to the FFA necessary for the development of perceptual expertise with nonface categories. Future studies should consider these possibilities.

CONCLUSIONS

Visual processing, which typically appears unimpaired among people with ASD, is often overlooked, with attention tending to focus more on the numerous deficiencies, especially in the social and affective domains, present in the profile of people with ASD. However, the abnormal pattern of performance within the visual domain among people with ASD may provide important insights that could contribute not only to our understanding of the face processing deficit in ASD, but also of the social impairments experienced by this group more generally. Research on ASD should take into account the strong possibility that autistic phenotypes result from interactions between biology and experience. This is not to say that changes in experience can fully and necessarily mitigate a biological predisposition toward ASD. However, behaviors characteristic of ASD should not be assumed merely to reflect biological differences or even differences within a single domain such as social processing. In the case of face processing, we suggest that deficits characteristic of ASD are likely the result of complex interplays between abnormalities in both sensory and emotional processing, and how these alter everyday experience and behaviors during development. To the degree that this is true, efforts to change behavior and experience early in life may have potential for minimizing the debilitating symptoms of ASD.

REFERENCES

Allison, T., Puce, A., & McCarthy, G. (2000). Social perception from visual cues: Role of the STS region. *Trends in Cognitive Sciences, 4*(7), 267–278.

Amaral, D. G., & Price J. L. (1984). Amygdalo-cortical projections in the monkey (Macaca fascicularis). *Journal of Comparative Neurology, 230*(4), 465–496.

American Psychiatric Association. (2000). *Diagnostic and statistical manual of mental disorders: DSM-IV-TR*. Washington, DC.

Anderson, G. (2008). The potential role for emergence in autism. *Autism Research, 1,* 18–30.

Aylward, E. H., Minshew, N. J., Goldstein, G., Honeycutt, N. A., Augustine, A. M., Yates, K. O., Barta, P. E., & Pearlson, G. D. (1999). MRI volumes of amygdala and hippocampus in non-mentally retarded autistic adolescents and adults. *Neurology, 53*(9), 2145–2150.

Bachevalier, J., & Loveland, K. A. (2006). The orbitofrontal-amygdala circuit and self-regulation of social-emotional behavior in autism. *Neuroscience and Biobehavioral Review, 30*(1), 97–117.

Bailey, A. J., Braeutigam, S., Jousmaki, V., & Swithenby, S. J. (2005). Abnormal activation of face processing systems at early and intermediate latency in individuals with autism spectrum disorder: a magnetoencephalographic study. *European Journal of Neuroscience, 21*(9), 2575–2585.

Bailey, A., Le Couteur, A., Gottesman, I., Bolton, P., Simonoff, E., Yuzda, E., & Rutter, M. (1995). Autism as a strongly genetic disorder: Evidence from a British twin study. *Psychological Medicine, 25*(1), 63–77.

Baranek, G. T. (1999). Autism during infancy: A retrospective video analysis of sensory-motor and social behaviors at 9–12 months of age. *Journal of Autism and Developmental Disorders, 29*(3), 213–224.

Baron-Cohen, S., & Belmonte, M. K. (2005). Autism: A window onto the development of the social and the analytic brain. *Annual Review of Neuroscience, 28*, 109–126.

Baron-Cohen, S., Campbell, R., Karmiloff-Smith, A., Grant, J., & Walker, J. (1999). Are children with autism blind to the mentalistic significance of the eyes? *British Journal of Psychology, 13*, 379–398.

Bauman, M., & Kemper, T. L. (1985) Histoanatomic observations of the brain in early infantile autism. *Neurology, 35*, 866–874.

Bauman, M., & Kemper T. L. (1994) Neuroanatomic observations of the brain in autism. In: *The neurobiology of autism* M. Bauman & T. L. Kemper (Eds.), pp. 119–145. Baltimore, MD: Johns Hopkins UP.

Behrmann, M., Avidan, G., Leonard, G. L., Kimchi, R., Luna, B., Humphreys, K., & Minshew, N. (2006). Configural processing in autism and its relationship to face processing. *Neuropsychologia, 44*(1), 110–129.

Behrmann, M., Thomas, C., & Humphreys, K. (2006). Seeing it differently: Visual processing in autism. *Trends in Cognitive Sciences, 10*(6), 258–264.

Bentin, S., & Deouell, L. Y. (2000). Structural encoding and identification in face processing: ERP evidence for separate mechanisms. *Cognitive Psychology, 17*(1–3), 35–55.

Bentin, S., Allison, T., Puce, A., Perez, E., & McCarthy, G. (1996). Electrophysiological studies of face perception in humans. *Journal of Cognitive Neuroscience, 8*(6), 551–565.

Blair, R. J., Frith, U., Smith, N., Abell, F., & Cipolotti, L. (2002). Fractionation of visual memory: Agency detection and its impairment in autism. *Neuropsychologia, 40*(1), 108–118.

Blakemore, C., & Campbell, F. W. (1969a). Adaptation to spatial stimuli. *Journal of Physiology, 200*(1), 11P–13P.

Blakemore, C., & Campbell, F. W. (1969b). On the existence of neurones in the human visual system selectively sensitive to the orientation and size of retinal images. *Journal of Physiology, 203*(1), 237–260.

Boucher, J. & Lewis, V. (1992). Unfamiliar face recognition in relatively able autistic children. *Journal of Child Psychology and Psychiatry, 33*(5), 843–859.

Brian, J. A., & Bryson, S. E. (1996). Disembedding performance and recognition memory in autism/PDD. *Journal of Child Psychology and Psychiatry and Allied Disciplines, 37*(7), 865–872.

Bushnell, I. W., Sai, F., & Mullin, J. T. (1989). Neonatal recognition of the mother's face. *British Journal of Developmental Psychology, 7*(1), 3–15.

Campbell, F. W., & Robson, J. R. (1968). Application of Fourier analysis to the visibility of gratings. *Journal of Physiology 197*, 551–566.

Carey, S. (1996). Perceptual categorization and expertise. In R. Gelman & T. Kit-Fong Au (Eds.), *Perceptual and cognitive development* (pp. 49–69). San Diego, CA: Academic Press.

Carey, S., & Diamond, R. (1994). Are faces perceived as configurations more by adults than by children? *Visual Cognition, 1*, 253–274.

Cassia, V. M., Turati, C., & Simion, F. (2004). Can a nonspecific bias toward top-heavy patterns explain newborns' face preference? *Psychological Science, 15*(6), 379–383.

Carver, L. J., Dawson, G., Panagiotides, H., Meltzoff, A. N., McPartland, J., Gray, J., & Munson, J. (2003). Age-related differences in neural correlates of face recognition during the toddler and preschool years. *Developmental Psychobiology, 42*(2), 148–159.

Castelli, F., Frith, C. D., Happé, F., & Frith, U. (2002). Autism, Asperger syndrome and brain mechanisms for the attribution of mental states to animated shapes. *Brain, 125*, 1839–1849.

Celani, G., Battacchi, M. W., & Arcidiacono, L. (1999). The understanding of the emotional meaning of facial expressions in people with autism. *Journal of Autism and Developmental Disorders, 29*(1), 57–66.

Cheung, O. S., Richler, J. J., Palmeri, T. J., & Gauthier, I. (2008). Revisiting the role of spatial frequencies in the holistic processing of faces. *Journal of Experimental Psychology: Human Perception and Performance, 34*(6), 1327–1336.

Critchley, H. D., Daly, E. M., Bullmore, E. T., Williams, S. C., Van Amelsvoort, T., Robertson, D. M., et al. (2000). The functional neuroanatomy of social behaviour: Changes in cerebral blood flow when people with autistic disorder process facial expressions. *Brain, 123*(11), 2203–2212.

Curby, K. M., Schyns, P., Gosselin. F., & Gauthier, I. (2003, May). *Spatial frequency use in Asperger's syndrome*. Annual meeting of the Vision Science Society, Sarasota, FL.

Dalton, K. M., Nacewicz, B. M., Johnstone, J., Schaefer, H. S., Gernsbacher, B. A., Goldsmith, H. H., Alexander, A. L., & Davidson, R. J. (2005). Gaze fixation and the neural circuitry of face processing in autism. *Nature Neuroscience, 8*, 519–526.

Dawson, G., Carver, L., Meltzoff, A. N., Panagiotides, H., McPartland, J., & Webb, S. J. (2002). Neural correlates of face and object recognition in young children with autism spectrum disorder, developmental delay, and typical development. *Child Development, 73*(3), 700–717.

Dawson, G., Webb, S. J., Carver, L., Panagiotides, H., & McPartland, J. (2004). Young children with autism show atypical brain responses to fearful versus neutral facial expressions of emotion. *Developmental Science, 7*(3), 340–359.

Dawson, G., Webb, S. J., & McPartland, J. (2005). Understanding the nature of face processing impairment in autism: Insights from behavioral and electrophysiological studies. *Developmental Neuropsychology, 27*(3), 403–424.

de Haan, M., Johnson, M. H., Maurer, D., & Perrett, D. I. (2001). Recognition of individual faces and average face prototypes by 1- and 3-month-old infants. *Cognitive Development, 16*(2), 659–678.

de Haan, M., & Nelson, C. A. (1999). Brain activity differentiates face and object processing by 6-month-old infants. *Developmental Psychology, 34*, 1114–1121.

Deruelle, C., Rondan, C., Gepner, B., & Tardif, C. (2004). Spatial frequency and face processing in children with autism and Asperger syndrome. *Journal of Autism and Developmental Disorders, 34*(2), 199–210.

Deruelle, C., Rondan, C., Salle-Collemiche, X., Bastard-Rosset, D., & Da Fonséca, D. (2008). Attention to low- and high-spatial frequencies in categorizing facial identities, emotions and genders in children with autism. *Brain and Cognition, 66*, 115–123.

De Valois, R. L., & De Valois, K. K. (1988). *Spatial vision*. New York: Oxford University Press.

Eckhorn, R., Reitboeck, H. J., Arndt, M., & Dicke, P. (1990). Feature linking via synchronization among distributed assemblies: Simulations of results from cat visual cortex. *Neural Computation, 2*(3), 293–307.

Eger, E., Schyns, P. G., & Kleinschmidt, A. (2004). Scale invariant adaptation in fusiform face-responsive regions. *NeuroImage, 22*(1), 232–242.

Eimer, M. (1998). Does the face-specific N170 component reflect the activity of a specialized eye processor? *NeuroReport, 9*(13), 2945–2948.

Eimer, M. (2000a). Event-related brain potentials distinguish processing stages involved in face perception and recognition. *Clinical Neurophysiology, 111*(4), 694–705.

Eimer, M. (2000b). Effects of face inversion on the structural encoding and recognition of faces: Evidence from event-related brain potentials. *Cognitive Brain Research, 10*(1–2), 145–158.

Eimer, M. (2000c). Attentional modulation of event-related brain potentials sensitive to faces. *Cognitive Neuropsychology, 17*(1–3), 103–116.

Eimer, M., & Holmes, A. (2002). An ERP study on the time course of emotional face processing. *NeuroReport, 13*(4), 427–431.

Farah, M. J., Wilson, K. D., Drain, M., & Tanaka, J. N. (1998). What is "special" about face perception? *Psychological Review, 105*(3), 482–498.

Fredrickson, B. L., & Branigan, C. (2005). Positive emotions broaden the scope of attention and thought-action repertoires. *Cognition & Emotion, 19*(3), 313–332.

Freire, A., Lee, K., & Symons, L. A. (2000). The face-inversion effect as a deficit in the encoding of configural information: Direct evidence. *Perception, 29*, 159–170.

Frith, U. (1989). *Autism: Explaining the enigma.* Oxford, UK: Basil Blackwell.

Gauthier, I., & Tarr, M. J. (2002). Unraveling mechanisms for expert object recognition: Bridging brain activity and behavior. *Journal of Experimental Psychology: Human Perception and Performance, 28*(2), 431–446.

Gauthier, I., Curby, K. M., Skudlarski, P., & Epstein, R. A. (2005). Individual differences in FFA activity suggest independent processing at different spatial scales. *Cognitive, Affective and Behavioral Neuroscience, 5*(2), 222–234.

Gauthier, I., Curran, T., Curby, K. M., & Collins, D. (2003). Perceptual interference supports a non-modular account of face processing. *Nature Neuroscience, 6*(4), 428–432.

Gauthier, I., Skudlarski, P., Gore, J. C., & Anderson, A. W. (2000). Expertise for cars and birds recruits brain areas involved in face recognition. *Nature Neuroscience, 3*(2), 191–197.

Gauthier, I., Tarr, M. J., Anderson, A. W., Skudlarski, P., & Gore, J. C. (1999). Activation of the middle fusiform 'face area' increases with expertise in recognizing novel objects. *Nature Neuroscience, 2*(6), 568–573.

George, N., Evans, J., Fiori, N., Davidoff, J., & Renault, B. (1996). Brain events related to normal and moderately scrambled faces. *Cognitive Brain Research, 4*, 65–76.

Geschwind, D. H., & Levitt, P. (2007). Autism spectrum disorders: Developmental disconnection syndromes. *Current Opinions in Neurobiology, 17*(1), 103–111.

Goffaux, V., Gauthier, I., & Rossion, B. (2003). Spatial scale contribution to early visual differences between face and object processing. *Cognitive Brain Research, 16*(3), 416–424.

Goffaux, V., & Rossion, B. (2006). Faces are "spatial"—holistic face perception is supported by low spatial frequencies. *Journal of Experimental Psychology: Human Perception and Performance, 32*(4), 1023–1039.

Goren, C. C., Sarty, M., & Wu, P. Y. K. (1975). Visual following and pattern discrimination of face-like stimuli by newborn infants. *Pediatrics, 56*(4), 544–549.

Gray, C. M., König, P., Engel, A. K., & and Singer, W. (1989). Oscillatory responses in cat visual cortex exhibit inter-columnar synchronization which reflects global stimulus properties. *Nature, 338*, 334–336.

Grelotti, D. J., Klin, A. J., Gauthier, I., Skudlarski, P., Cohen, D. J., Gore, J. C., Volkmar, F. R., & Schultz, R. T. (2005). fMRI activation of the fusiform gyrus and amygdala to cartoon characters but not to faces in a boy with autism. *Neuropsychologia, 43*(3), 373–385.

Grice, S. J., Spratling, M. W., Karmiloff-Smith, A., Halit, H., Csibra, G., de Haan, M., & Johnson, M. H. (2001). Disordered visual processing and oscillatory brain activity in autism and Williams syndrome. *NeuroReport, 12*(12), 2697–2700.

Happé, F., & Frith, U. (2006). The weak coherence account: Detail-focused cognitive style in autism spectrum disorders. *Journal of Autism and Developmental Disorders, 36*(1), 5–25.

Hobson, R. P., Ouston, J., & Lee, A. (1988). What's in a face? The case of autism. *British Journal of Psychology, 79,* 441–453.

Howard, M. A., Cowell, P. E., Boucher, J., Broks, P., Mayes, A., Farrant, A., & Roberts, N. (2000). Convergent neuroanatomical and behavioural evidence of an amygdala hypothesis of autism. *NeuroReport, 11*(13), 2931–2935.

Jemel, B., Mottron, L., & Dawson, M. (2006). Impaired face processing in autism: Fact or artifact? *Journal of Autism and Developmental Disorders, 36*(1), 91–106.

Johnson, K. J., & Fredrickson, B. L. (2005). "We All Look the Same to Me": Positive emotions eliminate the own-race bias in face recognition. *Psychological Science, 16*(11), 875–881.

Johnson, M. H., Dziurawiec, S., Ellis, H., & Morton, J. (1991). Newborns' preferential tracking of face-like stimuli and its subsequent decline. *Cognition, 40*(1–2), 1–19.

Jolliffe, T., & Baron Cohen, S. (1997). Are people with autism and Asperger syndrome faster than normal on the Embedded Figures Test? *Journal of Child Psychology and Psychiatry and Allied Disciplines, 38*(5), 527–534.

Joseph, R. M., & Tanaka, J. (2003). Holistic and part-based face recognition in children with autism. *Journal of Child Psychology and Psychiatry and Allied Disciplines, 44*(4), 529–542.

Juranek, J., Filipek, P. A., Berenji, G. R., Modahl, C., Osann, K., & Spence, M. A. (2006). Association between amygdala volume and anxiety level: Magnetic resonance imaging (MRI) study in autistic children. *Journal of Child Neurology, 21*(12), 1051–1058.

Kanwisher, N., McDermott, J., & Chun, M. M. (1997). The fusiform face area: A module in human extrastriate cortex specialized for face perception. *Journal of Neuroscience, 17,* 4302–4311.

Keil, A., Müller, M. M., Ray, W. J., Gruber, T., & Elbert, T. (1999). Human gamma band activity and perception of a gestalt. *The Journal of Neuroscience, 19*(16), 7152–7161.

Klin, A., Jones, W., Schultz, R., Volkmar, F., & Cohen, D. (2002). Visual fixation patterns during viewing of naturalistic social situations as predictors of social competence in individuals with autism. *Archives of General Psychiatry, 59*(9), 809–816.

Klin, A., Sparrow, S. S., de Bildt, A., Cicchetti, D. V., Cohen, D. J., & Volkmar, F. R. (1999). A normed study of face recognition in autism and related disorders. *Journal of Autism and Developmental Disorders, 29*(6), 499–508.

Langdell, T. (1978). Recognition of faces: An approach to the study of autism. *Journal of Child Psychology and Psychiatry and Allied Disciplines, 19*(3), 255–268.

Maestro, S., Muratori, F., Cavallaro, M. C., Pei, F., Stern, D., Golse, B., & Palacio-Espasa, F. (2002). Attentional skills during the first 6 months of age in autism spectrum disorder. *Journal of the American Academy of Child and Adolescent Psychiatry, 41*(10), 1239–1245.

McPartland, J., Dawson, G., Webb, S. J., Panagiotides, H., & Carver, L. J. (2004). Event-related brain potentials reveal anomalies in temporal processing of faces in autism spectrum disorder. *Journal of Child Psychology and Psychiatry, 45*(7), 1235–1245.

Milner, P. M. (1974). A model for visual shape recognition. *Psychological Review, 81*(6), 521–535.

Morton, J. & Johnson, M. H. (1991). CONSPEC and CONLERN: A two-process theory of infant face recognition. *Psychological Review, 98*(2), 164–181.

Mottron, L., Burack, J. A., Stauder, J. E. A., & Robaey, P. (1999). Perceptual processing among high-functioning persons with autism. *Journal of Child Psychology and Psychiatry and Allied Disciplines, 40*(2), 203–211.

Mottron, L., Dawson, M., Soulieres, I., Hubert, B., & Burack, J. (2006). Enhanced perceptual functioning in autism: An update, and eight principles of autistic perception. *Journal of Autism and Developmental Disorders, 36*(1), 27–43.

Mundy, P., Sigman, M., Ungerer, J., & Sherman, T. (1986). Defining the social deficits of autism: The contribution of non-verbal communication measures. *Journal of Child Psychology and Psychiatry, 27*(5), 657–669.

Nacewicz, B. M., Dalton, K. M., Johnstone, T., Long, M. T., McAuliff, E. M., Oakes, T. R., Alexander, A. L., & Davidson, R. J. (2006). Amygdala volume and nonverbal social impairment in adolescent and adult males with autism. *Archives of General Psychiatry, 63*(12), 1417–1428.

Nelson, C. A., & de Haan, M. (1996). Neural correlates of infants' visual responsiveness to facial expression of emotion. *Developmental Psychobiology, 29*(7), 577–595.

Njiokiktjien, C., Verschoor, A., de Sonneville, L., Huyser, C., Op het Veld, V., & Toorenaar, N. (2001). Disordered recognition of facial identity and emotions in three Asperger type autists. *European Child and Adolescent Psychiatry, 10*(1), 79–90.

O'Roak, B., & State, M. (2008). Autism genetics: Strategies, challenges, and opportunities. *Autism Research, 1*, 4–17.

Osterling, J., & Dawson, G. (1994). Early recognition of children with autism: A study of first birthday home videotapes. *Journal of Autism and Developmental Disorders, 24*(3), 247–257.

Osterling, J. A., Dawson, G., & Munson, J. A. (2002). Early recognition of 1-year-old infants with autism spectrum disorder versus mental retardation. *Developmental Psychopathology, 14*(2), 239–251.

Ozonoff, S., Rogers, S. J., & Pennington, B. F. (1991). Asperger's syndrome: Evidence of an empirical distinction from high-functioning autism. *Journal of Child Psychology and Psychiatry and Allied Disciplines, 32*(7), 1107–1122.

Pasley, B. N., Mayes, L. C. & Schultz, R. T. (2004). Subcortical discrimination of unperceived objects during binocular rivalry. *Neuron, 42*, 163–172.

Pelphrey, K. A., Morris, J. P., & McCarthy, G. (2005). Neural basis of eye gaze processing deficits in autism. *Brain, 128*(5), 1038–1048.

Pelphrey, K. A., Sasson, N. J., Reznick, J. S., Paul, G., Goldman, B. D., & Piven, J. (2002). Visual scanning of faces in autism. *Journal of Autism and Developmental Disorders, 32*(4), 249–261.

Pierce, K., Haist, F., Sedaghat, F., & Courchesne, E. (2004). The brain response to personally familiar faces in autism: Findings of fusiform activity and beyond. *Brain, 127*(Pt. 12), 2703–2716.

Pierce, K., Müller, R. A., Ambrose, J., Allen, G., & Courshesne, E. (2001). Face processing occurs outside the fusiform "face area" in autism: Evidence from functional MRI. *Brain, 124*, 2059–2073.

Plaisted, K. C., Swettenham, J., & Rees, L. (1999). Children with autism show local precedence in a divided attention task and global precedence in a selective attention task. *Journal of Child Psychology and Psychiatry and Allied Disciplines, 40*(5), 733–742.

Rebai, M., Poiroux, S., Bernard, C., & Lalonde, R. (2001). Event-related potentials for category-specific information during passive viewing of faces and objects. *International Journal of Neuroscience, 106*(3–4), 209–226.

Rinehart, N. J., Bradshaw, J. L., Moss, S. A., Brereton, A. V., & Tonge, B. J. (2000). Atypical interference of local detail on global processing in high-functioning autism and Asperger's disorder. *Journal of Child Psychology and Psychiatry and Allied Disciplines, 41*(6), 769–778.

Ristic, J., Mottron, L., Friesen, C. K., Iarocci, G., Burack, J. A., & Kingstone, A. (2005). Eyes are special but not for everyone: The case of autism. *Cognitive Brain Research, 24*(3), 715–718.

Rodriguez, E., George, N., Lachaux, J. P., Martinerie, J., Renault, B., & Varela, F. J. (1999). Perception's shadow: Long-distance synchronization of human brain activity. *Nature, 397,* 430–433.

Rojas, D. C., Smith, J. A., Benkers, T. L., Camou, S. L., Reite, M. L., & Rogers, S. J. (2004). Hippocampus and amygdala volumes in parents of children with autistic disorder. *American Journal of Psychiatry, 161*(11), 2038–2044.

Rossion, B., Gauthier, I., Tarr, M. J., Despland, P. A., Linotte, S., Bruyer, R., & Crommelinck, M. (2000). The N170 occipito-temporal component is enhanced and delayed to inverted faces but not to inverted objects: An electrophyiological account of face-specific processes in the human brain. *NeuroReport, 11,* 1–6.

Rotshtein, P., Vuilleumier, P., Winston, J., Driver, J., & Dolan, R. (2007). Distinct and convergent visual processing of high and low spatial frequency information in faces. *Cerebral Cortex, 17*(11), 2713–2724.

Schultz, R. T. (2005). Developmental deficits in social perception in autism: The role of the amygdala and fusiform face area. *International Journal of Developmental Neuroscience, 23*(2–3), 125–141.

Schultz, R. T., Chawarska, K., & Volkmar, F. R. (2006). The social brain in autism: Perspectives from neuropsychology and neuroimaging. In S.O. Moldin & J. L. R. Rubenstein (Eds.), *Understanding autism: From basic neuroscience to treatment.* Boca Raton, FL: CRC Press, 323–348.

Schultz, R. T., Gauthier, I., Klin A., Fulbright, R., Anderson, A., Volkmar, F., Skudlarski, P., Lacadie, C., Cohen, D. J., & Gore, J. C. (2000). Abnormal ventral temporal cortical activity during face discrimination among individuals with autism and Asperger syndrome. *Archives of General Psychiatry, 57*(3), 331–340.

Schultz, R. T., Grelotti, D. J., Klin, A., Kleinman, J., Van der Gaag, C., Marois, R., & Skudlarski, P. (2003). The role of the fusiform face area in social cognition: Implications for the pathobiology of autism. *Philosophical Transactions of the Royal Society London B, Biological Sciences, 358*(1430), 415–427.

Schultz, R. T., Hunyadi, E., Connors, C., & Pasley, B. (2005, June). *fMRI study of facial expression perception in autism: The amygdala, fusiform face area and their functional connectivity.* Paper presented at the annual meeting of the Organization for Human Brain Mapping, Toronto, Canada.

Schumann, C. & Amaral, D. G. (2006). Stereological analysis of amygdala neuron number in autism. *The Journal of Neuroscience, 26*(29), 7674–7679.

Schumann, C. M., Hamstra, J., Goodlin-Jones, B. L., Lotspeich, L. J., Kwon, H., Buonocore, M. H., Lammers, C. R., Reiss, A. L., & Amaral, D. G. (2004). The amygdala is enlarged in children but not adolescents with autism; the hippocampus is enlarged at all ages. *Journal of Neuroscience, 24,* 6392–6401.

Sergent, J. (1986). Microgenesis of face perception. In H. D. Ellis, M. A. Reeves, F. Newcombe, and A. W. Young (Eds.), *Aspects of Face Processing.* Dordrecht, The Netherlands: Martinus Nijhoff.

Shah, A., & Frith, U. (1983). An islet of ability in autistic children: A research note. *Journal of Child Psychology and Psychiatry and Allied Disciplines, 24*(4), 613–620.

Shah A., & Frith, U. (1993). Why do autistic individuals show superior performance on the block design task? *Journal of Child Psychology and Psychiatry, 34*(8), 1351–1364.

Shulman, G. L., Sullivan, M. A., Gish, K., & Sakoda, W. J. (1986). The role of spatial-frequency channels in the perception of local and global structure. *Perception, 15*(3), 259–273.

Shulman, G. L., & Wilson, J. (1987). Spatial frequency and selective attention to local and global information. *Perception, 16*(1), 89–101.

Simion, F., Valenza, E., Umilta, C., & Dalla Barba, B. (1998). Preferential orienting to faces in newborns: A temporal-nasal asymmetry. *Journal of Experimental Psychology: Human Perception and Performance, 24*(5), 1399–1405.

Sparks, B. F., Friedman, S. D., Shaw, D. W., Aylward, E. H., Echelard, D., Artru, A. A., Maravilla, K. R., Giedd, J. N., Munson, J., Dawson, G., & Dager, S. R. (2002). Brain structural abnormalities in young children with autism spectrum disorder. *Neurology, 59*(2), 184–192.

Tanaka, J. W., & Farah, M. J. (1993). Parts and wholes in face recognition. *Quarterly Journal of Experimental Psychology, 46A*, 225–245.

Tanaka, J. W., & Sengco, J. A. (1997). Features and their configuration in face recognition. *Memory & Cognition, 25*(5), 583–592.

Tantam, D., Monaghan, L., Nicholson, H., & Stirling, J. (1989). Autistic children's ability to interpret faces: A research note. *Journal of Child Psychology and Psychiatry, 30*, 623–630.

Tarr, M. J., & Gauthier, I. (2000). FFA: A flexible fusiform area for subordinate-level visual processing automatized by expertise. *Nature Neuroscience, 3*(8), 764–769.

Teunisse, J. P., & de Gelder, B. (2003). Face processing in adolescents with autistic disorder: The inversion and composite effects. *Brain and Cognition, 52*(3), 285–294.

Thioux, M., Stark, D. E., Klaiman, C., & Schultz, R. T. (2006). The day of the week when you were born in 700 ms: Calendar computation in an autistic savant. *Journal of Experimental Psycholology: Human Perception and Performance, 32*(5), 1155–1168.

Treffert, A. D. (1989). *Extraordinary people.* New York: Harper & Row.

Trepagnier, C., Sebrechts, M. M., & Peterson, R. (2002). Atypical face gaze in autism. *CyberPsychology & Behavior, 5*(3), 213–217.

van der Geest, J. N., Kemner, C., Verbaten, M. N., & van Engeland, H. (2002). Gaze behavior of children with pervasive developmental disorder toward human faces: A fixation time study. *Journal of Child Psychology and Psychiatry, 43*(5), 669–678.

Volkmar, F., Lord, C., Bailey, A., Schultz, R. T., & Klin, A. (2004). Autism and pervasive developmental disorders. *Journal of Child Psychology and Psychiatry, 45*(1), 135–170.

Vuilleumier, P., Armony, J. L., Driver, J., & Dolan, R. J. (2003). Distinct spatial frequency sensitivities for processing faces and emotional expressions. *Nature Neuroscience, 6*(6), 624–631.

Vuilleumier, P., Richardson, M. P., Armony, J. L., Driver, J., & Dolan, R. J. (2004). Distant influences of amygdala lesion on visual cortical activation during emotional face processing. *Nature Neuroscience, 7*(11), 1271–1278.

Wang, L., Mottron, L., Peng, D., Berthiaume, C. & Dawson, M. (2007). Local bias and local-to-global interference without global deficit: A robust finding in autism under various conditions of attention, exposure time, and visual angle. *Cognitive Neuropsychology, 24*(5), 550–574.

Weeks, S. J., & Hobson, R. P. (1987). The salience of facial expression for autistic children. *Journal of Child Psychology and Psychiatry, 28*(1), 137–151.

Willenbockel, V., Fiset, D., Chauvin, A., Blais, C., Argin, M.,Tanaka, J. W., Bub, D. N., & Gosselin, F. (in press). Does face inversion change spatial frequency tuning?

Winston, J. S., Vuilleumier, P., & Dolan, R. J. (2003). Effects of low-spatial frequency components of fearful faces on fusiform cortex activity. *Current Biology, 13*(20), 1824–1829.

Wing, L., & Gould, J. (1979). Severe impairments of social interaction and associated abnormalities in children: Epidemiology and classification. *Journal of Autism and Developmental Disorders, 9*(1), 11–29.

Wolf, J. M., Tanaka, J. W., Klaiman, C., Cockburn, J., Herlihy, L., Brown, C, South, M., McPartland, J., Kaiser, M. D., Phillips, R., & Schultz, R. T. (in press). Specific impairment of face processing abilities in children with autism spectrum disorder using the Let's Face It! skills battery. *Autism Research.*

Wolf, J. M., Tanaka, J. W., Klaiman, C., Koenig, K., Cockburn, J., Herlihy, L., Brown, C., Stahl, S. S., South, M., McPartland, J., & Schultz, R. T. (2008). *Let's Face It! A computer-based intervention for strengthening face processing skills in individuals with autism spectrum disorders.* International Meeting for Autism Research, London, England.

Yin, R. K. (1969). Looking at upside-down faces. *Journal of Experimental Psychology, 81*(1), 141–145.

Young, A. W., Hellawell, D., & Hay, D. (1987). Configural information in face perception. *Perception, 10*, 747–759.

6

Congenital and Acquired Prosopagnosia: Flip Sides of the Same Coin?

Marlene Behrmann, Galia Avidan, Cibu Thomas, and Kate Humphreys

"... I have always been a rather extreme introvert, uncomfortable in groups of people and in social activities. I sort of tend to want to be a hermit. I've even wondered if I tend to be agoraphobic. However, I find it relaxing to go window shopping in a mall. A crowd of a hundred strangers is more relaxing than a dozen neighbors whom I am supposed to know ..." These comments were made by a woman, Helen. In response to this, Helen's niece, who may also have difficulties in recognizing faces, added "except for the danger that a neighbor may be in that crowd."

"After talking with all my family members, kids and friends today, I found that a great way to describe my facial recognition problem was like this: I have a Toyota Scion, color thunder gray. If I were in a parking lot and were looking for my car and there were 20 thunder gray Toyota Scions, I wouldn't know which one was mine unless I looked inside and saw my stuff, or I saw my "blessed are the peacemakers" sticker on the back or the dirt on it because I hadn't washed it, etc. That is how I look at faces where the rest of you look at faces and just know which one is which. I have to see the difference in the face or else it is just like all the others. If I didn't find anything distinctive on the face or the Scion, I would have to listen to the person talk or try my key on all of them to find mine. Today we were driving through a parking lot of a grocery store near our condo and my husband said hello to a lady. I asked him who that was and he said she lived across the hall from us. Yes, she has only lived there about 3 months but I have seen her at least 20 times and yet I didn't recognize her. I guess she wasn't my Toyota Scion." This reflection was sent to us by Emma who has participated in many of our studies.

BACKGROUND

The coupled comments by Helen and her niece and by Emma (fictitious names, of course) reflect some of the major characteristics of congenital prosopagnosia (CP), a disorder that has received considerable attention recently. Jane and Emma are individuals who suffer from CP, a lifelong difficulty in face processing in the absence of any obvious sensory, neural

167

(no obvious lesion or brain alteration), or cognitive disorder. Aside from the intrigue associated with a failure to recognize faces (see for example, Oliver Sacks' *The Man Who Mistook his Wife for a Hat*), the reason that CP has attracted so much current interest is that it appears to be far more prevalent than has been previously assumed. In one recent series of studies, incidence figures in the range of 2% of the Caucasian population have been suggested, based on screening questionnaires addressing face recognition abilities and on a semistructured interview (Kennerknecht et al., 2006; Kennerknecht, Plumpe, Edwards, & Raman, 2007). Out of the 689 individuals screened in these studies, CP was detected in 17, yielding a prevalence rate of 2.47%. Interestingly, and in accordance with previous studies showing a familiar factor in CP, all indexed CP individuals in this study had an affected first-degree relative. This relatively high incidence prompted these researchers to examine the incidence of CP in other ethnic groups and, using the same procedure that they had adopted previously but now at Banaras Hindu University in Varanasi, India, they identified one female student who had several other affected family members (Kennerknecht et al., 2007). The epidemiological evidence as well as prior pedigree and segregation studies indicate that CP is compatible with an autosomal-dominant mode of trans-mission with a point mutation as the basis of the disorder (monogenic disorder) (Grüter et al., 2007). The possibility of a definable genetic mechanism in CP is intriguing and exciting, and data from fairly large pedigrees are becoming available—for example, a very recent study docu-ments the impairment in face recognition in 10 members of a single family (Duchaine, Germine, & Nakayama, 2007), and another study describes the mode of inheritance in multiple families with multiple affected members (Grüter et al., 2008). The comments by Jane and her niece (no additional information is available in this particular family, as far as we are aware) cited at the beginning of this chapter are clearly compatible with the growing evidence that CP has a familial component, and many of the participants we have tested also report having affected family members. CP has also affected some well-known celebrities, such as the famous primatologist, Jane Goodall, and this too has added to its popular interest (Grüter & Grüter, 2007).

Aside from the intrigue associated with this particular disorder, CP offers a unique window into the scientific study of the psychological and neural mechanisms mediating face recognition. Studies of individuals with acquired prosopagnosia (AP) are well known but individuals with AP are rather rare, and it is usually the case that the disorder arises from a fairly large lesion, so inferring brain–behavior correspondences is difficult in these cases. The presence of a fairly substantial number of individuals with the congenital form of prosopagnosia allows more comprehensive exploration of the affected underlying behavioral and neural systems. Indeed, in the last decade, perhaps as a result of the availability of Internet access for recruiting appropriate participants, there has been an increasing number of studies conducted with individuals with CP, and these have addressed a host of outstanding issues. However, many questions remain (see also Harris & Aguirre, 2007). For example, to what extent is this disorder really *selective* for faces? Is the deficit restricted to the *recognition* of faces, or is it more extensive, affecting the *discrimination* of faces too? Are *other aspects of face processing* such as emotional expression processing also affected, or is the deficit more circumscribed? Might there be some *covert or implicit processing* of faces even in the absence of overt recognition? And similar open questions remain with regard to the underlying neural system including the extent to which *different brain regions* are necessary and/or sufficient for face processing and the *relative computational contribution* of these different areas. Questions about the extent of rehabilitation potential also exist and are just beginning to be addressed with some systematicity.

One immediate question, and the focus of the current chapter, is the extent to which CP is really analogous to the acquired form of prosopagnosia (AP), which has been more fully investigated and described over a longer period of time. Since the early work of Bodamer (1947), in which he described two individuals who suffered face-selective deficits after marked brain damage in the Second World War, many detailed reports of individuals with AP have been published. In obvious and marked distinction with CP, these AP individuals suffer from prosopagnosia following an explicit insult to the brain (for example, following a traumatic brain injury, tumor, or vascular accident), and the site of damage is now rather well characterized (Barton, 2003, 2008; Barton, Press, Keenan, & O'Connor, 2002; Bouvier & Engel, 2006). Another obvious difference between the two forms of agnosia is the familial aspect that is so prominent in CP but not relevant in the case of AP. A final difference concerns the point at which the deficit becomes apparent to the individual. In the AP case, the recognition of the failure to recognize faces occurs quite dramatically and suddenly as the individual, who was premorbidly normal and had presumably had a typical course of development, becomes aware of the failure to recognize faces following the brain damage. In the CP case, the course of development is not normal, and there is not one single point in time in which there is a dramatic change in recognition ability. Also, given the absence of explicit testing or evaluation of face recognition ability (unlike, say developmental dyslexia, which is often diagnosed when a child enters school and undergoes formal evaluation), the individual may not become aware of the deficit for a long time, perhaps even into adulthood. The delayed awareness of the face recognition difficulty is likely to be especially true in those individuals with affected family members where the pattern of recognition failure might not be that uncommon. It is also the case that whereas the loss of the recognition ability tends to have catastrophic emotional consequences for the AP patients, this strong emotional response is less evident in CP.

In this chapter, we compare and contrast the detailed behavioral and neural signatures of congenital and the acquired form of prosopagnosia. Much is to be gained from this comparison—if indeed the disorders are flip sides of the same coin, many findings from the years of study of AP can be automatically ported to CP, and the access to larger samples of CP individuals facilitates the acquisition of additional data, which might then have bearing on AP. Additionally, understanding the extent to which the acquisition and breakdown of a cognitive skill are mirrors of each other is of great scientific interest in and of itself.

Does Acquisition and Breakdown Follow the Same Path?

The idea that developmental acquisition mirrors the breakdown of a cognitive skill has a long history and is perhaps best explored in the comparison between language acquisition and breakdown, as in aphasia (Avrutin, Haverkort, & van Hout, 2001). The key idea is that the order of language development is reversely mirrored by the order of language loss, with the implication that the later the acquisition of a process, the more susceptible the process is to loss (something like the adage "last in, first out"). The acquisition of face-processing skills is analogous to the case of language acquisition and, in this way, one might compare and contrast the processes that are impaired following a lesion with the sequential order of the development of face processing. The case of CP is somewhat different from either the acquired form or the normal developmental sequence in that in CP all of the necessary cognitive skills to support normal face processing are not acquired, despite ample opportunity for this to happen. The question essentially remains the same, however—are the relative vulnerabilities and preservations the same in both CP and AP even though in the former the skills were not acquired, and in the latter, the skills were lost?

If a similar trajectory of acquisition (normal, CP) and breakdown (AP) is observed, this might point to some fundamental sequence of acquisition or ordering of the componential processes and might shed light on the developmental trajectory associated with the processes of face recognition. In addition to the example of language acquisition and aphasia alluded to above, many existing studies suggest that a wide variety of developmental disorders mirror the pattern manifest in the adult patients with acquired brain damage. One notable example is developmental dyslexia in which the difficulties encountered by children learning to read for the first time share many of the same difficulties most prominently experienced by premorbidly normal readers who become dyslexic following brain damage sustained in adulthood (Brambati et al., 2006; McGrath, Smith, & Pennington, 2006).

In this chapter, we review the evidence for a correspondence between CP and AP. To our knowledge, there are very few studies that directly compare CP and AP and so, in addition to reviewing these comparison studies, we consider each literature separately, indicating, as far as possible, the commonalities and differences. We acknowledge up front that there is considerable heterogeneity both among CP (Duchaine, Yovel, Butterworth, & Nakayama, 2006; Harris, Duchaine, & Nakayama, 2005; Le Grand et al., 2006; Minnebusch, Suchan, Ramon, & Daum, 2007) and among AP individuals (Barton, 2008; De Renzi, 1986; De Renzi, Faglioni, Grossi, & Nichelli,

1991), and so definitive conclusions about the common and invariant properties of each, although desirable, may be unlikely. In the course of these comparisons, we make reference to some of our own recent studies but also refer to studies from related investigations in other laboratories.

BEHAVIORAL PROFILE OF CP AND AP

Explicit Face Recognition and Perception

Given that the definition of AP and CP is primarily based on a failure to recognize faces, by definition, both groups exhibit problems in explicitly recognizing other individuals (and, in extreme cases, even family members or themselves in photographs). In general, the problem seems not to be one of detecting the presence of a face (for example, detecting the presence of a face in a scene or among nonfaces), but rather, it is in assigning individual identity to the face. CP individuals are notoriously unconfident about their ability to individuate a face (see comments at the beginning of the chapter), and individuals from both groups often comment that faces, although classifiable as faces per se, lack a sense of familiarity.

A brief review of the available studies suggests that there is quite a wide range of severity of both AP and CP, but direct measurements of the abilities of the two groups are still difficult given the different types of assessment tools that have been used to diagnose the disorders. Whereas some studies primarily use questionnaires as an initial screening device (Carbon, Grüter, Weber, & Leuschow, 2007; Grüter et al., 2007; Grüter et al., 2008), others use measures that require some face learning (old–new matching of some learned faces) (Duchaine and Nakayama, 2005) while still others, ourselves included, use sets of famous faces to assess recognition at the outset and then follow up with measures of face matching/discrimination (Avidan, Thomas & Behrmann, 2008; Behrmann, Avidan, Marotta, & Kimchi, 2005). At this stage, then, there is no clear comparison of whether there are severity or even bias or sensitivity differences among the AP and CP individuals. Fortunately, many researchers are starting to use similar tests and, in time, we will likely have a good means by which to make comparisons amongst individuals. Whereas there is growing consensus that standardized face processing tests such as the Benton Facial Recognition Test (Benton, Sivan, Hamsher, Varney, & Spreen, 1983) and the Warrington recognition memory for faces may not be sufficiently sensitive (Duchaine & Nakayama, 2004; Duchaine & Weidenfeld, 2003), especially for individuals with CP, tests such as the Cambridge Face Memory Test and the Cambridge Face Perceptual Test are being used more frequently and normative data have been collected (Duchaine & Nakayama, 2006), making this a promising avenue for all. It will be critical to examine both the qualitative as well as quantitative distributions of the two populations, AP and CP, on such measures, and it will also be useful to acquire a verbal protocol from the individuals in which they report their strategies and introspections.

Whether the difficulty in face recognition in AP and CP is associated with a more perceptual or a more memorial process also remains open. In some of our previous work, we have argued that the difficulty in AP and CP extends beyond the recognition of faces to include problems in face discrimination, and that both types of individuals experience difficulties deriving an intact percept of a face even in the absence of the requirement to match the face to a long-term representation (Behrmann & Avidan, 2005; Behrmann, Avidan, et al., 2005). For example, we compared the ability of five CP and three AP individuals to make same/different judgments on pairs of novel faces presented for an unlimited exposure duration on a computer screen. The two faces in the pair could be the same or different, and when they differed, they could differ in that each face was a different gender ("gender" condition) or both faces were the same gender but different individuals. The latter condition is likely to be more taxing perceptually. We found that both AP and CP sets of individuals were markedly impaired, relative to the control counterparts (96% accuracy), in discriminating between the pair of novel faces, and that the two types of individuals were probably not that different from each other in their face discrimination abilities (Behrmann, Avidan, et al., 2005) (see Figure 6.1). While the AP individuals were somewhat *less accurate* (70%) than the CP (85%) group, the AP group responded significantly *more quickly* than the CP group, suggesting that these two populations may be trading speed for accuracy with differential weighting on the former or latter. This same pattern was true when the two groups made same/different judgments on novel faces presented upright or inverted (see Figure 6.2) (see also, Barton, Radcliffe, Cherkasova, & Edelman, 2007). Both AP and CP groups lacked the typical or expected superiority for upright over inverted faces, but again they traded speed for accuracy with AP being less accurate but faster than CP, and CP showing the reverse pattern. Similar findings comparing two adults, one with AP (prosopagnosia following closed head injury at age 6) and one with CP (no history of neurological disorder), revealed problems not just in recognition but in face matching of upright and inverted faces and in matching parts of faces versus parts of houses

Figure 6.1 Mean reaction time (RT) for controls, AP and CP individuals (and 1 SE) to discriminate between pairs of faces that differ in gender or that share gender but differ at the individual level.

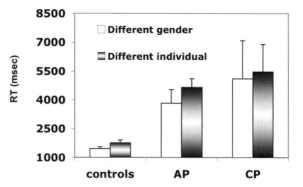

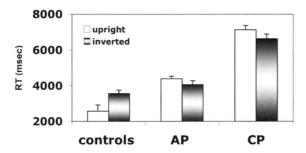

Figure 6.2 Mean reaction time (RT) for controls, AP, and CP individuals (and 1 SE) to discriminate between pairs of faces presented upright or inverted.

(de Gelder & Rouw, 2000), although some of the details of the profiles are different across the two individuals.

It is also true, however, that there have been occasional case reports of both AP and CP individuals where the problem appears to lie not in the perceptual end of face processing but in establishing the long-term representation of faces. The term "prosopamnesia" is sometimes used to describe individuals with preserved face perception, preserved memory for material other than faces (including visual material), and preserved recognition of premorbidly known faces, along with the failure to acquire new face representations. One such case of acquired prosopamnesia shows normal performance on taxing face perception tasks, a normal face inversion effect, and the ability to learn visual material other than faces (Tippett, Miller, & Farah, 2000). His recognition of faces learned before the head injury was reasonably good, but he failed to recognize the face of any individual who had become famous after his injury. Prosopamnesia can be congenital, too—in the one existing case report (to our knowledge), the prosopamnesic individual, C, performs well on simple and complex object tasks and can discriminate well between familiar and unfamiliar faces but cannot learn new faces (Williams, Berberovic, & Mattingley, 2007). She did, however, perform poorly on the Benton face recognition task when faces had to be matched across vantage point, and it is possible that she employed a featural matching strategy, which is ineffective across vantage point. It may be the case that this reliance on this strategy precludes the efficient and normal acquisition of new face representations (but one might wonder then how she acquired the representations she possesses that allows her to differentiate familiar from unfamiliar faces). Prosopamnesia, in its purest form, may bear some similarities to the associative form of prosopagnosia (De Renzi et al., 1991). However, prosopamnesics, hypothetically, may be able to recognize faces of those previously known but be unable to learn any new faces in an anterograde fashion. In contrast, the associative prosopagnosic individuals may be unable even to recognize individuals known to them prior to the onset of the face impairment as they cannot gain access to their long-term representations of any faces despite the intact pre-existing percept.

As is evident from this overview, there are similarities but also some differences between AP and CP both in encoding and as well as in learning new faces, but the extent to which these exist remains to be clarified. It will be particularly advantageous to be able to do a direct comparison between these two samples in future studies. Much of the outcome will likely depend on the measurement tools chosen and on the inclusion criteria adopted by different studies. Perhaps the only tentative conclusion possible at present is that there are patients with CP whose impairments are probably as severe as those with AP, and there are probably both acquired and congenital forms of all types of prosopagnosia (apperceptive, associative, prosopamnesic), although this is still somewhat speculative and remains to be definitively verified. Also, understanding the exact nature of acquisition, say in individuals with the congenital prosopamnesic form of CP in which some, but not all, representations are acquired (or acquirable) is likely to be highly informative and perhaps can even shed light on methods for retraining and intervention in CP and AP.

Implicit Face Recognition

A particular interesting question and one that has both theoretical import as well as possible implications for forms of intervention is whether, despite the deficit in explicit recognition, individuals with CP and AP evince implicit knowledge for faces they fail to identify overtly. In contrast with the few studies conducted in CP, there are several studies designed to explore the nature and extent of implicit processing in AP (for example, Barton, Cherkasova, & Hefter, 2004; Schweinberger & Burton, 2003). Most of these studies attest to the presence of implicit processing as revealed using a variety of measures, including skin conductance response (SCR) (Tranel & Damasio, 1985), event-related potentials (Bobes, Lopera, Comas, Galan, Carbonell, Bringas, and Valdes-Sosa, 2004; Renault, Signoret, Debruille, Breton, & Bolgert, 1989), eye movement patterns (Rizzo, Hurtig, & Damasio, 1987) and behavioral paradigms. Whether individuals with CP reveal implicit processing is especially interesting given that an assumption of many models of face processing is that implicit processing emerges from a system in which pre-existing face representations are intact but inaccessible from visual input (Burton, Young, Bruce, Johnston, & Ellis, 1991; De Haan, Bauer, & Greve, 1992). In CP, clearly there are few, if any, pre-existing face representations in place (and where they exist, they do not seem to support intact explicit recognition), but implicit processing may still be possible.

As mentioned above, very few studies have examined implicit face processing in CP, and the evidence itself is not clear-cut [note that there is one existing study that compared acquired with developmental prosopagnosics on various covert tasks, but all developmental individuals had some form of brain damage acquired early on in life (Barton Cherkasova, & O'Connor, 2001)]. Using behavioral measures, for example, Bentin, Degutis, D'Esposito & Robertson found no implicit processing in one of their CP subjects (1999) and only weak, indirect evidence for implicit processing in their second subject (2007). Similarly, De Haan and Campbell (1991) found no clear evidence for implicit processing in a single developmental prosopagnosic subject (whom we would label CP given the absence of a neurological history). However, in contrast, in a child with developmental prosopagnosia with no neurological or psychiatric background, Jones and Tranel (2001) reported an increased amplitude of skin conductance responses (SCR) for familiar compared to unknown faces, which was similar to that of controls. Also, more recently, Bate et al. (2008) reported an eye movement-based memory effect (fewer fixations and reduced regional sampling for famous compared to novel faces) in a CP individual, AA, even for those famous faces AA failed to explicitly recognize.

To assess the extent of implicit processing in CP further, in a recent investigation (Avidan & Behrmann, 2008), we employed an identity matching task with familiar (famous, as determined by an independent set of observers) and unknown faces. This task is similar to that used by De Haan, Young, & Newcombe (1987) in a patient with AP. In this paradigm, participants make same/different judgments on the identity of two sequentially presented faces. Unknown to the subject, the pairs of stimuli fall into three conditions: Both pictures in the pair are identical (same picture–same identity; for example, the identical picture of Bill Clinton is repeated twice); the two pictures differ, but they are both pictures of the same individual (different pictures–same identity; for example, two different photographs of Bill Clinton), and the two pictures are different, but they are of two different individuals (different pictures–different identity; for example, a picture of Bill Clinton and a picture of Elvis Presley). As is probably clear, the first and the third of the conditions are easier than the middle condition given that making same/different judgments on identical images or on rather different images may be done on the basis of perceptual similarity. The more taxing condition is the middle one in which the response is "same" but the input images are different, and it is in this condition that any effects of familiarity might be most evident and illuminating. Important to note again is that the familiarity of the face is orthogonal to the task being performed, and hence, we can assess the influence of familiarity on the speed and/or accuracy of identity matching in an implicit fashion.

The results indicated that, like control subjects, CP individuals made identity judgments faster on famous than on the nonfamous/unfamiliar faces. More specifically, as shown in Figure 6.3, the CP individuals, again like the controls, performed better on familiar than unfamiliar faces in the "different pictures–same identity" condition. This is particularly interesting and strongly suggestive of implicit processing. Unlike the two other conditions, in which the identity match might be accomplished on the basis of same/different geometry alone, identity here has to be abstracted from the face given that the two instances of the face are different. Deriving identity then is not straightforward, and better performance on famous than nonfamous faces in this condition is indicative of implicit identity processing. Importantly, we also confirmed that the CP individuals failed to recognize those very faces for which they showed facilitated identity judgments.

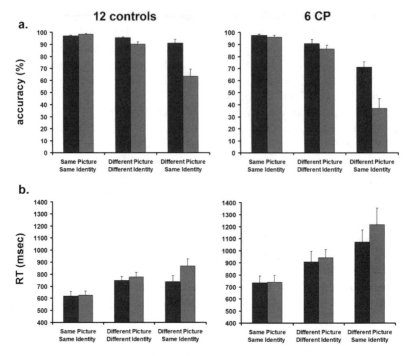

Figure 6.3 Implicit processing task including three conditions: same picture–same identity, different picture–different identity and different picture–same identity. (a) Mean accuracy of controls (left panel) and CPs (right panel). (b) Median reaction time for controls and CPs. Overall, both controls and CPs were more accurate and faster in response to the famous faces (black bars) compared to unknown faces (gray bars). The "different picture, same identity" condition was the most difficult condition, particularly for the unknown faces, as evident in both lowest accuracy and slowest RT. Used with permission from G. Avidan, C. Thomas, and M. Behrmann, "An integrative approach to understanding the psychological and neural basis of congenital prosopagnosia," in M. Jenkin & L. Harris (Eds.), *Cortical mechanisms of vision*, 2009, Cambridge University Press, pp. 209–235.

One mechanism that might support implicit processing in both AP and CP is not the pre-existing presence of intact long-term face representations (given that this is unlikely in CP) but the presence of partial, degraded representations. While these partial representations, perhaps acquired gradually and with difficulty in CP and not fully normal, may not be sufficiently precise or elaborated for explicit identification of an individual, they may suffice for the kind of same/ different task described here, which may not be as taxing and for which the partial representations may be adequate. Taken together, the presence of implicit processing in both AP and CP further attests to their similarities.

Emotional Expression Recognition

In addition to the ability to extract identity from a face, face processing enables the observer to derive information about gender, health, age, and emotional state, among other attributes. The question is whether either AP and/or CP can continue to derive such information despite the failure to process identity. According to many models of face recognition, different systems may be responsible for decoding the identity of the face and the emotional expression of a face (Gobbini & Haxby, 2006), although the extent to which emotion and identity recognition are truly dissociable is somewhat contentious (Ganel, Valyear, Goshen-Gottstein, & Goodale, 2005). Despite profoundly impaired identity recognition, normal facial emotion recognition has been documented in many studies of CP (Bentin, Deouell, & Soroker, 1999; Duchaine, Germine, et al., 2007a; Duchaine, Parker, & Nakayama, 2003; Nunn, Postma, & Pearson, 2001). Several studies of AP, however, have reported poor emotion processing in their patients (Sergent & Signoret, 1992; Takahashi, Kawamura, Hirayama, Shiota, & Isono, 1995). For example, in one study, Humphreys, Donnelly, & Riddoch (1993) investigated facial identity, gender, and expression recognition in two AP patients when the stimuli were either static photographs or moving point-light images. The two patients showed different specific patterns of impairments, but both were impaired at emotional expression recognition. One patient (HJA) was highly impaired at judging gender and expressions from photographs but performed at normal levels when making expression judgments from point-light image movies. The other patient (GK) was poor at judging expressions from both static and moving images. Whether there are differences in AP and CP or whether the differing profiles are a result of the different ways in which emotion processing was measured remains somewhat open.

To examine possible differences in emotion expression recognition further, we compared the performance of three CP individuals, two AP individuals and control subjects on a fine-grained expression task, covering all six basic facial expressions (anger, disgust, fear, happiness, sadness, surprise), and incorporating both unambiguous and more subtle expressions, following the procedures of Young et al. (1997) (Humphreys, Avidan, & Behrmann, 2007). Grayscale photographs of an individual face (Ekman & Friesen, 1976) showing the different expressions were morphed in all possible pairwise combinations at 20% moprh intervals (e.g., 90% fear, 10% surprise; 70% fear, 30% surprise, etc., for the fear–surprise continuum), and the task was to decide which of the six basic expressions each image most resembled.

While the results from the CP participants were indistinguishable from those of the age- and gender-matched comparison individuals, both AP individuals were markedly impaired. All CP individuals were well within 2 standard deviations of the comparison group mean for both accuracy (see Figure 6.4) and speed, and this was true for all six expressions. Where they made errors, the most common confusions were those also made by the controls—for example, confusing fear with surprise. In contrast, both AP individuals showed severe deficits, particularly at recognizing anger, disgust, and sadness (with one of them additionally impaired at recognizing fear). They were slow to recognize all expressions (with the exception of sadness, for which one of the two AP individuals was at the borderline). The types of

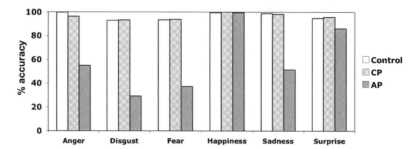

Figure 6.4 Mean percent accuracy for controls, AP, and CP individuals in a six-choice emotion recognition experiment for faces that are unambiguous (90:10 morph) that express the six basic emotional expressions. Note the low accuracy for the AP for anger, disgust, fear, and sadness. (adapted with permission from K. Humphreys, N. Minshew, G. Leonard, & M. Behrmann, 2007, "A fine-grained analysis of facial expression processing in high functioning adults with autism," *Neuropsychologia* 45(4), 685–95)

errors they made were also less predictable; for example, anger was confused with surprise. These findings suffice to indicate the difference between AP and CP on emotional expression recognition. Whether this holds across a larger sample of the individuals is uncertain, but this is one domain where the differences between AP and CP seem robust.

What might give rise to the big differences in AP and CP in emotion recognition? One possible explanation is that the lesion in AP is so large that it also encompasses regions of cortex mediating the recognition of emotion, such as superior temporal sulcus (Gobbini & Haxby, 2006). Thus, areas involved in processing identity and areas involved in processing emotion are both adversely affected. However, many researchers have argued that emotion and identity processing are not separate, and both may be supported by the activation of the fusiform face area; for example, even when participants directed their attention to the identity of the displayed face, fusiform activation was affected by the emotional expression of the face (Ganel et al., 2005). If identity and emotion are both mediated by the fusiform area, it is not hard to understand why a lesion to this region in AP gives rise to both deficits. It is more puzzling then how individuals with CP acquire normal expression recognition in the absence of identity processing. One possibility is that if they are impaired at extracting more global or holistic aspects of the face during perception (see below), then focusing on individuals' features may suffice for emotion recognition, such as the downturn of the edge of the mouth for sadness or widening of the eyes for surprise, but not for identity which requires a more configural representation. These are rather wild speculations and clearly much more remains to be done to address some of these issues.

Configural Processing

As mentioned above, there may be many ways by which information about a face can be processed, and it has been suggested that a breakdown in configural processing might lie at the crux of the deficits in AP and CP. There are considerable data to support the idea that configural processing is important for the ability to recognize faces (Maurer, Le Grand, & Mondloch, 2002), although there is ongoing uncertainty about exactly what constitutes configural processing (Gauthier and Tarr, 2002). The crucial idea, however, is that it is insufficient to process just the features themselves, like the eyes, nose, and mouth, and that the spatial relations and second-order statistics also need to be computed to support recognition.

Several studies have explored the extent to which a breakdown in configural processing is apparent in AP and CP. In one study, the ability to process upright and inverted faces and the ability to process parts of a face in and out of the face context were compared in two individuals, one with AP and one with CP (de Gelder & Rouw, 2000; note that Barton et al., 2003, compare adult-acquired and child-acquired forms of prosopagnosia but not CP). This study found that there was a difference between the two. Specifically, while the AP patient showed an "inverted inversion effect" (Farah, Wilson, Drain, & Tanaka, 1995) and "face context inferiority effect," the CP patient showed neither. The authors interpreted this to mean that while both participants were using part-based processing, in the upright case for the AP individual, there was interference from a damaged "configural" processor, so performance was actually better when stimuli were inverted and this mechanism was not triggered (de Gelder & Rouw, 2000). In the CP case, there was no apparent operation of a damaged configural processor and so no subsequent interference either.

What constitutes configural processing and how it should be assessed, however, remain controversial. Using a rather different approach, Carbon and colleagues (2007) measured the time needed to report the grotesqueness of a Thatcherized face, as a function of the orientation of the face in 14 individuals with CP and matched controls. The control individuals showed a clear sigmoidal function depending on rotation from the upright orientation, but the CP group showed a much weaker sigmoid trend, closely approximately a more linear function. The authors interpret these findings as evidence for impaired configural processing and consider this as a diagnostic indicator of the failure of face processing in CP.

Another measure often adopted to assay configural processing is the extent to which the observer is sensitive to changes in the spatial distance between features of the face versus changes to the features themselves (Maurer et al., 2002; Mondloch, Maurer, & Ahola, 2006). Barton and colleagues (Barton, 2009; Barton et al., 2002) have reported that whereas their control subjects easily and efficiently detected alterations in interocular distance or distance between the nose and mouth of the faces, the AP patients performed more poorly, especially with faces that had changes to the eye configuration. Patients with anterior temporal lobe lesions were less affected than those with fusiform lesions, and the researchers in this study associate the failure to derive facial structure primarily with lesions to the fusiform area. Under fairly similar experimental conditions, in which either the spacing between the parts (spacing task) or the parts (parts task) themselves were altered, however, CP individuals manifest a different result, showing lower performance than controls on both the spacing and the part tasks (Yovel & Duchaine, 2006). This raises the possibility that the difficulty in prosopagnosia may extend beyond the configural domain and affect the processing of the component parts, too.

Several recent studies have also suggested that not only do individuals with AP process parts rather than wholes, but also that, unlike normal observers who typically focus primarily on the eyes of a face, AP individuals do not. For example, patient PS used the lower part of the face, including the mouth and external contours when trying to recognize a face (Caldara et al., 2005; Rossion et al., 2009). The differential weighting of the lower part of the face, in contrast with the upper part that is typically used, is also supported in a study of two AP individuals who were unable to detect featural and configural differences in the eye region of a face but performed normally in evaluating size and spacing differences in the mouth region (Bukach, Le Grand, Kaiser, Bub, & Tanaka, 2008). These findings not only point to a different strategy in prosopagnosia in dealing with the components of the face but also suggest that the eyes are disproportionately reduced in salience, relative to the controls.

A completely different approach in which the ability to assemble an integral whole from disparate parts was assessed in a study that we conducted with individuals with AP and those with CP. To examine whether the failure to derive a configuration was more general than that associated with faces, we tested CP, AP, and control subjects on a hierarchical letter task (Navon, 1977) in which one of four stimuli appeared centrally for unlimited duration on the computer screen, and subjects indicated via button press whether the stimulus was a "H" or an "S." The four stimuli consisted of two congruent stimuli, in which the identity of the global letter and the local letters was congruent (global H made of small Hs and global S made of small Ss) and two incongruent stimuli in which the global and local identities differed (global H made of small Ss and global S made of small Hs). In separate blocks of trials, subjects identified the letter at the global or local level. As evident in Figure 6.5, both the AP and CP individuals show a pattern that differs from the controls (and note that there are different controls for each of the AP and CP groups to accommodate the differences in age, gender, etc.). The AP controls (top row, left panel) exhibit an advantage for global over local letters (faster for the former than the latter) and increased interference for global-to-local report in the inconsistent condition. Two AP individuals are slower in RT than the controls: one of them, SM, does show a global advantage (top row, right panel) whereas the other, RN, does not (bottom row, left panel). On subsequent testing with more fine-grained stimuli, we showed that SM, although not normal in configural processing, is eventually able to derive the global configuration with sufficient exposure duration and enough perceptual support (i.e., multiple local items that help configure the whole). RN, the

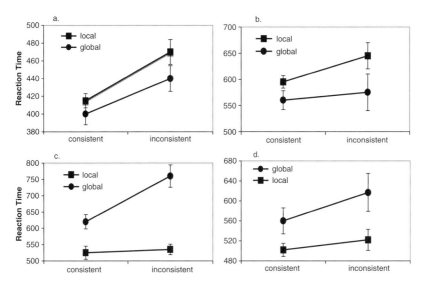

Figure 6.5 RT for means for (a) controls; (b) AP patient, SM; and (c) AP patient, RN. (d) CP group for global and local identification as a function of consistency.

more severe of the two, however, is unable to derive any benefit from the global whole under any circumstances. The pattern seen in the CP individuals (bottom row, right panel) is very similar to that observed in the AP individual, RN, and suggests that these individuals might have difficulty configuring local elements into a more unified and holistic representation. A recent report with a single case of an individual with integrative congenital prosopagnosia has replicated these results and reported that this individual has marked difficulties deriving a global representation of nonface stimuli (Bentin, Degutis, D'Esposito, & Robertson, 2007).

A second experiment with both of these prosopagnosic populations, as well as the controls, using a microgenetic approach to map out the evolution of the holistic percept, confirms that the AP and CP group are not normally able to derive a global whole from disparate elements and continue to show a bias or advantage for the elements across a protracted time course, while the controls derive a holistic representation rather rapidly and efficiently (especially when there are multiple small elements in the display, affording a surface texture). Interestingly and surprisingly, not all CP individuals show the local bias (Duchaine, Yovel, & Nakayama, 2007), and the mean of the 14 individuals who participated in this study show a pattern that is not statistically significant from that of the controls. It is unclear why there is this large discrepancy in the two data sets given the relatively minor changes in experimental procedures across the two studies. What remains to be determined is whether the two sets of CP individuals perform similarly on other tests of face recognition (hence similar measures need to be collected on both) as well as on other perception and nonface recognition tasks. Whether the differences are a further manifestation of the heterogeneity of the population is a possibility, although the clear division between the two samples makes this seem unlikely. Another possibility is that there are differences in severity of the sample. More standard testing of the individuals across different labs will help resolve some of these issues, and hopefully, we will clarify whether the differences are quantitative (in severity) or whether there are indeed qualitatively different subgroups in CP. Clearly, there is much that remains to be done and many discrepancies that need to be resolved.

Eye Movements in AP and CP

Closely related to issues concerning the encoding of faces and possible differences in perceptual representations is the question of how the face is fixated by observers and whether the AP and CP show similar eye movement patterns to those of controls. A number of studies have already examined the eye movements of individuals with AP during their perception of faces but, for the most part, have not revealed any major or dramatic differences in the patterns of eye movements between the AP and control counterparts in terms of the number, duration, location, and sequence of eye movements (Lê, Raufaste, Roussel, Puel, & Demonet, 2003). This may not be that surprising given that these individuals had normal face processing skills premorbidly and might well have acquired the normal patterns of eye movements prior to the onset of brain damage. One difference reported, however, was that the AP individuals did not evince normal sequential dependence of fixations for unfamiliar faces—the familiar faces appear to have activated existing schema and trajectories, but novel faces did not seem to engage the same scanpath (Barton et al., 2007; Rizzo et al., 1987). That there was differentiation for familiar versus unfamiliar faces is interesting and is compatible with the findings of covert or implicit processing in CP, as reviewed above.

   To date, there is one study of the eye movements in CP that reports that the CP individuals fixated more external features of the face and had a more dispersed gaze pattern than the control subjects and that this was true for the perception of both familiar and unfamiliar faces (Schwarzer et al., 2006). It seems that for the CP individuals, the internal features of the face do not constitute the highly informative regions, and they search the external features for cues to the individual's identity. The study reference above by Bate et al. (2008) also employed eye tracking in a case of CP but the emphasis was mostly on the extent to which the pattern of eye movements reflects implicit processing of face recognition.

Summary: Behavioral Profile of AP and CP

Although an impairment in face processing is de facto required for the diagnosis of CP, face processing is not monolithic and can involve, for example, detecting whether a face is present among nonface stimuli, determining whether two faces are the same or different, or recognizing the individual identity of a face (Grill-Spector, Knouf, & Kanwisher, 2004; Liu, Harris, & Kanwisher, 2002). In addition, whether the same processes are implicated for faces as for other nonface stimuli (i.e., whether the mechanisms are domain specific or more general) remains to be determined (McKone Kanwisher, & Duchaine, 2007). Exactly what processes are adversely impacted in AP and in CP and whether they are the same processes or not is still somewhat unclear. Perhaps the clearest finding to date is the deficit in emotion expression recognition in most AP individuals with preservation in most CP individuals. The extent to which the deficits in recognition and discrimination are associated in AP and in CP and the relative severity of each are yet to be established. There are also several unresolved issues concerning the extent to which there is a breakdown in configural processing in prosopagnosia, both AP and CP, whether this is correlated or even causal in the face-processing deficit, and whether there are differences in AP and CP in their eye movement trajectories in scanning a face. It is indeed the case that the systematic investigation of CP is still in its infancy, and so many issues remain open. From a scientific point of view, this affords researchers wonderful opportunities to embark on a new series of studies to uncover in the clearest and best-targeted fashion the nature and extent of the deficit in CP and its relationship to AP.

NEURAL PROFILE OF CP AND AP

Only a small number of studies have conducted neural investigations of CP, although an increasing number of studies are being undertaken and published at present. The studies fall primarily into one of two methodological approaches: electrophysiological (ERP and MEG) or neuroimaging (structural and functional MRI).

Electrophysiology Studies

With regard to the electrophysiological studies, there is a reasonably long tradition of using event-related potentials to examine a very specific electrophysiological marker, a negative event-related potential at occipitotemporal scalp sites between 130 and 200 ms (N170) that is larger when elicited by faces than by any other visual object category. The N170 for faces is highly sensitive to orientation, and is delayed and enhanced for inverted over upright faces, as well as for faces with a missing outer contour. The N170 appears to reflect relatively early stages of face processing, possibly relating to structural encoding, and is unaffected by semantic or familiarity aspects of the face (e.g., Bentin & Deouell, 2000). A similar waveform signature, the M170, has also been documented using magnetoencephalography (MEG), and it too may serve as a marker that is selective for face processing (Liu et al., 2002). To date, only a few ERP studies have been conducted with individuals with prosopagnosia, and the findings are somewhat mixed.

Many studies conducted with individuals with CP have revealed a reduction in face selectivity in the N170 or M170 component, although there is some individual variability in this pattern. Although an N170 can be detected in cases with CP, and it is of equal magnitude to that seen in the normal controls, it seems not to be specific to faces and is elicited with equivalent amplitude by other nonface stimuli, too (Bentin et al., 1999, 2007; Kress & Daum, 2003). In the single study using MEG (Harris et al., 2005), the M170 response was indistinguishable from the profile obtained from the controls in two out of five individuals, but there was no face-selective response in the remaining three. In a recent ERP study, three CP subjects showed reliable N170 amplitude differences between faces and nonface stimuli, whereas one individual showed significantly reduced amplitude differences between faces and nonface objects. The heterogeneity is also evident in a recent report in which three out of four congenital prosopagnosic individuals (they are referred to as developmental prosopagnosics in the paper, but there is no lesion or any other alteration evident on conventional MRI scan) show a reliable N170 amplitude difference between faces and nonface objects whereas this is not the case for the fourth individual (Minnebusch et al., 2007). Finally, a single case study of an individual with difficulties in integrating local elements (see above) and with CP failed to show the typical N170 preference for faces (Bentin et al., 2007)

The status of the N170 in individuals with AP is also not clear. Individuals with AP typically do not evince the enhanced N170 at the temporal electrodes, say for faces compared with houses, nor do they show the differential waveform for upright over inverted faces (de Gelder & Stekelenburg, 2005; Eimer & McCarthy, 1999). In one AP individual, in contrast with the controls, there was no enhanced negativity, associated with N170, at the lateral temporal electrodes (Eimer & McCarthy, 1999), and this was taken as evidence for a problem in the structural encoding of faces. Surprisingly, however, a later study with one AP individual reported robust N170 potentials following fairly extensive damage bilaterally to the ventral temporal cortex (Bobes et al., 2004). Because the N170 to nonface objects was not examined in this same individual, however, it leaves open the question about how selective the N170 really is in this case.

Taken together, conclusions from the electrophysiological investigations are probably premature, and the heterogeneity among the findings is most evident. It seems that the findings from AP are perhaps clearer (although the absence of nonface experiments with the patient by Bobes et al., 2004, makes the interpretation tricky). The CP studies reveal much more heterogeneity with respect to the status of the physiological markers, the N170 and M170. Whether this is a consequence of the differences among individuals in the samples or different experimental procedures or whether this is indeed the case remains to be determined. What is clear is that the face-processing deficits are not necessarily correlated with the presence or absence of face-specific N170.

Neuroimaging: Functional

There is similar ambiguity concerning the results obtained from neuroimaging studies, at least in the case of CP. The findings from the AP individuals seem more consistent. For example, in two individuals with lesions that affected the fusiform gyrus per se, face-selective activation was observed, not in the normal fusiform face area but either more posteriorly in the right hemisphere or posteriorly in the left hemisphere (Marotta, Behrmann, & Genovese, 2001). In contrast, normal FFA activation was observed in a woman with AP and tissue loss in the right inferior lateral occipital lobe and the left medial temporal lobe, mainly in the fusiform gyrus. Despite the fact that the left occipital face area (OFA) was affected, a normal pattern of face selectivity was observed in the right FFA (Rossion et al., 2003; Schiltz et al., 2006; Sorger, Goebel, Schiltz, & Rossion, 2007). A similar finding has been reported by Steeves and colleagues (Steeves et al., 2006) in which a normal pattern of face-related activation was noted both in FFA and in the STS in an AP patient with damage to the OFA (see also Steeves et al., 2009). However, in two other individuals with brain damage sustained during childhood (GA, RP), there was reduction or elimination of face selectivity (Hadjikhani & De Gelder, 2002), and similar activations for faces and houses were found in the fusiform face area (the pre-eminent area for face processing, FFA). In fact, there was no face-selective activation in any area along the ventral visual pathway even when a permissive statistical threshold was used.

The functional imaging results are also inconsistent with respect to CP. Some individuals do not show face-related activation (Bentin et al., 2007; Hadjikhani & De Gelder, 2002) whereas others apparently do. For example, in a group of four CP individuals, we reported a normal pattern of fMRI activation in the fusiform gyrus (FFA) and in other ventral occipitotemporal (VOT) areas, in response to faces, buildings, and other objects, shown both as line drawings and as more natural images (Avidan et al., 2005; see Figure 6.6). These same individuals also showed a normal pattern of adaptation (reduced BOLD signal for repeated over nonrepeated stimuli) for faces and for other objects throughout ventral temporal cortex. We have replicated these results in two additional CP individuals using the same protocol (Avidan, Thomas & Behrmann, 2008). Like these individuals, subject YT, who showed reduced face selectivity in the ERP study, reported above exhibited face-related activation in ventral visual cortex that mirrored that of normal individuals in terms of site of activation, activation profile, and hemispheric laterality (Hasson, Avidan, Deouell, Bentin, & Malach, 2003). Avidan and Behrmann (2009) have recently replicated these findings in six individuals with CP, all of whom have difficulties in perceptual discrimination as well as face recognition. Importantly, these individuals evince adaptation for faces in the FFA, but do not reveal activation of other regions shown by the control subjects (such as left posterior cingulate and medial frontal

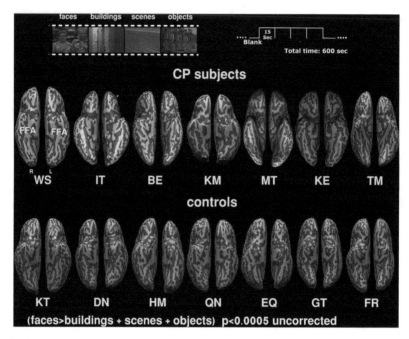

Figure 6.6 Functional maps of the conventional face and object mapping experiment. Face and building activation maps are shown for each of the CP subjects (top row) and for four representative control subjects (bottom row). Note that all CP subjects exhibit similar activation patterns to the control groups. Used with permission from G. Avidan, C. Thomas, & M. Behrmann, "An integrative approach to understanding the psychological and neural basis of congenital prosopagnosia," in M. Jenkin, & L. Harris (Eds.), *Cortical mechanisms of vision*, 2008, Cambridge University Press, pp. 209–235 (see color Plate 5).

cortex), sites previously documented in other studies of repetition priming with faces.

The imaging studies conducted to date have been with the more apperceptive or perceptual forms of CP. A very recent imaging study on a CP individual with prosopamnesia demonstrated normal attenuation of the PPA and FFA activation to houses and familiar faces (reduced signal following repeated but not following nonrepeated stimuli), respectively, but no adaptation in the BOLD signal to unfamiliar faces. These findings suggest that in developmental prosopamnesia, the FFA cannot maintain stable representations of new faces for subsequent recall or recognition. The lack of FFA adaptation to unfamiliar faces is especially interesting. As alluded to previously in the earlier discussion on prosopamnesia, an open question is how the initial representations (that show adaptation for familiar faces) are acquired in the first place in these individuals and why new face representations ones are not acquired. This issue is also closely related to the possibility of intervention or training and the potential for learning in individuals with prosopamnesia and with prosopagnosia, more generally, and this is discussed in greater detail below.

Neuroimaging: Structural

A last thread of evidence concerning the neural underpinnings of CP comes from a few studies that have attempted to examine structural alterations in the cortex of those with CP. Although almost all the studies endorse the absence of any obvious structural changes on conventional MRI (and, in fact, this is one of the criteria for inclusion in the CP group), two studies have indicated the presence of volumetric differences in the temporal cortex of CP individuals, relative to controls. CP individual, YT (see above, too), had a smaller right temporal lobe than the controls (Hasson et al., 2003). This was replicated in a group of six CP subjects in whom detailed volumetric measurement uncovered a smaller right anterior fusiform region and a larger right anterior and middle temporal gyrus (Behrmann, Gao, Avidan & Black, 2007). No differences are observed in the hippocampus or parahippocampal region, suggesting that it is not the entire temporal cortex that is reduced but rather the fusiform gyrus, the pre-eminent structure for face processing, specifically. Importantly, too, the reduction in anterior fusiform is significantly negatively correlated with the severity of the face recognition impairment (less volume, greater impairment). This finding is particularly intriguing in light of the recent reports of face-selective (and even selectivity for individual faces) activation in anterior inferior temporal cortex, as revealed in functional imaging of both humans and nonhuman primates (Rajimehr, Young & Tootell, 2009).

TREATMENT

Unsurprisingly, given the complexity of the disorder, there have been very few systematic and theoretically motivated attempts to rehabilitate individuals with prosopagnosia, and direct comparisons between AP and CP in terms of outcome are not yet possible. The existing studies, however, are both interesting and cautious illuminating. One such study (Behrmann, Marotta, Gauthier, Tarr, & McKeeff, 2005) attempted to retrain an individual with AP using the now well-established regimen for training individuals to become Greeble experts (Gauthier & Tarr, 1997). Of great interest in the study of Greeble expertise is that individuals who have acquired such expertise evince activation in the fusiform face area (FFA), the pre-eminent area involved in face processing (Kanwisher, McDermott, & Chun, 1997). The AP individual did manage to learn to identify some Greebles, even at an individual level (i.e., associating a name with a specific Greeble that shared both the main body and appendage orientation with other Greebles but was uniquely defined by its own appendages) and even showed some generalization to untrained Greebles. This is of much interest in and of itself as it demonstrates the ability of an AP individual to acquire new visual representations. Surprisingly and somewhat shockingly, along with the improvement in Greebles, this AP individual exhibited a significant reduction in his ability to discriminate faces. Moreover, a comparison between a pre- and post-intervention functional MRI scan, in which face selectivity was explored, revealed that there was a post-intervention reduction in the number of voxels that showed some face-selective responses prior to intervention, and there was a concomitant increase in the number of voxels that showed Greeble selectivity. These findings were taken as evidence that, in a neural system that is compromised, there is competition for representation, and optimizing the neural system for representing Greebles diminished its ability to represent faces.

Intervention studies in CP are few in number. One study, although not a rehabilitation study per se, trained a CP individual to recognize Greebles (Duchaine, Dingle, Butterworth, & Nakayama, 2004). In this study, a man with severe prosopagnosia completed training with a set of Greebles, using a modified training regimen of the kind used by Gauthier and Tarr (1997). Surprisingly, this individual performed normally throughout the standard Greeble training procedure. Given the individual's prosopagnosia, these findings were taken as evidence that face recognition and Greeble recognition rely on separate mechanisms. It seems, however, that before this conclusion can be reached definitively, a similar training regimen with faces needs to be undertaken—if, indeed, the same individual fails to learn the faces under similar circumstances in which he succeeded in Greeble learning, a stronger conclusion might be proposed. At present, however, whether faces and non-face stimuli, even those closely related to faces, are processed by different mechanisms remains to be determined.

Finally, a recent exciting paper reports a very promising approach for rehabilitation in CP. This paper describes the performance of a single CP individual who underwent a simple configural training paradigm in which she learned to discriminate faces on the basis of spacing between the internal components of the face (Degutis, Bentin, Robertson, & D'Esposito, 2007). The individual showed improved face identification both on experimental tasks as well as in every day life. Moreover, the improvement was accompanied by marked changes in connectivity and activity in ventral occipital temporal cortex as well as in the selectivity of the N170 on an ERP paradigm. This very encouraging finding suggests that it is configural processing that is impaired in CP, and hence, intervening at this level may have the maximal leverage for bringing about change. Furthermore, addressing this core configural deficit may lead to clear behavioral and neural changes that support normal face recognition.

CONCLUSION

The study of prosopagnosia continues to provide a unique window into understanding the psychological and biological mechanisms supporting face processing, although many of the findings remain puzzling and inconsistent, and moreover, very similar studies yield somewhat different findings even just within AP and CP. Reaching conclusions about similarities in psychological and neural profile across the two forms of the disorder is all the more difficult given the inconsistencies even within one domain. What can account for the within-group differences? One obvious conclusion and the one we are left with at this stage is that both AP and CP are extremely heterogeneous. While this conclusion may be true, we arrive at it primarily by default, as we have no way to make sense of the differences. A more satisfying outcome, however, would be a compelling explanation for why and when these differences manifest. Critically, in order to start down this path, consensus on the diagnosis and inclusion criteria for CP is required. Whether the individuals included in a sample of CP individuals fall in the tail of the normal distribution or whether they are truly outside of the distribution must be clearly determined at the outset, and some agreement as to what constitutes CP is urgently needed. Of course, to do this, one needs robust and reliable measures, and there are now several that might serve this role (Duchaine & Nakayama, 2006). Self-report does not suffice, as there is at least one case in which a family member included himself in the sample by self-report, but objective measures did not support this self-characterization (De Haan, 1999).

Whether the mechanisms that are affected in the acquired form of the disorder and the mechanisms that are not developed in the congenital form of the disorder are one and the same is also, unfortunately, not yet clear. Comprehensive and direct comparisons of these populations, employing the same experimental procedures, are not yet available, although there are some studies beginning to bear fruit on this topic. As above, these comparisons can only be meaningful if systematic inclusion criteria and a clear definition of what constitutes prosopagnosia are laid out.

While there seem to be some similarities across AP and CP in the findings to date, there are also some differences. Of course, the failure to recognize faces is a common characteristic. It seems that deriving information about the emotional expression of a face may be better in CP than in AP, although not every CP individual evinces this pattern (Jones & Tranel, 2001; Nunn et al., 2001). It is also the case that some AP and some CP individuals seem to show difficulties that extends beyond face processing, implicating other visual categories as well, as well as other modalities (such as voice recognition [von Kriegstein et al., 2006]). Finally, ERP and MEG profiles are both normal and abnormal in CP but not normal in AP, and this is true for the BOLD pattern in CP and AP, too. Lastly, the lesion site in AP may be more circumscribed and easier to identify, but there may well be parallel structural changes in CP.

Both AP and CP continue to be intriguing disorders, and the anecdotes provided by these individuals shed light on their experiences:

"In most instances I realize that a face is familiar but am unable to place it. Generally I say neutral things that fail to give me away, and then I wait to see if the other person brings up some matter that will lead me to recognition. Sometimes nothing will come up, and I make inoffensive small talk that I know will not give me away. When that happens I wonder for days thereafter who the other person was . . . . There are times I wish I could sport some commonly accepted symbol like the white cane associated with blindness, but then what one might call face blindness must look utterly trivial compared to genuine blindness. Meanwhile I contemplate possible moves of my own. The time may well be ripe for a prosopagnosia support group. And it may also be time to make sure that prosopagnosiacs [sic] are entitled to the same rights as other disabled people: it would make sense, for example, to require nametags (above all legibly lettered ones!) at all federally funded public gatherings. Most important of all, we should all work toward increased research funding that may eventually enable successful surgical or pharmacological interventions for those with an improperly functioning fusiform gyrus. Passivity is no longer a viable option: Prosopagnosiacs [sic] of the world, unite!"

(from "Recognition Envy," written by an individual who has participated in some recent studies of ours, 2007).

ACKNOWLEDGMENTS

The research reported here was supported by a grant from the National Institutes of Mental Health (MH54246) and by a grant from the McDonnell Foundation to the Perceptual Expertise Network. We thank Bruno Rossion for his helpful comments.

REFERENCES

Avidan, G. and Behrmann, M. (2009). Functional MRI reveals compromised neural integrity of the face processing network in congenital prosopagnosia, *Current Biology*, doi:10.1016/j.cub.2009.04.060

Avidan, G. and Behrmann, M. (2008). Implicit familiarity processing in congenital prosopagnosia, *Journal of Neuropsychology*, 2, 141–164.

Avidan, G., Hasson, U., Malach, R., & Behrmann, M. (2005). Detailed exploration of face-related processing in congenital prosopagnosia. 2. Functional neuroimaging findings. *Journal of Cognitive Neuroscience*, 17, 1150–1167.

Avidan, G., Thomas, C. and Behrmann, M. (2008). An integrative approach to understanding the psychological and neural basis of congenital prosopagnosia. In M. Jenkins and L. Harris (Eds.) Cortical Mechanisms of Vision, Cambridge University Press, 209–235.

Avrutin, S., Haverkort, M., & van Hout, A. (2001). Language acquisition and language breakdown. *Brain and Language*, 77, 269–273.

Barton, J. J. S. (2003). Disorders of face perception and recognition. *Neurologic Clinics, 21*, 521–548.

Barton, J. J. S. (2008). Structure and function in acquired prosopagnosia: lessons from a series of 10 patients with brain damage. *J Neuropsychol*, 2(Pt 1), 197–225.

Barton, J. J. S. (2009). What is meant by impaired configural processing in acquired prosopagnosia? *Perception*, 38, 242–260.

Barton, J. J. S., Cherkasova, M.V., & Hefter, R. (2004). The covert priming effect of faces in prosopagnosia. *Neurology*, 63, 2062–2068.

Barton, J. J. S., Cherkasova, M., & O'Connor, M. (2001). Covert recognition in acquired and developmental prosopagnosia. *Neurology*, 57, 1161–1168.

Barton, J. J., Cherkasova, M. V., Press, D. Z., Intriligator, J. M., & O'Connor, M. (2003). Developmental prosopagnosia: a study of three patients. *Brain and Cognition*, 51(1), 12–30.

Barton, J. J. S., Press, D. Z., Keenan, J. P., & O'Connor, M. (2002). Lesions of the fusiform face area impair perception of facial configuration in prosopagnosia. *Neurology*, 58, 71–78.

Barton, J. J. S., Radcliffe, N., Cherkasova, M. V., & Edelman, J. A. (2007). Scan patterns during the processing of facial identity in prosopagnosia. *Experimental Brain Research*

Bate, S., Haslam, C., Tree, J. J., & Hodgson, T. L. (2008). Evidence of an eye movement-based memory effect in congenital prosopagnosia. *Cortex*, 44(7), 806–819.

Behrmann, M., & Avidan, G. (2005). Congenital prosopagnosia: Face-blind from birth. *Trends in Cognitive Sciences*, 9, 180–187.

Behrmann, M., Avidan, G., Marotta, J. J., & Kimchi, R. (2005). Detailed exploration of face-related processing in congenital prosopagnosia. 1. Behavioral findings. *Journal of Cognitive Neuroscience*, 17, 1130–1149.

Behrmann, M., Gao, F., Avidan, G. and Black, S. E. (2007). Neurostructural alterations in congenital prosopagnosia, *Cerebral Cortex*, 17, 10, 2354–2363.

Behrmann, M., Marotta, J., Gauthier, I., Tarr, M. J., & McKeeff, T. J. (2005). Behavioral change and its neural correlates in visual agnosia after expertise training. *Journal of Cognitive Neuroscience*, 17, 554–568.

Bentin, S., Degutis, J. M., D'Esposito, M., & Robertson, L. C. (2007). Too many trees to see the forest: Performance, event-related potential, and functional magnetic resonance imaging manifestations of integrative congenital prosopagnosia. *Journal of Cognitive Neuroscience*, 19, 132–146.

Bentin, S., & Deouell, L. (2000). Structural encoding and identification in face processing: ERP evidence for separate mechanisms. *Cognitive Neuropsychology*, 17(1-3), 35–54.

Bentin, S., Deouell, L. Y., & Soroker, N. (1999). Selective visual streaming in face recognition: Evidence from developmental prosopagnosia. *Neuroreport*, 10, 823–827.

Benton, A. L., Sivan, A. B., Hamsher, K., Varney, N. R., & Spreen, O. (1983). *Contributions to neuropsychological assessment* (2nd ed.). Oxford, UK: Oxford University Press, Inc.

Bobes, M. A., Lopera, F., Comas, L. D., Galan, L., Carbonell, F., Bringas, M. L., and Valdes-Sosa, M. (2004). Brain potentials reflect residual face processing in a case of prosopagnosia. *Cognitive Neuropsychology*, 21, 7, 691–718.

Bodamer, J. (1947). Die Prosop-agnosie. *Archiv für Psychiatrie und Nervkrankheiten*, 179, 6–53.

Bouvier, S. E., & Engel, S. A. (2006). Behavioral deficits and cortical damage loci in cerebral achromatopsia. *Cerebral Cortex*, 16, 183–191.

Brambati, S. M., Termine, C., Ruffino, M., Danna, M., Lanzi, G., Stella, G., et al. (2006). Neuropsychological deficits and neural dysfunction in familial dyslexia. *Brain Res*, 1113(1), 174–185.

Bukach, C. M., Le Grand, R., Kaiser, M. D., Bub, D. N., & Tanaka, J. W. (2008). Preservation of mouth region processing in two cases of prosopagnosia. *J Neuropsychol*, 2(Pt 1), 227–244.

Burton, A. M., Young, A. W., Bruce, V., Johnston, R. A., & Ellis, A. W. (1991). Understanding covert recognition. *Cognition*, 39, 129–166.

Caldara, R., Schyns, P., Mayer, E., Smith, M. L., Gosselin, F., & Rossion, B. (2005). Does prosopagnosia take the eyes out of face representations? Evidence for a defect in representing diagnostic facial information following brain damage. *J Cogn Neurosci, 17*(10), 1652–1666.

Carbon, C. C., Grüter, T., Weber, J. E., & Leuschow, A. (2007). Faces as objects of non-expertise: Processing of Thatcherized faces in congenital prosopagnosia. *Perception, 36*(11), 1635–1645.

de Gelder, B., & Rouw, R. (2000). Configural face processes in acquired and developmental prosopagnosia: evidence for two separate face systems? *NeuroReport, 11,* 3145–3150.

de Gelder, B., & Stekelenburg, J. J. (2005). Naso-temporal asymmetry of the N170 for processing faces in normal viewers but not in developmental prosopagnosia. *Neuroscience Letters, 376,* 40–45.

Degutis, J. M., Bentin, S., Robertson, L. C., & D'Esposito, M. (2007). Functional plasticity in ventral temporal cortex following configural training with faces in a congenital prosopagnosic. *Journal of Cognitive Neuroscience, 19,* 1790–1802.

De Haan, E. H. (1999). A familial factor in the development of face recognition deficits. *Journal of Clinical and Experimental Neuropsychology, 21,* 312–315.

De Haan, E. H., & Campbell, R. (1991). A fifteen year follow-up of a case of developmental prosopagnosia. *Cortex, 27,* 489–509.

De Haan, E. H., Young, A., & Newcombe, F. (1987). Face recognition without awareness. *Cognitive Neuropsychology, 4,* 385–415.

De Haan, E. H. F., Bauer, R. M., & Greve, K. W. (1992). Behavioral and physiological evidence for covert face recognition in a prosopagnosic patient. *Cortex, 28,* 77–95.

De Renzi, E. (1986). Current issues in prosopagnosia. In H. Ellis, M. A. Jeeves, F. Newcombe, & A. W. Young (Eds.), *Aspects of face processing.* Dordrecht, The Netherlands: Martinus Nijhoff.

De Renzi, E., Faglioni, P., Grossi, D., & Nichelli, P. (1991). Apperceptive and associative forms of prosopagnosia. *Cortex, 27,* 213–221.

Duchaine, B. C., Dingle, K., Butterworth, E., & Nakayama, K. (2004). Normal Greeble learning in a severe case of developmental prosopagnosia. *Neuron, 43,* 466–473.

Duchaine, B. C., Germine, L., & Nakayama, K. (2007). Family resemblance: Ten family members with prosopagnosia and within-class object agnosia. *Cognitive Neuropsychology, 24,* 419–430.

Duchaine, B. C., & Nakayama, K. (2004). Developmental prosopagnosia and the Benton Facial Recognition Test. *Neurology, 62,* 1219–1220.

Duchaine, B. C., & Nakayama, K. (2005). Dissociations of face and object recognition in developmental prosopagnosia. *Journal of Cognitive Neuroscience, 17,* 249–261.

Duchaine, B. C., & Nakayama, K. (2006). The Cambridge Face Memory Test: Results for neurologically intact individuals and an investigation of its validity using inverted face stimuli and prosopagnosic participants. *Neuropsychologia, 44,* 576–585.

Duchaine, B. C., Parker, H., & Nakayama, K. (2003). Normal recognition of emotion in a prosopagnosic. *Perception, 32,* 827–838.

Duchaine, B. C., & Weidenfeld, A. (2003). An evaluation of two commonly used tests of unfamiliar face recognition. *Neuropsychologia, 41,* 713–720.

Duchaine, B., Yovel, G., Butterworth, E. J., & Nakayama, K. (2006). Prosopagnosia as an impairment to face-specific mechanisms: Elimination of the alternative hypotheses in a developmental case. *Cognitive Neuropsychology, 23,* 714–747.

Duchaine, B. C., Yovel, G., & Nakayama, K. (2007). No global processing deficit in the Navon task in 14 developmental prosopagnosics. *Social Cognitive and Affective Neuroscience, 2*(2), 104–113.

Eimer, M., & McCarthy, R. A. (1999). Prosopagnosia and structural encoding of faces: Evidence from event-related potentials. *NeuroReport, 10,* 255–259.

Ekman, P., & Friesen, W. L. (1976). *Pictures of facial affect.* Palo Alto, CA: Consulting Psychologist Press.

Farah, M. J., Wilson, K. D., Drain, H. M., & Tanaka, J. R. (1995). The inverted face inversion effect in prosopagnosia: Evidence for mandatory, face-specific perceptual mechanisms. *Vision Research, 35,* 2089–2093.

Ganel, T., Valyear, K. F., Goshen-Gottstein, Y., & Goodale, M. A. (2005). The involvement of the "fusiform face area" in processing facial expression. *Neuropsychologia, 43,* 1645–1654.

Gauthier, I., & Tarr, M. J. (1997). Becoming a "Greeble" expert: Exploring mechanisms for face recognition. *Vision Research, 37,* 1673–1682.

Gauthier, I., & Tarr, M. J. (2002). Unraveling mechanisms for expert object recognition: Bridging brain activity and behavior. *Journal of Experimental Psychology: Human Perception and Performance, 28,* 431–446.

Gobbini, M. I., & Haxby, J. V. (2006). Neural systems for recognition of familiar faces. *Neuropsychologia, 45,* 32–41.

Grill-Spector, K., Knouf, N., & Kanwisher, N. (2004). The fusiform face area subserves face perception, not generic within-category identification. *Nature Neuroscience 7,* 555–562.

Grüter, M., Grüter, T., Bell, V., Horst, J., Laskowski, W., Sperling, K., Halligan, P. W., Ellis, H. D. and Kennerknecht, I. (2007). Hereditary prosopagnosia: the first case series. *Cortex, 43*(6), 734–749.

Grüter, T., Grüter, M., & Carbon, C. C. (2008). Neural and genetic foundations of face recognition and prosopagnosia. *J Neuropsychol, 2*(Pt 1), 79–97.

Grüter, T., & Grüter, M. (2007). Prosopagnosia in biographies and autobiographies. *Perception, 36,* 299–301.

Hadjikhani, N., & De Gelder, B. (2002). Neural basis of prosopagnosia. *Human Brain Mapping, 16,* 176–182.

Harris, A. M., & Aguirre, G. K. (2007). Prosopagnosia. *Current Bioliogy, 17,* R7–8.

Harris, A. M., Duchaine, B. C., & Nakayama, K. (2005). Normal and abnormal face selectivity of the M170 response in developmental prosopagnosics. *Neuropsychologia, 43,* 2125–2136.

Hasson, U., Avidan, G., Deouell, L. Y., Bentin, S., & Malach, R. (2003). Face-selective activation in a congenital prosopagnosic subject. *Journal of Cognitive Neuroscience, 15,* 419–431.

Humphreys, G. W., Donnelly, N., & Riddoch, M. J. (1993). Expression is computed separately from facial identity, and it is computed separately for moving and static faces: Neuropsychological evidence. *Neuropsychologia, 31,* 173–181.

Humphreys, K., Avidan, G., & Behrmann, M. (2007). A detailed investigation of facial expression processing in congenital prosopagnosia as compared to acquired prosopagnosia. *Experimental Brain Research, 176,* 356–373.

Jones, R. D., & Tranel, D. (2001). Severe developmental prosopagnosia in a child with superior intellect. *Journal of Clinical and Experimental Neuropsychology, 23,* 265–273.

Kanwisher, N., McDermott, J., & Chun, M. M. (1997). The fusiform face area: A module in human extrastriate cortex specialized for face perception. *Journal of Neuroscience, 17,* 4302–4311.

Kennerknecht, I., Grüter, T., Welling, B., Wentzek, S., Horst, J., Edwards, S. and Grueter, M. (2006). First report of prevalence of non-syndromic hereditary prosopagnosia (HPA). *American Journal of Medical Genetics A, 140*, 1617–1622.

Kennerknecht, I., Plumpe, N., Edwards, S., & Raman, R. (2007). Hereditary prosopagnosia (HPA): The first report outside the Caucasian population. *Journal of Human Genetics, 52*, 230–236.

Kress, T., & Daum, I. (2003). Event-related potentials reflect impaired face recognition in patients with congenital prosopagnosia. *Neuroscience Letters, 352*, 133–136.

Lê, S., Raufaste, E., Roussel, S., Puel, M., & Demonet, J. F. (2003). Implicit face perception in a patient with visual agnosia? Evidence from behavioral and eye tracking analyses. *Neuropsychologia, 41*, 702–712.

Le Grand, R., Cooper, P. A., Mondloch, C. J., Lewis, T. L., Sagiv, N., de Gelder, B. and Maurer, D. (2006). What aspects of face processing are impaired in developmental prosopagnosia? *Brain and Cognition, 16*, 1584–1594.

Liu, J., Harris, A., & Kanwisher, N. (2002). Stages of processing in face perception: An MEG study. *Nature Neuroscience, 5*, 910–916.

Marotta, J. J., Behrmann, M., & Genovese, C. (2001). A functional MRI study of face recognition in patients with prosopagnosia. *NeuroReport, 12*, 959–965.

Maurer, D., Le Grand, R., & Mondloch, C. J. (2002). The many faces of configural processing. *Trends in Cognitive Sciences, 6*, 255–260.

McGrath, L. M., Smith, S. D., & Pennington, B. F. (2006). Breakthroughs in the search for dyslexia candidate genes. *Trends in Molecular Medicine, 12*, 333–341.

McKone, E., Kanwisher, N., & Duchaine, B. C. (2007). Can generic expertise explain special processing for faces? *Trends in Cognitive Sciences, 11*, 8–15.

Minnebusch, D. A., Suchan, B., Ramon, M., & Daum, I. (2007). Event-related potentials reflect heterogeneity of developmental prosopagnosia. *European Journal of Neuroscience, 25*, 2234–2247.

Mondloch, C. J., Maurer, D., & Ahola, S. (2006). Becoming a face expert. *Psychological Science, 17*, 930–934.

Navon, D. (1977). Forest before trees: The precedence of global features in visual perception. *Cognitive Psychology, 9*, 353–383.

Nunn, J. A., Postma, P., & Pearson, R. (2001). Developmental prosopagnosia: Should it be taken at face value? *Neurocase, 7*, 15–27.

Rajimehr, R., Young, J. C., & Tootell, R. B. (2009). An anterior temporal face patch in human cortex, predicted by macaque maps. *Proc Natl Acad Sci U S A, 106*(6), 1995–2000.

Renault, B., Signoret, J. L., De Bruille, B., Breton, F., & Bolgert, F. (1989). Brain potentials reveal covert facial recognition in prosopagnosia. *Neuropsychologia, 27*, 905–912.

Rizzo, M., Hurtig, R., & Damasio, A. R. (1987). The role of scanpaths in facial recognition and learning. *Annals of Neurology, 22*, 41–45.

Rossion, B., Caldara, R., Seghier, M., Schuller, A. M., Lazeyras, F., & Mayer, E. (2003). A network of occipito-temporal face-sensitive areas besides the right middle fusiform gyrus is necessary for normal face processing. *Brain, 126*, 2381–2395.

Rossion, B., Kaiser, M. D., Bub, D., & Tanaka, J. W. (2009). Is the loss of diagnosticity of the eye region of the face a common aspect of acquired prosopagnosia? *J Neuropsychol, 3*(Pt 1), 69–78.

Schiltz, C., Sorger, B., Caldara, R., Ahmed, F., Mayer, E., Goebel, R. and Rossion, B. (2006). Impaired face discrimination in acquired prosopagnosia is associated with abnormal response to individual faces in the right middle fusiform gyrus. *Cerebral Cortex, 16*, 574–586.

Schwarzer, G., Huber, S., Gruter, M., Gruter, T., Gross, C., Hipfel, M., & Kennerknecht, I. (2007). Gaze behaviour in hereditary prosopagnosia. *Psychol Res, 71*(5), 583–590.

Schweinberger, S. R., & Burton, A. M. (2003). Covert recognition and the neural system for face processing. *Cortex, 39*, 9–30.

Sergent, J., & Signoret, J.-L. (1992). Functional and anatomical decomposition of face processing: Evidence from prosopagnosia and PET study of normal subjects. *Philosophical Transactions of the Royal Society London B, 335*, 55–62.

Sorger, B., Goebel, R., Schiltz, C., & Rossion, B. (2007). Understanding the functional neuroanatomy of acquired prosopagnosia. *NeuroImage, 35*, 836–852.

Steeves, J. K., Culham, J. C., Duchaine, B. C., Pratesi, C. C., Valyear, K. F., Schindler, I. Humphrey, G. K., Milner, A. D. and Goodale, M. A. (2006). The fusiform face area is not sufficient for face recognition: Evidence from a patient with dense prosopagnosia and no occipital face area. *Neuropsychologia, 44*, 594–609.

Steeves, J., Dricot, L., Goltz, H. C., Sorger, B., Peters, J., Milner, A. D., et al. (2009). Abnormal face identity CODING in the middle fusiform gyrus of two brain-damaged prosopagnosic patients. *Neuropsychologia*.

Takahashi, N., Kawamura, M., Hirayama, K., Shiota, J., & Isono, O. (1995). Prosopagnosia: A clinical and anatomical study of four patients. *Cortex, 31*, 317–329.

Tippett, L. J., Miller, L. A., & Farah, M. J. (2000). Prosopamnesia: A selective impairment in face learning. *Cognitive Neuropsychology, 17*, 241–255.

Tranel, D., & Damasio, A. R. (1985). Knowledge without awareness: An autonomic index of facial recognition by prosopagnosics. *Science, 228*, 1453–1454.

von Kriegstein, K., Kleinschmidt, A., & Giraud, A. L. (2006). Voice recognition and cross-modal responses to familiar speakers' voices in prosopagnosia. *Cereb Cortex, 16*(9), 1314–1322.

Williams, M. A., Berberovic, N., & Mattingley, J. B. (2007). Abnormal fMRI adaptation to unfamiliar faces in a case of developmental prosopamnesia. *Current Biology 17*, 1259–1264.

Young, A. W., Rowland, D., Calder, A. J., Etcoff, N. L., Seth, A., & Perrett, D. I. (1997). Facial expression megamix: Tests of dimensional and category accounts of emotion recognition. *Cognition, 63*, 271–313.

Yovel, G., & Duchaine, B. (2006). Specialized face perception mechanisms extract both part and spacing information: Evidence from developmental prosopagnosia. *Journal of Cognitive Neuroscience, 18*, 580–593.

7

Modeling Perceptual Expertise

Thomas J. Palmeri and Garrison W. Cottrell

> *To have one's hunches about how a simple combination of processes will behave repeated dashed by one's own computer program is a humbling experience that no experimental psychologist should miss. Surprises are likely when the model has properties that are inherently difficult to understand, such as variability, parallelism, and nonlinearity—all, undoubtedly, properties of the brain.*
>
> Hintzman, 1990

INTRODUCTION

In this chapter we delineate what we believe to be the important characteristics of perceptual expertise that a complete model should try to capture, motivate why computational models are important for any complete understanding of perceptual expertise, and then describe several models that have been constructed to account for visual object processing, perceptual categorization, and face processing. Models are evaluated in terms of their ability to account for the phenomena of perceptual expertise. A challenge in developing a comprehensive computational model of perceptual expertise is that the range of empirical phenomena, many of which are described in the various chapters in this volume, are at the intersection of so many fundamental areas of perception and cognition. This implies that any complete understanding of the various facets of perceptual expertise requires a theoretical coupling across a number of traditionally distinct areas of visual perception and visual cognition.

Radiologists, ornithologists, birders, firefighters, and other specialists are noted for their remarkable ability to rapidly recognize, categorize, and identify objects and events in their domain of expertise. Understanding the unique abilities of experts can certainly have important real-world implications for enhancing the development of expertise in the workplace. However, we believe that understanding perceptual expertise has implications beyond simply characterizing the behavior of individuals with idiosyncratic skills in highly specialized domains (Palmeri et al., 2004). Mechanisms of perceptual expertise may also explain some of the unique aspects of everyday domains such as recognizing faces (Diamond & Carey, 1986; Gauthier & Tarr, 2002), words (McCandliss, Cohen, & Dehaene, 2003), or letters (Wong & Gauthier, 2006). We view perceptual expertise as the logical end point of the normal trajectory of learning, rather than an idiosyncratic skill. This allows us to exploit studies of experts to understand the general principles and limits of human learning and plasticity. Furthermore, viewing faces, words, and letters as domains of perceptual expertise may yield new insights into how abnormal brain development or brain damage can lead to the perceptual and cognitive deficits seen in autism, dyslexia, prosopagnosia, and other conditions, and may lead to breakthroughs in education and treatment.

This theoretical view of perceptual expertise is mirrored in our approach to developing computational models. A comprehensive computational theory of the development of perceptual expertise remains elusive. However, viewing perceptual expertise as the end point of the trajectory of normal learning suggests that we should ultimately look to various computational models from literatures such as object recognition, face recognition, perceptual categorization, automaticity, and skill learning as theoretical starting points. Indeed, we believe that the development of perceptual expertise should be explored first within the context of extant models of normal visual cognition. Of course, this is a hypothesis, not an axiom. We may ultimately discover that specialized domains of expertise require specialized domain-specific computational models. However, to this point, we have not needed to make that assumption.

We begin by delineating what we believe to be the core phenomena of perceptual expertise (largely taken from Palmeri et al., 2004) that a comprehensive model should account for. We then briefly review some general issues in modeling, followed by consideration of models of object processing, perceptual categorization, and face processing as models of perceptual expertise. Of course, no model can account for all of the characteristics of perceptual expertise (although significant progress has been made). At the end of the chapter, we will briefly discuss ways in which some of these models might be theoretically integrated.

THE CORE FEATURES OF PERCEPTUAL EXPERTISE

There are a number of behavioral and neural characteristics that distinguish novices and experts, many of which are discussed in other chapters in this volume. It goes without saying that experts know more than novices about their domain of expertise. They can verbalize more properties, describe more relationships, make more inferences, and so forth (e.g., Ericsson et al., 2006; Kim & Ahn, 2002; Murphy & Wright, 1984; Johnson & Mervis, 1997). This is, after all, what makes them experts. Our focus here is on behavioral and neural changes in visual cognition that underlie *perceptual* expertise. Here we provide a brief summary of some of the phenomena that any comprehensive computational theory of the development of perceptual expertise must ultimately account for:

- Novices often rely on explicitly verbalized category knowledge in the form of rules or ideal cases that are acquired from reference manuals or explicit instruction (e.g., Allen & Brooks, 1991) or that are created through induction (e.g., Johansen & Palmeri, 2002). By contrast, although experts have more verbal knowledge about a domain, expert categorization often seems removed from explicit and conscious deliberation (e.g., Brooks, Norman, & Allen, 1991; Sloman, 1996). What accounts for this shift from conscious deliberation to more automatic decisions?

- Novices are slow and deliberate in their decisions, perhaps reflecting their use of explicit rules and strategies. The development of expertise is accompanied by a marked speedup in processing, originally characterized by the power law of practice (Newell & Rosenbloom, 1981; but see Heathcote, Brown & Mewhort, 2000; Rickard, 1997; Palmeri, 1999). What causes this increase in the speed of decisions with perceptual expertise?

- One important aspect of this speedup is the so-called "entry level shift" (Jolicoeur, Gluck, & Kosslyn, 1984; Tanaka & Taylor, 1991). For novices, categorizations at the basic level ("dog" or "bird") are faster than categorizations at either a superordinate ("animal" or "plant") or a subordinate level ("robin" or "terrier"). The fastest level of categorization is often described as the entry-level into conceptual knowledge. For experts, there is an entry-level shift whereby subordinate-level categorizations are made as quickly as basic-level categorizations (Johnson & Mervis, 1997; Tanaka & Taylor, 1991). Does this shift reflect a qualitative change in how expert categories are processed, or is it a manifestation of a more continuous quantitative change in the efficiency of processing over learning (Joyce & Cottrell, 2004; Mack, Wong, Gauthier, Tanaka, & Palmeri, 2007; Tong et al., 2008)?

- Novices and experts show different patterns of interference. Novices are easily distracted whereas experts may be able to simultaneously engage in other tasks while making expert decisions. Part of this apparent lack of interference may be because experts no longer use explicit verbalizable routines, so concurrent verbal activity does not interfere with performance. But when experts engage in tasks that tap the same representational resources used for other domains of expertise, they suffer interference in ways unseen in novices (Gauthier & Curby, 2005; Gauthier, Curran, Curby, & Collins, 2003; Rossion et al., 2004; see also Curby & Rossion, this volume). What accounts for these different patterns of interference in experts and novices?

- Novices can attend to part of a complex object while ignoring irrelevant parts. By contrast, experts show interference from irrelevant variation in an unattended part. For example, in a part-matching task—adapted from work in the face recognition literature (Young, Hellawell, & Hay, 1987)—subjects are asked to attend to the top part of a whole object. After a brief delay, a second object is shown with the irrelevant bottom either matching or mismatching the bottom of the first object. When judging whether the top is the same or different, novices are unaffected by the irrelevant bottom, whereas experts show facilitation when the irrelevant bottom would lead to the same decision, and interference when the irrelevant bottom would lead to a different decision (Cheung, Richler, Palmeri, & Gauthier, 2008; Gauthier et al., 2003; Richler et al., 2008). However, the direction of this interference depends upon the objects of expertise—for example, Chinese readers do not suffer this interference when viewing Chinese characters, while novices do (Hsiao & Cottrell, 2008). What causes this nominal processing cost associated with expertise, and what explains when the expert will show this cost?

- Experts generalize their knowledge. Experts can learn to categorize and identify new objects more quickly than novices, and can discriminate novel objects better than novices, at least so long as the new objects are similar to other objects in their domain of expertise (i.e., they vary systematically in the same way as other learned objects; Gauthier & Tarr, 1997, 2002; Tanaka, Curran, & Sheinberg, 2005).

- The ability of experts to generalize is also limited in specific ways (Palmeri, 1997). Experience is often limited to particular viewpoints. In much the same way that face recognition is impaired by inversion, expert object recognition is impaired by inversion as well (Diamond & Carey, 1986). For example, experts are highly sensitive to changes in the configuration of features, but only when objects are presented in a familiar orientation (Maurer, LeGrand, & Mondloch, 2002; Mondloch, LeGrand, & Maurer, 2002; Gauthier & Tarr, 1997). What does this limited generalization and sensitivity to orientation or viewpoint imply about how experts represent their perceptual knowledge?

- Finally, experts show different patterns of brain activity than novices. For example, with fMRI it has been shown that the fusiform face area (FFA) is not just involved in face recognition but is activated by objects of expertise in real-world experts such as birders (Gauthier, Skudlarski, Gore, & Anderson, 2000; Xu, 2005; but see Grill-Spector, Knouf, Kanwisher, 2004) and by objects of expertise created in the lab (Gauthier & Tarr, 1997, 2002). Similarly, event-related potential (ERP) markers for face recognition, such as the N170, which shows highest amplitude for faces, also show higher amplitude when observing objects of visual expertise over objects that are not (Tanaka & Curran, 2001; but see Scott, Tanaka, Sheinberg, & Curran, 2006). Why are brain areas that are devoted to one domain of expertise, in this case faces, recruited for another domain of expertise? What is different about an expert domain such as letter perception, which recruits different brain areas entirely (Gauthier, Tarr, et al., 2000; Wong & Gauthier, 2006)?

No single computational model can, at present, account for all of the various behavioral aspects of the development of perceptual expertise. At the same time, some models do speak to certain aspects of expertise, and a comprehensive computational theory may be possible by combining complementary models (or lessons learned from those models). This chapter provides an overview of models from visual object processing, perceptual categorization, and face recognition that we believe provide insights into the mechanisms underlying the development of perceptual expertise. At the end of the chapter, we sketch some possible avenues for theoretical integration toward a comprehensive model of perceptual expertise. Ultimately, we need a model that captures the long-term dynamics of learning throughout the development of expertise, the short-term dynamics of novice and expert decisions, and the dynamic interplay of the various brain structures that are recruited at various stages of expertise and how those brain structures are molded by experience.

SOME WHAT'S, WHY'S, AND HOW'S OF MODELING

First, what is a model? Definitions vary widely. For our purposes, we define a model as a theory that has been formalized in terms of mathematical equations or computer simulations. An advantage of formalization beyond mere verbal description is that it forces the theorist to be explicit about all components of the theory, allowing those theories to be clearly articulated, rigorously evaluated, and potentially falsified (e.g., Hintzman, 1990). Intuitions about how components of a theory interact are often overly simplistic or downright wrong. Thus, models often generate new and novel predictions regarding empirical work that would otherwise be unavailable.

There are many varieties of models (e.g., Luce, 1995). There are *statistical models* of data, such as structural equation modeling, multidimensional scaling, factor analysis, principal components analysis, or nonlinear regression. Statistical models can be applied to any data from any domain, at least so long as those data abide by the assumptions underlying the valid use of those models. As models of data, statistical models do not explain why the data was observed. They analyze what was observed. There are *normative models*, such as optimal control theory, Bayesian decision theory, and expected utility theory. Normative models attempt to explain what should be done in a particular situation based on various optimality considerations. To the extent that individuals deviate from optimality, these models fail to explain what people actually do, although often the real issue here is determining what the individual's utilities are. There are *artificial intelligence* and *machine learning models* for computer vision, face recognition, expert reasoning and problem solving, and spoken language recognition. These models attempt to mirror the complex behavior of humans and may even make use of what is known about the processes underlying human perception and cognition, but ultimately they aim to see, hear, or reason as well as people, or even better than people, irrespective of whether the underlying mechanisms bear any resemblance to human mental and neural processes.

Our focus is on *process models* of cognition and perception. They attempt to explain how and why people think, remember, and perceive the way they do. They formally instantiate hypotheses about the mechanisms that lead to observed behavior and are often grounded in neurally inspired computational mechanisms. The somewhat counterintuitive goal of these models is to make the same errors people make, to be slow when people are slow and fast when people are fast, and to be able to mimic the effects of brain damage and mental illness. While process models have different goals than statistical models, normative models, and artificial intelligence models, the initial development of a process model may be closely related to those models. For example, it could be possible to develop a process model that mechanistically instantiates Bayesian decision theory and then see if this model accounts for human behavior, or an existing process model that accounts well for human behavior may end up being related mathematically to Bayesian decision theory years after the model was first developed (e.g., Myung, 1994). Sometimes whole classes of models may be unknowingly related; it took many years for the field to fully realize the intimate relationship between neural networks and statistical models (e.g., Bishop, 1995).

So why model?

Models Rush in Where Theories Fear to Tread

Theories are relatively high-level verbal descriptions of the processes underlying behavior. As such, they are often vague about specific mechanisms, which can make it difficult to make a priori predictions based upon them. However, using machine learning or statistical techniques, one can often create a *working model* of the process involved, even in cases where there is no theory. These can then be examined in order to gain insights into how the process might work. For example, an early class of face processing models was built from "eigenfaces" extracted using principal components analysis[1], a well-known statistical analysis technique (O'Toole, Abdi, Deffenbacher, & Valentin, 1993; Turk & Pentland, 1991). Figure 7.8 shows some eigenfaces, which served as the features for the model. These whole-face templates are

---

[1] Eigenfaces are whole-face templates that arise from finding the directions of maximum variance in a data set of faces. In particular, they encode the strongest *covariances* between the pixels in a set of faces. More formally, they are the principal eigenvectors of the covariance matrix of the data. For example, in a data set of male and female faces, the first principal component, or the first eigenface, will often correspond to the distinction between male and female. In a data set of Asian and Caucasian faces, the first principal component may correspond to the difference between Asians and Caucasians. It is interesting to note here that neural network models developed around the same time are formally equivalent to these eigenface models (Cottrell & Metcalfe, 1991; Fleming & Cottrell, 1990; Furl, Phillips, & O'Toole, 2002; Golomb, Lawrence, & Sejnowski, 1991).

clearly holistic features. Each face is represented by its correlation with the eigenfaces, giving a vector of numbers that can be matched with a set of stored representations with labels (e.g., identity or emotion). The label of the closest stored face is the label chosen by the model. The original face can be reconstructed as a weighted sum of these eigenfaces. In other words, faces are a point in this high-dimensional eigenspace (the number of dimensions corresponds to the number of eigenfaces used). In this sense, they are one of the first computational instantiations of Valentine's "face space" account of face processing (Valentine, 1991), and provide insights into how a face space might arise, and how holistic effects can be accounted for (more on this later).

Models Can Make Counterintuitive Predictions

Our opening quote by Hintzman (1990) makes this point well. Hintzman's own work showed that behavior that seems to clearly indicate some form of abstraction from specific experiences could actually emerge from a simple learning mechanism with no abstractions in the model whatsoever, just memory for specific experiences (Hintzman, 1986; see also Medin & Schaffer, 1978; McClelland & Rumelhart, 1985; Nosofsky, 1984) (more on this later, too). The behavioral abstraction of the model arose from the mechanism that accessed and used specific memories. Thus, models can be intuition pumps for alternative conceptualizations of hypothetical mechanisms and how they might work.

Models Can Be Manipulated in Ways People (and Animals) Cannot

A computational model allows the modeler to explore "what if" questions that cannot be easily explored with humans and that would be difficult or impossible to explore, even with animal models. By performing these experiments that may go beyond the parameters that are reasonable for the human brain or beyond real-world experience, one can begin to see why things are the way they are. For example, with models we can explore systematically the effects of manipulations such as variations in cortical architecture (e.g., hemispheric vs. "monolithic" brain models, Shillcock & Monaghan, 2001), variations in processing resources (e.g., variations in number of hidden, Plaut et al., 1996), variations in the environment (e.g., What if our parents were cans, cups, or books instead of humans? i.e., Is there something special about face expertise versus visual expertise in general? Joyce & Cottrell, 2004; Sugimoto & Cottrell, 2001; Tong et al., 2008), or variations in brain damage within the very same "brain" (e.g., Hinton & Shallice, 1991; Plaut et al., 1996; Plunkett & Juola, 1999).

Models allow us to explore the effects of a far denser space of potential brain lesions and brain damage than possible with our limited neuropsychological samples. Extremely rare disorders seen in single cases may be attributable to the tails of a distribution of cases seen in an extremely large sample of possible cases (e.g., Thomas & de Wet, 1998). Or extreme cases may correspond to behaviorally distinct regimes. For example, Plunkett and Juola (1999) showed by lesioning their model of past tense formation that one could get behavior that appeared as if "the rule system" was broken, and other behavior that appeared as if "the rote memory system" was broken, even though their model had neither of these components. Such behavioral dissociations and double dissociations are often interpreted as evidence for modules that map directly onto the particular behaviors that are preserved or damaged. However, while modular accounts certainly do predict dissociations and double dissociations, models (combined with simple logic) show that the arrow of implication only goes in one direction: observing dissociations and double dissociations does *not* imply a modular organization (Palmeri & Flanery, 2002; Palmeri & Gauthier, 2004; Plaut, 1995; Plunkett & Juola, 1999; Thomas & de Wet, 1999). Only by having an explicit computational model is it possible to explore how brain damage might affect behavior by breaking the model in various ways (e.g., Dailey & Cottrell, 1999), providing a more comprehensive theoretical account of the deleterious effects of brain damage and mental illness on behavior (e.g., Treat et al., 2007).

Models Can Be Analyzed in Ways People (and Animals) Cannot

For example, in neurocomputational models, one can perform single-cell recordings from "birth" to "death" and fully map out the receptive and projective fields of every unit in the network. We can selectively ablate and restore parts of the network, even down to the single-unit level, to assess their contribution to processing. We can measure responses at different layers of processing to find the best match to human data (e.g., which level accounts for a particular judgment: perceptual processing, object representation, or categorization, Dailey et al., 2002). In general, with any model, we can analyze the interactions between components at a level of detail unavailable in biological preparations.

In this way, models can also generate new theories, in that they may allow the theorist to see formal relations between different aspects of behavior that might not be obvious at first blush (e.g., Logan, 2004). We also remark here that models that are formalized to account for data from one domain can often be extended to apply to data from other domains. Indeed, one might argue that such generalization is the hallmark of a "good" model. As we will see in this chapter, some models of face and object processing can be extended to perceptual expertise more generally (e.g., Joyce & Cottrell, 2004). Models of categorization, identification, and automaticity have also been combined into a more general model of perceptual categorization and perceptual expertise (see Palmeri et al., 2004).

Of course, modeling is not all wine and roses. One common criticism of models goes something like "with enough parameters to tweak, a model can predict anything." This is a valid criticism when a model has too many free parameters relative to the number of degrees of freedom in the data. And too many free parameters can also risk overfitting, where the model accounts not only for stable quantitative and qualitative effects, but also the random variability—the "noise"—in the data as well. In addition, it's true that just as underspecified verbal theories are unfalsifiable, underspecified or weakly constrained computational models risk being unfalsifiable as well. The source of this common criticism may partly stem from the way modeling results are commonly portrayed in the literature. Often the focus is on a particular parameterization of a particular model that fits a particular pattern of observed data. In that sense, these are often more like cases of "postdiction" rather than prediction (e.g., Roberts & Pashler, 2000), or at least they can be (perhaps falsely) interpreted that way. On the one hand, demonstrations of the sufficiency of a particular formal model can be important in showing that a hypothetical mechanism *can* work, even if that mechanism seems counter-intuitive at first blush. On the other hand, demonstrating sufficiency is only the first step.

The fact that most models have free parameters doesn't mean that those models are unconstrained. Models may produce similar qualitative predictions for a wide range of (plausible) parameter values, demonstrating that the pattern of behavior is inherent in the model structure rather than in a specific choice of parameter values (e.g., Johansen & Palmeri, 2002; Pitt, Kim, Navarro, & Myung, 2006). Sometimes model parameters can be chosen a priori to have values that correspond to a range of values that have been measured, either through neurophysiology, psychophysics, or scaling techniques (e.g., Boucher et al., 2007; Nosofsky, 1992b). Specific parameter values may also be chosen because they can be shown to be optimal in some way (Nosofsky, 1998). Parameter-free predictions can also be generated by first fitting the model to one part of the data, such as training data in the case of learning models, and then model predictions with fixed parameters can be compared to observed data that are outside the range of the training data (e.g., Busemeyer & Wang, 2000; Dailey et al., 2002). It's up to the modeler to go through these extra steps.

Perhaps more vexing is that multiple models can produce the same behavior; indeed, there are an infinite number of possible models that can produce the same input–output behavior (Moore, 1956). This is where model selection, and even model competition, may come in. One criterion is to select models based upon an application of Ockham's razor—simpler models that account for the data are to be preferred to more complex ones. Complexity can be measured in, for example, the number of parameters of the model, or models may be nested within one another. Various statistical tests can weigh whether additional complexity leads to a significantly better account of the data. While as a first-order approximation, the more constraints there are on a model's parameters, or the fewer free parameters a model has, the simpler the model is, in actuality, quantifying model flexibility and model falsifiability can get quite complicated (e.g., see Pitt et al., 2002). If competing models are of comparable complexity, and they account for the same set of data, then the models must be weighed on the basis of their predictions. Some of the best modeling work adopts a strong inference approach (Platt, 1964) by designing critical experiments that contrast the predictions of competing models (e.g., Ashby & Waldron, 1999; Nosofsky & Palmeri, 1997).

MODELS OF OBJECT PROCESSING

One approach to developing a model of perceptual expertise is to first turn to models of generic object processing and ask how those models might account for the development of perceptual expertise after the right kind and the right amount of learning has taken place. Of course, this assumes that perceptual expertise can be seen as the end point of the trajectory of normal learning, which need not be the case. However, if we can do so without making any additional assumptions, then by Ockham's razor, we should. In this section, we begin by briefly describing the problems that models of object processing try to solve. We then turn to a number of extant models of object processing and discuss how those models might account for the development of perceptual expertise.

How do we know that an object is the same object we have seen before? Or at least how do we know that it is the same kind of an object that we have seen before? At first glance, what could be simpler? We just open our eyes and we know what things are and whether we recognize them or not. Of course, these naïve intuitions belie the tremendous computational challenges facing our visual system with every glance at the world around us. The dynamic, ever-changing world conspires to present a dramatically different stimulus to our eyes, even though the very same physical object may be present in front of us. Somehow, our visual system overcomes this tremendous variation in visual information to create a stable perception of the world. Three-dimensional objects seem stable as we move around, as objects move around, and as the lighting changes. But how does the visual system allow us to perceive this stability when the two-dimensional images falling onto our retinae are changing so dramatically? This is known as the *invariance problem*.

Almost all solutions to the problem of visual object recognition begin by generally characterizing visual processing as a form of dimensionality reduction. The retinal representation has extremely high dimensionality in that each of the 120 million or so photoreceptors can (semi) independently encode a different local aspect of the visual scene. The visual system transforms this high-dimensional stimulus representation into the activation of a million nerve fibers. While this is hardly low dimensional, it is relative to the dimensionality of the retinal stimulation. However, once the cortex is reached, the dimensionality increases again, around 100-fold. This high-dimensional representation allows the cortex to extract many independent features from the input that are relatively sparse (meaning, a small fraction of the neurons fire) and distributed. These independent features are then used to recognize objects. Different theories propose varying solutions to the problem of creating a low-dimensional object representation, differing markedly in the form of that representation, and in how great a dimensionality reduction is assumed. Most stop there and do not consider the dimensionality expansion that occurs (although ongoing work on "overcomplete" independent components analysis is suggesting ways this might be done).

Some of the earliest models of object processing assumed that the fundamental goal of vision was to create a faithful description of the objects in the world, in a sense reconstructing the three-dimensional structure of objects and their spatial relations within visual representations. One of the most intuitive proposals for constructing such representations, originally put forth by Marr and Nishihara (1978; Marr, 1982), assumes that every given object can be described in terms of generic three-dimensional primitives and their spatial relations. This idea was adopted by Biederman (1987) and implemented as a neural network simulation by Hummel and Biederman (1992), in the "recognition-by-components" (RBC) theory. RBC assumes a small vocabulary of three-dimensional primitives called "geons" and specifies the rules, based upon "viewpoint invariant properties" for extracting geons from images (see Figure 7.1). The key idea is that the geons have properties that are invariant to some distortion and viewing angle, thereby directly addressing two of the twin challenges facing vision. This represents an extreme dimensionality reduction: different views of an object and different exemplars within an object class all map onto the same configuration of three-dimensional geon primitives.

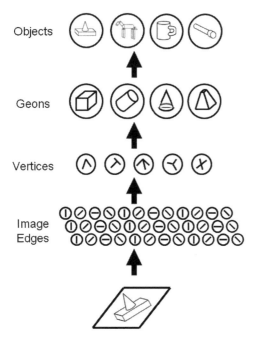

Figure 7.1 Recognition-by-components (Biederman, 1987; Hummel & Biederman, 1992) assumes that a retinal image is initially described in terms of its edges. A variety of nonaccidental primitive features are extracted from this edge description, such as "L" junctions, "Y" junctions, and other properties. Combinations of various viewpoint-invariant primitives signal the presence of one of the small number of geons. Viewpoint-invariant object recognition involves recognizing the particular combination and relative configuration of the viewpoint invariant geon representations extracted from a complex object.

In the context of RBC, any basic-level visually defined category may be uniquely represented by a small subset of geons in particular spatial configurations. For example, a wide variety of birds are made up of roughly the same parts—head, body, wings, beak—perhaps with the exception of atypical birds like penguins. The problem of basic-level categorization is solved because all birds map onto the same structural description. Of course, if these structural descriptions lack metric information about the relative sizes of geons and the quantitative location of geons with respect to one another, which early versions of RBC did, then within-category discrimination is nearly impossible. That is, if one believes that visual expertise is just an end point of normal object recognition, it is unclear how this theory could be generalized to that situation. More recent versions have added a separate pathway for metric information in order to solve the problem of face recognition, but the evidence for two distinct recognition pathways in the brain is weak or nonexistent. In any case, it is unclear how such a model would account for *any* of the phenomena of perceptual expertise.

These structural description models have been challenged based on other objections (e.g., Edelman, 1997, 1999). Specifically, a variety of laboratories have shown that object recognition depends on experience with particular views of an object (e.g., Bülthoff & Edelman, 1992; Tarr, 1995; Tarr & Pinker, 1989). Viewpoint-invariant recognition derives from experience with multiple views (Tarr, Kersten, & Bülthoff, 1998), not because object representations are inherently viewpoint independent, as suggested by RBC and its variants. These and other results led to an alternative class of object processing models based on stored representations of previously experienced views of objects (see Figure 7.2). These theories often begin with a very different assumption of the goals of vision. Rather than assuming that we need to reconstruct the three-dimensional world inside our heads, view-based approaches typically stress the importance of generalization from past to present experiences (Edelman, 1999; Shepard, 1994). Considering that we are vanishingly unlikely to ever experience the same situation twice, and that similar objects often give rise to similar consequences, survival demands that we recognize the similarities (Shepard, 1987). So one solution is to create representations that preserve the similarity structure between objects even if those representations do not encode three-dimensional structure explicitly (Edelman, 1999).

View-based models solve the problem of viewpoint invariance by generalizing according to the similarity between the current representation of an object and the stored representations of objects in memory, without any need for explicit image transformations (e.g., Poggio & Edelman, 1990; Reisenhuber & Poggio, 1999; Serre, Oliva, & Poggio, 2007). Models of this sort account well for experimental patterns of interpolation between learned views and limited extrapolation beyond learned views (Bülthoff & Edelman, 1992; Edelman & Bülthoff, 1992). The most recent instantiations of view-based models (e.g., Jiang et al. 2006; Reisenhuber & Poggio, 1999, 2000) incorporate a number of neurobiological constraints in terms of

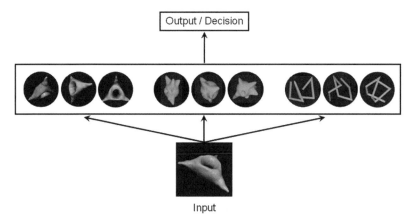

Figure 7.2 View-based models assume that objects are represented in terms of stored views. Interpolation to new views differing from experienced views in terms lighting, viewpoint, and other factors is based on similarity to stored views. In the model illustrated in the figure, an input image is matched against the stored views depicted for three different objects. The output depends on what the model is trained to reproduce. It can be trained to generate a canonical view of an object plus information about the pose of the viewed image (e.g., Poggio & Edelman, 1990). Or it can be trained to categorize, identify, or recognize the viewed image.

computations that are performed and the hierarchy of transformations performed by earlier stages of visual processing (illustrated later in Figure 7.9). One of the appealing aspects of using similarity as a means to invariance is that the same kind of mechanism can account for how we generalize across both viewing and category variation (more on the latter later). While invariance over view can be achieved by encoding multiple views of individual objects, invariance over kind can be achieved by encoding multiple views of multiple objects of that kind. Given sufficient views of objects from multiple classes, both view and class invariance can be achieved.

Unlike the RBC model, view-based models can be naturally extended to account for aspects of perceptual expertise. For example, if one has a lot of experience with certain classes of objects, for example, faces, the model would store many representations of views of the same face. This dense representation would clearly lead to the ability to finely discriminate between faces, while discrimination would be poorer for the more sparse representations of other objects (Palmeri et al., 2004). Thus, view-based accounts provide a language for thinking about the kind of perceptual learning that takes place with expertise. Perceptual experts are better able to visually discriminate between objects within their domain of expertise, even if those objects are unfamiliar (Tanaka, Curran, & Sheinberg, 2005). To the extent that experts have learned a wide range of views from a wider range of objects, they have a larger "vocabulary" of stored images from which to encode a new shape and represent its similarity to other objects. But the extent of this increase in perceptual discriminability is limited to the range of objects experts have had experience with (Gauthier & Tarr, 1997), and view-based models naturally account for the limited extrapolation beyond the experienced set (see also Palmeri, 1997).

Models like this can account for perceptual speedups by assuming an inverse relationship between response time and categorization certainty, with certainty proportional to the density of the (correctly labeled) representations[2]. Furthermore, if the label stored with the representations corresponds to the subordinate level, this would also account for the entry level shift with expertise, as the density of subordinate-level representations would be greater than category-level ones. Also, it is clear that if most representations are in a canonical orientation, then inversion effects should fall out of the representation. It is less clear how they would account for the difference in interference patterns between novices and experts, the shift from rule-based behavior to similiarity-based, or fMRI results showing the use of similar regions of cortex for different areas of expertise. Finally, if a view-based model uses full-image representations, then it would seem that all objects should show holistic responses, not just objects of expertise.

Ullman, Vidal-Naquet, and Sali (2002; Ullman, 2007) suggested an alternative model of object processing that in some sense combines elements of structural description models and view-based models. They showed that view-based features of "intermediate complexity" best account for basic-level classification, where the particular features and their size were determined by the mutual information between the patch and the category label (see Figure 7.3). For faces, these features might include what we would generally call the "parts" of a face such as the eyes, nose, or mouth, and for a car these might include "parts" like the wheel or the driver's side window. It is important to emphasize that these are not parts in any way like geons are parts. These are viewpoint-dependent view-based fragments. They are generally not full images, although full-image representations can be part of the suite of image features. Moreover, spatial relationships between these parts are not explicitly encoded, but if the local context is preserved and local features overlap, there is an implicit representation of configural information. So generic object recognition at the basic level may be view based, and it need not depend on full images of objects. Moreover, it is tempting to speculate about the relationship between these view-based fragments and the kinds of ad hoc feature sensitivities seen in neurons in TEO (Tanaka, 1996, 2002; see also Serre et al., 2007). Neither correspond directly to what we might typically think of as a distinct object part, or to anything like a geon.

---

[2] Ultimately, of course, any complete account of the time-course of perceptual expertise demands models that incorporate true temporal dynamics, not simply correlating time with some other nontemporal measure.

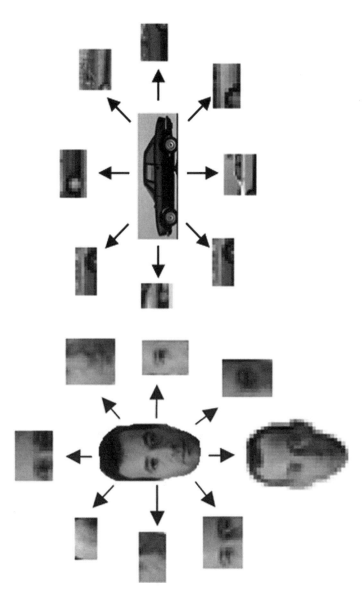

Figure 7.3 Illustration of view-based visual features of intermediate complexity maximize delivered information with respect to a basic-level category of objects. The figure shows examples of face fragments and car fragments (adapted with permission from S. Ullman, M. Vidal-Naquet, & E. Sali, 2002, "Visual features of intermediate complexity and their use in classification," *Nature Neuroscience*, 5(7) © 2002 Nature Publishing Group). Zhang and Cottrell (2005) found somewhat larger and more complex view-based visual features for subordinate identification.

The approach proposed by Ullman et al. (2002) was intended to be a solution to basic-level classification—classifying an object as a face or a car—not more subordinate-level classifications—classifying an object as Barack Obama or a Toyota Prius. But recently, Zhang and Cottrell (2005) extended this approach to discover the image features that have maximal informativeness for subordinate-level classification. What they found was that these image features were larger and more complex than the features Ullman et al. reported for basic-level classifications. For example, for face individuation, these features included an eye and a nose, or an eye with part of the nose and mouth. Thus, it is possible that accounting for the emergence of configural and holistic effects with expertise requires assembling hierarchies of features, not simply relating them in a single level of spatial relations (e.g., Gauthier & Tarr, 2002; Maurer, Le Grand, & Mondloch, 2002). Holistic effects emerge with perceptual expertise as larger and more complex view-based fragments, or even entire images, are learned.

MODELS OF PERCEPTUAL CATEGORIZATION

To recognize an object is to decide that its perceptual representation is similar to an object representation created and stored during some previous experience with that object. But to identify or categorize an object, its perceptual representation must be compared with a knowledge representation that summarizes what is known about the identity or category of that object. Ultimately, models of object processing and models of perceptual categorization both aim to explain how people recognize, identify, and categorize objects. But whereas models of object processing typically emphasize the nature of the perceptual representations created by high-level vision, models of perceptual categorization have focused more on the nature of the knowledge representations and decision processes underlying recognition, identification, and categorization (Palmeri & Gauthier, 2004). Perceptual categorization models often begin with relatively simplified assumptions about how objects are represented, commonly assuming that objects are represented in a multidimensional psychological space (Ashby, 1992) with visually similar objects close together in that space and visually dissimilar objects far apart in that space (similar multidimensional representations were adopted by "face space" theories discussed in the next section, e.g., Valentine, 1991). These multidimensional object representations are not chosen arbitrarily in a post hoc manner; they are typically derived a priori from known psychophysical mappings between physical and psychological dimensions or using various psychological scaling techniques (e.g., Nosofsky, 1992b). So while object processing models differ in how objects are perceptually represented, categorization models often assume the same multidimensional perceptual representations of objects. Categorization models differ in how knowledge about an object's identity and category are represented.

One key dimension on which categorization models differ is the abstraction of the category representations. A hallmark of visual cognition is generalization; even young children know when two visually similar but distinct objects are members of the same category. One solution to the problem of generalizing from specific experiences is to create knowledge representations that are themselves abstract generalizations. An early solution was to assume that conceptual knowledge is organized into abstract semantic networks or conceptual hierarchies (Anderson, 1976; Collins & Quillian, 1969) that link one kind of thing with another kind of thing. In a related vein, early theories assumed that people learn new categories by forming abstract logical rules, and research focused on what kinds of rules people found more or less difficult to learn (e.g., Bruner, Goodnow, & Austin, 1956; Hunt, Marin, & Stone, 1966; see also Goodman, Tenenbaum, Feldman, & Griffiths, 2008; Nosofsky & Palmeri, 1998). Subsequent research instead assumed that people learned abstract category representations based on prototypes—statistical central tendencies of experienced category exemplars—rather than rules (e.g., Homa, 1978; Minda & Smith, 2000; Posner & Keele, 1968; Reed, 1972). Both rule-based and prototype-based theories assume that because category knowledge can be applied abstractly, the underlying category knowledge representations must themselves be abstract (Figure 7.4).

This solution is similar to the solution to the invariance problem in object recognition proposed by Biederman (1987). Objects differ in viewpoint. RBC achieves viewpoint invariance by constructing abstract perceptual representations that are invariant over object view. Objects from the same category look different. Prototype and rule models achieve class invariance by constructing abstract category representations that are invariant over category instance. But in the same way that view-based models of object processing can achieve viewpoint invariance using viewpoint-dependent representations (Bülthoff & Edelman, 1992; Poggio & Edelman, 1990; Tarr & Pinker, 1989), so-called "exemplar-based" models of categorization can achieve class invariance using instance-specific representations (Hintzman, 1986; Medin & Schaffer, 1978; Nosofsky, 1984); both "views" and "exemplars" are representations tied to specific object experience. Computationally, there is a common solution to recognizing an object from a novel viewpoint and categorizing a novel instance of a category using experience-specific representations (Edelman, 1999).

As the name implies, exemplar models of categorization assume that categories are represented in terms of the specific exemplars that have been experienced. The perceptual representation of an object to be classified activates these stored exemplars depending on its similarity to those exemplars, with similarity a decreasing function of distance in multidimensional psychological space. The probability of classifying the object into a particular category depends on how similar it is to exemplars of that category relative to its similarity to exemplars of other categories (for details see Kruschke, 1992; Lamberts, 2000; Medin & Schaffer, 1978; Nosofsky, 1984; Nosofsky, 1992a). Exemplar models naturally account for many phenomena thought to

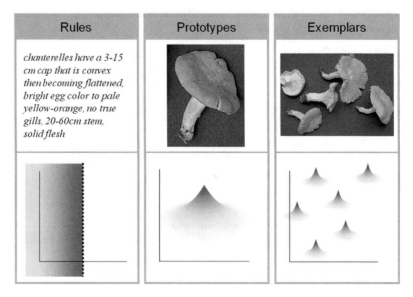

| Rules | Prototypes | Exemplars |

chanterelles have a 3-15 cm cap that is convex then becoming flattened, bright egg color to pale yellow-orange, no true gills, 20-60cm stem, solid flesh

Figure 7.4 Illustration of rule-based, prototype-based, and exemplar-based category representations. Verbal rules for categorizing edible chanterelle from similar nonedible or even poisonous mushrooms can be quite complex (top row). As an illustration of a simple one-dimensional rule, the space of objects is carved into those defined by the rule in gray shading and everything else (bottom row). The most prototypical chanterelle (top row) would be an average of experienced exemplars. The prototype lies in the center of the space of category examples, with the generalization gradient around the prototype defining the typicality (bottom row). Knowledge of chanterelles can also be represented by the range of examples that have been experienced (top row). Categorization is determined by the similarity to stored exemplars in the space of possible objects (bottom row).

demonstrate the formation of abstract rules or prototypes (e.g., Busemeyer, Dewey, & Medin, 1984; Hintzman, 1986; Nosofsky, 1986; Shin & Nosofsky, 1992); for example, category prototypes are well classified because they are similar to many stored exemplars, without any need to additionally store an abstracted prototype explicitly (Palmeri & Nosofsky, 2001). A large body of research demonstrated the theoretical success of exemplar-based models in accounting for a range of categorization and related phenomena (e.g., Estes, 1994; Kruschke, 1992; Lamberts, 1995, 2001; Nosofsky, 1988; Nosofsky & Palmeri, 1997; Figure 7.5 illustrates the formal relationships between various models). Computationally, the exemplar representations in many exemplar models of categorization (e.g., Kruschke, 1992) are quite similar to the view representations in view-based models of object processing (e.g., Poggio & Edelman, 1990; Riesenhuber & Poggio, 1999). [3] As such, exemplar models of

---

[3] Exemplar models have also recently been shown to be computationally similar to certain popular machine learning algorithms (Jäkel, Schölkopf, Wichmann, 2007, 2008).

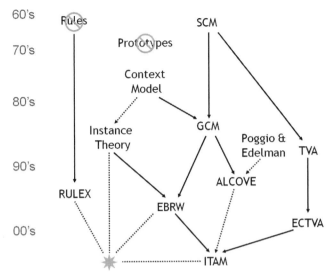

Figure 7.5 A family tree expressing the relations between a class of computational models over time. Models connected by solid lines have formal mathematical relationships. Models connect by dotted lines share computational principles. Important aspects of the development of perceptual expertise can be explained by conjoining aspects of rule-based categorization models like RULEX, theories of automaticity like instance theory, and exemplar-based categorization models like EBRW. These models also bear important formal relations to models of visual attention like ITAM. SCM = similarity choice model (Luce, 1959; Shepard, 1957); context model (Medin & Schaffer, 1978); GCM = generalized context model (Nosofsky, 1984, 1986); instance theory (Logan, 1988; Poggio and Edelman, 1990); TVA = theory of visual attention (Bundesen, 1990); ALCOVE = attention learning COVEring theory (Kruschke, 1992); RULEX = RULe-plus-EXception model (Nosofsky, Palmeri, & McKinley, 1994); EBRW = exemplar-based random walk model (Nosofsky & Palmeri, 1997; Palmeri, 1997); ECTVA = executive control of TVA (Logan & Gordon, 2001); ITAM = instance theory of attention and memory (Logan, 2002).

categorization share many of the same qualities—and shortcomings—of view-based models of object processing in terms of accounting for core phenomena of perceptual expertise as described in the last section.

Some defining characteristics of perceptual expertise entail comparisons between categorization and subordinate-level identification. On the one hand, categorization and identification seem diametrically opposed, with identification highlighting discrimination between stimuli and categorization rendering discriminable stimuli equivalent. Indeed, early work by Shepard and colleagues (Shepard & Chang, 1963; Shepard, Hovland, & Jenkins, 1961) suggested that the same exemplar generalization mechanism could *not* account jointly for categorization and identification performance. But Nosofsky (1984, 1986, 1987) showed how exemplar models could naturally account for both kinds of decisions using the same exemplar representations. The key insight was that exemplar generalization could be task dependent, unlike the task-independent exemplar generalization assumed by Shepard. Specifically, Nosofsky assumed that some psychological dimensions could be weighted more heavily than others depending on their diagnosticity for categorization (see also Kruschke, 1992; Lamberts, 2000; Nosofsky & Kruschke, 1992). Whereas all dimensions may be important for discriminating objects for purposes of identification, certain dimensions may be more (or less) relevant than others for categorizing objects; this makes exemplars that differ along nondiagnostic dimensions more similar than exemplars that differ along diagnostic dimensions. In addition to accounting for relations between identification and categorization, this dimensional weighting (called "dimensional selective attention" in these models) is necessary for exemplar models to account for the time course of learning categories; models without dimensional weighting have difficulty accounting for category learning (Nosofsky, Gluck, Palmeri, McKinley, & Glauthier, 1994; Nosofsky & Palmeri, 1996). Many models of object processing (e.g., Riesenhuber & Poggio, 1999) also lack this dimensional weighting and assume task-independent generalization (Jiang et al., 2007), so it is quite possible that they will be unable to account for the full gamut of object categorization data either.

The flexibility imbued by dimensional selective attention in exemplar models seems to fly in the face of the limits on selective attention seen with perceptual expertise. While novices can attend selectively to part of a complex object, experts show interference from variation in an irrelevant part. Experts represent objects holistically. Perhaps what's key to resolving this paradox is that most experiments demonstrating holistic processing have made irrelevant (temporarily) a part of an object that has always in the past been diagnostic for identification or categorization. From a subject's perspective, for decades both the top and bottom parts of a face have been important for face recognition; for car experts both the top and the bottom of a car have always been relevant for telling apart car models. Now in the experiment, they are told that the bottom is no longer relevant for some decision they are asked to do (for the next few minutes). Like novices they are able to do the task, and attend to the top while ignoring the bottom. However, selective attention is never perfect, especially for spatially contiguous parts. Decades of experience have caused long-term exemplar representations of faces or cars to include both the top and the bottom because both parts are critical to successful identification or categorization of faces or cars. So even a small failure to ignore the irrelevant part can end up having a large effect on observed behavior, manifested by an interference by the irrelevant part for experts. It's likely that the flexibility in selective attention cannot override extensive past experience that has created more permanent representations (see Gauthier & Palmeri, 2002; Palmeri et al., 2004), but this dynamic in exemplar models between extensive past experience and current task demands has not yet been fully explored.

Understanding dynamics has to play a key role in fully understanding perceptual expertise. Experts are fast. Several core features of perceptual expertise involve significant speedups in processing. Unlike many other models of categorization and object processing, exemplar-based models of categorization have taken time seriously (e.g., Cohen & Nosofsky, 2003; Lamberts, 2000; Logan, 1988; Nosofsky & Palmeri, 1997; Palmeri, 1997; see also Ashby et al., 2007). These models make specific assumptions about the time for perceptual processing, the time it takes to match perceptual representations with stored representations in memory and how those times change with experience, and the time to accumulate evidence from these matches in order to make rapid perceptual decisions.

For example, the exemplar-based random walk (EBRW) model (Nosofsky & Palmeri, 1997; Palmeri, 1997) assumes that when an object is presented, its perceptual representation is used as a probe of stored exemplars. These stored exemplars race to be retrieved with rates proportional to their similarity to the presented object. The winning exemplar provides incremental evidence for a particular categorization decision. Retrieval is noisy, so multiple exemplar retrievals are needed to obtain reasonably accurate decisions. The results of these multiple retrievals are accumulated over time, with each potential decision associated with a different accumulator. Whichever accumulator reaches its threshold first determines which decision is made and when it is made. EBRW is a member of a family of stochastic (noisy) accumulator models (random walk models and diffusion models) that provide excellent accounts of things like speed–accuracy tradeoffs and shapes of response time distributions (e.g., Ratcliff, 1978; Ratcliff & Rouder, 1998), and these models appear to have some grounding as the neural basis of perceptual decisions (Boucher et al., 2007; Schall, 2004; Smith & Ratcliff, 2004). What distinguishes EBRW from more general diffusion-type models is that it provides a specific theory of the evidence that drives the stochastic accumulation of evidence to a threshold.

Objects that are hard to categorize, because they are similar to objects in other categories, are categorized slowly. According to EBRW, confusable objects will tend to retrieve objects from multiple competing categories, causing a stochastic accumulation that vacillates between competing alternatives, causing longer response times. But even difficult-to-categorize objects will be categorized more quickly and more accurately as people develop perceptual expertise. EBRW assumes that with more and more experience with exemplars, more and more exemplar information is stored in memory (Logan, 1988). As more exemplar information is stored in memory, the right exemplars are retrieved (Lamberts, 2000; Nosofsky & Alfonso-Reese, 1999). Exemplar retrieval also takes place ever more rapidly. More rapid retrieval causes more rapid accumulation of evidence to a threshold and faster decisions. EBRW naturally accounts for the ubiquitous power law of learning observed throughout the skill learning and expertise literatures (Logan, 1988, 1992; Newell & Rosenbloom, 1981; Palmeri, 1997; but see Heathcote et al., 2000; Palmeri, 1999; Rickard, 1997). With the sharpening of exemplar representations that comes with experience (Nosofsky, 1987), EBRW naturally accounts for the relative speedups in basic-level categorization versus subordinate-level identification seen over the development of perceptual expertise. The entry-level shift with expertise emerges directly from quantitative changes in exemplar representations rather than any qualitative shift in processing strategies (Mack et al., 2007; Palmeri et al., 2004).

While exemplar models have provided compelling accounts of a range of phenomena, there has been growing interest in reexamining the potential role of more abstract forms of category representation, such as rules or prototypes (but see Nosofsky & Johansen, 2000). Various hybrid theories (see Figure 7.6) have been proposed that involve mixtures of rules and exemplars (e.g., Anderson & Betz, 2001; Erickson & Kruschke, 1998; Johansen & Palmeri, 2002; Noelle & Cottrell, 1996; Nosofsky, Palmeri, & McKinley, 1994; Palmeri, 1997; Smith, Patalano, & Jonides, 1998; Thomas, 1998), prototypes and exemplars (e.g., Anderson, 1990; Love, Medin, &

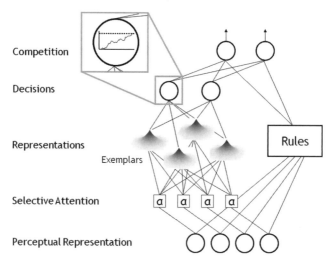

Figure 7.6 An illustration of a broad class of categorization models (e.g., Ashby et al., 1998; Erickson & Kruschke, 1992; Johansen & Palmeri, 2002; Kruschke, 1992; Nosofsky & Palmeri, 1997; Palmeri, 1997). Objects are represented along multiple perceptual dimensions and features (Perceptual Representation). Categories can be represented using exemplars or rules. Along the exemplar route, dimensions can be selectively attended according to their diagnosticity (e.g., Gauthier & Palmeri, 2002; Kruschke, 1992). As such, exemplars are activated according to their similarity to the presented object, but with diagnostic dimensions carrying more weight than nondiagnostic dimensions (Nosofsky, 1984). Depending on the model, exemplars are associated with learned categories by weights tuned using Hebbian or error-driven learning mechanisms. Categorization decisions can be driven by a variety of accumulation of evidence models (e.g., Nosofsky & Palmeri, 1997; Smith & Ratcliff, 2004). A variety of processes can be used to resolve the competition between rule-based and exemplar-based categorization decisions.

Gureckis, 2004; Smith & Minda, 1998), and various kinds of linear and nonlinear decision boundaries (e.g., Ashby, Alfonso-Reese, Turken, & Waldron, 1998; see also Ashby, Ennis, & Spiering, 2007). Let us consider the possible interplay between abstract knowledge and more specific knowledge as it might play out in a domain of perceptual expertise. We can imagine that a novice searching the woods for prized Chanterelle mushrooms must refer to a set of fairly complex rules for telling them apart from many visually similar, yet quite poisonous species, such as the Jack O'Lantern mushroom (Phillips, 1991). Although these rules may become internalized, categorizing mushrooms as edible versus poisonous (without requiring reference to a field guide) may still appear to involve deliberate use of explicit rule-based knowledge. With experience, however, a mushroom gatherer eventually seems to shift from this potentially slow, deliberate, attention-demanding mode of categorizing to a far more rapid and automatic mode of processing that seems to characterize more expert-like performance (it's likely that after finding the mushroom at a glance, they may still check whether they are correct by using the well-known rules since the consequences of misclassification could be dire). Understanding the kinds of representational changes that allow someone to become a skilled mushroom gatherer who can recognize the prized Chanterelle so quickly and effortlessly without needing to make recourse to explicit rules is a key question of perceptual expertise. These hybrid categorization models have attempted to explicitly understand these changes in category knowledge.

One way of thinking about these shifts is to view categorization as just another domain in which people develop cognitive skills with experience. According to Logan's (1988) instance theory, automaticity in a range of skills is attributed to a shift from strategic and algorithmic processes, such as the use of explicit rules, to the retrieval of exemplars from memory. Automaticity is a memory phenomenon. Exemplars are memories. Could such shifts characterize the development of expertise in perceptual categorization whereby people initially use simple rules to categorize objects but eventually come to rely on similarity-based retrieval of exemplars? Palmeri (1997, 1999; see also Palmeri et al., 2004) found evidence for shifts from rules to exemplars in a paradigm in which subjects were supplied an explicit rule for initially classifying objects into different categories. In a different paradigm, Brooks and colleagues (Allen & Brooks, 1991; Regehr & Brooks, 1993) found evidence for intrusions of similarity-based retrieval even when subjects were supplied an explicit categorization rule. But in many experimental paradigms and in many real-world situations, people are not supplied categorization rules prior to learning about categories of objects. Johansen and Palmeri (2002) found that in situations where no explicit rule is provided, people still seem to adopt an analytic strategy of developing simple rules at the outset of category learning. However, over the course of learning, these rules eventually give way to processes more akin to similarity-based exemplar retrieval. According to this view, because much of expert performance is based on similarity, generalization to new objects can be rather limited. Experts may sometimes be able to turn to rules when exposed to truly novel objects in novel situations, but then performance may not have the automaticity and fluency that often distinguishes experts from novices.

MODELS OF FACE RECOGNITION

Much of the research described throughout this volume begins with the hypothesis that what makes faces special is not that they are faces per se, but that faces are a domain of perceptual expertise; needless to say, this is seen as a controversial hypothesis by some researchers (Farah et al., 1998; McKone, Kanwisher, & Duchaine, 2007; Robbins & McKone, 2007), as addressed in some detail in other chapters. Starting with the hypothesis that expert face processing shares important computational principles with other domains of perceptual expertise, models of face processing and face recognition can be a fruitful starting point for a computational under-standing of other domains of perceptual expertise. Face recognition differs from common object recognition in the type of problem: object recognition typically requires *ignoring* within-class variability, in order to recognize all of the variants of a class, while face recognition requires paying a great deal of attention to within-class variability, because that is the signal that separates the individual members of the class. One could therefore imagine treating face recognition as another type of object recognition, just one level down the hierarchy of objects, but in this case, all of the objects share overall shape and parts. This is what makes the classic RBC theory far from able to account for expertise.

We will begin this section by describing some classic and more recent models of face recognition and then turn to work that makes direct links between face recognition and other kinds of expert recognition within the same general processing architecture.

There are at least three kinds of face recognition models: psychological models, computer vision models, and models that try to combine these approaches to generate computational cognitive models of face recognition. Within the latter class, there are models that emphasize the relationship to the brain, and attempt neural plausibility, while others abstract away from the neural architecture.

We will start with the best-known psychological model of face recogni-tion, the classic Bruce and Young (1986) model (Figure 7.7). While it is not a computational process model, it serves as a useful starting point and gave rise to a later implementation. Bruce and Young's model, which they termed a "functional"[4] model, was designed to account for a wide range of behavioral and neuropsychological data. They began by distinguishing seven different

---

[4] Here, "functional" means that the model tries to account for all of the functions required, but the model is not computational in the sense that it is not implemented on a computer.

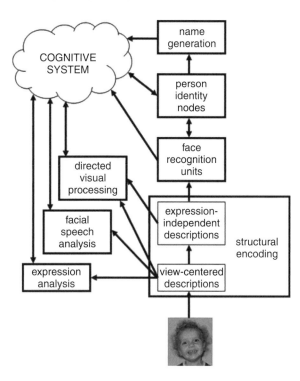

Figure 7.7 Illustration of the Bruce and Young model (reproduced with permission from Bruce & Young, 1986, © The British Psychological Society).

"codes" or representations that were necessary in order for their model to account for this data. In the model, face processing starts with a pictorial code, corresponding to Marr's (1982) "primal sketch." This is followed by a view-based code, analogous to Marr's "2.5D sketch", useful for face recognition memory of unfamiliar faces, recognition of facial expressions, and visual speech coding, all of which branch off at this point. For identifying known faces, the view-centered description is further transformed into an expression-independent representation, corresponding to some extent to Marr's "3D object representation" level, allowing the recognition of familiar faces in new situations (e.g., in novel lightings, orientations, etc.). However, the structural codes were considered to be very different than those posited by Marr, who was interested in visual object recognition; in face recognition, within-class discrimination is the primary problem. Hence, the structural encoding must have fine-grained configural information encoded. The structural encoding stage then activates face recognition units, which allow for recognition of a face as known, without necessarily recognizing who it is. This is the job of the person identity units, which activate semantic information about the person and the name unit for the person.

These various levels were deemed necessary to account for a great deal of data. For example, prosopagnosics would have damage somewhere along the stream that activated the face recognition units, without damage to the person identity nodes, since they can recognize people from voice or other means. The name units were differentiated from other semantic units because information about a person can be accessed without accessing their name. This model and its later implementations (Burton & Bruce, 1993; Burton et al. 1990; Burton et al., 1999) have continued to have a major influence on theories of and experiments in face recognition. However, no learning mechanism was included in the model, so it is hard to say how it would account for the acquisition of perceptual expertise.

Another influential psychological model is Tim Valentine's face space model (Valentine, 1991). His idea was that faces are represented as points in a high-dimensional space (which could be the equivalent of the structural encoding stage of the Bruce and Young model). In terms of a computational model, these dimensions could each correspond to a feature, and the actual point then specifies values for each feature. These kinds of representations are akin to the multidimensional representations used in many of the perceptual categorization models described in the previous section (e.g., Ashby, 1992; Lamberts, 1995, 2000; Nosofsky & Palmeri, 1997). Thinking of faces in this way leads to consideration of clusters in that space, for example, for unfamiliar-race faces versus familiar-race faces. Valentine posited that unfamiliar-race faces were clustered in a less differentiated ball in the face space, while familiar-race faces were more differentiated, explaining the so-called "other-race effect" (ORE) in face recognition. This model is highly compatible with current computational models that use patterns of activation over a set of units to represent faces. Indeed, such models have been used to explain the ORE in much the same way as Valentine envisioned it (e.g., Haque & Cottrell, 2005; O'Toole, Deffenbacher, Valentin, & Abdi, 1994).

Another influential psychological model is that of Farah, Wilson, Drain, and Tanaka (1998), in which they posited holistic representations for faces. The idea of a holistic representation is that the features of a face are connected in some way with one another, achieving a more important status than the representations of the individual parts. While they were somewhat agnostic concerning the actual form of this representation—it could correspond to whole-face templates or it could correspond to strong connectivity between the parts of a single face—the holistic representation can be used to explain the whole-face superiority effect. This effect, similar to the word superiority effect, corresponds to the ability of subjects to better discriminate a nose in the context of a face than a nose in isolation.

Computational models of face identification (in contrast with the face categorization models noted above) began with Takeo Kanade's doctoral thesis in 1973. His model was the first to actually use real images as inputs. It recognized faces by measuring distances between face features. Unlike many modern models, it actually had a top-down component that reanalyzed the face if there was not a good enough match. The next generation of models began with Kohonen's neural network model (Kohonen et al., 1977), which essentially used singular value decomposition to learn a map from pixels to names; another way of thinking about this model is that it was a linear neural network that learned to map from faces to names. This results in an appearance-based, holistic model. He showed that he could recognize faces in novel orientations by training the system on multiple orientations. This model thus was one of the first to show how an appearance-based model could generalize by interpolating between learned views.

The next set of models all began around 1990 when there was a sudden burst of interest in the use of principal components analysis (PCA) to represent faces. Turk and Pentland's (1991) "eigenface" model used principal components of gray scale images to learn a representation of faces (see Figure 7.8). These

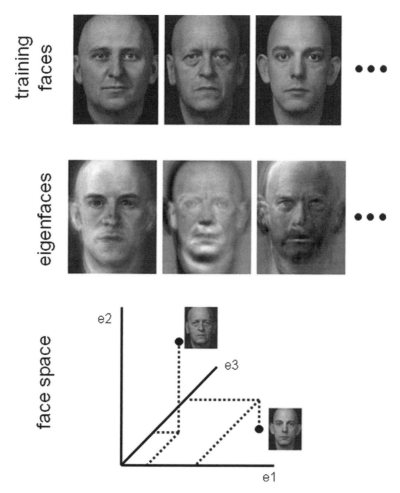

Figure 7.8 Examples of training faces (top row) and the first three eigenfaces (middle row) found using PCA (Adapted with permission from M. N. Dailey, G. W. Cottrell, and T. A. Busey, 1998, "Eigenfaces for familiarity," In *Proceedings of the Twentieth Annual Cognitive Science Conference*, © 1998 Lawrence Erlbaum Associates.). Faces are represented in terms of a linear combination of eigenfaces, generating a multidimensional face space representation (bottom row).

models are holistic in the sense that a face is represented by a weighted combination of whole-face features, that is, eigenfaces. Once the eigenfaces were extracted from a set of images, novel images could be categorized by projecting them onto the eigenfaces, and then labeling them with the identity of the closest projection from the training set (Figure 7.8). A version of this model won portions of Defense Advanced Research Projects Agency's (DARPA's) face recognition bake-off (Face Recognition Technology, FERET) in 1994 and 1995. A number of similar models based on neural networks were developed at this time, but they were considered cognitive models, and we discuss them below. In that section, we also discuss some of the interesting cognitive modeling properties of eigenfaces.

The model that performed the best overall in the FERET 1994 and 1995 tests was von der Malsburg's system (Okada et al., 1998). It used a deformable template that was fitted over the face. At each node of the template was the response of a set of Gabor filters (wavelets), which can be thought of as a kind of "zip code" for that portion of the face. There was one such template for each person in the training set. The links between the nodes can be thought of as "springs" that were stretched when matching a new face, which gave the model the ability to match faces that were displayed in quarter and full profile. It was this ability to match rotated faces that gave this system the edge over eigenfaces, which had no method for deforming them in order to match such rotations. This fitting process must be repeated for each template in the database, which is computationally more expensive than the nearest-neighbor technique used in the eigenface system. Given that the training faces were frontal, it is unclear how the eigenface method could be adapted to this test, without learning in advance how faces are transformed by rotations out of the image plane.

Around this same time, cognitive models based on PCA or their neural network equivalent, autoencoder networks, were being developed (Cottrell & Metcalfe, 1991; Fleming & Cottrell, 1990; Hancock et al., 1996; O'Toole et al., 1993). What was demonstrated in these early models is that there is a neurally plausible architecture for extracting principal components (eigenfaces when applied to faces) and that these representations are sufficient for a number of face processing tasks when used with a discriminative classifier, including identity, gender, and emotion classification (Padgett & Cottrell, 1997). These models made contact with the psychological literature in a variety of ways. For example, the other-race effect (ORE) was explained in a manner very close to that envisioned by Valentine by encoding a greater proportion of one race versus the other in an autoassociative matrix (O'Toole et al., 1994). The matrix then reproduced the less-represented-race faces with less fidelity than the faces of the more frequently encoded race. Padgett and Cottrell (1998) compared their model's categorization of morph stimuli to human responses, and by comparing internal representations, showed that the model could discriminate facial expressions better near a category boundary, as people do (Young et al., 1997). The PCA approach has also been combined with an interactive activation and competition version of the Bruce and

Young (1986) model to create a model that can explain face priming effects, such as Stan Laurel's face priming Oliver Hardy's, as well as face repetition effects (Burton et al., 1999). O'Toole and her colleagues have extended the idea of statistical analysis of 2D faces, as represented by PCA, to 3D face representations, and demonstrated the psychological validity of the representation through adaptation effects (Blanz et al., 2000).

More recently, neurophysiologically realistic models of general object processing (Riesenhuber & Poggio, 1999) have been applied to face recognition (Jiang et al., 2006). By so doing, these models make explicit the hypothesis that computations performed in the context of recognizing faces are qualitatively the same as those for recognizing common objects. As shown in Figure 7.9, this model starts with model cells similar to simple cells and has layers that alternate between layers of cells that encode complex cell responses by combining the responses of simple cells using a "max" operation, and layers of cells that combine the max cell responses into shape representations with linear rules. At the uppermost layer, cells with a Gaussian response function are trained to respond to particular individuals. While the model is illustrated for a face recognition problem, the basic structure of the model is identical for nonface object recognition as well. The training is via a brute force search of thousands of parameter settings until some are found that give response profiles that are not significantly different from the desired responses. After this training, the model has view-tuned units that have responses in quantitative agreement with human response profiles on the same data. This kind of modeling gives a proof of concept that such models can show both configural and featural effects without an explicit encoding of either. However, this kind of result can also be obtained by PCA models of face processing (Zhang & Cottrell, 2006), which use a more realistic training mechanism of learning the statistical structure of faces from the responses of Gabor filters used to model V1. However, the Jiang et al. model then makes predictions concerning the tuning and connectivity properties of FFA neurons that can be checked experimentally. Indeed, Jiang et al. (2007) use an fMRI-RA (rapid adaptation) paradigm to test the model's prediction that there should be an asymptote to discrimination performance that occurs when the population of neurons in the FFA responding to the two faces becomes disjoint. Thus, using a combination of computational modeling, fMRI, and behavioral techniques, they found that both human face discrimination performance and FFA activation can be quantitatively explained by a simple shape-based model in which human face discrimination is based on a sparse code of tightly tuned face neurons.

We now turn to a series of models developed originally by Fleming and Cottrell (1990) and Cottrell and Metcalfe (1991). The models reached their mature form in Dailey and Cottrell (1999) and then were further elaborated upon over the next 10 years by Cottrell and colleagues, although we will simply refer to these variants as "the model." Whereas Jiang et al. (2006) originated from a model of object processing (Riesenhuber & Poggio, 1999) that was later extended to face recognition, this model originated as a model of face

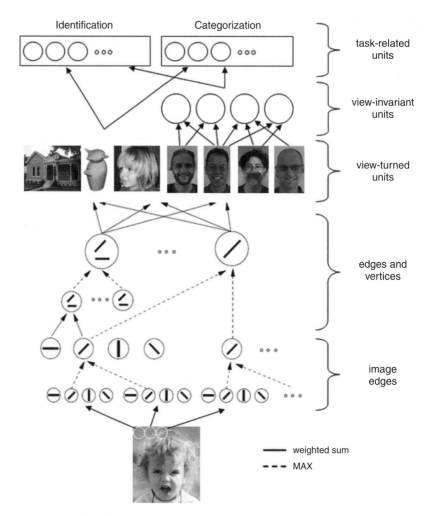

Figure 7.9 Illustration of the network architecture of the object and face recognition model developed by Riesenhuber and Poggio (1999, 2000; reproduced with permission from Jiang et al., 2006). An image is initially processed by a hierarchy of levels that extract edges and vertices, representing visual areas V1–V4 in cortex. Scale and translation invariance is performed by layers that calculated a weighted sum of inputs (solid lines) and layers that compute the unit with maximal activity (dotted lines). These feed into high-level view-tuned and view-invariant representations in IT. Task-specific units for making categorization and identification decisions are assumed to be in prefrontal cortex. Reprinted from X. Jiang, E. Rosen, T. Zeffiro, J. VanMeter, V. Blanz and M. Riesenhuber, 2006, "Evaluation of a Shape-Based Model of Human Face Discrimination Using fMRI and Behavioral Techniques," *Neuron*, 50(1), pp. 159–172. Copyright 2006. Used with permission from Elsevier.

recognition that was later extended to object recognition and perceptual expertise. The common theoretical insight is that qualitatively the same computational principles account for both object recognition and face recognition.

The basic structure is that of a neural network with four processing layers (Figure 7.10). The first layer represents the processing by V1, which is modeled as Gabor filters of five scales and eight orientations. The second

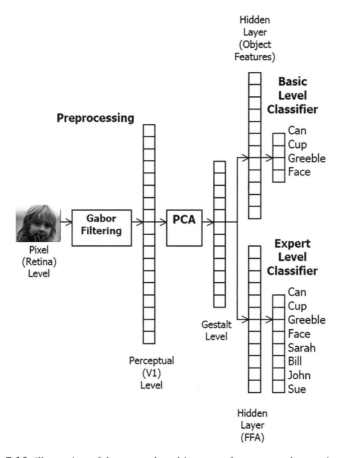

Figure 7.10 Illustration of the network architecture of a perceptual expertise model developed by Cottrell and colleagues (adapted with permission from Tong, Joyce, & Cottrell, 2005). The retinal image is preprocessed by a bank of Gabor wavelet filters at a number of different spatial scales and orientations to approximate the processing that occurs in early visual areas. The result is submitted to principal components analysis to reduce the dimensionality to a PCA projection (note that the PCA layer is "trained" on a different set of images from those used to test other predictions of the model). The resulting PCA representation is labeled as the Gestalt level in the figure. This representation is associated with basic-level and subordinate-level categories via a hidden layer representation, with weights trained using standard back-propagation. In this particular instantiation of the model, there are separate basic- and expert-level subnetworks, with the expert-level subnetwork hypothesized as a model FFA.

layer uses principal components to extract covariances from the Gabor filters and reduce the dimensionality of the representation. This can be thought of as the structural description layer from the Bruce & Young model and may correspond to later occipital layers. The next layer is an adaptive hidden layer trained by back-propagation to learn features that are appropriate for the task, and corresponds to either FFA when the model is trained at an expert level, or object layers in the ventral stream when trained to categorize. While back-propagation itself is not thought to be neurally plausible, more biologically realistic training methods exist that give rise to similar representations (Plaut & Shallice, 1993). This adaptive layer is often divided into several separate areas that are considered to be separate cortical areas competing to solve the tasks given to them, an assumption that was explicitly modeled by Dailey & Cottrell (1999). The fourth layer represents the output of the model, providing category or individual labels to the inputs, and likely corresponds to frontal areas (Palmeri & Gauthier, 2004; Riesenhuber & Poggio, 1999). The level of differentiation at this layer determines the fineness of the hidden layer features needed to discriminate the categories. Structurally, both the Cottrell model and a recent extension of the Riesenhuber and Poggio model (Serre et al., 2007) propose an initial stage of image filtering, followed by unsupervised learning of visual representations, followed by supervised learning of object categorizations.

One of the first issues addressed by this model was how the FFA develops in the first place (Dailey and Cottrell, 1999; see Figure 7.10). In their model, the banks of Gabor filters of different scales were treated as separate input channels. The representation of each scale was processed by a channel-specific PCA, so there was a low–spatial frequency input channel, up through a high–spatial frequency input channel, and PCA captured the covariances within each channel. It is well known that babies have poor contrast sensitivity in higher spatial frequencies, so using this scheme they could model the developmentally appropriate lower spatial frequency input to the cortex by attenuating the input from the higher spatial frequencies. The model then consisted of competing representations, which can be conceptualized as modeling the left and right hemispheres, one receiving relatively low spatial frequencies and one receiving relatively high spatial frequencies (Ivry & Robertson, 1998). The model was then trained to either categorize four classes of 12 objects each (five images per object) at a basic level, or to individuate one of the classes into its 12 identities, while continuing to simply categorize the other three classes of stimuli. To explain the differentiation of cortical areas for different tasks, the model assumed that different cortical areas competed for task through a gating network that fed more error back to the classifier with the lowest error—a rich-get-richer approach (this is also known as a "mixture of experts" model). Experiments using these differing levels of classification, as well as identical versus differential spatial frequency inputs, demonstrated that only in the case of different spatial frequency inputs to the two hidden layers, and the task of face identification, was there consistent specialization of one of the networks for face processing.

Consistent with behavioral data, the network receiving the lower spatial frequencies was always superior in the face identification task. Differential damage to the model produced prosopagnosia and object agnosia. Further experiments demonstrated that networks using lower spatial frequencies generalized to new images of the trained individuals much better than networks using high spatial frequencies, explaining why the specialization occurred, as better generalization also implies faster learning. They concluded that the model supported the hypothesis that something resembling a face processing "module" could arise as a natural consequence of the infant's developmental environment—poor visual acuity coupled with the goal of individuating people's faces—without being innately specified.

In terms of how this model accounts for the core features of perceptual expertise, we start with the last one, that experts tend to show activity in the fusiform face area (FFA) for objects of expertise, even after only 10 hours of training in the lab (Gauthier et al., 2000). If this is true, then the question arises as to why the FFA, an area that must start out as a face area in typically developing children, becomes recruited for other expertise tasks. One suggestion is that the FFA is the location of a *process*—fine-level discrimination of homogeneous categories. However, this is an analgesic answer—it makes us feel better, but it just covers up the problem by giving it a name. A modeler wants to know *how* this happens—what is the mechanism? In a series of papers, Cottrell and colleagues have addressed this as a question that can be solved by modeling (Joyce & Cottrell, 2004; Sugimoto & Cottrell, 2001; Tong et al., 2005; Tong et al., 2008). Following Dailey and Cottrell (1999), the model assumes that there are two networks (corresponding to two cortical areas) that have competed such that one becomes specialized for categorizing objects at the basic level (modeling LOC or other visual processing areas), and the other is specialized for the subordinate/expert level (i.e., it corresponds to the FFA). Aside from their tasks, the two networks have identical processing resources in their hidden layers. Despite this, the model displays the entry-level shift in response times—RT's (modeled as the uncertainty of the output) are just as fast for expert-level responses as for basic-level ones as in humans (Gauthier & Tarr, 1997). These two networks are then placed in a competition to learn a new category of objects at the expert level. The consistent result is that the expert network always learns the new expertise category first. This occurs even if the first category of expertise is not faces; hence, there is nothing special about faces per se. Indeed, a model trained to individuate donuts learns to individuate swords faster than a basic-level categorizer. Thus, the rather fanciful conclusion is that if our parents were donuts, the fusiform donut area would win the competition for new categories of expertise.

The model can then be analyzed to determine why the expert network won. The analysis reveals that the expert network spreads the stimuli into broader regions of representational space. That is, as in the Valentine model, faces are spread out in representational space, while objects are localized. This makes sense given that we need to ignore within-class variability in order to categorize an object, while we need to amplify to within-class variability in order to individuate members of a category. The mapping from the inputs to the hidden units amplifies variability for expert objects, and this spreading transformation generalizes to new objects. Thus, the expert network has a head start in differentiating new objects from one another. The model also predicts that there will be relatively greater within-class variability in neural responses within the FFA as compared to object recognition areas, a prediction that can be tested neurophysiologically.

In terms of the other core features of perceptual expertise, the model accounts for speedups in processing due to the development of expertise. This phenomenon can be explained in terms of the connection strengths to the correct outputs growing with learning. The correct outputs are then turned on with less uncertainty, which leads to faster response times. The entry-level shift is explained in a similar fashion, combined with the non-linearity in the outputs. As the connection strengths to the correct output are increased, the activity of the correct output increases, but it reaches a maximum level, so that uncertainty cannot be reduced beyond a floor. Hence, the subordinate-level category outputs reach the same level of activity as the category-level outputs and can go no further, so the corresponding response times are the same. Thus, this model shows that the entry-level shift can be explained as a continuous, quantitative change in the efficiency of processing over learning (Joyce & Cottrell, 2004). We should note that while the model accounts well for speedups with expertise, the model itself has no inherent temporal dynamics; response times are assumed to be inversely related to categorization certainty.

The model also shows the same pattern as experts in being unable to ignore variation in an unattended part (Cottrell et al., 2002). Specifically, the model can be modified to "pay attention" to half of the face by simply attenuating the input from part of the face. In these circumstances, the model shows interference from unattended parts of the face and also shows the same specific interaction between changes in identity and expression that is seen in human subjects (Calder et al., 2000). This form of holistic processing can be explained in terms of the whole-face templates that are developed at the PCA level (while this layer is like the eigenfaces in other models, in this model, it is "eigen-Gabor-faces," but the principle is the same). Suppose the model is presented with George Bush's face in the upper half of the input, and Al Gore's face in the lower half of the input. If there is a template (principal component) that preferably matches Al Gore's face, it will be partially matched by the input, and so will fire at a reduced level and pass this activation on to later layers. However, there is no way for these later layers to "know" what part of the input was matched – this template is voting for *all* of Al Gore's face, including his eyes, and so there is interference in recognizing the top half of the input as George Bush.

The model is also able to account for the way that experts generalize their knowledge, given the way they are trained to categorize the objects

(Nguyen & Cottrell, 2005). Specifically, subjects will fail to improve their discrimination of new examples of a category of objects when they have been trained only to give the same label (i.e., categorize) that set of objects (Tanaka, Curran, & Sheinberg, 2005). However, when they are trained to the individual level (in this case, the species of a type of bird, owls or wading birds), they then improve their discrimination in a graded fashion depending on the similarity of the novel examples to the trained categories. As with the explanation of the recruitment of the FFA for new objects of expertise, the result is explained in terms of within-class versus between-class variance in the representations required for basic-level categorization versus expert-level categorization. The internal representations are more differentiated for objects of expertise, and when new examples of the expert category are presented, they are more or less differentiated, depending upon their similarity to the trained expert class. On the other hand, when a large number of objects are categorized as "the same" by being given the same label (e.g., "owls" or "wading birds"), then the internal representations of those objects are pushed closer together by the learning mechanism and hence are less differentiated.

Finally, the model is impaired by inversion in the same way human subjects are (Ge et al., 2006; Mondloch et al., 2002). This can be explained entirely by the principal components level of the model (McCleery et al., 2008; Zhang & Cottrell, 2006). The principal components are sensitive to the orientation of the training data. If most of the training data is upright, and the objects of expertise have quite different statistics when inverted, the representation of inverted objects is relatively undifferentiated. The model is able to explain the difference in priming effects between inverted Chinese characters and faces, two types of expertise (McCleery et al., 2008), as well as the *development* of the sensitivity to configural, featural, and contour differences between upright and inverted faces (Zhang & Cottrell, 2006).

This model has not been tested against the data on the transition from verbalizable rules to automated processing, but connectionist mechanisms exist for making this transition (Noelle & Cottrell, 1996). Furthermore, the interference patterns seen in n-back tasks between different areas of expertise (Gauthier & Curby, 2005; Gauthier et al., 2003) have not been investigated. Adding residual activation patterns to the units in the model to implement the role of previous processing might accomplish this, but at this point, this is mere speculation. Even with the success of the model so far, it is important to systematically explore what phenomena it can't account for.

SUMMARY AND CLOSING THOUGHTS

What makes an expert an expert? Experts perceive objects in their area of expertise better than novices. Do they perceive differently? Experts know more than novices; that's what makes them experts, after all. They have a deeper and more fine-grained understanding about objects in their area of expertise. Is their knowledge fundamentally different from what novices know, or do they just know more and do they know it better? Experts make faster and more accurate decisions than novices. Are experts using information to make decisions in a way that novices simply cannot? Or are experts using that information more effectively?

Although perception, knowledge, and decisions by experts could be qualitatively different from novices—in that the mechanisms underlying expertise might operate under completely different principles from those underlying novice performance—computational models allow us to explore whether qualitative changes in behavior might emerge from quantitative changes in perception and memory over the course of learning. A number of key expertise effects can indeed be explained by using models of normal object recognition and perceptual categorization that learn representations, select representations, strengthen representations, and sharpen representations, without having to invoke qualitative changes. From a neural perspective, it is far easier to envision incremental changes in the brain from those that support novice object recognition to those that support expert object recognition than it is to envision creating a new special-purpose module for an expert domain. That certainly could happen, especially over the course of evolution or maybe over the course of development, and expertise does take a long time to develop (e.g., Ericsson & Lehmann, 1996; Ericsson et al., 2006). But so far we have not needed to invoke this kind of modular restructuring to explain many of the important behavioral or neural changes that take place over the development of perceptual expertise.

One basic question that seems not fully resolved is the specific locus for changes that take place with perceptual expertise. For example, are holistic processing effects that emerge with expertise best explained by changes in how objects are perceived, how decisions are made about those objects, or some combination of the two (Cheung et al., 2008; Richler et al., 2008)? We could also ask whether perceptual expertise is driven by changes in how we perceive objects or what we know and remember about objects, but the boundaries between perception and memory are rather fuzzy (e.g., Palmeri & Tarr, 2008). Category representations are strongly influenced by the particular category exemplars that have been experienced, and object representations are strongly influenced by the particular views of objects that have been experienced—so what you know about a category of objects and how you perceive objects from a well-known category depends on some kind of memory for what you've seen before. Open questions remain regarding issues such as how densely the space of experienced exemplars is represented (e.g., Ashby & Waldron, 1999; Palmeri et al., 2004), whether view-based representations are full templates (e.g., Riesenhuber & Poggio, 1999), view-based parts (e.g., Ullman et al., 2002), or somewhere in between (Zhang & Cottrell, 2005), and the extent to which representations are localist (e.g., Ashby & Waldron, 1999; Kruschke, 1992) versus distributed (e.g., Dailey & Cottrell, 1999).

Models need to take time seriously. As we documented, many of the key phenomena of perceptual expertise involve time. It is not sufficient to simply correlate the output activations of a model with mean observed response times. Trade-offs between speed and accuracy are far more complex and far more interesting (e.g., Lamberts, 2000; Mack et al., 2007, 2008). There are important details in distributions of response times that are not captured by simply examining the mean or the median RT (e.g., Townsend, 1990), so models should produce distributions of RTs (e.g., Lamberts, 2000; Nosofsky & Palmeri, 1997; Palmeri, 1999). Behavior changes with the temporal dynamics of the stimulus (e.g., Grill-Spector & Kanwisher, 2005; Mack et al., 2008), so models need to be dynamic. The precise timing of neural events is the cornerstone of neurophysiological studies (e.g., Anderson & Sheinberg, 2008; Mruczek & Sheinberg, 2008) and ERP studies (e.g., Scott et al., 2006; Tanaka & Curran, 2001), and techniques are emerging to significantly improve the temporal resolution of fMRI (e.g., Dux, Ivanoff, Asplund, & Marois, 2006). Process models must not only account for the timing of behavior, but the precise timing revealed by the neural markers as well (e.g., see Boucher et al., 2007). While efforts have been made to develop models of perceptual categorization and perceptual decision making that take time seriously, many object processing models are static (e.g., Dailey & Cottrell, 1999; Riesenhuber & Poggio, 1999). Given the growing body of cognitive neuroscience data on the timing of object recognition and how it changes with perceptual expertise, models of high-level vision need to incorporate these temporal dynamics.

Despite the plethora of models we have reviewed in this chapter, there is a surprising amount of theoretical convergence toward a comprehensive computational model of perceptual expertise. Over the years, research in object recognition and perceptual categorization has approached questions of visual cognition with somewhat surprising independence yet has arrived at theories that share important properties (Palmeri & Gauthier, 2004). A challenge will be putting the pieces together. The model of object recognition proposed by Riesenhuber and Poggio (1999; Serra et al., 2007) shares important computational principles of exemplar category representations as models of categorization proposed by Nosofsky, Kruschke, and others (e.g., Kruschke, 1992; Nosofsky & Kruschke, 1992). Categorization models have stressed the critical importance of learned selective attention to diagnostic properties of objects relevant to particular categorizations (e.g., Nosofsky, 1984, 1986) and have played close attention to how perceptual decisions are made (e.g., Lamberts, 2000; Nosofsky & Palmeri, 1997), neither of which have been the focus of object processing models. Object processing models have tried to make reasonable assumptions about lower-level visual processing (Dailey & Cottrell, 1999; Riesenhuber & Poggio, 1999, 2001), whereas categorization models typically start with representations suggested by careful psychophysical scaling studies without worrying about how those representations arise, probably at their detriment.

A comprehensive model of perceptual expertise must incorporate all of these various components. It's probably clear from our review that we believe this comprehensive model of perceptual expertise will also be a comprehensive model of normal object recognition and categorization as well, with expertise merely the end point of normal learning. One challenge in this endeavor is balancing the need for a model that spans perception, memory, and decisions, accounts for existing data, and predicts new results with an honest appraisal of the complexity that might encumber such an omnibus model. While having a model that works in the real world and behaves like people do is the goal of machine learning, artificial intelligence, and robotics, it's not the ultimate goal of psychology and neuroscience. Arguably, having a model that really "works" on real images in real time has an advantage over one that is more theoretical. But if such a model is burdened with so many ad hoc processing assumptions and freely tuned parameters in order to make it "work," then it fails as a viable and testable theory that can be falsified. Our challenge then is to balance these competing goals as we move toward more powerful and comprehensive theories of perceptual expertise.

REFERENCES

Allen, S. W., & Brooks, L. R. (1991). Specializing the operation of an explicit rule. *Journal of Experimental Psychology: General, 120,* 3–19.

Anderson, J. R. (1976). Language, memory, and thought. Hillsdale, NJ: Erlbaum.

Anderson, J. R. (1990). The adaptive character of thought. Hillsdale, NJ: Erlbaum.

Anderson, J. R., & Betz. J. (2001). A hybrid model of categorization. *Psychonomic Bulletin & Review, 8,* 629–647.

Anderson, B., & Sheinberg, D. L. (2008). Effects of temporal context and temporal expectancy on neural activity in inferior temporal cortex. *Neuropsychologia, 46*(4), 947–957.

Ashby, F. G. (1992). Multidimensional models of perception and cognition. Hillsdale, NJ, Lawrence Erlbaum Associates, Inc.

Ashby, F. G., Alfonso-Reese, L. A., Turken, A. U., & Waldron, E. M. (1998). A formal neuropsychological theory of multiple systems in category learning. *Psychological Review, 105,* 442–481.

Ashby, F. G., Ennis, J. M., & Spiering, B. J. (2007). A neurobiological theory of automaticity in perceptual categorization. *Psychological Review, 114,* 632–656.

Ashby, F. G., & Waldron, E. M. (1999). On the nature of implicit categorization. *Psychonomic Bulletin & Review, 6,* 363–378.

Biederman, I. (1987). Recognition-by-components: A theory of human image understanding. *Psychological Review, 94,* 115–147.

Bishop, C. M. (1995). Neural networks for pattern recognition. London: Oxford University Press.

Blanz, V., O'Toole, A. J., Vetter, T., & Wild, H. A. (2000). On the other side of the mean: The perception of dissimilarity in human faces. *Perception, 29,* 885–891.

Boucher, L., Palmeri, T. J., Logan, G. D., & Schall, J. D. (2007). Interactive race model of countermanding saccades. *Psychological Review, 114,* 376–397.

Brooks, L. R., Norman, G. R., & Allen, S. W. (1991). Role of specific similarity in a medical diagnostic task. *Journal of Experimental Psychology: General, 120,* 278–287.

Bruce, V., & Young, A. (1986). Understanding face recognition. *British Journal of Psychology, 77,* 305–327.

Bruner, J. S., Goodnow, J. J., & Austin, G. A. (1956). A study of thinking. Oxford, England: Wiley.

Bülthoff, H. H., & Edelman, S. (1992). Psychophysical support for a two-dimensional view interpolation theory of object recognition. *Proceedings of the National Academy of Sciences, 89,* 60–64.

Bundesen, C. (1990). A theory of visual attention. *Psychological Review, 97,* 523–547.

Burton, A. M., & Bruce, V. (1993). Naming faces and naming names: Exploring an interactive activation model of person recognition. *Memory, 1,* 457–480.

Burton, A. M, Bruce, V., & Hancock, P. J. B. (1999). From pixels to people: A model of familiar face recognition. *Cognitive Science, 23,* 1–31.

Burton, A. M., Bruce, V., & Johnston, R. A. (1990). Understanding face recognition with an interactive activation model. *British Journal of Psychology, 81,* 361–380.

Busemeyer, J. R., Dewey, G. I., & Medin, D. L. (1984). Evaluation of exemplar-based generalization and the abstraction of categorical information. *Journal of Experimental Psychology: Learning, Memory, and Cognition, 10,* 638–648.

Busemeyer, J. R., & Wang, Y. (2000). Model comparisons and model selections based on the generalization criterion methodology. *Journal of Mathematical Psychology, 44,* 171–189.

Calder, A. J., Young, A. W., Keane, J., & Dean, M. (2000). Configural information in facial expression perception. *Journal of Experimental Psychology: Human Perception and Performance, 26,* 527–551.

Cheung, O. S., Richler, J. J., Palmeri, T. J., & Gauthier, I. (2008). Revisiting the role of spatial frequencies in the holistic processing of faces. *Journal of Experimental Psychology: Human Perception and Performance, 34,* 1327–1336.

Cohen, A. L., & Nosofsky, R. M. (2003). An extension of the exemplar-based random-walk model to separable-dimension stimuli. *Journal of Mathematical Psychology, 47,* 150–165.

Collins, A. M., & Quillian, M. R. (1969). Retrieval time from semantic memory. *Journal of Verbal Learning and Verbal Behavior, 8,* 240–247.

Cottrell, G. W., Branson, K., & Calder, A. J. (2002). Do expression and identity need separate representations? In *Proceedings of the 24th Annual Cognitive Science Conference, Fairfax, Virginia.* Mahwah, NJ: Lawrence Erlbaum.

Cottrell, G. W., & Metcalfe, J. (1991). EMPATH: Face, gender and emotion recognition using holons. In R. P. Lippman, J. Moody, & D. S. Touretzky (Eds.), *Advances in neural information processing systems, Vol. 3* (pp. 564–571), San Mateo, CA: Morgan Kaufmann.

Dailey, M. N., & Cottrell, G. W. (1999). Organization of face and object recognition in modular neural network models. *Neural Networks, 12,* 1053–1073.

Dailey, M. N., Cottrell, G. W., & Busey, T. A. (1998). Eigenfaces for familiarity. In *Proceedings of the Twentieth Annual Cognitive Science Conference.* Madison, WI, Mahwah: Lawrence Erlbaum.

Dailey, M. N., Cottrell, G. W., Padgett, C., & Adolphs, R. (2002). Empath: A neural network that categorizes facial expressions. *Journal of Cognitive Neuroscience, 14,* 1158–1173.

Diamond, R., & Carey, S. (1986). Why faces are and are not special: An effect of expertise. *Journal of Experimental Psychology: General, 115,* 107–117.

Dux, P. E., Ivanoff, J. G., Asplund, C. L., & Marois, R. (2006). Isolation of a central bottleneck of information processing with time-resolved fMRI. *Neuron, 52,* 1109–1120.

Edelman, S. (1997). Computational theories of object recognition. *Trends in Cognitive Sciences, 1,* 296–304.

Edelman, S. (1999). *Representation and recognition in vision.* Cambridge, MA: MIT Press.

Edelman, S., & Bülthoff, H. H. (1992). Orientation dependence in the recognition of familiar and novel views of three-dimensional objects. *Vision Research, 32,* 2385–2400.

Ericsson, K. A., Charness, N., Feltovich, P., & Hoffman, R. R. (2006). *Cambridge handbook of expertise and expert performance.* Cambridge: Cambridge University Press.

Ericsson, K. A., & Lehmann, A. C. (1996). Expert and exceptional performance: Evidence of maximal adaptations to task constraints. *Annual Review of Psychology, 47,* 273–305.

Erickson, M. A., & Kruschke, J. K. (2002). Rule-based extrapolation in perceptual categorization. *Psychonomic Bulletin and Review, 9,* 160–168.

Erickson, M. A., & Kruschke, J. K. (1998). Rules and exemplars in category learning. *Journal of Experimental Psychology: General, 127,* 107–140.

Estes, W. K. (1994). *Classification and Cognition.* London: Oxford University Press.

Farah, M. J., Wilson, K. D., Drain, M., & Tanaka, J. N. (1998). What is "special" about face perception? *Psychological Review, 105,* 482–498.

Fleming, M., & Cottrell, G. W. (1990). Categorization of faces using unsupervised feature extraction. *Proceedings of the International Joint Conference on Neural Networks, 2,* 65–70.

Frank, M. J., & Claus, E. D. (2006). Anatomy of a decision: Striato-orbitofrontal interactions in reinforcement learning, decision making and reversal. *Psychological Review, 113,* 300–326.

Furl, N., Phillips, P. J., & O'Toole, A. J. (2002). Face recognition algorithms as models of the other race effect. *Cognitive Science, 96,* 1–19.

Gauthier, I., & Curby, K.M., (2005). A perceptual traffic-jam on highway N170: Interference between face and car expertise. *Current Directions in Psychological Science, 4,* 30–33.

Gauthier, I., Curran, T., Curby, K. M., & Collins, D. (2003). Perceptual interference supports a non-modular account of face processing. *Nature Neuroscience, 6,* 428–432.

Gauthier, I., & Palmeri, T. J. (2002). Visual neurons: Categorization-based selectivity. *Current Biology, 12,* R282–R284.

Gauthier, I., Skudlarski, P., Gore, J. C., & Anderson, A. W. (2000). Expertise for cars and birds recruits brain areas involved in face recognition. *Nature Neuroscience, 3,* 191–197.

Gauthier, I., & Tarr, M. J. (1997). Becoming a "greeble" expert: Exploring mechanisms for face recognition. *Vision Research, 37,* 1673–1682.

Gauthier, I., & Tarr, M. J. (2002). Unraveling mechanisms for expert object recognition: Bridging brain activity and behavior. *Journal of Experimental Psychology: Human Perception & Performance, 28,* 431–446.

Gauthier, I., Tarr, M. J., Moylan, J., Skudlarski, P., Gore, J. C. & Anderson, A. W. (2000). The fusiform "face area" is part of a network that processes faces at the individual level. *Journal of Cognitive Neuroscience, 12,* 495–504.

Ge, L., Wang, Z., McCleery, J., & Lee, K. (2006). Activation of face expertise and the inversion effect. *Psychological Science, 17*(1), 12–16.

Golomb, B. A., Lawrence, D. T., & Sejnowski, T. J. (1991). Sexnet: A neural network identifies sex from human faces. In R. P. Lippman, J. Moody, & D. S. Touretzky (Eds.), *Advances in neural information processing systems, Vol. 3* (pp. 572–577), San Mateo, CA: Morgan Kaufmann.

Goodman, N. D., Tenenbaum, J. B., Feldman, J., & Griffiths, T. L. (2008). A rational analysis of rule-based concept learning. *Cognitive Science, 32,* 108–154.

Grill-Spector, K., & Kanwisher, N. (2005). Visual recognition: As soon as you know it is there, you know what it is. *Psychological Science, 16,* 152–160.

Grill-Spector, K., Knouf, N., & Kanwisher, N. (2004). The fusiform face area subserves face perception, not generic within-category identification. *Nature Neuroscience, 7,* 555–562.

Hancock, P. J. B., Burton, A. M., & Bruce, V. (1996). Face processing: Human perception and principal components analysis. *Memory & Cognition, 24,* 26–40.

Haque, A., & Cottrell, G. W. (2005). Modeling the other race advantage. In *Proceedings of the 27th Annual Cognitive Science Conference, La Stresa, Italy.* Mahwah, NJ: Lawrence Erlbaum.

Heathcote, A., Brown, S., & Mewhort, D. J. K. (2000). Repealing the power law: The case for an exponential law of practice. *Psychonomic Bulletin & Review, 7,* 185–207.

Hinton, G. E., & Shallice, T. (1991). Lesioning an attractor network: Investigations of acquired dyslexia. *Psychological Review, 98,* 74–95.

Hintzman, D. L. (1986). "Schema abstraction" in a multiple-trace memory model. *Psychological Review, 93,* 411–428.

Hintzman, D. L. (1990). Human learning and memory: Connections and dissociations. *Annual Review of Psychology, 41,* 109–139.

Hsiao, J., & Cottrell, G. W. (2008). Not all expertise is holistic, but it may be leftist: The case of Chinese character recognition. *Psychological Science, 10,* 998–1006.

Homa, D. (1978). Abstraction of ill-defined form. *Journal of Experimental Psychology: Human Learning and Memory, 4,* 407–416.

Hummel, J. E., & Biederman, I. (1992). Dynamic binding in a neural network for shape recognition. *Psychological Review, 99,* 480–517.

Hunt, E. B., Marin, J., & Stone, P. J. (1966). *Experiments in induction.* New York: Academic Press.

Ivry, R., & Robertson, L. C. (1998). The two sides of perception. Cambridge, MA: MIT Press.

Jäkel, F., Schölkopf, B., & Wichmann, F. A. (2007). A tutorial on kernel methods for categorization. *Journal of Mathematical Psychology, 51,* 343–358.

Jäkel, F., Schölkopf, B., & Wichmann, F. A. (2008). Generalization and similarity in exemplar models of categorization: Insights from machine learning. *Psychonomic Bulletin & Review, 15,* 256–271.

Jiang, X., Rosen, E., Zeffiro, T., VanMeter, J., Blanz, V., & Riesenhuber, M. (2006). Evaluation of a shape-based model of human face discrimination using fMRI and behavioral techniques. *Neuron, 50,* 159–172.

Jiang, X., Bradley, E., Rini, R.A., Zeffiro, T., VanMeter, J., & Riesenhuber, M. (2007). Categorization training results in shape- and category-selective human neural plasticity. *Neuron, 53,* 891–903.

Johansen, M. K., & Palmeri, T. J. (2002). Are there representational shifts during category learning? *Cognitive Psychology, 45,* 482–553.

Johnson, K. E., & Mervis, C. B. (1997). Effects of varying levels of expertise on the basic level of categorization. *Journal of Experimental Psychology: General, 126,* 248–277.

Jolicoeur, P., Gluck, M. A., & Kosslyn, S. M. (1984). Pictures and names: Making the connection. *Cognitive Psychology, 16,* 243–275.

Joyce, C., & Cottrell, G. W. (2004). Solving the visual expertise mystery In H. Bowman & Labiouse, C. (Eds.), *Connectionist models of cognition and perception II: Proceedings of the eighth neural computation and psychology workshop.* Hackensack, NJ: World Scientific.

Kanade, T. (1973). *Picture processing system by computer complex and recognition of human faces.* Unpublished doctoral thesis, Department of Information Science, Kyoto University.

Kim, N. S., & Ahn, W. (2002). Clinical psychologists' theory-based representations of mental disorders predict their diagnostic reasoning and memory. *Journal of Experimental Psychology: General, 131,* 451–476.

Kohonen, T., Lehtio, P., Oja, E., Kortekangas, A., & Makisara, K. (1977). Demonstration of pattern processing properties of the optimal associative mappings. In *Proceedings of the International Conference on Cybernetics and Society: IEEE,* Washington, D.C.

Kruschke, J. K. (1992). ALCOVE: An exemplar-based connectionist model of category learning. *Psychological Review, 99,* 22–44.

Lamberts, K. (1995). Categorization under time pressure. *Journal of Experimental Psychology: General, 124,* 161–180.

Lamberts, K. (2000). Information-accumulation theory of speeded categorization. *Psychological Review, 107,* 227–260.

Logan, G. D. (1988). Toward an instance theory of automatization. *Psychological Review, 95,* 492–527.

Logan, G. D. (1992). Shapes of reaction time distributions and shapes of learning curves: A test of the instance theory of automaticity. *Journal of Experimental Psychology: Learning, Memory and Cognition, 18,* 883–914.

Logan, G. D. (2002). An instance theory of attention and memory. *Psychological Review, 109,* 376–400.

Logan, G. D. (2004). Cumulative progress in formal theories of attention. *Annual Review of Psychology, 55,* 207–234.

Logan, G. D., & Gordon, R. D. (2001). Executive control of visual attention in dual-task situations. *Psychological Review, 108,* 393–434.

Love, B. C., Medin, D. L., & Gureckis, T. M. (2004). SUSTAIN: A network model of category learning. *Psychological Review, 111,* 309–332.

Luce, R. D. (1959). *Individual choice behavior.* New York: Wiley.

Luce, R. D. (1995). Four tensions concerning mathematical modeling in psychology. *Annual Reviews of Psychology, 46,* 1–26.

Mack, M. L., Gauthier, I., Sadr, J., & Palmeri, T. J. (2008). Object detection and basic-level categorization: Sometimes you know it is there before you know what it is. *Psychonomic Bulletin & Review, 15,* 28–35.

Mack, M. L., Richler, J. J., Palmeri, T. J., & Gauthier, I. (in press). Categorization. To appear in G. G. Berntson & J. T. Cacioppo (Eds.), *Handbook of neuroscience for the behavioral sciences.*

Mack, M. L., Wong, A. C.-N., Gauthier, I., Tanaka, J. W., & Palmeri, T. J. (2007). Unraveling the time-course of perceptual categorization: Does fastest mean first? *Proceedings of the Twenty-Ninth Annual Meeting of the Cognitive Science Society.* New York: Erlbaum.

Marr, D. (1982). *Vision: A computational investigation into the human representation and processing of visual information.* San Francisco, CA: Freeman.

Marr, D., & Nishihara, H. K. (1978). Representation and recognition of the spatial organization of three-dimensional shapes. *Proceedings of the Royal Society of London, Series B, Biological Sciences, 200,* 269–294.

Maurer, D., LeGrand, R. L., & Mondloch, C. J. (2002). The many faces of configural processing. *Trends in Cognitive Sciences, 6,* 255–260.

McCandliss, B. D., Cohen, L., & Dehaene, S. (2003). The visual word form area: Expertise for reading in the fusiform gyrus. *Trends in Cognitive Sciences, 7,* 293–299.

McCleery, J. P., Zhang, L., Ge, L., Wang, Z., Christiansen, E. M., Lee, K., and Cottrell, G.W. (2008). The roles of visual expertise and visual input in the face inversion effect: Behavioral and neurocomputational evidence. *Vision Research, 48,* 703–715.

McClelland, J. L., & Rumelhart, D. E. (1985). Distributed memory and the representation of general and specific information. *Journal of Experimental Psychology: General, 114,* 159–188.

McKone, E., Kanwisher, N., & Duchaine, B. (2007). Can generic expertise explain special processing for faces? *Trends in Cognitive Sciences, 11,* 8–15.

Medin, D. L., & Schaffer, M. M. (1978). A context theory of classification learning. *Psychological Review, 85,* 207–238.

Minda, J. P., & Smith, J. D. (2000). Prototypes in category learning: The effects of category size, category structure, and stimulus complexity. *Journal of Experimental Psychology: Learning, Memory, and Cognition, 27,* 775–799.

Mondloch, C. J., LeGrand, R., & Maurer, D. (2002). Configural face processing develops more slowly than featural face processing. *Perception, 31,* 553–566.

Moore, E. F. (1956). Gedanken-experiments on sequential machines. *Automata Studies, Annals of Mathematical Studies, 34,* 129–153.

Mruczek, R., & Sheinberg, D. L. (2008). Activity of inferior temporal cortical neurons predicts recognition choice behavior and recognition time during visual search. *Journal of Neuroscience, 27*(11), 2825–2836.

Murphy, G. L., & Wright, J. C. (1984). Changes in conceptual structure with expertise: Differences between real-world experts and novices. *Journal of Experimental Psychology: Learning, Memory, and Cognition, 10,* 144–155.

Myung, I. J. (1994). Maximum entropy interpretation of decision bound and context models of categorization. *Journal of Mathematical Psychology, 38,* 335–365.

Newell, A., & Rosenbloom, P. S. (1981). Mechanisms of skill acquisition and the law of practice. In J. R. Anderson (Ed.), *Cognitive skills and their acquisition* (pp. 1–55). Hillsdale, NJ: Erlbaum.

Nguyen, N., & Cottrell, G. W. (2005). *Owls and wading birds: Generalization gradients in expertise.* Proceedings of the 27th Annual Cognitive Science Conference, La Stresa, Italy. Mahwah, NJ: Lawrence Erlbaum.

Noelle, D. C., & Cottrell, G. W. (1996). *Modeling interference effects in instructed category learning.* Paper presented at the 18th Annual Conference of the Cognitive Science Society, La Jolla, CA.

Nosofsky, R. M. (1984). Choice, similarity, and the context theory of classification. *Journal of Experimental Psychology: Learning, Memory and Cognition, 10,* 104–114.

Nosofsky, R. M. (1986). Attention, similarity, and the identification–categorization relationship. *Journal of Experimental Psychology: General, 115,* 39–57.

Nosofsky, R. M. (1987). Attention and learning processes in the identification and categorization of integral stimuli. *Journal of Experimental Psychology: Learning, Memory, and Cognition, 13,* 87–108.

Nosofsky, R. M. (1992a). Exemplar-based approach to relating categorization, identification, and recognition. In F. G. Ashby (Ed.), *Multidimensional models of perception and cognition.* Scientific psychology series (pp. 363–393). Hillsdale, NJ, England: Lawrence Erlbaum Associates, Inc.

Nosofsky, R. M. (1992b). Similarity scaling and cognitive process models. *Annual Review of Psychology, 43,* 25–53.

Nosofsky, R. M. (1998). Optimal performance and exemplar models of classification. In M. Oaksford and N. Chater (Eds.), *Rational models of cognition,* London: Oxford University Press.

Nosofsky, R. M., & Alfonso-Reese, L. A. (1999). Effects of similarity and practice on speeded classification response times and accuracies: Further tests of an exemplar-retrieval model. *Memory & Cognition, 27,* 78–93.

Nosofsky, R. M., Gluck, M., Palmeri, T. J., McKinley, S. C., & Glauthier, P. (1994). Comparing models of rule-based classification learning: A replication and extension of Shepard, Hovland, and Jenkins (1961). *Memory & Cognition, 22,* 352–369.

Nosofsky, R. M., & Johansen, M. K. (2000). Exemplar-based accounts of "multiple-system" phenomena in perceptual categorization. *Psychonomic Bulletin & Review, 7,* 375–402.

Nosofsky, R. M., & Kruschke, J. K. (1992). Investigations of an exemplar-based connectionist model of category learning. In D. L. Medin (Ed.), *The Psychology of Learning and Motivation,* Vol. 28 (pp. 207–250). San Diego, CA: Academic Press.

Nosofsky, R. M., & Palmeri, T. J. (1996). Learning to classify integral-dimension stimuli. *Psychonomic Bulletin & Review, 3,* 222–226.

Nosofsky, R. M., & Palmeri, T. J. (1997). An exemplar-based random walk model of speeded classification. *Psychological Review, 104,* 266–300.

Nosofsky, R. M. (1998). Optimal performance and exemplar models of classification. In M. Oaksford & N. Chater, (Eds.), *Rational Models of Cognition.* London: Oxford University Press.

Nosofsky, R. M., & Palmeri, T. J. (1998). A rule-plus-exception model for classifying objects in continuous-dimension spaces. *Psychonomic Bulletin & Review, 5,* 345–369.

Nosofsky, R. M., Palmeri, T. J., & McKinley, S. C. (1994). Rule-plus-exception model of classification learning. *Psychological Review, 101,* 53–79.

Okada, K., Steffans, J., Maurer, T., Hong, H., Elagin, E., Neven, H., & Malsburg, C. v. d. (1998). The Bochum/USC face recognition system and how it fared in the FERET phase III test. In H. Wechsler, P. J. Phillips, V. Bruce, F. F. Soulie, and T. S. Huang (Eds.), *Face recognition: From theory to applications* (pp. 186–205), Berlin: Springer-Verlag.

O'Toole, A. J., Abdi, H., Deffenbacher, K., & Valentin, D. (1993). Low-dimensional representation of faces in higher dimensions of the face space. *Journal of the Optical Society of America, 10,* 405–411.

O'Toole, A. J., Deffenbacher, K., Valentin, D., & Abdi, H. (1994). Structural aspects of face recognition and the other-race effect. *Memory & Cognition, 22,* 208–224.

Padgett, C., & Cottrell, G. W. (1997). Representing face images for emotion classification. In M. C. Mozer, M. I. Jordan, & T. Petsche (Eds.), *Advances in neural information processing systems 9* (pp. 894–900). Cambridge, MA: MIT Press.

Padgett, C., & Cottrell, G. W. (1998). A simple neural network models categorical perception of facial expressions. In *Proceedings of the Twentieth Annual Cognitive Science Conference.* Madison, WI, Mahwah, NJ: Lawrence Erlbaum.

Palmeri, T. J. (1997). Exemplar similarity and the development of automaticity. *Journal of Experimental Psychology: Learning, Memory, and Cognition, 23,* 324–354.

Palmeri, T. J. (1999). Theories of automaticity and the power law of practice. *Journal of Experimental Psychology: Learning, Memory, and Cognition, 25,* 543–551.

Palmeri, T. J., & Flanery, M. A. (2002). Memory systems and perceptual categorization. In B. H. Ross (Ed.), *The psychology of learning and motivation* (Vol. 41, pp. 141–189), New York, NY: Academic Press.

Palmeri, T. J., & Gauthier, I. (2004). Visual object understanding. *Nature Reviews Neuroscience, 5,* 291–303.

Palmeri, T. J., & Nosofsky, R. M. (2001). Central tendencies, extreme points, and prototype enhancement effects in ill-defined perceptual categorization. *The Quarterly Journal of Experimental Psychology, 54,* 197–235.

Palmeri, T. J., & Tarr (2008). Object recognition and long-term visual memory for objects. In S. Luck & A. Hollingsworth (Eds.), *Visual memory.* London: Oxford University Press.

Palmeri, T. J., Wong, A. C. N., & Gauthier, I. (2004). Computational approaches to the development of perceptual expertise. *Trends in Cognitive Sciences, 8,* 378–386.

Phillips, R (1991). *Mushrooms of North America.* Boston, MA: Little, Brown and Company.

Pitt, M. A., Kim, W., Navarro, D. J., & Myung, J. I. (2006). Global model analysis by parameter space partitioning. *Psychological Review, 113,* 57–83.

Pitt, M. A., Myung, I. J., & Zhang, S. (2002). Toward a method of selecting among computational models of cognition. *Psychological Review, 109,* 472–491.

Platt, J. R. (1964). Strong inference. *Science, 146,* 347–353.

Plaut, D. C. (1995). Double dissociation without modularity: Evidence from connectionist neuropsychology. *Journal of Clinical and Experimental Neuropsychology, 17,* 291–321.

Plaut, D. C., McClelland, J. L., Seidenberg, M. S., and Patterson, K. (1996). Understanding normal and impaired word reading: Computational principles in quasi-regular domains. *Psychological Review, 103,* 56–115.

Plaut, D. C., & Shallice, T. (1993). Deep dyslexia: A case study of connectionist neuropsychology. *Cognitive Neuropsychology, 10,* 377–500.

Plunkett, K., & Juola, P. (1999) A connectionist model of English past tense and plural morphology. *Cognitive Science, 23,* 463–490.

Poggio, T., & Edelman, S. (1990). A network that learns to recognize three-dimensional objects. *Nature, 343,* 263–266.

Posner, M. I., & Keele, S. W. (1968). On the genesis of abstract ideas. *Journal of Experimental Psychology, 77,* 353–363.

Ratcliff, R. (1978). A theory of memory retrieval. *Psychological Review, 85,* 59–108.

Ratcliff, R., & Rouder, J. N. (1998). Modeling response time for decisions between two choices. *Psychological Science, 9,* 347–356.

Ratcliff, R., & Smith, P. L. (2004). A comparison of sequential sampling models for two-choice reaction time. *Psychological Review, 111,* 333–367.

Reed, S. K. (1972). Pattern recognition and categorization. *Cognitive Psychology, 3,* 382–407.

Regehr, G., & Brooks, L. R. (1993). Perceptual manifestations of an analytic structure: The priority of holistic individuation. *Journal of Experimental Psychology: General, 122,* 92–114.

Richler, J., Gauthier, I., Wenger, M., & Palmeri, T. J. (2008). Holistic processing of faces. *Journal of Experimental Psychology: Learning, Memory, and Cognition, 34,* 328–342.

Rickard, T. C. (1997). Bending the power law: A CMPL theory of strategy shifts and the automatization of cognitive skills. *Journal of Experimental Psychology: General, 126,* 288–311.

Riesenhuber, M., & Poggio, T. (1999). Hierarchical models of object recognition in cortex. *Nature Neuroscience, 2,* 1019–1025.

Riesenhuber, M., & Poggio, T. (2000). Models of object recognition. *Nature Neuroscience, 3*(Suppl.), 1199–1204.

Robbins, R. A., & McKone, E. (2007). No face-like processing for objects-of-expertise in three behavioural tasks. *Cognition, 103,* 34–79.

Roberts, S., & Pashler, H. (2000). How persuasive is a good fit? A comment on theory testing. *Psychological Review, 107,* 358–367.

Rossion, B., Kung, C.-C., & Tarr, M. J. (2004). Visual expertise with nonface objects leads to competition with the early perceptual processing of faces in the human occipitotemporal cortex. *Proceedings of the National Academy of Sciences, 101,* 14521–14526.

Schall, J. D. (2004). On building a bridge between brain and behavior. *Annual Review of Psychology, 55,* 23–50.

Scott, L., Tanaka, J. W., Sheinberg, D., & Curran, T. (2006). A reevaluation of the electrophysiological correlates of expert object processing. *Journal of Cognitive Neuroscience, 18,* 1453–1465.

Serre, T., Oliva, A., & Poggio, T. (2007). A feedforward architecture accounts for rapid categorization. *Proceedings of the National Academy of Science, 104,* 6424–6429.

Shepard, R. N. (1957). Stimulus and response generalization: A stochastic model relating generalization to distance in psychological space. *Psychometrika, 22,* 325–345.

Shepard, R. N. (1987). Toward a universal law of generalization for psychological science. *Science, 237,* 1317–1323.

Shepard, R. N. (1994). Perceptual-cognitive universals as reflections of the world. *Psychonomic Bulletin and Review, 1,* 2–28.

Shepard, R. N., & Chang, J. J. (1963). Stimulus generalization in the learning of classifications. *Journal of Experimental Psychology, 65,* 94–102.

Shepard, R. N., Hovland, C. I., & Jenkins, H. M. (1961). Learning and memorization of classifications. *Psychological Monographs, 75* (13, Whole No. 517).

Shillcock, R., & Monaghan, P. (2001). The computational exploration of visual word recognition in a split model. *Neural Computation, 13,* 1171–1198.

Shin, H. J., & Nosofsky, R. M. (1992). Similarity-scaling studies of dot-pattern classification and recognition. *Journal of Experimental Psychology: General, 121,* 278–304.

Sloman, S. A. (1996). The empirical case for two systems of reasoning. *Psychological Bulletin, 119,* 3–22.

Smith, J. D., & Minda, J. P. (1998). Prototypes in the mist: The early epochs of category learning. *Journal of Experimental Psychology: Learning, Memory, and Cognition, 24,* 1411–1436.

Smith, E. E., Patalano, A. L., & Jonides, J. (1998). Alternative mechanisms of categorization. *Cognition, 65,* 167–196.

Smith, P. L., & Ratcliff, R. (2004). Psychology and neurobiology of simple decisions. *Trends in Neurosciences, 27,* 161–168.

Sugimoto, M., & Cottrell, G. W. (2001). Visual expertise is a general skill. In *Proceedings of the 23rd Annual Cognitive Science Conference, Edinburgh, Scotland,* pp. 994–999. Mahwah, NJ: Lawrence Erlbaum.

Tanaka, K. (1996). Inferotemporal cortex and object vision. *Annual Review of Neuroscience, 19,* 109–139.

Tanaka, K. (2002). Neuronal representation of object images and effects of learning. In M. Fahle & T. Poggio (Eds.), *Perceptual learning* (pp. 67–82). Cambridge, MA: MIT Press.

Tanaka, J. W., & Curran, T. (2001). A neural basis for expert object recognition. *Psychological Science, 12,* 43–47.

Tanaka, J. W., Curran, T., & Sheinberg, D. (2005). The training and transfer of real-world, perceptual expertise, *Psychological Science, 16,* 141–151.

Tanaka, J. W., & Taylor, M. (1991). Object categories and expertise: Is the basic level in the eye of the beholder? *Cognitive Psychology 23,* 457–482.

Tarr, M. J. (1995). Rotating objects to recognize them: A case study on the role of viewpoint dependency in the recognition of three-dimensional objects. *Psychonomic Bulletin & Review, 2,* 55–82.

Tarr, M. J., Kersten, D., & Bülthoff, H. H. (1998). Why the visual recognition system might encode the effects of illumination. *Vision Research, 38,* 2259–2275.

Tarr, M. J., & Pinker, S. (1989). Mental rotation and orientation-dependence in shape recognition. *Cognitive Psychology, 21,* 233–282.

Thomas, M. S. C. & de Wet, N. M. (1998). Stochastic double dissociations in distributed models of semantic memory. In G. Humphreys & D. Heinke (Eds.), *Proceedings of the 5th Neural Computation and Psychology Workshop.* London: Springer.

Thomas, R. D. (1998). Learning correlations in categorization tasks using large, ill-defined categories. *Journal of Experimental Psychology: Learning, Memory and Cognition, 24,* 119–143.

Tong, M. H., Joyce, C. A., & Cottrell, G. W. (2005). Are Greebles special? Or, why the Fusiform Fish Area would be recruited for sword expertise (if we had one). In *Proceedings of the 27th Annual Cognitive Science Conference, La Stresa, Italy.* Mahwah, NJ: Lawrence Erlbaum.

Tong, M. H., Joyce, C. A., & Cottrell, G.W. (2008). Why is the fusiform face area recruited for novel categories of expertise? A neurocomputational investigation. *Brain Research.*

Townsend, J. T. (1990). The truth and consequences of ordinal differences in statistical distributions: Toward a theory of hierarchical inference. *Psychological Bulletin, 108,* 551–567.

Treat, T. A., McFall, R. M., Viken, R. J., Kruschke, J. K., Nosofsky, R. M., & Wang, S. S. (2007). Clinical-cognitive science: Applying quantitative models of cognitive processing to examination of cognitive aspects of psychopathology. In R. W. J. Neufeld (Ed.), *Advances in clinical-cognitive science: Formal modeling and assessment of processes and symptoms* (pp. 179–205). Washington, DC: APA Books.

Turk, M., & Pentland, A. (1991). Eigenfaces for recognition. *Journal of Cognitive Neuroscience, 3,* 71–86.

Ullman, S. (2007). Object recognition and segmentation by a fragment-based hierarchy. *Trends in Cognitive Sciences, 11,* 58–64.

Ullman, S., Vidal-Naquet, M., & Sali, E. (2002). Visual features of intermediate complexity and their use in classification. *Nature Neuroscience, 5,* 682–687.

Valentine, T. (1991). A unified account of the effects of distinctiveness, inversion and race in face recognition. *Quarterly Journal of Experimental Psychology, 43A,* 161–204.

Wong, C.-N., & Gauthier, I. (2006). An analysis of letter expertise in a levels-of-categorization framework. *Visual Cognition 15*(7), 854–879.

Xu, Y. (2005). Revisiting the role of the fusiform and occipital face areas in visual expertise. *Cerebral Cortex, 15,* 1234–1242.

Young, A. W., Hellawell, D., & Hay, D. C. (1987). Configurational information in face perception. *Perception, 16,* 747–759.

Young, A. W., Rowland, D., Calder, A. J., Etcoff, N. L., Seth, A., & Perrett, D. I. (1997). Facial expression megamix: Tests of dimensional and category accounts of emotion recognition. *Cognition, 63,* 271–313.

Zhang, L., & Cottrell, G. W. (2005). Holistic processing develops because it is good. In B. G. Bara, L. Barsalou, & M. Bucciarelli (Eds.), *Proceedings of the 27th Annual Cognitive Science Conference.* Mahwah, NJ: Lawrence Erlbaum.

Zhang, L., & Cottrell, C. (2006). Look Ma! No network: PCA of Gabor filters models the development of face discrimination. In *Proceedings of the 28th Annual Cognitive Science Conference, Vancouver, BC, Canada.* Mahwah, NJ: Lawrence Erlbaum.

8

Competition between Face and Nonface Domains of Expertise

Kim M. Curby and Bruno Rossion

INTRODUCTION

We are confronted daily by the capacity-limited nature of human information processing. For example, talking on a cellular phone while driving makes
it more difficult to pay attention to the road, suggesting that these tasks
compete for overlapping limited processing resources. Measurements of
interference between concurrently performed tasks can provide insight into
the nature of the underlying neural substrates. For example, the reduction in
the amount of visual information that can be kept in mind by a concurrent
visual, but not verbal, task provides evidence for the independence of visual
and verbal short-term memory systems (Baddeley & Hitch, 1974). Given the
long-standing debate about whether the system supporting our expert face
processing skills is modular, that is, dealing with faces only and independently from non-face object processes (e.g., Bodamer, 1947; Ellis & Young,
1989; Yin, 1969), an important question is whether face and nonface domains
of expertise compete for common expert processes. If the cognitive system
underlying face processing is domain specific so that it responds only to faces
as suggested by some (e.g., Farah, Wilson, Drain, & Tanaka, 1995; Kanwisher,
2000; Nachson, 1995), then this competition should not occur. However, if
this system is domain general, responding to other classes of visual stimuli
with which we have substantial expertise, then acquiring expertise with a
nonface category should increase interference or competition for this capacity across face and nonface domains of expertise.

There is already much evidence consistent with the proposal that face and
nonface expert processing are supported by a domain-general system.
Perceptual experts show similar visual short-term memory advantages, behavioral inversion effects, and holistic processing for nonface objects of expertise and faces (Curby & Gauthier, 2007; Curby, Glazek, & Gauthier, 2009;
Diamond & Carey, 1986; Gauthier & Tarr, 1997, 2002). These holistic
processes recruited for face and nonface objects of expertise render the
features within an object inseparable from their context (Tanaka & Farah,
1993). For example, the features within a stimulus, such as the eyes, and their
relations, such as the distance between the two eyes, are processed interactively. Nonface objects of expertise also appear to recruit brain areas
responding preferentially to faces in the fusiform gyrus, providing a potential

neural locus for this holistic processing (Gauthier, Skudlarski, Gore, & Anderson, 2000; Gauthier, Tarr, Anderson, Skudlarski, & Gore, 1999; Xu, 2005). In addition, expertise effects for nonface objects are found in the first face-sensitive responses of the human brain as identified by event-related potential (ERP) studies (Busey & Vanderkolk, 2005; Rossion, Gauthier, Goffaux, Tarr, & Crommelinck, 2002; Tanaka & Curran, 2001). The expertise account of these neural markers suggests that nonface objects (e.g., cars) can be processed by experts within the same system as faces because similar holistic processes are involved (Tarr & Gauthier, 2000). However, studies supporting this account only reveal similarity in processing and proximity of neural substrates: It remains possible that nonface objects of expertise are processed in a system that is similar and neighboring, but that does not interact with a face-specific system. Therefore, the domain specificity of face processes is still an open question.

The time course of processing is another important factor when considering whether the processing of face and nonface objects of expertise share resources. It is possible that face and object expertise recruits the same neural substrate, but at different stages of processing. For example, faces may recruit the "fusiform face area" (FFA) in a feed-forward manner, whereas activation in this area for nonface objects of expertise may come predominantly from feedback connections from higher-level processing areas. A spatial overlap without a temporal overlap would suggest important differences in the manner in which face and nonface objects of expertise are processed. This would also raise important questions about what constitutes a modular system or, more specifically, whether modular systems must be domain specific across time. For example, it is conceivable that a brain area such as the FFA might perform different functions at different stages of processing. Early responses in the FFA to feed-forward information may predominantly reflect perceptual processing of faces, whereas responses after re-entrant input has reached this area may reflect higher-level processing such as that triggered by the social or reward attributes of the stimulus (Schultz et al., 2003). Therefore, an overlap that occurs in both space and time would provide stronger evidence for a common processing system and mechanism for face and nonface objects of expertise. The temporal limitations of fMRI render such questions, namely whether the activation in response to face and nonface objects of expertise occur in the same time frame, almost impossible to examine through this method.

The greater temporal resolution of techniques such as event-related brain potentials (ERPs) or event-related magnetic fields (ERMFs) make these procedures ideally suited to address questions about the temporal overlap between face and nonface expert processing. However, these methods, ERPs in particular, are not without their own limitations. Visual potentials recorded on the human scalp, such as the N170/VPP complex, which is much larger to faces than any other object category (Bentin, Allison, Puce, Perez, & McCarthy, 1996; Jeffreys, 1996; Joyce & Rossion, 2005) and whose amplitude is modulated by perceptual expertise (Busey & Vanderkolk,

2005; Rossion et al., 2002; Tanaka & Curran, 2001), are assumed to have a number of underlying sources. Thus, it is possible that the N170 evoked in response to objects of expertise may have a different set of sources than that in response to faces. Therefore, these effects of expertise found on the N170 in response to objects may arise not from face-related holistic processes, but instead from different processes occurring at approximately the same latency and with an overlapping scalp potential, as argued by some (McKone & Kanwisher, 2005; Robbins & McKone, 2006).

Recent reports of the capacity-limited nature of the system supporting face processing have provided a potential method for probing both the spatial and temporal nature of the overlap between face and nonface expert processing (Bindemann, Burton, & Jenkins, 2005; Jenkins, Lavie, & Driver, 2003; Palermo & Rhodes, 2002): If face and nonface objects of expertise recruit overlapping resources, the concurrent processing of these items should be more vulnerable to capacity limitations relative to the simultaneous processing of face and nonface objects of nonexpertise. Therefore, by pairing high–temporal resolution neuroimaging techniques such as ERPs with behavioral paradigms where the processing of faces and objects of expertise occur concurrently, cognitive neuroscientists can address the issue of the functional overlap of the systems supporting different-category expert processing.

In this chapter, we discuss a number of recent studies that use these paradigms to provide insight into the question of the domain specificity of face perception. To anticipate, these studies using interference paradigms suggest a functional overlap between face and nonface expert processing that occurs at the perceptual level. These findings lead to intriguing predictions about the potential for long-term interference between such processing. Evidence for such long-term interference effects between the development of expertise with face and nonface objects and their implications are also discussed.

CAPACITY LIMITATIONS OF THE FACE PROCESSING SYSTEM

Interference between face and nonface expert processing would be expected if holistic face processing is capacity limited, and this limitation is shared across face and nonface expert processing. This section outlines existing evidence suggesting that face processing is capacity limited, thus providing the foundation upon which interference studies between face and nonface expertise are based.

Evidence from Distractor Interference Paradigms

Most studies explore the capacity of face processing mechanisms indirectly. They operate under the assumption that a distractor stimulus or a secondary task will interfere with the processing of a central stimulus, providing that (1) it recruits overlapping capacities, and (2) the central task does not recruit the entire face processing capacity. A number of studies have measured the impact of the *congruency* between a distractor and target in order to estimate category-specific perceptual capacity limitations (Bindemann et al., 2005; Jenkins et al., 2003). For example, in a sex categorization task, if the target is a female face, a distractor taking the form of a male face would constitute an *incongruent* event, whereas the presentation of a female distractor face would be a *congruent* event. Using this general paradigm, a recent study provided evidence that our processing capacity for faces may be as little as one item. When making a sex or semantic judgment about a face, participants experienced distractor congruency effects when the distractor was a word but not when it was another face (Bindemann et al., 2005). Importantly, when the target was a word, distractor congruency effects were present regardless of whether the distractor was a face or a word (Bindemann et al., 2005). Based on the absence of interference from a distractor face on a central face judgment, the authors of the study suggested that visual face processing is capacity limited, with no more than *one* face processed at a time.

In contrast, other studies have reported evidence that the capacity for face processing is greater than one. Jenkins and colleagues (2003) demonstrated that when subjects performed an occupation judgment about a centrally presented famous individual's name, the influence of a famous face distractor depended on whether it was congruent (i.e., a politician's face with a politician's name) or incongruent (i.e., politician's face with a pop star's name). As expected, performance was worse when the distractor was incongruent versus when it was congruent. Notably, however, the presence of a task-irrelevant additional unknown face diluted this distractor congruency effect, although the presence of other stimuli did not influence this effect. The dilution of the distractor effect by the presentation of an additional unknown face suggests that we can in fact process more than one face at a time. Although the Bindemann and Jenkins studies lead to different conclusions about the precise capacity of face processing mechanisms, they both agree that not only do faces draw on a limited capacity resource, but that this resource is face specific.

Although a number of studies suggest that the presence of additional faces in one's visual field can interfere with the processing of a central face, it is unclear from these studies whether this interference occurs during perceptual encoding or at later processing stages. More specifically, it is unclear whether observers can actually encode multiple faces at once, which then compete with each other at later output stages leading to the observed interference effect. Alternatively, the distractor interference might instead reflect the sharing of limited resources insufficient to encode multiple faces at once, thus suggesting that the interference occurs at a perceptual level. This distinction is critical for interpretations with regard to the capacity-limited nature of face processing and its consequences for nonface expert processing.

Evidence from ERP studies suggests that this interference occurs at a perceptual level: The occipito-temporal N170 potential elicited in response to a laterally presented face is considerably reduced in amplitude when participants fixate on a centrally presented face as compared to when they fixate on a nonface central stimulus (phase-scrambled face, Jacques & Rossion, 2004; see Figure 8.1). This reduction in the amplitude of the N170 holds even when the target stimulus is presented at the fovea and the distractor is presented laterally (Jacques & Rossion, 2006). Notably, this effect takes place on the earliest face-selective response in the brain, occurring only 130 ms after the face is presented (N170, 130–200 ms), suggesting that the interference occurs during the perceptual processing of the faces rather than during later stages. More specifically, the modulation of the N170 potential is consistent with a significant overlap and competition in the neural representations used for different individual faces. Presumably, such overlap would lead to perceptual capacity limitations because neural resources required to encode face representations would become more scarce with increasing face load, as each face stimulus would compete for more and more of the same neurons.

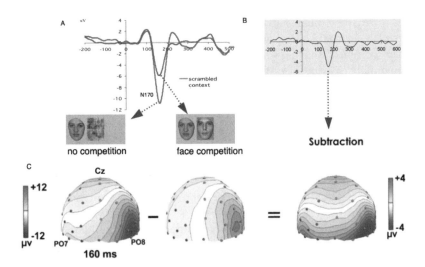

Figure 8.1 (A) ERP waveforms at right occipitotemporal sites (here PO8 electrode) following the onset of a face stimulus presented in the left visual field, either when subjects fixate another face stimulus (face competition) or a phase-scrambled stimulus of equal size and luminance. The N170 is substantially reduced in amplitude when subjects are fixating the face stimulus, illustrating the competition effect within the face domain. (B) Subtraction between the two waveforms, showing that the competition effect starts at about 130 ms following stimulus onset. (C) Topographical maps of the back of the head for the electrical potentials observed at 160 ms in the two conditions and the result of their subtraction. Note that the topography of the competition effect is highly similar to the original N170 scalp distribution (figure adapted with permission from Jacques & Rossion, 2004, "Concurrent processing reveals competition between visual representations of faces, *NeuroReport 15*(15), 2417–2421. © 2004 Lippincott Williams & Wilkins/Wolters-Kluwer Health) (See color Plate 6).

The observation of a reduction in the amplitude of the N170 potential for faces perceived in the context of a face distractor relates to several single-cell recording studies in the monkey brain: When two visual stimuli are present at the same time within a neuron's receptive field, the response of the neuron appears to be a weighted average of the responses to the individual stimuli when presented alone (Moran & Desimone, 1985; Reynolds, Chelazzi, & Desimone, 1999). That is, if a preferred visual stimulus for a cell is presented together with a poor visual stimulus, the cell's response is reduced compared to that elicited by the single good stimulus. This sensory suppressive interaction among multiple visual stimuli has been observed at the single-cell level in several visual areas in the ventral stream of the monkey brain (V2, V4, IT; Miller, Li, & Desimone, 1993; Moran & Desimone, 1985; Reynolds et al., 1999; Rolls & Tovee, 1995) and is generally interpreted as an expression of competition for neural representation (Desimone, 1998; Kastner & Ungerleider, 2001). In the inferotemporal cortex, it was described for neurons responding preferentially to faces (Miller et al., 1993; Rolls & Tovee, 1995). In the same vein, fMRI studies performed on human subjects reported a reduction of BOLD signal in several extrastriate visual areas of the ventral stream (V2, V4, TEO, TE) when complex shapes where presented simultaneously compared to sequentially (Kastner, De Weerd, Desimone, & Ungerleider, 1998; Kastner & Ungerleider, 2001). Thus, the results outlined in this section from studies using distractor interference paradigms are well grounded in the basic physiological properties of the visual system.

Evidence from Other Interference Paradigms

Studies using other paradigms, such as visual search, have also provided evidence consistent with an early perceptual capacity limitation for face processing. However, such studies suggest a larger capacity limit than that suggested by those studies using distractor interference paradigms. One such study utilizing a visual search paradigm found evidence that 2–4 faces can be perceived during one 200 ms fixation (Nasanen & Ojanpaa, 2004). This finding suggests either that faces are processed *very* rapidly or that more than one face can be processed in parallel, and thus that the capacity for face processing mechanisms is indeed greater than one. Consistent with this latter interpretation, there is evidence that visual processing in the inferotemporal cortex can occur in parallel, but only during the very early stages of processing (Rousselet, Thorpe, & Fabre-Thorpe, 2004). The capacity of this parallel system is relatively unknown. Therefore, the larger capacity limit for faces found in this search task (compared to that reported in studies using distractor interference paradigms) may reflect this very early processing limit, while other studies demonstrating a smaller perceptual capacity may reflect later perceptual processing stages. Thus, the amount of sharing of this limited perceptual capacity across images may vary from little (Jenkins et al., 2003) to none (Bindemann et al., 2005) depending on the task.

Further evidence for the capacity-limited nature of the perceptual processing of faces is provided by the failure of a target face to "pop-out" from an array of faces (Purcell, Stewart, & Skov, 1996). The phenomenon of "pop-out"—when the time to find a target among an array of distractors is independent of the number of items to be searched—is believed to reflect preattentive processing that is immune to attentional capacity limits (Treisman & Gelade, 1980; Wolfe, Cave, & Franzel, 1989). Notably, though, observers experience a pop-out effect when searching for a face among nonface objects (Hershler & Hochstein, 2005). Some suggest that this pop-out effect may be due to low-level properties of face stimuli (VanRullen, 2006). However, others interpret this finding as consistent with previous studies suggesting that face processing is supported by a domain-specific, but capacity-limited mechanism.

Dual-task paradigms have also been used to explore capacity limitations, specifically assessing the degree to which two tasks interfere. In such paradigms, as the name implies, participants are required to perform two tasks concurrently. One such paradigm was used to demonstrate that face processing is perceptually limited: Palermo and Rhodes (2002) showed that the holistic encoding of a central face was reduced when participants concurrently performed a matching task on two flanking faces. The degree of holistic processing of the central face was measured using a paradigm similar to that used by Tanaka and Farah (1993); holistic processing was operationalized as the advantage for matching a face part encoded in the context of a whole face compared to when it was encoded in isolation. Tanaka and Farah (1993) found that holistic processing of faces is limited to those in an upright orientation, and thus it is noteworthy that holistic processing of the central face in this task appeared to be unaffected when the flanking faces were presented upside-down (Palermo & Rhodes, 2002). The results of this study demonstrate that interference between concurrently processed faces is not only found when two face stimuli are simply detected or perceived, but also when they actively recruit certain perceptual processes in the context of a deliberate task.

PERCEPTUAL PROCESS SHARING BETWEEN FACE AND NONFACE EXPERT PROCESSING

Evidence from Distractor Interference Paradigms

As outlined in the previous section, there is much evidence to suggest that face processing is capacity limited. Therefore, if face and nonface objects of expertise recruit overlapping processing resources, then these same general paradigms used to explore the capacity-limited nature of face processing should also reveal interference between face and nonface expert processing. Participants who possess expertise with a nonface category should experience greater capacity limitations (interference) when processing face and nonface objects of expertise concurrently, relative to novice observers processing the same face and nonface objects concurrently.

This hypothesis can be tested, for example, using the ERP distractor interference paradigm described earlier (Jacques & Rossion, 2004, 2006). This is possible because the reduction in the amplitude of the N170 in response to a target face stimulus due to the ongoing processing of another face stimulus most likely arises from regions in the cortex where "face-specific" activity is found, or, more specifically, where faces and nonface objects are functionally segregated. Notably, the onset of the reported N170 amplitude difference between faces and other objects (e.g., Bentin et al., 1996; Rossion et al., 2000) has a similar latency as the onset of the competition effect between individual faces (Jacques & Rossion, 2004, 2006). Moreover, the competition effect has a very similar distribution on the scalp as a classical N170 response to faces, suggesting that the locus of the competition effect largely lies in the occipitotemporal regions that participate in generating the N170 (Figure 8.1). Finally, both the N170 amplitude advantage for faces over objects (e.g., Bentin et al., 1996; Rossion, Joyce, Cottrell, & Tarr, 2003) and the competition effect between concurrently presented faces are larger in the right hemisphere, in agreement with the prominent role of this hemisphere in face processing (e.g., Hillger & Koenig, 1991; Sergent & Signoret, 1992).

If expertise leads to an overlap in the processes recruited for face and nonface objects, interference between the concurrent processing of face and nonface objects of expertise (as detected using the distractor interference paradigm) should increase with the development of expertise with the nonface object category. To address this question, Rossion, Kung, & Tarr (2004) used an established lab-based expertise training protocol to train participants to become experts with a category of novel objects, namely Greebles (Gauthier & Tarr, 1997). The N170 elicited by laterally presented faces was measured while participants were fixating on nonface objects (either Greebles or control stimuli of equivalent complexity). All participants were tested before expertise training with the Greebles set, at the middle of training, and following their reaching of an expertise level defined by a criterion used in previous behavioral studies (Gauthier & Tarr, 1997; Gauthier, Williams, Tarr, & Tanaka, 1998). Following expertise training with the nonface object category, there was a substantial reduction in this N170 amplitude (~20% of signal) at occipitotemporal sites where the response to faces was maximal (Figure 8.2). Thus, the N170 amplitude in response to faces was strongly modulated as a consequence of expertise training with novel nonface objects. The reduction was specific to the object category trained (Greebles) but was not tied to specific items: The N170 amplitude reduction in response to faces was equally large whether participants focused on novel or unfamiliar individual Greebles. In addition, the effects of expertise were gradual: There was already a substantial face N170 reduction midway through training. Thus, the increase in the degree of interference between the processing of face and nonface objects with expertise training provides strong support for the role of learning in the functional reorganization of occipitotemporal cortices.

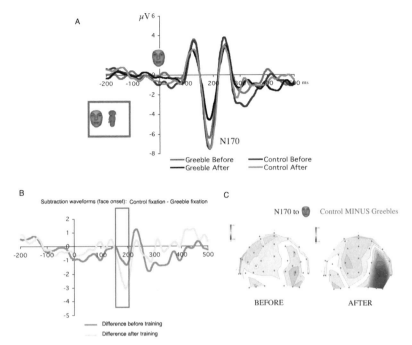

Figure 8.2 (A) competition effect between Greebles and faces. The waveforms (average of four right occipitotemporal channels) follow the presentation of a lateralized face stimulus while participants fixate either a central Greeble or a control object. Following expertise training with the Greebles, there was a substantial and specific reduction of amplitude of the N170 in response to faces when participants fixate a stimulus from the Greeble category (novel or old, see Rossion, Kung, & Tarr, 2004). (B) Subtraction waveforms, showing the competition effect, that is, the reduction of the N170 for faces while fixating Greebles as compared to control objects (yellow waveform is the result of the subtraction between green and black traces displayed above). The red rectangle represents the time window used to display topographical maps of the back of the head on (C). All waveforms are recorded in response to faces and thus show a strong modulation of the N170 amplitude to this category following training with nonface objects (adapted with permission from Rossion, Kung, & Tarr, 2004, "Visual expertise with nonface objects leads to competition with the early perceptual processing of faces in the human occipitotemporal cortex," PNAS 101(40), pp. 14521–14526, ©2004 National Academy of Sciences (See color Plate 7).

More recently, Rossion, Collins, Goffaux, & Curran (2007) utilized a similar distractor interference paradigm to explore the question of interference between face and nonface domains of expertise in real-world experts, specifically participants with expertise at visually recognizing cars. Consistent with the findings from the study using lab-trained experts, the reduction in the amplitude of the N170 elicited by laterally presented faces while participants were fixating on pictures of cars relative to control stimuli (fixation cross and scrambled cars) was larger among car experts than car

novices (Figure 8.3). This observation indicates that naturally developed
long-term visual expertise with nonface objects can interfere with face processes at the perceptual level. Thus, perceptual expertise appears to lead to a
functional overlap in the neural networks supporting the processing of face
and nonface objects of expertise.

Notably, in both of these studies that report interference between the
processing of face and nonface expert categories, the effect was much
larger in the right hemisphere, reinforcing the idea of an overlap with the
right dominant face processes, and in line with the localization of

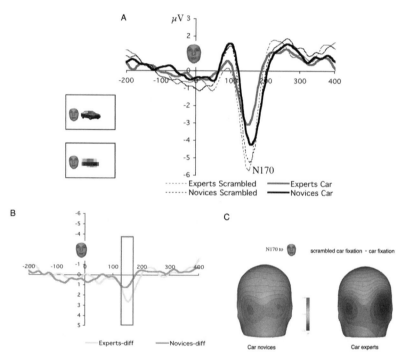

Figure 8.3 Competition effect between cars and faces. (A) The waveforms (T6 – right
occipitotemporal channel) follow the presentation of a lateralized face stimulus while
participants fixate either the picture of a car or a scrambled car (stimuli on the left).
Relative to novices, car experts show a substantial and specific reduction of amplitude of
the N170 in response to faces when they fixate novel cars (see Rossion, Collins, Goffaux, &
Curran, 2007). (B) Subtraction waveforms, showing the competition effect, that is, the
reduction of the N170 for faces while fixating cars as compared to scrambled cars for car
experts and novices. The red rectangle represents the time window used to display
topographical maps of the back of the head on C. All waveforms are recorded in
response to faces and thus show a strong modulation of the N170 amplitude to this
category following training with nonface objects (adapted with permission from Rossion
et al., 2007, "Long-term expertise with artificial objects increases visual competition with
early face categorization processes," *Journal of Cognitive Neuroscience*, 19(3), 543–555,
Copyright 2007 MIT Press) (See color Plate 8).

previous effects of visual expertise in neuroimaging studies (e.g., Gauthier et al., 2000; Gauthier, Curby, Skudlarski, & Epstein, 2005; Gauthier & Tarr, 2002; Xu, 2005). The reduction of the N170 amplitude for faces was substantial in the two studies, contradicting the claim that facelike effects of visual expertise are generally small and/or nonreplicable (McKone & Kanwisher, 2005; McKone, Kanwisher, & Duchaine, 2007). Moreover, the link between visual expertise and the face N170 effect was reinforced by complementary analyses showing a highly significant correlation between the amount of visual expertise with cars, as measured in an independent behavioral task, and the N170 reduction for faces during the interference paradigm (Rossion et al., 2007). This indicates that visual expertise with nonface objects, and thus interference with face processes, is not all-or-none, but rather a matter of degree.

Beyond observations of sensory suppressive interactions between visual stimuli at the single-cell level or in fMRI, the interest of these competition effects observed in ERP studies is two-fold. First and most interestingly, they show that competition between different object shapes (i.e., a car and a face stimulus) can be dramatically increased with visual expertise and thus is not entirely dependent on the visual structure of the stimuli. Second, by virtue of the excellent temporal resolution offered by ERP recordings and the spatial sampling of the whole system, they demonstrate that visual competition between faces and objects of expertise takes place as early as 130 ms after the onset of the stimuli, during a limited time window, and in occipitotemporal areas. Overall, these observations indicate that the neurofunctional processes involved in processing objects of visual expertise directly compete with those recruited to process faces at the perceptual level.

Evidence from Dual-Task Paradigms of Shared Holistic Processes

In these ERP studies, the subject's task is simple: to detect laterally presented faces while nonface objects of expertise (or control stimuli) are attended to. This simple orthogonal task is used to maintain attention, while ensuring that general attentional factors do not play a role in the effects observed (for further arguments against spatial or selective attention accounts of these effects, see discussion sections in Rossion, Kung, & Tarr, 2004; Rossion et al., 2007; as well as empirical evidence by Jacques & Rossion, 2007). However, the visual expertise hypothesis suggests that the modulation of the N170 in response to faces by a distractor object of expertise does not only occur because of an overlap in the way that face and nonface objects of expertise are merely seen or detected, but because of shared specific *processes*. What kind of early perceptual process would be recruited selectively for both faces and objects of expertise? It has long been suggested by many authors that one fundamental characteristic of our face processing system is that it treats faces holistically (Galton, 1879). There have been many definitions of holistic (and configural) face processing in the literature, but a simple and widely accepted definition is that facial features are integrated rather than being processed and represented independently (Sergent, 1984; Tanaka & Farah, 1993; Young, Hellawell, & Hay, 1987). Perhaps the best evidence for holistic processing of faces comes from the so-called face composite effect first described by Young and colleagues (1987). This effect was reported as the slowing down at naming the top half of a familiar face (cut below the eyes) when it is aligned with the bottom part of another face, as compared with the naming when the same top and bottom parts are offset laterally (i.e., mis-aligned) (Young et al., 1987). Over the years, it has been used with unfamiliar faces in individual discrimination tasks (Endo, Masame, & Maruyama, 1989; Goffaux & Rossion, 2006; Hole, 1994; Hole, George, & Dunsmore, 1999; Le Grand, Mondloch, Maurer, & Brent, 2004; Michel, Rossion, Han, Chung, & Caldara, 2006; Robbins & McKone, 2006) to demonstrate that facial features (here the two halves of the face) cannot be perceived in isolation, that is, they interact with each other during face processing. A functional locus of the effect is thought to be at early perceptual encoding stages for faces, being larger for low-spatial frequency faces (Goffaux & Rossion, 2006), and taking place primarily in the FFA with a right hemisphere advantage (Schiltz & Rossion, 2006).

There is evidence that faces are processed more holistically than other nonface objects in novices (Farah, Wilson, Drain, & Tanaka, 1998; Tanaka & Farah, 1993; Tanaka & Gauthier, 1997). However, visual expertise with nonface objects such as Greebles leads to enhanced holistic processing of these stimuli (Gauthier & Tarr, 1997, 2002; but see Robbins & McKone, 2006), raising the question as to whether these processes enter in competition for faces and nonface objects of expertise.

A dual task paradigm was developed to specifically test whether interference between the concurrent processing of face and nonface objects of expertise occurs at least in part due to competition for limited-capacity holistic processes (Curby & Gauthier, 2001; Gauthier, Curran, Curby, & Collins, 2003). In this interleaved two-back visual short-term memory task, car experts and car novices were required to process a face and a car in an overlapping manner (Figure 8.4); participants had to keep a face in mind while they processed the interleaved car and vice versa. All the images used in this task were composite images made by aligning the tops and bottoms of different cars or faces. Participants made same/different matching judgments about *only* the bottom halves of the images; the task-irrelevant (top) parts were either congruent (e.g., the two tops were different, and the correct response for the bottom judgment was "different") or incongruent (e.g., the two tops were different, and the correct response for the bottom judgment was "same"). Notably, the degree to which the congruency of the task-irrelevant part impacted performance on the task provided a means for measuring the degree of holistic processing of the faces in the car context. In order to specifically test for a trade-off between the *holistic* processing of faces and cars that is related to participants' expertise with cars, the degree of holistic processing of the cars was manipulated in two conditions: The

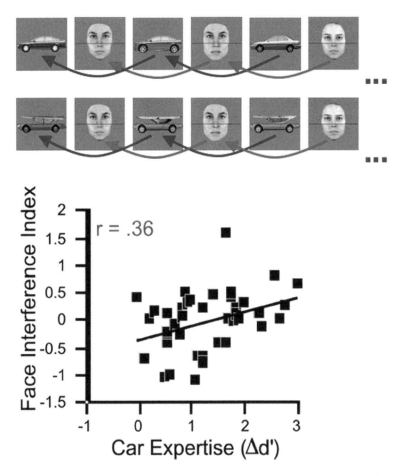

Figure 8.4 (A) diagram of the two-back task used to measure the interference effect of the cars on holistic face processing. Composites of faces and cars made of the top and bottom of different objects were alternately presented. Subjects were instructed to attend only to the bottom half of all the objects for the entire experiment and, for each one, to make a two-back judgment on whether the bottom part matched that of the last object from the same category. Normal faces (configurally intact) were interspersed with either normal cars (top row) or cars with a transformed configuration with the top half inverted (bottom row). (B) A scatter plot shows the correlation between the behavioral face interference index (i.e., holistic processing of faces in the context of normal cars minus holistic processing of faces in the context of configurally modified cars) and car expertise. The greater one's car expertise, the greater the reduction in holistic face processing in the normal car context relative to the configurally modified car context. (Figure adapted with permission from Gauthier et al., 2003, "Perceptual interference supports a non-modular account of face processing," *Nature Neuroscience*, 6(4), 428–432.) (See color Plate 9).

interleaved cars were either in a normal or modified configuration (i.e., their top halves were inverted) (Figure 8.4). Critically, disrupting the configuration of nonface objects of expertise (or faces) reduces the degree of holistic processing for these items (Gauthier et al., 2003; Gauthier & Tarr, 2002). Therefore, the interleaved cars in a modified configuration should compete less with the faces, relative to the interleaved cars in an intact configuration, for holistic processing resources.

The pattern of performance by experts and novices in this interleaved two-back task provided evidence for a functional overlap between holistic processes for face and nonface objects of expertise (Curby & Gauthier, 2001; Gauthier et al., 2003). Specifically, there was evidence of a trade-off between holistic processing of faces and cars that was related to expertise with cars; among experts, faces processed concurrently with cars in a normal configuration were processed less holistically than those processed in the context of cars in a modified configuration (tops inverted). Importantly, confirming the validity of the car manipulation, cars in the modified configuration were processed less holistically by experts and therefore presumably competed less for holistic processing resources. Notably, the degree to which the holistic processing of faces was impacted by the format of the cars was correlated with individuals' level of expertise with cars (Figure 8.4). Thus, the level of interference between the processing of these categories depended on the degree to which the car task recruited a holistic processing strategy; the level of interference depended both on one's visual expertise with cars and also whether the cars were intact (Curby & Gauthier, 2001). Therefore, the results of this study provide evidence of a functional overlap between the holistic processing of face and nonface objects of expertise.

This interference between holistic processes for faces and cars was also reflected in the N170 potential: the greater a participant's expertise with cars, the greater the N170 amplitude difference between faces presented among normal cars and faces presented among transformed cars (Figure 8.5; Gauthier et al., 2003). That is, the concurrent processing of intact cars, but not configurally modified cars, decreased the face N170 in car experts relative to that in car novices. Again, the expertise effect was located mainly on right occipitotemporal sites (Figure 8.5), as in the other studies showing more general competition effects between face and nonface objects of expertise (Rossion et al., 2004; 2007; Figure 8.2).

The demonstration of a functional overlap between face and nonface expert processing at perceptual stages (occipitotemporal N170) in the context of a dual-task paradigm is important as it provides further evidence that the interference between face and nonface expert processing measured using distractor interference paradigms is unlikely to arise through attentional confounds. Most notably, though, not only does it suggest that there is a behavioral consequence of this interference, but it also ties the source of such interference to the overlap in the early holistic processes recruited for face and nonface domains of expertise.

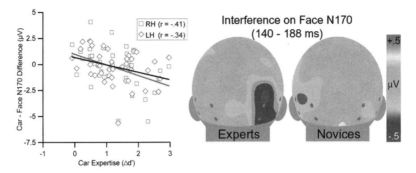

Figure 8.5 (A) A scatter plot shows the correlation between the electrophysiological face interference index (i.e., N170 amplitude for faces processed in the context of normal cars minus N170 amplitude for faces processed in the context of configurally modified cars) and car expertise. The greater one's car expertise, the greater the reduction in the N170 to faces processed in the normal car context relative to those processed in the configurally modified car context. (B) Electrophysiological map of the interference effect between face and cars illustrating the right hemisphere dominance of this effect. (Figure adapted with permission from Gauthier et al., 2003.) (See color Plate 10).

EVIDENCE FOR LONG-TERM INTERFERENCE BETWEEN FACE AND NONFACE EXPERT PROCESSING

The demonstration of interference between the processing of face and non-face objects of expertise leads to some intriguing questions regarding the long-term effects of dual expertise. Does such interference only occur when face and nonface objects of expertise are processed concurrently or are there long-term consequences of this resource overlap? More specifically, does the development of perceptual expertise with a nonface category reduce the resources available for face processing on a larger timescale?

A number of neurophysiological studies have demonstrated a clear effect of experience (or the absence thereof) on the organization of visual cortex. For example, Hubel, Wiesel, and LeVay (1977) demonstrated that preventing visual stimulation to one eye leads to a rewiring of monocular (eye-specific) columns in visual cortex in monkeys. Similarly, there are reports of an astounding degree of plasticity in somatosensory cortex in the brains of rodents, primates, and other animals (Buonomano & Merzenich, 1998; Feldman & Brecht, 2005; Kaas, Merzenich, & Killackey, 1983; Merzenich, Kaas, Wall, Nelson et al., 1983; Merzenich, Kaas, Wall, Sur et al., 1983). Elbert and colleagues (1995) have demonstrated that this plasticity is possible in the normal intact human brain even in the absence of the deprivation of experience. A group of string instrument musicians were found to have an increased representation for the little finger of the left hand, which correlated with the age at which the person started training (Elbert, Pantev, Wienbruch, Rockstroh, & Taub, 1995). Musicians, more generally, were also shown to have an increased representation for tones, pitch, and timbre in the auditory cortex (Pantev et al., 1995; Pantev, Engelien, Candia, & Elbert, 2001; Pantev et al., 1998). In addition to these functional differences, there have been reports of structural differences (white matter: Bengtsson et al., 2005; corpus callosum: Schlaug, Jancke, Huang, Staiger, & Steinmetz, 1995) that are believed to be a result of musicians' extensive experience and the resulting development of their specialized skills. Therefore, such demonstrations of experience-induced plasticity in the intact human brain suggests that the extensive experience required to develop perceptual expertise with an object domain could also potentially lead to a dynamic long-term reorganization of cortical areas. It is conceivable that such reorganization could lead to a trade-off between different expert categories that compete for the same limited processing capacity.

The first hints that a functional trade-off may occur between face and nonface expert processing were provided by Gauthier and colleagues (Gauthier et al., 1999). In their study, participants were scanned before, during, and after completing a lab-based expertise training paradigm with Greebles. In addition to the hypothesized finding of a training-related increase in upright Greeble-selective activation in the right middle fusiform area, there was an accompanying trend for a *decrease* in upright face-selective activation in this same region. More recent work, outlined below, suggests that this trend could reflect the early stages of experience-induced functional reorganization of this area.

A more recent training study with the patient SM who has visual agnosia with concomitant prosopagnosia provides support for the possibility of long-term interference between face and nonface object processing. Over the period of expertise training with Greebles, SM demonstrated a similar trade-off between face and nonface expert categories; SM's growing Greeble-selective activation in the fusiform region with training was accompanied by decreasing face selectivity in this same region (Behrmann, Marotta, Gauthier, Tarr, & McKeeff, 2005). However, presumably because SM's face system was already compromised through his acquired brain lesion in this region, this trade-off had severe consequences. SM's pattern of behavioral performance over the training period mimicked that of the fMRI results; SM's training-related performance increase in tasks with Greebles was coupled with decreasing performance in face perception tasks. SM's training with Greebles, however, did lead to some benefits; coupled with SM's improved ability to recognize novel Greebles was an improved ability to recognize common objects. Closer inspection of the fMRI data provided evidence consistent with a trade-off between the resources recruited for Greeble and face processing; areas of the brain that had once been face selective were no longer so after training and became more Greeble selective. These findings are consistent not only with the possibility of a dynamic reorganization of temporal cortex after extensive training, but also with the possibility that sharing and competition for resources between face and nonface processing can have long-term consequences.

Studies with real-world bird experts have also provided evidence consistent with the speculation put forth in this section. In a recent study, Kung

(2006) reported experiencing more difficulty locating a face-selective region in participants who were bird experts compared to those who were novices; using a standard method, an FFA could be localized in only four out of nine bird experts, whereas it was easily located in all nine novices. Kung (2006) proposed that the difficulty in defining a face-selective region among the expert group might be a result of a long-term dynamic reorganization of temporal cortex, resulting from these participants' extensive experience with birds. Consistent with this possibility, the degree of face-selective activation in or close to the FFAwas negatively related to performance in a behavioral measure of expertise with birds. This correlation was present across four different task comparisons (one- or two-back identity matching, one-back spatial location judgment, or passive viewing). Thus, supplementing studies reporting long-term interference between face and nonface objects of expertise in lab-trained participants, Kung's (2006) studies provided evidence of long-term interference in a group of real-world experts.

Notably, the possibility that there is long-term interference between face and nonface processing after the development of perceptual expertise with a nonface category is in conflict with a strong process map model of fusiform cortex. A strong process map model would only predict interference between face and nonface processing when the processing of the items from these two categories overlaps in time. Specifically, if brain regions in this area of cortex are defined in terms of processes rather than object categories and/or geometries, the development of expertise with a nonface category should not impact processing of faces as the same processes could presumably be used by both. Observations of long-term interference between face and nonface expert processing suggest that face and, for example, Greeble expertise, are coded by separate populations within the same area, and that visual expertise increases the representation for Greebles at the expense of the representation for faces. Interestingly, this would be akin to the competition between representations of different fingers in primary somatosensory cortex after a change in the relative stimulation of different fingers, such as in the case of string instrument musicians. Thus, the presence of long-term interference between face and nonface object domains of expertise would suggest that brain regions in the fusiform cortex are defined in terms of both processes and object category/geometry.

The studies reported in this section provide tantalizing hints suggesting the possibility of a long-term dynamic reorganization of temporal cortex after expertise training. This possibility would have profound consequences for our current understanding of the effects of learning in the brain. However, further work, with more rigorous pre- and posttraining comparisons and the use of high-resolution fMRI (Grill-Spector, Sayres, & Ress, 2006), is required to adequately test the validity of this hypothesis. In addition, studies utilizing single-cell neurophysiological recordings of pre- and posttraining activity could also provide much insight into the possibility of experience-induced long-term reorganization in the occipitotemporal cortex.

THE ROAD AHEAD: CLARIFYING THE NEUROFUNCTIONAL MECHANISMS UNDERLYING THE PERCEPTUAL COMPETITION BETWEEN FACE AND NONFACE OBJECTS OF EXPERTISE

In this chapter, we have outlined a number of studies that not only complement each other but also provide convincing evidence for a functional overlap between the processing of face and nonface objects of expertise. However, it is important to note that although there is evidence consistent with a functional overlap between face and nonface expert processing, two very important and related questions at the core of this overlap still remain unanswered: (1) *At what degree of resolution are the processes for faces and objects of expertise interfering?* and (2) *What are the neurofunctional mechanisms underlying this competition between face and expert processing?*

Spatial Resolution Issues and Neural Mechanisms of Interference Effects

The first question refers to the multiple levels of organization of the human brain (Churchland & Sejnowski, 1988), from synapses to networks of brain areas. In this chapter, we have reviewed recent evidence that there is competition between the processing of face and nonface objects of expertise at the systems level. These findings speak directly against a strong face modularist position that posits that the face processing system is functionally isolated or encapsulated. The data have been collected using behavioral and electrophysiological recordings in humans, with the results suggesting that the competition between face and expertise domains takes place at the perceptual level. A direct interpretation of these observations is that the development of expertise with nonface object categories (cars, Greebles) leads to an overlap of representations and processes for these nonface objects and faces. At what level of organization does this sharing take place? Are face-selective cells in the inferotemporal cortex (Gross, Roche-Miranda, & Bender, 1972; Perrett, Rolls, & Caan, 1982) becoming responsive to nonface object categories through expertise training? Or, alternatively, do these interference effects reflect the strengthening of inhibitory connections between anatomically distinct populations of neurons? Thus, the precise neural mechanisms underlying the interference between the processing of face and nonface objects of expertise are unclear.

The first hypothesis is that the same populations of neurons responding selectively to faces in occipitotemporal areas start responding to nonface objects (i.e., cars) with the development of visual expertise. The face N170 potential is thought to originate from multiple brain areas located in the occipitotemporal cortex, including the fusiform gyrus, the superior temporal sulcus, and the middle and inferior temporal gyri (e.g., Henson et al., 2003; Herrmann, Ehlis, Muehlberger, & Fallgatter, 2005) where cortical surface potentials in response to faces—N200s—have been observed at roughly the same latency (Allison, Puce, Spencer, & McCarthy, 1999). Single-cell recordings in the monkey inferotemporal cortex show that cells in these areas are organized into columns that may be highly selective to face stimuli (e.g., Desimone, 1991; Perrett, et al., 1982; Tanaka, 1996; Tsao, Freiwald, Tootell, & Livingstone, 2006). However, it is yet unclear whether these neurons are tuned to respond to faces only (i.e., are "domain-specific"), or if they may also fire in response to members of a nonface object category following extensive visual experience with this category. Responses of single neurons in the monkey IT can be tuned to novel, visually similar objects—bars or "amoeba" shapes—following expertise training (Baker, Behrmann, & Olson, 2002; Logothetis & Pauls, 1995), and these neurons appear to share a number of properties with face-selective neurons such as viewpoint selectivity (Logothetis, Pauls, Bülthoff, & Poggio, 1994; Logothetis, Pauls, & Poggio, 1995) and a strong sensitivity to the removal of parts of the stimulus (Logothetis & Pauls, 1995). However, recordings in these studies are made in more anterior and ventral areas of IT than in the regions where most face-selective cells have been reported, and the response of these cells to face stimuli is unknown.

Since different faces are represented by the same population of neurons in a distributed coding system (Rolls, 1992), the similarity between the N170 competition effects found within the face domain (Jacques & Rossion, 2004, 2006, 2007) and those found between faces and nonface objects of expertise (Rossion et al., 2004, 2007) supports this hypothesis of an overlap of representations at the cellular level. Moreover, instances of long-term interference effects described previously in the section "Evidence for Long-Term Interference between Face and Nonface Expert Processing" (Behrmann, Marotta, Gauthier, Tarr, & McKeeff, 2005; Gauthier et al., 1999; Kung, 2006), which suggest that face processes suffer from the development of visual expertise with nonface objects, also support this view: A substantial part of the face representations would no longer be tuned selectively to faces, leading to a decrease in performance and neural activation for faces even without the concurrent presentation of nonface objects.

A second hypothesis is that the competition between objects of expertise and faces may be due to competitive interactions from distinct but neighboring populations of cells through local lateral inhibitory connections (Allison, Puce, & McCarthy, 2002; Waltz & Stanfill, 1988). In the monkey brain, local inhibition contributes to generating the response specificity of IT neurons to complex stimuli. Furthermore, blocking inhibition in IT neurons mostly reveals the responses of a cell to new stimuli differing from a preferred stimulus in systematic ways along certain parameters (contrast, shape, etc.), suggesting that local competition between preferred stimuli at the single-cell level is not randomly organized, but depends on the object features (Waltz & Stanfill, 1988). This mechanism would be difficult to reconcile with findings suggestive of long-term interference between face and nonface expert processing described in the previous section but fits with the observation that the competition is larger when the two domains (faces and nonface objects of expertise) are presented concurrently rather than sequentially (Rossion et al., 2007).

In summary, the competition effects described in this chapter between faces and objects of expertise may result from the recruitment of face cells for nonface objects of expertise, or from an increase in local competition generated from distinct populations of cells coding for objects of expertise, following extensive visual expertise training. Given the evidence summarized here, our view would be that both mechanisms are possibly at work. In the novice brain, faces and nonface objects may be represented by separate populations of neurons organized in clusters of columns, at a spatial resolution level below that of a functional area such as the FFA (Allison, et al., 1999; Tsao et al., 2006; Wang, Tanaka, & Tanifuji, 1996). However, this functional organization of high-level visual areas would remain relatively plastic in the adult brain, such that visual expertise with certain classes of objects would both (1) increase the tuning of neuronal populations within the same area for these objects at the expense of the face representations and (2) increase the competition through inhibitory connections between representations for nonface objects of expertise and faces. Future studies coupling interference paradigms with high spatial resolution methods such as fMRI or optical imaging are needed to clarify this issue. As far as the face modularity debate is concerned, it does not matter much whether competition effects reflect the recruitment of an overlapping set of neurons or rather inhibitory mechanisms between neighbor populations of neurons. What matters is that these effects take place *within the same functional area*, indicating that they concern clusters of neurons that are degenerate, that is, that can potentially carry the same function (Leonardo, 2005; Tononi, Sporns, & Edelman, 1999), and thus these findings are inconsistent with the face modularist view.

Functional Mechanisms

Through what functional mechanisms does the development of visual expertise lead to increased competition between the processing of face and nonface objects? Even though this view is somewhat simplistic, holistic processing, in the sense of a stronger interdependence of features, is a main candidate. There is evidence not only that faces are processed more holistically than other nonface objects in general (Farah, et al., 1998; Tanaka & Farah, 1993; Tanaka & Gauthier, 1997), but also that visual expertise with nonface objects leads to a shift to a more holistic processing strategy (Diamond & Carey, 1986; Gauthier & Tarr, 1997). Most importantly, some studies reviewed here show that measures of holistic processing reflect interference between concurrently processed faces and nonface objects of expertise (Curby & Gauthier, 2001; Gauthier et al., 2003). However, much future work with more compelling evidence is required to confirm these observations (Robbins & McKone, 2006). In addition, before the potential of holistic processing to account for the functional overlap between face and nonface expertise can be properly assessed, a clear understanding of the mechanism responsible for face holistic processing effects is necessary (e.g., the composite effect forming the basis of the interference index used in the dual-task paradigm; Gauthier et al., 2003). Currently, the concept of holistic face processing is not only defined differently by different groups, but it all too often is described in terms of the end product rather than the actual mechanism underlying this phenomenon. For example, one of the most widely accepted definitions of holistic processing describes the inseparability of features from their context in holistic representations (Farah et al., 1998). This definition was responsible for inspiring over a decade of insightful work on face processing, but an important unanswered question is how this interdependence between features and their context arises. Such attempts to understand the mechanism rather than just the consequences of holistic processing are a worthy direction for future research and will provide much insight not only into the functional basis of the overlap between face and nonface expert processing, but also into perceptual expertise more generally.

REFERENCES

Allison, T., Puce, A., & McCarthy, G. (2002). Category-sensitive excitatory and inhibitory processes in human extrastriate cortex. *Journal of Neurophysiology, 88*(5), 2864–2868.

Allison, T., Puce, A., Spencer, D. D., & McCarthy, G. (1999). Electrophysiological studies of human face perception. I: Potentials generated in occipitotemporal cortex by face and non-face stimuli. *Cerebral Cortex, 9*, 415–430.

Baddeley, A. D., & Hitch, G. J. (1974). Working memory. In G. H. Bower (Ed.), *The psychology of learning and motivation, 8*, (pp. 47–89) New York: Academic Press.

Baker, C., Behrmann, M., & Olson, C. R. (2002). Impact of learning on representation of parts and wholes in monkey inferotemporal cortex. *Nature Neuroscience, 5*(11), 1210–1216.

Behrmann, M., Marotta, J., Gauthier, I., Tarr, M. J., & McKeeff, T. J. (2005). Behavioral change and its neural correlates in visual agnosia after expertise training. *Journal of Cognitive Neuroscience, 17*(4), 554–568.

Bengtsson, S. L., Nagy, Z., Skare, S., Forsman, L., Forssberg, H., & Ullen, F. (2005). Extensive piano practicing has regionally specific effects on white matter development. *Nature Neuroscience, 8*(9), 1148–1150.

Bentin, S., Allison, T., Puce, A., Perez, E., & McCarthy, G. (1996). Electrophysiological studies of face perception in humans. *Journal of Cognitive Neuroscience, 8*(6), 551–565.

Bindemann, M., Burton, A. M., & Jenkins, R. (2005). Capacity limits for face processing. *Cognition, 98*(2), 177–197.

Bodamer, J. (1947). Die Prosop-Agnosie. *Archiv für Psychiatrie und Nervenkrankheiten, 179*, 6–54.

Buonomano, D. V., & Merzenich, M. M. (1998). Cortical plasticity: from synapses to maps. *Annual Review of Neuroscience, 21*, 149–186.

Busey, T. A., & Vanderkolk, J. R. (2005). Behavioral and electrophysiological evidence for configural processing in fingerprint experts. *Vision Research, 45*(4), 431–448.

Churchland, P. S. & Sejnowski, T. J. (1988). Neural representations and neural computation. In L. Nadel (Ed.), *Biological computation*. Cambridge, MA: MIT Press.

Curby, K. M., & Gauthier, I. (2001, November). *Interference between car and face expertise*. Paper presented at the OPAM workshop, Orlando, Florida.

Curby, K. M., & Gauthier, I. (2007). A visual short-term memory advantage for faces. *Psychonomic Bulletin and Review, 14*, 620–628.

Curby, K. M., Glazek, K., & Gauthier, I. (2009). A visual short-term memory advantage for objects of expertise. *Journal of Experimental Psychology: Human Perception and Performance, 35*(1), 94–107.

Desimone, R. (1991). Face-selective cells in the temporal cortex of monkeys. *Journal of Cognitive Neuroscience, 3*(1), 1–8.

Desimone, R. (1998). Visual attention mediated by biased competition in extrastriate visual cortex. *Philosophical Transactions of the Royal Society London B, Biological Sciences, 353*(1373), 1245–1255.

Diamond, R., & Carey, S. (1986). Why faces are and are not special: An effect of expertise. *Journal of Experimental Psychology: General, 115*(2), 107–117.

Elbert, T., Pantev, C., Wienbruch, C., Rockstroh, B., & Taub, E. (1995). Increased cortical representation of the fingers of the left hand in string players. *Science, 270*(5234), 305–307.

Ellis, H. D. & Young, A. W. (1989). Are faces special? In A. W. Young & H. D. Ellis (Eds.), *Handbook of research on face processing* (1–26). Amsterdam: North Holland.

Endo, M., Masame, K., & Maruyama, K. (1989). Interference from configuration of a schematic face onto the recognition of its constituent parts. *Tohoku Psychologica Folia, 48*(1–4), 97–106.

Farah, M. J., Wilson, K. D., Drain, H. M., & Tanaka, J. R. (1995). The inverted face inversion effect in prosopagnosia: Evidence for mandatory, face-specific perceptual mechanisms. *Vision Research, 35*(14), 2089–2093.

Farah, M. J., Wilson, K. D., Drain, M., & Tanaka, J. N. (1998). What is "special" about face perception? *Psychological Review, 105*(3), 482–498.

Feldman, D. E., & Brecht, M. (2005). Map plasticity in somatosensory cortex. *Science, 310*(5749), 810–815.

Galton, F. (1879). Composite portraits, made by combining those of many different persons into a single resultant figure. *The Journal of the Anthropological Institute of Great Britain and Ireland, 8*, 132–144

Gauthier, I., Curby, K. M., Skudlarski, P., & Epstein, R. A. (2005). Individual differences in FFA activity suggest independent processing at spatial scales. *Cognitive, Affective, and Behavioral Neuroscience, 5*(2), 222–234.

Gauthier, I., Curran, T., Curby, K. M., & Collins, D. (2003). Perceptual interference supports a non-modular account of face processing. *Nature Neuroscience, 6*(4), 428–432.

Gauthier, I., Skudlarski, P., Gore, J. C., & Anderson, A. W. (2000). Expertise for cars and birds recruits brain areas involved in face recognition. *Nature Neuroscience, 3*(2), 191–197.

Gauthier, I., & Tarr, M. J. (1997). Becoming a "Greeble" expert: Exploring mechanisms for face recognition. *Vision Research, 37*(12), 1673–1682.

Gauthier, I., & Tarr, M. J. (2002). Unraveling mechanisms for expert object recognition: Bridging brain activity and behavior. *Journal of Experimental Psychology: Human Perception and Performance, 28*(2), 431–446.

Gauthier, I., Tarr, M. J., Anderson, A. W., Skudlarski, P., & Gore, J. C. (1999). Activation of the middle fusiform "face area" increases with expertise in recognizing novel objects. *Nature Neuroscience, 2*(6), 568–573.

Gauthier, I., Williams, P., Tarr, M. J., & Tanaka, J. (1998). Training "Greeble" experts: A framework for studying expert object recognition processes. *Vision Research, 38*(15/16), 2401–2428.

Goffaux, V., & Rossion, B. (2006). Faces are "spatial"—holistic face perception is supported by low spatial frequencies. *Journal of Experimental Psychology: Human Perception and Performance, 32*(4), 1023–1039.

Grill-Spector, K., Sayres, R., & Ress, D. (2006). High-resolution imaging reveals highly selective nonface clusters in the fusiform face area. *Nature Neuroscience, 9*(9), 1177–1185.

Gross, C. G., Roche-Miranda G. E., & Bender, D. B. (1972). Visual properties of neurons in the inferotemporal cortex of the macaque. *Journal of Neurophysiology, 35*, 96–111.

Henson, R. N., Goshen-Gottstein, Y., Ganel, T., Otten, L. J., Quayle, A., & Rugg, M. D. (2003). Electrophysiological and haemodynamic correlates of face perception, recognition and priming. *Cerebral Cortex, 13*(7), 793–805.

Herrmann, M. J., Ehlis, A. C., Muehlberger, A., & Fallgatter, A. J. (2005). Source localization of early stages of face processing. *Brain Topography, 18*(2), 77–85.

Hershler, O., & Hochstein, S. (2005). At first sight: a high-level pop out effect for faces. *Vision Research, 45*(13), 1707–1724.

Hillger, L. A., & Koenig, O. (1991). Separable mechanisms in face processing: Evidence from hemispheric specialization. *Journal of Cognitive Neuroscience, 3*(1), 42–58.

Hole, G. J. (1994). Configurational factors in the perception of unfamiliar faces. *Perception, 23*(1), 65–74.

Hole, G. J., George, P., & Dunsmore, V. (1999). Evidence for holistic processing of faces viewed as photographic negatives. *Perception, 28*, 341–359.

Hubel, D. H., Wiesel, T. N., & LeVay, S. (1977). Plasticity of ocular dominance columns in monkey striate cortex. *Philosophical Transactions of the Royal Society London B, Biological Sciences, 278*(961), 377–409.

Jacques, C., & Rossion, B. (2004). Concurrent processing reveals competition between visual representations of faces. *NeuroReport, 15*(15), 2417–2421.

Jacques, C., & Rossion, B. (2006). The time course of visual competition to the presentation of centrally fixated faces. *Journal of Vision, 6*(2), 154–162.

Jacques, C., & Rossion, B. (2007). Electrophysiological evidence for temporal dissociation between spatial attention and sensory competition during human face processing. *Cerebral Cortex, 17*(5), 1055–1065.

Jeffreys, D. A. (1996). Evoked potential studies of face and object processing. *Visual Cognition, 3*(1), 1–38.

Jenkins, R., Lavie, N., & Driver, J. (2003). Ignoring famous faces: Category-specific dilution of distractor interference. *Perception and Psychophysics, 65*(2), 298–309.

Joyce, C., & Rossion, B. (2005). The face-sensitive N170 and VPP components manifest the same brain processes: The effect of reference electrode site. *Clinical Neurophysiology, 116*(11), 2613–2631.

Kaas, J. H., Merzenich, M. M., & Killackey, H. P. (1983). The reorganization of somatosensory cortex following peripheral nerve damage in adult and developing mammals. *Annual Review of Neuroscience, 6*, 325–356.

Kanwisher, N. (2000). Domain specificity in face perception. *Nature Neuroscience, 3*(8), 759–763.

Kastner, S., De Weerd, P., Desimone, R., & Ungerleider, L. G. (1998). Mechanisms of directed attention in the human extrastriate cortex as revealed by functional MRI. *Science, 282*(5386), 108–111.

Kastner, S., & Ungerleider, L. G. (2001). The neural basis of biased competition in human visual cortex. *Neuropsychologia, 39*(12), 1263–1276.

Kung, C.-C. (2006). Prolonging the FFA debate: Reevaluating recent studies and new evidence for the flexible and multimodal fusiform gyrus. Unpublished Doctorial Dissertation, Brown University.

Le Grand, R., Mondloch, C. J., Maurer, D., & Brent, H. P. (2004). Impairment in holistic face processing following early visual deprivation. *Psychological Science, 15*(11), 762–768.

Leonardo, A. (2005). Degenerate coding in neural systems. *Journal of Comparative Physiology A: Neuroethology, Sensory, Neural, and Behavioral Physiology, 191*(11), 995–1010.

Logothetis, N. K., & Pauls, J. (1995). Psychophysical and physiological evidence for viewer-centered object representations in the primate. *Cerebral Cortex, 5*(3), 270–288.

Logothetis, N. K., Pauls, J., Bülthoff, H. H., & Poggio, T. (1994). View-dependent object recognition in monkeys. *Current Biology, 4*(5), 401–414.

Logothetis, N. K., Pauls, J., & Poggio, T. (1995). Shape representation in the inferior temporal cortex of monkeys. *Current Biology, 5*(5), 552–563.

McKone, E., & Kanwisher, N. (2005). Does the human brain process objects of expertise like faces? A review of the evidence. In S. Dehaene, J.-R. Duhamel, M. D. Hauser, & G. Rizzolatti (Eds.), *From monkey brain to human brain* (pp. 339–356). Cambridge, MA: MIT Press.

McKone, E., Kanwisher, N., & Duchaine, B. C. (2007). Can generic expertise explain special processing for faces? *Trends in Cognitive Sciences, 11*(1), 8–15.

Merzenich, M. M., Kaas, J. H., Wall, J., Nelson, R. J., Sur, M., & Felleman, D. (1983). Topographic reorganization of somatosensory cortical areas 3b and 1 in adult monkeys following restricted deafferentation. *Neuroscience, 8*(1), 33–55.

Merzenich, M. M., Kaas, J. H., Wall, J. T., Sur, M., Nelson, R. J., & Felleman, D. J. (1983). Progression of change following median nerve section in the cortical representation of the hand in areas 3b and 1 in adult owl and squirrel monkeys. *Neuroscience, 10*(3), 639–665.

Michel, C., Rossion, B., Han, J., Chung, C. S., & Caldara, R. (2006). Holistic processing is finely tuned for faces of one's own race. *Psychological Science, 17*(7), 608–615.

Miller, E. K., Li, L., & Desimone, R. (1993). Activity of neurons in anterior inferior temporal cortex during a short-term memory task. *Journal of Neuroscience, 13*(4), 1460–1478.

Moran, J., & Desimone, R. (1985). Selective attention gates visual processing in the extrastriate cortex. *Science, 229*, 782–784.

Nachson, I. (1995). On the modularity of face recognition: The riddle of domain specificity. *Journal of Clinical and Experimental Neuropsychology, 17*(2), 256–275.

Nasanen, R., & Ojanpaa, H. (2004). How many faces can be processed during a single eye fixation? *Perception, 33*(1), 67–77.

Palermo, R., & Rhodes, G. (2002). The influence of divided attention on holistic face perception. *Cognition, 82*, 225–257.

Pantev, C., Bertrand, O., Eulitz, C., Verkindt, C., Hampson, S., Schuierer, G., & Elbert, T. (1995). Specific tonotopic organizations of different areas of the human auditory cortex revealed by simultaneous magnetic and electric recordings. *Electroencephalography and Clinical Neurophysiology, 94*(1), 26–40.

Pantev, C., Engelien, A., Candia, V., & Elbert, T. (2001). Representational cortex in musicians. Plastic alterations in response to musical practice. *Annals of the New York Academy of Sciences, 930*, 300–314.

Pantev, C., Oostenveld, R., Engelien, A., Ross, B., Roberts, L. E., & Hoke, M. (1998). Increased auditory cortical representation in musicians. *Nature, 392*(6678), 811–814.

Perrett, D. I., Rolls, E. T., & Caan, W. (1982). Visual neurones responsive to faces in the monkey temporal cortex. *Experimental Brain Research, 47*, 329–342.

Purcell, D. G., Stewart, A. L., & Skov, R. B. (1996). It takes a confounded face to pop out of a crowd. *Perception, 25*(9), 1091–1108.

Reynolds, J. H., Chelazzi, L., & Desimone, R. (1999). Competitive mechanisms subserve attention in macaque areas V2 and V4. *Journal of Neuroscience, 19*(5), 1736–1753.

Robbins, R., & McKone, E. (2006). No face-like processing for objects-of-expertise in three behavioural tasks. *Cognition, 103*(1), 34–79.

Rolls, E. T. (1992). Neurophysiological mechanisms underlying face processing within and beyond the temporal cortical visual areas. *Philosophical Transactions of the Royal Society London B: Biological Sciences, 335*(1273), 11–20.

Rolls, E. T., & Tovee, M. J. (1995). The responses of single neurons in the temporal visual cortical areas of the macaque when more than one stimulus is present in the receptive field. *Experimental Brain Research, 103*, 409–420.

Rossion, B., Collins, D., Goffaux, V., & Curran, T. (2007). Long-term expertise with artificial objects increases visual competition with early face categorization processes. *Journal of Cognitive Neuroscience, 19*(3), 543–555.

Rossion, B., Gauthier, I., Goffaux, V., Tarr, M. J., & Crommelinck, M. (2002). Expertise training with novel objects leads to left lateralized face-like electrophysiological responses. *Psychological Science, 13*(3), 250–257.

Rossion, B., Gauthier, I., Tarr, M. J., Despland, P. A., Linotte, S., Bruyer, R., & Crommelinck, M. (2000). The N170 occipito-temporal component is enhanced and delayed to inverted faces but not to inverted objects: An electrophyiological account of face-specific processes in the human brain. *NeuroReport, 11*, 1–6.

Rossion, B., Joyce, C. A., Cottrell, G. W., & Tarr, M. J. (2003). Early lateralization and orientation tuning for face, word, and object processing in the visual cortex. *Neuroimage, 20*(3), 1609–1624.

Rossion, B., Kung, C. C., & Tarr, M. J. (2004). Visual expertise with nonface objects leads to competition with the early perceptual processing of faces in the human occipitotemporal cortex. *Proceedings of the National Academy of Sciences U S A, 101*(40), 14521–14526.

Rousselet, G. A., Thorpe, S. J., & Fabre-Thorpe, M. (2004). How parallel is visual processing in the ventral pathway? *Trends in Cognitive Science, 8*(8), 363–370.

Schiltz, C., & Rossion, B. (2006). Faces are represented holistically in the human occipito-temporal cortex. *Neuroimage, 32*(3), 1385–1394.

Schlaug, G., Jancke, L., Huang, Y., Staiger, J. F., & Steinmetz, H. (1995). Increased corpus callosum size in musicians. *Neuropsychologia, 33*(8), 1047–1055.

Schultz, R. T., Grelotti, D. J., Klin, A., Kleinman, J., Van der Gaag, C., Marois, R., & Skudlarski, P. (2003). The role of the fusiform face area in social cognition: Implications for the pathobiology of autism. *Philosophical Transactions of the Royal Society London B, Biological Sciences, 358*(1430), 415–427.

Sergent, J. (1984). An investigation into component and configural processes underlying face perception. *British Journal of Psychology, 75*(2), 221–242.

Sergent, J., & Signoret, J. L. (1992). Implicit access to knowledge derived from unrecognized faces in prosopagnosia. *Cerebral Cortex, 2*, 389–400.

Tanaka, J. W., & Curran, T. (2001). A neural basis for expert object recognition. *Psychological Science, 12*(1), 43–47.

Tanaka, K. (1996). Inferotemporal cortex and object vision. *Annual Review of Neuroscience, 19*, 109–139.

Tanaka, J. W., & Farah, M. J. (1993). Parts and wholes in face recognition. *Quarterly Journal of Experimental Psychology, 46A*, 225–245.

Tanaka, J. W., & Gauthier, I. (1997). Expertise in object and face recognition. In R. L. Goldstone & P. G. Schyns (Eds.), *Mechanisms of perceptual learning* (Vol. 36, pp. 83–125). San Diego, CA: Academic Press.

Tarr, M. J., & Gauthier, I. (2000). FFA: A flexible fusiform area for subordinate-level visual processing automatized by expertise. *Nature Neuroscience, 3*(8), 764–769.

Tononi, G., Sporns, O., & Edelman, G. M. (1999). Measures of degeneracy and redundancy in biological networks. *Proceedings of the National Academy of Sciences U S A, 96*(6), 3257–3262.

Treisman, A. M., & Gelade, G. (1980). A feature-integration theory of attention. *Cognitive Psychology, 12*, 97–136.

Tsao, D. Y., Freiwald, W. A., Tootell, R. B., & Livingstone, M. S. (2006). A cortical region consisting entirely of face-selective cells. *Science, 311*(5761), 670–674.

VanRullen, R. (2006). On second glance: Still no high-level pop-out effect for faces. *Vision Research, 46*(18), 3017–3027.

Waltz, D. L., & Stanfill, C. (1988). *Artificial intelligence related research on the connection machine.* Paper presented at the Proceedings of the International Conference on Fifth Generation Computational Systems, Tokyo, Japan.

Wang, G., Tanaka, K., & Tanifuji, M. (1996). Optical imaging of functional organization in the monkey inferotemporal cortex. *Science, 272*, 1665–1668.

Wolfe, J. M., Cave, K. R., & Franzel, S. L. (1989). Guided search: An alternative to the feature integration model for visual search. *Journal of Experimental Psychology: Human Perception and Performance, 15*, 419–433.

Xu, Y. (2005). Revisiting the role of the fusiform face area in visual expertise. *Cerebral Cortex, 15*(1234–1242).

Yin, R. K. (1969). Looking at upside-down faces. *Journal of Experimental Psychology, 81*(1), 141–145.

Young, A. W., Hellawell, D., & Hay, D. (1987). Configural information in face perception. *Perception, 10*, 747–759.

9

The Locus of Holistic Processing

Olivia S. Cheung and Isabel Gauthier

INTRODUCTION

When you see a big smile on someone's face, you may expect to also see dimples or scrunched eyes. If the smile is replaced by a plain expression, the scrunched eyes also appear to have changed. Any change to a face part influences our perception and interpretation of other face parts. This holistic, interactive processing of parts is thought to be special for faces (Tanaka & Farah,1993; Young, Hellawell, & Hay, 1987) and objects of expertise (Gauthier, Curran, Curby, Collins, 2003; Gauthier & Tarr, 1997, 2002) because we do not have such strong associations for the parts of other common objects. As illustrated in Figure 9.1, it is probably much easier to see that the handles of the two cups are identical than to see that the two face top parts are the same. These examples demonstrate the holistic nature of face processing, as opposed to the part-based nature of common object processing (Biederman, 1987).

This chapter reviews the literature on the locus of holistic processing. It is often assumed that holistic processing has a perceptual locus. However, since perception as a mental construct can only be inferred rather than directly measured, researchers must analyze perceptual processes or representations from observers' responses. Before producing a response, a decisional process is required to interpret the percept and select a response based on the task at hand (Ashby & Townsend, 1986). Therefore, both perceptual and decisional processes may alter the way the observer responds to a perceptual event. Unfortunately, decisional mechanisms have largely been neglected by researchers who are interested in face perception. Recently, several studies have examined the contributions of perceptual and decisional processes in the holistic effects that characterize face perception, and revealed consistent decisional influences (Richler, Gauthier, Wenger, & Palmeri, 2008; Wenger & Ingvalson, 2002, 2003). Thus, there is a need to reconsider the processing loci of holistic effects.

The first section, "*Holistic Processing of Faces*," outlines the operational definitions of holistic processing and reviews the paradigms that are frequently employed to study holistic processing, including the inversion paradigm, the whole–part paradigm, and the composite paradigm. Several major research questions on holistic processing addressed with these paradigms are also discussed. Importantly, we suggest that a basic theory of holistic processing that explains the locus of the interactions of facial features is still lacking. The second section, "*Evidence for the Perceptual and Decisional Loci of Holistic*

Figure 9.1 Example of faces with identical top parts and cups with identical handles. Because of the holistic nature of face processing, it is more difficult to recognize that the face top parts are the same than to see that the cup handles are identical.

Processing," discusses two methods that can be used to examine perceptual and decisional influences on holistic processing in the existing literature. The first method compares the magnitude of holistic effects induced by manipulations during perceptual encoding and decisional judgment stages in different tasks. By separating the effects arising from perceptual encoding and the decisional judgment stages, it is shown that manipulations at the decisional stage alone can influence the magnitude of holistic effects. These results thus suggest a possible decisional locus of holistic processing. The second method utilizes signal detection measures to examine perceptual and decisional effects by assessing discriminability and response bias from accuracy data. Response biases are readily obtained in various studies intended to study perceptual effects in holistic processing (Davidoff & Donnelley, 1990; Farah, Wilson, Drain, & Tanaka, 1998; Hole, 1994). These findings provide additional support for decisional influences on holistic processing. Crucially, the locus of holistic processing can also be investigated within the general recognition theory framework (Ashby & Townsend, 1986), which distinguishes the influences of perceptual and decisional interaction of face parts in cases where conventional behavioral holistic measures fail to separate them (Richler, Gauthier, et al., 2008). The third section, *"General Recognition Theory,"* discusses the varieties of psychological interactions between parts of an object that can contribute to holistic effects, as distinguished by general recognition theory, and the analyses used for revealing these interactions. This line of research supports the importance of a decisional locus in holistic processing (Farivar & Chaudhuri, 2003; Richler, Gauthier, et al., 2008; Wenger & Ingvalson, 2002, 2003). The fourth section, *"Evaluations, Implications and Future Directions,"* evaluates the evidence so far on the locus of holistic processing and ends by discussing future directions for the investigation of holistic processing.

HOLISTIC PROCESSING OF FACES

Over a hundred years ago, Galton (1879) reported an intriguing demonstration that an image formed by superimposing several individual faces appeared as a natural though slightly blurred face rather than a mere combination of face parts from different individuals. This demonstration suggests that faces are recognized by the overall impression of all parts instead of separate parts. Since all faces share the same basic configuration (such as two eyes above a nose that is above a mouth), the precise spatial relationships among parts become critical in distinguishing individual faces (Diamond & Carey, 1986; Friere, Lee, & Symons, 2000; Leder & Bruce, 1998; 2000; Leder, Candrian, Huber, & Bruce, 2001; Le Grand, Mondloch, Maurer, & Brent, 2004; Mondloch, Le Grand, & Maurer, 2002; Murray, 2004; Murray, Rhodes, & Schuchinsky, 2003; Rhodes, Brake, & Atkinson, 1993; Searcy & Bartlett, 1996). It is suggested that facial features and their spatial information are processed in a holistic, interactive manner (Macho & Leder, 1998; Sergent, 1984; Tanaka & Sengco, 1997; Thomas, 2001). Because of the integrative nature of features and the spatial relations among them, selective attention to part of a face is extremely difficult (Hole, 1994; Young et al., 1987). According to one influential hypothesis, face parts and configural information among parts are encoded and represented as a unitary whole, whereas other objects (e.g., houses) are represented only with respect to their parts (Farah, Tanaka, & Drain, 1995; Farah et al., 1998; Tanaka & Farah, 1993; Tanaka & Sengco, 1997). Alternatively, perceptual representations of faces may not be holistic, but judgment of a face part may be affected by the presence of other face parts in the whole, resulting in holistic effects (Richler, Gauthier, et al., 2008; Wenger & Ingvalson, 2002).

A main characteristic of holistic processing is its vulnerability to changes in stimulus orientation. Recognition performance is disproportionally impaired when faces are upside down, compared to when other everyday objects that are normally seen in the upright orientation are inverted (Yin, 1969). Yin proposed that inversion impairs face recognition, which relies on a "general impression of the whole picture" (p.145), more than object recognition, which depends on discrimination of features. This idea was supported in a study showing that the large inversion effect for faces is caused by the disruption of encoding holistic representations (Farah et al., 1995). Subsequent studies have used the inversion effect to infer holistic processing (Carey, Diamond, & Woods, 1980; Rossion et al., 1999; Sagiv & Bentin, 2001; Schwarzer, 2000), or used inverted faces as control stimuli to contrast with the holistic processing of upright faces (e.g., Boutet, Gentes-Hawn, & Chaudhuri, 2002; Farah et al., 1998; Palermo & Rhodes, 2002; Robbins & McKone, 2003). However, the inversion effect remains an indirect measure of holistic processing.

Two direct measures of holistic processing are the whole–part paradigm and the composite paradigm. The rationale of the whole–part paradigm is that if parts of a stimulus are explicitly represented, then recognition of parts alone should be as good as that within the context of other parts (Joseph & Tanaka, 2003; Leder & Carbon, 2005; Michel, Caldara, & Rossion, 2006; Palmer, 1977; Palermo & Rhodes, 2002; Pellicano & Rhodes, 2004; Tanaka & Farah, 1993; Tanaka & Sengco, 1997). In a whole–part task, observers are asked to identify facial features either embedded in whole faces that differ only in the target features (whole condition) or in isolation (part condition). Holistic processing is demonstrated by the better performance for identifying facial features in the whole than part condition, indicating that representations of facial features become contextually dependent on the whole (Tanaka & Farah, 1993)[1]. Also, face recognition is impaired when the spatial relationships among features are different from study to test (Le Grand et al., 2004; Mondloch et al., 2002; Tanaka & Sengco, 1997), suggesting that at least part of the representation for a face is based on the relations of features in the whole context.

The composite paradigm reveals holistic processing in terms of an interference effect, as the task-irrelevant parts on a face influence the processing of the target parts (Carey & Diamond, 1994; Hole, 1994; Young et al., 1987). This result suggests that faces in meaningful configurations are processed as wholes. In this task, composites are formed by combining the top and bottom parts of different individual faces. Observers are asked to attend to one part of the composite and ignore the other part. In one version of the composite task, termed the *complete design* (Gauthier & Bukach, 2007; see Figure 9.2), the congruency of the relations of the top and bottom parts between study and test is manipulated (Cheung, Richler, Palmeri, & Gauthier, 2008; Farah et al., 1998; Gauthier et al., 2003; Richler, Gauthier, et al., 2008; Richler, Tanaka, Brown, & Gauthier, 2008). The task-relevant and task-irrelevant parts can each be the same or different, resulting in congruent relations (both top and

---

[1] One caveat is that the whole–part effect is only obtained when observers first study whole faces: better performance for parts than wholes is observed when observers first study parts (Leder & Carbon, 2005). Therefore, the whole–part effect might reflect a study–test compatibility effect instead of revealing a true advantage for integrated, holistic representations.

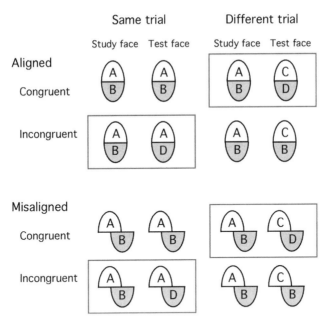

Figure 9.2 Schematic of the trial types used in the two versions of composite task, with different letters representing different identities and task-relevant parts in white and task-irrelevant parts in gray. The necessary trials in the *complete design* include congruent and incongruent trials of aligned composites (top panel), whereas trials with misaligned composites (bottom panel) may also be included. The boxes indicate the trials included in the *partial design*.

bottom parts are the same between the study and test items or both are different) and incongruent relations (one of the parts is the same between study and test, but the other part is different). In this task, holistic processing is revealed by better discriminability (usually measured by d') for congruent than incongruent trials, indicating a failure of selective attention to parts in whole faces even when observers are instructed to only attend to the task-relevant parts. The congruency effect is typically found for upright, aligned face parts and is reduced for various stimulus transformations such as inversion or misalignment of parts (Farah et al., 1998; Richler, Tanaka, et al., 2008; Wenger & Ingvalson, 2002). Another common version of the composite paradigm is termed the *partial design* (Gauthier & Bukach, 2007) and contains only half of the trials from the *complete design*. The partial design follows the paradigm used by Young and colleagues (1987), where the face parts of each composite are either spatially aligned or misaligned, and the task-irrelevant parts are always different across study and test faces. Typically, identification performance of the target parts is worse (lower hit rates and slower response times) when the two parts are aligned than when misaligned (e.g., Boutet et al., 2002; Carey & Diamond, 1994; Goffaux & Rossion, 2006; Hole, 1994; Le Grand et al., 2004; Robbins & McKone, 2007;

Weston & Perfect, 2005; Young et al., 1987). These results are typically interpreted to reveal that aligned face parts are recognized as a whole face because the different task-irrelevant parts produce interference on the recognition of the target parts[2].

Holistic processing has been a major topic of focus in research on face recognition. Studies have investigated various aspects of holistic processing, such as whether it is specific for faces or whether it develops through perceptual expertise and so might occur for other kinds of objects (see Chapter 2), its developmental course (see Chapter 3), whether it is automatic or demands attentional resources (see Chapter 8), and its neural correlates with electrophysiological and neuroimaging techniques (see Chapters 1 and 6). These issues are briefly discussed below.

The whole–part effect and the composite effect are robust for upright faces and are reduced or absent for inverted faces, scrambled faces, and common or novel objects (Farah et al., 1998; Robbins & McKone, 2007; Tanaka & Farah, 1993; Tanaka & Sengco, 1997; Young et al., 1987; but see Davidoff & Donnelly, 1990). However, holistic effects are not unique to faces; they can also be found for other object categories when observers have acquired perceptual expertise (Diamond & Carey, 1986; Gauthier & Curby, 2005; Gauthier & Tarr, 1997, 2002; Gauthier, Williams, Tarr, & Tanaka, 1998; Gauthier et al., 2003), especially in the case of expertise that requires recognizing individual exemplars in a category. These findings argue against the idea that holistic processing is face specific. It has also been suggested that holistic processing for faces may take about 4 years to develop (Carey & Diamond, 1977; de Heering, Houthuys, & Rossion, 2007; Pellicano & Rhodes, 2003), and that it is not broadly tuned to all faces of different races (e.g., Chance, Turner, & Goldstein, 1982; Goldstein & Chance, 1980; Michel, Caldara, & Rossion, 2006; Michel, Rossion, Han, Chung, & Caldara, 2006). This is consistent with the idea that holistic processing for both faces and objects may be acquired through similar processes.

The acquisition of perceptual expertise can alter processing in a variety of ways, but critically, expertise tends to result in some degree of automaticity (e.g., Schiffrin & Schneider, 1977; Schneider & Shiffin, 1977). Because most individuals are experts with faces, holistic processing may be automatically engaged when faces are perceived (Boutet et al., 2002). For example, when observers are instructed to selectively attend to part of a whole face, the task-irrelevant part is nonetheless processed (Hole, 1994; Leder & Carbon, 2005; Young et al., 1987). Moreover, while divided attention to objects during the encoding of faces does not affect holistic face processing (Boutet et al., 2002), in contrast, divided attention to other upright faces reduces holistic

---

[2] Caution should be taken to interpret the results from the partial design because such results (i.e., differences in hit rates) may be driven by response biases rather than true differences in perceptual discriminability (e.g., Cheung et al., 2008; Richler, Tanaka, et al., 2008). More elaborate discussion on this issue can be found in the fourth section of this chapter.

processing of a target face. This suggests that holistic processing has a domain-specific limited attentional capacity that may be limited to one upright face at a time (Bindemann, Burton, Jenkins, 2005; Bindemann, Jenkins, Burton, 2007; Boutet & Chaudhuri, 2001; Palermo & Rhodes, 2002).

Holistic processing also accompanies two important neural signatures of face perception. In electrophysiological studies, a larger amplitude of the N170, a negative-going component occurring around 170 ms after the stimulus onset recorded from the occipitotemporal sites in the right hemisphere, is found for faces and objects of expertise, which are processed holistically, compared with other objects (Bentin, Allison, Puce, & Perez, 1996; Carmel & Bentin, 2002; Tanaka & Curran, 2001). Inverted faces or objects of expertise, for which holistic processing is disrupted, cause a delay in the N170 component (Rossion et al., 1999; Rossion et al., 2000; Rossion, Gauthier, Goffaux, Tarr, & Crommelinck, 2002). While dividing attention among several upright faces reduces the whole–part effect of a target face (Palermo & Rhodes, 2002), the N170 amplitude for a target face is also reduced if the target face is simultaneously presented with other upright faces or objects of expertise (Jacques & Rossion, 2004, 2006a, 2006b; Rossion, Kung, & Tarr, 2004; see also Gauthier et al., 2003), suggesting a close relation between holistic processing and the N170. Holistic processing is also correlated with the selective activation of the fusiform "face" area (FFA) and the occipital "face" area (Gauthier & Tarr, 2002; Rotshtein, Geng, Driver, & Dolan, 2007; see also Schiltz & Rossion, 2006).

Surprisingly, although many empirical findings about holistic processing have accumulated, the notion of holistic processing itself remains imprecise (Wenger & Townsend, 2001). Specifically, the operational definitions of holistic processing, such as an advantage for part recognition in whole faces rather than in isolation (Tanaka & Farah, 1993), or failures of selective attention to parts (Young et al., 1987), lack a theoretical basis explaining how the multiple facial features and their configural relations may interact (O'Toole, Wenger, & Townsend, 2001; Wenger & Ingvalson, 2002; Wenger & Townsend, 2001). A large portion of the face literature has suggested or assumed that holistic processing is a perceptual effect (e.g., Farah et al., 1998; McKone, Kanwisher, & Duchaine, 2007; Robbins & McKone, 2007) and ignores the possibility that it might occur at other stages of processing. However, since the observable responses only reflect the final product of processing, psychological interactions may occur during different stages of processing, including perceptual or decisional processes (Ashby & Townsend, 1986). It is possible that holistic, interactive effects of face processing may take place during the perceptual processes (e.g., Farah et al., 1998; Tanaka & Farah, 1993; Tanaka & Sengco, 1997). This could stem from an advantage to the individuation of highly similar faces to represent facial features and their spatial relations as wholes (Zhang & Cottrell, 2005, but see Zhang & Cottrell, 2004). Alternatively, it is also possible that the representations of features are independent, but that interactions may occur during the decisional processes when an interpretation or a judgment about the percept is required (Richler, Gauthier, et al., 2008; Wenger & Ingvalson, 2002, 2003). In the real world, the top and bottom parts of a face always represent one individual, thus it is likely that the interpretation or decision for the identity of a part will change if there is a change of identity of another part.

The second section, "*Evidence for the Perceptual and Decisional Loci of Holistic Processing*," discusses attempts to separate the perceptual and decisional influences on holistic processing in past studies that used the inversion, whole–part, or composite tasks. However, since these tasks do not specifically attempt to study the interaction of features during the different stages of processing, these proposed methods remain indirect in teasing apart when such interactions occur. The third section discusses the general recognition theory framework that can be applied to directly investigate the interactions among multiple facial features during the perceptual and decisional processes.

EVIDENCE FOR THE PERCEPTUAL AND DECISIONAL LOCI OF HOLISTIC PROCESSING

In the majority of the face literature, it is suggested that holistic processing occurs during perceptual encoding (Bartlett & Searcy, 1993; Boutet et al., 2002; Carey & Diamond, 1994; Farah et al., 1998; Hole, 1994; Hole, George, & Dunsmore, 1999; Joseph & Tanaka, 2003; McKone et al., 2007; Palermo & Rhodes, 2002; Pellicano & Rhodes, 2003; Robbins & McKone, 2007; Sagiv & Bentin, 2001; Schwarzer & Massaro, 2001; Tanaka, Kiefer, & Bukach, 2004), which enables holistic representations to be stored in memory (Lewis & Glenister, 2003; Tanaka & Farah, 1993). These conclusions are based on the use of matching or memory tasks that involve a perceptual comparison between stimuli. By this account, judgments about face parts cannot be made independently because the representation of faces does not include independent representations of parts. However, the decisional component involved in these tasks is often overlooked. As will be discussed throughout this chapter, it is possible for parts to be represented independently and yet for decisions about them not to be independent (perhaps because of a history of regularities in our judgments of face parts). In this section, two methods that can be used to examine the perceptual and decisional effects in the conventional behavioral tasks are discussed.

Experimental Manipulations during the Study and Test Phases

It is difficult to completely disentangle perceptual and decisional stages in perceptual judgments because perceptual representations may be modified by how they are interpreted, and interpretations of perceptual representations may be influenced by additional incoming perceptual information (Vogel, Luck, & Shapiro, 1998). Here, perceptual and decisional processes are discussed as two separate stages for brevity of discussion. Perceptual and decisional processes may be separated according to the point where the necessary perceptual representation of a stimulus for a particular task has been formed and the interpretation of a perceptual representation for selection of a response is to be initiated. In a same–different judgment task with sequentially presented faces, the perceptual processes end when the representations of faces (or facial features) for a particular trial are formed. The decisional processes include interpretations of whether the perceptual representations of the study and test faces indicate a same or different identity. With these definitions, the relative influences of the perceptual and decisional processes may be observed within learning and sequential matching tasks. During the study phase of a learning or sequential matching task, the perceptual representational processes on the study item are critical. Since no response is required yet, the decisional processes are less important. During the test phase, a perceptual representation of the test item has to be formed. Additionally, the decisional process becomes relatively more important because a response has to be selected for the test item (Ashby & Townsend, 1986; Sternberg, 1969). Thus, the effects resulting from manipulations during the study phase may be interpreted as mostly perception based, whereas those resulting from manipulations during the test phase may be interpreted as reflecting stronger influences from decisional processes.

The relative roles of perceptual or decisional processes are difficult to differentiate in tasks where the manipulations at the study phase and the test phase are the same (e.g., both the study and test stimuli were in the same orientations, Carey & Diamond, 1977; Yin, 1969). But for studies that used different manipulations at study and test, the relative importance of perceptual or decisional processes can be observed based on *when* the manipulation is introduced. We will first discuss evidence for a perceptual locus revealed by manipulations at study, then evidence for decisional components revealed by manipulations at test. We also address concerns about ambiguity over whether certain effects occur solely at a decisional locus because the stimuli at test still have to perceptually encoded before a decision is made, and any mismatch in stimulus representations between study and test may be related to perceptual processes. Nonetheless, we suggest that this method of comparing the effects induced by manipulations at study or test provides at least some indications for decisional influences on holistic processing.

Perceptual Locus Revealed by Manipulations at Study

Several studies examined the effects of stimulus manipulations at study and revealed evidence that supports a perceptual locus for holistic processing. For instance, Farah et al. (1995) found that the inversion effect for whole faces during the test phase is stronger when whole faces rather than scattered face parts were presented during the study phase. The reduced inversion effect in the scattered part condition suggests that the inversion effect may rely on encoding of holistic representations at study. The relative importance of perceptual processes over decisional processes in holistic processing is also revealed in a study by Yin (1969), suggesting that the inversion effect can be induced by both study and test manipulations, but the effect is stronger when the faces are inverted at study compared to that at test. In one experiment, he manipulated the orientation of faces at either study or test. He found a larger inversion effect when observers studied inverted faces and were tested with upright faces, compared with when observers studied upright faces and were tested with inverted faces. In addition, the alignment effect in the composite paradigm was found when upright face composites were presented at both study and test, but it was eliminated when inverted face composites were studied and upright face composites were presented at test (Boutet et al., 2002). This finding also supports the idea that encoding of holistic representations of upright faces may be important for obtaining an alignment effect, suggesting that the perceptual stage may be the locus of the inversion and alignment effects.

Decisional Locus Revealed by Manipulations at Test

Other studies with stimuli manipulated at test suggest that perceptual encoding of whole faces may not be necessary to produce holistic effects (e.g., a large inversion effect, or an alignment or congruency effect in the composite paradigm), indicating that the locus of holistic processing may not be perceptual. Rather, decisional processes, such as evaluations or decision making on perceptual representations, may have a stronger influence in producing holistic effects. For instance, the magnitude of the inversion effect is not solely determined by encoding of upright, whole faces. Moscovitch and Moscovitch (2000) reported a larger inversion effect for face parts rather than whole faces presented at test: the accuracy of naming famous people was lower for upside-down fractured face parts than inverted intact faces. Also, perceptual representations of wholes at study are not necessary to produce an alignment effect, and it is possible that interference during the decisional processes may produce such effect. In an experiment by Young et al. (1987), observers first learned names for only the top parts of a few unfamiliar faces. Since only the top parts of the faces were shown, holistic representations could not be formed for those faces. During the test phase, the observers were presented with a composite face composed of a learned top part and a task-irrelevant bottom part that was not shown before, either aligned or misaligned with the learned top part. An alignment effect was found, with slower response times for naming parts of aligned than misaligned composites. Similarly, encoding of whole faces in a normal configuration is also not critical to obtain a congruency effect (Richler, Tanaka, et al., 2008). In a sequential matching task, Richler, Tanaka, et al. presented only the target parts at study, thus no representations of whole faces could be formed. During test, target parts were either aligned or misaligned with task-irrelevant parts. Although the task-irrelevant parts did not contain any useful information to match with the target parts, performance was worse for aligned than misaligned composites, suggesting that it was very difficult to ignore the task-irrelevant parts at test when they were aligned with the target parts. Therefore, the interference between face parts at test is sufficient to produce a composite effect. Richler, Tanaka, et al. (2008) also found that regardless of the configuration of parts presented during the study phase (whether they were aligned or misaligned), comparable congruency effects were obtained as long as aligned face composites were presented at test, showing that the face configuration at study may not be critical in producing a congruency effect. However, the congruency effect was significantly reduced with misaligned compared to aligned parts at test, regardless of whether aligned or misaligned composites were studied. Taken together, these findings suggest that encoding of perceptual representations of wholes may not be crucial in holistic processing. Instead, holistic effects may occur in postperceptual, decisional processes during evaluations of perceptual representations (e.g., the matching of a top part of a composite may be affected by whether the bottom part is the same or different from a study face).

Concerns Regarding Inferences of Decisional Effects

Although manipulations at test in sequential matching tasks have demonstrated strong influences on holistic processing, those manipulations during the test phases could have affected both perceptual and decisional processes. In particular, since the perceptual representations are incompatible between the study and test stimuli in several studies (Moscovitch & Moscovitch, 2000; Richler, Tanaka, et al., 2008; Young et al., 1987), one could argue that the reduction of the magnitude of alignment and congruency effects may due to the mismatch in the perceptual representations instead of the decisional processes of interpreting the perceptual representations or selecting a response. For instance, Leder and Carbon (2005) demonstrated that the whole–part effect is sensitive to whether the formats of the study and test items match. Specifically, the whole–part effect, as revealed by better matching performance when the target parts at test were embedded in wholes than when they were presented in isolation, was only obtained when observers first studied whole faces. Critically, the whole–part effect was reversed when observers first studied parts instead of whole faces. It is possible that the mismatch of perceptual representations alone, when parts are misaligned or changed, could account for the cost of manipulations at test (Richler, Tanaka, et al., 2008; Young et al., 1987). However, if a manipulation at test affects holistic processing more than a manipulation at study, when there is no mismatch between the formats of the study and test stimuli, a decisional influence can be inferred.

The relative influence of the decisional component has been isolated in a recent study that kept the representations of the study and test stimuli comparable (Cheung & Gauthier, in press). In a dual task paradigm, a working memory task of faces was inserted in between the study and test phases of a sequential matching composite task (see Figure 9.3). Observers were instructed to match only the top parts of the composites. In the load-at-study condition, study items of the working memory task were presented before a study composite, which was followed by a test item of the working

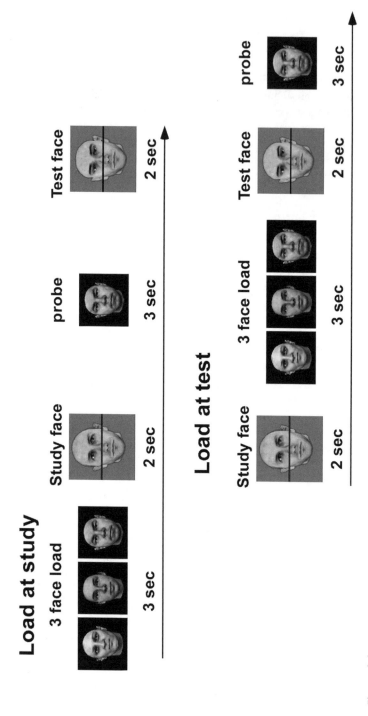

Figure 9.3 Schematic of the load-at-study condition (top panel) and the load-at-test condition (bottom panel) in Cheung and Gauthier (in press). Copyright © by the American Psychological Association. Adapted with permission.

memory task, then by a test composite. In the load-at-test condition, a study composite was presented before study items of the working memory task, which were followed by a test composite, then by the test item of the working memory task. Thus, the representations encoded in the composite task were analogous in both conditions. Compared to a no load condition, both working memory load conditions reduced the congruency effect for the composites, suggesting interference on holistic processing with the presence of a face working memory load. Importantly, the congruency effect was reduced further by the working memory load at test than at study. This finding provides strong evidence that decisional processes have a larger impact on holistic processing than perceptual processes.

Summary

To summarize, it is possible to observe the relative roles of perceptual and decisional processes by examining the effects arising from either the encoding stage or the decisional judgment stage. The idea that the perceptual encoding stage may be important for holistic processing is supported by several findings. For instance, inversion during the study phase appears to have a larger impact than inversion during the test phase on face processing (Farah et al., 1995). Inverted faces at study also reduce the alignment effect in the composite task (Boutet et al., 2002). In contrast, other findings indicate that face parts in meaningful configurations presented at test were processed as a whole regardless of whether holistic representations were encoded during study. Because perceptual effects should be strongest at study than at test because no comparison has to be made during study, the lack of effects by manipulations at study argues against a perceptual locus for holistic processing. For instance, a larger inversion effect was found for face parts than for whole faces at test (Moscovitch & Moscovitch, 2000), and additional task-irrelevant face parts at test produce interference even when only a single part was encoded at study, and result in the alignment effect and the congruency effect in the composite paradigm (Richler, Tanaka, et al., 2008; Young et al., 1987). When the formats of stimuli at study and test were equated, the congruency effect was further influenced by a face working memory load at test rather than at study (Cheung & Gauthier, in press). These findings indicate the importance of the decisional stage in holistic processing.

Signal Detection Measures Reveal Perceptual and Decisional Effects

One method to directly tease apart perceptual and decisional effects is to employ signal detection theory (Green & Swets, 1966; Swets, 1996). The classical signal detection theory is a means to discern discriminability and potential response bias in a task where observers are asked to distinguish signal from noise. The rationale of signal detection theory is that the discrimination of signals depends on the strength of the signal (discriminability) and the observer's strategy in choosing a response (response bias). Because of intrinsic variability in the perceptual system, the perceptual effect of an identical stimulus may differ across trials. Over trials, the varied perceptual effects of signal and noise form two probability distributions. Discriminability of signal from noise is indicated by the distance between these distributions. Also, signal detection theory emphasizes that the observer actively produces a decision rather than passively making a response. If an observer were not biased toward choosing either response, the location of response criterion would fall halfway in between the two probability distributions. However, given the same stimuli, one observer may be liberal in reporting detection of signals, whereas another observer may be conservative in judging the presence of a signal unless he or she is very certain about it. Thus, the location of response criterion may vary across observers or experimental conditions. Performance is based on both the discriminability and the response criterion.

In perceptual matching or recognition tasks, observers may be required to discriminate learned faces from new faces. Applying signal detection theory to such tasks, two probability distributions of percepts would be formed, one for learned faces and another for new faces. The discriminability of distinguishing learned faces from new faces would depend on the distance between their probability distributions. The location of the response criterion would depend on the strategy of observers. Here, it is of particular interest whether the experimental manipulations of holistic processing such as inversion or alignment would influence either discriminability or response criterion in face matching or recognition tasks.

In the face literature, response times and accuracy rates have been the main measures reported. Signal detection measures are seldom mentioned. This is critical because the holistic effects that have been attributed to perceptual processes could instead have been identified with decisional processes if response biases had been examined. Fortunately, some studies that examine holistic processing in same–different judgment tasks provide the accuracy rates in all conditions, which are necessary for post-hoc examination of discriminability and response bias measures. The results are summarized in Table 9–1.

Across various tasks, robust response biases are consistently observed in the different assessments of holistic processing. As illustrated in Table 9.1, there is a difference in response bias between upright and inverted composites when task-irrelevant parts were always different (Hole, 1994): observers were more likely to respond "different" to upright than to inverted composites, indicating that observers' response strategies became more conservative for upright than inverted composites with the presence of interference from the different task-irrelevant parts. In contrast, their discriminability appeared to be less affected by the orientation manipulation. This result suggests that conflicting information from the irrelevant part of a composite may be more likely to affect decisional judgment on (but not the perceptual representation of) the target part in upright than in inverted faces. Moreover, in Davidoff and Donnelly (1990), when upright faces were presented, observers were more likely to respond "same" to whole than part probes at test in a

Table 9–1   Post hoc discriminability (d') and response criterion (c) measures in studies involving the inversion (Hole, 1994) and whole–part (Davidoff & Donnelly, 1990) manipulations.

	D'	C
Hole (1994), Experiment 1, 2, and 3		
Top/bottom composites 2 sec		
Upright faces	1.745	.2275
Inverted faces	1.915	−.0075
Top/bottom composites 80 ms		
Upright faces	1.625	.1725
Inverted faces	1.535	−.0975
Left/right composites 80 ms		
Upright faces	1.745	.2475
Inverted faces	1.58	−.135
Davidoff & Donnelly (1990), Experiment 2		
Exposure time: 250 ms		
Wholes at test	1.445	−.2475
Parts at test	.844	−.102
Exposure time: 2 sec		
Wholes at test	2.626	−.163
Parts at test	1.724	.188

Note: A higher d' value indicates better discriminability. A positive c value indicates a tendency to respond "different," and a negative c value indicates a bias to respond "same."

sequential matching task. It is likely a study–test compatibility effect in response bias (as also shown in accuracy, Leder & Carbon, 2005) because the "same" whole probes at test were identical to the study stimuli (whole faces) while the "same" part probes were only parts of the study stimuli. Furthermore, participants are more likely to respond "different" for aligned than for misaligned composites (Cheung et al., 2008; Richler, Gauthier, et al., 2008; Richler, Tanaka, et al., 2008). It is possible that the frequent variation of part combinations in those studies resulted in a bias to respond "different" to aligned composites, which are holistically processed, more often than to misaligned composites, which rely more on part-based processing than aligned composites. Additionally, there is also a bias shift in the selective attention paradigm in Farah et al. (1998), as reported by Wenger & Ingvalson (2002), with observers more likely to respond "different" when the features were incongruent compared to when they were congruent, presumably because the incongruent facial information led observers to believe that the faces looked more different than those with congruent facial information. Similar response biases of responding "different" to incongruent compared to congruent trials for upright faces were also reported in Cheung et al. (2008) and Richler, Tanaka, et al. (2008). Other manipulations on face composites, such as spatial frequency filtering, also lead to differential response biases (Cheung et al., 2008). To conclude, response bias differences between conditions that are randomized within an experiment are prominent across many manipulations in various same–different judgment tasks that assessed holistic processing, indicating that the holistic effects may at least in part result from changes in the decisional processes. However, it is noteworthy that holistic effects can still be obtained using a forced-choice task where observers' response criterion is assumed to be to be unbiased (e.g., the whole–part effect, Pellicano & Rhodes, 2003; Tanaka & Farah, 1993; Tanaka & Sengco, 1997; the alignment effect, Teunisse & de Gelder, 2001). Nonetheless, the consistent response biases in the same–different judgment task should not be ignored because they suggest multiple influences that can contribute to holistic effects.

Importantly, response biases cannot be identified with a decisional stage of processing, as biases could occur as part of any process, perceptual or decisional. That is, one can conceive of a perceptual process that would be biased to perceive the world in a certain way, and of a decisional process that can bias the decisions it makes based on evidence received from the perceptual processes, depending on the outcome of different types of errors. The two mechanisms would have similar effects in standard signal detection analysis. One distinction, however, is that the perceptual bias would be expected to be relatively stable and automatic, either innate or slowly adjusting to the statistics of the world. In contrast, the decisional bias could be more obviously influenced by strategy and context. Indeed, recent work suggests important contextual effects on holistic processing. Objects that are not processed holistically can show a larger congruency effect if they are processed within the context of a trial together with an aligned face, which is processed holistically, than in the context of a misaligned face, not processed holistically (Richler, Bukach, & Gauthier, 2009). In sum, there is some evidence from contextual effects across categories supporting a decisional locus of holistic processing.

Section Summary

In summary, decisional influences are suggested on holistic processing of faces, as revealed by comparing effects induced by the manipulations at study or at test, the assessment of discriminability and response bias using signal detection measures, and contextual effects. However, the essence of holistic processing is the interactions among features, which are not directly captured by the methods described in the previous sections. Critically, classical signal detection measures only assess discriminability and response criterion for two stimulus states (e.g., whether the composites are congruent or incongruent). This method does not provide information about more complicated stimulus states, such as how the top and bottom parts of two faces in a same–different judgment task may interact. Specifically, there are two possible stimulus states (same or different) for two face parts (top or bottom).

Therefore, a more complex version of signal detection theory, namely multi-dimensional detection analysis within the framework of the general recognition theory (Ashby & Townsend, 1986), becomes necessary.

GENERAL RECOGNITION THEORY

Holistic processing indicates that parts of a stimulus are processed in an interactive manner. The perceptual and decisional interactions of parts can be addressed in the general recognition theory framework (Ashby & Townsend, 1986). General recognition theory uses a multidimensional version of signal detection theory. According to general recognition theory, different parts of a stimulus can be defined as different dimensions in a multidimensional perceptual space. For composite stimuli with two parts, each stimulus can be represented as a point in a perceptual space along two dimensions: a value on one dimension for the top part, and a value on the other dimension for the bottom part. In a same–different judgment task, the parts may either be the same or different. Thus, there are two states (same or different) along the top or bottom dimensions, forming a two-by-two perceptual space. Because of variability in the perceptual system, the same stimulus is represented as a different point in perceptual space at every encounter. Over trials, the points form a probability distribution of the percept. Four distributions of percepts would be formed for the different combinations of top and bottom parts: same-same, same-different, different-same, or different-different. Figure 9.4a illustrates a schematic of these distributions in a multidimensional perceptual space. Figure 9.4b illustrates a simplified visual representation of these distributions, where the equal density cross-sections of these three-dimensional distributions are drawn. The

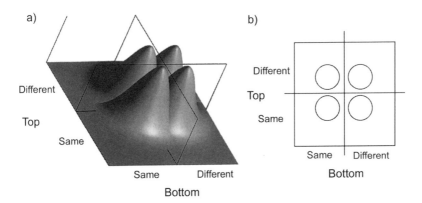

Figure 9.4 Schematic diagrams of (a) a two-dimensional perceptual space with the perceptual distributions of four stimuli, and (b) equal density cross-sections of the distributions in (a). The black lines represented the response criteria. Copyright 2008 by the American Psychological Association. Reproduced with permission.

shape of each cross-section illustrates the variability corresponding to each of the two dimensions and any covariance between dimensions. The importance of the shape of these cross-sections will be discussed later.

Schematics of examples of three types of psychological interactions described in the general recognition theory are depicted in Figure 9.5. According to the general recognition theory, discriminability between percepts is indicated by the distance between the perceptual distributions. If the perceptual distributions of the dimensions do not interact, the distances between the distributions of one dimension (e.g., top-same and top-different) across the states of the other dimension (when the bottom parts are the same and when they are different) would be equal. If the two dimensions

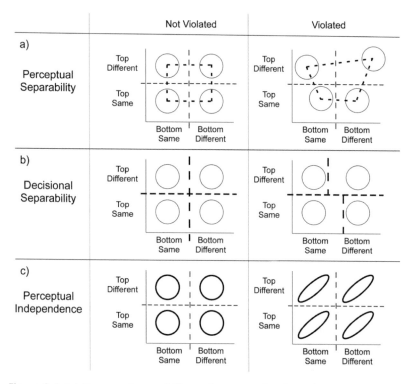

Figure 9.5 (a) Perceptual separability and an example of a violation of perceptual separability. Perceptual separability is violated when the shape of the connected centers of the distributions is not rectangular. (b) Decisional separability and an example of a violation of decisional separability. Decisional separability is violated when the locations of the response criterions do not fall halfway between the distributions or are not parallel to the perceptual dimension axes. (c) Perceptual independence and an example of a violation of perceptual independence. Perceptual independence is violated when there is no violation in decisional separability, and there is systematic noise that is correlated between two dimensions. Copyright © 2008 by the American Psychological Association. Adapted with permission.

do not interact, the centers of the four distributions should be connected into a rectangle. Conversely, if the perceptual distributions of the dimensions interact, the distances would not be equal, and the shape of the connected perceptual distributions would not be a rectangle. For example, the distance of the distributions of the bottom parts may be closer when the top parts are the same, but they may be farther away from each other when the top parts are different. This type of perceptual interaction is termed a violation of *perceptual separability* (Ashby & Townsend, 1986).

As illustrated in classical signal detection theory, observers can employ different strategies in selecting responses about the percepts. If the observer is not biased, the lines representing the response criteria fall halfway between the two perceptual distributions of each dimension and should be perpendicular to the perceptual dimension axes. If there were a bias toward a particular response for one dimension (e.g., bottom parts) depending on the state of another dimension (e.g., whether the top parts are the same or different), the location or slope of the corresponding response criterion would shift. Because of various possible interactions of response biases, the response criterion may be linear or nonlinear, and they can be orthogonal or non-orthogonal to the perceptual dimension axes. This type of decisional interaction, when the response criterion for one dimension (part) is not independent of values on the other dimension, is termed a violation of *decisional separability* (Ashby & Townsend, 1986).

In addition, within this framework, when decisional interactions have been ruled out for both parts, it becomes possible to test for another type of perceptual interaction whereby, for a given stimulus, the perceptual effect on one dimension correlates with that on another dimension. For example, for a composite that has the same top and bottom parts as a previously studied face, the "sameness" of its top part may correlate with the "sameness" of its bottom part. This type of perceptual interaction is referred to as a violation of *perceptual independence* (Ashby & Townsend, 1986). Graphically, if there is perceptual independence, the shape of a perceptual distribution is a circle. If there is a violation of perceptual independence for a perceptual distribution, its shape is an ellipse, indicating a correlation between dimensions.

To determine whether the face parts interact in a perceptual or decisional manner in the general recognition theory framework, it is necessary to acquire responses for all parts in every trial (Macho, 2007). This requires a considerable amount of data in a difficult task for observers, but it appears critical since simulations have demonstrated that the congruency effect taken as evidence for holistic processing in standard composite tasks could stem from either perceptual or decisional sources. Therefore, in a complete identification task with composite stimuli, observers have to perform judgments for both top and bottom parts within each trial and select one of four responses: both top and bottom parts are the same, top part is the same and bottom part is different, top part is different but bottom part is the same, or both top and bottom parts are different. Thus, responses for both parts can be analyzed by *multidimensional signal detection analyses* (MSDA; Kadlec, 1995, 1999; Kadlec & Townsend, 1992a, 1992b). MSDA contain many sets of statistical tests since the comparisons conducted include all possible combinations of the different states of the dimensions. Critically, MSDA include two types of tests that are basically extended signal detection measures and that are important in drawing conclusions about any interactions of stimulus parts. The first type of tests, *the marginal analyses*, reveal any violations of perceptual or decisional separability by assessing whether the d' and c values of a dimension (e.g., tops) depends on the state of another dimension (e.g., bottoms). The second type of tests, *the conditional analyses*, reveal any violations of perceptual independence or decisional separability by assessing whether the d' and c values of a dimension depend on whether a participant correctly responded in a particular state of the other dimension. These results are then confirmed by other sets of tests that assess the independence of response probability on the state of the other dimension. Readers who are interested in more details and the rationale of these tests should refer to Kadlec and Townsend (1992a, 1992b) and Kadlec (1995, 1999).

Recent studies using the complete identification task and MSDA to examine the locus of holism of face judgments have revealed some evidence of violations of perceptual separability, although the evidence has been inconsistent, suggesting that occasionally the discriminability of the state of a part depends on whether the other part is same or different (Farivar & Chaudhuri, 2003; Richler, Gauthier, et al., 2008; Wenger & Ingvalson, 2003). Importantly, these studies consistently revealed violations of decisional separability, indicating that the response criterion for reporting the state of a face part always changes depending on the state of the other face part (Farivar & Chaudhuri, 2003; Richler, Gauthier, et al., 2008; Wenger & Ingvalson; 2002; 2003). It has been suggested that the strongest form of holistic representation should be revealed by a violation of perceptual independence, where the parts of a face are statistically correlated with each other (Wenger & Ingvalson, 2002). However, the only evidence supporting the presence of violations of perceptual independence in a face task was found when decisional separability was assumed (Thomas, 2001). Since violations of decisional separability are consistently obtained in other studies with faces (Farivar & Chaudhuri, 2003; Richler, Gauthier, et al., 2008; Wenger & Ingvalson; 2002; 2003), evidence for perceptual independence may not be valid. Together, these findings suggest that holistic processing has a reliable decisional locus, while additional perceptual effects should not be ruled out.

One may be concerned that the measures in the general recognition theory may not be directly applied to the traditional face literature because the complete identification task is quite different from other composite tasks that assess holistic processing. In the conventional composite tasks, observers are asked to selectively attend to target face parts rather than respond to both

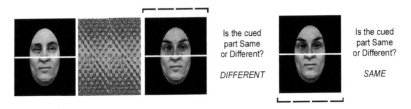

Figure 9.6 Schematic of the *sequential response task* of the composite paradigm used in Richler, Gauthier, et al. (2008). Copyright © 2008 by the American Psychological Association. Adapted with permission.

face parts as in the complete identification task. To resolve this issue, Richler, Gauthier, et al. (2008) created a new version of the composite task, the *sequential response task*, to link the selective attention task with the complete identification task (see Figure 9.6). In the sequential response task, observers first make a judgment about one part of the composites. This procedure is identical to that in the selective attention task, and it is possible to measure congruency effects from the responses to the first parts. After the response to the first part, the other part of the composites is cued and requires a response. Thus, the information needed for MSDA is obtained. Richler et al. found comparable congruency effects between the selective attention task and the first response in the sequential response task. Furthermore, MSDA applied on the data from the sequential response task revealed the same results as in those from the complete identification task, which showed consistent decisional interactions and less consistent effects of perceptual interactions, depending on the state of the other parts. Thus, the use of the general recognition theory framework with MSDA in the complete identification task is comparable to the traditional face literature and proves to be a powerful tool to assess how stimulus parts interact, which the conventional behavioral tasks could not assess.

Moreover, the sequential response task with MSDA has proven to be useful in teasing apart the interactions of features in manipulations that are known to influence holistic processing. For example, misalignment of parts in the selective attention task is known to disrupt holistic processing. In Richler, Gauthier, et al. (2008), the sequential response task replicated a reduction of congruency effects due to misalignment. In addition, misalignment also reduced the decisional interactions of parts, which was reflected by a smaller degree of response criterion difference between the different states (same or different) of the other parts. In contrast, there was less consistent evidence for violations of perceptual separability. Violations of perceptual separability also did not consistently vary across the misalignment manipulations. These findings provide further evidence for the usefulness of the sequential response task in connecting the traditional face literature with the general recognition theory framework and reveal that holistic processing has a strong decisional component.

EVALUATIONS, IMPLICATIONS AND FUTURE DIRECTIONS

Evaluations of Methods

This chapter has discussed three methods that may be used to reveal whether the locus of holistic processing is perceptual or decisional. It is important to emphasize that two of these methods reveal primarily the effects of the experimental manipulations. First, it is useful to examine the relative importance of experimental manipulations during the study or test phase in learning or matching tasks when accuracy data necessary for signal detection measures are not available. Second, signal detection theory provides a stronger test compared to the first method and can separate two different sources (affecting sensitivity and response bias, respectively) affecting judgments in tasks measuring holistic processing. However, neither of these methods directly speaks to the locus of inter-actions of facial features, which is the essence of holistic processing. General recognition theory, on the other hand, is useful as a method of separating such effects because of its multidimensional nature. Three types of psychological independence are specified in the general recogni-tion theory framework: perceptual independence, perceptual separability, and decisional separability. A perceptual locus is revealed by a violation of either perceptual independence or perceptual separability. A decisional locus is revealed by a violation of decisional separability. The power of these measures is that they can differentiate perceptual and decisional effects that could not be distinguished within standard signal detection theory analyses. It is critical that the outcome of all methods used to date concur in suggesting that holistic processing effects get at least some contribution from postperceptual processes. But if researchers are inter-ested in the locus of interactions of stimulus features, the application of general recognition theory should be considered.[3]

Implications and Future Directions

It is essential to clarify the locus of holistic processing because it has important implications for various aspects of the study of face and object perception, including the fundamental nature of the interactions between features, how the processing of faces and objects differs during each processing stage, and the proper use of designs and analyses in behavioral tasks to measure holistic processing. These implications will be discussed in turn.

---

[3] Note that recent work (Mack, Richler, Gauthier, & Palmeri, 2007; Richler, Mack, Gauthier, & Palmeri, 2007) suggests that results from MSDA may not unmistakably relate to the constructs in general recognition theory, and the conclusions from MSDA on the locus of holistic processing depend on the assumptions of the theory and method. Further work is in progress to address these issues (Mack et al., 2007; Richler et al., 2007).

Nature of Psychological Interactions in Face Perception

An influential hypothesis regarding holistic processing has been the holistic representation hypothesis suggested by Tanaka, Farah, and colleagues, which suggests that holistic processing results from encoding representations of wholes into memory (Farah et al., 1998; Tanaka & Farah, 1993, 2003; Tanaka & Sengco, 1997). This chapter has discussed three ways to inspect perceptual and decisional effects in holistic processing, including the locus of manipulations, signal detection measures, and multidimensional signal detection analyses in the general recognition theory framework. All three methods indicate that holistic processing is not merely a perceptual effect but also has a decisional locus. However, since these methods did not specify *how* the interactions during perceptual and decisional processes take place, this issue needs to be addressed in future research.

It is possible to speculate on how facial features may be processed interactively. One possibility is that representations for configural information may emerge from explicit representations of individual features (Pomerantz et al., 2003; Sergent, 1984). For example, when identifying faces that share very similar features (e.g., faces of identical twins), discrimination may critically rely on perceptual representations that encompass several features and their configural information (e.g., Le Grand, Mondloch, Maurer, & Brent, 2001, 2003; Mondloch, et al. 2002). Moreover, the extended experience of using all the features and the spatial distance among features to distinguish individual faces may lead to larger attentional windows, leading observers to represent more features in a perceptual unit. Alternatively, it may instead encourage people to adopt a decisional strategy that makes use of the information from all available features even if the features are independently represented. For example, all features in a face tend to reflect the same emotions simultaneously. After prolonged experience of seeing a smile and scrunched eyes co-occur, it is likely that an expectation for both features to convey similar information may facilitate recognition. Scrunched eyes may not be interpreted in the same way when they appear with an emotionless mouth, presumably because the co-occurrence of these two pieces of information is not expected. Similarly, for a face composite consisting of two parts from different individuals, people usually regard that composite as a new identity different from the original faces. It is likely that the perceptual system naturally interprets that if the identity of a face part is changed, the identities of other face parts must also have changed. Future research is necessary to explore how the perceptual and decisional effects in holistic processing may occur.

Experimental Designs and Analyses for Holistic Processing

Because of the consistent evidence for some decisional effects in holistic processing, researchers should be careful about choosing the tasks and analytical measures that allow assessment of response biases in the investigation of holistic processing. Recently, there has been controversy about the appropriate task designs and statistical analyses over the composite paradigm (Gauthier & Bukach, 2007; McKone et al., 2007; McKone & Robbins, 2007; Robbins & McKone, 2007). Two main types of composite tasks, the *complete* and *partial* designs, are frequently used in the literature (Gauthier & Bukach, 2007). In both designs, holistic processing is inferred from failures of selective attention to parts. In a complete composite design, the task-relevant and task-irrelevant parts can be same or different, and the congruency of top and bottom parts across study and test is manipulated (see Figure 9.2). Holistic processing is indicated by a congruency effect, with better performance for congruent than incongruent trials. Since same and different trials for congruent and incongruent trial types are included, the discriminability and response bias in terms of congruency can be assessed. Additionally, alignment can be independently manipulated in the complete design (Richler, Tanaka, et al., 2008). In contrast, in the partial design, the task-irrelevant parts in the composites are always different from study to test. Holistic processing is implied by an alignment effect, with better performance with misaligned than aligned composites. It is possible to calculate discriminability and response bias in the partial design in terms of alignment. However, in many studies that adopted the partial design, the accuracy data from same and different trials were analyzed separately with an emphasis on the *same* trials (e.g., Goffaux & Rossion, 2006; Le Grand et al., 2004; Michel, Rossion, Han, Chung, & Caldara, 2006; Robbins & McKone, 2007). Moreover, the responses are confounded with congruency in this design: the "same" trials always contain incongruent information (i.e., target parts are the same but task-irrelevant parts are different) and "different" trials are congruent (i.e., target and task-irrelevant parts are both different). Due to the consistent observations of response biases for the different manipulations in the composite task (congruency: Farah et al., 1998; Wenger & Ingvalson, 2002; 2003; congruency and alignment: Cheung et al., 2008; Richler, Gauthier, et al., 2008; Richler, Tanaka, et al., 2008; orientation: Hole, 1994; spatial frequency filtering: Cheung et al., 2008), response biases affecting the partial design can be misinterpreted as discriminability effects. For example, Goffaux and Rossion (2006) suggested that holistic processing is mainly supported by low-spatial frequencies but not high-spatial frequencies because the alignment effect was significantly larger for low-passed filtered faces than for high-passed filtered faces. Note that their analyses emphasized the *same* trials in the partial design and are vulnerable to response bias. Indeed, using a complete composite design, Cheung et al. (2008) found similar alignment effects with the trials included by Goffaux and Rossion (2006) but found no difference in the congruency effects between the low-passed or high-passed filtered faces with all trials in the complete design. These results indicate that both high- and low-passed filtered faces are processed holistically. Crucially, a response bias of responding "same" was found for both aligned and misaligned high-passed filtered faces, but there was a larger bias to respond "different" for aligned than misaligned low-pass filtered faces, suggesting that the differential alignment effects among the spatial frequency conditions in Goffaux and Rossion arose from response bias. Thus, it is necessary to include a full design that allows measurement of perceptual discriminability and response bias in terms of congruency (and alignment) for further investigation of holistic processing. Again, while it is difficult to map directly the construct of response bias onto that of a decisional effect, it is critical to distinguish manipulations that affect how well people can discriminate whether face parts are identical or not (such as misalignment of the parts) from manipulations that only affect people's willingness to respond "same" regardless of the evidence.

Implications for the Investigation of Face and Object Recognition

The finding of a decisional locus of holistic processing raises many important theoretical questions regarding face and object recognition. For face perception, how the processing stages are organized still requires further research. It is speculative that perceptual and decisional processes may be discrete and that facial features are independently represented. Rather, there could be reciprocal influences of these two processes so that decisional processes may modify perceptual or memory representations to become more "holistic". In addition, the role of attention in holistic processing should be addressed. Attention may play a more critical role during the decisional than during the perceptual processes. This is possible because attentional manipulations during encoding did not affect holistic processing (Boutet et al., 2002), but those during matching reduced it (Palermo & Rhodes, 2002). Likewise, the limited capacity of holistic processing in working memory may also be due to a larger limitation of decisional rather than perceptual mechanisms (Cheung & Gauthier, in press). Furthermore, holistic and configural effects of face perception may have different loci. Because holistic face processing appears to mature by age 4 (de Heering et al., 2007; Pellicano & Rhodes, 2003) but the sensitivity to configural information in face processing may take 10 years to develop (Mondloch et al., 2002), it is possible that perceptual and decisional effects involved in these two types of processing are different.

Since holistic processing appears to have strong decisional influences, face and object processing may differ mainly in terms of decisional rather than perceptual processes (but see Wenger & Ingvalson, 2002). Perhaps the features of faces and objects are independently represented, but the interpretations of representations are more holistic for face than for object parts because of experienced use of all parts in a face for discriminating individual faces. If this is true, changes in decisional effects should be observed during the development of perceptual expertise of other object categories, whereas there should be little or no changes in perceptual effects.

Also, holistic effects in face processing may be compared with the word superiority effect (Reicher, 1969), in which a target letter is better recognized when it is presented within a word than in isolation. Since these "holistic" effects in face and word recognition are comparably influenced by different manipulations (Martelli, Majaj, & Pelli, 2005), it would be interesting to investigate whether the "holistic" effects in word recognition might also arise from a decisional locus.

Future research may address whether the neural signatures of holistic processing, the N170 component and the activations in face-selective area such as the fusiform "face" area (FFA), are correlated with different aspects of performance (such as discriminability and response bias) in face perception tasks. For instance, it is speculative that the N170 may reflect a perceptual decisional effect rather than a pure perceptual effect. Another potential candidate ERP component that might reflect the decisional effects is the N250, which is sensitive to judgment of stimulus familiarity or repetition (e.g., Itier & Taylor, 2004; Schweinberger, Pfutze, & Sommer, 1995; Tanaka, Curran, Porterfield, & Collins, 2006). Similarly, it would be interesting to investigate whether the recruitment of the FFA and other face-selective areas correlates with the discriminability or response bias measures in holistic processing. Recently, it has been shown that perceptual similarity and response bias both correlate with activity in the left anterior ventral fusiform area during object recognition, suggesting a strong decisional effect in differentiating similar object representations (Joseph & Farley, 2004). A speculation is that certain face-selective areas may also reflect response biases in holistic processing. Several studies have shown correlations between the activations in the FFA and measures of behavioral face inversion effect (in accuracy, Yovel & Kanwisher, 2005), and between the FFA activations and behavioral measures of expertise (in discriminability, Gauthier et al., 2000; Gauthier, Curby, Skudlarski, & Epstein, 2005; Gauthier & Tarr, 2002; Xu, 2005). However, direct tests of the relationship between face-selective activity and the decisional measures of holistic processing have yet to be conducted.

CONCLUSION

Human observers are actively involved in perceiving the world, and perception can be subject to decisional influences. The locus of holistic processing of faces is shown to have a consistent decisional component, although it is much more difficult to rule out that there is also a perceptual component at play. The issue of decisional effects in holistic processing demands more attention from the field. It has only been a recent effort to investigate the role of the decisional processes in face holistic processing (Cheung et al., 2008; Cheung & Gauthier, in press; Richler, Gauthier, et al., 2008; Wenger & Ingvalson, 2002; 2003). The precise nature of these decisional effects and their influences in many aspects of face and object recognition related to holistic processing remain to be addressed. Nonetheless, this issue raises a serious challenge to behavioral experimental designs that neglect response bias when examining holistic processing. The clarification of the locus of holistic effects may reduce confusions in the literature regarding experimental designs and analyses. Crucially, there has been little attempt in developing a process theory of holistic processing, one that can account for the differences between face and object processing, for the acquisition of holistic processing and for the range of behavioral phenomena reviewed in this chapter. While they are not models of processing, the signal detection theory and general recognition theory offer measures for distinguishing perceptual and decisional effects and also provide important constraints for future process theories of holistic processing, and face and object perception in general.

REFERENCE

Ashby, F. G., & Townsend, J. T. (1986). Varieties of perceptual independence. *Psychological Review, 93*(2), 154–179.

Bartlett, J. C., & Searcy, J. (1993). Inversion and configuration of faces. *Cognitive Psychology, 25*(3), 281–316.

Bentin, S., Allison, T., Puce, A., & Perez, E. (1996). Electrophysiological studies of face perception in humans. *Journal of Cognitive Neuroscience, 8*(6), 551–565.

Biederman, I. (1987). Recognition-by-components: A theory of human image understanding. *Psychological Review, 94*(2), 115–147.

Bindemann, M., Burton, A. M., & Jenkins, R. (2005). Capacity limits for face processing. *Cognition, 98*(2), 177–197.

Bindemann, M., Jenkins, R., & Burton, A. M. (2007). A bottleneck in face identification: Repetition priming from flanker images. *Experimental Psychology, 54*(3), 192–201.

Boutet, I., & Chaudhuri, A. (2001). Multistability of overlapped face stimuli is dependent upon orientation. *Perception, 30*(6), 743–753.

Boutet, I., Gentes Hawn, A., & Chaudhuri, A. (2002). The influence of attention on holistic face encoding. *Cognition, 84*(3), 321–341.

Carey, S., & Diamond, R. (1977). From piecemeal to configurational representation of faces. *Science, 195*(4275), 312–314.

Carey, S., & Diamond, R. (1994). Are faces perceived as configurations more by adults than by children? *Visual Cognition, 1*(2/3), 253–74.

Carey, S., Diamond, R., & Woods, B. (1980). Development of face recognition: A maturational component? *Developmental Psychology, 16*(4), 257–269.

Carmel, D., & Bentin, S. (2002). Domain specificity versus expertise: Factors influencing distinct processing of faces. *Cognition, 83*(1), 1–29.

Chance, J. E., Turner, A. L., & Goldstein, A. G. (1982). Development of differential recognition for own- and other-race faces. *Journal of Psychology: Interdisciplinary and Applied, 112*(1), 29–37.

Cheung, O. S., & Gauthier, I. (in press). Selective interference on the holistic processing of faces in working memory. *Journal of Experimental Psychology: Human Perception and Performance.*

Cheung, O. S., Richler, J. J., Palmeri, T. J., & Gauthier, I. (2008). Revisiting the role of spatial frequencies in the holistic processing of faces. *Journal of Experimental Psychology: Human Perception and Performance 34*(6), 1327–1336.

Davidoff, J., & Donnelly, N. (1990). Object superiority: A comparison of complete and part probes. *Acta Psychologica, 73*(3), 225–243.

de Heering, A., Houthuys, S., & Rossion, B. (2007). Holistic face processing is mature at 4 years of age: Evidence from the composite face effect. *Journal of Experimental Child Psychology, 96*(1), 57–70.

Diamond, R., & Carey, S. (1986). Why faces are and are not special: An effect of expertise. *Journal of Experimental Psychology: General, 115*(2), 107–117.

Farah, M. J., Tanaka, J. W., & Drain, H. M. (1995). What causes the face inversion effect? *Journal of Experimental Psychology: Human Perception and Performance, 21*(3), 628–634.

Farah, M. J., Wilson, K. D., Drain, M., & Tanaka, J. N. (1998). What is "special" about face perception? *Psychological Review, 105*(3), 482–498.

Farivar, R., & Chaudhuri, A. (2003). "I can't see your eyes well 'cause your nose is too short": An interactivity account of face processing. In *Proceedings of the Twenty-Fifth Annual Conference of the Cognitive Science Society* (pp. 378–383). Boston, MA: Cognitive Science Society.

Freire, A., Lee, K., & Symons, L. A. (2000). The face-inversion effect as a deficit in the encoding of configural information: Direct evidence. *Perception, 29*(2), 159–170.

Galton, F. (1879). Composite portraits, made by combining those of many difference persons into a single resultant figure. *The Journal of the Anthropological Institute of Great Britain and Ireland, 8*, 132–144.

Gauthier, I., & Bukach, C. (2007). Should we reject the expertise hypothesis? *Cognition, 103*(2), 322–330.

Gauthier, I., & Curby, K. M. (2005). A perceptual traffic jam on highway n170: Interference between face and car expertise. *Current Directions in Psychological Science, 14*(1), 30–33.

Gauthier, I., Curby, K. M., Skudlarski, P., & Epstein, R. A. (2005). Individual differences in FFA activity suggest independent processing at different spatial scales. *Cognitive, Affective and Behavioral Neuroscience, 5*(2), 222–234.

Gauthier, I., Curran, T., Curby, K. M., & Collins, D. (2003). Perceptual interference supports a non-modular account of face processing. *Nature Neuroscience, 6*(4), 428–432.

Gauthier, I., & Tarr, M. J. (1997). Becoming a "greeble" expert: Exploring mechanisms for face recognition. *Vision Research, 37*(12), 1673–1682.

Gauthier, I., & Tarr, M. J. (2002). Unraveling mechanisms for expert object recognition: Bridging brain activity and behavior. *Journal of Experimental Psychology: Human Perception and Performance, 28*(2), 431–446.

Gauthier, I., Williams, P., Tarr, M.J., & Tanaka, J.W. (1998). Training "greeble" experts: A framework for studying expert object recognition processes. *Vision Research, 38*(15–16), 2401–2428.

Goffaux, V., & Rossion, B. (2006). Faces are "spatial"—holistic face perception is supported by low spatial frequencies. *Journal of Experimental Psychology: Human Perception and Performance, 32*(4), 1023–1039.

Goldstein, A. G., & Chance, J. E. (1980). Memory for faces and schema theory. *Journal of Psychology: Interdisciplinary and Applied, 105*(1), 47–59.

Green, D. M., & Swets, J. A. (1966). *Signal detection theory and psychophysics.* New York: John Wiley & Sons, Inc.

Hole, G. J. (1994). Configurational factors in the perception of unfamiliar faces. *Perception, 23*(1), 65–74.

Hole, G. J., George, P. A., & Dunsmore, V. (1999). Evidence for holistic processing of faces viewed as photographic negatives. *Perception, 28*(3), 341–359.

Itier, R. J., & Taylor, M. J. (2004). Effects of repetition learning on upright, inverted and contrast-reversed face processing using ERPs. *NeuroImage, 21*(4), 1518–1532.

Jacques, C., & Rossion, B. (2004). Concurrent processing reveals competition between visual representations of faces. *NeuroReport: For Rapid Communication of Neuroscience Research, 15*(15), 2417–2421.

Jacques, C., & Rossion, B. (2006a). The speed of individual face categorization. *Psychological Science, 17*(6), 485–492.

Jacques, C., & Rossion, B. (2006b). The time course of visual competition to the presentation of centrally fixated faces. *Journal of Vision, 6*(2), 154–162.

Joseph, J. E., & Farley, A. B. (2004). Cortical regions associated with different aspects of object recognition performance. *Cognitive, Affective and Behavioral Neuroscience, 4*(3), 364–378.

Joseph, R. M., & Tanaka, J. (2003). Holistic and part-based face recognition in children with autism. *Journal of Child Psychology and Psychiatry, 44*(4), 529–542.

Kadlec, H. (1995). Multidimensional signal detection analyses (MSDA) for testing separability and independence: A Pascal program. *Behavior Research Methods, Instruments and Computers, 27*(4), 442–458.

Kadlec, H. (1999). Statistical properties of d' and beta estimates of signal detection theory. *Psychological Methods, 4*(1), 22–43.

Kadlec, H., & Townsend, J. T. (1992a). Implications of marginal and conditional detection parameters for the separabilities and independence of perceptual dimensions. *Journal of Mathematical Psychology, 36*(3), 325–374.

Kadlec, H., & Townsend, J. T. (1992b). Signal detection analyses of dimensional interactions. In F. G. Ashby (Ed.), *Multidimensional models of perception and cognition* (pp.188–227). Hillsdale, NJ: Lawrence Erlbaum Associates.

Le Grand, R., Mondloch, C. J., Maurer, D., & Brent, H. P. (2001). Early visual experience and face processing. *Nature, 410*(6831), 890.

Le Grand, R., Mondloch, C. J., Maurer, D., & Brent, H. P. (2003). Expert face processing requires visual input to the right hemisphere during infancy. *Nature Neuroscience, 6*(10), 1108–1112.

Le Grand, R., Mondloch, C. J., Maurer, D., & Brent, H. P. (2004). Impairment in holistic face processing following early visual deprivation. *Psychological Science, 15*(11), 762–768.

Leder, H., & Bruce, V. (1998). Local and relational aspects of face distinctiveness. *The Quarterly Journal of Experimental Psychology A: Human Experimental Psychology, 51A*(3), 449–473.

Leder, H., & Bruce, V. (2000). When inverted faces are recognized: The role of configural information in face recognition. *The Quarterly Journal of Experimental Psychology A: Human Experimental Psychology, 53A*(2), 513–536.

Leder, H., Candrian, G., Huber, O., & Bruce, V. (2001). Configural features in the context of upright and inverted faces. *Perception, 30*(1), 73–83.

Leder, H., & Carbon, C. C. (2005). When context hinders! Learn-test compatibility in face recognition. *The Quarterly Journal of Experimental Psychology A: Human Experimental Psychology,58A*(2), 235–250.

Lewis, M. B., & Glenister, T. E. (2003). A sideways look at configural encoding: Two different effects of face rotation. *Perception, 32*(1), 7–14.

Macho, S. (2007). Feature sampling in detection: Implications for the measurement of perceptual independence. *Journal of Experimental Psychology: General, 136*(1), 133–153.

Macho, S., & Leder, H. (1998). Your eyes only? A test of interactive influence in the processing of facial features. *Journal of Experimental Psychology: Human Perception and Performance, 24*(5), 1486–1500.

Mack, M. L., Richler, J. J., Gauthier, I., & Palmeri, T. J. (2007). Comparing the loci of holistic processing in people and models [Abstract]. *Journal of Vision, 7*(9):507, 507a, http://jounralofvision.org/7/9/507, doi:10.1167/7.9.507.

Martelli, M., Majaj, N. J., & Pelli, D. G. (2005). Are faces processed like words? A diagnostic test for recognition by parts. *Journal of Vision, 5*, 58–70.

McKone, E., Kanwisher, N., & Duchaine, B. C. (2007). Can generic expertise explain special processing for faces? *Trends in Cognitive Sciences, 11*(1), 8–15.

McKone, E., & Robbins, R. (2007). The evidence rejects the experience hypothesis: Reply to Gauthier & Bukach. *Cognition, 103*(2), 331–336.

Michel, C., Caldara, R., & Rossion, B. (2006). Same-race faces are perceived more holistically than other-race faces. *Visual Cognition, 14*(1), 55–73.

Michel, C., Rossion, B., Han, J., Chung, C. S., & Caldara, R. (2006). Holistic processing is finely tuned for faces of one's own race. *Psychological Science, 17*(7), 608–615.

Mondloch, C. J., Le Grand, R., & Maurer, D. (2002). Configural face processing develops more slowly than featural face processing. *Perception, 31*(5), 553–566.

Moscovitch, M., & Moscovitch, D. A. (2000). Super face-inversion effects for isolated internal or external features, and for fractured faces. *Cognitive Neuropsychology, 17*(1/2/3), 201–219.

Murray, J. E. (2004). The ups and downs of face perception: Evidence for holistic encoding of upright and inverted faces. *Perception, 33*(4), 387–398.

Murray, J. E., Rhodes, G., & Schuchinsky, M. (2003). When is a face not a face? The effects of misorientation on mechanisms of face perception. In M. A. Peterson & G. Rhodes (Eds.), *Perception of faces, objects and scenes: Analytic and holistic processing* (pp. 75–91). Oxford, UK: Oxford University Press.

O'Toole, A. J., Wenger, M. J., & Townsend, J. T. (2001). Quantitative models of perceiving and remembering faces: Precedents and possibilities. In M. J. Wenger & J. T. Townsend (Eds.), *Computational, geometric, and process perspectives on facial cognition* (pp.1–38). Mahwah, NJ: Erlbaum.

Palermo, R., & Rhodes, G. (2002). The influence of divided attention on holistic face perception. *Cognition,82*(3), 225–257.

Palmer, S. E. (1977). Hierarchical structure in perceptual representation. *Cognitive Psychology,9*(4), 441–474.

Pellicano, E., & Rhodes, G. (2003). Holistic processing of faces in preschool children and adults. *Psychological Science, 14*(6), 618–622.

Pomerantz, J. R., Agrawal, A., Jewell, S. W., Jeong, M., Khan, H., & Lozano, S. C. (2003). Contour grouping inside and outside of facial contexts. *Acta Psychologica, 114*(3), 245–271.

Reicher, G. M. (1969). Perceptual recognition as a function of meaningfulness of stimulus material. *Journal of Experimental Psychology, 81*(2), 275–280.

Rhodes, G., Brake, S., & Atkinson, A. P. (1993). What's lost in inverted faces? *Cognition, 47*(1), 25–57.

Richler, J. J., Bukach, C. M., & Gauthier, I. (2009). Context influences holistic processing of nonface objects in the composite task. *Attention, Perception and Psychophysics, 71*(3), 530–540.

Richler, J. J., Gauthier, I., Wenger, M. J., & Palmeri, T. J. (2008). Holistic processing of faces: Perceptual and decisional components. *Journal of Experimental Psychology: Learning, Memory and Cognition, 34*(2), 328–342.

Richler, J. J., Mack, M. L., Gauthier, I., & Palmeri, T. J. (2007). Distinguishing between perceptual and decisional sources of holism in face processing. *Proceedings of the Twenty-Ninth Annual Meeting of the Cognitive Science Society*, 1427–1432.

Richler, J. J., Tanaka, J. W., Brown, D. D., & Gauthier, I. (2008). When does selective attention to face part fails? *Journal of Experimental Psychology: Learning, Memory and Cognition 34*(6) 1356–1368.

Robbins, R., & McKone, E. (2003). Can holistic processing be learned for inverted faces? *Cognition, 88*(1), 79–107.

Robbins, R., & McKone, E. (2007). No face-like processing for objects-of-expertise in three behavioural tasks. *Cognition, 103*(1), 34–79.

Rossion, B., Delvenne, J. F., Debatisse, D., Goffaux, V., Bruyer, R., Crommelinck, M., et al. (1999). Spatio-temporal localization of the face inversion effect: An event-related potentials study. *Biological Psychology, 50*(3), 173–189.

Rossion, B., Gauthier, I., Goffaux, V., Tarr, M. J., & Crommelinck, M. (2002). Expertise training with novel objects leads to left-lateralized facelike electrophysiological responses. *Psychological Science, 13*(3), 250–257.

Rossion, B., Gauthier, I., Tarr, M. J., Despland, P., Bruyer, R., Linotte, S., et al. (2000). The n170 occipito-temporal component is delayed and enhanced to inverted faces but not to inverted objects: An electrophysiological account of face-specific processes in the human brain. *NeuroReport: For Rapid Communication of Neuroscience Research, 11*(1), 69–74.

Rossion, B., Kung, C. C., & Tarr, M. J. (2004). Visual expertise with nonface objects leads to competition with the early perceptual processing of faces in the human occipitotemporal cortex. *Proceedings of the National Academy of Sciences, 101*(40), 14521–14526.

Rotshtein, P., Geng, J. J., Driver, J., & Dolan, R. J. (2007). Role of features and second-order spatial relations in face discrimination, face recognition, and individual face skills: Behavioral and functional magnetic resonance imaging data. *Journal of Cognitive Neuroscience, 19*(9), 1435–1452.

Sagiv, N., & Bentin, S. (2001). Structural encoding of human and schematic faces: Holistic and part-based processes. *Journal of Cognitive Neuroscience, 13*(7), 937–951.

Schneider, W., & Shiffrin, R. M. (1977). Controlled and automatic human information processing: I. Detection, search, and attention. *Psychological Review, 84*(1), 1–66.

Schiltz, C., & Rossion, B. (2006). Faces are represented holistically in the human occipito-temporal cortex. *NeuroImage, 32*(3), 1385–1394.

Schwarzer, G. (2000). Development of face processing: The effect of face inversion. *Child Development, 71*(2), 391–401.

Schwarzer, G., & Massaro, D. W. (2001). Modeling face identification processing in children and adults. *Journal of Experimental Child Psychology,79*(2), 139–161.

Schweinberger, S. R., Pfutze, E. M., & Sommer, W. (1995). Repetition priming and associative priming of face recognition: Evidence from event-related potentials. *Journal of Experimental Psychology: Learning, Memory, and Cognition, 21*(3), 722–736.

Searcy, J. H., & Bartlett, J. C. (1996). Inversion and processing of component and spatial-relational information in faces. *Journal of Experimental Psychology: Human Perception and Performance, 22*(4), 904–915.

Sergent, J. (1984). An investigation into component and configural processes underlying face perception. *British Journal of Psychology, 75*(2), 221–242.

Shiffrin, R. M., & Schneider, W. (1977). Controlled and automatic human information processing: II. Perceptual learning, automatic attending and a general theory. *Psychological Review,84*(2), 127–190.

Sternberg, S. (1969). The discovery of processing stages: Extensions of Donders' method. *Acta Psychologica, 30,* 276–315.

Swets, J. A. (1996). *Signal detection theory and roc analysis in psychology and diagnostics: Collected papers.* Mahwah, NJ: Lawrence Erlbaum Associates.

Tanaka, J. W., & Curran, T. (2001). A neural basis for expert object recognition. *Psychological Science, 12*(1), 43–47.

Tanaka, J. W., Curran, T., Porterfield, A. L., & Collins, D. (2006). Activation of preexisting and acquired face representations: The n250 event-related potential as an index of face familiarity. *Journal of Cognitive Neuroscience, 18*(9), 1488–1497.

Tanaka, J. W., & Farah, M. J. (1993). Parts and wholes in face recognition. *The Quarterly Journal of Experimental Psychology A: Human Experimental Psychology, 46A*(2), 225–245.

Tanaka, J. W., & Farah, M. J. (2003). The holistic representation of faces. In M. A. Peterson, & G. Rhodes (Eds.), *Perception of faces, objects and scenes: Analytical and holistic processes* (pp. 53–74). Oxford, UK: Oxford University Press.

Tanaka, J. W., Kiefer, M., & Bukach, C. M. (2004). A holistic account of the own-race effect in face recognition: Evidence from a cross-cultural study. *Cognition, 93*(1), B1–B9.

Tanaka, J. W., & Sengco, J. A. (1997). Features and their configuration in face recognition. *Memory and Cognition, 25*(5), 583–592.

Teunisse, J. P., & de Gelder, B. (2001). Impaired categorical perception of facial expressions in high-functioning adolescents with autism. *Child Neuropsychology, 7*(1), 1–14.

Thomas, R. D. (2001). Perceptual interactions of facial dimensions in speeded classification. *Perceptual & Psychophysics, 63,* 625–650.

Vogel, E. K., Luck, S. J., & Shapiro, K. L. (1998). Electrophysiological evidence for a postperceptual locus of suppression during the attentional blink. *Journal of Experimental Psychology: Human Perception and Performance, 24*(6), 1656–1674.

Wenger, M. J., & Ingvalson, E. M. (2002). A decisional component of holistic encoding. *Journal of Experimental Psychology: Learning, Memory & Cognition, 28*(5), 872–892.

Wenger, M. J., & Ingvalson, E. M. (2003). Preserving informational separability and violating decisional separability in facial perception and recognition. *Journal of Experimental Psychology: Learning, Memory, and Cognition, 29*(6), 1106–1118.

Wenger, M. J., & Townsend, J. T. (2001). *Faces as gestalt stimuli: Process characteristics.* In M. J. Wenger & J. T. Townsend (Eds.), *Computational, geometric, and process perspectives on facial cognition* (pp. 229–284). Mahwah, NJ: Erlbaum.

Weston, N. J., & Perfect, T. J. (2005). Effects of processing bias on the recognition of composite face halves. *Psychonomic Bulletin and Review, 12*(6), 1038–1042.

Xu, Y. (2005). Revisiting the role of the fusiform face area in visual expertise. *Cerebral Cortex, 15*(8), 1234–1242.

Yin, R. K. (1969). Looking at upside-down faces. *Journal of Experimental Psychology, 81*(1), 141–145.

Young, A., Hellawell, D., & Hay, D. (1987). Configural information in face perception. *Perception, 16*(6), 747–759.

Yovel, G., & Kanwisher, N. (2005). The neural basis of the behavioral face-inversion effect. *Current Biology, 15*(24), 2256–2262.

Zhang, L., & Cottrell, G. W. (2004). When holistic processing is not enough: Local features save the day. In *Processing of the 26th Annual Cognitive Science Conference* (pp. 1506–1511). Chicago, IL: Mahwah: Lawrence Erlbaum.

Zhang, L., & Cottrell, G. W. (2005). Holistic processing develops because it is good. In *Proceedings of the 27th Annual Cognitive Science Conference* (pp. 2428–2433). La Stresa, Italy: Mahwah: Lawrence Erlbaum.

10

The Case for Letter Expertise

Karin H. James, Alan C.-N. Wong, and Gael Jobard

Visual letter recognition is a type of perceptual expertise resulting from our extensive experience with printed material. We perceive letters at an amazing speed during reading, and efficient letter perception has been shown to be the basis for successful reading performance in psychophysical and neuropsychological studies (Arguin, Fiset, & Bub, 2002; Helenius, Tarkiainen, Cornelissen, Hansen, & Salmelin, 1999; Legge et al., 2007; McClelland, 1976; Nazir, Jacobs, & O'Regan, 1998; Pelli, Farell, & Moore, 2003; Pelli et al., 2007; Saffran & Coslett, 1998). Letter perception can also be distinguished from perception of other shapes and objects, as indicated by the recruitment of selective neural substrates (Cohen et al., 2000; Flowers et al., 2004; James, James, Jobard, Wong, & Gauthier, 2005; James & Gauthier, 2006; Longcamp, Anton, Roth, & Velay, 2003; Peterson, Fox, Snyder, & Raichle, 1990; Polk & Farah, 1998; Puce, Allison, Asgari, Gore, & McCarthy, 1996; Pugh et al., 1996; Tarkiainen, Helenius, Hansen, Cornelissen, & Salmelin, 1999; Wong, Jobard, James, James, & Gauthier, 2009) and association with specific behavioral phenomena (e.g., Gauthier & Tarr, 2002; Sanocki, 1987, 1988, 1991a,b,c; Wong & Gauthier, 2007).

What makes letter processing different from that of other objects, and what factors contribute to the specialized mechanisms underlying letter perception? Certainly, language forms a large part of what makes letter perception different from the perception of other objects. After all, we learn letters for the purpose of reading and only for that purpose. It is not surprising, therefore, that the majority of research on letter perception has been performed in the context of word recognition and reading, focusing on different linguistic processes (e.g., Johnson & Pugh, 1994; McClelland, 1976; Perfetti, Liu, & Tan, 2005; Reicher, 1969) or on the perceptual units used to recognize words (Carreiras, Alvarez, & De Vega, 1993; Healy, 1994; Prinzmetal, Treiman, & Rho, 1986; Rey, Ziegler, & Jacobs, 2000; Spoehr & Smith, 1973). Nevertheless, as will be discussed in this chapter, a substantial part of the unique nature of letter perception can also be explained in a framework of visual object recognition.

Recently, the object recognition field has witnessed an increasing interest in the topic of perceptual expertise with a variety of objects such as faces, cars, birds, dogs, fingerprints, novel objects, and so forth (Busey & Vanderkolk, 2005; Gauthier, Curran, Curby, & Collins, 2003; Gauthier, Skudlarski, Gore, & Anderson, 2000; Gauthier, Tarr, et al., 2000; Tanaka & Curran, 2001). Although considerable progress has been made to understand the nature of perceptual expertise, much less is known about how expert letter perception compares with other types of perceptual expertise and object perception in general. To better understand these relationships, it may be fruitful to consider different aspects of visual letter recognition, including the stimulus properties, task demands, and so forth, involved in letter recognition in daily reading experiences. In this chapter we will begin by describing how letter perception relates to reading before outlining the evidence supporting neural selectivity for letter processing. We will then discuss potential reasons for the specialized neural mechanisms devoted to letters, in terms of both the interaction between letter processing and other modalities, and, in greater detail, the specific perceptual nature of letter perception.

LETTER PERCEPTION AND WORD READING

Learning to recognize individual letters is the very first ability that children are trained to acquire when learning to read, and it is crucial for successful reading. A seemingly simple activity such as reading these introductory lines already required the reader to perceive and recognize several hundreds of letters in a matter of just a few seconds. In natural situations such as this, however, letters are not perceived in isolation because they do not convey meaning on their own; rather, they are combined to be recognized as words. The idea that word recognition is the goal of reading has led some researchers to consider that letters may not be the perceptual unit that is used for reading. Instead of recognizing each letter individually, embedded within a letter string, some researchers have argued that we may rely on the identification of perceptual units formed of several letters.

Supraletter Perceptual Units

In a seminal experiment, Reicher and Wheeler demonstrated an experimental effect known as the "Word Superiority Effect" (WSE) (Reicher, 1969; Wheeler, 1970). In this experiment, stimuli were briefly exposed, followed by a visual mask, and subjects had then to perform a forced choice task pertaining to the identity of a letter present at a certain place in the target letter string (e.g., WORK tested at the fourth position for K/D). The choice between two letters that formed candidates similar in nature (words or nonwords) ensured that the lexical status could not interfere with subject's accuracy. Reicher thus showed that although the subject's decisions concerned the identity of a single letter, performance was facilitated when the target letter was perceived in the context of a word rather than in the context of a nonword or in isolation. By demonstrating that knowledge about a perceived word could be better than that of its constituent letters, these results suggest that in the context of reading, the perceptual unit most available to the reader may not be individual letters. One may question the perceptual origin of the WSE and argue that it could be the mere consequence of a top-down influence of either lexical semantic or phonological processing. Such an interpretation is, however, challenged by work that has replicated this WSE with words, pseudowords (e.g., "thap") and nonwords (e.g., "yibv"), showing increasing context facilitation for letters in nonwords, followed by pseudowords and finally words (Adams, 1979). The fact that a "WSE" can be obtained in the context of letter strings devoid of meaning indicates that its origin cannot be semantic, while the phonological hypothesis is brought into question by the effect showing with unpronounceable stimuli such as the nonwords. The WSE would therefore be related to a perceptual stage of word reading, in which orthographic units of various natures could help the recognition of single letters. The gradual growth of facilitation from nonwords to words observed by Adams confirms this because these stimuli present increasingly more familiar letter combinations. In fact, several reading experiments advocated the role of prelexical units composed of several letters but that were smaller than words. For example, graphemes have an effect on letter processing: letters are harder to detect when they are embedded in complex rather than simple graphemes (e.g., is there "an 'o' in boat ?" vs. "is there an 'o' in rope?") (Rey et al., 2000; see also Drewnowski & Healy, 1977, and Healy, 1994). This result indicates that after being exposed to words, graphemes are easier to access than letters because subjects exhibit more difficulties when they have to segment the stimuli to accurately detect the presence of a target letter. Similar results with different paradigms have also shown a role in reading of different orthographic units such as open bigrams[1] (Whitney & Berndt 1999), syllables (Carreiras et al., 1993; Mewhort & Beal, 1977; Prinzmetal et al., 1986; Rapp, 1992; Spoehr & Smith, 1973), or onsets and rimes (Treiman, 1994; Treiman and Chafetz, 1987).

Although these results all demonstrate that perceptual units relying on several letters (from bigrams to whole words) do play a role in reading and seem to be more readily available to the reader than letters, they do not necessarily imply that letter identification is not critical to reading. In fact, systems that can lead to the recognition of supraletter units are more or less explicitly described as intervening after the identification of single letters.

The Contribution of Individual Letters to Reading

The two main families of reading models (dual route and connectionist models) rely on a perceptual, orthographic stage in which words would be represented as an ordered sequence of abstract identities of letters constituting an "abstracted word shape" (Coltheart, Rastle, Perry, Langdon, & Ziegler, 2001; Paap, Newsome, McDonald, & Schvaneveldt, 1982; Rumelhart & McClelland, 1982; Seidenberg & McClelland, 1989). An interesting aspect of the conceptualization adopted by most recent reading models

---

[1] Defined as ordered pairs of letters coding for a given word: "take" would be coded by the units TA, TK, TE, AK, AE, and KE.

is that individual letter recognition is the starting point of correct lexical access. The central role of letters during reading has been recently demonstrated by Pelli and colleagues by presenting letters and words embedded in noise, and estimating performance as a function of word length (Pelli et al., 2003). They found that in these degraded conditions, the effect of word length was much larger than WSE. While human recognition performance suffered a five-fold decrease with a five-letter word compared with a letter, WSE only improved performance by a factor of 1.3. This suggests that even if the word context is useful, its effect on letter perception may be rather small compared with factors such as the length of the word that all fell into fovea during a fixation. Concordant reports have been recently published that demonstrated that the number of letters that can be correctly identified within a single fixation is a critical factor that determines the reading speed of subjects (Legge et al., 2007; Pelli et al., 2007).

Another interesting line of research to study the contribution of letters to reading has been the use of letter confusability, defined as the extent to which a letter can be confused with another. A measure of this confusability is obtained by presenting letters in degraded presentation conditions and by collecting subject's answers concerning the identity of the stimulus exposed (Bouma, 1971; Gilmore, Hersh, Caramazza, & Griffin, 1979; Loomis, 1982; Townsend, 1971; Van Der Heijden, Malhas, & Van Der Roovart, 1984). These studies result in confusability matrices that show what letters are harder to be uniquely identified, and with which letters they are more susceptible to be confused. Not surprisingly, results demonstrate that letters sharing visual features (such as curves, or vertical or horizontal lines) are much more likely to be confused with one another. Similarly, presenting a visually similar prime results in greater letter naming times than presenting visually dissimilar primes (Arguin and Bub, 1995). While these studies indicate that some letters are easier to perceive in isolation than others, some researchers sought to evaluate whether letter confusability had an impact on word recognition. Using words constructed with low- and high-confusability letters, several studies showed that letter confusability had no effect during word reading (Arguin et al., 2002; Cosky, 1976).

The lack of letter confusability effects in word reading may seem in contradiction with the above results showing that the best predictor of correct word identification is the ease with which we can recognize the individual letters. We believe these two results are actually complementary and illustrate the direction of the dependence between words and letters. The experiments of Pelli et al. (2003) degrade the perception of letters themselves in a quite drastic way and therefore target the initial perceptive stages of reading, leaving few chances for activation to propagate to higher levels of perception (that of supraletter units). In that sense, these results demonstrate quite convincingly how critical the perception of letters is to reading. The manipulation of letter confusability however, renders the perception of letters more difficult without introducing any perceptual degradation. In other words, in a situation where visually similar stimuli can be activated with some degrees of imprecision, supraletter units may intervene to help disambiguating the letters perceived.

Behavioral patterns exhibited by individuals with dyslexia prove to be quite informative concerning the role of letters in reading. For example, the hallmark feature of letter-by-letter reading (LBL) in dyslexia is an abnormal increase of reading times as a function of word length—this increase is not as extreme in the typical reader. Although individuals that are LBL readers adopt a strategy that relies on the identification of single letters in a sequential fashion, it has been shown that a deficit in letter perception is very likely to be the cause of LBL reading in dyslexia (Behrmann & Shallice, 1995). According to these authors, skillful word reading would depend in the first place on the efficiency of the processes involved in letter identification. A compatible conclusion has been obtained by Fiset that proposed that letter processing deficits would have an impact particularly on the parallel letter identification that takes place during word reading and that requires perception of several letters simultaneously without fixating on them individually (Fiset, Arguin, Bub, Humphreys, & Riddoch, 2005). Complementary experiments showed that when individuals with dyslexia were required to process single letters in the context of a word (that is, in a way that is compatible with a sequential processing of individual letters) the effect of word length was not modulated by the confusability of letters. When these same individuals processed words shown in a horizontal format, the word length effect could be eliminated by using gradually less confusable letters as their number in the word increased. These last results would therefore lend further support to the fact that the most critical deficit affecting LBL readers would be the parallel identification of letters, a process that would be more difficult when more confusable letters are present. Such a process would be instantiated during word reading.

While it does seem to rely on individual letter recognition, reading is a complex activity: high-level processes related to linguistics and supraletter orthographical processing modulate the coarse identification of letters. Although issues concerning letter recognition have often been debated in the larger framework of reading, the studies above argue for processing that differs substantially between the perception of letters embedded in words and in isolation. Such a distinction has to be kept in mind for the researcher interested in discovering the specificity of letter recognition as a visual object because it may require studying letter processing outside the activity of recognizing words. As we will now see, the distinction outlined above between isolated letters and letters strings finds its counterpart at the cerebral level when we consider the specificity of letter processing.

CEREBRAL SELECTIVITY FOR THE VISUAL PERCEPTION OF LETTERS

Selectivity for Letter Strings or Word Forms

About a century ago a case study was reported of a patient who suffered from a left inferior occipitotemporal lesion and lost the ability to recognize letters and words, while having no trouble speaking, writing, or recognizing other visual material (Dejerine, 1892, as cited in Bub et al., 1993). Although Dejerine interpreted this pure alexia as a specific blindness to the visually presented letters, later works focused on the visual processes involved in reading through the recognition of word forms. Word forms have been regarded as perceptual units with distinct representations, and a visual word form system has been proposed for the parsing of letter strings into familiar units for further analyses (Carr & Pollatsek, 1985; Warrington & Shallice, 1980). Recent neuroimaging studies have identified a visual word form area (VWFA) in the left inferior occipitotemporal region, including parts of the left fusiform gyrus, which may be responsible for such processes (Cohen et al., 2000). This region has been shown to play a critical role in reading and responds more to various strings of letters, such as words, pseudowords, and consonant strings than to other shapes (Cohen et al., 2003; Joubert et al., 2004; Tagamets, Novick, Chalmers, & Friedman, 2000; Vigneau, Jobard, Mazoyer, & Tzourio-Mazoyer, 2005). Importantly, the neural response in this region is invariant to changes in location, case, and font (Cohen & Dehaene, 2004; Cohen et al., 2000; McCandliss, Cohen, & Dehaene, 2003), indicating some level of abstraction needed to recognize letter strings despite perceptual variations.

The nature of selectivity of the VWFA has generated much discussion. Some studies showed that perceiving words and consonant strings activated the VWFA more than perceiving checkerboards (Cohen et al., 2003), geometric symbols (Tagamets et al., 2000), textures and faces (Puce et al., 1996), faces and buildings (Hasson, Levy, Behrmann, Hendler, & Malach, 2002), and digit strings (Polk et al., 2002). Consistent with this, intracranial recordings in the bilateral posterior fusiform gyrus have found a larger N200 component for letter strings (in the form of words, pronounceable pseudowords, or consonant strings) than for cars and butterflies (Allison, McCarthy, Nobre, Puce, & Belger, 1994; Nobre, Allison, & McCarthy, 1994). Other studies, however, failed to show a greater engagement of the VWFA during the perception or naming of objects than of words (Moore & Price, 1999; Price & Devlin, 2003).

Selectivity for Single Letters

Relatively few studies have directly tackled the question of selectivity for individual letters. The question of how letters are processed used to be addressed through the generalization of results obtained using letter strings, and some researchers suggested that the region responsible for the recognition of letters may actually be a subregion of the visual word form area (Dehaene et al., 2004).

Recently, some studies using isolated letters have shown a degree of cerebral selectivity for these simple stimuli. At an electrophysiological level, an EEG study showed that an early negative component occurring at about 170 ms after stimulus onset was enhanced with single, familiar characters compared with unknown characters or pseudoletters at posterior channels

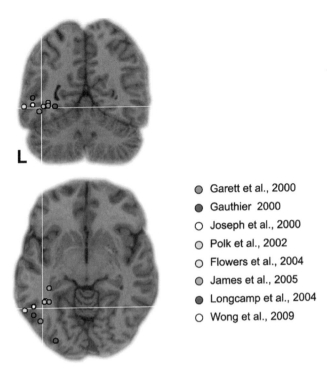

○ Garett et al., 2000
● Gauthier 2000
○ Joseph et al., 2000
○ Polk et al., 2002
○ Flowers et al., 2004
◉ James et al., 2005
● Longcamp et al., 2004
○ Wong et al., 2009

Figure 10.1 Schematic of approximate peak % BOLD signal change activation for letters recorded across several experiments. For coronal section, Talairach Y = (−50); for transverse section, Talairach Z = (−4). Note that activation peaks are quite variable but are all left lateralized and fall either on the fusiform gyrus or middle temporal gyrus (See color Plate 11).

(Wong et al., 2005). Concordant with this result, an MEG study has also shown an early component at about 150–200 ms that is larger for single letters than geometric shapes (Tarkiainen et al., 1999). In functional imaging studies (see Figure 10.1), isolated letters elicited higher activation in the left fusiform gyrus than oblique lines (Longcamp et al., 2003), faces (Gauthier, Tarr, et al., 2000), Chinese characters (James et al., 2005), and simple objects (James & Gauthier, 2006). Further, the left occipitotemporal region was recruited more when attention was paid to letters compared with colors and symbols (Flowers et al., 2004), and a correlation could be observed between the activity level of this region and the performance of discrimination between letters and symbols (Garrett et al., 2000).

Although varying to some extent from one study to another, the localizations of the identified "letter sensitive area" are all situated in the occipitotemporal junction that also hosts the VWFA, and the question remains as to how these two regions relate. A recent study that addressed the selectivity for words together with isolated letters indicated, however, that these stimuli may recruit separate neural substrates (James et al., 2005). We found that the region showing selectivity for single letters but not letter strings was situated in a fusiform region anterior to the VWFA, while the region showing selectivity for strings but not single letters overlapped with the VWFA.

INTERACTION WITH OTHER COGNITIVE SYSTEMS

Neuroimaging results have shown that our perceptual expertise with letters is subtended by a cerebral region located in the visual processing stream. Letters are a special kind of visual object whose identification may trigger activation in systems devoted to other modalities than vision, and we will now consider the possible impact of this interaction on the letter area.

Interactions with the Linguistic System

Writing systems are all designed to enable the translation of what are initially auditorily encoded items to be transferred into the visual modality. As such, letters are meant to cooperate with other cognitive systems pertaining to phonology or semantics, to activate words. In most models of reading, two ways of accessing words are usually implemented. The letter-to-sound is referred to as the grapho-phonological route, also called "indirect" because words meanings are mediated by their pronunciation. The word–meaning association (also called lexico-semantic route) is called "direct" since an orthographic representation of the word is directly mapped onto its signification. A meta-analysis of 35 neuroimaging studies of word and nonword reading suggested that these two possible ways to access words have a common starting point in the left ventral occipitotemporal region for the direct (lexico-semantic) and indirect (graphophonological) routes of reading (Jobard, Crivello, & Tzourio-Mazoyer, 2003). The meta-analysis identified activation peaks for direct route contrasts (words > pseudowords, Kanji[2] words > Kana words and Kanji words > fixation, lexical or semantic decision > phonological decision, irregular words > regular words) and indirect route contrasts (the opposite of the direct route contrasts). It was indeed found that the left ventral occipitotemporal region contained peaks for both routes. Hence, it seems that all the stages subsequent to the visual analysis of letter strings rely on left-lateralized networks, independently of the two possible routes used to process them. Other studies have also shown that characters in alphabetic and nonalphabetic writing systems recruit highly overlapping regions in the left occipitotemporal cortex (Bolger, Perfetti, & Schneider, 2005; Wong et al., 2009) and cause enhancement of the same early electrophysiological component (Wong et al., 2005), despite the greater reliance on the indirect route for alphabetic languages for their regular grapheme-to-phoneme correspondence. The need to communicate with regions involved in various components of the

---

[2] Kanji and Kana refer to two different writing systems used in Japan. Kanji are ideograms that are sometimes arbitrarily associated to a meaning, while Kana refer to syllables of the Japanese language.

linguistic system may therefore constitute a constraint related to the hemisphere in which the letter-selective area can establish.

Sensorimotor Interactions

Recent research has suggested that visual perception of objects may access stored information that is multimodal, depending upon how we learn and experience the given object. For example, visual identification of objects that we interact with motorically not only involves visual processing but also automatically activates motor areas of the brain (Bartolomeo et al., 2002; Boronat et al., 2004; Buccino et al., 2005; Chao & Martin, 2000; Grezes & Decety, 2002; James et al., 2006; Kato et al., 1999; Longcamp et al., 2005; Mecklinger et al., 2002; James & Atwood, 2008). Presumably this activation is due to our sensorimotor experience with the objects, as the motor cortices are not engaged when we perceive objects with which we do not usually interact motorically, such as faces, animals, and buildings (Grezes & Decety, 2002).

We not only learn letters visually, but we also learn to write them, which may establish letter-specific motor programs. We have recently found that simply perceiving letters activates motor regions of the brain, and writing letters (without seeing them) activates visual areas of the brain (James & Gauthier, 2006; see also Longcamp et al., 2005), resulting in a letter processing "network" (Figure 10.2). Recent work has shown that handwriting perception activates motor cortices more than print perception (Longcamp et al., 2006). The neural activation to individual letters that we do not see to

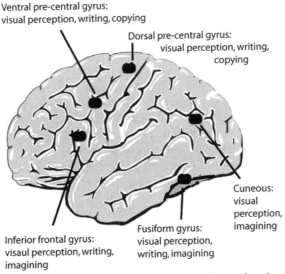

Figure 10.2 Schematic of a sensorimotor network of neural activation patterns found to letters but not to other, similar shapes (used with permission from K. H. James and I. Gauthier, 2006, "Letter processing automatically recruits a sensory-motor brain network," *Neuropsychologia* (4), with permission of Elsevier).

letter strings (James et al, 2005) can be explained in terms of motor efferents. That is, we write words letter-by-letter, and therefore, we may have a motor program associated with individual letters but not with words per se (independently of the constituant letters). Furthermore, we have also shown that other forms such as pseudoletters (letter-like symbols) activate letter-selective areas of the brain only after writing training (James & Atwood, 2009, see also Longcamp et al., 2008). That is, practice writing pseudoletters results in left fusiform gyrus and left precentral gyrus activation that is not apparent after typing training or visual-only training on the same pseudoletters. The selective processing that we, and others, have observed for letter perception may be due partly to the involvement of the motor system in processing these stimuli. In fact, we have recently seen the emergence of a letter-selective area in the left fusiform gyrus in preliterate children as they learn how to print letters that is not present if children are exposed to letters with visual only practice (James, in press). These results suggest that the development of the ventral "letter area" may be reliant upon, at least partially, our writing experience (James & Gauthier, 2006).

THE PERCEPTUAL SPECIFICITIES OF LETTERS

Apart from the fact that letter identification uniquely necessitates the cooperation of visual with linguistic and sensorimotor processes, letters are also unique as visual objects in regard to their perceptual characteristics. Three aspects of perceptual processing could contribute to the special nature of letters: spatiotemporal properties, task demand, and geometry of individual letters.

Spatiotemporal Properties

Co-occurrence

The fact that letters tend to occur together in space and time has been suggested as a reason why letters form a special category of objects. Polk and colleagues (Polk & Farah, 1998; Polk et al., 2002) offered a co-occurrence hypothesis to account for neural selectivity for letters. According to this account, letter selectivity is a result of the close occurrence of letters in terms of time and spatial location (with themselves but not with other object types) in the environment, captured by correlation-based mechanisms of neural learning. Their network model makes some natural predictions about letter representations in the brain. First, segregated cortical areas for letters should be more common and robust than other object categories, like digits, because letters appear more frequently with each other than digits occur with each other. Also, separate neural substrates should be recruited by different object categories because co-occurrence occurs much more frequently within, than between categories (Polk & Farah, 1995).

Nonetheless, some fMRI results are hard to reconcile with the idea that co-occurrence alone can account for neural selectivity for letters. First, with fixation as a baseline, Polk and colleagues observed a high degree of overlap between letter- and digit-selective areas, despite the low co-occurrence of letters and digits for most people. Similarly, using unfamiliar characters as baseline, our recent fMRI work used unfamiliar characters as control and found an overlap of activations not only between letters and digits (James et al., 2005), but also between Roman and Chinese characters in bilinguals (Wong et al., 2009). Such findings seem to contradict the co-occurrence model's predictions and suggest that co-occurrence is not likely the only cause for the neural selectivity for letter perception, at least not at the coarse scale in the order of millimeters. However, other properties accompanying the spatiotemporal co-occurrence of letters may play a role, as discussed below.

Regularity in Orientation

Letters tend to appear not only in clusters close in space and time but also with a coherent style (as in words and passages). Given that reading requires fast letter perception, it would be advantageous to utilize such regularity to help meet the high demand on speed. Behavioral studies have shown that regularity of, for example, orientation, across different letter instances is extracted, leading to more efficient letter and word perception (e.g., Jolicoeur, 1990). Triplets of uppercase letters were presented, and participants named the letters with a higher accuracy when the orientation was regular for the three letters (e.g., all rotated for 60° clockwise, i.e., 60°) than when the orientation changed. Orientation change was less detrimental when it was gradual and along a fixed direction than when it was random, even with the average disorientation of the letters controlled for the two conditions. These results suggest that identification of a letter is sensitive to the relative orientation of other neighboring letters.

Sensitivity to the regularity in orientation has also been shown for novel characters (Gauthier & Tarr, 1997), though only among structurally similar ones that presumably belong to the same "basic-level" (Rosch, Mervis, Gray, Johnson, & Boyes-Braem, 1976) category. In that study, participants first learned to name two-dimensional line shapes in a canonical orientation. Later, they were asked to name the same shapes presented one by one in several different orientations presented in random order. A typical view sensitivity pattern was found, with performance the best at the canonical view and deteriorating more with larger view difference from the canonical view. The viewpoint cost was greatly reduced when orientations were blocked, suggesting the use of orientation information of an object to facilitate subsequent identification. This orientation priming effect, however, only eliminated the viewpoint cost for similar shapes (e.g., ╪ and ╪) but not between less similar shapes (e.g., ╫ and ╪), which indicates that orientation tuning may occur only for objects within the same basic-level category. Another study also found that orientation priming did not occur between objects from different basic-level categories; for example, a 60° horse does not facilitate subsequent recognition of a 60° chair (McKone & Grenfell, 1999).

Here we see one important difference between the orientation priming patterns for letters and common objects. Whereas orientation priming does not occur across basic levels for objects, it exists for letters that differ greatly in shape and thus constitute different basic-level categories (e.g., B, V, C). One likely reason involves our differential experience with letters and objects. The prolonged experience of perceiving clusters of letters in the same orientation may result in the formation of transletter features, or strengthening of connections between units representing different letters in the same orientation, both of which would lead to orientation priming.

Regularity in Font

Apart from orientation, font also occurs with a high regularity in texts. It has been demonstrated that letters are identified faster within a string with the same font compared with a string with mixed fonts (Sanocki, 1987, 1988, 1991b, 1992). A recent study suggested that such font tuning effects may occur only for certain type of font changes (aspect ratio) and may depend on expertise (Gauthier et al., 2006). That is, font tuning effects were found only with familiar characters (e.g., Roman letters for English readers, Roman letters or Chinese characters for Chinese readers) but not novel ones (e.g., Chinese characters for English readers).

It is a reasonable postulate that the use of regularity in font or style for letters in text can be one of those characteristics that make letter perception different from the perception of other objects. Although there are also cases where objects appear in a coherent style (e.g., different types of furniture in a particular designing style), such regularity may not be used as extensively as for letters for several reasons. First, regularity in style occurs more frequently for letters (almost every time one sees a text) than for other objects. More importantly, there is a higher demand for speed on letter perception (as a result of a large number of letters to be processed during reading) than on object perception, resulting in a larger driving force for the visual system to utilize whatever is useful in the stimuli (such as font regularity) to increase efficiency in letter perception.

Different mechanisms underlying font tuning have been suggested. One involves the explicit, separate representation of information about letter identity and style. According to some accounts, a letter contains both a letter concept and font parameters (Hofstadter & McGraw, 1995; Sanocki, 1988). A letter concept is an abstract description of the parts of a letter and how they are connected (e.g., a "p" has a post and a loop attached to its upper right). Font parameters describe the variations in the parts (e.g., length of the post and curvature of the loop in "p"). During reading, to recover the letter concepts and thus efficiently recognize the letters, one has to also establish the parameter values for the styles and factor them out from the letter description. Such parameter value establishments cost time, and it would help to have a regular font and style since no new parameters need to be determined. In other words, with font regularity in a text, one would be able to utilize the font information of the current letter to facilitate abstraction of letter concept information of subsequent letters. Computational studies in the field of optical character recognition (OCR) have also suggested that performance of OCR programs deteriorates with font variations, and that explicit extraction of font information improves recognition accuracy (Baird & Nagy, 1994; Chaudhuri & Garain, 2001). This is analogous to some studies suggesting that extraction of certain speaker characteristics (e.g., pitch) facilitates speech recognition (e.g., Hariharan & Viikki, 2002).

Contrary to the abstractionist view mentioned above, one can also explain font tuning in terms of retrieval of exemplars or instances in memory (Logan, 1988). It was suggested that the same letter in different fonts is represented and stored as different instances (Sanocki, 1992). Texts with regular fonts will improve letter recognition because the greater similarities of same-font letters (as opposed to different-font letters) result in the currently perceived letter activating representations of other letters of the same font to a greater extent. A similar nonabstractionist, instance-based account has also been suggested for handling speaker variability in speech recognition (Goldinger, 1998; Pisoni, 1993).

The instance-based account is more consistent with behavioral and neural findings. In an identification task with backward-masked strings, it was found that accuracy was lowered when a change in size or style occurred. Importantly, the reduction in performance was the same whether the size, the style, or both size and style changed (Sanocki, 1991c). In another study where participants judged if a string contained all letters or one nonletter, one subset of letters was first presented and later a new subset was used without any warning. Performance was lowered when a new set of letters in the same font was used, to a similar extent as when a new set of letters in a new font or the same set of letters in a new font was used (Sanocki, 1992). In other words, keeping the font unchanged did not reduce the costs of switching to a new set of letters. These findings suggest that font-specific letter instances are represented as separate entities. Neuroimaging work also supports the possibility of exemplar representations for letters. The letter-selective areas in the ventral occipitotemporal cortex showed more adaptation to the same letter presented repeatedly in the same font compared with the same letter presented consecutively in different fonts (Gauthier, Tarr, et al., 2000). These studies provide support for the storage of exemplars instead of the separated representations of letter concepts and font parameters.

Task Demand

Generalization across Cases

Different cases exist in certain writing systems (e.g., Latin, Greek, Cyrillic, and Armenian alphabets) but not others (e.g., Arabic, Hebrew, and Georgian alphabets, Kanji, and Kana). Case generalization, the ability to name or perceive two examples of a letter presented in a different case at the same efficiency as two different letters presented in the same case, has been demonstrated repeatedly in priming experiments (e.g., Bowers et al., 1991; Bowers, Vigliocco, & Haan, 1998; Evett & Humphreys, 1981). However, in naming tasks, letters of different case are named more slowly than two identical letters presented in the same case (e.g. Posner, Boies, Eichelman, & Taylor, 1969, Posner & Boies, 1971), indicating imperfect generalization. This being said, the demand for case generalization has historically been thought to be somewhat unique to letter perception.

Two lines of research have addressed the representations for letters in different cases (e.g., Coltheart, 1981; Posner, 1978; Posner & Boies, 1971; Posner et al., 1969; Rynard & Besner, 1987). Posner and colleagues postulated two types of codes, visual codes and phonetic (name) codes, for the representation of letters. For instance, while "A" and "a" are represented by two different visual codes, they share the same phonetic codes (Posner, 1978; Posner & Boies, 1971; Posner & Mitchell, 1967; Posner et al., 1969). Based on the results that response time in a name match task was faster for physically identical (e.g., AA) pairs than pairs with the same name but differing visually (e.g., Aa), Posner and colleagues postulate that the visual code is computed followed by the phonetic code, which allows for generalization of letter recognition across cases. Follow-up studies by other labs have also offered support for a level of phonetic letter representation, in that naming performance was worse for phonologically similar letter pairs like "D" and "p" than phonological dissimilar pairs like "F" and "h" (Dainoff & Haber, 1970; Ellis, 1981; Marmurek, 1985).

The idea of the phonetic nature of the name code has been challenged by researchers arguing instead that an abstract letter identity is the representation for the same letter across cases. Besner and colleagues asked participants to perform speeded classification on two simultaneously presented letter strings based on physical matches (i.e., respond "same" only to the same strings in the same case but not in different cases) (Besner & Coldheart et al., 1984). In different trials, it was harder to say "different" when the strings shared the same abstract letter identities (e.g., HILE/hile) and differed in case, compared with the condition when the strings shared the same phonological code but differed in spelling (e.g., HILE/hyle). In other studies, no phonological effect has been found (Arguin and Bub 1995; Boles and Eveland, 1983). In a letter-matching task, response time was similar in the different conditions with either phonologically similar (e.g., "A" and "j") or dissimilar pairs (e.g., "A" and "z"). It has also been suggested that the phonological effects found in some earlier studies (Dainoff and Haber, 1970; Ellis, 1981) were purely a result of the use of reversible letters (e.g., "p," the mirror image of which is another letter, "q") in the phonologically confusable condition (Bigsby, 1988). This provides support for the notion that letter abstraction does not require an intermediary based on phonology.

Neuropsychological studies have also identified patients who failed to name letters but could match the upper and lower cases of the same letter

(Bigsby, 1990; Coltheart, 1981; Mycroft, Hanley, & Kay, 2002; Rynard & Besner, 1987). Recently, an fMRI study revealed that a posterior portion of the fusiform area showed masked priming of letters across cases, suggesting that the area may be responsible for representing abstract letter identities (Dehaene et al., 2004).

Contrary to what has been suggested above, one could argue that the demand for case generalization may not play a large role in the recruitment of specialized mechanisms for letter perception. The rationale is that the mechanisms underlying case generalization may not be distinct from similar processes that occur for object recognition in general. Imaging studies have located common areas in the occipitotemporal cortex not only for Roman letters but also for characters that do not involve case, such as Chinese and Japanese characters (Bolger et al., 2005; Wong et al., in press). In addition, in most cases of reading, letters appear in the same case (except for the initial letter of a proper noun or the initial word of a sentence). The demand for treating the upper- and lowercase versions of letters as the same may not be that high. In fact, case can provide important information about syntax (e.g., capital letters at the beginning of a statement) and meanings (e.g., to indicate an emphasis), and sensitivity to case changes within a word is often found (Mayall, Humphrey, & Olson, 1997). Also, the underlying mechanisms for case generalization may not be any different from other processes related to object perception, such as 3-D viewpoint generalization. Different views of an object have been shown to vary to a greater degree than similar views of different objects. For example, image analyses have shown a larger difference between different views of a face than the same view of different faces (Ullman, 1989). One way to recognize different views of an object is to arbitrarily assign the different view-specific representations of an object to the same category in memory. Generalization of object recognition to familiar and novel views could be achieved by a system with object units receiving a weighted sum of inputs from a few view-specific units (Bülthoff & Edelman, 1992; Poggio, 1990; Wong & Hayward, 2005). Neurons in the inferotemporal cortex are also able to associate pairs of visually distinct patterns (Sakai & Miyashita, 1991). Research is needed to determine whether similar mechanisms are used for assigning the same letter in different cases to the same category.

Resolution Demand

There are two different views concerning the resolution demand required for letter perception. Some suggest that letter perception is an extreme case of object perception requiring a high resolution. Others regard letter perception as not particularly demanding in terms of analyses of detail.

The idea of letter perception requiring a high resolution comes from studies of eccentricity biases associated with different object categories (Hasson et al., 2002; Hasson, Harel, Levy, & Malach, 2003; Levy, Hasson, Avidan, Hendler, & Malach, 2001; Levy, Hasson, Harel, & Malach 2004; Malach, Levy, & Hasson, 2002). Accordingly, a continuum exists such that at one extreme there are substrates with a foveal bias and thus the capacity for object analyses at high resolutions, while at the other extreme substrates manifest a peripheral bias and low spatial resolutions. Evidence comes from studies showing that areas selective for different object categories seem to follow the distribution of the areas showing preference for foveal or peripheral presentation, with letter- and face-selective areas overlapping with the fovea-bias regions whereas building-selective areas with the periphery-biased regions (more details discussed in the next section). Words and letters represent the extreme case of object perception requiring high resolution and foveation, even more so than face recognition. Therefore, letters engage regions that are even more fovea-biased than faces.

In contrast with the view described above, one can regard letter perception as a less demanding task than face perception in terms of analysis of detail (Wong & Gauthier, 2007). We learn the optimum procedure for letter recognition with repeated experience at an early age. The recognition demands that are placed on the visual system for letter recognition are quite different than those for other types of objects. For instance, our usual task during object recognition is to simply recognize that a chair is a chair so that we may sit down. Recognizing that a chair is a chair requires that we realize that it is not a bed, or a table—a decision that requires distinguishing objects that are very different in their overall shape. This type of decision has been called one of "basic-level discrimination" (Rosch et al., 1976). We can also distinguish one chair from another—which may require a finer-grained analysis of features, rather than distinguishing overall shape. This is often called "subordinate-level" categorization and is based more on second-order relations among parts, such as distances from one part to another as well as size and shape of individual parts. While basic-level categorization is the default task demand during recognition of the majority of common objects, subordinate-level categorization is thought to underlie most face recognition tasks (Gauthier, Tarr, et al., 2000). Letter recognition, though also a type of perceptual expertise, requires decisions to be made at the basic level. That is, many letters are of very different overall shapes, requiring one to disregard slight variations in second-order similarities (e.g., individual differences in how the lower case "b" is written). Extensive experience with characters in a particular writing system results in a greater ability to discriminate and use basic-level differences in images while efficiently filtering out subordinate-level noise like font and handwriting (Gauthier et al., 2006). Such difference in recognition demand leads to opposite phenomena associated with letter and face perception: whereas expertise with a character set is associated with a larger basic-level advantage (better performance for basic- than subordinate-level recognition), expertise with faces is typically linked to a shrink in this advantage (Wong & Gauthier, 2007). Similarly, Zhang and Cottrell have shown that a network trained for discriminating among letters was not as good as a face discrimination network in performing a fine-grained discrimination task on blob patterns (each with four blobs forming a Y-shape-like configuration) that differ in small shifts in the blob locations

(Zhang & Cottrell, 2004). These suggest that letter perception requires a lower resolution than face perception.

The basic-/subordinate-level account and the eccentricity bias theory characterize letter and face perception differently because they focus on different aspects of object perception. According to the eccentricity bias theory, the conclusion that letter perception requires a higher resolution than face perception is based on these premises and findings: (1) The changes in the ventral occipitotemporal region have to be continuous from low resolution in the medial portion to high resolution in the lateral portion; (2) letter-selective areas are more lateral than face-selective areas; and (3) letters appear smaller than faces in general, and their perception thus requires a higher resolution. The levels-of-categorization account, however, stresses the difference in within-category homogeneity between letters, other objects, and faces. It does not consider the size differences between letters and faces as they appear in daily-life situations. Nor does it assume continuous biases for processes along the ventral occipitotemporal region. Further work could help resolve the differences by teasing apart the effects of different factors like size and within-category homogeneity.

Constraints from a Fixed Letter Set

Another unique aspect of letter processing concerns the limited number of instances and features involved in perception and recognition. Letters or characters in a particular writing system consist of a limited number of features combined in different ways. An expert system can possibly utilize this characteristic to limit the features to be considered during letter perception. A study by Rouder suggested such possibility (Rouder, 2001). He examined the effect of the number of alternatives on the efficiency of line length identification and letter identification. Results demonstrated that having fewer alternatives to choose from facilitated line length identification but not letter identification. While Rouder (2001) gives no account for this difference, one explanation lies in our expertise with letters. For identification of unfamiliar stimuli like lines of different lengths, having fewer alternatives may increase efficiency by drawing attention to certain length values. For letters, however, we are used to identifying one letter out of the 26 alternatives in real-life contexts. The prolonged experience of considering all features or letters useful for this task may render us less flexible. So even when there are fewer alternatives and fewer features can be considered, we cannot take advantage of this, and identification thus does not benefit from fewer alternatives.

That letter perception involves a limited set of items differentiates it from the perception of other objects, where the set is open. As described above, such a set property provides various constraints to facilitate letter perception. Various types of connections between different features' nodes are likely to capture such information. The word-to-letter-level and the letter-to-feature-level constraints are achieved by the feedback connections, while the Rouder results are likely contributed by lateral connections among features and obligatory use of stored exemplars (Logan, 1988). The rich connectivity between and within levels may be a reason for the segregation of neural substrates for letter perception.

CONCLUSION

Letter perception has been heavily studied in the context of reading, and relatively less emphasis has been placed on the underlying visual mechanisms in letter processing. This chapter is aimed at discussing the mechanisms involved in visual letter perception that may distinguish it from processing of other objects and other types of perceptual expertise. The selectivity of certain neural substrates for letter perception may be explained by a comprehensive consideration of the stimulus characteristics, and experience associated with letter perception. Letter perception requires putting perceptually dissimilar instances such as the same letter in different fonts and cases into the same category, in contrast with face perception requiring discrimination among highly similar instances. In addition, the emphasis on speed for letter perception may have urged an experienced reader to utilize the regularities (e.g., in terms of font type) available in texts. Our motor and linguistic experiences with letters also may require neural processing that is different from that of some other objects and faces. One postulate is that the high-level visual system, as reflected in ventral occipitotemporal processing, contains different units with different pre-existing biases. Some parts of the high-level visual system are associated with certain objects because of the representations and processes suitable for the stimulus characteristics and perceptual demands for those objects. Experience plays a role in forming such associations between certain objects and neural substrates. In the end, a good theory of perceptual expertise with objects should not only explain the computational and implementation similarities and differences among expertise with different objects, but also predict what behavioral and neural markers are associated with object expertise.

REFERENCES

Adams, M. J. (1979). Models of word recognition. *Cognitive Psychology, 2,* 133–176.

Allison, T., Ginter, H., McCarthy, G., Nobre, A. C., Puce, A., Luby, M., et al. (1994). Face recognition in human extrastriate cortex. *Journal of Neurophysiology, 71(2),* 821–825.

Allison, T., McCarthy, G., Nobre, A., Puce, A., & Belger, A. (1994). Human extrastriate visual cortex and the perception of faces, words, numbers, and colors. *Cerebral Cortex, 4(5),* 544–554.

Arguin, M., & Bub, D. (1995) Priming and response selection processes in letter classification and idenfication tasks. *Journal of Experimental Psychology: Human Perception and Performance 21,* 1199–1219.

Arguin, M., Fiset, S., & Bub, D. (2002). Sequential and parallel letter processing in letter-by-letter dyslexia. *Cognitive Neuropsychology, 19,* 535–555.

Baird, H. S., & Nagy, G. (1994). *A self-correction 100-font classifier.* In Vincent, L.M & Pavlidis, T (Eds.) Document Recognition (Proceedings Volume, pp. 106–115), SPIE digital Library.

Bartolomeo, P., Bachoud-Levi, A.-C., Chokron, S., & Degos, J. D. (2002). Visually- and motor-based knowledge of letters: Evidence from a pure alexic patient. *Neuropsychologia, 40,* 1363–1371.

Beauregard, M., Chertkow, H., Bub, D., Murtha, S., Dixon, R., & Evans, A. (1997) The neural substrates for concrete, abstract, and emotional word lexica: A positron emission tomography, *Journal of Cognitive Neuroscience 9,* 441–461.

Bentin, S., Allison, T., Puce, A., Perez, E., & et al. (1996). Electrophysiological studies of face perception in humans. *Journal of Cognitive Neuroscience, 8(6),* 551–565.

Behrmann, M., & Shallice, T. (1995). Pure alexia: A nonspatial visual disorder affecting letter activation. *Cognitive Neuropsychology 12,* 409–454.

Biederman, I., Mezzanotte, R. J., & Rabinowitz, J. C. (1982). Scene perception: Detecting and judging objects undergoing relation violations. *Cognitive Psychology, 14,* 143–177.

Bigsby, P. (1990). Abstract letter identities and developmental dyslexia. *British Journal of Psychology, 81,* 227–263.

Binder, J. R., McKiernan, K. A., Parsons, M. E., Westbury, C. F., Possing, E.T., Kaufman, J. N., & Buchanan, L. (2003). Neural correlates of lexical access during visual word recognition, *Journal of Cognitive Neuroscience 15,* 372–393.

Bolger, D. J., Perfetti, C. A., & Schneider, W. (2005). Cross-cultural effect on the brain revisited: Universal structures plus writing system variation. *Human Brain Mapping, 25,* 92–104.

Bouma, H. (1971). Visual recognition of isolated lower-case letters. *Vision Research, 11,* 459–474.

Bowey, J. A. (1990) Orthographic onsets and rimes as functional units of reading. *Memory & Cognition,12,* 419–427.

Bowers, J. S., Vigliocco, G., & Haan, R. (1998). Orthographic, phonological, and articulatory contributions to masked letter and word priming. *Journal of Experimental Psychology: Human Perception & Performance, 24(6),* 1705–1719.

Bub, D. N., Arguin, M., & Lecours, A. R. (1993). Jules Dejerine and his interpretation of pure alexia. *Brain and Language, 45(4),* 531–559.

Bukach, C. M., Gauthier, I., & James, T. W. (2006a). The influence of semantics on perception: An fMRI study of greeble matching following social and inanimate trait-association learning. *Perceptual Expertise Network Workshop* XII. Longboat Key, FL.

Bukach, C. M., Gauthier, I., & Tarr, M. J. (2006b). Beyond faces and modularity: The power of an expertise framework. *Trends in Cognitive Sciences, 10(4),* 159–166.

Busey, T. A., & Vanderkolk, J. R. (2005). Behavioral and electrophysiological evidence for configural processing in fingerprint experts. *Vision Research, 45,* 431–448.

Bülthoff, H. H., & Edelman, S. (1992). Psychophysical support for a two-dimensional view interpolation theory of object recognition. *Proceedings of the National Academy of Sciences USA, 89,* 60–64.

Carlson, T. A., Schrater, P., & He, S. (2003). Patterns of activity in the categorical representations of objects. *Journal of Cognitive Neuroscience, 15,* 704–717.

Carr, T. H., & Pollatsek, A. (1985). Recognizing printed words: A look at current models. In D. Besner, T. G. Waller, & G. E. MacKinnon (Eds.), *Reading research: Advances in theory and practice* (Vol. 5, pp. 2–82). New York: Academic Press.

Carreiras, M., Alvarez, C. J. Y., & De Vega, M. (1993). Syllable frequency and visual word recognition in Spanish. *Journal of Memory and Language, 13,* 766–780.

Changizi, M. A., & Shimojo, S. (2005). Character complexity and redundancy in writing systems over human history. *Proceedings of the Biological Society, 272,* 267–275.

Chaudhuri, B. B., & Garain, U. (2001). Extraction of type style-based meta-information from imaged documents. *International Journal on Document Analysis and Recognition, 3,* 138–149.

Cohen, L., & Dehaene, S. (2004). Specialization within the ventral stream: The case for the visual word form area. *NeuroImage, 22,* 466–476.

Cohen, L., Dehaene, S., Naccache, L., Lehericy, S., Dehaene-Lambertz, G., Henaff, M. A., et al. (2000). The visual word form area: Spatial and temporal characterization of an initial stage of reading in normal subjects and posterior split-brain patients. *Brain, 123(Pt. 2),* 291–307.

Cohen, L., Jobert, A., Le Bihan, D., & Dehaene, S. (2004). Distinct unimodal and multimodal regions for word processing in the left temporal cortex. *NeuroImage, 23,* 1256–1270.

Cohen, L., Lehericy, S., Cohochon, F., Lemer, C., Rivaud, S., & Dehaene, S. (2002). Language-specific tuning of visual cortex? Functional properties of the visual word form area. *Brain, 125,* 1054–1069.

Cohen, L., Martinaud, O., Lemer, C., Lehericy, S., Samson, Y., Obadia, M., Slachevsky, A., & Dehaene, S, (2003). Visual word recognition in the left and right hemispheres: anatomical and functional correlates of peripheral alexias. *Cerebral Cortex 13,* 1313–1333.

Coltheart, M. (1981). Disorders of reading and their implications for models of normal reading. *Visible Language, 15,* 245–286.

Coltheart, M., Rastle, K., Perry, C., Langdon, R., & Ziegler, J. (2001) DRC: A dual route cascaded model of visual word recognition and reading aloud. *Psychological Review 108,* 204–256.

Cosky, M. J. (1976) The role of letter recognition in word recognition. *Memory & Cognition 4,* 207–214.

Cox, D., & Savoy, R. (2003). Functional magnetic resonance imaging (fMRI) "brain reading": Detecting and classifying distributed patterns of fMRI activity in human visual cortex. *Neuroimage, 19,* 261–270.

Dainoff, M., & Haber, R. N. (1970). Effect of acoustic confusability on levels of processing. *Canadian Journal of Psychology, 24,* 98–108.

Dehaene, S., Cohen, L., Sigman, M., & Vinckier, F. (2005). The neural code for written words: A proposal. *Trends in Cognitive Sciences, 9(7),* 335–341.

Dehaene, S., Jobert, A., Naccache, L., Ciuciu, P., Poline, J.-B., Le Bihan, D., et al. (2004). Letter binding and invariant recognition of masked words. *Psychological Science, 15(5),* 307–313.

Dehaene, S., Le Clec'H, G., Poline, J. B., Le Bihan, D., & Cohen, L. (2002). The visual word form area: À prelexical representation of visual words in the fusiform gyrus. *NeuroReport, 13,* 321–325.

Downing, P. E., Chan, A. W., Peelen, M. V., Dodds, C. M., & Kanwisher, N. (2005). Domain specificity in visual cortex. *Cerebral Cortex, 24,* 2005.

Downing, P. E., Jiang, Y., Shuman, M., & Kanwisher, N. (2001). A cortical area selective for visual processing of the human body. *Science, 293(5539),* 2470–2473.

Drewnowski, A., & Healy, A. F. (1977) Detection errors on the and and: Evidence for reading units larger than the word. *Memory & Cognition, 20,* 636–647.

Ellis, N. (1981). A lexical encoding deficiency: Experimental evidence. In G. T. Pavlidis & T. R. Miles (Eds.), *Dyslexia research and its applications to education.* Chichester, UK: Wiley.

Epstein, R., Harris, A., Stanley, D., & Kanwisher, N. (1999). The parahippocampal place area: Recognition, navigation, or encoding? *Neuron, 23*(1), 115–125.

Epstein, R., & Kanwisher, N. (1998). A cortical representation of the local visual environment. *Nature, 392*(6676), 598–601.

Evett, L. J., & Humphreys, G. W. (1981). The use of abstract graphemic information in lexical access. *Quarterly Journal of Experimental Psychology: Human Experimental Psychology, 33A*, 325–350.

Fiset, D., Arguin, M., Bub, D., Humphreys, G. W., & Riddoch, M. J. (2005) How to make the word-length effect disappear in letter-by-letter dyslexia. *Psychological Science 16*, 535–541.

Flowers, D. L., Jones, K., Noble, K., VanMeter, J., Zeffiro, T. A., Wood, F. B., et al. (2004). Attention to single letters activates left extrastriate cortex. *Neuroimage, 21*(3), 829–839.

Garrett, A. S., Flowers, D. L., Absher, J. R., Fahey, F. H., Gage, H. D., Keyes, J. W., et al. (2000). Cortical activity related to accuracy of letter recognition. *NeuroImage, 11*(2), 111–123.

Gauthier, I. (2000). What constrains the organization of the ventral temporal cortex? *Trends in Cognitive Sciences, 4*(1), 1–2.

Gauthier, I., Curran, T., Curby, K. M., & Collins, D. (2003). Perceptual interference supports a non-modular account of face processing. *Nature Neuroscience, 6*(4), 428–432.

Gauthier, I., Skudlarski, P., Gore, J. C., & Anderson, A. W. (2000). Expertise for cars and birds recruits brain areas involved in face recognition. *Nature Neuroscience, 3*(2), 191–197.

Gauthier, I., & Tarr, M. J. (1997). Orientation priming of novel shapes in the context of viewpoint-dependent recognition. *Perception, 26*, 51–73.

Gauthier, I., & Tarr, M. J. (2002). Unraveling mechanisms for expert object recognition: Bridging brain activity and behavior. *Journal of Experimental Psychology: Human Perception and Performance, 28*(2), 431–446.

Gauthier, I., Tarr, M. J., Moylan, J., Anderson, A. W., Skudlarski, P., & Gore, J. C. (2000). The fusiform "face area" is part of a network that processes faces at the individual level. *Journal of Cognitive Neuroscience, 12*(3), 495–504.

Gauthier, I., Wong, A. C.-N., Hayward, W. G., & Cheung, O. S.-C. (in press). Font-tuning associated with expertise in letter perception. *Perception.*

Gilmore, G. C., Hersh, H., Caramazza, A., & Griffin, J. (1979). Multidimensional letter similarity derived from recognition errors. *Perception & Psychophysics, 25*, 425–431.

Goldinger, S. D. (1998). Echoes of echoes? An episodic theory of lexical access. *Psychological Review, 105*, 251–279.

Grill-Spector, K., Sayres, R., & Ress, D. (2006). High-resolution imaging reveals highly selective non-face clusters in the fusiform face area. *Nature Neuroscience, 9*, 1177–1185.

Hariharan, R., & Viikki, O. (2002). An integrated study of speaker normalisation and hmm adaption for noise robust speaker-independent speech recognition. *Speech Communication, 37*, 349–361.

Hasson, U., Harel, M., Levy, I., & Malach, R. (2003). Large-scale mirror-symmetry organization of human occipito-temporal object areas. *Neuron, 37*, 1027–1041.

Hasson, U., Levy, I., Behrmann, M., Hendler, T., & Malach, R. (2001). Eccentricity bias as an organizing principle for human high order object areas. *Neuron, 25,* 213–225.

Hasson, U., Levy, I., Behrmann, M., Hendler, T., & Malach, M. (2002). Eccentricity bias as an organizing principle for human high order object areas. *Neuron, 34,* 479–490.

Haxby, J. V., Gobbini, M. I., Furey, M. L., Ishai, A., Schouten, J. L., & Pietrini, P. (2001). Distributed and overlapping representations of faces and objects in ventral temporal cortex. *Science, 293*(5539), 2425–2430.

Healy, A. F. (1994) Letter detection: A window to unitization and other cognitive processes in reading text. *Psychonomic Bulletin & Review 1,* 333–344.

Helenius, P., Tarkiainen, A., Cornelissen, P., Hansen, P. C., & Salmelin, R. (1999). Dissociation of normal feature analysis and deficient processing of letter-strings in dyslexic adults. *Cerebral Cortex, 9*(5), 476–483.

Hofstadter, D. R., & McGraw, G. E., Jr. (1995). Letter spirit: Esthetic perception and creative play in the rich microcosm of the roman alphabet. In D. R. Hofstadter (Ed.), *Fluid concepts and creative analogies* (pp. 407–466). New York: BasicBooks.

Hollingworth, A., & Henderson, J. M. (1998). Does consistent scene context facilitate object perception? *Journal of Experimental Psychology: General, 127*(4), 398–415.

Ishai, A., Ungerleider, L. G., Martin, A., Schouten, J. L., & Haxby, J. (1999). Distributed representation of objects in the human ventral visual pathway. *Proceedings of the National Academy of Sciences USA, 96,* 9379–9384.

James, K. H. (in press). Sensori-motor experience leads to changes in visual processing in the developing brain. *Developmental Science.*

James, K. H., & Atwood, T. P (2009). The role of sensori-motor learning in the perception of letter-like forms: Tracking the causes of neural specialization for letters. *Cognitive Neuropsychology, 26(1),* 91–101.

James, K. H., & Gauthier, I. (2006). Letter processing automatically recruits a sensory-motor brain network. *Neuropsychologia, 44,* 2937–2949.

James, K. H., James, T. W., Jobard, G., Wong, A. C.-N., & Gauthier, I. (2005). Letter processing in the visual system: Different activation patterns for single letters and strings. *Cognitive, Affective, and Behavioral Neuroscience, 5*(4), 452–466.

Jobard, G., Crivello, F., & Tzourio-Mazoyer, N. (2003). Evaluation of the dual route theory of reading: A metaanalysis of 35 neuroimaging studies. *NeuroImage, 20,* 693–712.

Johnson, N. F., & Pugh, K. R. (1994). A cohort model of visual word recognition. *Cognitive Psychology, 26,* 240–346.

Jolicoeur, P. (1990). Orientation congruency effects on the identification of disoriented shapes. *Journal of Experimental Psychology: Human Perception and Performance, 16*(26), 351–364.

Jordan, T. R., Thomas, S. M., & Scott-Brown, K. C. (1999). The illusory-letters phenomenon: An illustration of graphemic restoration in visual word recognition. *Perception, 28,* 1413–1416.

Joubert, S., Beauregard, M., Walter, N., Bourgouin, P., Beaudoin, G., Leroux, J. M., Karama, S. and Lecours, A. R. (2004). Neural correlates of lexical and sublexical processes in reading, *Brain and Language, 89,* 9–20.

Kanwisher, N., McDermott, J., & Chun, M. M. (1996). A module for the visual representation of faces. *NeuroImage, 3*(3, Suppl.), S361.

Kanwisher, N., McDermott, J., & Chun, M. M. (1997). The fusiform face area: A module in human extrastriate cortex specialized for face perception. *Journal of Neuroscience, 17,* 4302–4311.

Kanwisher, N., & Yovel, G. (2006). The fusiform face area: A cortical region specialized for the perception of faces. *Philosophical Transactions of the Royal Society B, 361,* 2109–2128.

Kimchi, R., & Hadad, B.-S. (2002). Influence of past experience on perceptual grouping. *Psychological Science, 13*(1), 41–47.

Legge, G. E., Cheung, S. -H., Yu, D., Chung, S. T. L., Lee, H.-W., & Owens, D. P. (2007). The case for the visual span as a sensory bottleneck in reading. *Journal of Vision, 7*(2), 9, 1–15.

Levy, I., Hasson, U., Avidan, G., Hendler, T., & Malach, R. (2001). Center-periphery organization of human object areas. *Nature Neuroscience, 4,* 533–539.

Levy, I., Hasson, U., Harel, M., & Malach, R. (2004). Functional analysis of the periphery effect in human building related areas. *Human Brain Mapping, 22,* 15–26.

Logan, G. D. (1988). Toward an instance theory of automatization. *Psychological Review, 95*(4), 492–527.

Logothetis, N. K., & Pauls, J. (1995). Psychophysical and physiological evidence for viewer-centered object representations in the primate. *Cerebral Cortex, 5*(3), 270–288.

Logothetis, N. K., & Sheinberg, D. L. (1996). Visual object recognition. *Annual Review of Neuroscience, 19,* 577–621.

Loomis, J. M. (1982) Analysis of tactile and visual confusion matrices. *Perception & Psychophysics,* 41–52.

Longcamp, M., Anton, J.-L., Roth, M., & Velay, J.-L. (2003). Visual presentation of single letters activates a premotor area involved in writing. *NeuroImage, 19*(4), 1492–1500.

Longcamp, M., Bouchard, C., Gilhodes, J.-C., Anton, J.-L., Roth, M., Nazarian, B., & Velay, J,-L. (2008). Learning through hand- or typewriting influences visual recognition of new graphic shapes: Behavioral and functional imaging evidence. *Journal of Cognitive Neuroscience, 17,* 1234–1236.

Lupker, S. J. (1979). On the nature of perceptual information during letter perception. *Perception and Psychophysics, 25*(4), 303–312.

Malach, R., Levy, I., & Hasson, U. (2002). The topography of high-order human object areas. *Trends in Cognitive Sciences, 6,* 176–184.

Marmurek, H. H. C. (1985). Evidence against the computation of abstract letter identities in visual processing. *Canadian Journal of Psychology, 39*(4), 536–545.

Mayall, K., Humphreys, G. W., Mechelli, A., Olson, A., and Price, C. J. (2001). The effects of case mixing on word recognition: Evidence from a PET study. *Journal of Cognitive Neuroscience, 13,* 844–853.

Mayall, K., Humphrey, G. W., & Olson, A. (1997). Disruption to word or letter processing? The origins of case-mixing effects. *Journal of Experimental Psychology: Learning, Memory, and Cognition, 23*(5), 1275–1286.

McCandliss, B. D., Cohen, L., & Dehaene, S. (2003). The visual word form area: Expertise for reading in the fusiform gyrus. *Trends in Cognitive Sciences, 7*(7), 293–299.

McClelland, J. L. (1976). Preliminary letter identification in the perception of words and nonwords. *Journal of Experimental Psychology: Human Perception and Performance, 2*(1), 80–91.

McClelland, J. L., & Rumelhart, D. L. (1981). An interactive activation model of context effects in letter perception. Part 1. An account of basic findings. *Psychological Review, 88,* 375–407.

McKone, E., & Grenfell, T. (1999). Orientation invariance in naming rotated objects: Individual differences and repetition priming. *Perception and Psychophysics, 61*(8), 1590–1603.

McKone, E., Kanwisher, N., & Duchaine, B. C. (2007). Can generic expertise explain special processing for faces? Trends in Cognitive Sciences, *11*, 8–15.

Mewhort, D. J. K., & Beal, A. L. (1977). Mechanisms of word identification. *Journal of Experimental Psychology: Human Perception and Performance, 3*(4), 629–640.

Moore, C. J., & Price, C. J. (1999). Three distinct ventral occipitotemporal regions for reading and object naming. *NeuroImage, 10*(2), 181–192.

Mycroft, R., Hanley, J. R., & Kay, J. (2002). Preserved access to abstract letter identities despite abolished letter naming in a case of pure alexia. *Journal of Neurolinguistics, 15*, 99–108.

Nazir, T. A., Jacobs, A. M., & O'Regan, J. K. (1998). Letter legibility and visual word recognition. *Memory and Cognition, 26*(4), 810–821.

Nobre, A. C., Allison, T., & McCarthy, G. (1994). Word recognition in the human inferior temporal lobe. *Nature, 372*(6503), 260–263.

O'Toole, A. J. O., Jiang, F., Abdi, H., & Haxby, J. V. (2005). Partially distributed representations of objects and faces in ventral temporal cortex. *Journal of Cognitive Neuroscience, 17*(4), 580–590.

Palmer, S. E. (1977). Hierarchical structure in perceptual representation. *Cognitive Science, 9*, 441–474.

Paap, K. R., Newsome, S. L., McDonald, J. E., & Schvaneveldt, R. W. (1982). An activation-verification model for letter and word recognition: The word superiority effect. *Psychological Review, 89*(5), 573–594.

Peelen, M. V., & Downing, P. E. (2005). Selectivity for the human body in the fusiform gyrus. *Journal of Neuroscience, 193*, 603–608.

Pelli, D. G., Farell, B., & Moore, D. C. (2003). The remarkable inefficiency of word recognition. *Nature, 423*, 752–756.

Pelli, D. G., Tillman, K. A., Freeman, J., Su, M., Berger, T. B., & Majaj, N. J. (2007) Crowding and eccentricity determine reading rate. *Journal of Vision, 7*(2), 20, 1–36.

Perani, D., Cappa, S. F., Schnur, T., Tettamanti, M., Collina, S., Rosa, M. M., and Fazio, F. (1999). The neural correlates of verb and noun processing—A PET study. *Brain, 122*, 2337–2344.

Perfetti, C. A., Liu, Y., & Tan, L. H. (2005). The lexical constituency model: Some implications of research on Chinese for general theories of reading. *Psychological Review, 112*(1), 43–59.

Perrett, D. I., Oram, M. W., & Ashbridge, E. (1998). Evidence accumulation in cell populations responsive to faces: An account of generalisation of recognition without mental transformations. *Cognition, 67*(1,2), 111–145.

Peterson, S. E., Fox, P. T., Snyder, A. Z., & Raichle, M. E. (1990). Activation of extrastriate and frontal cortical areas by visual words and word-like stimuli. *Science, 249*(4972), 1041–1044.

Pisoni, D. B. (1993). Long-term memory in speech perception: Some new findings on talker variability, speaking rate and perceptual learning. *Speech Communication, 13*(1–2), (Special Issue), 109–125.

Poggio, T. (1990). Regularization algorithms for learning that are equivalent to multilayer networks. *Science, 247*, 978–982.

Poggio, T., & Bizzi, E. (2004). Generalization in vision and motor control. *Nature, 431*, 768–774.

Poggio, T., & Edelman, S. (1990). A network that learns to recognize three-dimensional objects. *Nature, 343,* 263–266.

Polk, T. A., & Farah, M. J. (1995). Brain localization for arbitrary stimulus categories: A simple account based on Hebbian learning. *Proceedings of the National Academy of Sciences of the United States of America, 92*(26), 12370–12373.

Polk, T. A., & Farah, M. J. (1998). The neural development and organization of letter recognition: Evidence from functional neuroimaging, computational modeling, and behavioral studies. *Proceedings of the National Academy of Sciences USA, 95*(3), 847–852.

Polk, T. A., Stallcup, M., Aguirre, G. K., Alsop, D. C., D'Esposito, M., Detre, J. A., et al. (2002). Neural specialization for letter recognition. *Journal of Cognitive Neuroscience, 14*(2), 145–159.

Posner, M. I. (1978). Chronometric explorations of mind. Hillsdale, NJ: Erlbaum.

Posner, M. I., & Boies, S. J. (1971). Components of attention. *Psychological Review, 78,* 391–408.

Posner, M. I., Boies, S. J., Eichelman, W. H., & Taylor, R. L. (1969). Retention of visual and name codes of single letters. *Journal of Experimental Psychology: Monographs, 79*(1, Pt. 2).

Posner, M. I., & Mitchell, R. F. (1967). Chronometric analysis of classification. *Psychological Review, 74*(5), 392–409.

Price, C. J., & Devlin, J. T. (2003). The myth of the visual word form area. *Neuroimage, 19,* 473–481.

Price, C. J., Winterburn, D., Giraud, A. L., Moore, C. J., & Noppeney, U. (2003). Cortical localisation of the visual and auditory word form areas: A reconsideration of the evidence. *Brain and Language, 86,* 272–286.

Prinzmetal, W., Treiman, R., & Rho, S.H. (1986). How to see a reading unit. *Journal of Memory and Language, 25,* 461–475.

Puce, A., Allison, T., Asgari, M., Gore, J. C., & McCarthy, G. (1996). Differential sensitivity of human visual cortex to faces, letter strings, and textures: A functional magnetic resonance imaging study. *Journal of Neuroscience, 16*(16), 5205–5215.

Pugh, K. R., Shaywitz, B. A., Shaywitz, S. E., Constable, R. T., Skudlarski, P., Fulbright, R. K., et al. (1996). Cerebral organization of component processes in reading. *Brain, 119*(4), 1221–1238.

Rapp, B. (1992). The nature of sublexical orthographic organization: The bigram trough hypothesis examined. *Journal of Memory and Language,* 31, 33–53.

Rees, G., Russell, C., Frith, C. D., and Driver, J. (1999). Inattentional blindness versus inattentional amnesia for fixated but ignored words. *Science, 286,* 2504–2507.

Reicher, G. M. (1969). Perceptual recognition as a function of the meaningfulness of the stimulus material. *Journal of Experimental Psychology, 81,* 275–280.

Rey, A., Ziegler, J. C., & Jacobs, A. M. (2000). Graphemes are perceptual reading units. Cognition 75, 1–12.

Riesenhuber, M., & Poggio, T. (1999). Hierarchical models of object recognition in cortex. *Nature Neuroscience, 2*(11), 1019–1025.

Rosch, E., Mervis, C. B., Gray, W. D., Johnson, D. M., & Boyes-Braem, P. (1976). Basic objects in natural categories. *Cognitive Psychology, 8,* 382–439.

Rossion, B., Curran, T., & Gauthier, I. (2002). A defense of the subordinate-level expertise account for the n170 component. *Cognition, 85,* 189–196.

Rossion, B., Kung, C.-C., & Tarr, M. J. (2004). Visual expertise with nonface objects leads to competition with the early perceptual processing of faces in the human occipitotemporal cortex. *Proceedings of the National Academy of Sciences USA, 101,* 14521–14526.

Rouder, J. N. (2001). Absolute identification with simple and complex stimuli. *Psychological Science, 12*(4), 318–322.

Rousselet, G. A., Thorpe, S. J., & Fabre-Thorpe, M. (2004). How parallel is visual processing in the ventral pathway? *Trends in Cognitive Sciences, 8*(8), 363–370.

Rumelhart, D. E., & McClelland, J. L. (1982). An interactive activation model of context effects in letter perception: Part 2. The contextual enhancement effect and some tests and extensions of the model. *Psychological Review, 89,* 60–94.

Rynard, D., & Besner, D. (1987). Basic processes in reading: On the development of cross-case letter matching without reference to phonology. *Bulletin of the Psychonomic Society, 25,* 361–368.

Saffran, E. M., & Coslett, H. B. (1998). Implicit vs. letter-by-letter reading in pure alexia: A tale of two systems. *Cognitive Neuropsychology, 15,* 141–166.

Sakai, K., & Miyashita, Y. (1991). Neural organization for the long-term memory of paired associates. *Nature, 354,* 152–155.

Sanocki, T. (1987). Visual knowledge underlying letter perception: Font-specific, schematic tuning. *Journal of Experimental Psychology: Human Perception and Performance, 13*(2), 267–278.

Sanocki, T. (1988). Font regularity constraints on the process of letter recognition. *Journal of Experimental Psychology: Human Perception and Performance, 14*(3), 472–480.

Sanocki, T. (1991a). Effects of early common features on form perception. *Perception and Psychophysics, 50*(5), 490–497.

Sanocki, T. (1991b). Intra- and interpattern relations in letter recognition. *Journal of Experimental Psychology: Human Perception and Performance, 17*(4), 924–941.

Sanocki, T. (1991c). Looking for a structural network: Effects of changing size and style on letter recognition. *Perception, 20*(4), 529–541.

Sanocki, T. (1992). Effects of font- and letter-specific experience on the perceptual processing of letters. *American Journal of Psychology, 105*(3), 435–458.

Sanocki, T. (1993). Time course of object identification: Evidence for a global-to-local contingency. *Journal of Experimental Psychology: Human Perception and Performance, 19*(4), 878–898.

Schwarzlose, R. F., Baker, C. I., & Kanwisher, N. (2005). Separate face and body selectivity on the fusiform gyrus. *Journal of Neuroscience, 25*(47), 11055–11059.

Seidenberg, M. S., & McClelland J. L. (1989). A distributed, developmental model of word recognition and naming. *Psychological Review,* 523–568.

Spoehr, K. T., & Smith, E. E. (1973) The role of syllables in perceptual processing. *Cognitive Psychology,* 21–34.

Tagamets, M. A., Novick, J. M., Chalmers, M. L., & Friedman, R. B., (2000). A parametric approach to orthographic processing in the brain: An fMRI study. *Journal of Cognitive Neuroscience, 12,* 281–297.

Tanaka, J. W., & Curran, T. (2001). A neural basis for expert object recognition. *Psychological Science, 12*(1), 43–47.

Tarkiainen, A., Helenius, P., Hansen, P. C., Cornelissen, P. L., & Salmelin, R. (1999). Dynamics of letter string perception in the human occipitotemporal cortex. *Brain, 122*(Pt. 11), 2119–2132.

Tarr, M. J., & Gauthier, I. (2000). FFA: A flexible fusiform area for subordinate-level visual processing automatized by expertise. *Nature Neuroscience, 3*(8), 764–769.

Townsend, J. T. (1971). Theoretical analysis of an alphabetic confusion matrix. *Perception & Psychophysics*, 40–50.

Treiman, R. (1994) To what extent do orthographic units in print mirror phonological units in speech? *Journal of Psycholinguistic Research, 23*, 91–110.

Treiman, R., & Chafetz, J. (1987) Are there onset- and rime-like units in written words? In *The psychology of reading. Attention and Performance* (M. Coltheart, Ed.), pp. 281–298.

Ullman, S. (1989). Image understanding. Norwood, NJ: Ablex Publishing Co.

Van Der Heijden, A. H. C., Malhas, M. S. M., & Van Der Roovart, B. P. (1984). An empirical interletter confusion matrix for continuous-line capitals. *Perception & Psychophysics, 35*, 85–88.

Vigneau, M., Jobard, G., Mazoyer, B., & Tzourio-Mazoyer, N. (2005). Word and non-word reading: What role for the visual word form area? *NeuroImage, 27*, 694–705.

Warrington, E. K., & Shallice, T. (1980). Word-form dyslexia. *Brain, 103*, 99–112.

Weisstein, N., & Harris, C. S. (1974). Visual detection of line segments: An object-superiority effect. *Science, 186*, 752–755.

Wheeler, D. D. (1970). Processes in word recognition. *Cognitive Psychology, 1*, 59–85.

Whitney, C. & Berndt, R. (1999). A new model of letter string encoding: Simulating right neglect dyslexia. *Progress in Brain Research, 121*, 142–163.

Wong, A. C.-N., & Gauthier, I. (2007). An analysis of letter expertise in a levels-of-categorization framework. *Visual Cognition, 15*(7), 854–879.

Wong, A. C.-N., Gauthier, I., Woroch, B., Debuse, C., & Curran, T. (2005). An early electrophysiological response associated with expertise in letter perception. *Cognitive, Affective, and Behavioral Neuroscience, 5*(3), 306–318.

Wong, A. C.-N., & Hayward, W. G. (2005). Constraints on view combination: Effects of self-occlusion and difference between familiar views. *Journal of Experimental Psychology: Human Perception and Performance, 31*, 110–121.

Wong, A. C.-N., Jobard, G., James, K. H., James, T. W., & Gauthier, I. (2009). Expertise with characters in alphabetic and non-alphabetic writing systems engage the same occipito-temporal area. *Cognitive Neuropsychology, 26*(1), 101–120.

Xu, Y. (2005). Revisiting the role of the fusiform face area in visual expertise. *Cerebral Cortex, 15*(8), 1234–1242.

Yovel, G., & Kanwisher, N. (2004). Face perception: Domain specific, not process specific. *Neuron, 44*, 889–898.

Zhang, L., & Cottrell, G. W. (2004). *Seeing blobs as faces or letters: Modeling effects on discrimination.* Paper presented at the 2004 International Conference on Development and Learning, La Jolla, CA.

Plate 1. Arcimboldo's *The Vegetable Gardener*, circa 1590. Upright, the face formed by this configuration of vegetables is easily perceived as a face, but inverted it looks merely like a bowl of vegetables randomly arranged. Used with permission from Bridgeman Art Library (See Figure 1.1)

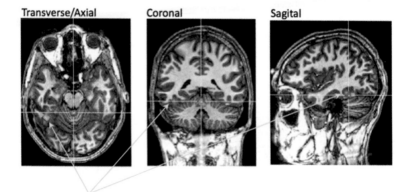

Transverse/Axial   Coronal   Sagittal

Right FFA

Plate 2. The right fusiform face area (FFA, in yellow-red), as defined in an individual subject using a typical functional localizer (contrast between perception of faces vs. objects) (See Figure 1.5)

Plate 3. Do these objects "look like faces"? (See Figure 2.2)

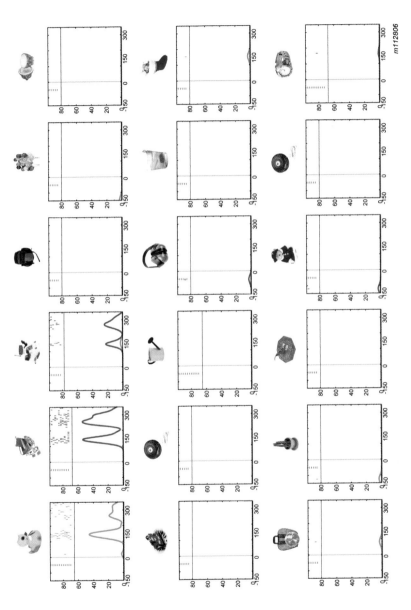

m112806

Plate 4. Simultaneous recording from two nearby cells (electrodes approximately 0.5 mm apart) in monkey inferior temporal cortex reveals high selectivity for a variety of objects during a passive viewing task. The 18 panels each indicate the response of the two neurons to the images shown above. One cell responds almost exclusively to the figure of the rubber duck and the other to the wheelchair and, to a lesser extent, the robot. Each horizontal tick left of the vertical line at zero marks a single trial (necessary, as many trials include no spikes). Data from Anderson and Sheinberg (unpublished) (See Figure 2.5)

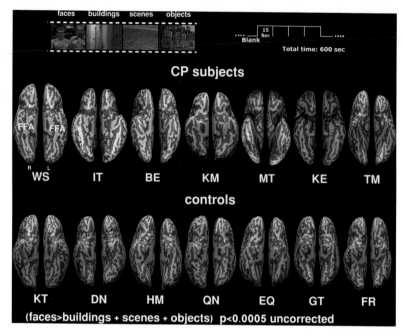

Plate 5. Functional maps of the conventional face and object mapping experiment. (See Figure 6.6)

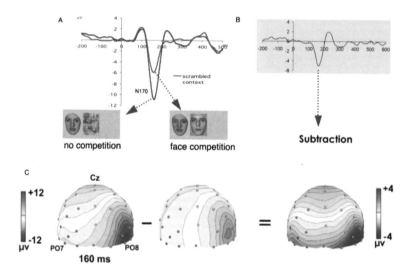

Plate 6. (A) ERP waveforms at right occipitotemporal sites (here PO8 electrode) following the onset of a face stimulus presented in the left visual field, either when subjects fixate another face stimulus (face competition) or a phase-scrambled stimulus of equal size and luminance. (B) Subtraction between the two waveforms, showing that the competition effect starts at about 130 ms following stimulus onset. (C) Topographical maps of the back of the head for the electrical potentials observed at 160 ms in the two conditions and the result of their subtraction. (See Figure 8.1)

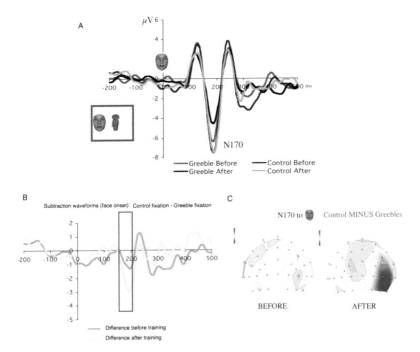

Plate 7. (A) competition effect between Greebles and faces. (B) Subtraction waveforms, showing the competition effect, that is, the reduction of the N170 for faces while fixating Greebles as compared to control objects (yellow waveform is the result of the subtraction between green and black traces displayed above). The red rectangle represents the time window used to display topographical maps of the back of the head on (C). (See Figure 8.2)

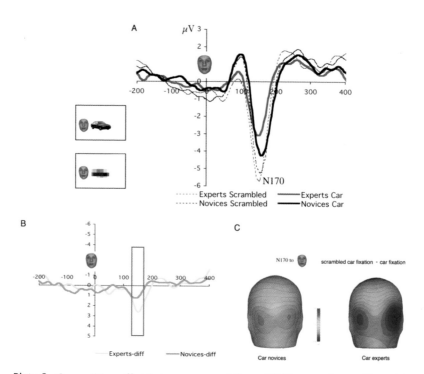

Plate 8. Competition effect between cars and faces. (A) The waveforms (T6 – right occipitotemporal channel) follow the presentation of a lateralized face stimulus while participants fixate either the picture of a car or a scrambled car (stimuli on the left). (B) Subtraction waveforms, showing the competition effect, that is, the reduction of the N170 for faces while fixating cars as compared to scrambled cars for car experts and novices. The red rectangle represents the time window used to display topographical maps of the back of the head on (C). (See Figure 8.3)

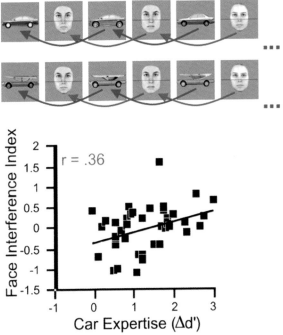

Plate 9. (A) diagram of the two-back task used to measure the interference effect of the cars on holistic face processing. (B) A scatter plot shows the correlation between the behavioral face interference index (i.e., holistic processing of faces in the context of normal cars minus holistic processing of faces in the context of configurally modified cars) and car expertise. (See Figure 8.4)

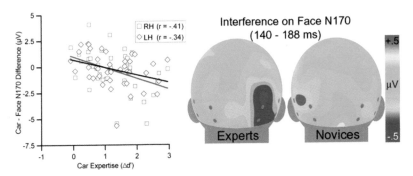

Plate 10. (A) A scatter plot shows the correlation between the electrophysiological face interference index (i.e., N170 amplitude for faces processed in the context of normal cars minus N170 amplitude for faces processed in the context of configurally modified cars) and car expertise. The greater one's car expertise, the greater the reduction in the N170 to faces processed in the normal car context relative to those processed in the configurally modified car context. (B) Electrophysiological map of the interference effect between face and cars illustrating the right hemisphere dominance of this effect. (Figure adapted with permission from Gauthier et al., 2003.) (See Figure 8.5)

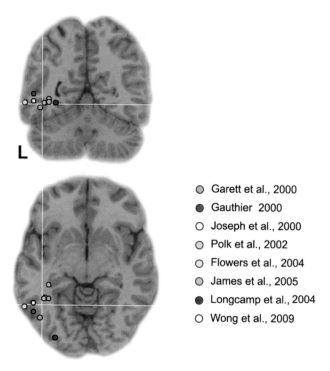

○ Garett et al., 2000
● Gauthier 2000
○ Joseph et al., 2000
○ Polk et al., 2002
○ Flowers et al., 2004
◎ James et al., 2005
● Longcamp et al., 2004
○ Wong et al., 2009

Plate 11. Schematic of approximate peak % BOLD signal change activation for letters recorded across several experiments. For coronal section, Talairach Y = (−50); for transverse section, Talairach Z = (−4). Note that activation peaks are quite variable but are all left lateralized and fall either on the fusiform gyrus or middle temporal gyrus (See Figure 10.1)

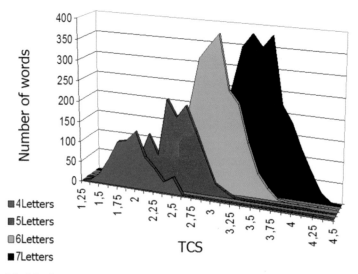

Plate 12. The frequency distribution of total confusability scores for different word lengths (See Figure 12.2)

11

Perceptual and Conceptual Interactions in Object Recognition and Expertise

Thomas W. James and George S. Cree

INTRODUCTION

Visual object recognition is a fundamental cognitive operation performed countless times each day. Yet despite the ease with which we are able to recognize familiar objects in our environment, object recognition is extremely complicated, and the computations necessary to recognize objects have eluded cognitive modelers for decades. This complexity can be observed in the fact that engaging in even the simplest of object recognition tasks recruits widespread regions of the cortex (for review, see Grill-Spector, 2003).

Curiously, even though many of the regions active during object recognition lie outside of traditional visual cortex, object recognition is, to a large extent, thought of as a mainly visual process. Most (if not all) current theories of general object recognition are based almost solely on data from visual experiments (Biederman, 2000; Deco & Rolls, 2004; Grossberg, 1999; Humphreys & Forde, 2001; Tarr & Bulthoff, 1998). Furthermore, since the early 1980s, object recognition has often been considered a bottom-up process that occurs separately from other cognitive operations (Marr, 1982; Pylyshyn, 1999). But object recognition involves much more than dissecting an object into its visual features; we rapidly, and often involuntarily, access nonvisual information about the object as well.

What role does this nonvisual information play in object recognition? One could argue that access to this "semantic" information comes only after the visual processes have finished, and this would be consistent with the theory that object recognition is visually driven and that semantic memory is a cognitive capacity separate from vision. But we will argue that conceiving of object recognition as solely visual misrepresents the flexible and adaptive nature of the mechanisms that support it.

We believe that perceptual and conceptual processes and representations are integrated into a distributed sensorimotor system that underlies both object recognition *and* semantic memory. In the rest of the chapter we will discuss evidence that object recognition is best conceived of within a framework wherein both conceptual influences and multisensory interactions play a central role in object recognition. A majority of the data that we discuss will focus on what has been learned from the study of people who have become experts through training in the lab, or are already recognized experts in the domain of interest. We will first consider the interface of perceptual and conceptual processing, and how the two interact. We will then turn to structure within the visual/semantic pathways and review evidence for the existence of highly interactive, modality-specific processing streams.

EXPERTISE, AND PERCEPTUAL AND CONCEPTUAL PROCESSES FOR OBJECT RECOGNITION

In the past 15 years we have witnessed a shift away from the traditional view of conceptual representation as amodal, verbal, and proposition-like, to the view that thinking is firmly grounded in modality-specific processing channels, and concepts are represented in brain regions contiguous with, and perhaps even overlapping, the sensory pathways through which information is acquired (for example, see Barsalou, 1999). These pathways have been described as a continuum, varying in how much, and what sort of, top-down processing has been applied to the bottom-up input, and the degree of productivity afforded by the resultant representations (Goldstone & Barsalou, 1998). This change in viewpoint has brought about a search for new behavioral paradigms that allow us to explore both the representations and computations that occur throughout these processing channels.

One promising approach is to explore how processing and representation change as one gains perceptual and/or conceptual experience with a set of objects. For us, this idea was inspired by the perceptual expertise approach to studying object recognition in which one studies the processing and representational changes that occur as participants gain experience in dealing with closed-class sets of complex visual objects, such as Greebles (Gauthier & Tarr, 1997, 2002). Examples of this kind of approach also exist in the concepts and categorization literature, and the literature that examines experts in knowledge-rich domains, for instance, chess or medicine.

In the concepts and categorization literature, there have been numerous studies designed to look at how the goals and demands of categorization influence perceptual processing. Researchers have examined, for example, how knowledge influences the interpretation of visual features (Wisniewski & Medin, 1994), and how information about the concepts to be acquired influences the creation of new perceptual features (Shyns, Goldstone, & Thibaut, 1998). Within categorization learning paradigms, using small sets of stimuli, Goldstone and colleagues have been able to address several interesting phenomena, including sensitization of existing perceptual dimensions, sensitization of novel perceptual dimensions, perceptual reorganization, and unitization (for review, see Goldstone, Steyvers, Spencer-Smith, & Kersten, 2000).

In the study of experts in knowledge-rich domains there have been many studies looking at how perceptual abilities change as people gain experience within their domain of expertise. There is considerable evidence, for example, that experts parse the perceptual features of the world differently than do novices, this having been demonstrated in the domains of chess (De

Groot, 1966), radiology (Myles-Worsley, Johnston, & Simons, 1988), sexing day old chicks (Biederman & Shiffrar, 1987), and beer tasting (Peron & Allen, 1988), to name a few prominent examples. Although insightful, the approaches taken in this literature are limited for our purposes because they rarely involve the use of object classes that allow for systematic manipulation of the perceptual components of the objects of expertise, and the knowledge that is associated with those objects.

In the next section we will discuss evidence from two different paradigms used in our labs that reveal how conceptual knowledge can influence perceptual processing, even in tasks that have traditionally been thought to be primarily perceptual in nature.

Behavioral Studies with Experts

One approach to understanding the cognitive and neural mechanisms underlying object recognition is to explore how behavioral and neural activation measures change as participants gain experience identifying exemplars from a set of highly visually similar objects (e.g., Greebles; Gauthier & Tarr, 1997; see also Chapter 8 of this volume). This work has shown that regions of the fusiform gyrus once thought to be specialized for processing faces (e.g., fusiform face area; FFA) can be engaged by objects for which the goals of learning, and types of visual processing, are similar to faces. That is, the FFA is recruited for identification of highly visually similar object classes for which one has expertise at the individual level. The evidence suggests that the critical process is configural or holistic; it is a process that allows the learner to discriminate among exemplars by learning more than just the specific parts. Of perhaps greatest importance, they learn the arrangements of those parts in relation to one another (Gauthier & Tarr, 2002). Support for this hypothesis comes from studies using inversion or midpoint misalignment with face, dog, bird, car, fingerprint, and Greeble experts (Busey & Vanderkolk, 2005; Diamond & Carey, 1986; Gauthier, Skudlarski, Gore, & Anderson, 2000).

One factor that has not been studied in relation to the recruitment of holistic processing for expert object recognition is the role of conceptual or semantic knowledge. In laboratory visual-expertise training tasks, conceptual information is not made available—although some learners do create their own semantic associations during training (personal communication, Isabel Gauthier). It is likely that extant experts associate a great deal of nonperceptual semantic information with their perceptual representations of a stimulus class, yet the amount of semantic information that they acquire, its nature, and the method by which it is assimilated is rarely measured. The relationships built between nonperceptual and perceptual features of objects may act to strengthen learning of perceptual features, either in a holistic or a feature-based manner. For example, if a learner understands why the parts, or the configuration of parts, vary as they do, and why specific combinations of parts are likely to occur together, then this may make the learning problem substantially easier. Knowledge of genetics, and why specific combinations of morphological traits are likely to occur together, is an example of such knowledge.

Consider, for example, the rock hyrax, a small animal that to the untrained eye appears visually similar to the groundhog. An appropriately trained biologist is not fooled by the surface visual similarity and can point out that the clubbed foot of the rock hyrax serves as an obvious visual cue to the fact that it is more closely genetically related to the elephant than to the groundhog. Examples of such knowledge include an understanding of the relation between genetics and the emergence of combinations of morphological traits within and across species. Birds provide a domain in which to test whether or not semantic knowledge acquired during learning affects the recruitment of holistic processing because there are both enthusiasts, known as birders, and scholars, known as ornithologists. Although both share a passion for birds, their learning goals are different and may play an important role in the knowledge represented, and how that information is processed. Birders often identify birds in the field, in suboptimal conditions, and under time pressure. This may lead them to rely heavily on information about shape and distinctive visual features. Additionally, although they possess knowledge about habitats, flying patterns, and feeding habits, it is reasonable to suppose that the knowledge is of a different sort than that possessed by ornithologists. Specifically, birders may lack knowledge that links morphological traits to conceptual knowledge. Ornithologists, on the other hand, are more likely to have rich, detailed knowledge about birds due to extensive book-based research and hands-on experience. Most importantly, they have been specially trained to understand the rich variation in morphological traits across species, and how and why those traits are related to other properties, many of which may not be visually present on the exterior of the bird. Thus, morphological traits may serve as visual anchors around which ornithologists organize their knowledge about birds. If true, then ornithologists may be capable of recognizing birds in an analytic, parts-based fashion, rather than, or perhaps in addition to, holistically.

Ozubko, Cree, and Bub (2005) reported two experiments designed to test these ideas. Experiment 1 tested depth of conceptual knowledge about birds by probing knowledge of bird taxonomies. It was reasoned that ornithologists should perform the best, given their extensive book-based training with birds, followed by birders, and finally novices. Experiment 2 tested memory for pictures of inverted versus upright birds. It is well documented that recognition of many stimulus classes thought to be processed holistically, such as faces, is impaired if the images are inverted (Yin, 1969). Therefore, individuals recognizing birds in a holistic manner should perform worse with inverted birds than upright birds. It was predicted that birders would be most likely to process birds holistically, and so should have the worst memory for inverted birds. Ornithologists, in comparison, were predicted to perform equally well for inverted and upright birds, due to their reliance on parts-based processing.

Twenty-three novices, 16 birders, and five ornithologists participated in the study. The novices self-reported having no specialized knowledge or interest in birds, the birders all had at least 10 years of birding experience (average 26 years of experience with birds), and the ornithologists were all practicing professionals from either the Royal Ontario Museum or the University of Guelph (average 31 years of experience with birds).

Eighty images of birds local to the Toronto area were selected from the Sibley Guide to Birds (Sibley, 2000). For Experiment 1, the Patuxent Bird Identification Infocenter (Gough, Sauer, & Iliff, 1998) was used to classify the birds into biologically related families. Twenty-four triads were constructed such that two of the birds looked similar to one another whereas the third looked different. For consistent triads, the two visually similar birds were also biologically related, whereas the dissimilar bird was unrelated. For inconsistent triads, the two birds that looked similar were not biologically related, and the visually dissimilar bird was related to one of the other two. For Experiment 2, 60 of the bird images were used, 48 of which were of unique bird species and 12 of which were repetitions of species already selected. For the 12 repeated species, juvenile, breeding plumage, and/or female pictures of the species were selected, whereas the other birds were all adult, nonbreeding plumage, male birds.

In Experiment 1 participants were told that three birds would be presented, one near the top of the screen, one near the left, and one near the right. The bird on the top was called the host bird. Participants were told to press the "Z" key if they believed that the bird on the left was more similar to the host than the other bird, and to press the "/" key if they believed that the bird on the right was most similar. The few participants that asked what criteria to use when deciding on similarity (a subset of the ornithologists) were told by the experimenter to "use whatever criterion you think is best."

In Experiment 2 participants were told that images of birds would be presented on the screen, one at a time. They were informed that there would be a memory test and were instructed to remember the individual bird images, and not just species names, as they were warned that different images of the same bird species would appear at test. This technique was adapted from Diamond and Carey (1986), who used it to prevent experts from using mnemonic techniques. Thirty-six images of different birds were shown to participants during the study phase. No bird species was repeated. Images were presented one at time, and presented for 3 s with a 0.5 s interstimulus interval where the screen was blank. The first six and last six images were used as buffers to reduce primacy and recency effects and were not used at test. The images were presented in a randomized order, half inverted, the other half upright. After the study phase, bird images were shown on the screen, two at a time, and participants were instructed to press the "Z" key if they believed they had seen the bird on the left at study, and the "/" key if they believed they had seen the bird on the right. Birds were presented in the same orientation at study and test and were paired with one other bird in the same orientation. In every pair, one of the birds had been presented at study and one had not. Of the birds not present at study, 12 were the same species as birds seen at study, and were highly visually similar, but were not the same image.

The performance of novices, birders, and ornithologists in Experiment 1 can be seen in Figure 11.1. The degree to which participants correctly classified birds in inconsistent triads can be viewed as a measure of the degree to which participants were relying on conceptual knowledge of birds, and not on visual similarities. Conservative, nonparametric tests (i.e., the Mann-Whitney and Wilcoxon Signed Ranks tests) were used to analyze the data because inspection revealed that both the assumptions of homogeneity of variance and normality were violated. Mann-Whitney tests were used to look for differences between the groups. Birders performed significantly better than novices on inconsistent triads, $U = 11.0$, $p < .001$, but no difference was found for consistent triads, $U = 176.0$, $p = .832$. Ornithologists performed significantly better than novices on inconsistent triads, $U = 0$, $p < .001$, but no difference was found for consistent triads, $U = 55.0$, $p = .908$. Finally, ornithologists and birders were found to behave similarly on both inconsistent triads, $U = 19.5$, $p = .091$, and consistent triads, $U = 40.0$, $p = 1.00$. These results suggest that, in general, both birders and ornithologists possess more knowledge of bird taxonomy than novices, and, contrary to our predictions, that birders and ornithologists possess similar levels of conceptual knowledge about birds. This suggests that both birders and ornithologists are quite knowledgeable when it comes to taxonomic conceptual knowledge regarding birds.

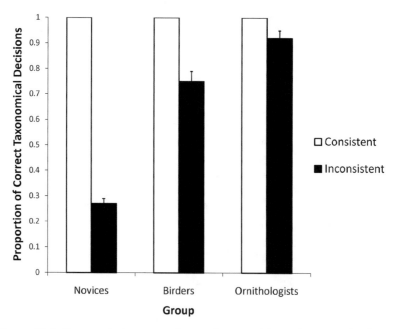

Figure 11.1 Taxonomical accuracy for consistent and inconsistent triads of birds from Experiment 1 (behavioral). Consistent triads have no error bars because the standard error for the Novice, Birders, and Ornithologists were 0.003, 0, and 0, respectively.

The second experiment examined the memory of participants for inverted versus upright birds. The recognition accuracy of the three groups can be seen in Figure 11.2. A Mann-Whitney test was conducted to examine possible differences between novices and birders. A significant difference was found between the two groups for both inverted birds, $U = 80.50$, $p = .002$, and for upright birds, $U = 9.0$, $p < .001$. Therefore, as expected, birders were found to have better recognition accuracy for birds than novices, regardless of whether the birds were inverted or upright. A second Mann-Whitney test examined the differences between novices and ornithologists for both inverted birds, $U = 5.50$, $p < .001$, and for upright birds, $U = 1.5$, $p < .001$. Ornithologists, therefore, also demonstrated better recognition accuracy for inverted and upright birds than novices. In general, these two results confirm that birders and ornithologists were "expert" groups insomuch as both birders and ornithologists had an easier time remembering birds than novices.

A more theoretically interesting difference was also found between birders and ornithologists in the second experiment. A significant difference was found for inverted birds, $U = 15.5$, $p = .04$, but not for upright birds, $U = 39.0$, $p = .968$. This suggests that although birders and ornithologists had similar recognition accuracy for upright birds, birders had poorer recognition accuracy for inverted birds than did ornithologists. Even more interestingly, whereas birders may have performed significantly worse when birds were inverted, ornithologists may have been unaffected. To test this hypothesis, a

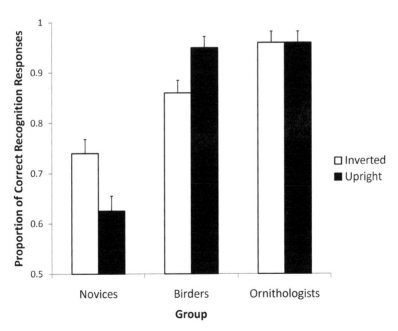

Figure 11.2 Recognition accuracy for inverted and upright birds from Experiment 2 (behavioral).

Wilcoxon Signed Ranks test was used to examine the difference between ornithologists' recognition accuracy for inverted versus upright birds. No significant difference was found in recognition accuracy for ornithologists for these two stimulus types, $Z = 0$, $p = 1.00$. However, a second test was used to examine the difference between birders' recognition accuracy for inverted versus upright birds, and a significant difference was found, $Z = -2.338$, $p = .019$. These results suggest that ornithologists were unaffected by the orientation of the birds, performing similarly regardless of whether the bird was inverted or upright, but birders were affected by the orientation of the birds, performing worse when birds were inverted. Thus, birders showed a typical "inversion" effect, but ornithologists did not. The results held even when one considered only the trials on which a very highly visually similar distractor of the same species was present, suggesting that a labeling strategy was not in play.

Configural processing is considered a hallmark of visual expertise. However, only birders in this study demonstrated a reliable inversion effect, which is a marker of configural processing. Ornithologists, who are also experts with birds, did not demonstrate evidence of configural processing, by way of an inversion effect. These data speak against the idea that visual perceptual expertise necessarily leads to a reliance on just configural processing. But, if configural processing does not necessarily arise from visual expertise, in what circumstances does it arise, and in what cases do experts engage other visual object recognition mechanisms?

One possibility is that configural processing is engaged for objects for which people have very little conceptual knowledge. Greeble training is one example. However, the results of Experiment 1 suggest that things may not be this simple, as birders and ornithologists may have similar levels of conceptual knowledge for local birds. It would therefore be difficult to argue that configural processing arises due to a lack of semantic knowledge, because, to the extent that it was tested, both birders and ornithologists appear to have similar background knowledge about birds.

An alternate idea, and one that has been developed elsewhere by other authors (Bukach, Gauthier, & Tarr, 2006; James, James, Jobard, Wong, & Gauthier, 2005), is that different types of experts have different goals that recruit different perceptual processes. For example, although birders and ornithologists may have similar semantic knowledge about birds, they may have different perceptual goals. Birders may be primarily interested in being able to quickly identify birds in the field. Once a birder spots a bird in the field, they have limited time to identify it before it leaves. Thus, birders may have more utilitarian, quick identification goals when it comes to birds. They may therefore adopt a more holistic method of processing birds out of necessity. However, ornithologists, who may spend more time examining birds in textbooks or in laboratories, may not be interested in being able to quickly identify birds, but instead be interested in being able to draw fine-grained distinctions between similar-looking birds who differ on only a few attributes. Goals such as these could bias ornithologists to process birds in a more part-based, analytic manner than birders. Overall, configural processing may arise in situations where individuals seek to simply identify members of a stimulus class, whereas analytic processing may be more likely to arise in situations where experts seek to make classifications of members of a class based on access to conceptual knowledge.

There are a number of important caveats that must accompany these data. First, the sample of ornithologists is very small, and it is important that these results be confirmed in a larger sample before firm conclusions can be drawn. Second, although Experiment 1 was designed to be a difficult task, it is possible that it was actually too easy for these participants. Further analyses of the data revealed that some birders demonstrated taxonomic knowledge as good as, if not better than, some ornithologists, whereas others demonstrated near-novice levels. A ceiling effect may also have been responsible for the fact that ornithologists did not significantly outperform birders. That is, ornithologists may possess more taxonomical knowledge than birders, but because the task was easy enough for some birders to achieve perfect scores, ornithologists were unable to perform better than birders. It will be important to probe for other kinds of conceptual knowledge about birds in the three groups before conclusions can be drawn about whether birders and ornithologists have comparable conceptual knowledge about birds (which seems unlikely). Third, the Sibley guide is a very popular birding book, and so it is possible that the participants were familiar with these pictures. With all that being said, it is still interesting that the inversion effect was not found in the ornithologists, and it will be interesting to see if this finding holds in future work.

fMRI Studies of Conceptual Learning

The above experiments showed that both birders and ornithologists use nonvisual information learned about birds to make classification decisions. Although there has been considerable work documenting the brain networks involved in the perceptual aspects of expert categorization, little is known about the brain networks that support the use of conceptual knowledge for decision making. To investigate this question, some researchers have compared the brain activation produced by common as opposed to novel objects, with the assumption that brain regions activated more by common objects are being recruited to process the semantic information associated with those objects. Two studies that used this method (Martin, 1999; Vuilleumier, Henson, Driver, & Dolan, 2002) revealed a common focus of activation in the inferior frontal cortex, suggesting that this region is involved in processing semantic information as opposed to visual information. One concern with this method, however, is that novel objects may produce different patterns of activation simply because they are less familiar visually. This problem was addressed in one study (Leveroni et al., 2000) in which participants were familiarized with novel faces before testing. Activation with these newly learned faces was compared to activation with famous faces. Similar to the other two studies, Leveroni, et al. (2000) found greater activation in the inferior frontal cortex for famous faces, compared with familiar nonfamous faces. These findings suggest that the inferior frontal cortex provides a significant contribution to the processing of nonvisual information associated with objects.

Another method for investigating the neural substrates of visual and nonvisual contributions to object recognition is to compare the effects of perceptual and conceptual priming. In neuroimaging, priming effects usually manifest as decreased activation with a repeated stimulus (repetition priming), or to a similar stimulus (for review, see Schacter & Buckner, 1998; Wiggs & Martin, 1998). Perceptual priming effects arise when the manipulation of the stimulus between study and test is restricted to the perceptual attributes of the stimulus, for instance, a chair seen from two different viewpoints. Conceptual priming takes place between stimuli that are related conceptually. For instance, chairs, couches, and stools are perceptually distinct but are conceptually related because they are all used for sitting. Two studies that compared conceptual and perceptual priming (Koutstaal et al., 2001; Vuilleumier et al., 2002) found a common site of activation in the inferior frontal cortex that was affected by conceptual priming, but not perceptual priming. One concern with this method, however, is that conceptually similar items are often perceptually similar (e.g., a stool is more similar to a chair than to a lamp) and consequently, a conceptual priming effect may actually reflect a combination of conceptual and perceptual factors, or perhaps perceptual factors alone.

Despite the methodological concerns with the two sets of studies reviewed above, the findings converge to suggest that an important neural-processing site for nonvisual information associated with objects exists in the inferior frontal cortex. Using a third methodology for dissociating visual and nonvisual contributions to object recognition, we recently provided further evidence that the inferior frontal cortex is important for the processing of nonvisual information (James & Gauthier, 2004). In this experiment, subjects associated verbal information with sets of objects (Figure 11.3). In the semantic condition (SEM), the information was a nickname, such as Carl, and three nonvisual semantic features, such as strong, soft, and friendly. In the name condition (NAM), the information was a first, middle, and last name, such as Michael Francis Sutherland. Thus, each object in these two conditions could be individuated by the verbal information with which it was associated. In the SEM condition, however, this information not only individuated the objects, but it also carried strong semantic associations. Two significant benefits of our conceptual learning paradigm over existing methods of studying semantic associations are: (1) The conditions are equated on familiarity, and (2) the semantic features and the visual features of the objects are related arbitrarily, and therefore are not confounded.

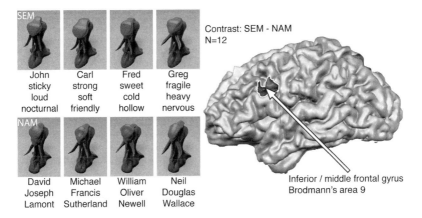

				Contrast: SEM - NAM
John	Carl	Fred	Greg	N=12
sticky	strong	sweet	fragile	
loud	soft	cold	heavy	
nocturnal	friendly	hollow	nervous	
David	Michael	William	Neil	Inferior / middle frontal gyrus
Joseph	Francis	Oliver	Douglas	Brodmann's area 9
Lamont	Sutherland	Newell	Wallace	

Figure 11.3 Stimuli and results for the Semantic (SEM) and Name (NAM) conditions from Experiment 1 (fMRI).

During neuroimaging, subjects performed a same/different perceptual match task on pairs of objects from within the same condition shown at a learned orientation. Because of the ease of performing the perceptual match task, it was highly improbable that subjects explicitly attempted to recall the verbal information that was associated with the objects to help individuate them. It is more likely that they relied only on the visual information. Despite not explicitly using the verbal information, a comparison of the SEM and NAM conditions showed significantly greater activation of the inferior frontal cortex for the SEM condition (Figure 11.3).

This finding converges with the studies described above to suggest that the inferior frontal cortex plays a role in processing semantic associations with object stimuli. Semantic associations are recruited during object recognition, even when the information is not necessary to perform the task. It is worthwhile mentioning that the novel semantic associations in this study were developed over a period of a few days, yet our findings converge with evidence from objects for which semantic associations were developed over a lifetime of experience. Therefore, the role that the inferior frontal cortex plays in processing semantic associations seems to be flexible with respect to the learning of new information.

Conclusions

The evidence described here suggests that experts can make use of both perceptual and conceptual information to classify objects. Conceptual information appears to be recruited even for tasks that are traditionally thought to be primarily perceptual. The findings also strengthen the claim that the learning goal at least partially determines the type of perceptual processes that are recruited during learning. That is, experts will use the perceptual features of objects in ways that maximize their chances of success, given a particular goal.

The combination of different kinds of knowledge, and goals, may lead to the engagement of different perceptual processes in experts. For instance, given a wealth of conceptual information with which to aid identification, preliminary evidence suggests that birders and ornithologists may recruit different perceptual processes in pursuit of their task goals. Finally, our findings converge with other methodologies, showing that an area of the inferior frontal cortex is automatically recruited during object recognition. Although activation in this area has been described by others as related to the retrieval of semantic information, we prefer to think of activation in this region as recruitment of an executive process that is responsible for engaging and binding task- and stimulus-class-specific perceptual processes. This process is recruited more strongly when multiple sources of information must be engaged, such as with object classes for which there is significant semantic knowledge.

KNOWLEDGE TYPES

A growing body of evidence supports the claim that some important components of conceptual knowledge, specifically the knowledge associated with the perceptual and functional attributes of object concepts, is represented as distributed patterns of activity across multiple modality-specific processing pathways in the brain. This idea is not new (Lissauer, 1890), but the data required to support it have become much more readily available with the advent of modern neuroimaging techniques. The basic claim is that cognition is embodied, grounded in both perception and action, and that conceptual knowledge is stored in brain regions that overlap with those involved in acquiring and using that knowledge (Barsalou, 1999; Damasio, 1989; Warrington & Shallice, 1984). These brain regions are specialized for processing specific types of information (e.g., form, color, taste, function, etc.), and thus conceptual knowledge for a concept is distributed across these regions to the extent that each knowledge type is relevant to the representation of that concept (e.g., taste is salient for foods, but not vehicles). Current research is focused on determining which modality-specific pathways are important in conceptual representation, how they differ from perceptual representations, and where they are in the brain.

Neuroimaging studies have provided a wealth of evidence supporting the idea that perceptual and conceptual knowledge are stored in distinct, over-lapping brain regions, and that different types of knowledge are stored in different modality-specific processing pathways (for review, see Martin, 2007). In one of the first such studies (Martin, Haxby, Lalonde, Wiggs, & Ungerleider, 1995), participants were presented with either black and white pictures of common objects, or the written names of those objects, and were asked to generate words for action or color associates. Generating actions, relative to colors, led to heightened activity in several regions that were common for both pictures and words, including left middle temporal gyrus (pMTG) just anterior to the primary visual motion processing area. Color word generation, relative to action words, activated the fusiform gyrus anterior to regions associated with color and object perception. More recent work has extended these findings showing that as the task becomes less perceptual and more conceptual (e.g., verifying properties of concepts presented in written form), activation can be observed extending from early occipital areas into temporal areas thought to be involved in processing conceptual knowledge (Beauchamp, Haxby, Jennings, & DeYoe, 1999; Simmons, Ramjee, McRae, Martin, & Barsalou, 2006). This overlap has been observed for several types of knowledge, including visual, auditory, tactile, and gustatory information (Goldberg, Perfetti, & Schneider, 2006).

Analysis of Feature Norms

A useful source of information about the modalities important in object concept representations, and how salient each knowledge type is for different categories of concepts, is analysis of the verbal features people use to describe concrete nouns. If, for example, when participants were asked to list the features of specific objects, they used a large number of color features for fruits and vegetables relative to other object categories, then this could be interpreted as evidence that color information is especially salient and important in the representation of fruits and vegetables. Thus, the strategy in this kind of research is to develop a taxonomy of knowledge types, to classify the features provided by participants into those knowledge types, and to develop a measure that reflects the importance of each knowledge type in each object category. Some taxonomies can be purely statistical descriptions of the data, whereas other taxonomies may be created within specific theoretical constraints. Cree and McRae (2003) classified a large set of verbal feature production norms for 541 concepts into two different knowledge type taxonomies. The first taxonomy came from an independent source (Wu & Barsalou, personal communication) and was a cognitively inspired, statistical analysis of how objects are described and used in language. The second taxonomy was constrained by neuropsychological and neuroimaging evidence regarding possible brain-based modality-specific sensorimotor processing pathways, and included nine knowledge types: visual form and surface properties, visual color, visual motion, sound, smell, taste, touch, function, and encyclopedic knowledge. Cree and McRae used hierarchical cluster analyses to examine the relative salience of the different knowledge types in concepts from each of 34 different categories. Remarkably similar results were found using the two knowledge type taxonomies. Of most interest, they found that the groupings of categories observed in the cluster analyses reflected the patterns of impairment observed across patients with category-specific semantic deficits. The most striking result was that the categories clustered roughly into three major domains: animals, fruits and vegetables, and nonliving things. These are also the three major clusters of categories likely to be impaired/spared in patients (Capitani, Laiacona, Mahon, & Caramazza, 2003). Furthermore, in the cluster analysis, the musical instruments category clustered with living things, and foods clustered with nonliving things. These two patterns were again similar to what is often observed in the patient literature (for summary, see Cree & McRae, 2003). These findings validated the brain-based knowledge type taxonomy that had been employed, and they provided support for the idea that conceptual knowledge may be distributed across these knowledge types in the brain such that damage to specific clusters of knowledge type pathways could lead to the patterns of impairment observed in patients. Thus, feature norms should provide a valuable tool for designing experiments that can probe for the existence of modality-specific sensorimotor knowledge type pathways in the brain using verbal features.

fMRI Studies of Feature Learning

In an earlier section, we described a conceptual learning paradigm in which words describing semantic features were associated with novel objects during learning. This conceptual learning paradigm provides a unique methodology for exploring the brain regions involved in representing modality-specific sensorimotor conceptual knowledge. In addition to the benefits of the conceptual learning paradigm described above—(1) the conditions are equated on familiarity, and (2) the semantic features and the visual features of the objects are related arbitrarily and therefore not confounded—there is another benefit of using conceptual learning to study knowledge types. As described in the preceding section, most categories of objects are represented across several knowledge types. This makes studying knowledge types with common objects difficult because all categories of objects are described by several types of knowledge. The conceptual learning paradigm removes this constraint because the types of knowledge that are associated with a set of objects are arbitrary. Thus, a set of objects can be trained with information from one, and only one, knowledge type, or can purposefully be trained with combinations of knowledge types. In the following paragraphs, we describe two experiments in which we attempted to isolate the neural substrates involved in modality-specific semantic processing using the conceptual learning paradigm.

In our first experiment (James & Gauthier, 2003), subjects associated verbal information from two separate knowledge types with two sets of objects. One set of objects was trained with auditory or "sound" features (SND) and the other set of objects was trained with visual motion or "action" features (ACT; Figure 11.4). According to the neural systems knowledge type taxonomy described above, cortical regions involved in the perceptual processing of sounds should be involved in processing semantic sound features. Likewise, cortical regions involved in the perceptual processing of biological motion should be involved in processing semantic action features.

During neuroimaging, subjects performed "localizer" tasks aimed at locating brain regions involved in processing environmental sounds and brain regions involved in processing biological motion. For the sound localizer, environmental sounds were compared with the same sounds phase scrambled in Fourier space. An area of the superior temporal gyrus (STG) showed greater activation for intact than scrambled sounds (Figure 11.4). For

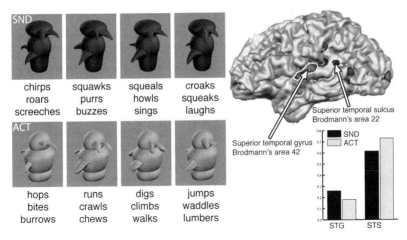

Figure 11.4 Stimuli and results for the Auditory (AUD) and Action (ACT) conditions from Experiment 2 (fMRI). Height of bars indicate percent signal change in superior temporal gyrus (STG; primary & secondary auditory cortex) and superior temporal sulcus (STS).

the biological motion localizer, point-light displays of people performing various movements were compared with scrambled point-light displays. An area of the posterior superior temporal sulcus (STSp) showed greater activation for intact than scrambled biological motion displays.

The subjects also performed a same/different perceptual matching task on pairs of objects from the same learning set. Again, even though the subjects did not explicitly use the verbal information to individuate the objects and aid their performance on the perceptual matching task, a comparison of the different learning conditions produced significant differences in brain activation. In the STG, the SND condition produced significantly greater activation than the ACT condition; in the STSp, the ACT condition produced significantly greater activation than the SND condition (Figure 11.4).

In our second experiment, we attempted to broaden the scope of the neural systems knowledge type taxonomy to categories other than sensorimotor. Much of our conceptual knowledge of the world, and especially of other human beings, is affective or social in nature. We are able to readily perceive affective nuances in facial and vocal expression and in body posture. Our social interactions with individuals, or groups of other humans, are influenced by our previous experiences with those individuals or groups. To investigate the possible neural substrates underlying these social semantic feature types, we had subjects associate social personality traits with one set of objects, and inanimate properties with another set of objects (Figure 11.5). Our intention was to make the first set of objects seem like living creatures to the subjects, complete with unique personalities, and social predispositions. The second set of objects would seem like nonliving statues (or perhaps bookends or doorstops), but again, with characteristics that made each one unique.

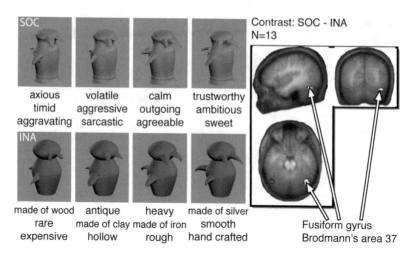

Figure 11.5 Stimuli and results for the Social (SOC) and Inanimate (INA) conditions from Experiment 3 (fMRI). Clockwise from the top-left are sagittal, coronal, and axial slices of an average structural MRI.

Our hypothesis was based on the work of Shultz and colleagues (Schultz et al., 2003). By comparing a social attribution task with a control task, they were able to show the brain networks involved in social information processing. Although many of these brain regions overlap with other work on social cognition (Adolphs, 2001), the key contribution of their study was the finding that the fusiform gyrus is involved in social attribution. The fusiform gyrus is best known for its specialized role in the recognition of faces (Kanwisher, McDermott, & Chun, 1997), and other objects of expertise (Gauthier, Skudlarski, Gore, & Anderson, 2000), but it is worthwhile considering its role in social cognition, and how the processes recruited for social cognition may overlap with the processes recruited for perceptual and conceptual expertise. If, as we argue, objects are not just processed using visual information, but also conceptual knowledge associated with the object, then perhaps the fusiform gyrus does not represent a purely perceptual stage in visual processing, but instead represents a conceptual stage of object processing.

Based on this premise, we were not surprised when we compared objects trained with social traits with objects trained with inanimate characteristics and found that the fusiform gyrus evoked stronger activation with social objects (Figure 11.5). Although there is considerable evidence that parts of the fusiform gyrus are heavily recruited for perceptual processing, our findings converge with others to suggest that the fusiform gyrus may be involved in more than just perceptual processing. Specifically, areas of the fusiform gyrus may be specialized for processing the social and affective importance of objects.

Our results also suggest that the view of cognition embodied only in sensorimotor processes is likely too limited. This bias probably comes from the heavy focus on object concepts in most behavioral, neuroimaging, and feature norming studies of semantic memory. By including the neural systems involved in affective and social cognitive processes, perhaps we edge closer to explaining conceptual processing in full.

Conclusions

The evidence reported here converges on the idea that knowledge can be categorized into different types and that these types are represented and/or processed in different neural structures. Thus, knowledge types are a useful construct for understanding the organization of semantic memory. Furthermore, at this stage of our understanding, using knowledge types based on neural-processing systems may be more predictive, in terms of elucidating mind/brain functioning, than knowledge types based on more abstract cognitive categories.

SUMMARY

In this chapter we have presented one view, supported by convergent empirical findings of behavioral and neuroimaging experiments, of the relationships between perceptual and conceptual cognitive and neural processes. The results of these experiments have prompted us to make two controversial claims, for which there is growing support. First, early visual perceptual processes are coupled with other higher-level processes involved in the representation of object concepts. That is, vision is not encapsulated from other cognitive processes. Second, the neural processes involved in conceptual processing are organized according to a sensorimotor framework. That is, the sensorimotor neural machinery involved in perceptual processing is also involved in conceptual processing. Although the number of studies supporting these arguments is growing, a complete understanding of the complex interplay of conceptual and perceptual processing, both on the cognitive and the neural level, will require much more investigation.

ACKNOWLEDGMENTS

This research was supported by grants from the NSF, NIH, JSMF, NSERC, and CIHR. Daniel Bub deserves special credit for suggesting the birder/ornithologist comparison, and Jason Ozubko for collecting the associated data as part of an honors thesis project at UTSC. The fMRI studies were developed under the mentorship of Isabel Gauthier. Bob Shultz and Cindy Bukach were instrumental in the development and analysis of the social cognition fMRI study. Lu Bukach, Danielle Brown, and Danielle Nikolaiczyk helped with fMRI data collection. We are appreciative of the helpful comments and advice given by Karin Harman James, and other members of the Perceptual Expertise Network.

REFERENCES

Adolphs, R. (2001). The neurobiology of social cognition. *Current Opinion in Neurobiology, 11*, 231–239.

Barsalou, L. W. (1999). Perceptual symbol systems. *Behavioral and Brain Sciences, 22*, 577–660.

Beauchamp, M. S., Haxby, J. V., Jennings, J. E., & DeYoe, E. A. (1999). An fMRI version of the Farnsworth-Munsell 100-Hue test reveals multiple color-sensitive areas in human ventral occipitotemporal cortex. *Cerebral Cortex, 9*, 257–263.

Biederman, I. (2000). Recognizing depth-rotated objects: a review of recent research and theory. *Spatial Vision, 13*(2–3), 241–253.

Biederman, I., & Shiffrar, M. M. (1987). Sexing day-old chicks: A case study and expert systems analysis of a difficult perceptual-learning task. *Journal of Experimental Psychology: Learning, Memory, & Cognition, 13*, 640–645.

Bukach, C. M., Gauthier, I., & Tarr, M. J. (2006). Beyond faces and modularity: the power of an expertise framework. *Trends in Cognitive Sciences, 10*(4), 159–166.

Busey, T. A., & Vanderkolk, J. R. (2005). Behavioral and electrophysiological evidence for configural processing in fingerprint experts. *Vision Research, 45*(4), 431–448.

Capitani, E., Laiacona, M., Mahon, B., & Caramazza, A. (2003). What are the effects of semantic category-specific deficits? A critical review of the clinical evidence. *Cognitive Neuropsychology, 20*, 213–261.

Cree, G. S., & McRae, K. (2003). Analyzing the factors underlying the structure and computation of the meaning of chipmunk, cherry, chisel, cheese, and cello (and many other such concrete nouns). *Journal of Experimental Psychology: General, 132*(2), 163–201.

Damasio, A. R. (1989). Time-locked multiregional retroactivation: A systems-level proposal for the neural substrates of recall and recognition. *Cognition, 33*(1–2), 25–62.

Deco, G., & Rolls, E. T. (2004). A neurodynamical cortical model of visual attention and invariant object recognition. *Vision Research, 44*(6), 621–642.

De Groot, A. (1966). Perception and memory versus thought: Some old ideas and recent findings. In B. Kleinmuntz (Ed.), *Problem Solving: Research, method, and theory*. New York: Wiley.

Diamond, R., & Carey, S. (1986). Why faces are and are not special: An effect of expertise. *Journal of Experimental Psychology: General, 115*, 107–117.

Gauthier, I., Skudlarski, P., Gore, J. C., & Anderson, A. W. (2000). Expertise for cars and birds recruits brain areas involved in face recognition. *Nature Neuroscience, 3*(2), 191–197.

Gauthier, I., & Tarr, M. J. (1997). Becoming a "Greeble" expert: exploring mechanisms for face recognition. *Vision Research, 37*(12), 1673–1682.

Gauthier, I., & Tarr, M. J. (2002). Unraveling mechanisms for expert object recognition: bridging brain activity and behavior. *Journal of Experimental Psychology: Human Perception and Performance, 28*(2), 431–446.

Goldberg, R. F., Perfetti, C. A., & Schneider, W. (2006). Perceptual knowledge retrieval activates sensory brain regions. *Journal of Neuroscience, 26*, 4917–4921.

Goldstone, R. L., & Barsalou, L. W. (1998). Reuniting perception and conception. *Cognition, 65*, 231–262.

Goldstone, R. L., Steyvers, M., Spencer-Smith, J., & Kersten, A. (2000). Interactions between perceptual and conceptual learning. In E. Diettrich & A. B. Markman (Eds.), *Cognitive dynamics: Conceptual change in humans and machines*. Mahwah, New Jersey: Lawrence Erlbaum Associates.

Gough, G. A., Sauer, J. R., & Iliff, M. (1998). Patuxent Bird Identification Infocenter (Version 97.1). Laurel, MD: Patuxent Wildlife Research Center.

Grill-Spector, K. (2003). The neural basis of object perception. *Current Opinion in Neurobiology, 13*, 1–8.

Grossberg, S. (1999). The link between brain learning, attention, and consciousness. *Conscious Cognition, 8*(1), 1–44.

Humphreys, G. W., & Forde, E. M. E. (2001). Hierarchies, similarity, and interactivity in object recognition: "Category-specific" neuropsychological deficits. *Behavioral and Brain Sciences, 24*(3), 453–509.

James, K. H., James, T. W., Jobard, G., Wong, C.-N., & Gauthier, I. (2005). Letter processing in the visual system: Different activation patterns for single letters and strings. *Cognitive, Affective and Behavioral Neuroscience, 5*(4), 452–466.

James, T. W., & Gauthier, I. (2003). Auditory and action semantic features activate sensory-specific perceptual brain regions. *Current Biology, 13*, 1792–1796.

James, T. W., & Gauthier, I. (2004). Brain regions engaged during visual judgments by involuntary access to novel semantic information. *Vision Research, 44*, 429–439.

Kanwisher, N., McDermott, J., & Chun, M. M. (1997). The fusiform face area: a module in human extrastriate cortex specialized for face perception. *Journal of Neuroscience, 17*, 4302–4311.

Koutstaal, W., Wagner, A. D., Rotte, M., Maril, A., Buckner, R. L., & Schacter, D. L. (2001). Perceptual specificity in visual object priming: functional magnetic resonance imaging evidence for a laterality difference in fusiform cortex. *Neuropsychologia, 39*, 184–199.

Leveroni, C. L., Seidenberg, M., Mayer, A. R., Mead, L. A., Binder, J. R., & Rao, S. M. (2000). Neural systems underlying the recognition of familiar and newly learned faces. *The Journal of Neuroscience, 20*(2), 878–886.

Lissauer, H. (1890). Ein Fall von Seelenblindheit nebst einem Beitrag zur Theorie derselben. *Archiv fur Psychiatrie, 21*, 222–270.

Marr, D. (1982). *Vision: a computational investigation into the human representation and processing of visual information.* New York: W.H. Freeman.

Martin, A. (1999). Automatic activation of the medial temporal lobe during encoding: lateralized influences of meaning and novelty. *Hippocampus, 9*, 62–70.

Martin, A. (2007). The representation of object concepts in the brain. *Annual Review of Psychology, 58*, 25–45.

Martin, A., Haxby, J. V., Lalonde, F. M., Wiggs, C. L., & Ungerleider, L. G. (1995). Discrete cortical regions associated with knowledge of color and knowledge of action. *Science, 270*, 102–105.

Myles-Worsley, M., Johnston, W. A., & Simons, M. A. (1988). The influence of expertise on X-ray image processing. *Journal of Experimental Psychology: Learning, Memory and Cognition, 14*(3), 553–557.

Ozubko, J., Cree, G. S., & Bub, D. (2005). *Not all visual experts are created equal.* Paper presented at the Fifteenth Annual Meeting of the Canadian Society for Brain, Behavior and Cognitive Science.

Peron, R. M., & Allen, G. L. (1988). Attempts to train novices for beer flavor discrimination: A matter of taste. *The Journal of General Psychology, 115*, 403–418.

Pylyshyn, Z. (1999). Is vision continuous with cognition? The case of impenetrability of visual perception. *Behavioral and Brain Sciences, 22*, 341–423.

Schacter, D. L., & Buckner, R. L. (1998). Priming and the brain. *Neuron, 20*(2), 185–195.

Schultz, R. T., Grelotti, D. J., Klin, A., Kleinman, J., Van der Gaag, C., Marois, R., et al. (2003). The role of the fusiform face area in social cognition: implications for the pathobiology of autism. *Philosophical Transactions of the Royal Society of London: Series B, 358*, 415–427.

Shyns, P. G., Goldstone, R. L., & Thibaut, J.-P. (1998). Development of features in object concepts. *Behavioral and Brain Sciences, 21*, 1–54.

Sibley, D. A. (2000). *The Sibley Guide to Birds*. New York: Algred A. Knopf, Inc.

Simmons, W. K., Ramjee, V., McRae, K., Martin, A., & Barsalou, L. W. (2006). fMRI evidence for an overlap in the neural bases of color perception and color knowledge. *Neuroimage, 31*, S182.

Tarr, M. J., & Bulthoff, H. H. (1998). Image-based object recognition in man, monkey and machine. *Cognition, 67*(1–2), 1–20.

Vuilleumier, P., Henson, R. N., Driver, J., & Dolan, R. J. (2002). Multiple levels of visual object constancy revealed by event-related fMRI of repetition priming. *Nature Neuroscience, 5*(5), 491–499.

Warrington, E. K., & Shallice, T. (1984). Category-specific semantic impairments. *Brain, 107*, 829–854.

Wiggs, C. L., & Martin, A. (1998). Properties and mechanisms of perceptual priming. *Current Opinion in Neurobiology, 8*, 227–233.

Wisniewski, E. J., & Medin, D. L. (1994). On the interaction of theory and data in concept learning. *Cognitive Science, 18*, 221–281.

Yin, R. K. (1969). Looking at upside-down faces. *Journal of Experimental Psychology, 81*, 141–145.

12

Lessons from Neuropsychology

Daniel Bub

INTRODUCTION

Neuropsychological evidence from brain-damaged cases may offer valuable clues on the organization of mental processes, especially when combined with results from methodologies applied to normal individuals. In principle, a synthesis derived from convergent approaches holds obvious appeal. In practice, analyses of impaired performance do not extend so easily beyond their own circumscribed domain. Consider acquired or congenital disorders of face recognition (prosopagnosia); to what extent has the disorder yielded insights that might clarify the results of neuroimaging studies conducted with normal observers? The answer, perhaps surprisingly, is: not especially much.

There are cogent reasons for the limited interaction between the two potential sources of evidence on the cortical network mediating face recognition (see Rossion, 2008, for a recent discussion). Neuroimaging research has emphasized the right fusiform gyrus (the FFA) as an important part of a distributed network that derives the structure and identity of faces. But the functional details of the components that make up the network, the architecture and flow of information between them, are not yet within reach. At present, the evidence from cases of impaired face recognition merely adds to the mystery. Prosopagnosia as a clinical symptom indicates only that there is difficulty identifying faces and implies nothing about the underlying cause of the impairment. Cases showing documented cortical lesions differ widely in severity and in the location of the brain damage. An equal degree of variability can be seen in their performance on tasks designed to arrive at some interpretation of the functional deficit (see for example, Sergent and Signoret, 1992a). Furthermore, it is not the case that prosopagnosia is necessarily associated with an absent signal to faces in the FFA, even though this is the very region emphasized as a crucial part of the face recognition network in most studies with normal observers. For example, case DF has damage affecting the lateral occipital complex in both hemispheres yet shows FFA activation when passively viewing faces compared to viewing scenes as a baseline (Steeves et al., 2006). A similar result is described by Rossion et al. (2003) for patient PS. The FFA plays some role then, in face recognition, but the evidence from prosopagnosia implies that the region's contribution can only be understood within a larger conceptual framework that encompasses a network of specialized processes.

Could a sufficiently detailed analysis of prosopagnosia help clarify the nature of discrete components within a complex architecture for identifying faces? My goal in this chapter is to describe some of the challenges inherent in such a venture, taking a rather unusual point of departure. I will delay any discussion of methodological issues that confront analyses of prosopagnosia. Instead, I begin by considering another disorder, letter-by-letter (LBL) reading, for my purposes more suited to highlighting the puzzles and para-doxes that emerge in any attempt to understand the subtleties of a higher-level perceptual disorder. LBL reading is an acquired form of dyslexia in previously literate adults, associated with damage to the left occipitotemporal cortex (e.g., Leff et al., 2001). Patients retain their ability to write and spell, but are incapable of reading even short familiar words without a laborious and apparently sequential approach to identifying their constituent letters (e.g., Bub, Arguin, and Lecours, 1993). The basic characteristics of the syndrome are (a) very slow response times in even the simplest reading task (e.g., identifying short, familiar words), (b) an overwhelming effect of word length on reading performance, and (c) normal writing and spelling. Four letter words are read more slowly than three-letter words, and each extra letter brings with it an additional processing burden, delaying the time to visual identification by 1/2 second or more.

Why take LBL reading, rather than prosopagnosia, as a prime example of the pitfalls that arise when we attempt to forge a link between a high-level perceptual impairment and brain-based evidence from normal performance? The syndrome has a number of features that render it paradigmatic. We know that the elements affecting the patient's performance are letters, the individual constituents of words. When we turn to faces and prosopagnosia, the notion of incremental levels of difficulty becomes blurred. What are the relevant variables that affect face recognition in prosopagnosia? This is a much harder, theory-laden question to entertain than the same enquiry applied to LBL reading. In addition, the way in which word length affects performance seems to provide a straightforward clue about the mechanism the patient is relying on to identify a word: the more letters, the slower the reading speed. Does not this result straightforwardly indicate a sequential mode of processing, different from the normal rapid (and presumably, parallel) integration of letters into a word? In prosopagnosia, the constituents of the face that are attended and the means by which they are integrated, if at all, are not so clear. It is often remarked that prosopagnosics attempt to identify faces in a piecemeal, analytic fashion (Mayer and Rossion, 2007), but this inference must be arrived at indirectly, by assuming that some aspect of performance, say the way the patient responds to a change in the orientation of a face from upright to inverted, is consistent with the notion that holistic levels of processing are impaired.

A third reason that LBL reading provides an apt illustration of the chal-lenges facing an integrative approach is the ostensible link between the syndrome and functional imaging research with normal readers. Models of reading include a mechanism that translates abstract letter identities into higher-level perceptual units made up of letter sequences. The processes responsible for deriving these units from print are collectively referred to as the "visual word-form" (VWF) system, in brain-based terms, a cortical system that ". . . . is thought to play a pivotal role in informing other temporal, parietal and frontal areas of the identity of the letter string, for the purpose of both semantic access and phonological retrieval" (Dehaene, Cohen, Sigman, and Vinckier, 2005, p. 335). The nature of the orthographic units represented in the VWF is open to debate, but reasonable candidates are pairs of letters or bigrams (Grainger and Whitney, 2004), and perhaps even sequences larger than these, such as letter triplets (e.g., a sequence like STR) and quadrigrams (Vinckier et al., 2007).

Functional imaging research has led to the view that a portion of the middle left fusiform gyrus represents the neural correlate of the VWF, and the region is currently designated as the "visual word form area" (VWFA; Cohen et al., 2002). The claims regarding the computational role of this cortical area are quite specific: The VWFA in the left fusiform gyrus extracts letter identities that are invariant across changes in case and integrates strings of letters into an ordered sequence that constitutes the spelled form of the word (Dehaene et al., 2005; Kleinschmidt and Cohen, 2006). Of particular interest, the nature of LBL reading is taken as evidence confirming this interpretation of the functional status of the middle left fusiform gyrus. It is the behavioral characteristics of the syndrome, as well as the location of the brain lesions in selected cases, that are held to support the idea that the left fusiform gyrus represents the VWFA. Because word length has such a massive impact on reading speed, it seems reasonable to infer that patients have lost direct access to higher level orthographic elements normally derived by the VWF system, and that word identification from print is taking place by laborious attention to individual letters. Furthermore, the left posterior brain lesions in LBL reading are deemed consistent with either a ". . . disruption of the VWFA itself, or from impaired projections to or from this system" (Cohen et al., 2004; p. 1769).

The argument, as plausible as it seems at first glance, has not gone unchallenged. In a provocative article, entitled "The myth of the visual word form system," Price and Devlin (2003) note that the VWFA is active in normal subjects engaged in tasks that have nothing to do with reading (e.g., naming pictures or colors). They endorse a view of the left middle fusiform gyrus as an association area that integrates information from different domains but that is not dedicated specifically to the analysis of visual word form. Legge (2007) summarizes our current understanding as follows: The theoretical construct of visual word form representations, independent of any arguments from neuroanatomy or neurophysiology, is fully compatible with bottom-up models of word reading. As for the domain-specific role attributed to the left fusiform cortex, "It remains to be seen whether this brain region is uniquely dedicated to processing text stimuli, and whether it is truly a first stage in visual word decoding in reading" (p. 98).

In evaluating the nature of the VWFA, a label that Price and Devlin (2003) dismiss as premature at best and false at worst, an accurate interpretation of

LBL reading takes on critical importance. Whatever the functional status of the lesions responsible for the impairment, presumably this much is clear: The nature of LBL reading seems fully compatible with the assumption that patients are confined to a laborious analysis of individual letters, and so the VWFA plays no causal role in their performance (Cohen et al., 2004). Or does it? In what follows, I will provide a detailed discussion of what lies beneath the surface of a syndrome that appears disarmingly simple if we take its defining features at face value.

My purpose is to show that the seemingly obvious in this instance conceals a witch's brew of subtleties and complications that ultimately force us to confront a paradox. There is in fact enough evidence to suggest that the vast majority of LBL readers are not simply reading by analyzing the identity of each letter in sequence, and their performance is much more consistent with the view that multiple letters are still being mapped in parallel to higher level orthographic representations. But then, how do we explain the fact that the greater the number of letters, the more time required to identify the word? Surely this result can only be accommodated if we hold to the view that LBL reading is just what it seems: each letter contributes individually to the time taken to read a word? The only way to resolve the dilemma is to show that the effect of word length has somehow been misunderstood. It is not the number of letters but some other as yet hidden variable (highly correlated with array length) that must be the true basis for the observed impact of word length on performance. If this variable were controlled for, the effect of length on LBL reading should vanish. I describe evidence that isolates this mystery variable and in so doing, I show that there is no firm basis for the idea that the VWF system is sufficiently disrupted by posterior left hemisphere damage so as to play no causal role in LBL reading.

There are some general implications that can be gleaned from a more nuanced reinterpretation of LBL reading, one that fits more accurately with the evidence at hand. I reconsider the inferences from functional imaging experiments conducted with LBL readers, and the logic invoked to relate the syndrome to specific claims about the VWFA. I argue that the actual results permit no firm conclusions on the status of this cortical area. I then turn to prosopagnosia, a much more variable and complex disorder than LBL reading, and I discuss some important methodological requirements that must be satisfied in order to avoid the pitfalls that obscure legitimate inferences about functional organization from the performance of brain damaged cases.

A BRIEF HISTORY OF LBL DYSLEXIA: SOME HINTS OF A PUZZLE

The name of this syndrome is the modern term for what has more traditionally been labeled as pure alexia or alexia without agraphia. A classic case, presented by Dejerine to the Biological Society in Paris in 1892 (see Bub, Arguin, and Lecours, 1993, for a summary), included many of the theoretical assumptions embraced more recently. Dejerine's model of pure alexia assumed that in addition to centers in the left hemisphere for decoding auditory words (Center A or Wernicke's center) and producing them in spoken form (Center B or Broca's center), there must be a center for the representation of visual words (Center V), established by perceptual expertise ("par l'éducation de l'oeil ").

Center V, according to Dejerine, is the functional component that enables a reader to identify visual letters and letter combinations as abstract linguistic codes, and without its activity the visual system can only analyze letters as meaningless shapes. In the extreme form of pure alexia, the patient is unable to identify even single letters, but this degree of impairment is unusual. More typically, Dejerine observed, the deficit does not extend to the identification of individual letters, and patients remain capable of deciphering words by laboriously attending to each letter in sequence (Dejerine and Pélissier, 1914). For Dejerine, pure alexia entailed a disconnection between Center V and the visual cortices in each hemisphere (see Figure 12.1). Because the center is preserved (though inaccessible via inputs from either visual cortex), the patient retains the ability to write and spell through spared access to Center V from other language zones (i.e., from components B and A representing the sound of the word). Modern incarnations of Dejerine's theory generally assume that Center V is specific to reading, and that spelling and writing are mediated by other language components (e.g., Cohen et al., 2003).

The term "letter-by-letter reading," first suggested by Patterson and Kay (1982), is perhaps unfortunate, because it implies an interpretation of the syndrome that may turn out to be false. Some initial evidence raised the possibility that there must be more to LBL reading than a strictly sequential analysis of individual letters. A number of patients were able to extract partial

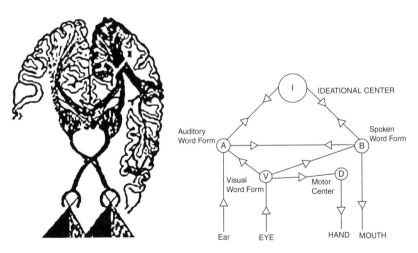

Figure 12.1 Dejerine's neuroanatomical diagram depicting the disconnection (marked with an X) between the visual cortices and the areas subsequently responsible for evoking the visual word form. His functional diagram with V (the visual word form), A (Wernicke's area), and B (Broca's area) is shown on the right.

meaning from written words under task conditions that made it extremely unlikely that they were relying on a sequential approach to reading. For example, some LBL readers can distinguish between words and pseudowords and are able to decide on the semantic category of a word (say, living versus nonliving) at better than chance levels of accuracy even when the targets are presented too briefly for them to identify explicitly (Coslett and Saffran, 1989; Coslett, Saffran, Greenbaum, and Schwartz, 1993; Shallice and Saffran, 1986).

Case DM (Bub and Arguin, 1995) illustrates the reality of the phenomenon: His naming latencies for three-letter words were over two seconds on average and more than three and a half seconds for six letter words. Reaction time increased by 0.5 second for every additional increase in word length by one letter. He was only able to identify 10% of common four-letter words presented briefly (e.g., for 100 milliseconds) and followed by a pattern mask, generally reporting only the first two letters. A chance remark first alerted us to the possibility that DM could extract some word-level information from print before resorting to a protracted analysis of letters. When presented with a task requiring him to distinguish between individual words (e.g., "garden") and nonsense words (e.g., "gardel"), he asked to our surprise whether we wished him to actually decipher the word, or to simply indicate whether it was real or nonsensical, a task he felt he could carry out without a demanding LBL strategy. Many experiments later, we were left with no doubt that DM did indeed retain some tacit reading process that allowed him to recognize a word as familiar, without full identification. The most striking result was obtained when we compared the effect of case alternation on two tasks, one requiring explicit word identification (naming the word) and another (distinguishing between words and pseudowords, a lexical decision task) that DM apparently could perform without LBL reading. Performance was very slow (more than 3 seconds on average) for the naming task, particularly when letter identification was rendered more difficult by case alternation, but lexical decisions were carried out more than twice as rapidly (well under 1.5 seconds on average), and with reasonable accuracy (around 80% for words and 90% for pseudowords). Case alternation did not reliably affect the speed or accuracy of lexical decisions.

Residual sensitivity to written words in some LBL readers does not evoke much confidence in the idea that the syndrome represents a complete failure to access visual word forms. It is possible to argue, though, that this form of implicit reading bears no real connection to normal left hemisphere modes of processing. Cohen et al. (2003), for example, endorse a proposal originally suggested by Coslett and Saffran (1989) that covert skills in LBL reading are mediated by right hemisphere mechanisms emerging only under conditions that prevent explicit attempts to read (say, if words are presented too briefly for a LBL approach and the patient is encouraged to guess). On this view the hypothesis is saved; covert right hemisphere reading is distinguished from the normal perceptual synthesis of visual word forms carried out by the left hemisphere. It is the latter function that has presumably been abolished in LBL reading.

ADDING TO THE PUZZLE

The Word Superiority Effect

The nature of explicit attempts to read individual words, then, becomes the central issue in LBL reading. How different in quality is explicit reading from the covert abilities documented in some cases? In particular, what informs us (leaving aside for now, the effect of word length on performance) that patients are invariably confined to a sequential analysis of individual letters? One kind of evidence that may clarify matters is the degree to which the patients' LBL reading performance is sensitive to word-level influences. A normal reader identifies letters in briefly presented words considerably better than letters in nonwords, even when memory demands are kept to a minimum and performance is controlled for guessing. Considerable empirical research and theoretical modeling work indicates that the normal word superiority effect (WSE) occurs because of interactive feedback between multiple letter elements extracted during early stages of processing and word-level representations (McClelland and Rumelhart, 1981). Thus, the individual elements of a briefly presented word like HAND are perceived more accurately than HANE, because the letter units in the former case have access to a familiar and specific visual word form, while the elements of the nonword must be retrieved from smaller units shared by words like HAVE, LANE, HAND, NONE, etc.

In the extreme, no analogous word superiority effect should be observed in patients who must arrive at the identity of each word or nonword by laboriously deciphering its letters in sequence. Of course, defining the limits of the effect in LBL reading becomes crucial if we are to have anything definite to infer about deviations from a strictly sequential approach to reading. Some advantage for words might be found simply because the patient has a better chance of arriving at the identity of a word than a nonword spelling pattern, based on partial letter information. For example, a word like HAND may be inferred on the basis of the first three letters, while no such constraints apply to a nonword like HANE. In addition, words may contain letter combinations like ND that are more common than corresponding letter pairings in nonwords. If the patient hazards a guess on a misperceived letter, responses may be guided by knowing the likelihood of a particular letter in a given position. If D after N, say is more common than E, the chances of guessing HAND using intuitions about letter probabilities would be greater than for guesses to HANE.

Fortunately, the literature on the word superiority effect in normal readers is replete with countermeasures developed to overcome these types of confound. Bowers, Bub, and Arguin (1996a) carried out a carefully designed analysis of the word superiority effect in patient IH, using four letter words varying in frequency of occurrence (Kucera and Francis, 1967) and pseudowords matched closely to the words in orthographic familiarity. Every pseudoword was generated to have the same summed bigram frequency as one of the target words. In addition, the pseudowords and words were matched for the density of their orthographic neighbors. We will see that this variable, neighborhood density, proves crucial in generating further constraints on the nature of LBL reading. It is defined simply as follows. Take any word (say four letters in length) and find all words sharing 3/4 letters with the target. The number of words that overlap in this way is the orthographic neighborhood (Coltheart, Davelaar, Jonasson, and Besner, 1977). Some words have few neighbors like FILM (FILL, FILE) while others like BEAT have many (HEAT, NEAT, BELT, BENT, BEST, BEAN, BEAR, BOAT, etc.). Matching words and pseudowords for the density of their neighborhoods as well as for summed bigram frequency reduces the possibility that any WSE observed in a LBL reader is merely the result of a piecemeal approach to letter identification based on the likelihood of their occurrence in particular positions in the string.

Words and pseudowords were presented in random order, each for a brief duration (83 milliseconds) followed by a pattern mask made up of overlaid X's and O's for 50 milliseconds. IH was asked to name the four letters appearing on the screen, an instruction designed to further reduce the tendency to guess (McClelland and Rumelhart, 1981). The pattern of results raised further doubts on the modal interpretation of LBL reading. Counting report of all four letters as correct, IH showed a clear WSE for common words and a consistent trend for words that were less familiar. Of interest, presenting words in mixed case (e.g., hANd) did not substantially diminish their advantage over pseudowords. This result is important because it demonstrates that like normal readers (Adams, 1979), IH's sensitivity to word-level representations must include an ability to process abstract letter identities, a function considered part of the left hemisphere's VWF system (Cohen et al., 2003).

Orthographic Neighborhood and Other Contextual Effects

This exploratory analysis of the WSE in a single case of LBL reading, though hardly definitive, calls for additional scrutiny of the view that performance is merely based on a sequential analysis of letters. IH could identify words better than matched pseudowords, implying access to higher-level contextual information, an outcome more consistent with the performance of a normal than a genuinely LBL reader. From the errors he made, there was no indication that his correct responses to words were driven by guesses about their identity. This strategy should yield a bias toward word responses even when pseudowords were displayed as targets. For example, perceiving HIN, and attempting to infer a word, IH might correctly produce HINT as a lucky guess, but the same approach would erroneously produce a word response to HINE. No such consistent error biases were observed. However, a more direct test for guessing revealed another important clue that raises further doubts about the actual nature of LBL reading.

Suppose we compare performance on familiar words taken from high and low density orthographic neighborhoods. A guessing strategy would produce better performance on a low-density word because its identity is much more constrained given a subset of the letters. If IH extracts BAB as the first three letters, for example, then BABY or BABE are the only alternatives while WOR could be WORN, WORK, WORD, WORE, WORM, and WORT (as in St. John's). In fact, there was a surprising trend for IH to be more accurate on briefly presented words with many (e.g., WORM) rather than few (e.g., BABY) orthographic neighbors! A subsequent, more detailed experiment confirmed this unexpected outcome (Arguin, Fiset, and Bub, 2002). We systematically varied neighborhood density, and measured naming latency and accuracy to four letter words matched as closely as possible for frequency, single-letter position, and bigram frequency. Words with many possible neighbors (8–13 neighbors) produced reliably faster reading speeds (around 1.5 seconds) than words with few neighbors (0–5 neighbors; average naming latency around 1.8 seconds). Error rates were also substantially higher for low-density words (around 25%) than high-density words (around 5%). In essence, the more guessable the word, the worse IH's performance!

There is an important possibility implied by these neighborhood effects, a general result verified subsequently in three additional cases of LBL reading (Arguin and Bub, 2005). Though counterintuitive, analogous effects are also typical of the normal reader; four-letter words from dense orthographic neighborhoods are identified more rapidly than four-letter words from sparsely populated neighborhoods (see Andrews, 1997, for a detailed review). Theoretical modeling of the benefit conferred by a dense neighborhood includes the assumption that words sharing letters with many other words generate high levels of concurrent activation in candidates that resemble the target word (McClelland and Rumelhart, 1981). The partially activated set of words forming the dense neighborhood ensures that letter clusters needed for identification receive more excitatory feedback than letters in a word from a sparse neighborhood (see Sears, Hino, and Lupker, 1995, for a discussion of theoretical interpretations of the N size effect). A further assumption, crucial for our purposes, is invoked by computational models of normal reading. In order for a large orthographic neighborhood to help rather than hinder the speed and accuracy of word recognition, many letters must be mapped at the same time (i.e., in parallel rather than serially) onto stored word-level representations (Seidenberg and McClelland, 1989).

Evidence from normal readers confirms the argument from theory, because sequential analysis of letters in the target word does not yield facilitation from the coactivation of many neighbors. Snodgrass and Mintzer (1993) presented words in a series of increasing fragments and found that accuracy was actually lower for words from larger neighborhoods, the opposite of the effect obtained when viewing conditions allow for perceptual integration over multiple letters. The same adverse impact of large neighborhoods on reading performance is observed when a single letter that distinguishes the target word from its neighbors is delayed by 100 milliseconds (Pugh, Rexer, Peter, and Katz, 1994; see also Carreiras, Perea, and Grainger, 1997).

The implications, as much as they seem at odds with the phenomenology of LBL reading, are hard to dismiss. Given the positive influence of a dense orthographic neighborhood on speed and accuracy in these readers, we cannot assume that the disorder reflects a complete destruction of the normal interface between letters and word forms. If there remains any doubt on the issue, consider the following: We have seen that normal readers show no benefit for words from higher density neighborhoods when letters are presented in a format (for example, in segments) that disrupts the parallel synthesis of multiple letters. If LBL readers also rely on the parallel uptake of letter information, their performance should be similarly affected by viewing conditions that enforce sequential processing. Indeed this is so! Fiset, Arguin, and McCabe (2006) have shown that the neighborhood effect in an LBL reader was completely abolished when letters making up the target word were presented sequentially in an incremental fashion from left to right, at a presentation rate derived from the slope of the word length function.

This result confirms the argument that letters in the word must be available simultaneously if higher-level orthographic effects are to exert their influence on LBL reading. Additional support for this claim comes from the demonstration that other word-level influences also require the simultaneous availability of multiple letters. LBL readers are better able to identify more common words that occur frequently in print than less common words. The same benefit occurs for high-imagery words like HAND compared to low-imagery words like FACT. These lexically based effects might plausibly be explained by assuming that LBL readers use their knowledge of meaning to augment partial information about the word derived from the sequential analysis of letter identities, a form of sophisticated guessing. But word-level effects of frequency and imageability, just like the effect of orthographic neighborhood, only occur if multiple letters are available for simultaneous viewing. They are abolished if letters are displayed in a left-to-right sequential order commensurate with the serial process ostensibly underlying the massive effect of word length on reading speed (Fiset et al., 2006).

Herein lies the curious paradox of LBL reading: a central aspect of performance—the fact that reading becomes progressively slower as word length increases—seems fully compatible with a sequential analysis of letters. Yet other evidence consistently belies this interpretation; LBL readers continue to demonstrate effects that require parallel processing of letters in words, and these effects are prevented under viewing conditions that enforce a genuinely sequential analysis of letters. But why then, if multiple letters are being processed in parallel, does the number of letters in the word exert such a huge impact on LBL reading? "Eliminate all other factors," Sherlock Holmes once famously remarked to Watson, "and whatever remains, however improbable, must be the truth." Clearly, what remains in the context of the present dilemma is the novel possibility that the effect of word length, though a defining feature of LBL reading, has somehow been misconstrued. Longer words are not harder to decipher just because they contain more letters for sequential analysis. The effect of length must be due to some other factor that covaries with the number of letters in a word. If this hidden variable can be isolated and held constant across changes in length, we should observe reading performance that, though very slow, no longer implies a strictly sequential LBL process; that is, identification time should not differ between longer and shorter words.

The Word Length Effect and Letter Confusability

In order to see what actually lies behind the massive susceptibility of LBL readers to the total number of letters in a word, notice that each individual letter is potentially confusable with other letters of the alphabet. It is easy to quantify the degree of confusability for each letter; under limited viewing conditions (brief presentation followed by a pattern mask) normal observers make errors identifying single letters, yielding an empirically derived confusion matrix. We define the confusability score of a given letter as its error probability when displayed very briefly and pattern masked, the likelihood the letter will be misidentified and so confused with the remaining letters of the alphabet. Published confusion matrices are generally limited to uppercase letters (Gilmore, Hersh, Caramazza, & Griffin, 1979; Loomis, 1982; Townsend, 1971; Van der Heijden, Malhas, & Van den Roovaart, 1984). Examining the pattern of error probabilities averaged from these matrices indicates that some capital letters yield many errors (e.g., B) and so have high confusability scores; others (e.g., L) are less confusable with remaining letters of the alphabet and so have substantially lower scores.

Words differ in the extent to which they comprise high or low confusability letters; a word like BARN, for example, is made up of letters with relatively high confusability scores while CULT has letters that are easier to identify. Surprisingly, even though it is the error scores of normal observers attempting to identify briefly displayed single letters that provides us with an estimate of their relative confusability, the time a skilled reader takes to identify a word does not depend on the confusability of its constituent letters (Arguin, Fiset, and Bub, 2002; Cosky, 1976). Presumably, the facility with which letters are perceived in normal word recognition under foveal viewing conditions prevents any measurable effect of confusability on reading.

There are excellent reasons, however, to assume that LBL reading would be highly sensitive to this factor. LBL readers will sometimes misidentify a letter when attempting to decipher a word, especially in severe cases. This tendency was observed by Patterson and Kay (1982), who noted that the cumulative error pattern revealed perceptual confusions that were driven by letter similarity (e.g., E misperceived as F). In LBL cases where reading is accurate (although of course very slow), the time to identify a word might also be affected by the perceptual confusability of the letters. A test of this assumption confirmed its validity; reading speed in four cases of LBL reading was tested using words made up of high- or low-confusability letters. The confusability score for each letter was obtained by averaging the error probabilities taken from published confusion matrices (Gilmore et al., 1979; Loomis, 1982; Townsend, 1971; Van der Heijden et al., 1984); high-confusability letters had values of 0.53 or higher, while low-confusability letters were 0.42 or lower. Words were all four letters in length and were matched across letter confusability for neighborhood size, bigram frequency, and word familiarity. Consistent with previous evidence, normal reading speed (naming latency) was unaffected for low-letter confusability (485 ms on average for low–letter confusability target words and 490 ms for high-confusability words). The average naming latencies of the four LBL readers, in contrast, was slowed by 225 ms (while error rates increased by 3.5%) with the increase in letter confusability (Arguin, Fiset, and Bub, 2002).

Additional evidence indicating abnormal effects of letter confusability on LBL reading can be seen by considering how this variable impacts the advantage that occurs for words from large orthographic neighborhoods. We have seen that LBL readers, like normal readers, are faster to identify words in dense orthographic neighborhoods. The effect of neighborhood, however, is modulated by letter confusability. Arguin at al. (2002) showed that the advantage of a dense neighborhood for LBL readers only occurs if the high-density words comprise low-confusability letters; the benefit associated with a high-density neighborhood is abolished if the target word consists of letters with high-confusability values. In normal readers, as we might expect, the benefit for words from large orthographic neighborhoods occurs regardless of letter confusability. Because we observe no facilitation in LBL readers when words with a large number of orthographic neighbors also contain letters of high visual confusability, it must be the case that enough imprecision occurs around the bottom-up activation of letters to interfere with the supportive effect generated by the activation of many orthographic neighbors. Of interest, an analogous result has been observed in normal readers when the visibility of words is reduced by moderate amounts of visual masking (Sears et al., 1995): a small cost (instead of the usual benefit) can then occur for words from dense neighborhoods. Sears and colleagues note that under these viewing conditions, readers will evoke a set of word candidates on the basis of partial letter information. For dense neighborhoods, many candidates emerge as consistent with the degraded letter inputs, increasing the possibility that readers will fail to arrive at the identity of the target.

If the fidelity of letter activation is compromised in LBL readers, how might an increase in confusability affect performance given words of varying length? There are two possibilities. (1) Greater confusability may add to the processing time of each letter in sequence, so the more letters, the larger the impact on reading speed. (2) The alternative is that confusability will increase the time to identify a word by a constant factor regardless of the number of letters. To borrow a useful metaphor from Legge (2007), who asked an analogous question about the impact on normal readers of a change from central to peripheral vision, word recognition may slow down the same way that a film takes longer to develop ("prolonged viewing"), or it may show evidence of a reduction in the number of letters that can be accurately processed in a given time ("shrinkage"). In fact, normal readers suffer shrinkage when words are displayed in the lower visual field (see Legge, 2007, for a discussion). But which of these alternatives, shrinkage or prolonged viewing, applies to the impact of letter confusability on LBL reading? The evidence in fact clearly favors prolonged viewing: Arguin, Fiset, and Bub

(2002) tested one case of LBL reading on three-, four-, five-, and six-letter words made up of letters that were high (0.54 or greater) or low in confusability (0.41 or lower). Words of the same length were matched pairwise on lexical frequency, neighborhood size, single-letter, and bigram frequencies across the two levels of letter confusability. The results indicated that long words were read much more slowly than short words (reading speed increased by nearly ½ second for each additional increase in length by one letter). Words that comprised high-confusability letters were read more slowly than words with less confusable letters, but this variable did not interact with word length. Short words were as much affected by the change in letter confusability as longer words.

We now have sufficient background clues to better understand the nature of the word length effect in LBL reading. The evidence does not suggest that increased letter confusability delays the processing of each letter in sequence. Rather, greater confusability slows the processing of many letters concurrently, regardless of the number of letters in the word. But why then, if readers continue to process letters in parallel, does the number of letters exert such a huge impact on their performance? The answer lies in the fact that as word length increases so too does the combined perceptual confusability of the letters. Let us define the Total Confusability Score (TCS) of a word as the sum of the confusability scores of the individual letters. Since the score for each individual letter provides a measure of its confusability with the remaining letters of the alphabet, the TCS yields an index of perceptual difficulty afforded by the letters of the word in combination. Each word has a TCS that will vary depending on the number and identity of its constituent letters. Figure 12.2 illustrates the frequency distribution of the summed

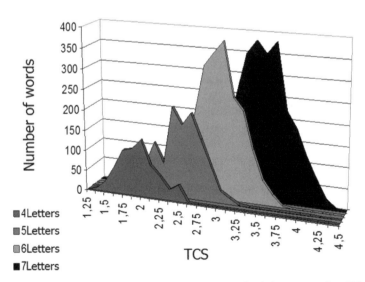

Figure 12.2 The frequency distribution of total confusability scores for different word lengths (See color Plate 12).

confusability scores for four-, five-, six-, and seven-letter words. The TCS, of course, increases on the average with word length (the more letters, the greater tends to be their summed confusability), though it is also clear that the distributions overlap to a certain degree; there are words that have the same TCS even though they have different lengths.

The following hypothesis then suggests itself, given how the TCS varies between shorter and longer words: It is not the mere number but the TCS, the summed confusability scores of the constituent letters, that affects the time to identify words in LBL readers. Hold the TCS constant, and LBL reading should no longer be sensitive to word length. Fiset, Arguin, Bub, Humphreys, and Riddoch (2005) carried out a test of this hypothesis on seven LBL readers. What lent the experiment particular significance was that six of the seven patients were cases previously documented in the literature as clear instances of LBL reading, with well-described lesions in the left temporo-occipital region (see Fiset et al. for details). These LBL readers were asked to read aloud two word lists (naming latencies were recorded), matched across word length for neighborhood size, word frequency, and bigram frequency, and intermixed randomly so as to prevent any strategic biases. List 1 comprised five-, six-, and seven-letter words with no attempt to control for the TCS across word length (and so the TCS increased systematically as the number of letters increased). List 2 also consisted of five-, six-, and seven-letter words, but the TCS was held constant across word length. List 1 yielded the typical word length effect documented in the literature: on average the slope of the word length function was 645 ms/letter (range 369–1035 ms/letter). List 2, by contrast, produced no effect of length at all (the average slope was -4 ms/letter). Only one of the seven LBL readers showed a modest effect of length after the TCS was controlled (165 ms/letter), and for this case the effect of length was nevertheless much reduced compared to words that varied in TCS across length (369 ms/letter).

Before concluding this section, a few loose ends need tidying. Notice that in order to match words of different lengths on their TCS, longer words must have letters with lower individual confusability scores than shorter words. Consider, for example, the words BEAST (confusability scores = 0.7, 0.6, 0.4, 0.5., 0.5) and CLIMATE (confusability scores = 0.2, 0.4, 0.3, 0.3, 0.4, 0.5, 0.6). Their TCS is the same (2.7), but the match requires that many letters in the word BEAST have larger confusability scores than letters in CLIMATE. Perhaps the absent effect of word length is simply an artifact? Individual letters in shorter words have higher confusability scores and so might be harder for LBL readers to decode than letters in longer words with lower confusability scores, counteracting the effect of word length. A number of control experiments convincingly rule out this possibility (see Fiset et al. for details). The most striking of these involved exactly the same two lists of words as before but presented in a format designed to disrupt parallel processing. The letters in each word were displayed on alternating lines (e.g., the word BAKER would have B K R on the top line and A E on the line below). The positioning of the letters requires integration of separate parts of the words in different spatial locations, a marked departure from the conventional format associated with skilled reading. If the impact of summed letter confusability on LBL readers is specifically determined by visual processes that continue to rely on the usual horizontal arrangement of characters, the novel mode of display should enforce a genuinely sequential analysis of letters. The effect of TCS on word length should therefore no longer be found.

The results averaged from the naming latencies of the seven LBL readers can be seen in Figure 12.3.

The left-hand panel indicates the absent effect of length when words are displayed in a conventional format with the TCS matched across word length, and the pronounced effect of length when the TCS is left to covary. The right-hand panel shows the LBL readers performance on the same words, but now presented in the novel two-line format. The word length is strongly present, regardless of whether words are matched or unmatched on their TCS. No patient showed any interaction between word length and matching condition; the average word length effect was 722 ms/letter (TCS matched) and 628 ms/letter (TCS unmatched).

We can encapsulate the results in the following way: If we think of the display format and the TCS as two variables that affect the performance of LBL readers, it is clear they do so in rather different ways. Controlling for TCS has a much bigger effect on the slope than the intercept of the word-length function, relative to a condition in which the TCS is allowed to covary with length. LBL readers are still very slow to identify words, but their

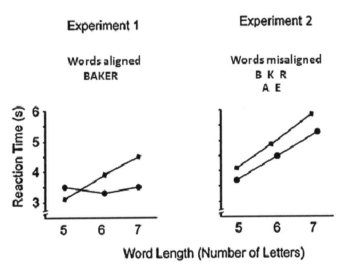

Figure 12.3 The word length effect in LBL readers (left panel) when the total confusability score (TCS) is matched (filled circles) or unmatched (filled triangles) across word length. The panel on the right shows the effect of length for same set of words when the letters are misaligned.

performance does not depend on the number of letters in the word. The change from a conventional to an unusual two-line display format affects the intercept of the word but not the slope. The same effect of length is obtained for typical and atypical displays, but reading is slower in general if words are arranged in an unusual spatial format. These different specific effects on the word length function suggest that LBL readers continue to use parallel letter analysis to identify words displayed in the normal way, but the speed of processing is limited by a low signal-to-noise ratio that occurs when attention is spread across the elements of the word. Longer words generate more noise unless the TCS is maintained as a constant factor over word length. When the conventional display format is broken by misaligning the letters, and integration across spatial regions compromised, LBL readers exhibit severe constraints on letter identification. The parallel mode of processing apparent when the TCS remains invariant is no longer manifest, and word identification is slowed by the unusual spatial arrangement of the letters.

IMPLICATIONS: REVISITING THE VWF SYSTEM

How discrepant is LBL reading from the mode of processing available to a skilled reader under typical viewing conditions? Put another way, has the cortical damage totally abolished the normal interface between letter analysis and the VWF system? Despite the misleading surface form of the disorder, the answer to the first of these questions is that LBL readers continue to display many of the hallmarks of skilled reading. It is clearly not the case that LBL reading is simply a slavish left-to-right processing of each letter in the array. To identify the word, LBL readers may attend to a subset of the letters that are difficult to resolve given partial information obtained by parallel processing in multiple letter locations. But this form of directed attention is more likely to be a guided search informed by feedback from word-level representations than a kind of reverse spelling process in which each letter is decoded sequentially. The answer to the second question follows directly from the response to the first. The left hemisphere posterior damage has imposed a lower signal-to-noise ratio on the parallel analysis of letter information, but there is plenty of evidence to suggest that the normal interaction between letters and words continues to exert a powerful influence on LBL reading.

Notwithstanding the remarkable subtlety of the disorder uncovered by detailed chronometric analyses, recent studies of LBL reading based on the methodology of functional imaging continue to opt for an interpretation of the disorder that is essentially the view articulated by Dejerine (1892). Consider for example, the following summary by Cohen et al. (2004) of their study of an LBL reader, using fMRI to draw inferences about the nature of the deficit: "As suggested before, letter-by-letter reading may result from a kind of serial spelling of stimuli by the right hemisphere to the left-hemispheric language system. Anatomical and functional data are compatible with this hypothesis" (p. 1327). What is the nature of the evidence from neuroimaging research taken to support the claim that "Letter-by-letter reading implies that the normal ability to identify letter strings in a quasi-parallel fashion is lost" (Cohen et al., 2004; p. 1329)?

The logic of the enterprise demands at least a basic understanding of the computational role mediated by various cortical regions activated when normal readers identify visual words (relative to proper baseline conditions), before there is any hope of interpreting departures from this modal pattern in LBL readers. The most recent evidence indicates a complex network of areas sensitive to the orthography of visual words. For example, Vinckier et al. (2007) presented skilled adult readers with letter strings that systematically approached the structure of real words. These authors compared activation yielded by strings of false fonts, infrequent or frequent letters in rare or common bigram combinations, letter strings of frequent bigrams containing rare or common quadrigrams, and real words. A gradient of activation was found in the occipitotemporal cortex, becoming more selective for larger orthographic segments toward the anterior fusiform region. But the inference that this region holds exclusive responsibility for the construction of a VWF is undermined by the fact that a very similar gradient of activation in response to varying orthographic structure was found in the left inferior frontoinsular cortex. Of interest, Pammer et al. (2004) have used magnetoencephalography (MEG) to show that activity in the VWFA lags behind activation in the left inferior frontal gyrus when subjects carry out a visual lexical decision task. Contrary to the assumption that the left fusiform cortex is the seat of the VWFA, the evidence seems more consistent with a complex interaction between anterior and posterior regions, the inferior frontal cortex even taking temporal precedence in the stream of processing.

In this context, the evidence from fMRI studies of LBL reading has few theoretical constraints that can be usefully applied to interpret the activation patterns associated with the syndrome and their departure from the norm. Patients often show some residual activity in regions close to the VWFA (relative to some baseline condition), atypically strong activation in the right hemisphere homologue of the VWFA, and extensive activation of the frontal cortex. The frontal activation is assumed to reflect the demands on working memory of an explicit LBL strategy: "A central component of letter-by-letter reading is the piecemeal assembly and identification of the target word, based on the serial recognition of letters. This may require a variety of operations, such as the storage in short term memory of an increasing set of letters, their phonological recoding, their combination into larger units, repeated access to the lexicon, etc" (Cohen et al., 2004; p. 1777). We have already seen, however, that some frontal activation in normal readers occurs very early and may involve processes that could well be part of the mechanism responsible for extracting higher level orthographic units from letters strings. It remains an open question then, how components of frontal activity in LBL reading are to be construed in the light of this possibility. The residual activity in the VWFA often found in LBL readers poses further interpretative challenges. The conventional stance is to simply dismiss it as epiphenomenal: "Residual top-down activations were observed in the VWFA, but they probably played no actual role in letter-by-letter reading" (Cohen et al., 2004; p. 1776). Given the complexity of the behavioral evidence, this form of reasoning appears to have little secure foundation.

There remains the fact that words may evoke greater activation in the right VWFA of LBL readers, whereas normal readers can show the reverse asymmetry, activation that favors the VWFA in the left hemisphere. It has been argued that the left VWFA constructs a representation of letter strings that abstracts away from upper- and lowercase (Dehaene et al., 2005) and spatial location (Cohen et al., 2002). The right VWFA by contrast is considered to be less selectively tuned to alphabetic stimuli, and to lack the facility of the left hemisphere in representing case invariant letter descriptions. These background considerations imply that LBL readers depend on a form of perception in the right hemisphere that does not readily extract the correspondence between upper- and lowercase letters, while normal readers have access to abstract letter identities in the left VWFA. Two points render this argument contentious. First, the asymmetrical activation produced by letters and words is not always found in functional imaging studies and may be particular to certain task conditions. Ben-Schachar, Dougherty, Deutsch, and Wandell (2007), for example, varied the amount of visual noise applied to words, false fonts, and line drawings and observed that cortical response functions showed greatest sensitivity to words in both the left and right VWFA. These authors point out that greater activation to words only occurs on the left when no noise is added to the stimuli. In addition, they argue that passive viewing of words may produce feedback signals from language cortex that enhance a left hemisphere VWF signal. Tasks that demand more attention tend to reduce the activation on the left, decreasing the asymmetry between the left and right VWFA. Since LBL reading is effortful, perhaps the abnormal reduction in left-sided activation under passive viewing is not especially diagnostic.

There is a second problem with the inference that LBL reading is based on a perceptual mechanism that cannot easily extract case-invariant letter identities. Bowers, Arguin, and Bub (1996b) explicitly tested the idea using a masked priming procedure to determine whether LBL reading can be affected by a briefly displayed word. We presented four-letter words very briefly (100 ms) as a priming event to an LBL reader (IH), followed immediately by a target word displayed for an unlimited duration. The task was simply to name the four-letter target as soon as possible. The question of interest was whether LBL reading could be speeded by a priming word (e.g., "bear") that matched the target word (BEAR) but differed in case. The results were clear: priming was highly specific in that it only occurred if the prime matched all four letters of the target. In addition, the magnitude of priming was unaltered by changes in case; same-case and cross-case priming effects were equivalent. Clearly then, at least some LBL readers gain fairly rapid access to case-invariant orthographic representations. This access is not sufficient to support fluent reading, but there is no easy convergence between the observable facts of performance and the interpretation arrived at through the methodology of functional imaging.

BEYOND LBL READING: LESSONS APPLICABLE TO FACE RECOGNITION AND PROSOPAGNOSIA

LBL reading as a syndrome provides an apt example of the challenges facing any attempt to interpret a higher level perceptual disorder in analytic terms that realistically map onto concepts derived from neuroimaging experiments. In general, the questions that arise in regard to this fascinating disorder are equally relevant to other complex perceptual deficits, including those responsible for prosopagnosia. The latter disorder, as noted earlier, poses an even greater interpretative challenge than LBL reading. How specific is the impairment to a particular domain? What is the nature of the perceptual elements affected by the lesion? What kinds of theoretical assumptions, developed for the special purpose of linking normal and impaired performance to brain activation, would facilitate a sophisticated approach to the problem? How does one deal with the fact that each neurological case is in a sense unique? It will not serve my purpose to provide a detailed review of the literature on prosopagnosia (see, for example, Mayer and Rossion, 2007). If we are still far from understanding the neural mechanisms underlying the ability to identify words, we are yet further from a detailed analysis of the mechanisms that determine the perception of faces. I wish instead to derive some general metatheoretical considerations, lessons learned from the attempt to uncover what lies beneath the surface of a complex impairment affecting one perceptual domain (visual words, or faces) more than others.

NOTING THE BACKGROUND ASSUMPTIONS

In any attempt to interpret a functional deficit, a set of background assumptions (usually implicit) on the suitability of a particular conceptual framework determines the kind of questions under consideration. Often, these assumptions are taken at face value, without a clear view of their limitations, though commitment to them inevitably lends a bias to the direction of subsequent research. Take for example, the tacit conceptual framework guiding the research on LBL reading. Much of the evidence I have described relies on an interactive-activation framework (McClelland and Rumelhart, 1981) in which letters as elements are mapped over processing cycles onto word-level orthographic representations, and top-down influences from words yield a variety of interesting perceptual effects in normal readers (for example, the neighborhood effect discussed previously). This framework provides much detail on the interactive effects of partially activated word units as letter identities unfold over time, but it is rather less explicit on the mechanisms of letter processing divorced from the contextual influences of words.

Application of the interactive-activation framework to LBL reading generated certain questions and controversies and stifled other, perhaps more profitable lines of investigation. For example, the perception of letters in words compared to random strings or letters in isolation yields the well-known word superiority effect (McClelland and Rumelhart, 1981) with certain definite characteristics in the normal reader (e.g., the effect under suitable conditions does not conform to the pattern expected if the observer were merely using sophisticated guesswork to infer the identity of the word). The performance of LBL readers using similar methods may reveal no obvious constraints on the word superiority effect (e.g., Bowers, Bub, & Arguin, 1996) even though words and letters must be displayed for longer durations than is needed for the same level of accuracy in normal readers, but the result will have nothing to say about the underlying perceptual impairment, except that it continues to support apparently normal top-down influences on letter identification (also see Berhmann, Plaut, and Nelson, 1998).

Consider, by contrast, a second quite different approach to perceptual aspects of reading (see Legge, 2007, for an excellent summary), an approach that at the time had little influence on our thinking about LBL reading. In this research program, reliant on psychophysical methods, the mechanisms of interest concern the perception of letters, either individually or in a short string, located in different parts of the visual field. One important goal of the enterprise is to arrive at a sufficient understanding of the perceptual bottleneck limiting the uptake of letter identities in discrete locations on the retina, in such a way so as to predict normal and low vision reading performance. The contextual feedback between word and letter perception, the dominant theme of the interactive-activation model, has little of direct import for the psychophysics of reading, except as an additional influence on more fundamental constraints (such as lateral masking or "crowding effects" in a visual array) that affect the identification of letters. Clearly, from this standpoint an important goal would be to better characterize the perceptual bottleneck of LBL readers prior to the activation of words. A further question concerns the specialized mechanisms that develop for processing individual letters. Recent experiments using fMRI show that identification of a letter presented in isolation activates different cortical regions than identification of (random) letter strings (James, James, Jobard, Wong, & Gauthier, 2005; see Chapter 10 for further discussion). In addition to understanding how brain damage affects the mechanism that transforms an array of letters into a visual word, the nature of cortical specialization for letters—as individual elements and as a string of characters—remains a critical part of the puzzle of LBL reading.

The conceptual framework best suited for analyzing disorders of face recognition is a similarly crucial step along the path to a successful interpretation of prosopagnosia. The literature on normal observers emphasizes the importance of holistic or configural processing, though the terms are used in different ways by different authors (see Maurer, Le Grand, and Mondloch, 2002, for an informative review). It seems natural to apply the distinction between featural and configural processing to prosopagnosia (for example, Levine and Calvanio, 1989), but it remains to be seen whether this approach applied to a variable disorder can yield new insights into the neural architecture of face recognition.

THE ROLE OF ASSOCIATED IMPAIRMENTS

A fundamental controversy in the literature regarding both LBL reading and prosopagnosia concerns the domain specificity of these disorders. Behrmann, Nelson, and Sekuler (1998), for example, show that LBL readers are abnormally slow in identifying pictures, and that their performance is influenced by visual complexity. They argue that ". . . the deficit giving rise to pure alexia is not restricted to orthographic symbols per se but rather is a consequence of damage to a more general purpose visual processing mechanism" (p. 1115). Gauthier, Behrmann, and Tarr (1999) likewise demonstrate that prosopagnosic cases are impaired on perceptual tasks that require subordinate-level discrimination between pairs of objects other than faces.

The interpretation of an association between impairment on one task (e.g., word identification) and another (object identification) has a controversial history in neuropsychology (see Bub, 2008, for a discussion). Posterior damage may affect cortical mechanisms that determine perception in several domains, but other than the fact that degree of impairment on one task correlates with degree of impairment on another, there are few rigorous demonstrations of a causal relationship (but see Patterson et al., 2006). What kind of evidence would indeed persuasively demonstrate that performance on Task A can explain performance on Task B? Consider an example from the psychophysics of reading (Legge, 2007): In attempting to define a perceptual bottleneck in letter identification that accounts for reading speed, Legge developed a task in which readers attempted to identify a letter, flanked on either side by another letter, in locations to the left and right of the midline. The visual span is defined as the area under the curve of the resulting inverted U-shaped function, which differs across individual subjects. The visual span predicts performance in a variety of reading tasks, but this correlation, though impressive, merely serves as the background to a series of more direct inferential tests. Thus, a variable that reduces the visual span like contrast reduction has a comparable effect on reading speed, improving the visual span by practice exerts a corresponding benefit on reading performance, the size of the visual span improves with development and there is a substantial correlation between this developmental change and reading speed, a variable that affects the visual span nonmonotonically has a similar nonmonotonic effect on reading speed, and so forth.

If we had similar detailed examples testing the causal link between associated impairments on different tasks in LBL readers or prosopagnosic cases, there would be much more to say on the question of domain specificity. What, though, might be the equivalent of a visual span task in the realm of face recognition? And consider also the following point: The visual span for reading is defined using letters as percepts but could presumably be measured with other symbols as content (say, false fonts or Chinese characters). Assuming we could predict reading performance from a visual span task using nonalphabetic characters instead of letters, how much more would we have learned about the nature of a fundamental perceptual constraint on the recognition of visual words? Reading requires attention to a horizontal array of elements, where the position of each element is crucial, and perception is limited by interference between adjacent items, particularly for positions outside a narrow foveal window. How similar are the processes involved to processing in other domains, like face and object recognition? To the extent that another task invokes similar cognitive demands, performance will be impaired in an LBL reader. Domain specificity, if it is to mean anything at all, surely must refer to processes that can generalize beyond a given task. A theoretically important question concerns the limits on such generalization.

COPING WITH VARIABILITY

LBL reading manifests quite uniformly between cases, but even this syndrome has variability. Some LBL readers may indeed by reading by a genuinely sequential analysis of letters (e.g., Rayner and Johnson, 2005) just as others show evidence for parallel processing. Prosopagnosics are even more diverse as a population. How does one go about drawing inferences given the variation that inevitably occurs between cases? A great deal of theoretical controversy emerges or vanishes, depending on the answer to this question. If each case is to serve as the basis for particular claims, then there is little hope of extrapolating away from individual variation to arrive at deeper organizing principles in regard to neurocognitive functional mechanisms. But the nature of invariance in a suitably defined population of prosopagnosics or LBL readers may apply to lawful differences between cases as well as to the commonalities in aspects of their performance (see Bub, 2008, for a more detailed discussion). Consider for example, two prosopagnosic cases recently documented in the literature: LR (Bukach, Bub, Gauthier, and Tarr, 2006), and PS (Caldara et al., 2005). These two cases are very different; LR's lesion involved the anterior and inferior portion of the right temporal lobe while PS had extensive lesions of the right inferior occipital cortex and left mid-fusiform gyrus. LR's perceptual abilities and powers of recollection are impressive; PS is not as capable in this regard. Nevertheless, both cases show the same remarkable abnormality in their performance on faces: they are severely impaired at discriminating differences in the eyes of unfamiliar faces but are quite normal at detecting differences in the mouth region. Rossion, LeGrand, Kaiser, Bub, and Tanaka (2007) suggest that the impairment on eye discrimination is secondary to a more general failure of holistic processing. If holistic processing involves a mechanism that integrates multiple facial features as a single perceptual representation, the diagnostic value of a face region made of multiple features (e.g., two eye features) will be more compromised than a single isolated feature such as the mouth. Despite surface variation, then, general principles governing a complex functional mechanism may yet be abstracted away from the diversity that occurs in a population of linked cases.

PONDERING FUNCTIONAL DEFICITS

In attempts to understand both prosopagnosia and LBL reading, a critical distinction is made between holistic and analytic processes. Normal readers, it is argued, extract higher level orthographic units from parallel letter identities ranging in size from bigrams to larger holistic units like quadri-grams and whole words (Shallice, 1988; Vinckier et al., 2007). Normal observers can identify faces configurally by relying on the spatial relationship between features (see Maurer, LeGrand, and Mondloch, 2002, for a summary). It is always tempting to interpret the result of brain damage as a reversion to simpler analytic procedures, on the assumption that more complex holistic mechanisms have been disrupted: an overreliance on letter analysis in the case of LBL readers, and on isolated facial features in proso-pagnosics (see Mayer and Rossion, 2007, for a review of this evidence).

There are several reasons why this line of thinking is an oversimplification. First, expert normal reading and face recognition is more reasonably con-sidered as an interaction between holistic and analytic procedures, not a relinquishing of analytic in favor of holistic perception. Foveal vision yields a perceptual window encompassing a certain number of elements that can be accurately identified, but fidelity quickly diminishes outside this region. Because the visual span shrinks from the fovea to the periphery, word length has little impact on normal reading speed if letters are presented at fixation, but length quickly becomes critically important when words require parafoveal vision (Legge, 2007).

Eye movements in expert reading efficiently update letter information that is not fully available during a single fixation. A similar integration of featural information with active holistic representations may occur in face recognition. An important consequence of brain damage to posterior cortical regions like the face fusiform area and the VWFA is the reduction in neural tissue specifically dedicated to foveal processing (Hasson, Levy, Behrmann, Hendler, and Malach, 2002). The result might be a slower and more error-prone interaction between holistic and featural processing, though not necessarily a complete abolition of configural ability.

There is a second reason to doubt that prosopagnosia inevitably reduces processing to a piecemeal analysis of local features. Some evidence indicates that individual cases retain configural abilities. For example, Sergent and Signoret (1992a) used multidimensional scaling of dissimilarity judgments to establish that the data in one prosopagnosic case "... were best fitted by the three dimensional Euclidean model, a solution also obtained in normal subjects and in another prosopagnosic patient ... and typical of configura-tional processing whereby the perception of faces relies on deriving an interaction among the features that are not treated independently of one another" (p. 380). Bukach et al. (2006) obtained more direct evidence for configural processing in case LR. Normal observers are slower and less accurate to recognize the top half of a face fused with the bottom half of a different face relative to a condition in which the top and bottom halves of the composite face are misaligned. The interfering effect of the integrated features on the ability to detect a difference in just the upper part of the face provides evidence for configural processing. LR shows a face composite effect (slower reaction time for judging that faces that have the same upper part when they differ in the lower part), despite the fact that he is more sensitive to the lower regions of the face (see the section "Coping with Variability").

Finally, some prosopagnosics show implicit abilities to extract knowledge of individual faces they cannot identify (e.g., Young and De Haan, 1988), an outcome analogous to covert word recognition in LBL reading. We have seen evidence to suggest that word-level knowledge tacitly available to the LBL reader can also influence performance in tasks that require explicit identification. A similar result can be observed in prosopagnosia (Sergent and Signoret, 1992b). Like LBL readers, prosopagnosics may not just be relying on a piecemeal analysis of isolated parts, and their performance could well reveal important insights on the interaction between holistic and analytic processes.

ACKNOWLEDGMENTS

The author acknowledges with deep gratitude the support of the Perceptual Expertise Network and the McDonnell Foundation.

REFERENCES

Adams, M. J. (1979). Models of word recognition. *Cognitive Psychology*, *11*, 133–176.

Andrews, A. (1997). The effect of orthographic similarity on lexical retrieval: Resolving neighbourhood conflicts. *Psychonomic Bulletin and Review*, *4*, 439–461,

Arguin, M., & Bub, D. (2005). Parallel processing blocked by letter similarity in letter by letter: A replication. *Cognitive Neuropsychology*, *22*, 589–602

Arguin, M., Fiset, S., & Bub, D. (2002). Sequential and parallel letter processing in letter-by-letter dyslexia. *Cognitive Neuropsychology*, *19*, 535–555.

Behrmann, M., Nelson, J., & Sekuler, E. B. (1998). Visual complexity in letter-by-letter-reading: "Pure" alexia is not pure. *Neuropsychologia*, *36*, 1115–1132.

Behrmann, M., Plaut, D. C., & Nelson, J. (1998). A literature review and new data supporting an interactive account of letter-by-letter reading. *Cognitive Neuropsychology*, *15*, 7–51.

Ben-Shachar, M., Dougherty, R. F., Deutsch, G. K., & Wandell, B. A. (2007). Differential sensitivity to words and shapes in ventral occipitotemporal cortex. *Cerebral Cortex 17*, 1604–1611.

Bowers, J. S., Bub, D., & Arguin, M. (1996). A characterization of the word superiority effect in pure alexia. *Cognitive Neuropsychology*, *13*, 415–441.

Bowers, J. S., Arguin, M., & Bub, D. (1996). Fast and specific access to orthographic knowledge in a case of letter-by-letter surface alexia. *Cognitive Neuropsychology*, *13*, 525–567.

Bub, D. (2008). Reflections on language evolution and the brain. *Cortex*, *44*, 206–217.

Bub, D., & Arguin, M. (1995). Visual word activation in pure alexia. *Brain and Language*, *49*, 77–103.

Bub, D., Arguin, M., & Lecours, A. R. (1993). Jules Dejerine and his interpretation of pure alexia. *Brain and Language, 45,* 531–559.

Bukach, C. M., Bub, D. N., Gauthier, I., & Tarr, M. J. (2006). Perceptual expertise effects are not all or none: Spatially limited perceptual expertise for faces in a case of prosopagnosia. *Journal of Cognitive Neuroscience, 18,* 48–63.

Caldara, R., Schyns, P., Mayer, E., Smith, M. L., Gosselin, F., & Rossion, B. (2005). Does prosopagnosia take the eyes out of face representations? Evidence for a defect in representing diagnostic facial information following brain damage. *Journal of Cognitive Neuroscience, 17,* 1652–1666.

Carreiras, M., Perea, M., & Grainger, J., (1997). Effects of the orthographic neighborhood in visual word recognition: Cross-task comparisons. *Journal of Experimental Psychology: Learning, Memory, & Cognition, 23,* 857–871.

Cohen, L., Henry, C., Dehaene, S., Molko, N., Lehéricy, S., Martinaud, O., Lemer, C., & Ferrieux, S. (2004). The pathophysiology of letter-by-letter reading. *Neuropsychologia, 42,* 1768–1780.

Cohen, L., Lehéricy, S., Chochon, F., Lemer, C., Rivard, S., & Dehaene, S. (2002). Language-specific tuning of visual cortex? Functional properties of the visual word form area. *Brain, 125,* 1054–1069.

Cohen, L., Martinaud, O., Lemer, C., Lehéricy, S., Samson, Y., Obadia, M., Slachevsky, A., & Dehaene, S. (2003). Visual word recognition in the left and right hemispheres: Anatomical and functional correlates of peripheral alexias. *Cerebral Cortex, 13,* 1313–1333.

Coltheart, M., Davelaar, E., Jonasson, J. T., & Besner, D. (1977). Access to the internal lexicon. In S. Dornic (Ed.), *Attention and performance VI* (pp. 535–555). London: Academic Press.

Cosky, M. J. (1976). The role of letter recognition in word recognition. *Memory and Cognition, 4,* 207–214.

Coslett, H. B., & Saffran, E. M. (1989). Evidence for preserved reading in "pure alexia". *Brain, 112,* 327–359.

Coslett, H. B., Saffran, E. M., Greenbaum, S., & Schwartz, H. (1993). Reading in pure alexia: The effect of strategy. *Brain, 116,* 21–37.

Dehaene, S., Cohen, L., Sigman, M., & Vinckier, F. (2005). The neural code for written words: A proposal. *Trends in Cognitives Sciences, 9,* 335–341.

Dejerine, J. (1892). Contribution à l'étude anatomo-pathologique et clinique des différentes variétés de cécité verbale. *Mémoires de la Société de Biologie, 4,* 61–90.

Dejerine, J., & Pélissier, P. (1914). Contribution a l'étude de la cécite verbale pure. *Encephale, 7,* 1–28.

Fiset, D., Arguin, M., Bub, D. N., Humphreys, G. W., & Riddoch, J. N. (2005). How to make the word length effect disappear in letter-by-letter dyslexia: Implications for an account of the disorder. *Psychological Science, 16,* 535–541

Fiset, D., Arguin, M., & McCabe, E. (2006). The breakdown of parallel letter processing in letter-by-letter dyslexia. *Cognitive Neuropsychology, 23,* 240–260.

Gilmore, G. C., Hersh, H., Caramazza, A., & Griffin, J. (1979). Multidimensional letter similarity derived from recognition errors. *Perception and Psychophysics, 25,* 425–431.

Grainger, J., & Whitney, C. (2004) Does the huamn mnid raed words as a wlohe? *Trends in Cognitive Sciences, 8,* 58–59.

Gauthier, I., Behrmann, M., & Tarr, M., J. (1999) Can face recognition really be dissociated from object recognition? *Journal of Cognitive Neuroscience, 11,* 349–370.

Hasson, U., Levy, I., Behrmann, M., Hendler, T., & Malach, M. (2002). Eccentricity bias as an organizing principle for human high order object areas. *Neuron, 34,* 479–490.

James, K. H., James, T. W., Jobard, G., Wong, A. C.-N., & Gauthier, I. (2005). Letter processing in the visual system: Different activation patterns for single letters and strings. *Cognitive, Affective, and Behavioral Neuroscience, 5,* 452–466.

Kleinschmidt, A., & Cohen, L. (2006). The neural bases of prosopagnosia and pure alexia: Recent insights from functional neuroimaging. *Current Opinion in Neurology, 19,* 386–391.

Kucera, M., & Francis, W. (1967). *Computational analysis of present-day American English.* Providence, RI: Brown University Press.

Leff, A. P., Crewes, H., Plant, G. T., Scott, S. K., Kennard, C., & Wise, R. J. (2001). The functional anatomy of single-word reading in patients with hemianopia and pure alexia. *Brain, 124,* 510–521.

Legge, G. E. (2007). *Psychophysics of reading in normal and low vision.* Lawrence Erlbaum Associates.

Levine, D. N., & Calvanio, R. (1989). Prosopagnosia: A defect in visual configural processing. *Brain and Cognition, 10,* 149–170.

Loomis, J. M. (1982). Analysis of tactile and visual confusion matrices. *Perception and Psychophysics, 31,* 41–52.

Maurer, D., Le Grand, R. & Mondloch, C. J. (2002). The many faces of configural processing. *Trends in Cognitive Sciences, 6,* 255–260.

Mayer, J., & Rossion, B. (2007). Prosopagnosia. In O. Godefroy and J. Bogousslavsky. *The behavioural and cognitive neurology of stroke* (pp. 315–334). Cambridge University Press, Cambridge, United Kingdom.

McClelland, J. L., & Rumelhart, D. E. (1981). An interactive activation model of context effects in letter perception. Part 1: An account of basic findings. *Psychological Review, 88,* 375–407.

Pammer, K., Hansen, P. C., Kringelbach, M. L., Holliday, I., Barnes, G., Hillebrand, A., Krish, D., Singh, K. D., & Cornelissen, P. L. (2004). Visual word recognition: The first half second. *NeuroImage, 22,* 1819–1825.

Patterson, K., & Kay, J. (1982). Letter-by-letter reading: Psychological descriptions of a neurological syndrome. *Quarterly Journal of Experimental Psychology, 34A,* 411–441.

Patterson, K., Lambon Ralph, M. A., Jefferies, E., Woolams, A., Jones, R., Hodges, J. R., & Rogers, T. T. (2006). "Presemantic" cognition in semantic dementia: Six deficits in search of an explanation. *Journal of Cognitive Neuroscience, 18,* 169–183.

Price, C. J., & Devlin, J. T. (2003). The myth of the visual word form area. *NeuroImage 19,* 473–481.

Pugh, K. R., Rexer, K., Peter, M., & Katz, L. (1994). Neighborhood effects in visual word recognition: Effects of letter delay and nonword context difficulty. *Journal of Experimental Psychology: Learning, Memory, and Cognition, 20,* 639–648.

Rayner, K., & Johnson, R. L. (2005). Letter-by-letter acquired dyslexia is due to the serial encoding of letters. *Psychological Science, 16,* 530–534.

Rossion, B. (2008). Constraining the cortical face network by neuroimaging studies of acquired prosopagnosia. *NeuroImage, 40,* 423–426.

Rossion, B., Caldara, R., Seghier, M., Schuller, A. M., Lazeyras, F., & Mayer, E. (2003). A network of occipito-temporal face-sensitive areas besides the right middle fusiform gyrus is necessary for normal face processing. *Brain, 126,* 2381–2395.

Rossion, B., Legrand, R., Kaiser, M., Bub, D., & Tanaka, J. (2007). Is the loss of diagnosticity of the eye region of the face a common aspect of acquired prosopagnosia? *Submitted for publication.*

Sears, C. R., Hino, Y., & Lupker, S. J. (1995). Neighbourhood size and neighbourhood frequency effects in visual word recognition. *Journal of Experimental Psychology, Human Perception and Performance, 21,* 876–900.

Seidenberg, M., & McClelland, J. (1989). A distributed developmental model of word recognition and naming. *Psychological Review, 96,* 523–568.

Sergent, J., & Signoret, J. L. (1992a). Varieties of functional deficits in prosopagnosia. *Cerebral Cortex, 2,* 375–388.

Sergent, J., & Signoret, J. L. (1992b). Implicit access to knowledge derived from unrecognized faces in prosopagnosia. *Cerebral Cortex, 2,* 389–400.

Shallice, T. (1988). *From neuropsychology to mental structure.* Cambridge University Press, Cambridge, United Kingdom.

Shallice, T., & Saffran, E. (1986). Lexical processing in the absence of explicit word identification: Evidence from a letter-by-letter reader. *Cognitive Neuropsychology, 4,* 429–458.

Snodgrass, J. G., & Mintzer, M. (1993). Neighborhood effects in visual word recognition: Facilitatory or inhibitory? *Memory & Cognition, 21,* 247–266.

Steeves, J. K., Culham, J. C., Duchaine, B. C., Pratesi, C. C., Valyear, K. F., Schindler, I., Humphrey, G. K., Milner, A. D., & Goodale, M. A. (2006). The fusiform face area is not sufficient for face recognition: Evidence from a patient with dense prosopagnosia and no occipital face area. *Neuropsychologia, 44,* 594–609.

Townsend, J. T. (1971). Theoretical analysis of an alphabetic confusion matrix. *Perception and Psychophysics, 9,* 40–50.

Van der Heijden, A. H. C., Malhas, M. S. M., & Van den Roovaart, B. P. (1984). An empirical interletter confusion matrix for continuous-line capitals. *Perception and Psychophysics, 35,* 85–88.

Vinckier, F., Dehaene, J., Jobert, A., Dubus, J. P., Sigman, M., & Cohen, L. (2007). Hierarchical coding of letter strings in the ventral stream: Dissecting the inner organization of the visual word-form system. *Neuron, 55,* 143–56.

Young, A.W., & De Haan, E. H. F. (1988). Boundaries of covert recognition in prosopagnosia. *Cognitive Neuropsychology, 5,* 317–336.

Endpiece

Isabel Gauthier

Suzie Dukic took over the role of PEN coordinator in 2003 and left PEN in December 2008 to pursue her own graduate work. Suzie has been an exceptional fit for our group: she cared about the science we do, and she excelled at making PEN a positive social environment that has facilitated our collaborations. In this parting song she penned (sic) for her final meeting, she captured PEN better than anyone (thanks Suzie!).

Lyrics by Suzie Dukic and Michael Mack
To the tune of "Dreadlock Holiday" (by 10cc)
This song was performed live by Suzie at the Hard Rock Hotel at PEN XVII.

I was walkin' down the street
Concentratin' on truckin' right
I heard a smart voice beside of me
And I looked round in a state of fright
I saw four scientists, one mad
The others from the gutter
They looked me up and down a bit
And turned to each other

I say
I don't like science oh no, I love it
I don't like research no no, I love it
They said, Don't walk away yet
You got to show some respect
We have our doctorates
And you're prosopagnosic

They said come back to the lab with us
They said we'll give you some dollars
I said I don't know my cars, man
And I'm afraid that I might holla
They said we like you, we want you
We need you for our research
You'll see faces and Greebles
While we record your blood flow properties
And EEGs . . . and I say:

I don't like science oh no, I love it
I don't like research no no, I love it

They said don't walk away yet
You got to show some respect
We've got millions in grants

And a posse of students
I hurried back to the Hard Rock
Sinkin' Pina Colada
I heard Gary beside me say
Would you like something harder
He said I've got it, you want it,
My models are the best, and if you try 'em
You'll like 'em, and wallow in the Research Holiday

Don't like the Hard Rock, oh no, I love her
Don't like Chicago, no no, I love her

He said don't you walk away yet

Got to show some respect,
Don't you walk away yet,
Cause you ain't seen the owls yet

Don't like the PIs, no no, I love them,
Don't like the trainees, ohhh, I love them,

I love the Science!

Author Index

Note: The locators with "f" denote a figure in that page.

Subject Index

Note: The locators with "f" denote a figure in that page.